Using 1-2-3® Release 4 for Windows, Special Edition

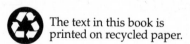

Rebecca Bridges Altman got her bachelor's degree in economics from Stanford University in 1981 and has run her own computer training and consulting business in Cupertino, California for 11 years. She has been a revision author for a number of Que books, including *Using 1-2-3 for Windows*; *Using 1-2-3 Release 3.1*, 2nd Edition; *Using 1-2-3 Release 2.2*, and *Using Symphony*, 2nd Edition. She has also authored books on PageMaker, Microsoft Works, Harvard Graphics, and Harvard Graphics for Windows.

Cathy Kenny is an assistant editor for *PC World* Lotus Edition. Before joining *PC World*, Kenny produced training materials for a microcomputer training company in Boston, MA. She has also served as technical editor on more than 100 books for Que and Howard W. Sams.

Joyce J. Nielsen is a senior product development specialist for Que Corporation. She received a B.S. degree in Quantitative Business Analysis from Indiana University. Nielsen formerly worked as a research analyst for a shopping mall developer, where she developed and documented 1-2-3 applications used nationwide. She is the author of *1-2-3 Release 4 for Windows Quick Reference*, *1-2-3 Release 2.4 Quick Reference*, and *1-2-3 Release 3.4 Quick Reference*; and contribuing author to many other Que titles such as *Using 1-2-3 Release 2.4*, Special Edition; *Using 1-2-3 Release 3.4*, Special Edition; and *1-2-3 Power Macros*.

Rob J. Perry is currently marketing manager for Lotus Development Corporation. Before this position, he was product manager for 1-2-3 for DOS Release 3.1 and Release 3.1+. Perry has been with Lotus for more than nine years and has been responsible for various other marketing efforts including international spreadsheet marketing, 1-2-3 upgrade programs, and marketing 1-2-3 for use on local area networks. Before joining Lotus in 1983, Perry was a technical consultant at Chase Econometrics/Interactive Data Corporation specializing in financial and econometric modeling applications. Perry was a technical editor for *Using 1-2-3 Release 3.1*. In his role as a 1-2-3 product manager, he has assisted many authors in developing and writing books on 1-2-3. Perry earned a bachelor of arts in economics from the University of Virginia in Charlottsville, VA.

Stephen W. Sagman is the president of a New York City-based company that provides training, courseware, documentation, and user interface consulting. He writes about personal computing in *PC/Computing*, *PC Week*, *Computer Shopper*, and *PC Magazine* and gives classes and seminars on desktop publishing, graphics, and multimedia. He is also the author of *Using Harvard Graphics 3.0*, *Using Windows Draw*, and *1-2-3 Graphics Techniques* from Que, the author of *Getting Your Start in Hollywood*, and a contributor to *Mastering CorelDraw 3*. He can be reached via CompuServe (72456,3325) or at CCM, Inc., 140 Charles St., New York, NY 10014.

Brian Underdahl is an author and independent consultant based in Reno, NV. He is the author of Que's best-selling *Upgrading to MS-DOS 5*; *Upgrading to MS-DOS 6*; *Using Quattro Pro for Windows*; *Que's Guide to XTree*; *1-2-3 for DOS Release 3.1+ Quick Reference*; and *Easy Paradox for Windows*. He was also a contributing author to Que's *Using Symphony*, Special Edition; *1-2-3 Beyond the Basics*; *1-2-3 for DOS Release 3.1+ QuickStart*; *1-2-3 Power Macros*; *Using 1-2-3 Release 3.1*; *Using 1-2-3 for DOS Release 3.1+*, Special Edition; *Using 1-2-3 for Windows*; and *Using 1-2-3 Release 2.4*, Special Edition. He also has served as technical editor for Que on *Using 1-2-3 Release 2.3*; *Batch File and Macros Quick Reference*; and *Computerizing Your Small Business*.

Christopher Van Buren is a veteran computer-book author with a dozen titles to his credit, including Que's *Using 1-2-3 for the Mac*; Que's *Using Excel 4 for the Mac*; *Spreadsheet Publishing with Excel for Windows*, by Ventana Press; and *The First Book of Excel for the Macintosh*, by Sams Publishing. Although Chris specializes in spreadsheets, he also has written about desktop publishing, graphics, operating systems, and integrated programs.

Bob Voges is a principal technical writer for Lotus Development Corporation. He has worked for Lotus for eight years, teaching and writing about 1-2-3. Before joining Lotus, he worked for Arthur Anderson & Co., where he began using and teaching 1-2-3 when it first shipped in 1983. He has a degree in accounting from Boston University and earned his Massachusetts CPA certificate in 1983.

Debbie Walkowski is a technical writer with a degree in scientific and technical communication. She has 12 years' experience in the computer industry writing documentation, designing user interfaces, and teaching computer courses. Debbie's company, The Writing Works, specializes in writing computer self-help books and providing writing services to companies such as Microsoft Corporation and Digital Equipment Corporation. She is the author of seven books on popular computer software including Microsoft Works, Microsoft PowerPoint, Microsoft Excel, Quicken, WordPerfect, and Lotus 1-2-3.

David C. Williamson is a consultant, instructor, and developer specializing in spreadsheet and database application programs for Productivity Point International, a training and consulting firm in San Antonio, Texas. Before his consulting career, Williamson spent 17 years in the semiconductor industry. He is coauthor of Que's *Using 1-2-3 Release 3.4*, Special Edition, and the technical editor for Que's *Easy 1-2-3 Macros*.

ACKNOWLEDGMENTS

Using 1-2-3 Release 4 for Windows, Special Edition, is the result of efforts by many talented and dedicated people. Que Corporation thanks the following people for their contributions to the revision of this book:

Authors **Rebecca Bridges Altman**, **Cathy Kenny**, **Joyce Nielsen**, **Rob Perry**, **Steve Sagman**, **Brian Underdahl**, **Chris Van Buren**, **Bob Voges**, **Debbie Walkowski**, and **Dave Williamson**, for adhering to the numerous instructions and guidelines, and for submitting high-quality material in record time.

Que publisher **David P. Ewing** for his valuable content suggestions.

Title manager **Don Roche Jr.** and product directors **Joyce Nielsen** and **Robin Drake** for greatly improving the overall outline and quality of this book, directing the authors, developing the text, and keeping this project on track through the development and editing stages.

Acquisitions editor **Sarah Browning** for assembling the team of authors and helping to keep this book on schedule; acquisitions coordinator **Debbie Abshier** for coordinating the technical editors; and vendor contact coordinator **Patty Brooks** for maintaining contact with Lotus and keeping Que informed of changes to the beta schedules.

Senior editor **Mike La Bonne** for his commitment to producing a high-quality book on a tight schedule. Editors **Tracy Barr**, **Elsa Bell**, **Andy Saff**, **Kathy Simpson**, and **Alice Martina Smith** for their editing skills, timeliness, and attention to detail.

Technical editors **Ed Hanley**, **Bob Holtz**, and **Steve Londergan** for their excellent technical review of this book.

The Que Production Department for producing a high-quality text and for ensuring a quick turnaround time.

Special thanks to **Candace Clemens** of Lotus Development Corporation for coordinating the software beta distribution among authors and Que staff.

CONTENTS AT A GLANCE

Appendixes

I Getting Started

2 Understanding the Graphical User Interface 45

II Building the Worksheet

III Printing Reports and Charts

10 Printing Reports 499

IV Managing Databases

V Customizing 1-2-3 for Windows

Appendixes

The Que Special Edition

Thank you for purchasing *Using 1-2-3 Release 4 for Windows*, Special Edition, the latest addition to Que's Special Edition series. The Special Edition line is the best-selling line of tutorial-references on popular computer software, from the world's leading publisher of computer books.

Since the introduction of the IBM PC, more than 10 years ago, the Using series of computer books from Que has been the favorite tool of PC users wanting to quickly learn how to become productive with their computers. In 1987 we realized that the growing complexity of the most popular software products had generated the need for even more comprehensive coverage than our Using books provided. In response to this need, we published the first *Using 1-2-3*, Special Edition. Since then we have published Special Editions on each of the most important software products in the industry.

From its inception, Que's Special Edition line has offered the clearest and most comprehensive coverage of the personal computer industry's flagship products. In every Special Edition from Que you can expect to find the following features:

- The most complete single-volume reference to your software

- Many step-by-step tutorials, examples and screen shots

- Functional use of color to bring to your attention helpful tips, notes, and warnings about use of your software

- Unique From Here cross-references at the end of major sections of each chapter, complete with page numbers, to help you quickly and easily find the information you need

- Q & A sections at the end of each chapter to help reinforce concepts and product capabilities learned in that chapter

Whenever you need the best book on personal computer software, look for the Special Edition from Que.

David P. Ewing
Publisher

Introduction

More than 10 years ago, the idea of using an electronic spreadsheet in business was little more than an intriguing possibility. Since then, the growing popularity of Lotus 1-2-3, the world's most popular software program, has made electronic spreadsheets a worldwide standard for people who want to make decisions more quickly and accurately.

When Lotus 1-2-3 was introduced, DOS was the major operating system for personal computers. As the computer industry has grown and matured, however, so have the needs of computer users. More powerful hardware, operating systems, and operating environments—such as Microsoft Windows—are in use today, as are more powerful software packages—such as 1-2-3 Release 4 for Windows.

Whether you are new to spreadsheets or are an experienced 1-2-3 user, this book is for you. Following the Que tradition, *Using 1-2-3 Release 4 for Windows*, Special Edition, leads you through the basics of spreadsheets and into the intermediate and advanced features of 1-2-3 Release 4 for Windows. This book provides the most extensive tutorial and reference coverage available for the new 1-2-3 Release 4 for Windows.

Que's unprecedented experience with 1-2-3 and 1-2-3 users has helped produce this high-quality, highly informative book. But a book such as *Using 1-2-3 Release 4 for Windows*, Special Edition, doesn't develop overnight. This book represents long hours of work from a team of expert authors and dedicated editors.

The experts who wrote and developed *Using 1-2-3 Release 4 for Windows*, Special Edition, know firsthand the many ways 1-2-3 is used every day. As Lotus product managers, consultants, trainers, and experienced 1-2-3 users, the authors of *Using 1-2-3 Release 4 for Windows*,

Special Edition, have used 1-2-3 and have taught others how to use 1-2-3 to build many types of applications—from accounting and general business applications to scientific applications. This experience, combined with the editorial expertise of the world's leading 1-2-3 publisher, brings you outstanding tutorial and reference information.

Que began revising the previous edition of this book immediately after Lotus software developers announced that they were planning a new version of 1-2-3. Even before the software was developed, Que's product development team began searching for the best group of 1-2-3 experts available. This team of authors had to be able to cover the powerful new program comprehensively, accurately, and clearly. The authors outlined the strategies needed to produce the best book possible on 1-2-3 Release 4 for Windows and analyzed the qualities that made previous editions of *Using 1-2-3* the most popular 1-2-3 books on the market. When Lotus announced 1-2-3 Release 4 for Windows, Que authors began updating the preceding edition of *Using 1-2-3 for Windows* to cover and explain the new features of Release 4.

NOTE   Because 1-2-3 Release 4 for Windows is a *major* upgrade of 1-2-3 for Windows Release 1 (affecting the command structure and many other areas of the product), this book has been written to focus *specifically* on 1-2-3 Release 4 for Windows. If you are using a previous version of 1-2-3 for Windows (Release 1.0, 1.0a, or 1.1), you should consider upgrading to 1-2-3 Release 4 for Windows to take advantage of the usability enhancements and other exciting new features of the product. (Release 1.1 is the most recent version of 1-2-3 for Windows before Release 4. Lotus made this jump to avoid confusion with 1-2-3 for DOS Releases 2.x and 3.x.)

In addition to the enhancements to this book based on the new features of 1-2-3 Release 4 for Windows, the design and overall structure of this book have also been greatly improved. User tips and cautions are emphasized with colored bars throughout the text. Special cross-references within chapters enable you to follow alternative learning paths by providing quick access to related topics in other chapters. The inside covers of *Using 1-2-3 Release 4 for Windows*, Special Edition, show the 1-2-3 Release 4 for Windows SmartIcon palettes and descriptions of the SmartIcons. Within the text, the actual SmartIcons appear in the margins to highlight text that describes and uses the SmartIcons. A pull-out card includes keyboard shortcuts, the parts of the 1-2-3 Release 4 for Windows screen, and additional SmartIcon palettes.

A new chapter on developing business presentations has been added to show you how to use spreadsheet-publishing techniques to create effective output for presentations. Another new chapter focuses on the

Version Manager, an exciting new feature of 1-2-3 Release 4 for Windows that makes it easier to keep track of changing information in worksheets. Another new chapter on integrating Lotus Windows applications has been added to show you how to combine into a single application the data-analysis powers of 1-2-3 Release 4 for Windows, the visual-representation capabilities of Freelance Graphics for Windows, and the presentation powers of Ami Pro for Windows.

Many chapters in this book have been restructured to make them even easier to follow than in previous editions. The final result of these efforts is a comprehensive tutorial and reference, written in the easy-to-follow style you expect from Que books.

Who Should Read This Book?

Using 1-2-3 Release 4 for Windows, Special Edition, is written and organized to meet the needs of a wide range of readers: those for whom 1-2-3 Release 4 for Windows is their first spreadsheet product and those experienced 1-2-3 users who have upgraded to 1-2-3 Release 4 for Windows.

If 1-2-3 Release 4 for Windows is your first spreadsheet product, this book helps you learn the basics so that you quickly can begin using 1-2-3 for your needs. The first three chapters teach you fundamental concepts of 1-2-3 Release 4 for Windows: an overview of the software features, the differences between and organization of the menus, special uses of the keyboard and mouse, and features of the 1-2-3 Release 4 for Windows screen.

If you are an experienced 1-2-3 user and have upgraded to 1-2-3 Release 4 for Windows, this book describes all the new features in 1-2-3 Release 4 for Windows as well as how to apply them.

Whether you are new to 1-2-3 or have upgraded to 1-2-3 Release 4 for Windows, *Using 1-2-3 Release 4 for Windows*, Special Edition, provides tips and techniques to help you get the most from the program.

Organization of This Book

If you browse quickly through this book, you can get a better sense of its organization and layout. The book is organized to follow the natural flow of learning and using 1-2-3 Release 4 for Windows.

Part I—Getting Started

Chapter 1, "An Overview of 1-2-3 Release 4 for Windows," covers the uses, features, and commands in 1-2-3 Release 4 for Windows that are the same as (or similar to) commands in other versions of 1-2-3. This chapter introduces the general concepts you need to understand 1-2-3 for Windows as a spreadsheet program; it also presents the program's major applications: creating worksheets, databases, charts, and macros.

Chapter 2, "Understanding the Graphical User Interface," teaches you how to use what may be a familiar program in a new environment. You learn how to manipulate and display multiple windows as well as use menus, dialog boxes, SmartIcons, and the mouse to improve your efficiency.

Chapter 3, "Learning Worksheet Basics," helps you begin using 1-2-3 for Windows for the first time and explains special uses of the keyboard and mouse, features of the screen display, and on-screen help. This chapter also introduces the concepts of worksheets and files and teaches you how to move the cell pointer around the worksheet, enter and edit data, and use the Undo feature.

Part II—Building the Worksheet

Chapter 4, "Using Fundamental Commands," teaches you how to use the 1-2-3 Release 4 for Windows command menus and the most fundamental commands for building worksheets. You learn how to save worksheet files, work with ranges, set column widths and row heights, copy and move data, protect and hide data, and find and replace data.

Chapter 5, "Changing the Format and Appearance of Data," shows you how to change the way data appears on the screen, including the way values, formulas, and text display. You also learn how to suppress the display of zeros and how to use named styles and style galleries to quickly format data.

Chapter 6, "Managing Files," covers the commands related to creating, saving, closing, opening, deleting, and listing files. You also learn how to combine values from separate files, change directories, and protect files. This chapter teaches you how to transfer files among different programs and how to send mail.

Chapter 7, "Using Functions," explains how to enter functions. The chapter provides a description of all the functions available in the following 1-2-3 Release 4 for Windows function categories: Calendar, Database, Engineering, Financial, Information, Logical, Lookup, Mathematical, Statistical, and Text.

Chapter 8, "Solving Formulas and Auditing Worksheets," introduces a new dimension of power to what-if analysis. Detailed examples show how to use Solver and Backsolver to find optimum solutions to problems. You learn to interpret Solver results and use functions with Solver. You also learn how to use the new Audit feature to examine formulas in worksheets.

Chapter 9, "Using the Version Manager," shows you how to use the new Version Manager feature to keep track of the changing information in worksheets—and how to share this information with others.

Part III—Printing Reports and Charts

Chapter 10, "Printing Reports," shows you how to specify a print range, preview reports before you print them, print reports of different sizes, and enhance reports with page-setup options. You also learn how to stop and suspend printing and how to print a text file to disk.

Chapter 11, "Using Charts and Graphics," teaches you how to create charts from worksheet data. This chapter covers all the options available to change the type of chart; label and title a chart; enhance a chart with colors, fonts, and grids; change the scale of a chart; and print a chart with worksheet data on the same page. You also learn how to draw objects in the worksheet and how to use and obtain clip art.

Chapter 12, "Developing Business Presentations," focuses on using spreadsheet-publishing techniques to create computer, slide, and overhead presentations. Examples include how to combine text, graphics, and clip art effectively on a single page.

Part IV—Managing Databases

Chapter 13, "Creating Databases," introduces the simplified 1-2-3 Release 4 for Windows database features and shows you how to create, modify, and maintain data records—including how to sort, locate, and extract data. This chapter also explains how to fill ranges with numbers and use the new Fill by Example feature to fill ranges with predetermined labels.

Chapter 14, "Understanding Advanced Data Management," covers some of the more advanced database features such as joining multiple databases, working with external databases, importing data, using cross tabs and aggregates, and creating what-if tables. You learn how to create frequency distributions, perform regression analysis, and analyze matrices.

Part V—Customizing 1-2-3 for Windows

Chapter 15, "Understanding Macros," is an introduction to the powerful macro capability in 1-2-3 Release 4 for Windows. This chapter teaches you how to create, name, and run macros, as well as how to protect and record macros. Also covered are how to add macro buttons to a worksheet, avoid common macro errors, and translate macros from earlier versions of 1-2-3 for Windows.

Chapter 16, "Using Macro Commands," explains the powerful macro commands available in the 1-2-3 Release 4 for Windows macro language. The chapter also includes a reference list of all the macro commands and some examples of their uses.

Chapter 17, "Using SmartIcons," shows you how to use the standard SmartIcons and how to customize SmartIcons by attaching your own macros to them.

Chapter 18, "Integrating Lotus Windows Applications," shows you how to use the Clipboard to perform basic copy-and-paste operations between applications. The chapter also explains how to use the more advanced DDE and OLE capabilities of Lotus Windows applications to dynamically link data between applications.

Appendixes

Appendix A, "Installing 1-2-3 Release 4 for Windows," explains how to install 1-2-3 Release 4 for Windows on your hardware and operating system and how to modify settings at a later time.

Appendix B, "Using the Dialog Editor," covers how to use the Lotus Dialog Editor to customize dialog boxes for your own applications.

Appendix C, "The Lotus Multibyte Character Set," presents tables of the Lotus Multibyte Character Set—characters not on the keyboard that can appear on-screen and that can be printed. These tables also include the compose sequence(s) used to create each character (if available).

Other Titles To Enhance Your Personal Computing

Although *Using 1-2-3 Release 4 for Windows*, Special Edition, is a comprehensive guide to 1-2-3 Release 4 for Windows, no single book can fill all your 1-2-3 and personal computing needs. Que Corporation publishes a full line of microcomputer books that complement this bestseller.

1-2-3 Release 4 for Windows Quick Reference is an affordable, compact reference to the most commonly used Release 4 procedures. This book is great to keep near your computer for those times when you need to know how to do a certain task (the book provides easy-to-follow steps for carrying out the task). This book also includes coverage of 1-2-3 Release 4 for Windows functions, macros, and SmartIcons.

There are several Que books that can help you learn and master your operating systems and environments. *Using Windows 3.1*, Special Edition, covers the Windows operating environment in detail; *Windows 3.1 QuickStart* quickly shows you the basics of Windows. *Using MS-DOS 6*, Special Edition, is an excellent comprehensive guide to the MS-DOS operating system. *Upgrading to MS-DOS 6* is directed at users upgrading to the latest version of MS-DOS. If you prefer to "get up and run" with DOS 6 fundamentals in a quick-and-easy manner, try Que's *MS-DOS 6 QuickStart*: this graphics-based tutorial helps you teach yourself the fundamentals of DOS 6.

All these books can be found in quality bookstores worldwide. In the United States, call Que at 1-800-428-5331 to order books or obtain further information.

Conventions Used in This Book

A number of conventions appear in *Using 1-2-3 Release 4 for Windows*, Special Edition, to help you learn the program. The following sections include examples of these conventions to help you distinguish among the different elements.

Special Typefaces and Representations

Elements printed in uppercase include range names (SALES), functions (@SUM), and cell references (A1..G20 and B:C4). Also presented in uppercase are DOS commands (CHKDSK) and file names (STATUS.WK4).

Special typefaces in *Using 1-2-3 Release 4 for Windows*, Special Edition, include the following:

Type	Meaning
italics	New terms or phrases when initially defined; function and macro-command syntax.
boldface	Information you are asked to type, including the first character of 1-2-3 Classic menu and Wysiwyg commands and the slash (/) and colon (:) that precede these commands.
<u>underscore</u>	1-2-3 Release 4 for Windows menu and dialog-box options that appear underlined on-screen.
`special type`	Direct quotations of words that appear on-screen or in a figure; menu command prompts.

In most cases, keys are represented as they appear on the keyboard. The arrow keys are usually represented by name (for example, *the up-arrow key*). The Print Screen key is abbreviated PrtSc; Page Up is PgUp; Insert is Ins; and so on. On your keyboard, these key names may be spelled out or abbreviated differently.

When two keys appear together with a plus sign, such as Shift+Ins, press and hold the first key as you press the second key. When two keys appear together without a plus sign, such as End Home, press and release the first key before you press the second key.

The function keys, F1 through F10, are used for special situations in 1-2-3. In the text, the function-key name and the corresponding function-key number usually are listed together, such as Edit (F2).

 NOTE   This paragraph format indicates additional information that may help you avoid problems or that should be considered in using the described features.

This paragraph format suggests easier or alternative methods of executing a procedure or discusses advanced techniques related to the topic described in the text.

T I P

CAUTION: This paragraph format cautions you of hazardous procedures (for example, activities that delete files).

WARNING: This paragraph format warns you that the procedure you're about to undertake could cause damage to your files, and perhaps your software.

Icons appear in the margin to indicate that the procedure described in the text includes instructions for using the appropriate SmartIcons in 1-2-3 Release 4 for Windows.

For Related Information sections are found in every chapter. These entries refer you to a specific section within a chapter.

Macro Conventions

Conventions that pertain to macros deserve special mention:

- Single-character macro names (Ctrl+*letter* combinations) appear with the backslash (\ ) and single-character name in lowercase: \a. The \ indicates that you press and hold the Ctrl key as you press the A key.

- Representations of direction keys such as {DOWN} and {NEXTSHEET}, function keys such as {CALC}, and editing keys such as {DEL} appear in uppercase letters and surrounded by curly braces.

- 1-2-3 for Windows macro commands are enclosed within curly braces—such as {GETLABEL} and {EDIT-COPY}—when used in a syntax line or within a macro; the same commands generally appear without braces in the text.

- The Enter key is represented by the tilde (~).

Getting Started

P A R T

1

OUTLINE

An Overview of 1-2-3 Release 4 for Windows

Since personal computers entered the business world over ten years ago, Lotus 1-2-3 has been one of the most popular software packages for PCs. Over 20 million people use 1-2-3 to solve business problems, analyze financial transactions, perform statistical analysis in engineering and production environments, and so on. Lotus 1-2-3 offers users an electronic worksheet, a database manager, business graphics, and a presentation-level report generator—all in one package.

1-2-3 Release 4 for Windows is similar to other versions of 1-2-3 in its basic functions, although Release 4 has many impressive enhancements. 1-2-3 Release 4 for Windows can be used for simple applications or very complex financial planning. The program organizes data and includes typical database functions such as those that sort, extract, and find data within 1-2-3 databases (as well as external disk-based databases such as dBASE, Paradox, Informix, the IBM OS/2 Database Manager, and SQL Server). With 1-2-3 Release 4 for Windows, you can produce graphic representations of financial and scientific data and add those graphics directly to the worksheet to create presentation-quality reports.

This chapter presents an overview of 1-2-3 for Windows. Features, commands, and uses common to all releases of 1-2-3 for Windows and those new to 1-2-3 Release 4 for Windows are covered. If you are upgrading from another release of 1-2-3, this chapter presents a general introduction to the new features and commands of 1-2-3 Release 4 for Windows that you will find helpful. Topics covered in this chapter include the following:

- The general capabilities of 1-2-3 Release 4 for Windows (an overview for readers new to 1-2-3, electronic spreadsheets, or personal computers)

- New features of 1-2-3 Release 4 for Windows (directed at readers upgrading from an earlier 1-2-3 release)

- The capability of 1-2-3 for Windows to link to other Windows applications

- The powerful what-if capabilities of Version Manager, Solver, and Backsolver

- The types of functions and commands included in 1-2-3 for Windows

- File-management capabilities of 1-2-3 for Windows

- The security features in 1-2-3 for Windows

- The new and greatly enhanced charting, graphics, and presentation capabilities of 1-2-3 for Windows

- The new and greatly enhanced database management tools unique to 1-2-3 Release 4 for Windows

- How to automate 1-2-3 for Windows operations by using the powerful macro command language

- The operating requirements for 1-2-3 for Windows

Using 1-2-3 in the Windows Environment

1-2-3 for Windows extends a new level of capability and performance to the personal computer user by using WYSIWYG (what-you-see-is-what-you-get) capabilities and other advanced features that take full advantage of the Microsoft Windows 3.0 and 3.1 operating environments.

In fact, many of the significant changes between 1-2-3 for Windows and other versions of 1-2-3 are changes made possible by the Windows environment. Except for 1-2-3 for OS/2 (which requires OS/2 and the Presentation Manager), other releases of 1-2-3 are character-based, which means that their on-screen display and graphics capabilities are limited. 1-2-3 for Windows breaks this barrier by running under a graphical user interface, which creates a more powerful and easy-to-use spreadsheet environment. (See Chapter 2, "Understanding the Graphical User Interface," for detailed explanations.)

Windows 3.0 and 3.1 give you wide varieties of colors and fonts so that you can organize data in easily identified ways and create presentation-quality graphics. Full mouse support gives you direct manipulation of objects; for example, you can size and move worksheet windows, select ranges, and execute commands with the mouse. A WYSIWYG display enables you to see data on-screen almost exactly as it appears when printed. Pull-down and cascade menus show where you are in the menu structure at all times.

Windows 3.0 and 3.1 also give 1-2-3 for Windows speed, power, and flexibility. The program's multitasking capabilities enable you to print one worksheet, recalculate another, and graph another—all at the same time. With Dynamic Data Exchange (DDE) and Object Linking and Embedding (OLE), you can link and embed 1-2-3 for Windows worksheets with other Windows applications. The ability to open multiple windows and applications enables you to view several worksheets at the same time or display the Help window while you work.

Comparing Release 4 with Earlier Versions

Release 4 is a major upgrade to both 1-2-3 for Windows Release 1.1 and the DOS versions of 1-2-3. 1-2-3 Release 4 for Windows offers all the traditional features of 1-2-3 plus the power of today's most popular operating environment, Windows 3.1. Release 4 includes many stunning new features, such as the following:

■ A redesigned user interface that is easy to use when working with and manipulating data in 1-2-3. Enhancements to the interface include in-cell editing, drag-and-drop, quick menus, an @function pull-down menu, worksheet tabs, an interactive status bar, and a customizable screen display.

■ Context-sensitive menus and SmartIcon palettes. The 1-2-3 main menu and SmartIcon palette change to reflect the current selection.

- The ability to create and edit charts and drawn objects directly in the worksheet.

- Menu-driven access to the 1-2-3 database management tools. Release 4 makes it easy to query and access data in a 1-2-3 database table or an external database table.

- DataLens drivers for dBASE, Paradox, and SQL database servers, IBM OS/2 Database Manager, and Informix.

- Over 120 new @functions and 200 new macro commands.

- The ability to manage and share worksheet information between individuals or among workgroups. The Version Manager enables individuals and workgroups to manage what-if analysis, track modifications to a worksheet, and effectively share information. Release 4 also enables you to share data using Object Linking and Embedding (OLE), Dynamic Data Exchange (DDE), and electronic mail.

- Multitasking through Windows 3.0 or 3.1.

- Support for any printer or display used by Windows 3.0 or 3.1.

- A guided tour and on-line tutorial.

The primary features of 1-2-3's earlier versions remain unchanged in Release 4. You can continue to use 1-2-3 for simple or complex financial applications; to organize, sort, extract, and find information; and to create graphs for use in analyzing data or in presentations.

1-2-3 for Windows supports all the features of 1-2-3 for DOS Release 3.1—and even includes the 1-2-3 Classic menu which consists of the Release 3.1 main and Wysiwyg menus. Three-dimensional worksheets, file linking, direct access to external data, and network support are completely supported and, in most cases, are enhanced in 1-2-3 for Windows.

In 1-2-3 for DOS Releases 1A through 2.4, you are limited to working with a single worksheet at a time. 1-2-3 for DOS Release 3.X and 1-2-3 for Windows take advantage of hardware technology and operating systems to break this barrier by providing up to 256 worksheets per file and the ability to have multiple files in memory at one time.

There are many advantages to working with multiple worksheets and worksheet files. First, this capability is an ideal tool for crafting consolidations—of regional sales, of departmental budgets, and so on. You easily can create formulas that reference cells in other worksheets and other files. These formulas are updated automatically whenever changes are made to any of the referenced worksheets.

The multiple worksheet capability also provides an alternative to scattering separate applications and macros over one large worksheet. Instead, you can reserve a separate sheet for each application—a worksheet on one, a database on another, and a macro library on a third. 1-2-3 Release 4 for Windows extends the multiple worksheet capability by providing *worksheet tabs* that make it easier to create new worksheets, navigate through the worksheets, and assign worksheet names to use in formulas and macros.

Understanding 1-2-3 for Windows Basics

1-2-3 for Windows, like other versions of 1-2-3, can be described as an *electronic accountant's pad* or an *electronic spreadsheet*. When you start 1-2-3 for Windows, the computer screen displays a grid of columns and rows into which you can enter text, numbers, or formulas as an accountant may on one sheet of a columnar pad. 1-2-3 for Windows extends this analogy further by offering true three-dimensional worksheets. You easily can page through the worksheets by using the worksheet tabs, and you can view up to three worksheets on-screen at a time.

In 1-2-3 for Windows, as in other versions of 1-2-3, the worksheet is the basis of the whole product. Whether you work with a database application or create graphs, you create everything within the structure of the worksheet. All commands and procedures are initiated from the 1-2-3 Release 4 for Windows menu, the 1-2-3 Classic menu, or the SmartIcon palette (see figs. 1.1, 1.2, and 1.3). Release 4 also enables you to access frequently used commands with quick menus (see fig. 1.3) and a live status bar. You create graphs from data entered in the worksheet and perform database operations on data organized into the worksheet's column-and-row format.

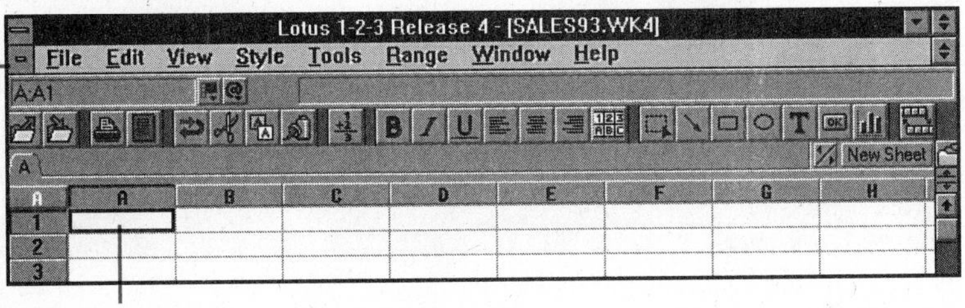

1-2-3 for Windows menu

Cell pointer

FIG. 1.1

The 1-2-3 for Windows menu.

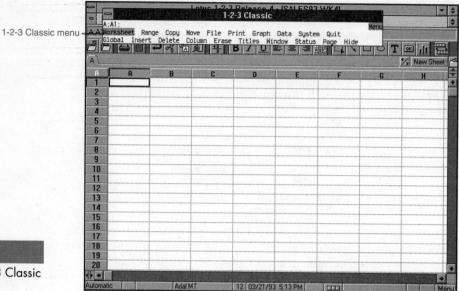

FIG. 1.2

The 1-2-3 Classic menu.

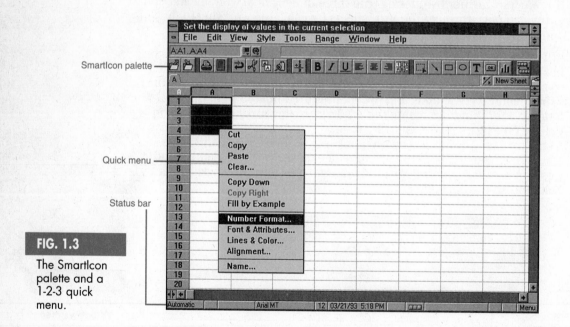

FIG. 1.3

The SmartIcon palette and a 1-2-3 quick menu.

One file can contain up to 256 worksheets and each worksheet is made up of 256 columns (labeled A through IV) and 8,192 rows (numbered consecutively). Each worksheet is identified by a letter followed by a colon. A: is the first worksheet; B: is the second; C: is the third; and so on (up to IV). 1-2-3 also uses worksheet tabs, which appear at the top of the worksheet, to identify each worksheet in the file. They are initially named A, B, C, and so on (up to IV), but you can assign specific names to the worksheet tabs by double-clicking the tab and typing a new name.

The intersections of rows and columns form *cells*; you enter data in cells. Each cell is identified by an address that consists of a worksheet letter (or worksheet name), column letter, and row number. If, for example, you enter data in the first worksheet, the fourth column, and the seventh row, you enter information in cell A:D7. If you assign the name Sales to worksheet A, the comparable cell address is Sales:D7.

As you work in the worksheet, 1-2-3 for Windows indicates the *current cell*—the cell in which you can enter data—with a highlighted rectangle. This highlighted rectangle is the *cell pointer*. When you enter data in a cell, the data appears directly in the cell as well as on the edit line. You move the cell pointer with the direction keys or the mouse.

Potentially, you can fill over two million cells in one worksheet—and you can include 256 worksheets in one file. Many users, however, never handle this much data—or do not have the necessary computer equipment. 1-2-3 for Windows requires at least 4M of random-access memory (RAM) on a computer with an 80386 or 80486 microprocessor to run in Windows 3.1 Standard mode. On a 80286 computer, you may need more RAM. In Windows 3.1 386 Enhanced mode, a 2MB swap file is recommended to run the program. For more information on minimum requirements, see the section "Understanding 1-2-3 Release 4 for Windows System Requirements," later in this chapter.

For Related Information

FROM HERE...

▶▶ "Learning the 1-2-3 for Windows Screen," p. 91.

▶▶ "Understanding Worksheets and Files," p. 100.

▶▶ "Moving around the Worksheet File," p. 108.

▶▶ "Entering Data into the Worksheet," p. 113.

▶▶ "Understanding the 1-2-3 for Windows Menus," p. 134.

▶▶ "Changing the Display of a Worksheet File," p. 161.

▶▶ "Using Charts and Graphics," p. 535.

▶▶ "Creating Databases," p. 639.

Creating Formulas

Because 1-2-3 for Windows is primarily for financial and scientific applications, its capability to use formulas is one of its most sophisticated
yet easy-to-use features. You can create a simple formula that adds the
values in two cells on the same worksheet, like this:

> +A1+B1

This formula indicates that the value stored in cell A1 is to be added to
the value stored in B1. The formula that adds the values in A1 and B1 is
recalculated if you enter new data. For example, if A1 originally contains the value 4 and B1 contains the value 3, the formula results in the
value 7. If you change the value in A1 to 5, the formula is recalculated to
result in 8.

You create formulas with symbols called *operators*: + (addition), –(subtraction), * (multiplication), and / (division). Logical formulas use *logical operators*: < (less than), > (greater than), and = (equal to). Operators
tell 1-2-3 for Windows the relationship between numbers.

The power of 1-2-3 for Windows formulas, however, is best showcased
by the program's capability to link data across worksheets and
worksheet files. By referencing cells in other worksheets and worksheet
files, formulas can calculate results from many worksheet applications.
To create a formula that links data across worksheets, you first specify
the worksheet in which the data is located (indicated by the letters A
through IV or by a defined worksheet name), followed by a colon (:),
and finally the cell address. The following example shows a formula
that links data across three worksheets (A, B, and D):

> +A:B3+B:C6+D:B4

If the formula links data across worksheet files, include the file name,
surrounded by double-angle brackets. For example:

> +A:C6+<<SALES1.WK4>>A:C5

T I P   If the files you want to link are open, click the mouse on the cells you
want to include in the formula. When you do this, 1-2-3 inserts the
file name, worksheet name, and cell address for you.

For Related Information

▶▶ "Linking Files with Formulas," p. 106.

▶▶ "Entering Formulas," p. 118.

▶▶ "Recalculating a Worksheet," p. 171.

▶▶ "Using Functions," p. 261.

FROM HERE...

Analyzing Worksheets with Version Manager, Solver, and Backsolver

Because formulas do not depend on a specific value in a cell, you can change a value in a cell and see what happens when the formulas are recalculated. This "what-if" capability makes 1-2-3 for Windows an incredibly powerful tool for many types of analysis. You can analyze the effect of an expected increase in cost of goods and determine what kind of product-price increases may be needed to maintain current profit margins.

With Release 4's Version Manager, you easily can play what-if by creating a series of *versions* of a single worksheet range that show the effects of certain changes in the data. One version, for example, can show the effect of an increase of the cost of goods without an accompanying increase in product price. Another version can show the expected effect of special advertising or product promotion. You assign a name to each version and then change each range (by substituting versions into the ranges) as needed to test various assumptions. You can group multiple versions of data in a *scenario* for distribution among colleagues.

NOTE You access the Version Manager through the <u>R</u>ange <u>V</u>ersion menu option. See Chapter 9, "Using the Version Manager," for more information.

The Solver utility revolutionizes 1-2-3's capability to perform what-if analysis. When you have a problem that involves a number of variables and has several possible results, Solver can explore all possible options and find all possible answers. To solve a what-if problem yourself, you enter the necessary numbers and formulas into the worksheet and then change various numbers until you reach the desired result. Solver does this work for you by performing all possible calculations within limits you specify. This utility uses symbolic (algebraic) and numeric analysis to solve linear and nonlinear problems.

The Backsolver utility solves problems by changing one or more variables that meet a specified goal. For example, to find out how much chocolate ice cream you need to sell to reach a profit of $1,000, you can use the Backsolver.

 NOTE You access Solver and Backsolver through the Range Analyze menu option. See Chapter 8, "Solving Formulas and Auditing Worksheets," for more information.

Using 1-2-3 for Windows Functions

If you could not calculate complex mathematical, statistical, logical, financial, and other types of formulas, you would find building applications in 1-2-3 for Windows quite difficult. 1-2-3 for Windows, however, provides more than 200 built-in formulas, called *functions* (or @functions) that enable you to create complex formulas for a wide range of applications, including business, scientific, and engineering. Instead of entering complicated formulas containing many operators and parentheses, you can use functions as a shortcut to creating such formulas.

All functions in 1-2-3 for Windows begin with the @ sign followed by the name of the function, such as @SUM, @RAND, and @ROUND. Many functions require you to enter *arguments*—the specifications the function needs to calculate the formula—after the function name. For example, to add the values contained in the range of cells A2 through H2, you can enter **@SUM(A2..H2)**. You also can use range names to specify arguments. For example, if range A2 through H2 is named SALES, you can enter **@SUM(SALES)**.

T I P Use the @function selector to quickly paste a function and its arguments in a cell. The @function selector is the icon with the picture of an @ sign, just below the 1-2-3 for Windows menu.

1-2-3 Release 4 for Windows includes ten categories of functions: calendar, database, engineering, financial, information, logical, lookup, mathematical, statistical, and text. See Chapter 7, "Using Functions," for more information on 1-2-3 functions and examples of the functions provided with 1-2-3 Release 4 for Windows.

Using 1-2-3 for Windows Menus

The 1-2-3 for Windows main menu is context sensitive. That is, the commands that appear in the menu change to reflect the current selection. For example, when you select a range of cells, the main menu displays the Range command. When you select a chart, the Chart command is displayed. And when you work with a 1-2-3 database, the Query command is displayed in the main menu. The SmartIcon palette provides easy access to common 1-2-3 for Windows commands. You can click the SmartIcon to access the command rather than choosing the command through the main menu. The SmartIcon palette also changes to reflect the current selection. For example, if you select a chart, the SmartIcon palette displays common charting commands. The SmartIcon palette is detailed in Chapter 17, "Using SmartIcons."

1-2-3 Release 4 also provides *quick menus* that appear when you click the right mouse button. These menus contain frequently used commands you can use with the current selection. For example, when you select a range of data and click the right mouse button, a menu appears with all the options you can use on that range of data (such as Copy, Number Format, and Fonts & Attributes). Figure 1.3 shows the quick menu that appears when you select a range and click the right mouse button.

In addition to the 1-2-3 for Windows main menu, Release 4 also offers the 1-2-3 Release 3.1 menu (called the *1-2-3 Classic menu*), which includes the 1-2-3 and Wysiwyg menus from 1-2-3 for DOS Release 3.1. The 1-2-3 Classic menu is provided primarily so that you can continue to use any of your existing 1-2-3 macros and so that you can continue to use command sequences you already know while you learn 1-2-3 for Windows. You access the 1-2-3 Release 3.1 menu and Wysiwyg menu the same way you do in DOS, press the slash key or the colon key respectively. Discussions in this book focus on the 1-2-3 for Windows menu instead of the 1-2-3 Classic menu.

Highlight a command in the 1-2-3 Classic menu and press F1 (Help) to find the equivalent 1-2-3 for Windows command.

T I P

The worksheet is the basis for all applications you create, modify, and print in 1-2-3 for Windows. You enter data in the form of text, numbers, and formulas. Through the menus, you format, copy, move, and print the data; create a graph from the data; and perform database operations on the data. You also can use commands to save and retrieve worksheet files, manage and change the files, and read and write files in formats different from the 1-2-3 for Windows worksheet file format.

You use some commands frequently when you create or modify a worksheet application. Other commands, such as specialized database commands, you may rarely or never use. The following sections introduce the commands you will probably use frequently—commands related to creating and modifying worksheet applications.

Using File Commands

The File menu provides commands that help you organize and maintain files, import and export data, print files, and open several files at the same time. With File commands, you can create a new worksheet, open an existing worksheet, or close the current worksheet. You can save worksheet files, combine disk files with files in memory, and extract data from the current worksheet. File commands can control network access to files and protect files to prevent unauthorized changes. In addition, the File menu provides quick access to the last five files you saved by displaying the file names at the bottom of the File menu.

You print worksheets using 1-2-3 for Windows File commands. Unlike DOS versions of 1-2-3, the 1-2-3 for Windows menu does not provide a single Print option for printing worksheets. Several File commands enable you to preview before printing, change page layout, and make printer selections.

FROM HERE...

For Related Information

▶▶ "Managing Files," p. 233.

▶▶ "Printing Reports," p. 499.

Using Edit Commands

The Edit menu's commands enable you to copy and move data; manipulate drawn objects; insert and delete ranges, columns, rows, and individual worksheets; and find and replace worksheet data.

You can use the Edit Copy and Edit Cut commands to copy and move text, numbers, and formulas to other areas within a worksheet, between multiple worksheet files, and among 1-2-3 for Windows worksheets and other Windows applications. These commands also enable you to create links between 1-2-3 for Windows worksheets and other Windows applications. By creating links between applications, you can make certain that reports and documents always contain the most current data.

When you use the Edit Copy and Edit Cut commands, the data is temporarily stored in the Windows Clipboard. You then can use the Edit Paste and Edit Paste Special commands to paste multiple copies of the data in the Clipboard to worksheets or other Windows applications.

You can copy data to adjacent cells in a highlighted range with the Copy Down and Copy Right commands. If you hold down the Shift key, you can use the Copy Up and Copy Left commands. Hold down the Alt key to use the Copy Back and Copy Forward commands. These commands save you hours of copying time by quickly copying data within a highlighted range.

Edit Clear deletes data, cell formatting, or both from a cell. When you choose Edit Clear, 1-2-3 displays a dialog box with three options: choose Cell to remove the contents of the cell and leave cell formatting intact; choose Styles to remove numeric formats, Wysiwyg formatting, and protection status from a cell and leave the cell contents intact; or choose Both to remove the cell contents and formatting from a cell. Edit Find & Replace enables you to find and replace characters in labels and formulas. The Edit Insert and Edit Delete commands enable you to insert and delete ranges, columns, rows, or individual worksheets.

For Related Information

FROM HERE...

▶▶ "Erasing Cells and Ranges," p. 157.

▶▶ "Deleting Cells, Rows, Columns, and Worksheets," p. 158.

▶▶ "Inserting Cells, Rows, Columns, and Worksheets," p. 160.

▶▶ "Moving Data," p. 175.

▶▶ "Copying Data," p. 178.

▶▶ "Finding and Replacing Data," p. 185.

▶▶ "Integrating Lotus Windows Applications," p. 935.

Using View Commands

The View commands enable you to control the screen display of 1-2-3 for Windows. You can specify whether or not to display the worksheet frame as well as such elements as the worksheet grid, scroll bars, SmartIcons, the edit line, and the status bar. Other commands enable you to change the display size of worksheet cells, split a worksheet window into two panes, and display three contiguous worksheets in perspective mode.

The View Freeze Titles command enables you to change the way data appears on-screen. You can, for example, freeze certain columns or rows so that they remain on-screen, even though you move the cell pointer to other areas of the worksheet. Such an arrangement can provide handy row and column titles as you move through a large worksheet.

FROM HERE...

For Related Information

▶▶ "Changing the Display of a Worksheet File," p. 161.

Using Style Commands

The Style commands control the appearance of worksheet data and printed reports. With the Style commands, you can change the way numbers and formulas appear in the worksheet—in Percent format, Currency format, Comma format, and so on. Other Style commands enable you to enhance worksheet data with lines and drop shadows, specify colors and shading, and assign fonts and attributes. You also can create up to 16 named styles that then can be used to quickly apply complete style sets to specified ranges; alternatively, you can select from a set of predefined 1-2-3 style templates.

T I P   Click the typeface and point-size selectors on the status bar to change the font size and typeface of selected data. For more information on using the status bar, see Chapter 3, "Learning Worksheet Basics."

The Style Alignment command controls the way data appears within a cell—both on-screen and on the printed output. You can, for example, change the alignment of labels and values in a range (both horizontally and vertically). You also can wrap text in a cell and align data across a range of cells.

Using the Style Protection command, you can protect certain areas of the worksheet so that you or other users do not accidentally change, erase, or overwrite data.

You also can use the Style commands to change the width of columns and the height of rows. Another Style command hides worksheets, columns, and rows to keep data confidential or to prevent data from printing. The Style Page Break command inserts or removes page breaks in printed reports.

The Style Worksheet Defaults command enables you to set the default styles for the worksheet (including the font, alignment, number format, and column width). Other options enable you to specify the text and background color in cells, display negative values in red, and turn Group mode on or off. By grouping worksheets, you can perform commands on multiple worksheets at the same time.

For Related Information

▶▶ "Grouping Worksheets," p. 139.

▶▶ "Setting Column Widths," p. 151.

▶▶ "Setting Row Heights," p. 155.

▶▶ "Protecting and Hiding Worksheet Data," p. 167.

▶▶ "Changing the Format and Appearance of Data," p. 191.

▶▶ "Using the Color Capabilities of 1-2-3," p. 612.

▶▶ "Emphasizing Text or Graphic Elements," p. 616.

Using Tools Commands

The Tools menu provides access to the charting, drawing, and database capabilities of 1-2-3, and enables you to run macros and change worksheet defaults.

The Tools Database Connect to External command accesses data in an *external database*—a file created and maintained by a database program such as dBASE IV. You can access data from an external table only if the necessary DataLens driver exists. 1-2-3 for Windows data management capabilities are covered in Chapter 14, "Understanding Advanced Data Management."

The Tools Audit command aids in documenting and tracking the logic used in a worksheet. For example, you can locate ranges referred to by a specific formula and locate formulas that refer to a specific range, as well as locate circular references, file links, and DDE links.

The Tools Spell Check utility enables you to locate and correct misspellings in a worksheet. The Tools User Setup command enables you to control whether 1-2-3 beeps when you make an error, whether Undo is enabled, whether 1-2-3 executes macros when files are retrieved, and whether the clock is displayed. Other options control the international settings used for punctuation, date and time formats, and the Recalculation method.

The Tools Macro command runs macros, records and plays back keystrokes, and helps debug macros by single-stepping and command-tracing. Tools Macro also enables you to display the Transcript window and assign a macro to a button in the worksheet.

The Tools SmartIcons command enables you to specify the position of the *SmartIcon palette*—a set of icons that execute worksheet commands when selected. You can create custom icons that execute command sequences you specify; you also can create custom SmartIcon palettes.

FROM HERE...

For Related Information

▶▶ "Checking Your Spelling," p. 127.

▶▶ "Solving Formulas and Auditing Worksheets," p. 419.

▶▶ "Using Charts and Graphics," p. 535.

▶▶ "Creating Databases," p. 639.

▶▶ "Understanding Advanced Data Management," p. 675.

▶▶ "Understanding Macros," p. 727.

▶▶ "Using Macro Commands," p. 773.

▶▶ "Using SmartIcons," p. 917.

Using Range Commands

The Range commands are used with single cells or ranges and appear in the 1-2-3 main menu when you select a cell or range of cells in the worksheet, as shown in figure 1.4.

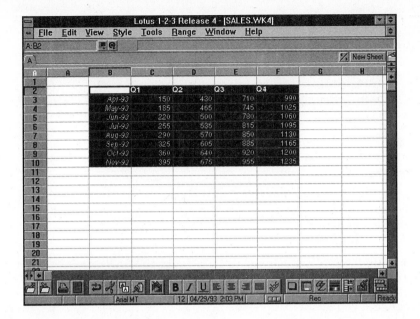

FIG. 1.4

The Range command appears in the main menu when you select a range of cells.

The Range Version command enables you to create, view, and manage different *versions* of data. For example, you can test typical business scenarios (such as a best and worst case) and save each set of data in a named version range. Versions can be grouped in *scenarios* and shared with other worksheet users.

With the Range Fill and Range Fill by Example commands, you can quickly fill a selected range with a sequence of values, dates, times, or percentages; these commands also enable you to fill a range based on what is already entered in the range. For example, if a cell contains the label Q1, the Range Fill by Example command fills the cells in the selected range with Q2, Q3, Q4, and so on, in sequence.

One of the most useful Range commands, Range Name, enables you to attach a name to a single cell or group of cells. By naming a range of cells, you can refer to that name rather than having to remember the cell address. For example, if the range of cells A1..A5 has the range name SALES, you can create a formula that totals the numbers in the named range instead of specifying the separate cells in the range. For example, you enter the function **@SUM** and in parentheses enter the *range name* of the cells: **@SUM(SALES)**. Range names also are useful for printing. Instead of specifying the exact cell addresses for an area you want to print, you can give that area a name and then enter the name when 1-2-3 asks you to indicate the part of the worksheet you want to print. If you use macros, range names have even more importance because they help ensure proper functioning of macros, even if worksheet layout changes.

T I P

To quickly select a named range in the current file, click the navigator and select a name from the list. The *navigator* is the icon just to the left of the @function selector icon, just below the 1-2-3 for Windows menu. For more information on using the navigator, see Chapter 4, "Working with Ranges."

Additional Range commands enable you to sort the data in a range; transpose rows, columns, and worksheets; and separate a range of labels into separate columns.

The Range Analyze commands enable you to access the Solver and Backsolver, create frequency distributions, and perform what-if and regression analyses.

FROM HERE...

For Related Information

▶▶ "Working with Ranges," p. 140.

▶▶ "Solving Formulas and Auditing Worksheets," p. 419.

▶▶ "Using the Version Manager," p. 463.

Using Chart Commands

The 1-2-3 for Windows Chart commands appear in the main menu when you select a chart in the worksheet (see fig. 1.5); they help you create and modify charts. The Chart commands enable you to change chart types, assign and plot individual data ranges, and add headings, legends, data labels, and grid lines to your charts.

T I P

Choose Tools Chart to create a chart from a worksheet selection.

The Chart Axis command enables you to customize the x-axis and y-axis of charts, including the titles, axis type, scale, and units.

Other Chart commands enable you to specify your own default chart settings and change the color and patterns of the data series in charts.

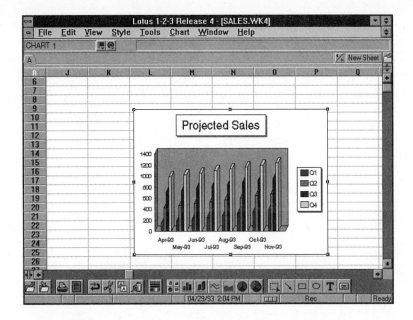

FIG. 1.5

The Chart command appears in the main menu when you select a chart.

For Related Information

▶▶ "Using Charts and Graphics," p. 535.

▶▶ "Developing Business Presentations," p. 597.

FROM HERE...

Using Query Commands

The Query command appears in the 1-2-3 main menu when you select 1-2-3 query tables (see fig. 1.6). The Query Set Criteria command helps you define criteria, limit the number of records displayed in a query table, and refresh the records in a query table. The Query Choose Fields command enables you to select the database fields used in the query table and create computed fields.

Choose Tools Database to create a 1-2-3 database query table.

T I P

	M	**N**	**O**	**P**	**Q**	**R**	**S**	**T**
1								
2								
3	FName	LName	Company	Address1	Address2	City	State	Zip
4	Jane	Smith	ABC Corp.	11 Granite street		Worcester	MA	08984
5	Peter	Reeve	Payne,LTD.	28 Spring St.	3rd Floor	Cambridge	MA	02122
6	Philip	Cane	Indian Relics	28 Marabar Lane	Suite 34	Gloucester	MA	98874
7	Julie	Ryan		12 Mosholu Ave	Apt 3B	Bronx	NY	45666
8	Michael	Londergan	Datacorp	197 Portland St.	2nd Floor	Boston	MA	02122

FIG. 1.6

The Query command appears in the main menu when you select a 1-2-3 database table.

Some Query commands enable you to assign a name to a query table, aggregate groups of values, sort the data in a query table, and rename fields used in the query table. With other Query commands, you can work with different database tables, join database tables, and replace the original records in a database table with edited records from a query table.

The Query Set Options command enables you to replace original records or exclude duplicate records from a query table, display sample data in the Set Criteria dialog box, and specify whether or not query tables are updated.

FROM HERE...

For Related Information

▶▶ "Creating Databases," p. 639.

▶▶ "Understanding Advanced Data Management," p. 675.

Using Transcript Commands

When you choose the Tools Macro Show Transcript command, 1-2-3 opens the macro Transcript window and displays the Transcript command in the main menu (see fig. 1.7). The Transcript Playback command enables you to run selected keystrokes as a macro. The Transcript Minimize on Run command reduces the window to an icon when you run recorded items as a macro. You can use the Edit commands to clear recorded keystrokes from the Transcript window and copy and move data between the Transcript and Worksheet windows. The Tools Macro command enables you to turn on Trace and Step mode and activate macro recording.

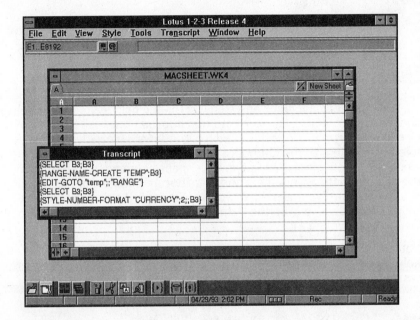

FIG. 1.7

The Transcript command appears in the main menu when you open the macro transcript window.

For Related Information

▸▸ "Recording Macros with the Transcript Window," p. 755.

FROM HERE...

Using Window Commands

The Window commands control the display of all open windows. Because 1-2-3 for Windows can have many open windows that display different worksheets, different files, the Help window, and the Transcript window, the Window commands help you place, size, and move windows for optimum versatility.

If several windows are open, selecting <u>W</u>indow also enables you to make a window active by choosing from a list containing up to nine window names.

For Related Information

▶▶ "Manipulating Windows," p. 69.

Using Help Commands

1-2-3 for Windows includes an extensive on-line help system. The <u>H</u>elp commands provide quick access to this information. 1-2-3 for Windows, like all other applications designed for Windows 3.0 or 3.1, enables you to copy help text to the Clipboard and later paste the text into the worksheet. You can, for example, copy macro command examples from the help text into a worksheet and incorporate portions of the sample macros in your own macros. If you use Windows 3.1, you can choose <u>H</u>elp Always on <u>T</u>op from the Help window to keep the Help window visible while you work.

You also can search for specific topics, find related items, and print any help topic.

T I P   Press F1 (Help) to receive context-sensitive help.

The 1-2-3 for Windows <u>H</u>elp <u>F</u>or Upgraders command displays a table of comparable 1-2-3 for Windows commands that replace Release 3.1 commands. The <u>H</u>elp <u>H</u>ow Do I? command presents a task-oriented approach to 1-2-3 for Windows operations.

The <u>H</u>elp <u>T</u>utorial command provides an on-line tutorial to help you learn basic 1-2-3 commands.

For Related Information

▶▶ "Using the 1-2-3 for Windows Help System," p. 99.

Managing 1-2-3 for Windows Files

The type of file you create most often in 1-2-3 for Windows is a worksheet file. 1-2-3 for Windows files are stored in a single file format with the WK4 extension. A worksheet file saves all the data, formulas, and text you enter into a worksheet, as well as the format of cells (including Wysiwyg formatting), the alignment of text, range names, and settings for ranges that are protected. 1-2-3 for Windows can read the following file formats:

- WKS files (1-2-3 Release 1A)—read-only

- WK1, FMT, and ALL files (1-2-3 Releases 2.01, 2.2, 2.3, and 2.4)

- WK3 and FM3 files (1-2-3 Releases 3, 3.1, 3.1+, 3.4, and 1-2-3 for Windows Release 1.1)

- WRK, WR1, and FMS files (Symphony)—read-only

- XLS files (Microsoft Excel Releases 2.0, 2.1, 2.2, 3.0, and 4.0)—read-only

- XLM files (Microsoft Excel Releases 2.0, 2.1, 2.2, 3.0, and 4.0)—read-only

NOTE   1-2-3 for Windows cannot use 1-2-3 for OS/2 files.

If you use Lotus Notes, you also can open and save 1-2-3 Release 4 shared (NS4) files containing versions and scenarios created with the Version Manager.

For Related Information

FROM HERE...

▶▶ "Understanding Worksheets and Files," p. 100.

▶▶ "Managing Files," p. 233.

▶▶ "Using the Version Manager," p. 463.

Protecting Worksheets and Files

In addition to providing a command that enables you to assign reservation status to a file, 1-2-3 for Windows enables you to assign a password to a file so that file retrieval is restricted to users who know that password. You may, however, want to give other users access to a worksheet file but restrict their ability to change or delete specific data in the file. With Style Protection and File Protect, you can lock areas of your worksheet from any changes.

FROM HERE...

For Related Information

▶▶ "Protecting and Hiding Worksheet Data," p. 167.

▶▶ "Protecting Files," p. 250.

Enhancing Worksheets with 1-2-3 Graphics

When 1-2-3 was first introduced, business users quickly recognized the advantages of being able to analyze worksheet data in instant graphs produced by the same worksheet program. Release 4 presents new chart features that give you even greater control over the appearance of charts.

You can create 12 types of charts with 1-2-3 Release 4: line, area, bar, pie, XY, high-low-close-open (HLCO), mixed (bar and line), radar, 3D line, 3D area, 3D bar, and 3D pie. You quickly can create a chart from a selected range of data in the worksheet; the chart is created and all elements (including titles, legends, and labels) are placed in a single step. Charts automatically update if any data is changed.

Beyond creating simple charts, 1-2-3 Chart commands enable you to enhance and customize charts. You can change the font and color of chart elements, label data points, change the display format of values, create a grid, and change the scaling along the x-axis or y-axis.

When a chart is selected, the main menu displays the Chart commands used to create and enhance graphs; the SmartIcon palette changes to display frequently used charting SmartIcons.

Some earlier versions of 1-2-3 provided the necessary tools for analyzing data in chart form but were primitive in their capacity to produce high-quality graphs on-screen and in printed form. The addition of such add-ins as Allways and Wysiwyg provided the capability to view charts in combination with the 1-2-3 worksheet—but it also required the use of two separate windows. 1-2-3 Release 4 produces presentation-quality charts right in the worksheet and also provides in-place chart editing. Simply click on a chart element to select it and use the Chart and Style commands to add such enhancements as color, designer frames, fonts, and text attributes.

The Tools Draw menu provides additional capabilities for enhancing worksheet charts. You can add lines, polylines, arrows, rectangles, arcs, ellipses, polygons, and text blocks to charts. Using the File Print command, you can print the worksheet data and chart together, or you can print a selected chart.

For Related Information

▶▶ "Using Charts and Graphics," p. 535.

▶▶ "Developing Business Presentations," p. 597.

FROM HERE...

Printing Reports and Charts

1-2-3 Release 4 for Windows offers significant improvements to printing functionality. In addition to printing worksheet ranges, you also can print a collection of worksheet ranges, selected charts or other drawn objects, the current worksheet, or an entire file. You can set the number of copies and customize page setup.

The File Print Preview command enables you to see a worksheet report before you print it. The margins, headers, footers, fonts, and graphics on each page display exactly as they print. With SmartIcons in the Print Preview window, you can cycle through all the pages, enlarge or reduce the display size, change the page setup, print the previewed data, and close the preview window.

The File Page Setup command provides features for aligning and customizing headers and footers and offers flexible ways to compress data for printing.

The File Print command enables you to use the Windows Print Manager and any print device supported by Windows 3.0 or 3.1 to take advantage of additional print functionality.

FROM HERE...

For Related Information

▶▶ "Printing Reports," p. 499.

Understanding 1-2-3 Database Management

1-2-3 provides true database management commands and functions so that you can sort, query, extract, and perform analysis on data and even access and manipulate data from an external database. One important advantage of 1-2-3 for Windows database functionality over independent database products is that 1-2-3's database commands are similar to the other commands used in the 1-2-3 program. As a result, you learn how to use the 1-2-3 database manager as you learn the rest of the 1-2-3 program.

After you build a database table (which is really no different than building any other worksheet application), you can perform a variety of functions on it. You accomplish some of these tasks by using standard 1-2-3 commands. For example, you can add a record to the database with the Edit Insert Row command. Editing the contents of a database record is as easy as editing any other cell: you move the cell pointer to that location and type.

When you need to manipulate the records in a database table, whether to find certain records or perform statistical analyses on the records, you define a *query*. Release 4 provides the Data Query Assistant to guide you through the process of building a 1-2-3 database. The Data Query Assistant presents a graphical approach to extracting information from a database, relying on dialog boxes rather than menu commands to guide you through the process.

The "Query by Box" technology uses drop-down menus and dialog boxes to build the criteria. Once a query has been formulated, you can save it and use it again. A query table enables you to manipulate a database without changing any of the data in the source database table. You can update the records in the database tables with any modifications made in the query table.

Although Release 4 has made it easier to query a database, you still have a wide range of options in defining criteria. Criteria can include complex formulas as well as simple numbers and text entries. You can join sets of criteria and change the relationship between one criteria and another with the AND and OR operators. You also can include wild-card characters to search for records that match certain characters in a field.

You can sort the data in a database as well as perform various kinds of analysis on the data. You can, for example, count the number of records in a database that match a specific criteria; compute the mean, variance, or standard deviation; and find the minimum and maximum values in a range. The capability to perform statistical analysis on a database is an advanced feature for database management systems on any microcomputer. 1-2-3 also has a special set of statistical functions that operate only on information stored in a database. Like the Query commands, the statistical functions use criteria to determine the records on which they are to operate.

1-2-3's capability to access external databases makes it a product well worth trying out. You can import records from another database such as Paradox into a 1-2-3 worksheet.

Release 4 includes new and updated DataLens drivers. DataLens is a unique Lotus technology that lets you read data from and write data to external tables without leaving 1-2-3. Whenever you need to communicate with an external table or other data source (such as an SQL Server), 1-2-3 uses a DataLens driver. Release 4 includes the following new and improved DataLens drivers:

- dBASE IV
- Paradox
- SQL Server
- IBM OS/2 Database Manager
- Informix
- Open Database Connectivity (ODBC)

If the right driver file exists and you establish a connection or link between 1-2-3 and an external database, you can perform several tasks: you can find and manipulate data in the external database and then work with that data in a worksheet; you can use formulas and database functions to perform calculations on the data in the external database; and you can create a new external database that contains data from the worksheet or from an existing external database.

For Related Information

▶▶ "Creating Databases," p. 639.

▶▶ "Understanding Advanced Data Management," p. 675.

FROM HERE...

Using Macros and the Macro Language

One of the most exciting features of 1-2-3 for Windows is its macro capability, with which you can automate and customize 1-2-3 for Windows for your applications. With macro commands, you can create—inside the 1-2-3 for Windows worksheet—programs to use for a variety of purposes. At the simplest level, macro programs automate a repetitive task and reduce the number of keystrokes you make for a 1-2-3 for Windows operation. At a more complex level, macro commands give you full-featured programming capabilities.

T I P Run 1-2-3 for Windows macros named with a backslash and a single letter by pressing Ctrl+*letter*—not Alt+*letter* as was true for versions of 1-2-3 for DOS.

With 1-2-3 for Windows, you use the Transcript window to record keystrokes in macro-instruction format. You can edit the keystrokes and copy the keystrokes as macros to the worksheet; alternatively, you can run the macro commands directly from the Transcript window. In addition to naming a macro with the backslash (\) and a single letter, you can name a macro with up to 15 characters.

After you name a macro, you activate the macro with one of three methods: press the Ctrl key and a letter key, press Run (Alt+F3) and select the macro name, or use the Tools Macro Run command. In addition, you can assign the macro keystrokes to a user-defined macro button or a custom SmartIcon so that all you have to do is click on the button or icon to run the macro. 1-2-3 also provides auto-executing macros, which automatically execute when you open the worksheet file that contains the macro.

1-2-3 Release 4 also provides a macro debugging capability. If a macro you have created does not function properly, you can *debug* (locate errors in) the macro by using Step mode and Trace. You will find that these debugging tools are most effective when you use them together. With Step mode, the macro runs one command at a time; the Trace window displays the macro command 1-2-3 is about to perform, making it easy for you to locate and correct the faulty code.

When you use the 1-2-3 for Windows macro commands, you discover the power available for your applications. For the applications developer, the macro commands are much like a programming language (such as BASIC). The programming process, however, is simplified significantly by the powerful features of the 1-2-3 for Windows spreadsheet, database, and graphics commands. Whether you use the 1-2-3 for Windows programming capability as a typing alternative or as a programming language, you soon discover that it simplifies and automates many 1-2-3 for Windows applications.

The 1-2-3 Release 4 for Windows macro language includes over 300 macro commands, many of which are new commands not included with earlier 1-2-3 releases; other commands offer improvements over earlier versions of macro commands. These commands enable macros to use the Clipboard, create and control DDE links, and control windows. Other macro commands let you create windows, menus, and dialog boxes for use with custom applications.

For Related Information

▶▶ "Understanding Macros," p. 727.

▶▶ "Using Macro Commands," p. 773.

FROM HERE...

Understanding 1-2-3 Release 4 for Windows System Requirements

Because 1-2-3 Release 4 for Windows contains many features not included in previous 1-2-3 releases, the program places the most demands on computer hardware. Because of the system architecture 1-2-3 Release 4 for Windows requires, many users may find that they cannot run 1-2-3 Release 4 for Windows on their current system. The program also requires much more memory than was required for other versions of 1-2-3. Table 1.1 lists the system requirements to run 1-2-3 Release 4 for Windows.

Table 1.1 1-2-3 Release 4 for Windows System Requirements

Published by:

Lotus Development Corporation
55 Cambridge Parkway
Cambridge, Massachusetts 02142
(617) 577-8500

System requirements:

System based on 80286, 80386, or 80486 architecture
EGA, VGA, SuperVGA, or IBM 8514 monitor
Available hard disk storage: 7M (or up to 15M for added features and
tutorials)
Random-access memory (RAM): 4M

Operating system:

Microsoft Windows 3.0 or higher
DOS Version 3.3 or higher

Optional hardware:

Mouse (recommended)
Printer (any printer supported by Windows 3.0 or 3.1)

Questions & Answers

This chapter provides an overview of the capabilities of electronic
spreadsheets and presents the basic functions and features of 1-2-3
Release 4 for Windows. Following are some questions commonly asked
about this basic information.

Q: I am upgrading from a DOS version of 1-2-3. Can I expect a steep
learning curve?

A: 1-2-3 Release 4 for Windows provides assistance for those upgrading from previous releases of 1-2-3. In addition to providing on-line
help, 1-2-3 for Windows also offers a guided tour and tutorials that
help you get up and running with 1-2-3 for Windows.

The 1-2-3 Tour is a 40-minute help session that aids you in learning worksheet basics as well as charting, drawing, working with
databases, and other major 1-2-3 features. The 1-2-3 Tour is available through a separate icon in the Windows Program Manager.

On-line tutorials also help you learn worksheet basics with quick
hands-on lessons. Each lesson varies from five to ten minutes; the
lessons are available from the 1-2-3 Help menu.

1-2-3 for Windows makes the transition easier for users of 1-2-3 for DOS by retaining the menu from 1-2-3 Release 3.1. The 1-2-3 Classic menu enables you to select most commands in the way you are accustomed. 1-2-3 also supplies the equivalent 1-2-3 for Windows commands. You need only highlight a command in the 1-2-3 Classic menu and press F1 (Help) to learn the equivalent 1-2-3 for Windows command.

Q: Can I use files created in previous releases of 1-2-3 in 1-2-3 for Windows Release 4?

A: You can open both .WK1 and .WK3 files in Release 4 and save them in their original format or as .WK4 files.

However, because 1-2-3 Release 4 has new features that are not available in prior releases of 1-2-3, that information will be lost when you save a Release 4 file as a .WK1 or .WK3 file. If you want to retain these features, save the file as a .WK4 file before you save it as .WK1 or .WK3 file.

Summary

1-2-3 Release 4 for Windows is an impressive sequel to earlier versions of 1-2-3, the program that revolutionized computing during the 1980s. 1-2-3 for Windows is a graphical spreadsheet that runs under DOS and Windows 3.0 or 3.1 and takes full advantage of the graphical user interface and Windows multitasking capability. The program supports features such as external data access, three-dimensional worksheets, network support, and file linking. 1-2-3 Release 4 for Windows also provides improved graphics, WYSIWYG display, full mouse support, and powerful new utilities.

The next chapter shows you how to use the Windows graphical user interface, the mouse, and the menus.

Understanding the Graphical User Interface

The graphical spreadsheet program 1-2-3 Release 4 for Windows runs under Microsoft Windows 3.1, a graphical user interface. Such an interface is easier to use than a character-based interface and provides a better on-screen display of text and graphics. When you apply the advantages of a graphical user interface to 1-2-3, you can accomplish the following tasks:

- Link to and use data from other Windows 3.1 applications

- Display graphs and worksheets at the same time—either in the same window or in separate ones

- Use multitasking to run 1-2-3 for Windows and other applications at the same time

- Incorporate graphic images from other Windows 3.1 applications in worksheets

- Execute other Windows 3.1 applications by using 1-2-3 for Windows macro commands

This chapter presents the components of the 1-2-3 Release 4 for Windows graphical user interface and shows you how to use them effectively. In this chapter, you learn how to do the following tasks:

- Start and exit 1-2-3 for Windows

- Use the mouse with 1-2-3 for Windows

- Change the size, position, and arrangement of windows

- Use pull-down, cascade, and quick menus

- Use dialog boxes

Understanding Microsoft Windows Basics

Microsoft Windows 3.1 is a powerful, easy-to-use extension to the MS-DOS operating system. If you are new to Windows 3.1, the following basic information should help you get started with Windows 3.1.

Windows 3.1 is a *graphical user interface* (GUI). A GUI combined with a PC that has an 80286, 80386, or 80486 processor offers new levels of power and ease of use compared to non-GUI operating environments (such as DOS). Windows 3.1 has two operating modes: *standard mode* and *386-enhanced mode*.

A mouse is highly recommended although not specifically required. Using Windows 3.1 and 1-2-3 for Windows is much easier with a mouse.

Windows 3.1 can run DOS programs and Windows programs (as a matter of fact, programs like 1-2-3 for Windows, Ami Pro, and PageMaker for Windows cannot run without Windows 3.1). Programs designed for Windows 3.1 have many advantages over non-Windows programs, including the capability to access much more memory than the 640K available to DOS-based programs.

One feature that makes Windows 3.1 programs easier to use is the nature of the GUI. Instead of typing commands to start and run a Windows 3.1 program, you can select the program's *application icon* (a small picture that represents the program). Figure 2.1 shows several typical Windows 3.1 application icons displayed in the Windows Applications group window.

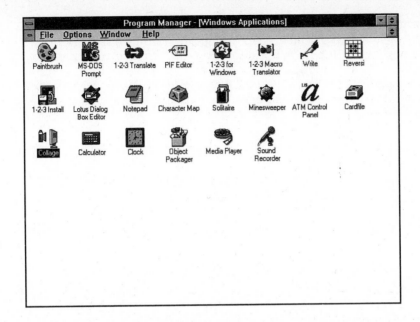

FIG. 2.1

Some typical
Windows 3.1
applications.

To run an application with a mouse, move the mouse pointer to the icon and double-click the left mouse button.

Running an application with the keyboard is slightly more complex. First, make certain that the window containing the icon is the active window—the window whose border is highlighted. If that window is not active, press Ctrl+Tab until the desired window is active (or select the group window name from the Window menu). Then use the direction keys to highlight the desired application icon (when an application icon is selected, its program name is displayed in reverse video). Finally, press Enter to run the program.

Starting 1-2-3 for Windows

If you have installed 1-2-3 for Windows according to the directions in Appendix A, the 1-2-3 for Windows program is stored in the C:\123R4W\PROGRAMS drive and directory. The 1-2-3 for Windows icons may be in a separate group window, called Lotus Applications, or located in the Windows Applications group window.

When you install 1-2-3 for Windows, the program's icon and the 1-2-3 Install icon are placed in their own group window instead of the Windows Applications group window (see fig. 2.2). If you choose to install the 1-2-3 for Windows Translate program, the Dialog Box Editor, Macro Translator, 1-2-3 Tour, the 1-2-3 IBM Database Catalog Tool, or the View Product Updates, these application icons are located in the same group window.

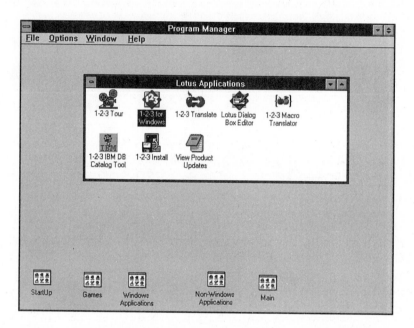

FIG. 2.2

The 1-2-3 for Windows application icons.

You may not want a separate group window for the 1-2-3 for Windows programs. You may find accessing 1-2-3 for Windows easier if you move the icons to the Windows Applications group window. Although you can have as many group windows as you like, too many groups clutter the Windows 3.1 Desktop. Reducing group windows to icons helps relieve the clutter, but you must restore the group-window icon before you can select its application icons. If you place major Windows 3.1 applications in the Windows Applications group window and do not reduce the group window to an icon, finding and running these programs is easier.

Windows 3.1 limits each group window to 40 applications items per group. You might want to restrict the Windows Applications group window to contain only major applications icons. You can use another window for secondary applications items. For instance, you might want to store the less frequently used applications, such as the Translate Utility and the View Product Updates programs, in the Lotus Applications group window.

Move the 1-2-3 for Windows application to the Startup group window to automatically run 1-2-3 whenever you start Windows.

T I P

The method you use to move the application icons depends on whether you have a mouse. To move the 1-2-3 for Windows icons to the Windows Applications group window by using a mouse, follow these steps:

1. Start Windows 3.1 by entering **WIN** at the DOS prompt.

2. If necessary, open the Windows Applications group window by double-clicking on its icon. Activate the Windows group window containing the 1-2-3 for Windows application icons (usually Lotus Applications) and use the mouse pointer to point to the 1-2-3 for Windows application icon.

3. Press and hold the left mouse button and drag the icon to an open position in the Windows Applications group window. Release the mouse button.

4. Repeat steps 2 and 3 for any additional icons you want to move (the 1-2-3 Install application icon, the 1-2-3 Translate icon, the Dialog Box Editor icon, the Macro Translator icon, the 1-2-3 Tour icon, the View Product Updates, or the 1-2-3 IBM Database Catalog Tool icon, if you installed these programs).

5. If you moved all the 1-2-3 application icons, delete the now-empty group window that contained the 1-2-3 for Windows application icons. To delete the window, click the mouse within the group window; then select File Delete by pressing Alt+F and then D, or, alternatively, press Del and then Enter to confirm the deletion.

6. If you chose not to move all the icons, you can delete them from the group window. Click the icon to select it; then select File Delete by pressing Alt+F and then D, or, alternatively, press Del and then Enter to confirm the deletion. If you want to keep the icons active, choose Close from the Control menu to close the group window.

To move the 1-2-3 for Windows icons to the Windows Applications group window by using the keyboard, follow these steps:

1. Start Windows 3.1 by entering **WIN** at the DOS prompt.

2. Activate the group window containing the 1-2-3 for Windows application icons (usually Lotus Applications) by pressing Ctrl+Tab until the window's title bar is highlighted.

3. Select the 1-2-3 for Windows icon using the direction keys.

4. Select File Move by pressing Alt+F and then M; alternatively, press F7 (Move). The Move Program Item dialog box (shown in fig. 2.3) appears. If the suggested destination in the To Group box is not the Windows Applications group window, use the up and down arrows to select the destination from the To Group list box; then press Enter.

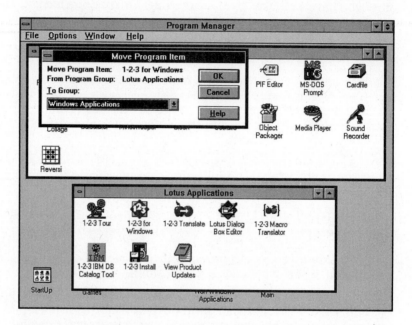

FIG. 2.3

The Move
Program Item
dialog box.

5. Repeat steps 3 and 4 to move other applicable icons (the 1-2-3 Install application icon, the 1-2-3 Translate icon, the Lotus Dialog Box Editor icon, the 1-2-3 Macro Translator icon, the 1-2-3 Tour icon, the View Product Updates icon, and the 1-2-3 IBM Database Catalog Tool icon) from the Lotus group window to the Windows Applications group window.

6. If you chose not to move all the icons, you can delete them from the group window. Click the icon to select it; then select File Delete by pressing Alt+F and then D, or, alternatively, press Del and then Enter to confirm the deletion. If you want to keep the icons active, choose Close from the Control menu to close the group window.

Starting 1-2-3 for Windows from the Program Manager

Whether or not you place the 1-2-3 for Windows icon in the Windows Applications group window, you start the program by double-clicking the mouse pointer on the application icon or by highlighting the icon with the direction keys and pressing Enter. If the 1-2-3 for Windows icon is contained in a group window that is itself an icon, you first must open the group-window icon before you can select the 1-2-3 for Windows application icon.

Before you can start 1-2-3 for Windows from the Program Manager, the group window that contains the 1-2-3 for Windows application icon must be active. To activate a group window, press Alt+Esc repeatedly until the Program Manager is in the foreground; press Ctrl+Tab as necessary (or click anywhere inside the window with the mouse) to select the window.

If you do not want to start 1-2-3 for Windows by selecting its application icon—perhaps because its group window has been reduced to an icon—you can use the Program Manager's File Run command. To start 1-2-3 for Windows by using this method, choose File Run. The Run dialog box appears. If you installed 1-2-3 according to the instructions in Appendix A, enter **C:\123R4W\PROGRAMS\123W.EXE** in the Command Line text box as shown in figure 2.4 and press Enter to start 1-2-3 for Windows.

> If you don't remember the drive and directory name of the program you want to run, click the Browse button in the Run dialog box to find and insert the program file's path name.

T I P

Starting 1-2-3 for Windows from DOS

Although 1-2-3 for Windows requires Windows 3.1, you can start 1-2-3 for Windows from the DOS command line if you pass the proper parameters to Windows 3.1. The basic syntax for starting any Windows 3.1 program from the DOS command line is as follows (the file extension is optional):

WIN /*mode drive:**path*\program.*extension*

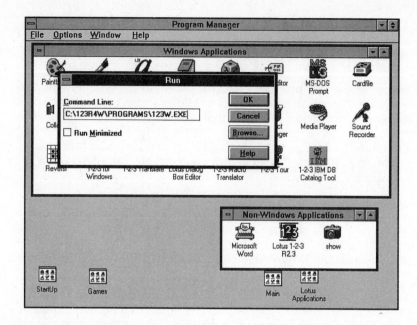

FIG. 2.4

Using the Run
dialog box to
start 1-2-3 for
Windows.

To start 1-2-3 for Windows from the command line by using the default
Windows 3.1 mode (which depends on your system), enter the following at the DOS prompt:

WIN C:\123R4W\PROGRAMS\123W.EXE

You also can open a 1-2-3 worksheet file by including the name of the
file in the prompt. To start 1-2-3 for Windows and open a specific
worksheet file from the command line, enter the following at the DOS
prompt:

WIN \123R4W\PROGRAMS\123W *path\filename.extension*

For example, to open a file named SALES.WK4 located in the FILES
subdirectory, enter the following at the DOS prompt:

WIN \123R4W\PROGRAMS\123W C:\FILES\SALES

If you often start 1-2-3 for Windows from the command line and you
use DOS 5, you may want to create a DOSKEY macro that enters the
proper commands. To create a DOS macro called 1234W, enter the
following:

**DOSKEY 1234W=C: $T CD \123R4W\PROGRAMS $T WIN
123W.EXE**

After creating this macro, you can start 1-2-3 for Windows by entering the following at the DOS prompt:

1234W

If you have not yet upgraded to DOS 5, you can create a small batch file to start 1-2-3 for Windows from the command line. To create this batch file, enter the following at the DOS prompt:

COPY CON 1234W.BAT
C:
CD \123R4W\PROGRAMS
WIN 123W.EXE

Press F6 and then Enter after the final line. The end-of-file character (^Z) is inserted at the end of the batch file.

 NOTE   1234W.BAT must be located in a directory specified by your PATH command.

After creating this batch file, you can start 1-2-3 for Windows by entering the following at the DOS prompt:

1234W

Using the Mouse

One of the most exciting 1-2-3 for Windows features is its mouse capabilities. As with the keyboard, the mouse enables you to choose commands and manipulate objects on-screen. You can perform many tasks more quickly with the mouse, such as moving through windows, setting column widths, and moving around in dialog boxes. Some tasks in 1-2-3 for Windows can be performed *only* with a mouse (such as using SmartIcons, selecting individual elements in a chart, selecting collections of data, and selecting one or more drawn objects). 1-2-3's quick menus are only available if you have a mouse.

Move the mouse pointer around the screen by moving the mouse on a flat surface with your hand. The mouse pointer moves in the same direction as your hand. Usually, the mouse pointer is in the shape of an arrow (see fig. 2.5). As you perform different tasks in 1-2-3 for Windows, the mouse pointer changes shape. In the Help window, for example, the mouse pointer becomes a hand with an extended index finger, indicating that you can select highlighted Help topics. Table 2.1 explains the various shapes of the mouse pointer.

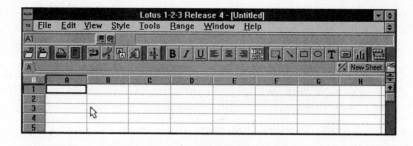

FIG. 2.5

The mouse pointer moves in the same direction as the mouse.

Table 2.1 Mouse Pointers

Shape	Description	Meaning
[1,2]	Black two-headed arrow	You can create or resize a window pane. If the mouse pointer is in a row or column heading and close to a grid line, you can widen a column or heighten a row.
[3]	Hand pointing left	You can select drawn objects.
[4]	Hand pointing up	The pointer is over a high-lighted Help topic or a macro button.
[5]	Hourglass	1-2-3 for Windows is in the middle of an operation and you cannot do anything with the mouse.
[6]	I-beam	The pointer is over data in a contents box or a text box; if you click on the box, you can edit or enter data.
[7]	Open hand	The pointer is over a worksheet range; you can drag the current selection or a copy of the current selection.
[8]	Pencil	You can use the pointer to create a freehand drawing.
[9]	Thin black cross	You can position a drawn object.

Shape	Description	Meaning
[10]	White arrow	You can perform normal operations, such as selecting ranges and menu commands.
[11]	White two-headed arrow	If the mouse pointer is on a window border, you can resize the window.
[12]	White four-headed arrow	If you choose Size or Move from the Control menu and the mouse pointer is on a window border, you can resize the window by using the keyboard.
[13]	Box with an arrow	You can select a worksheet range.
[14]	Closed fist	You can drag the current selection to a new location.
[15]	Closed fist with +	You can drag a copy of the current selection to a new location.
[16]	Cross and small chart	You can position a new chart on the worksheet.

Most mouse devices have a left and a right button. You use the left button to select cells and ranges, use menus, and enter information in dialog boxes. When the mouse pointer highlights a SmartIcon, pressing the right mouse button displays the SmartIcon's description. If you select a range of cells or an object in a chart, clicking the right mouse button displays a context-sensitive quick menu.

> **T I P**
>
> If a highlighted Help topic has a dotted underline, click and hold the left mouse button to read the topic. If the underline is solid, click the left button to read the topic.

Table 2.2 describes the mouse terminology you need to know as you read this book.

Table 2.2 Mouse Terminology

Term	Meaning
Point	Place the mouse pointer over the menu, cell, or data you want to select or move.
Click	Press and quickly release the left mouse button.
Double-click	Quickly press and release the left mouse button twice.
Drag	Press and hold the left mouse button and then move the mouse. This action, which is also called "click-and-drag," is usually performed to highlight a range of cells or to move an object.
Select	To select a range of cells, click and drag the mouse pointer over the range. To select an object, click the mouse pointer on the object.

Using the Control Menus

You use the 1-2-3 window to display and work with 1-2-3 for Windows worksheet files. The small rectangle in the upper-left corner of the screen is the *1-2-3 Control menu box* and accesses the *1-2-3 Control menu.* This menu is similar to the Control menu in all Windows 3.1 applications: it enables you to manipulate the size and position of the 1-2-3 window, close 1-2-3 for Windows, and switch to other Windows 3.1 applications (see fig. 2.6).

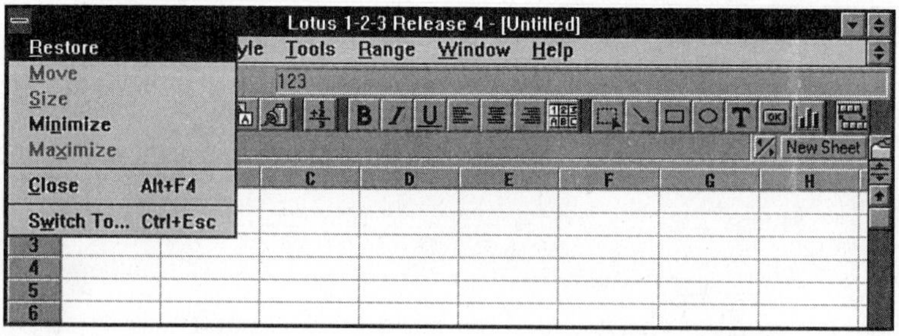

FIG. 2.6

The 1-2-3 for Windows Control menu.

The menu shown in figure 2.6 has seven options, but Move, Size, and Maximize are *dimmed* (or *grayed*); this means that their functions are currently unavailable. Because 1-2-3 for Windows is running as a full-screen application (that is, it is *maximized*) in this figure, the three grayed choices are inappropriate. If you are running 1-2-3 for Windows in a partial-screen window or have reduced it to an icon (that is, have *minimized* the window), different choices on this menu are dimmed, indicating that they are currently unavailable.

To access the 1-2-3 Control menu with the keyboard, press Alt and then the space bar. To select a command from the Control menu, type the underlined letter of the command; alternatively, use the arrow keys to highlight the command and then press Enter.

To access the 1-2-3 Control menu with the mouse, click on the 1-2-3 Control menu box and then click on the command you want to activate.

The *Worksheet Control menu* controls the size and position of the Worksheet window; it is accessed through the *Worksheet Control menu box*—the small rectangle in the upper-left corner of the Worksheet window. Although similar to the 1-2-3 Control menu, the Worksheet Control menu applies only to its own Worksheet window. The 1-2-3 Control menu's Switch To option (which switches between active Windows 3.1 applications) is replaced on the Worksheet Control menu by the Next option (which switches between active 1-2-3 Worksheet windows). Figure 2.7 shows the Worksheet Control menu.

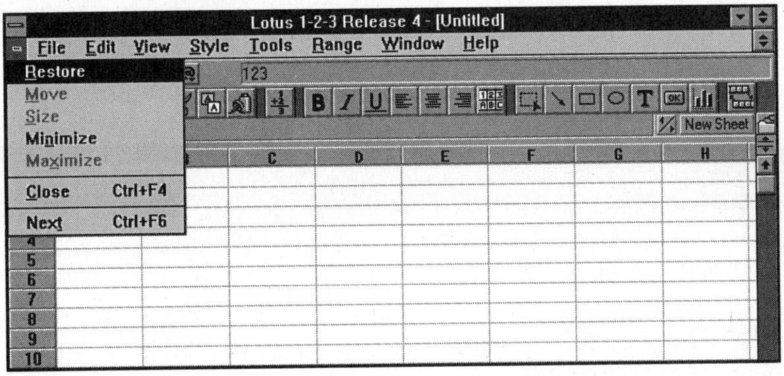

FIG. 2.7

The Worksheet Control menu.

> The 1-2-3 Control menu controls the 1-2-3 window; the Worksheet Control menu controls a single Worksheet window within the 1-2-3 window.
>
> **T I P**

To access the Worksheet Control menu with the keyboard, press Alt+- (hyphen). To select a command, type the underlined letter of the command; alternatively, use the arrow keys to highlight the command and then press Enter.

To activate the Worksheet Control menu with the mouse, click on the Worksheet Control menu box and then click on the command you want to activate.

To close the Worksheet Control menu by using the keyboard, press Esc twice. To close the Worksheet Control menu with the mouse, click anywhere outside the menu.

Using Command Menus

Almost every task you perform in 1-2-3 for Windows is part of a *command*. Commands help you analyze and organize data effectively, copy and move data, graph and format data, sort and manipulate databases, open and close worksheet files, and customize worksheets with colors and fonts.

Using the 1-2-3 for Windows Main Menu

Unlike other versions of 1-2-3, the 1-2-3 for Windows menus always appear on-screen. The commands that appear in the 1-2-3 for Windows main menu depend on what tool or utility you are using. For example, if you are working with a 1-2-3 database, the Query menu command replaces the Range menu command in the main menu. The menu you use most often is the 1-2-3 for Windows main menu. Other 1-2-3 for Windows menus are the Help window menu and the Transcript window menu.

1-2-3 for Windows also includes the 1-2-3 Classic menu. This menu is included primarily for macro compatibility with earlier 1-2-3 releases. To access the 1-2-3 Release 3.1 main menu, press the slash key (/) or press the colon key (:) to access the Wysiwyg menu. The 1-2-3 Classic menu, which is composed of the 1-2-3 for DOS Release 3.1 main and Wysiwyg menus, is not covered in this book.

To access a command on the main menu with the keyboard, first activate the menu by pressing the Alt or F10 (Menu) key. An inverse video highlight, the *menu pointer*, appears in the menu bar. Use the left and right arrows to move the menu pointer in the main menu.

You can choose a command with the keyboard in one of two ways: use the direction keys to select the menu item and then press Enter, or type the underlined letter of the menu item (usually the first letter).

When you activate the main menu and press the right- or left-arrow key, the menu pointer moves across the menu bar and highlights commands. When you reach the first or last item in the main menu, pressing the right- or left-arrow key activates the Control menus for the 1-2-3 window and the Worksheet window.

You can also perform common 1-2-3 and Windows 3.1 commands by using the accelerator keys. For instance, to save the current worksheet file, press and hold Ctrl and press S. When a command has an accelerator key, the key sequence is displayed to the right of the command name in the menu. A complete listing of keyboard shortcuts appears in Chapter 3, "Learning Worksheet Basics."

If you use the mouse to choose commands, you do not have to activate the main menu first. Just click the command you want to use.

Using Pull-Down Menus and Cascade Menus

All the commands on the 1-2-3 for Windows main menu lead to pull-down menus; many (but not all) pull-down menus lead to cascade menus. 1-2-3 for Windows uses *pull-down menus* to organize its first level of commands. If a command has an additional level of commands, a *cascade menu* appears beside the pull-down menu (see fig. 2.8). Cascade menus look and function just like pull-down menus.

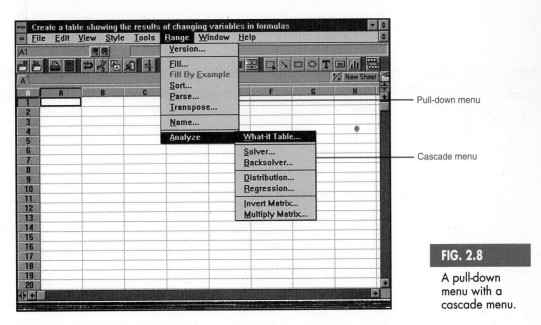

FIG. 2.8

A pull-down menu with a cascade menu.

Menu items can appear with a triangle, an *ellipsis* (...), or nothing beside them. If the menu item has a triangle, the item results in a cascade menu when selected. If the menu item has an ellipsis, 1-2-3 for Windows needs more information to complete the command and displays a *dialog box* for you to complete. If the menu item has no marker, the item is usually the last selection in the command sequence: if you click on the command (or highlight it and press Enter), 1-2-3 for Windows executes the selected command. Figure 2.9 displays a menu with several commands that have triangles and ellipses.

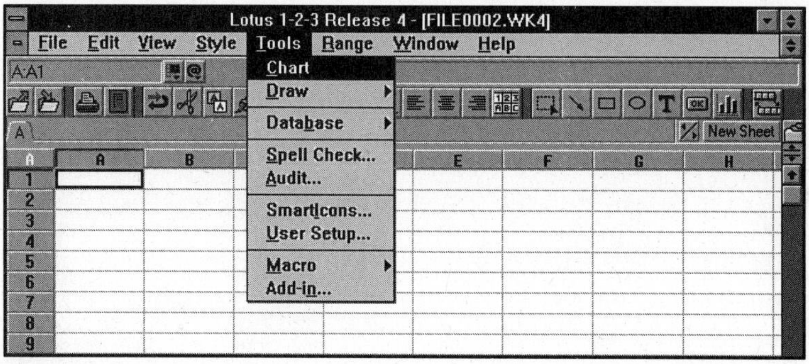

FIG. 2.9

A pull-down menu, showing commands with triangles and ellipses.

To select a command from a pull-down or cascade menu, use the up-arrow and down-arrow keys to move through the commands or type the underlined letter of the command you want to select. If you use a mouse, just click on the command.

You can cancel some commands by pressing Ctrl+Break or by pressing Esc. Depending on the command you have selected, the Esc key some-times cancels the command completely; sometimes, pressing Esc backs up one menu level at a time. With the mouse, click anywhere outside a menu to cancel the command (if a dialog box is displayed, click on the Cancel button in the dialog box).

Occasionally, a menu item on a pull-down or cascade menu appears in gray (that is, it is dimmed). As mentioned earlier, when a command appears in gray, you cannot choose that command. For example, the function of the Edit Paste command is to paste data from the Windows Clipboard to the worksheet. You cannot paste data from the Clipboard unless you have previously cut or copied data to the Clipboard. If you access the Edit menu and the Paste command appears in gray, this command is unavailable because there is no data in the Clipboard that can be pasted. Whether you choose this command with the keyboard or click on Paste with the mouse, nothing happens.

Using Quick Menus

1-2-3's context-sensitive quick menus contain frequently used commands that pertain to the currently selected item. You access a quick menu by selecting a range of data and then clicking the right mouse button. For instance, if you select a range of cells and click the right mouse button, 1-2-3 displays a quick menu that contains commands that you can apply to the range of cells. Figure 2.10 shows the quick menu that appears when you select a range of worksheet cells.

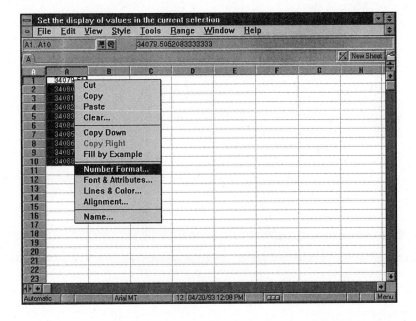

FIG. 2.10

A quick menu showing commands that you can apply to the highlighted range of data.

You choose commands from a quick menu in the same manner as you do from the 1-2-3 main menu. You can use the keyboard to move the menu highlight through the commands and press Enter to choose a command, or you can type the underlined character that appears in each command name. To choose the command by using the mouse, you click the command item.

For Related Information

▶▶ "Working with Command Menus," p. 135.

▶▶ "Using Quick Menus," p. 138.

FROM HERE...

Using Dialog Boxes

When 1-2-3 for Windows needs more information about a menu command, a *dialog box* is displayed. To execute the command, you must complete the dialog box and choose OK or press Enter. You also can cancel a command before it executes by choosing Cancel or pressing Esc to close the dialog box. The following sections explain how to use dialog boxes.

Understanding the Parts of a Dialog Box

A dialog box contains many sections so that you can read and enter information easily. 1-2-3 for Windows uses many dialog boxes that contain different parts; but every dialog box has a *title bar* and *command buttons* (see fig. 2.11). The title bar displays the name of the dialog box. When one dialog box appears in front of another, the title bar of the active dialog box is highlighted.

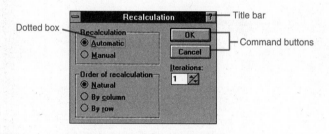

FIG. 2.11

A typical
dialog box.

When you choose a command button, you execute or cancel a command. To confirm the selections in a dialog box and execute the command the dialog box controls, you choose OK. To cancel the command and close the dialog box, choose Cancel or press Esc or Ctrl+Break.

The names on some buttons are followed by three periods (an ellipsis) to indicate that an additional dialog box appears if you select the button. Other buttons, such as OK and Cancel, execute a selection with no further action required.

A dialog box is composed primarily of *fields*; fields organize *options* (also called *choices*). Before you can specify an option, you first must select the field. The *dotted box* in a dialog box functions like the menu pointer: when an option is highlighted (shown in a dotted box) in a dialog box, you can select that option. When the dotted box appears in a command button, you can press Enter to execute the button.

 NOTE Not all fields have an underlined letter or can be surrounded by the dotted box. A field that has no underlined letter acts as a label for the choices below it. You do not have to worry about selecting these fields; you can bypass them and select the choices below them directly. When you select an option, the markers and the highlight move to show what you can select next.

You rarely need to fill in every field of a dialog box. For example, the dialog box shown in figure 2.11 has several options. To set just the type of recalculation, choose Automatic or Manual and then choose OK or press Enter to confirm the whole dialog box. You don't have to select an option from the Order of Recalculation area or specify a number in the Iterations text box to consider yourself finished with the dialog box.

Figures 2.12, 2.13, 2.14, and 2.15 show the types of fields 1-2-3 for Windows uses in its dialog boxes. The following sections describe these fields.

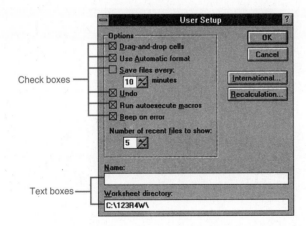

FIG. 2.12

A dialog box with check boxes and text boxes.

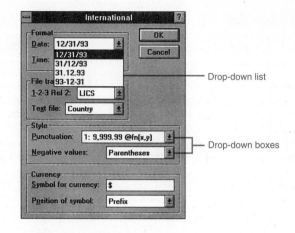

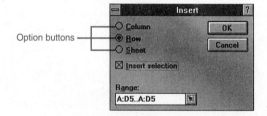

FIG. 2.13

A dialog box with drop-down boxes; notice that the Date option displays the drop-down list of choices.

FIG. 2.14

A dialog box with option buttons.

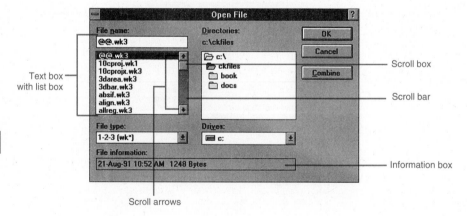

FIG. 2.15

A dialog box with list boxes.

Check Boxes

Check boxes turn choices on or off. If a choice is turned on, an X appears in the box.

To select or deselect a check box with the keyboard, press Alt and the underlined letter. Alternatively, select the field by using the Tab key and then use the direction keys to move through the choices. Then press the space bar to select the choice and put an X in the check box. If the check box already contains an X, pressing the space bar makes the X disappear and turns off the choice (*deselects* it).

If you use a mouse, click on a check box to turn it on or off. Check boxes can be selected or deselected regardless of the status of the other check boxes in the dialog box.

Option Buttons

Option buttons (also called *radio buttons*) indicate choices within a field of mutually exclusive items. You can select only one option button at a time in a field.

To select an option button with the keyboard, press Alt and the underlined letter. Or select the field by using the Tab key and then use the direction keys to move through the options. If you make a mistake, select another option button; 1-2-3 for Windows deselects the option button you selected by accident because only one option button in a group can be selected at a time.

Text Boxes

A *text box* is a box in which you type information, such as worksheet ranges or file names. 1-2-3 for Windows includes several types of text boxes in which you can type and edit text. Text boxes can appear with or without *list boxes* (described in the next section). When text boxes appear alone, you must enter information in the box. Usually, you type this information, but sometimes you can use the mouse to enter the information. For example, 1-2-3 for Windows often uses text boxes to ask for the range a command affects. You can specify a range by pointing with the mouse or by using the keyboard. To specify a range with the keyboard, type the range address; alternatively, you can use the arrow keys. The dialog box is removed from view as you select the range, and reappears when you press Enter. To use the mouse to select a range, click the Range selector icon at the far right of the text box to remove the dialog box from view and highlight the range. When you release the mouse button, the dialog box reappears.

Sometimes 1-2-3 for Windows fills in a text box with a suggested file name or path. To accept the suggestion, press Enter. To erase the suggestion and type your own entry, begin typing; the suggested information is erased. To edit the text box, press F2 (Edit) and then type the additional information. If you use the mouse, move the mouse pointer to the error location. When the mouse pointer changes from an arrow to an I-beam, click to display the cursor, use Del and Backspace to erase the incorrect characters, and then type the correct information. If you highlight some or all of the characters in the text box before you begin typing, those characters are replaced by the new characters you type.

List Boxes

List boxes display lists of choices. You can select only one choice from a list box. With the keyboard, use the direction keys to highlight the choice you want and then press Enter. With the mouse, click on your choice. A list box often has a text box on top that displays the choice highlighted in the list box. As you use the direction keys to highlight different choices, notice that the text box changes to reflect the new choices.

If a list box has more choices than it can display, you can scroll through the list box and see all the choices by using the direction keys and the PgUp, PgDn, Home, and End keys. If you use the mouse, click on the *scroll arrows* (the up and down arrows) or drag the *scroll box* in the *scroll bar* to scroll the list box.

Information Boxes

Information boxes display information about the current worksheet file. For example, in the Open File dialog box in figure 2.15, the information box called File Information tells you how many bytes of disk space the currently selected file occupies, as well as the date and time the file was created. You cannot type information in an information box.

Drop-Down Boxes

Drop-down boxes contain two or more choices. You display the choices in a drop-down box by clicking on the arrow at the right end of the drop-down box or by highlighting the drop-down box and pressing Alt+down arrow. To select an item from the drop-down box with the keyboard, press the first letter of the item or use the up and down arrow keys to move to the item. If you use a mouse, click on the item.

Navigating Fields

If you use the mouse in a dialog box, you do not need to select a field before specifying the choice you want; just click on the choice to select it. Moving around in a dialog box often is easier with the mouse. Table 2.3 describes how the direction keys work in a dialog box.

Table 2.3 Dialog Box Keys

Key	Action
←	Moves to the preceding choice in a field
→	Moves to the next choice in a field
↑	Moves to the preceding choice in a field; in a list box, highlights the item one level up
↓	Moves to the next choice in a field; in a list box, highlights the item one level down
Ctrl+Break	Cancels a dialog box
Del	Deselects a check box; in a text box, deletes text to the right of the cursor
End	Moves to the last choice in a list box
Enter	Completes the command and closes the dialog box
Esc	Closes the dialog box without completing the command; equivalent to selecting Cancel
Home	Moves to the first choice in a list box
PgDn	Scrolls down a list box
PgUp	Scrolls up a list box
Shift+Tab	Moves to the preceding field
Space bar	Toggles a selection in a check box

continues

Table 2.3 Continued

Key	Action
Tab	Moves to the next field
Alt+*letter*	Moves to and selects an option with the underlined *letter* you pressed
*letter	In a text box, moves to and selects an option with the first letter you press
Alt+ Space bar	Opens the Control menu of a dialog box (the Control menu contains commands to move and close the dialog box)

Moving a Dialog Box

Occasionally, a dialog box covers worksheet data you need to see to complete the command. To see the worksheet data, you have to move the dialog box.

You can use the keyboard to move a dialog box by pressing Alt+- (hyphen) to open the Control menu for the dialog box and then selecting Move (see fig. 2.16). A four-headed arrow appears in the dialog box; use the direction keys to move the box.

Dialog box control menu

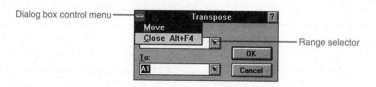

Range selector

FIG. 2.16

Moving a dialog box.

To move the dialog box with the mouse, move the mouse pointer to the dialog-box title bar, click on the title bar by pressing and holding the left mouse button, and drag the dialog box to another location.

If you use the range selector to specify a range in a dialog box, 1-2-3 for Windows temporarily removes the dialog box from the screen so that you can see data and select cells freely.

FROM HERE...

For Related Information

▶▶ "Working with Command Menus," p. 135.

Manipulating Windows

You can change the size and position of the 1-2-3 window or a Worksheet window by using the mouse or the keyboard. You can enlarge a window to fill the entire screen, reduce the window to a smaller size, or shrink the window to an icon.

Maximizing and Restoring Windows

When you *maximize* the 1-2-3 window, it fills the screen. When you maximize the Worksheet window and other windows within the 1-2-3 window, each window fills the work area of the 1-2-3 window.

The Control menu of each window has a Maximize command. To maximize a window with the keyboard, select the Maximize command from the appropriate Control menu. If you use the mouse to maximize a window, you don't need the Control menus. At the top right corner of the screen and of each window are a *Minimize button* and a *Maximize button* or a *Restore button*.

You click on a window's Maximize button to enlarge that window. When you maximize the 1-2-3 window or a Worksheet window, the Maximize button changes to the Restore button (the Restore button appears only when a window is maximized). In figure 2.17, the Worksheet window is maximized; the Restore button appears instead of the Maximize button. (The 1-2-3 window in this figure is slightly reduced from the maximized size so that you can see the 1-2-3 window's Maximize button.)

> Double-click on the title bar to maximize a window.   **T I P**

If you select the Restore command from the Control menu or click on the Restore button, 1-2-3 for Windows restores the window to its previous size—that is, the size it was before it was last maximized.

Minimizing Windows

To shrink the 1-2-3 window to an icon on the Desktop, select the Minimize command from the 1-2-3 Control menu or click on the Minimize button of the 1-2-3 window. If you are using another Windows application and want to run 1-2-3 for Windows in the background, you can minimize the 1-2-3 window or use Ctrl+Esc to switch to the other application.

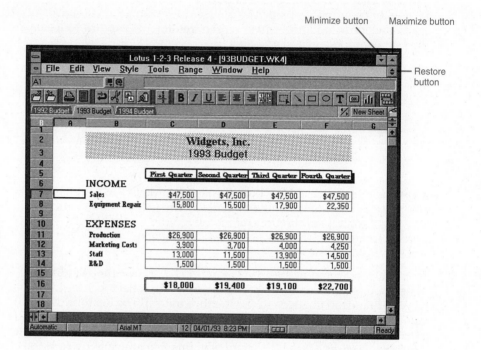

FIG. 2.17

The upper right corner of the window displays the Minimize and Maximize or Restore buttons.

You can shrink a Worksheet window in the 1-2-3 window to an icon by selecting the Minimize command from the Worksheet Control menu or by clicking on the window's Minimize button. Minimizing Worksheet windows can be useful if you are working with several utilities or worksheet files. Each type of window is identified by its own icon. For example, the Transcript window icon has a movie camera; the Worksheet window icon has a grid. Figure 2.18 shows examples of these icons.

Sizing Windows

To change the size of a window, use the Size command from the window's Control menu and the direction keys; alternatively, use the mouse. You also can control the display of Worksheet windows by using the Window Tile and Window Cascade commands.

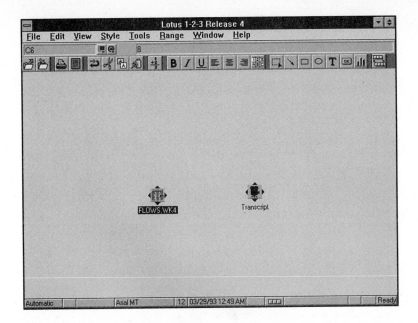

FIG. 2.18

Windows
reduced to icons.

To size the 1-2-3 window or a Worksheet window with the keyboard, select the Size command from the appropriate Control menu. When the mouse pointer changes to a four-headed white arrow, use the direction keys to move the arrow and resize the window. As you resize the window, an outline shows the size and shape of the window. Press the left and right arrows to change the window horizontally; press the up and down arrows to change the window vertically. Press Enter when you have sized the window as desired.

To size a window with the mouse, move the mouse pointer to the border you want to change. When the mouse pointer changes to a thick white double arrow, press and hold the left mouse button and drag the border to its new location.

Moving Windows

With the keyboard or mouse, you can move a window or its icon. With the keyboard, choose the Move command from the appropriate Control menu, use the direction keys to relocate the window or icon, and press Enter. An outline of the window or icon moves as you use the arrow keys. Moving a window is easier with the mouse: click on the title bar and drag the window to its new location. If the window is minimized, you can click on the window's icon and drag it to a new position.

Closing Windows

Each window's Control menu has a <u>C</u>lose command that enables you to close the 1-2-3 window or a Worksheet window. To close the 1-2-3 window with the mouse, double-click on the 1-2-3 Control menu box. To close a Worksheet window, double-click on the Worksheet Control menu box.

T I P   To quickly close the 1-2-3 window (or any Windows 3.1 application window), press Alt+F4 (Exit). To close a Worksheet window (or any Windows 3.1 document window), press Ctrl+F4 (Close).

If you have made any changes to a window and haven't saved them before you select the <u>C</u>lose command, a dialog box prompts you to save any files before closing the window (see fig. 2.19).

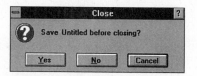

FIG. 2.19

The Close confirmation box.

Cascading Windows

Choose the <u>W</u>indow <u>C</u>ascade command or click on the Cascade Windows SmartIcon to arrange open windows so that they appear on top of one another, with only their title bars and the left edges of the windows showing (see fig. 2.20). The active window always appears on top. To use the keyboard to switch between cascaded windows, press Ctrl+F6 (Next). You can change the size and location of the cascaded windows as described in the preceding sections.

Tiling Windows

When you select <u>W</u>indow <u>T</u>ile or click on the Tile Windows SmartIcon, 1-2-3 for Windows sizes and arranges all open windows side by side, like floor tiles (see fig. 2.21). The active window's title bar has a dark background. To use the keyboard to switch between tiled windows, press Ctrl+F6 (Next). You can change the size and location of the tiled windows as described earlier in this chapter.

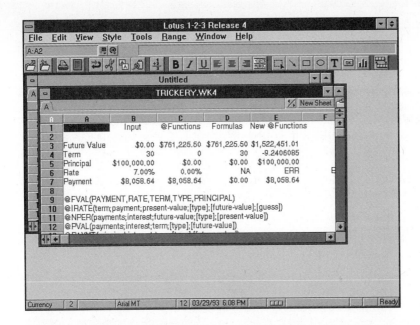

FIG. 2.20

Cascaded
windows.

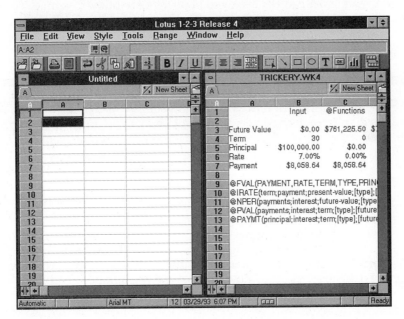

FIG. 2.21

Tiled windows.

Choosing a Window Display Mode

In addition to the cascade and tile display-mode options described in the preceding sections, 1-2-3 for Windows offers other choices for displaying Worksheet windows. You can, for example, split a Worksheet window into two panes either vertically or horizontally and maximize a Worksheet window to fill the entire work area. In addition, if you have multiple sheets in your worksheet file, you can display a three-dimensional view of your worksheet. With all these choices, you may find it difficult to choose the best display mode for your needs. The following guidelines may help you select the best display mode for your worksheets:

- Maximizing the window provides the largest visible work area.

- Tiling the windows enables you to view portions of several files at the same time.

- Cascading the windows provides a large visible work area for the current window (although not as large as a maximized window) and makes switching between files easy.

- A worksheet can be displayed in only one window at a time. To display two views of the same worksheet, use View Split Horizontal or View Split Vertical.

- If your worksheet contains multiple sheets, you can view three worksheets at the same time by using the View Split Perspective command.

The View Set View Preferences command enables you to further control the display of a worksheet window. Use this command to specify whether or not grid lines are displayed and to turn off the display of the edit line and status bar to maximize the 1-2-3 workspace.

Switching Windows

When you choose the Window command from the Worksheet Control menu, 1-2-3 for Windows lists up to nine open windows at the bottom of the Window menu; a check mark appears next to the active window's name. To make another window active, type the number displayed next to the window name, or click on the number in the menu with the mouse. If you have more than nine open windows, you can display the names of the additional windows by using the Window More Windows command (which appears only if more than nine windows are open).

You can make another window active without using the <u>W</u>indow menu. To cycle through the open windows in the 1-2-3 window, activating each window in turn, press Ctrl+F6 (Next). You also can activate a window by clicking anywhere inside that window.

Using the Task List

With the S<u>w</u>itch To command on the 1-2-3 Control menu, you can switch to the *Task List*, a Windows Program Manager utility that manages multiple applications. You can, for example, use the Task List to switch to the Print Manager so that you can pause or resume printing and remove print jobs from the print queue. To switch to the Task List with the keyboard, press Ctrl+Esc. Figure 2.22 shows the Task List window. For more information about the Task List, refer to your Windows documentation.

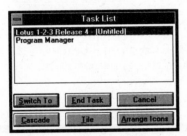

FIG. 2.22

The Windows 3.1 Task List window.

Press Alt+Tab to switch from application to application. If the application you switch to is reduced to an icon, the icon restores to a window when you release the Alt key.

T I P

For Related Information

▶▶ "Understanding Worksheets and Files," p. 100.

▶▶ "Understanding the 1-2-3 for Windows Menus," p. 134.

▶▶ "Changing the Display of a Worksheet File," p. 161.

▶▶ "Saving Files," p. 235.

▶▶ "Closing Files," p. 241.

FROM HERE...

Exiting from 1-2-3 for Windows

Windows 3.1 applications can open multiple document windows. You can, for example, have several different worksheet files open at the same time. 1-2-3 for Windows enables you to close individual Worksheet windows or to exit from 1-2-3 for Windows entirely—closing all open windows.

To exit from 1-2-3 for Windows and close all open windows at the same time, use the File Exit command or click on the End 1-2-3 Session SmartIcon.

To quit 1-2-3 for Windows and return to the Program Manager, use the following procedure with the keyboard:

1. Choose File Exit. If you have saved changes in active worksheet files, 1-2-3 closes. If you have not saved changes to active files, the confirmation box shown in figure 2.23 appears.

2. Select Yes to save the current worksheet file before exiting; select No to exit without saving the file; choose Cancel or press Enter to cancel the exit command and return to 1-2-3 for Windows. If you have multiple Worksheet windows open, select Save All to save all files before exiting.

FIG. 2.23

The Exit confirmation box.

You also can use the Windows 3.1 shortcut method of exiting 1-2-3 for Windows: Press Alt+F4 to make the Exit confirmation box appear. Make your selection as outlined in step 2.

To use the mouse to quit 1-2-3 for Windows and return to the Program Manager, double-click on the 1-2-3 Control menu box; the Exit confirmation box appears. Make your selection as outlined in step 2.

For Related Information

▶▶ "Saving Files," p. 235.

▶▶ "Closing Files," p. 241.

Questions & Answers

In this chapter, you learned the basic skills of working in a graphical environment. If you have any questions about any topic covered in this chapter and cannot find the answer in any of the help windows, scan this section.

Q: I cannot load Windows at the DOS prompt. What should I do?

A: Make sure that you are beginning with the proper directory. By default, this directory is C:\WINDOWS. You can use a word processing program or text editing program to add a PATH statement to your AUTOEXEC.BAT file to tell DOS which directories to search for external commands. A typical PATH statement looks like this:

```
PATH C:\DOS;C:\WINDOWS;C:\WORD
```

When it starts up, the computer searches the DOS directory, then the WINDOWS directory, and finally the WORD directory for any external commands you may type. For more details on the PATH statement, refer to your DOS documentation.

Q: I tried to load 1-2-3 for Windows by specifying a file name at the DOS prompt, but Windows didn't load the file. What went wrong?

A: When you name a file at the DOS prompt, Windows loads itself and then searches for the specified path and file name. If it cannot find either, an error message displays, and the Windows Program Manager is minimized and displayed at the lower left of the screen.

To load 1-2-3 for Windows, first double-click on the Program Manager to maximize it and then double-click on the 1-2-3 program icon; alternatively, select File Run and enter the file name in the Command Line text box.

Q: When I opened a new file, the worksheet I currently had opened disappeared. Where did it go?

A: When you open multiple worksheet windows in 1-2-3, each new window is placed on top of open windows. You can access the other worksheet files with the Window menu. To try it, choose Worksheet to open the Worksheet drop-down menu. At the bottom of the menu is a list of all worksheets that are currently open. Type the number to the left of the worksheet name or use the arrow keys to select the worksheet and press Enter.

You can also use the <u>N</u>ext command in the Worksheet Window control menu to switch between active windows. Press Alt+- to access the Worksheet Window Control menu and choose <u>N</u>ext; alternatively, press Ctrl+F6(Next) to switch active windows.

Q: When I start 1-2-3 the SmartIcon palette is not displayed. What happened to it?

A: The SmartIcon palette can be turned off to make more room on the desktop. To redisplay the SmartIcon palette choose <u>T</u>ools <u>S</u>martIcons, and select a location from the <u>P</u>osition drop-down box. For example, to display the SmartIcon palette at the bottom of the 1-2-3 Window, select <u>B</u>ottom. Click OK when you are finished to return to the worksheet.

You can also use the Status Bar to redisplay the SmartIcon palette. Click the SmartIcon button and choose the palette you want to display. 1-2-3 displays the palette in the position currently specified in the <u>T</u>ools <u>S</u>martIcon dialog box.

Q: When I start 1-2-3, several file names that I have previously loaded appear in a list at the bottom of the File menu. Is 1-2-3 loading these files?

A: 1-2-3 Release 4.0 for Windows stores up to the last five files you have opened at the bottom of the file menu. 1-2-3 does not automatically open any of these files. The files names are listed mainly for convenience. You can quickly open one of these files by choosing <u>F</u>ile and selecting one of the file names.

Q: When I double-click on the 1-2-3 for Windows icon to start the program, the following error message `MAIN123.EXE must be in your 1-2-3 program directory before you can run 1-2-3` appears. What happened to 1-2-3?

A: This message appears when Windows cannot find the file called 123W.EXE in the C:\123R4W\PROGRAMS subdirectory. When you install 1-2-3 for Windows, the 123W.EXE and MAIN123.EXE files are placed in the same subdirectory. If you move either of these files to a new location without moving the other, 1-2-3 does not load.

Move 123W.EXE back to the PROGRAMS subdirectory or move the MAIN123.EXE file to the same location as the 123W.EXE file to start 1-2-3.

Q: After moving programs to the Applications group window, the icons were jumbled into one area of the window. I resized the window and moved the icons manually, but wonder whether there is a quicker way to do this.

A: There are two ways to arrange icons in a group window. If you have already resized the group window, make sure that the window is still active and select Window Arrange Icons to arrange the icons in an orderly fashion. You also can arrange icons automatically whenever you resize a window. To do this, select Options Auto Arrange (when you do this, a check mark appears next to the command name, indicating that it is currently active). When you resize the window, the icons are automatically arranged. To turn off this feature, select the command again to remove the check mark.

To save your settings for subsequent Windows sessions, select Options Save Settings on Exit (a check mark appears next to the command).

Summary

In this chapter, you learned how to use the 1-2-3 for Windows graphical user interface. The chapter showed you how to use the mouse; change the size, position, and arrangement of windows; use the pull-down, cascade, and Control menus; and use dialog boxes. Because 1-2-3 for Windows was designed as a Windows 3.1 application, you easily can apply many of the same skills you learned in this chapter to other Windows 3.1 programs.

Chapter 3 introduces you to worksheet basics. You learn how to move the cell pointer in a worksheet, enter and edit data in a worksheet, and link worksheet files.

Learning Worksheet Basics

This chapter presents the skills you need for *Using 1-2-3 for Windows, Release 4*, Special Edition. Worksheet basics include entering data into worksheet cells, editing data, and moving around the worksheet. This chapter explains what worksheets are, how to use them, and how you can use several worksheets together. In addition, the chapter provides an overview of the 1-2-3 program and worksheet windows.

If you are familiar with electronic spreadsheets but are new to 1-2-3 for Windows, this chapter introduces you to 1-2-3 for Windows quickly. If you have upgraded from a previous version of 1-2-3 for Windows, this chapter gives you a quick view of many new features in Release 4.

In 1-2-3 for Windows, a spreadsheet is referred to as a *worksheet*—a two-dimensional grid of columns and rows that can be part of a three-dimensional *worksheet file*. Besides working with several worksheets in a file, you can work with several different worksheet files at the same time. You can, for example, link files by writing in one file formulas that refer to cells in another file.

This chapter shows you how to perform the following tasks:

- Use the 1-2-3 for Windows Help system
- Work with single and multiple worksheets
- Link worksheet files
- Move the cell pointer around the worksheet
- Enter and edit data
- Create formulas that sum the contents of columns and rows
- Use the Undo feature
- Use headings, explanations, and other labels to make a worksheet more understandable

T I P If you are familiar with 1-2-3 for DOS, see Chapter 4 for information on using the familiar / commands in 1-2-3 for Windows. If you used 1-2-3 Release 3, 3.1, 3.1+, or 3.4, you can use the skills you learned in those versions to manipulate three-dimensional worksheets and handle multiple files simultaneously in 1-2-3 for Windows.

Learning the 1-2-3 for Windows Keys

Figures 3.1 and 3.2 show the most common keyboard configurations for IBM and IBM-compatible personal computers. The enhanced keyboard now is the standard keyboard for all new IBM personal computers and most compatibles. Some compatibles, especially laptops, have different keyboards.

The keyboards are divided into four or five sections. The alphanumeric keys are in the center; the numeric keypad is on the right; and the function keys are on the left or across the top. The special keys are in various locations. The direction keys are in a separate section on the enhanced keyboard.

Most keys in the alphanumeric section match the keys of typewriters, and most maintain their usual functions in 1-2-3 for Windows. Several keys, however, have new and unique purposes or are not included in typewriter keyboards.

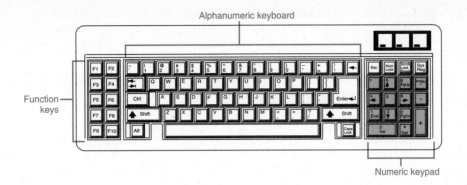

Alphanumeric keyboard

Function keys

Numeric keypad

FIG. 3.1

The original IBM AT keyboard.

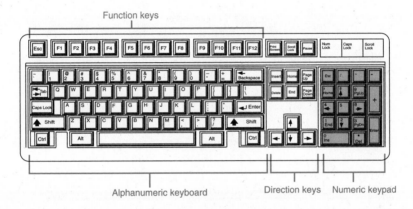

Function keys

Alphanumeric keyboard

Direction keys   Numeric keypad

FIG. 3.2

The IBM enhanced keyboard.

You use the keys in the numeric keypad (on the right side of the keyboard) to enter numbers or to move the cell pointer or cursor around the screen.

The function keys produce special actions. For example, you can use these keys to access 1-2-3 for Windows editing functions, calculate a worksheet, and call up Help messages. These keys are located across the top of the enhanced keyboard and on the left side of some keyboards.

The special keys include Del (Delete), Ins (Insert), Esc (Escape), Num Lock, Scroll Lock, Break, and Pause. These keys, which provide special actions, are located in different places on different keyboards. You use some of these keys alone or with Alt, Ctrl, or Shift to perform additional actions.

Only the enhanced keyboard has a separate section for the direction keys: Home, End, PgUp, PgDn, and the four arrow keys (up, down, left, and right). On the enhanced keyboard, you can use the numeric keypad to enter numbers and the separate direction keys to move around the worksheet.

The following sections list the 1-2-3 for Windows special functions provided by the different key sections. The meanings of these keys become clearer as the keys are explained in this chapter and later chapters.

The Accelerator Keys

The accelerator keys provide shortcut methods of executing common Windows and 1-2-3 for Windows commands. Table 3.1 describes the accelerator keys.

Table 3.1 Accelerator Keys

Key(s)	Action(s)
Alt+Backspace	Same as Edit Undo; reverses the effect of the last command or action that can be undone (see also Ctrl+Z)
Alt+F4	Same as File Exit; ends the 1-2-3 session, prompts you to save any unsaved files, and returns you to the Program Manager
Ctrl+Esc	Displays the Task List, which enables you to switch from one application to another
Ctrl+F4	Same as File Close; closes the current window and prompts you to save the file if it contains unsaved changes
Ctrl+F6	Same as choosing Next from the Control menu of a worksheet window; in 1-2-3 for Windows, makes the next open worksheet, graph, or transcript window active
Ctrl+Ins	Same as Edit Copy; copies selected data and related formatting from the worksheet to the Clipboard
Ctrl+O	Same as File Open; presents the Open File dialog box, in which you can specify a file to view on-screen
Ctrl+S	Same as File Save; saves the current file on disk under its current name
Ctrl+P	Same as File Print; presents the Print dialog box, which contains options for printing the current file

Key(s)	Action(s)
Ctrl+Z	Same as Edit Undo; reverses the effect of the last command or action that can be undone (see also Alt+Backspace)
Ctrl+X	Same as Edit Cut; removes the currently selected data and places it in the Clipboard for pasting
Ctrl+C	Same as Edit Copy; copies the currently selected data and places it in the Clipboard for pasting
Ctrl+V	Same as Edit Paste; places any Clipboard data in the active worksheet
Ctrl++	Same as Edit Insert; inserts cells, rows, columns, or sheets (depending on your selection) into the active worksheet
Ctrl+–	Same as Edit Delete; removes cells, rows, columns, or sheets (depending on your selection) from the active worksheet
Ctrl+*letter*	Same as Tools Macro Run; executes a macro in 1-2-3 for Windows (excludes the preassigned letters listed in this table)
Del	Same as Edit Clear; deletes selected data and related formatting without moving it to the Clipboard
Shift+Del	Same as Edit Cut; moves selected data and related formatting from the worksheet to the Clipboard (see also Ctrl+X)
Shift+Ins	Same as Edit Paste; copies selected data and related formatting from the Clipboard to the worksheet (see also Ctrl+V)

The Editing Keys

You use the editing keys to make changes in a cell or in a dialog box. Table 3.2 describes the editing keys.

Table 3.2 Editing Keys

Key(s)	Action(s)
→ or ←	Moves the cursor one character to the right or left
↑ or ↓	Completes the entry and moves the cell pointer up or down one cell if the entry is only one line in the control panel; if the entry is more than one line in the control panel, completes the entry and moves the cursor up or down one line
Backspace	Erases the character to the left of the cursor
Ctrl+←	Moves the cursor to the beginning of the preceding word
Ctrl+→	Moves the cursor to the beginning of the following word
Ctrl+PgUp or Ctrl+PgDn	Completes editing; in multiple worksheets, Moves the cell pointer forward or back one worksheet
Del	Erases the character to the right of the cursor or erases the highlighted selection
End	Moves the cursor after the last character in the entry
Enter	Completes editing and places the entry in the current cell
Esc	Erases all characters in the entry
F2 (Edit)	Switches 1-2-3 between Edit mode and Ready, Value, or Label mode
F9 (Calc)	Converts a formula to its current value (if 1-2-3 is in Edit or Value mode)
Home	Moves the cursor before the first character in the entry
PgUp or PgDn	Completes editing and moves the cell pointer up or down one worksheet screen

The File-Navigation Keys

You use the file-navigation keys to move among open files. Table 3.3 describes the file-navigation keys.

Table 3.3 File-Navigation Keys

Key(s)	Action(s)
Ctrl+End Home	Moves to the cell last highlighted in the first open file
Ctrl+End End	Moves to the cell last highlighted in the last open file
Ctrl+End, Ctrl+PgUp	Moves to the cell last highlighted in the next open file
Ctrl+End, Ctrl+PgDn	Moves to the cell last highlighted in the preceding open file
Ctrl+F6	Makes the next open worksheet, graph, or transcript window active

The Direction Keys

The direction keys move the cell pointer around the worksheet when 1-2-3 is in Ready mode. In Point mode, these keys move the cell pointer and specify a range in the worksheet. The keys in the numeric keypad, located on the right side of IBM AT-style keyboards, mainly move the cell pointer around the worksheet and through menu commands and options; in other words, they serve mainly as direction keys. When the Num Lock feature is on, however, these keys function as number keys. (For details about using the direction keys to move around the worksheet, see "Moving around the Worksheet File" later in this chapter.)

Table 3.4 describes the direction keys.

Table 3.4 Direction Keys

Key(s)	Action(s)
→ or ←	Moves right or left one column
↑ or ↓	Moves up or down one row
Ctrl+←	Moves left one worksheet screen
Ctrl+→ or Tab	Moves right one worksheet screen
Ctrl+Home	Moves to cell A:A1 in the current file

continues

Table 3.4 Continued

Key(s)	Action(s)
Ctrl+PgUp	Moves to the following worksheet
Ctrl+PgDn	Moves to the preceding worksheet
End+→ or End+←	Moves right or left to the next intersection between a blank cell and a cell that contains data
End+↑ or End+↓	Moves up to a cell that contains data and is next to a blank cell. Moves down to a cell that contains data and is next to a blank cell.
End Ctrl+Home	Moves to the bottom right corner of the current file's active area
End Ctrl+PgUp	Staying in the same row and column, moves back through worksheets to the next intersection between a blank cell and a cell that contains data
End Ctrl+PgDn	Staying in the same row and column, moves forward through worksheets to the next intersection between a blank cell and a cell that contains data
End Home	Moves to the bottom right corner of the worksheet's active area
Home	Moves to cell A1 in the current worksheet
PgUp or PgDn	Moves up or down one worksheet screen

The Alphanumeric Keys

Most of the alphanumeric keys perform the same actions as the corresponding keys on a typewriter. Some of these keys, however, have special meanings in 1-2-3 for Windows. Table 3.5 describes these special keys.

Table 3.5 Alphanumeric Keys

Key(s)	Action(s)
/ (slash) or < (less than)	Activates the 1-2-3 Classic menu
: (colon)	Activates the 1-2-3 Classic WYSIWYG menu
. (period)	When used in a range address, separates the address of the cell at the beginning of the range from the address of the cell at the end of the range; in Point mode, moves the anchor cell to another corner of the range
Alt	Used alone, activates the command menu; used with the function keys, provides additional functions
Alt+Backspace	Same as Edit Undo; cancels the last action or command you executed
Backspace	Erases the preceding character while you enter or edit data; erases a range address during prompts that suggest a range; displays the preceding Help screen while you are using the Help utility
Caps Lock	Shifts the letter keys to uppercase (unlike the shift-lock key on a typewriter, Caps Lock has no effect on numbers and symbols)
Ctrl	Used with several keys to change their functions; used with certain preassigned keys to invoke commands quickly (e.g., Ctrl+X); used with a letter key, invokes a macro
Enter	In a worksheet, enters typed data into a cell; in a dialog box, confirms the dialog-box settings and executes the command
Shift	Used with a letter, produces an uppercase letter; used with a number or symbol, produces the shifted character on that key; used with Num Lock and the numeric keypad, produces a direction key

The Function Keys

You use the 10 function keys—F1 through F10—to perform special actions in 1-2-3 for Windows. These keys are located across the top of the enhanced keyboard and on the left side of other keyboards (refer to figs. 3.1 and 3.2). The enhanced keyboard has 12 function keys, but 1-2-3 for Windows uses only the first 10. You can use the function keys alone or with the Alt, Shift, and Ctrl keys for additional features.

Table 3.6 describes the function keys.

Table 3.6 Function Keys

Key(s)	Action(s)
F1 (Help)	Displays a Help topic
F2 (Edit)	Places 1-2-3 in Edit mode so that you can edit an entry
F3 (Name)	Lists names of files, graphs, ranges, functions, macro keys, and advanced macro commands
F4 (Abs)	In Point or Value mode, changes the cell references in formulas from relative to absolute to mixed and back to relative; in Ready mode, anchors the cell pointer so that you can select a range
F5 (GoTo)	Moves the cell pointer to a cell, worksheet, or active file; equivalent to Edit Go To
F6 (Pane)	Moves the cell pointer between panes
F7 (Query)	Repeats the last Data Query command
F8 (Table)	Repeats the last Data What-if Table command
F9 (Calc)	In Ready mode, recalculates formulas; in Edit or Value mode, converts a formula to its current value
F10 (Menu)	Activates the 1-2-3 menu bar; equivalent to Alt
Alt+F1 (Compose)	Creates characters in 1-2-3 that you cannot enter directly from your keyboard
Alt+F2 (Step)	Turns Step mode on or off
Alt+F3 (Run)	Selects a macro to run
Alt+F6 (Zoom)	Enlarges the current horizontal, vertical, or perspective pane to the full size of the window or shrinks the pane to its original size
Alt+F7 (Add-In 1)	Starts an available 1-2-3 add-in assigned to the key
Alt+F8 (Add-In 2)	Starts an available 1-2-3 add-in assigned to the key
Alt+F9 (Add-In 3)	Starts an available 1-2-3 add-in assigned to the key

Learning the 1-2-3 for Windows Screen

The 1-2-3 for Windows screen display is divided into several parts: the control panel, SmartIcons, the worksheet window, and the status bar. Together, these parts enable you to work with and display worksheets and graphs.

Figure 3.3 shows the 1-2-3 for Windows screen with many of its components labeled.

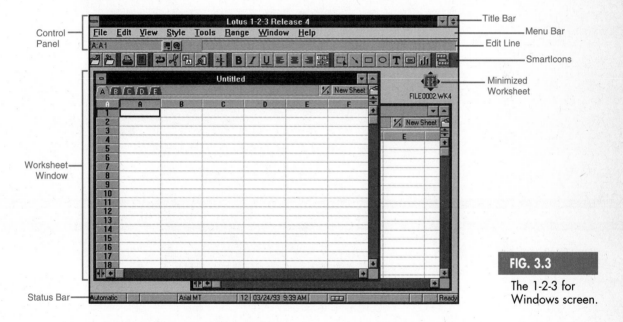

FIG. 3.3

The 1-2-3 for Windows screen.

The Control Panel

The control panel, which appears at the top of the program window, contains three segments: the *title bar*, which contains the program title, the Control menu box, and the Minimize, Maximize, and Restore buttons; the *menu bar*, which displays the 1-2-3 menus currently available; and the *edit line*, which displays information about the active cell and enables you to edit data in the worksheet. (For details about using the various elements of the title bar and the menu bar, refer to Chapter 2, "Understanding the Graphical User Interface.")

For Related Information

◀◀ "Understanding the Graphical User Interface," p. 45.

The edit line provides information about your worksheet and tools for entering data into the worksheet. Figure 3.4 shows each element of the edit line.

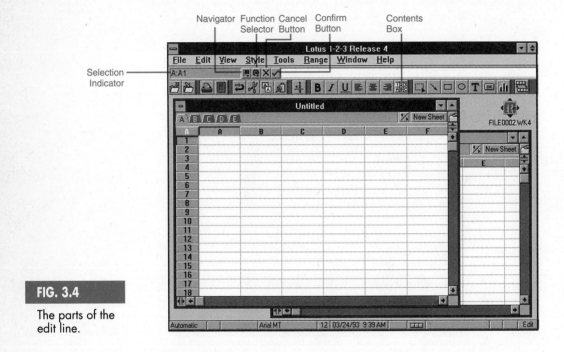

FIG. 3.4

The parts of the edit line.

The *selection indicator* displays the address of the current selection, which is the selected cell or range. A *cell address* consists of the worksheet letter followed by a colon, the column letter, and the row number. The address of the top left cell in the first worksheet, for example, is A:A1. While you are selecting a range, the contents box displays two addresses separated by two periods, which define opposite corners of the range.

The *navigator* is a pull-down list (simply click on the navigator to see the list) that displays all named ranges and objects in the worksheet. If you choose a name from this list while you are entering data into a cell (that is, while you are working in Edit mode), 1-2-3 places the selected name in the formula that you are entering. Otherwise, choosing a name from the navigator list selects (or jumps to) the named range or item.

The *@function selector* displays a list of functions available in 1-2-3. You can use this tool to insert functions into the formula you are currently typing or simply to remind yourself of functions available in 1-2-3. (For more information on the function selector, see Chapter 7, "Using Functions.")

For Related Information

▶▶ "Using Functions," p. 261.

FROM HERE...

You use the *Cancel button* and the *Confirm button* after you enter or edit information in a cell. When you finish entering data, you can click on the Cancel button to undo your entry and return the cell to its previous state. Clicking on the Confirm button accepts your entry and changes the cell accordingly. (You learn more about these tools in "Entering Data into the Worksheet" later in this chapter.)

At the right end of the edit line is the *contents box*. When you enter information into a 1-2-3 for Windows worksheet, the information appears both in the contents box and in the selected cell. When you highlight a cell, the cell's contents appear in the contents box. The difference between the information displayed in the contents box and the information displayed in the cell is that the cell displays the *result* of information that you enter. If you enter a formula, for example, the cell displays the result of the formula—not the formula itself. The contents box, on the other hand, displays the formula exactly as you entered it.

The SmartIcons

SmartIcons are tools that appear in the third line of the program window (below the edit line). Some SmartIcons are shortcuts for menu commands. One icon executes the File Save command; another adds an outline with a drop shadow. Other SmartIcons perform specialized actions that you cannot achieve with menu commands. One icon, for example, draws boxes in the worksheet.

The SmartIcons you see at the top of the screen are only a few of the many icons available in 1-2-3 for Windows. You can customize the icon set or choose icons from other sets. (For details about SmartIcon sets and customizing the icons, see Chapter 17, "Using SmartIcons.")

For Related Information

▶▶ "Customizing the SmartIcons," p. 921

1-2-3 for Windows usually displays the SmartIcons near the top of the screen, below the selection indicator and contents box. (You can control the SmartIcons palette location, however, by using the Tools SmartIcons command.)

The Worksheet Window

1-2-3 for Windows creates special files called *worksheet files*. Each application you create in 1-2-3 uses a worksheet file. When you open a worksheet file in 1-2-3, the file appears in a window called a *worksheet window*. You can open and view several worksheet windows at one time and even arrange them on-screen.

Figure 3.3 shows 1-2-3 with several worksheet windows in view, including one minimized worksheet window. Notice that all worksheet windows appear inside the *1-2-3 window*, in the space below the SmartIcons.

Each worksheet has its own title bar, which contains a Control menu, Minimize button, and Maximize or Restore button. If you have read Chapter 2, these elements should be familiar to you. You can use them to move and size the individual worksheet windows within the 1-2-3 program window. In figure 3.3, you can see two worksheet windows that have been moved and sized, plus a third worksheet that has been minimized. For more details about worksheets, see "Understanding Worksheets and Files" later in this chapter.

The Status Bar

The *status bar* is the bottom line of the screen. This bar displays information about the attributes of the current cell, such as the font applied to the cell and the number of decimal places used. As you move from cell to cell in the worksheet, the status bar may change to reflect the attributes of each cell as you select it.

The status bar also provides a quick method of changing cell attributes. Simply click any formatting attribute displayed in the status bar to display a list of options for that attribute. (Chapter 5, "Changing the Format and Appearance of Data," explains the formatting options available in the status bar. These options include number format, decimal places, font, point size, and date and time formats.)

For Related Information

▶▶ "Changing the Format and Appearance of Data," p. 191.

FROM HERE...

The status bar displays other information in the special indicators described in the following sections. Figure 3.5 shows each segment of the status bar.

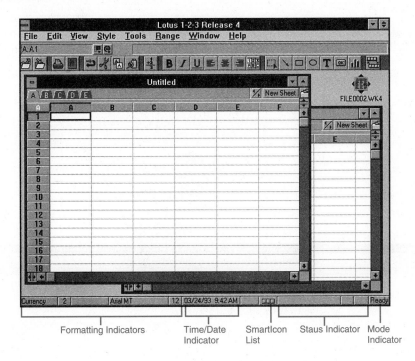

Formatting Indicators   Time/Date   SmartIcon   Staus Indicator   Mode
                         Indicator   List   Indicator

FIG. 3.5

Cell attributes displayed in the status bar.

NOTE   If you highlight two or more cells that contain different attributes, the status bar is blank, indicating that several attributes apply to the selection. If you choose a new attribute for the selection, the attribute applies to all the selected cells.

You can remove the status bar by using the View Set View Preferences command and deselecting the Status Bar option in the Preferences dialog box.

T I P

The Mode Indicators

The *mode indicator* appears at the right end of the status bar. This indicator tells you what mode 1-2-3 for Windows is in and what you can do next. When 1-2-3 for Windows is waiting for your next action, the mode indicator is Ready. When you change the information in a cell, the mode indicator changes to Edit.

Table 3.7 lists the mode indicators and their meanings.

Table 3.7 Mode Indicators	
Mode	**Description**
Edit	You pressed F2 (Edit) to edit an entry, selected Range Parse, or made an incorrect entry.
Error	1-2-3 is displaying an error message. Press F1 (Help) to get Help, or press Esc or Enter to clear the error message.
Find	You chose Tools Database Find Records.
Label	You are entering a label.
Menu	You pressed Alt, F10 (Menu), or the slash (/) key to choose a menu option. 1-2-3 is displaying a menu of commands.
Names	1-2-3 is displaying a list of range names, graph names, print-settings names, functions, macro commands, or external-table names.
Point	1-2-3 is prompting you to specify a range, or you are creating a formula by highlighting a range.
Ready	1-2-3 is ready for you to enter data or choose a command.
Value	You are entering a value.
Wait	1-2-3 is completing a command or process, such as saving a file.

The Status Indicators

1-2-3 for Windows displays *status indicators* at the right end of the status bar. The status indicators, such as Circ and Num, give you information about the state of the system.

Table 3.8 lists and explains these indicators.

Table 3.8 Status Indicators

Indicator	Description
Calc	You need to recalculate formulas by pressing F9 (Calc) or by clicking the Calc indicator in the status bar.
Caps	You pressed Caps Lock to type uppercase letters without using the Shift key.
Circ	You entered a formula that contains a circular reference. Click the Circ indicator in the status bar to jump to the circular reference.
Cmd	1-2-3 is running a macro.
End	You pressed the End key to use it with a direction key.
File	You pressed Ctrl+End to move between files.
Group	The current file is in Group mode.
Mem	The amount of available memory has fallen below 32K (kilobytes), or memory is divided into small blocks.
Num	You pressed Num Lock to use the numeric keypad to type numbers.
Pr	The current file is *protected*, which means that you cannot save changes to the file unless you get the file reservation.
Scroll	You pressed Scroll Lock so that ↑, ↓, ←, and → move the worksheet and the cell pointer.
Sst	1-2-3 is running a macro in Step mode.
Step	You pressed Alt+F2 (Record) and chose Step to run a macro in Step mode.
Zoom	After using View Split to create panes, you pressed Alt+F6 (Zoom) for a full-screen view of the current window.

For Related Information

▶▶ "Protecting and Hiding Worksheet Data," p. 167.

FROM HERE...

SmartIcon List

The Status Bar contains a special tool that helps you choose SmartIcon palettes. Just click on the SmartIcon tool to view a list of palettes. Choose the desired palette from the list and the screen changes to reflect your selection. You can change back again at any time by repeating the procedure.

FROM HERE...

For Related Information

▶▶ "Using the Standard SmartIcon Palettes," p. 919.

Time/Date Indicator

The Time/Date Indicator on the Status Bar shows you the current time and date according to the computer's internal clock. You can change the time and date using the Windows Control Panel. If you click on this indicator area, the time and date display will change to a row height and column width indicator. Click on this indicator to switch between the two displays.

Formatting Indicators

The left side of the Status Bar includes several formatting indicators. These indicators serve two purposes: First, they display information about the format of the active cell or block. (If the active block contains conflicting formats, then the indicator displays nothing for that format.) For example, if you click on cell A4, the font indicator will display the font currently active in cell A4. The second function these indicators serve is that they let you change the formats of the selected cell or block. Click on the indicator you want to change to view a list of additional selections. Next, choose from the list to change the format.

Because of their dual purpose, these indicators are more than just feedback for the current selection; they let you control the formatting of your worksheet on the spot. For more information about worksheet formatting and these indicators, refer to Chapter 5.

Using the 1-2-3 for Windows Help System

1-2-3 for Windows provides on-line, context-sensitive help at the touch of a key. You can be in the middle of any operation and press F1 (Help) to display one or more screens of explanations and advice on what to do next. To display the Help menu, choose Help from the menu bar or press F1. Then choose the Contents command.

The Help utility appears in a window that you can move and size like any other window. To move back and forth among windows, click the window you want to work in or press Alt+Tab. You may want to continue displaying the Help window while you work in 1-2-3; if so, choose the Always on Top command from the Help menu in the Help window.

You can press Help (F1) at any time, even while you execute a command or edit a cell. The help that you receive always is context-sensitive. If, for example, you are executing the Range commands and you press F1 (Help), 1-2-3 for Windows displays a Help window for the Range commands (see fig. 3.6).

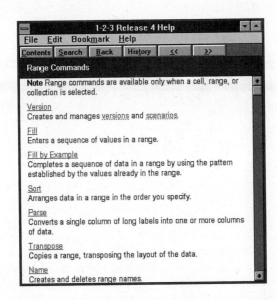

FIG. 3.6

A Help window for Range commands.

Certain Help topics appear in a color or intensity different from the rest of the Help window. If you place the mouse pointer on a colored topic, the pointer changes from an arrow to a hand with a pointing index finger. To see more information about one of these topics, click that topic.

The 1-2-3 Help utility conforms to Windows standards. One standard is that you always can jump to the contents page by clicking the Contents button. The History button moves backward through the topics you already viewed; the Back button moves to the last topic you viewed. You can browse through all Help windows in order by clicking the >> and << buttons to move forward or backward, respectively, through the windows.

Besides the Help buttons at the top of the window, the Help utility provides several useful menu commands. Two of the most useful commands are File Print Topic and Edit Copy. The first command prints the text of the current Help topic; the second copies all or part of the topic to the Windows Clipboard.

For further details on 1-2-3 for Windows features and commands, refer to Chapter 2, "Understanding the Graphical User Interface," and Chapter 4, "Using Fundamental Commands."

Understanding Worksheets and Files

When you start 1-2-3 for Windows, a blank worksheet (with the name Untitled) appears (see figure 3.7).

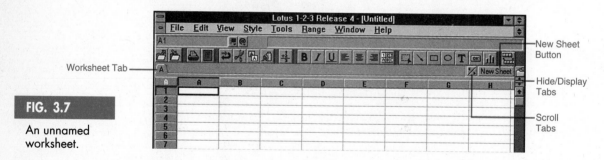

FIG. 3.7

An unnamed worksheet.

Notice that a *worksheet tab* containing the letter *A* appears at the top of the worksheet. You can add up to 255 more worksheets (also called *sheets*) to the worksheet file. Each additional worksheet is identified by a different letter. The identification scheme is similar to the scheme used for worksheet columns; columns are labeled A through Z and then AA through AZ, BA through BZ, and so on. Similarly, the first worksheet is A; the second is B; the 27th is AA; and so on. The sequence continues to IV, the 256th worksheet in the file. Together, these 256 worksheets are considered to be a *worksheet file*. You can enter data into one or more worksheets in a worksheet file and then save the work in a file on disk under a single file name. (See Chapter 6, "Managing Files," to learn more about files and saving your work.) After you save the worksheet file, the title bar displays the file name.

For Related Information

▶▶ "Managing Files," p. 233.

FROM HERE...

Figure 3.8 shows the worksheet file SALES.WK4, which contains two worksheets.

	Lotus 1-2-3 Release 4 - [SALES.WK4]						
File Edit View Style Tools Range Window Help							
A:B3	21880						

	A	B	C	D	E	F	G
1	Sales Consolidation						
2							
3	Women's hats	21,880					
4	Men's hats	8,750					
5							
6	Total hats sold	30,630					
7	Price per hat	$20					
8							
9	Total Sales	$612,600					
10	Less: Cost of goods sold	$393,810					
11							
12	Gross profit on sales	$218,790					
13							
14							
15							

FIG. 3.8

The SALES.WK4 worksheet file, containing two worksheets.

Opening and Saving Worksheet Files

Although a blank worksheet appears each time you start 1-2-3, you eventually will need to open other files. You also may need to start a new file and save it for future use. In 1-2-3, you can open a worksheet file at any time and even view two or more separate files at the same time.

The following sections explain the procedures for opening and saving worksheet files.

Opening New and Existing Files

You might decide to start a new worksheet file at some point, rather than add another worksheet to the existing file. To start a new, blank worksheet file, choose the File New command or click the Create File SmartIcon. 1-2-3 displays a new worksheet file without removing any existing files from the screen. The new worksheet file initially has only one worksheet. As shown earlier in this chapter, you can rearrange individual worksheet files (windows) and even minimize them.

You also can open worksheet files that you created and saved previously. To open an existing file, choose the File Open command or click the Open File SmartIcon. The Open File dialog box appears (see fig. 3.9).

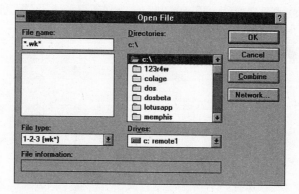

FIG. 3.9

The Open File dialog box.

Use the Drives and Directories lists to locate a file; its name should appear in the File Name list. Double-click the name to open the file. Alternatively, type the entire file name, including the directory path, in the File Name entry box, then click OK to open the file. (See Chapter 6, "Managing Files," for more information on opening and saving worksheet files.)

Saving Files

When you build a new worksheet file or make changes in an existing one, all the work exists only in the computer's memory. If you do not save new worksheets or changes before you quit 1-2-3 for Windows, you lose that work. (1-2-3 for Windows provides a warning, asking you whether you want to save the file before closing.)

When you save a file, you copy the file in memory to the disk and give the file a name. The file remains on disk after you quit 1-2-3 for Windows or turn off the computer.

To save changes in an existing file, choose File from the 1-2-3 for Windows main menu and then choose Save from the pull-down menu, or click the Save File SmartIcon. 1-2-3 automatically updates the file to include whatever alterations you made. If you are saving a new worksheet—one that has never been saved to disk—1-2-3 automatically assigns a name to the file. The file name will be in the form FILE*nnnn*, with *nnnn* representing a number (0001, 0002, and so on).

When you want to name a new file, or when you want to save an existing file under a new name while keeping the old file, use the File Save As command. 1-2-3 for Windows displays the Save As dialog box that enables you to save the file and to assign a password (see fig. 3.10). (For a complete discussion of saving files, see Chapter 6, "Managing Files.")

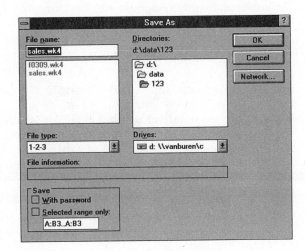

FIG. 3.10

The Save As dialog box.

Using Multiple Worksheets

Occasionally, you need only one worksheet to analyze and store data. At other times, however, you need to use multiple worksheets to organize data effectively.

Some applications are especially well suited to multiple worksheets. First, multiple worksheets are ideal for consolidations. If you need a worksheet that tracks data for several departments, you can create a separate worksheet for each department and store all the sheets as individual worksheets in the same file. Each worksheet is smaller (and easier to understand and use) than a large worksheet containing all the data for each department. You can enter into a cell in any worksheet a formula that refers to cells in the other worksheets.

Use multiple worksheets for any consolidations that contain separate parts, such as products, countries, or projects. Although you can accomplish many of these objectives by putting data in separate files, creating and maintaining separate files is more difficult than keeping all the data in a single multiple-worksheet file. (For a discussion of some of the advantages of using separate files, see "Linking Files with Formulas" later in this chapter.)

Another example of a multiple-worksheet file is a file in which each worksheet represents the activity for a month. Twelve worksheets contain the data for an entire year; and a 13th worksheet, placed before or after the others, represents a consolidation of data for all 12 months.

You also can use multiple worksheets to place separate sections of data in separate worksheets. You can, for example, place input areas, data ranges, formulas, assumptions, constants, and macros in separate worksheets. You then can customize each worksheet for a particular purpose. This technique of organizing data includes using global formats and setting column widths and row heights, as described in chapters 4 and 5.

Breaking your large applications into separate worksheets of a worksheet file has other advantages. As long as Group mode is not activated, you can change one worksheet without accidentally changing the others. If all the data is in one worksheet, you could insert or delete a row or column in one area and destroy part of another area that shares the same row or column. If you use multiple worksheets, however, you can insert and delete rows and columns anywhere without affecting other parts of the file.

Another common accident is writing over formulas in input areas. When you use multiple worksheets, you can separate input areas and formulas so that this error is less likely to occur.

Commands related to multiple worksheets include the following:

■ Insert one or more worksheets before or after the current worksheet by using the command Edit Insert Sheet. A fast way to insert a worksheet after the current worksheet is to click the New Sheet button under the worksheet title bar or to click the New Sheet SmartIcon.

■ Remove a worksheet, using the command Edit Delete Sheet, after activating the desired worksheet. You can delete selected worksheets quickly by clicking the Delete Sheet SmartIcon.

■ Move among the various worksheets by clicking their tabs.

■ Display up to three worksheets at one time, using the View Split Perspective command or the Perspective View SmartIcon. (Details about this command appear in the following section.)

- Display or hide the worksheet tabs by clicking the Tab button on the far right side of the worksheet window. You also can show or hide the tabs by choosing Set View Preferences from the View menu and then selecting or deselecting the Worksheet Tabs option from the Preferences dialog box.

- Group together several or all worksheets in a worksheet file so that some commands affect the whole group, not just the current worksheet, by using the command Style Worksheet Defaults and then specifying Group Mode from the dialog box that appears. (Details about grouping worksheets appear in Chapter 4, "Using Fundamental Commands.")

- Customize a worksheet's tab by double-clicking the tab and then typing the desired name. For example, you might name the sheets Jan, Feb, Mar, and so on. You can enter up to 255 characters, but it's best to use short, descriptive names.

Displaying Multiple Worksheets

You can use the View Split Perspective command or the Perspective View SmartIcon to view up to three worksheets in perspective view. (This command is covered in Chapter 4, "Using Fundamental Commands.") The default screen display is a window that shows part of one worksheet with other worksheets "behind" it, as shown by their tabs (refer to fig. 3.8).

For Related Information

▶▶ "Changing the Display of a Worksheet File," p. 161.

FROM HERE...

Figure 3.11 shows a perspective view of three worksheets. In this file, worksheet A is the consolidation worksheet; worksheet B contains data for Region 1; and worksheet C contains data for Region 2. (Worksheets D and E, which represent sales for regions 3 and 4, do not appear on-screen.)

If you use View Split Perspective to display more than one worksheet in a worksheet file, the current worksheet is the one that contains the cell pointer. You can determine the current worksheet in figure 3.11 in several ways. For example, the cell pointer is in worksheet A, and the cell address in the selection indicator begins with A:. In this figure, worksheet A is the current worksheet, and the current cell is A:B3.

To return to a display of one worksheet, use the command <u>V</u>iew C<u>l</u>ear Split. If you prefer to toggle between displaying three worksheets at one time and displaying only one of the worksheets, use the key combination Alt+F6 (Zoom).

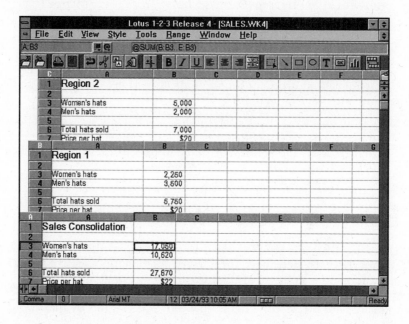

FIG. 3.11

A three-dimensional worksheet displayed with the <u>V</u>iew <u>S</u>plit Perspective command.

Linking Files with Formulas

Besides working with multiple worksheets in a worksheet file, you can work with several worksheet files. In a cell in one worksheet file, you can enter a formula that refers to cells in another worksheet file. This technique is called *file linking*.

File linking enables you to consolidate data in separate files. You can, for example, consolidate data from separate departments or cities by placing each department's data in a separate file.

A consolidation file can use formulas to combine the data from each file. The process also works in reverse; you can have a central database file and separate files to be distributed to the various departments. The department files can contain formulas that refer to data in the central database file.

You also can use the <u>E</u>dit Links commands or formula links to link a worksheet file to another worksheet file. (Chapter 6, "Managing Files," contains more detailed information on linking files with the <u>E</u>dit <u>L</u>inks commands.)

For Related Information

▸▸ "Combining Values from Separate Files," p. 246.

FROM HERE...

Figure 3.11 illustrated the use of multiple worksheets in a consolidation. Figure 3.12 shows the same consolidation with linked files.

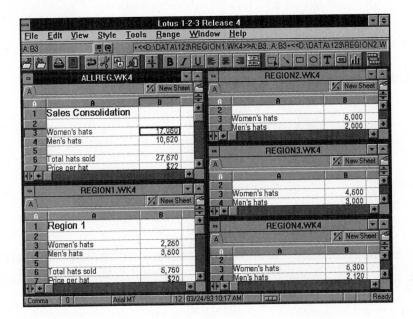

FIG. 3.12

Separate files linked with formulas.

The method you should use depends on the circumstances. If a different person updates each regional worksheet, you need separate files. If each regional worksheet is so large that you don't have enough memory to put all the regional worksheets into one file, you need separate files. If you have many small regional worksheets, using a multiple-worksheet file is preferable, because creating and editing formulas among worksheets is easier in a single worksheet file.

On the other hand, using linked worksheet files instead of one large multiple-worksheet file has advantages for certain applications:

- You can avoid creating a worksheet that is too large to fit into memory.

- You can link files that come from different sources.

- You can create in one file formulas that refer to cells in other files in memory or on disk.

- You can develop a separate file containing macros. (See Chapter 15, "Understanding Macros," for more information on creating macros.)

For more information about file linking with formulas, see "Entering Formulas that Link Files" later in this chapter.

Moving around the Worksheet File

You can enter data only at the location of the cell pointer. Because you can display only a small part of the worksheet at one time, you must know how to move the cell pointer to see other parts of the worksheet. The following sections focus on moving the cell pointer within a worksheet file and among worksheet files. Refer to tables 3.3 and 3.4 for summaries of the necessary commands.

Using the Direction Keys

The four arrow keys that move the cell pointer are located in the numeric keypad (or in the separate keypad on an enhanced keyboard). The cell pointer moves in the direction of the arrow on the key. If you hold down the arrow key, the cell pointer continues to move in the direction of the arrow key. When the cell pointer reaches the edge of the screen, the worksheet continues to scroll in the direction of the arrow.

You can use several other direction keys to move around the current worksheet a screen at a time. Press the PgUp or PgDn key to move up or down one screen. Press the Tab key or Ctrl+right arrow to move one screen to the right; press Shift+Tab or Ctrl+left arrow to move one screen to the left. The size of one screen depends on the size of the worksheet window.

Pressing the Home key moves the cell pointer directly to the *home position* (usually, cell A1 of the current worksheet). Pressing End and then Home moves the cell pointer to the last cell in the current worksheet. (In Chapter 4, you learn how to lock titles on-screen. Locked titles affect the location of the home position.)

Two direction keys—PgUp and PgDn—are especially important for moving around a worksheet file. Ctrl+PgUp moves the cell pointer to the following worksheet, and Ctrl+PgDn moves the cell pointer to the preceding worksheet. These key combinations also cause the cell pointer to cross file boundaries if the cell pointer is positioned on the last or first worksheet of a file.

End Ctrl+Home moves the cell pointer to the end of the active area of the last worksheet in a file (similar to End+Home in a single worksheet).

End Ctrl+PgUp and End Ctrl+PgDn move the cell pointer up or down through the worksheets to the next cell that contains data (similar to End+up arrow and End+down arrow in a single worksheet).

Using the Scroll Lock Key

The Scroll Lock key toggles the scroll feature on and off. When you press Scroll Lock, you activate the scroll feature. If you press Scroll Lock and then press an arrow key, the cell pointer stays in the current cell, and the entire worksheet moves in the direction of the arrow. If you continue to press the same arrow key when the cell pointer reaches the edge of the screen, the cell pointer remains next to the worksheet frame as the entire window scrolls.

Scroll Lock does not affect the other direction keys. If the cell pointer does not move the way that you expect, check to see whether you accidentally turned on Scroll Lock. If the Scroll status indicator appears at the bottom of the screen, press Scroll Lock again to turn off Scroll Lock.

To use the mouse to scroll the worksheet without moving the cell pointer, turn off Scroll Lock and then click one of the arrows in the scroll bars at the right and bottom edges of the worksheet. If you click an arrow one time, the worksheet scrolls one column or row in the direction of the arrow, and the cell pointer doesn't move. If you click an arrow and hold down the mouse button, the worksheet scrolls continuously in the direction of the arrow until you release the mouse button.

Using the End Key

When you press and release the End key, the End status indicator appears in the status bar. If you then press an arrow key, the cell pointer moves in the direction of the arrow and stops on the next cell that contains data. If no cell in the direction of the arrow contains data, the cell pointer stops at the edge of the worksheet. If no other data is in the worksheet and you press End and then the right-arrow key, for example, the cell pointer moves to the end of the worksheet. In short, the End key is used to move to the intersections of blank cells and cells that contain data.

End+→ or End+←	Moves right or left to the next intersection between a blank cell and a cell that contains data
End+↑ or End+↓	Moves up or down to a cell that contains data and is next to a blank cell

The End key works the same with the left- and up-arrow keys. In figure 3.13, pressing End and then the left-arrow key takes you to cell D4. From cell D4, pressing End and the up-arrow key takes you to cell D1 (the edge of the worksheet). After you press the End key, the End indicator stays on only until you press an arrow key or the End key again. If you press End by mistake, you can press End again to make the End status indicator disappear.

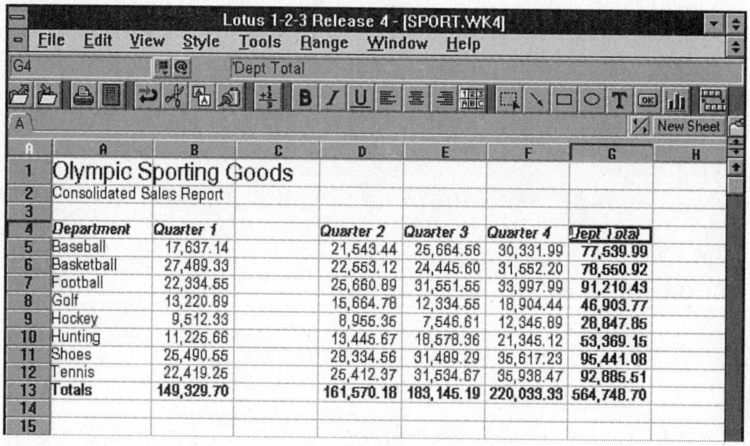

FIG. 3.13

The End key moves between blocks on the worksheet.

If you press End and then Home, the cell pointer moves to the last cell that contains data in the worksheet or in the active area. The *active area* includes all rows and all columns that contain data or cell formats. (Cell formatting is discussed in Chapter 5.) If you press the End key and then the Home key in the worksheet shown in figure 3.13, the cell pointer moves to cell G28—the end of the active area (see fig. 3.14). Although blank, cell G28 is the end of the active area, because entries appear in column G and row 28.

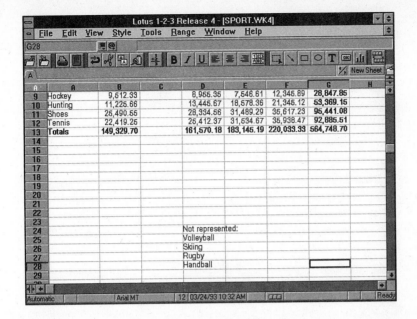

FIG. 3.14

Press End+Home
to move to the
bottom right
corner of the
worksheet's
active area.

Use the End and Home keys to find the end of the active area—
perhaps to add a section to the worksheet without interfering with
existing data—or to specify a print range.

T I P

Using the Goto Feature

The Goto feature enables you to jump directly to cells in the current
worksheet, to cells in other worksheets of the current worksheet file, or
to any cell in any worksheet of any other open worksheet file. You can
use *range names* with Goto so that you do not need to remember cell
addresses. A *range* is a rectangular group of cells and can be three-
dimensional, spanning several worksheets in a file. A range name designates a cell address; for example, you can give cell H11 the range name
TOT_POST_TAX. (For more information about ranges and range names,
see Chapter 4.)

You can access the Goto feature in two ways: press F5 (GoTo), or
choose the Edit Go To command. When you press F5 (GoTo) or choose
Edit Go To, the Go To dialog box prompts you for a range (see fig. 3.15).
When you enter a cell address or range name in the Range text box, the
cell pointer moves directly to this address.

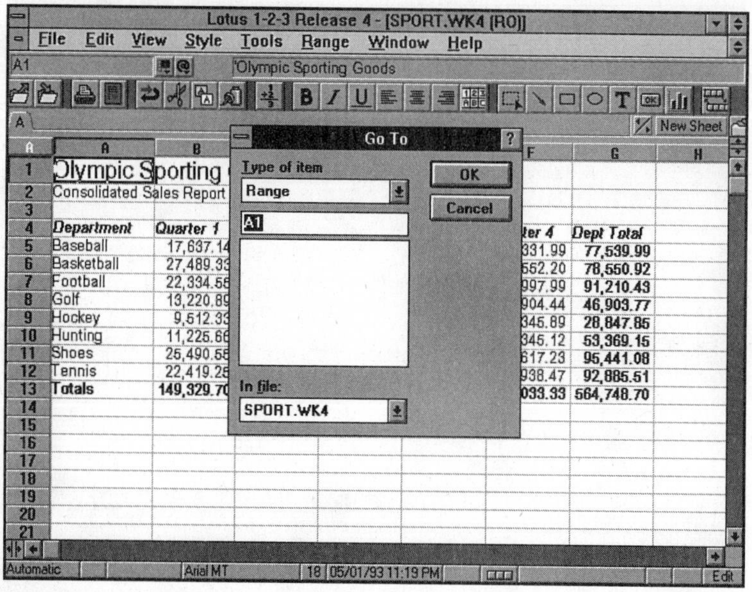

FIG. 3.15

The Go To
dialog box.

You don't need to type the cell address when you press F5 (GoTo). If you are moving to a range that you previously named with Range Name, simply highlight the range name in the list box. This box also contains the names of other open files; to move the cell pointer to another file, choose the file name from the In File list. All previously named ranges in the selected file appear in the Go To list box.

T I P You can jump to a range quickly by using the navigator in the edit line. All defined range names appear when you click this button. Click the range name to jump to that range.

To move to a specific worksheet in the chosen file, you need to type the worksheet letter and cell address. To move to cell B3 in worksheet C of the existing file, for example, type **C:B3** in the Range text box and press OK.

T I P An easier way to move to another worksheet file is to click the file (if the file is visible). If the file is hidden behind another window, press Ctrl+F6 repeatedly to cycle through the open windows until the file you want appears.

Entering Data into the Worksheet

To enter data into a worksheet, move the cell pointer to the appropriate cell, type the entry, and press Enter. As you type, the entry appears in the contents box of the edit line and in the cell. If you enter data into a cell that already contains information, the new data replaces the preceding entry. When you press Enter, the entry is complete.

Another way to enter information into a cell is to double-click on the cell. Double-clicking places the *cursor* (the flashing bar) in the cell, and you can begin typing.

If you plan to enter data into more than one cell, you do not need to press Enter and move the cell pointer to the next cell. You can enter data and move the cell pointer with one keystroke; press a direction key (for example, Tab, PgDn, or an arrow key) after typing the entry.

You can create two kinds of cell entries: label and value. A *label* is a text entry, and a *value* is a number or a formula. 1-2-3 for Windows determines the kind of cell entry from the first character you enter.

1-2-3 considers an entry to be a value (a number or a formula) if the entry begins with one of the following characters:

0 1 2 3 4 5 6 7 8 9 + – (@ # . $

If the entry begins with any other character, 1-2-3 considers the entry to be a label. When you type the first character, the mode indicator changes from Ready to Value or Label.

Entering Labels

Labels, which make the numbers and formulas in worksheets understandable, consist of the titles, row and column headings, and descriptive text that appears in your worksheets. A label can be a string of up to 512 characters.

> Avoid starting your worksheet in cell A1. Leaving an extra row or two at the top of the worksheet and an extra column at the left side makes your worksheets easier to read.
>
> T I P

When you enter a label, 1-2-3 for Windows adds a *label prefix* to the cell entry. 1-2-3 uses the label prefix to identify the entry as a label and to determine how to display and print the entry. By default, the program uses an apostrophe (') for a left-aligned label. To use a different label prefix, type one of the following prefixes as the first character of the label:

Prefix	Description
'	Left-aligned (the default)
"	Right-aligned
^	Centered
\	Repeating
		Nonprinting (the contents of the cell don't print)

The label prefix is not visible in the worksheet but appears in the contents box (see fig. 3.16).

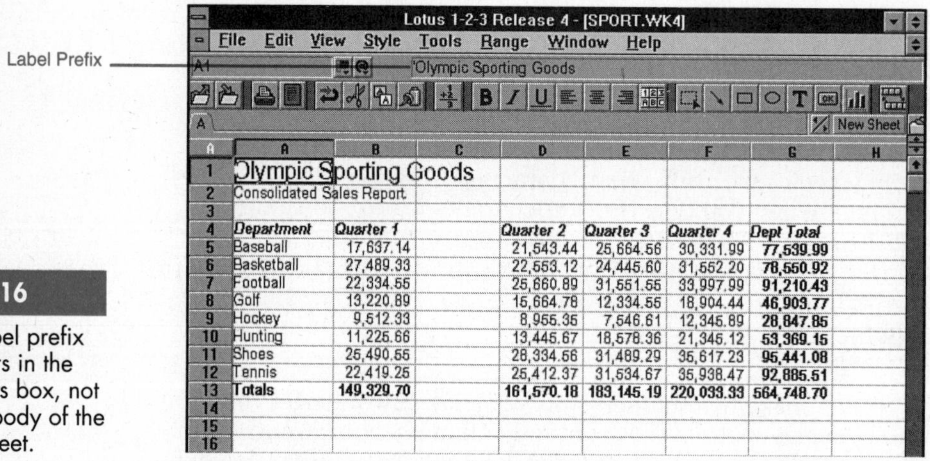

Label Prefix

FIG. 3.16

The label prefix appears in the contents box, not in the body of the worksheet.

For details on specifying alignment for the entire worksheet rather than for individual cells, see Chapter 5.

In figure 3.16, column A shows examples of the effects of different label prefixes so that you can compare how these prefixes display. Columns C through H show how you use these label prefixes in a typical worksheet.

Column headings, as shown in row 6, should align with the data in the columns. The heading in C6 is left-aligned to match the Item descriptions. When an entry fills the cell width, the alignments do not make a difference in the appearance of that cell. Because numbers and numeric formulas always are right-aligned, the headings above columns of numbers also generally are right-aligned.

In figure 3.16, the lines in row 5 are repeating labels, which fill the width of their cells. If you change the column width, 1-2-3 changes the length of a repeating label to fill the new column width.

If you want a label prefix character to appear as the first character of a label, you first must type a label prefix and then type another label prefix as the first character of the label. If you type **\015** in a cell, for example, the program displays 015015015015015015 as a repeating label. You first must type a label prefix—here, an apostrophe (')—and then type **\015**.

You also must type a label prefix if the first character of the label is a numeric character. If you do not type a prefix, when you type the numeric character, 1-2-3 for Windows switches to Value mode, because the program expects a valid number or formula to follow. If the label contains numbers and is a valid formula—for example, the telephone number **(317-555-6100)**—1-2-3 evaluates the entry as a formula. Similarly, if you type **9-30-92** to refer to a date, 1-2-3 evaluates the entry as a formula and displays the result –113. 1-2-3 considers a date entry of **9/30/92**, however, to be valid, and the program stores that entry as a date serial number. (See chapter 7 for more information on @Date functions and Date arithmetic.)

For Related Information

▶▶ "Using Calendar Functions," p. 268.

FROM HERE...

If a typed label such as an address (**338 Main Street**) results in an invalid formula, 1-2-3 for Windows refuses to accept the entry and switches to Edit mode. If 1-2-3 incorrectly evaluates a label as a formula, press F2 (Edit), press Home, type the label prefix, and then press Enter. If 1-2-3 for Windows beeps and places you in Edit mode, press Home, type the label prefix, and press Enter. (For a discussion of Edit mode, see "Editing Data in the Worksheet" later in this chapter.)

If a label is longer than a cell's width, 1-2-3 displays the label across all blank cells to the right of the cell. The data is not actually filling all these cells but is spilling across them. A long text entry may spill across several blank cells.

If the cells to the right of the label cell are not blank, 1-2-3 for Windows cuts off the display of the entry at the cell border. The program still stores the complete entry in the contents box, however, and displays the full entry when the cell is highlighted. To display the entire label in the worksheet, you can insert blank columns to the right of the cell containing the long label, or you can widen the column. Widening the column is easy when you use the mouse; simply click the column border to the right of the column letter and drag the border to the desired width.

T I P   Chapter 5 explains how to center text headings across several columns and provides other text-formatting tricks.

Entering Numbers

To enter a valid number in a worksheet, you can type any of the 10 digits (0 through 9) and certain other characters, as shown in the following table. The results in the Displayed/Stored column of the table are on the default column width (9) and the default font (12-point Arial MT).

Character	Example	Displayed/ Stored	Description
+ (plus)	+123	123	If the number is preceded by a plus sign, 1-2-3 for Windows doesn't store the plus sign.
– (minus)	–123	–123	If the number is preceded by a minus sign, 1-2-3 for Windows stores the number as a negative number.
()parentheses	(123)	–123	If the number is in parentheses, 1-2-3 for Windows stores the number as a negative number, displays the number preceded by a minus sign, and drops the parentheses.
$ (dollar sign)	$123	123	If the number is preceded by a dollar sign (unless the cell is formatted as Automatic or Currency), 1-2-3 for Windows doesn't store the dollar sign.

Character	Example	Displayed/ Stored	Description
. (period)	.123	0.123	You can include one decimal point, which 1-2-3 for Windows stores with the number.
, (comma)	123,456	123456	Three digits must follow each comma; 1-2-3 for Windows doesn't store the commas unless you formatted the cell as Automatic or Comma.
% (percent)	123%	1.23	If the number is followed by a percent sign, 1-2-3 for Windows divides the number by 100 and drops the percent sign unless you formatted the cell as Automatic or Percent.

1-2-3 for Windows stores only 18 digits of any number. If you enter a number with more than 18 digits, 1-2-3 rounds the number after the 18th digit. When displaying numbers on-screen, the program stores the complete number (up to 18 digits) but displays only what fits in the cell. If the number is too long to display in the cell, 1-2-3 for Windows tries to display as much of the number as possible. If the cell uses the default General format and the integer part of the number fits into the cell, 1-2-3 rounds the decimal characters that don't fit. If the integer part of the number doesn't fit in the cell, the program displays the number in *scientific (exponential) notation*. If the cell uses a format other than General or the cell width is too narrow to display in scientific notation and the number cannot fit into the cell, 1-2-3 for Windows displays asterisks.

You also can type a number in scientific notation. 1-2-3 stores a number in scientific notation only if it contains more than 20 digits. If you enter a number with more than 18 digits, 1-2-3 rounds the number to end with one or more zeros.

The following table shows examples of how 1-2-3 for Windows stores and displays numbers.

Entry	Stored	Displayed
123E3	123000	123000
123E30	1.23E+30	1.23E+30
123E–4	0.0123	0.0123
1.23E–30	1.23E–30	1.2E–30
12345678998765432198	12345678998765432200	1.2E+30

The appearance of a number in the worksheet depends on the cell's format, font, and column width. When you use the default font (12-point Arial MT) and the default column width (9), 1-2-3 displays the number 1234567890 as `1.2E+09`. If you use a column width of 11, however, 1-2-3 displays the number as entered. (For information on changing column widths, see Chapter 4.)

FROM HERE...

For Related Information

▶▶ "Setting Column Widths," p. 151.

Entering Formulas

The real power of 1-2-3 for Windows comes from the program's capability to calculate formulas. Formulas make 1-2-3 an electronic worksheet, not just a computerized way to assemble data. You enter the numbers and formulas into the worksheet, and 1-2-3 for Windows calculates the results of all the formulas. As you add or change data, you do not need to recalculate the worksheet to reflect the changes; 1-2-3 for Windows recalculates the data for you.

In the example shown in figure 3.17, if you change the value of Sales or Variable Costs, 1-2-3 for Windows recalculates Variable Margin.

FIG. 3.17

Results in the Variable Margin row reflect changes in the value of Sales or Variable Costs.

	A	B	C	D	E	F	G
1							
2		This Year	Last Year	% Change			
3	Sales	345,389.72	249,876.03	38.22%			
4	Variable Costs	199,045.00	151,678.09	31.23%			
5							
6	Variable Margin	146,344.72	98,197.94	49.03%			
7	Fixed Costs	81,456.00	73,459.23	10.89%			
8							
9	Profit Before Taxes	64,888.72	24,738.71	162.30%			
10	Taxes	82,893.53	59,970.25	38.22%			
11							
12	Profit After Taxes	147,782.25	84,708.96	74.46%			
13							
14							

Lotus 1-2-3 Release 4 - [FILE0001.WK4]

File Edit View Style Tools Range Window Help

A:B6   +B3-B4

New Sheet

You can enter formulas that perform calculations on numbers, labels, and other cells in the worksheet. Like a label, a formula can contain up to 512 characters. A formula can include numbers, text, operators, cell and range addresses, range names, and functions. A formula cannot include spaces except within a range name or text string.

You can create four kinds of formulas: numeric, string, logical, and function. *Numeric formulas* work with numbers, other numeric formulas, and numeric functions. *String formulas* work with labels, other string formulas, and string functions. *Logical formulas* are true-or-false tests for numeric or string values. This chapter covers these three kinds of formulas; formulas that contain functions are discussed in Chapter 7, "Using Functions."

Formulas can operate on numbers in cells. The formula 8+26 uses 1-2-3 for Windows as a calculator. A more useful formula involves cell references in the calculation. In figure 3.18, the formula in cell F16 is +B16+C16+D16+E16. The contents box shows the formula, and the worksheet shows the result of the calculation: 183. The result in cell F16 changes when you change any number in the other cells. This automatic-recalculation capability is the basis of the power of the 1-2-3 for Windows worksheet.

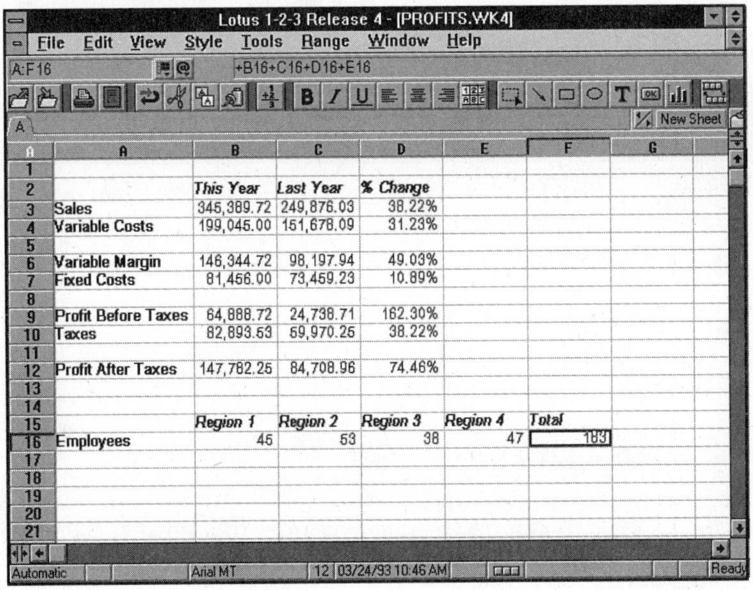

FIG. 3.18

The result, not the formula, appears in the worksheet.

Notice that the formula begins with a plus sign (+). If the formula begins with B16, 1-2-3 for Windows assumes that you are entering a label and performs no calculations.

 You can add a row or column of values quickly by placing the cell pointer in the blank cell at the bottom of a column (or at the right end of a row) and then clicking the Sum SmartIcon to calculate the result.

A *formula* is an instruction to 1-2-3 for Windows to perform a calculation. You use *operators* in numeric, string, and logical formulas to specify the calculations to be performed, and in what order. Table 3.9 lists the operators in the order in which 1-2-3 for Windows uses them.

Table 3.9 Operators and Their Order of Precedence

Operator	Operation	Precedence
^	Exponentiation	1
−, +	Negative, positive value	2
*, /	Multiplication, division	3
+, −	Addition, subtraction	4
=, <>	Equal to, not equal to	5
<, >	Less than, greater than	5
<=	Less than or equal to	5
>=	Greater than or equal to	5
#NOT#	Logical NOT	6
#AND#	Logical AND	7
#OR#	Logical OR	7
&	String formula	7

Using Operators in Numeric Formulas

You use numeric operators for addition, subtraction, multiplication, division, and *exponentiation* (raising a number to a power). The simplest kind of formula is a simple reference, such as the following:

> +C4

You can enter this formula, which simply duplicates (copies) the value of cell C4, into any cell except C4.

Another formula might read this way:

+C4+C5

This formula adds the values in two cells: C4 and C5.

You might include a *constant* value if needed, such as in the following example:

+C4+C5+100

In this formula, the value 100 is constant but the values in cells C4 and C5 are variable; those values depend on the numbers that currently are entered in those cells.

If a formula uses all the operators shown in table 3.9, 1-2-3 for Windows calculates the exponentials first and then works down the list. If two operators are equal in precedence, 1-2-3 can calculate either first. The order of precedence affects the result of many formulas. To override the order of precedence, use parentheses; 1-2-3 always calculates operations within a set of parentheses first.

Table 3.10 shows how 1-2-3 for Windows uses parentheses and the order of precedence to evaluate complex formulas. The examples use numbers instead of cell references to make the calculations easier to follow.

Table 3.10 Evaluating Complex Formulas in 1-2-3 for Windows

Formula	Evaluation	Result
5+3*2	(5+(3*2))	11
(5+3)*2	(5+3)*2	16
-3^2*2	-(3^2)*2	-18
-3^(2*2)	-(3^(2*2))	-81
5+4*8/4-3	5+(4*(8/4))-3	10
5+4*8/(4-3)	5+((4*8)/(4-3))	37
(5+4)*8/(4-3)	(5+4)*8/(4-3)	72
(5+4)*8/4-3	(5+4)*(8/4)-3	15
5+3*4^2/6-2*3^4	5+(3*(4^2)/6)(2*(3^4))	-149

Using Operators in String Formulas

The rules for string formulas are different from the rules for numeric formulas. A *string* is a label or a string formula. Only two string-formula operators exist, so you can perform only two operations with string formulas: repeat a string, or *concatenate* (join) two or more strings.

The simplest string formula uses only the plus sign (+) to repeat the string in another cell:

> +C4

In this example, cell C4 contains a text label, which is copied into the cell containing this formula.

The string-concatenation operator is the ampersand (&). Following is an example:

> +A4&B4

If cells A4 and B4 contain the text strings *19* and *94*, for example, the result of the formula is 1994.

The first operator in a string formula must be a plus sign; all other operators in the formula must be ampersands. If you do not use the ampersand but use any of the numeric operators, 1-2-3 for Windows considers the formula to be a numeric formula and will calculate the data in the cells as numeric values. A cell that contains a label has is considered to have a numeric value of 0 (zero).

If you use an ampersand in a formula, 1-2-3 for Windows considers the formula to be a string formula. If you also use any numeric operators (after the plus sign at the beginning), the formula results in ERR. The formulas +A3&B3+C3 and +A3+B3&C3, for example, result in ERR.

In many string formulas, you need to put a space between the various parts of the formula. You can insert a string directly into a string formula by placing the string inside double quotation marks (" "). If cells A4 and B4 contain the text *John* and *Doe*, for example, you can enter the formula **+A4&" "&B4** to get the result John Doe instead of JohnDoe.

To write more complex string formulas, you can use string functions. For a detailed discussion of these functions, see Chapter 7.

Using Operators in Logical Formulas

Logical formulas are true/false tests. A logical formula compares two values and returns 1 if the test is true or 0 if the test is false. This kind of formula is used mainly in database criteria ranges. (Logical formulas are covered in chapter 7.)

Pointing to Cell References

Formulas consist mainly of operators and cell references. The formula +C4+C5+C6+C7, for example, has four cell references. You can type each reference, but an easier way to enter them exists. When 1-2-3 for Windows expects a cell address, you can use the direction keys or the mouse to point to the cell or range. When you move the cell pointer, 1-2-3 for Windows changes to Point mode, and the address of the cell pointer appears in the formula in the contents box.

To point to a cell when entering a formula, you can use the arrow keys to move the cell pointer to the correct cell, or you can click on the cell. If this location marks the end of the formula, press Enter. If the formula contains more terms (or parts of the equation), type the next operator and continue the process until you finish; then press Enter.

You can type some addresses and point to others. You cannot tell in a completed formula whether the cell references were entered by typing or pointing.

In formulas, you also can refer to cells in other worksheets in the worksheet file. To refer to a cell in another worksheet, include the worksheet letter (or custom tab label) in the cell address. To refer to cell C4 in worksheet B, for example, type **+B:C4**. To point to a cell in another worksheet, type + and then use the direction keys, including Ctrl+PgUp and Ctrl+PgDn, to move the cell pointer to other worksheets. You also can click the Next Worksheet and Previous Worksheet SmartIcons.

Because typing an incorrect address in a formula is easy, pointing to a cell usually is faster and more accurate than typing the cell's address. The only time when typing an address is easier is when the cell reference is far from the current cell and you happen to remember the address. If you enter a formula in cell Z238 and want to refer to cell K23, typing **K23** may be faster than pointing to cell K23.

You also can use range names instead of cell addresses in formulas. Experienced 1-2-3 for Windows users rarely type cell addresses and frequently use range names.

Entering Formulas that Link Files

A formula can refer to cells in other files. This technique, described earlier, is known as *file linking with formula links*.

Figure 3.19 shows five files in memory. The formula in cell B3 in ALLREG.WK4 refers to cell B3 in the files named REGION1.WK4 through REGION4.WK4. This powerful feature enables you to consolidate data from separate files.

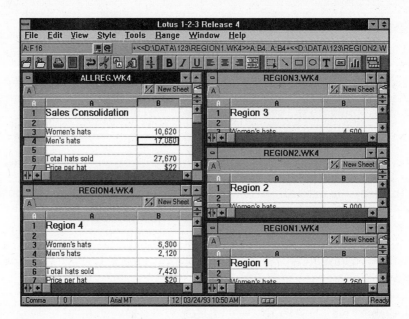

FIG. 3.19

A linking formula in cell B3 of ALLREG.WK4.

You can use formulas to link files in a network or another multiuser environment. If you believe that data in one or more of the linked files has changed since you read the file that contained the formula links, use the Edit Links command to update the formulas.

When you write a formula that refers to a cell in another file in memory, you can point to the cell as if it were a worksheet in the same file. 1-2-3 for Windows includes the path and file name as part of the cell reference. If the file is not in memory, you must type the entire cell reference, including the file name inside double angle brackets, such as in the following example:

+<<REGION1>>A:B3+<<REGION2>>A:B3+<<REGION3>>A:B3+<<REGION4>>A:B3

If the file is in another directory, you must include the entire path, as shown in the following example:

+<<C:\123W\DATA\REGION1.WK4>>A:B3

A formula that links files usually is long. If possible, when you build a formula that refers to a cell or range in another file, try to keep that file open so that you can point to the cells rather than type their addresses. (After you build the formulas, all the linked files do not need to be in memory at the same time.) Because formulas are longer and more complex with multiple worksheets and files, always try to use Point mode when you enter a formula.

When you retrieve a file containing formulas that refer to cells in another file, 1-2-3 for Windows reads the referenced cells from each linked file and recalculates each linked formula.

You can open the ALLREG.WK4 file without opening the REGION1.WK4 through REGION4.WK4 files (refer to fig. 3.19). As you open the file, 1-2-3 for Windows updates the formulas in ALLREG.WK4 that refer to cells in other files. You can update and save any of the REGION files; then, when you retrieve ALLREG.WK4, you get the correct consolidated data.

Correcting Errors in Formulas

If you accidentally enter a formula that 1-2-3 for Windows cannot evaluate, the program beeps, changes to Edit mode, and then usually moves the cursor to the place in the formula where the program encountered an error. You cannot enter an invalid formula into a worksheet. (For more information about changing a cell in Edit mode, see "Editing Data in the Worksheet" later in this chapter.)

Common errors that make a formula invalid are extra or missing parentheses, misspelled function names, and incorrect arguments in functions. Following are a few examples of common errors:

Formula	Error
+A1/(A2-A3	Missing right parenthesis
@SIM(A1..A3)	Misspelled @SUM function
@IF(A1>200,200)	Missing argument in function

If you cannot find, or do not know how to fix, the error in the formula, you can use the Help utility to check the format of the function. Before you can do anything else, you must clear the error. If you press Esc, you erase the entire entry. If you press Esc again, you return to Ready mode, but you lose the entire formula.

If you still cannot fix the error, convert the formula to a label. Because all labels are valid entries, this technique clears the error and enables you to continue working.

Follow these steps to convert a formula to a label, clear Edit mode, and return to Ready mode:

1. Press Home to move to the beginning of the formula.

2. Type an apostrophe (') as the label prefix. (1-2-3 for Windows accepts anything preceded by an apostrophe as a label.)

3. Press Enter.

You can use the Help utility again or look at another part of the worksheet that has a similar formula. When you find the error, correct the formula and remove the apostrophe.

Editing Data in the Worksheet

After you enter data in a cell, you may want to change the data. Perhaps you misspelled a word in a label or created an incorrect formula. You can change an existing entry in either of two ways: You can replace the contents of a cell by typing a new entry, or you can change part of a cell's contents by editing the cell.

To replace the contents of a cell, move the cell pointer to the cell you want to change, type the new data, and press Enter. To edit a cell's contents, move the cell pointer to the cell and press F2 (Edit) to enter Edit mode, or double-click the cell. You also can move the mouse pointer to the contents box; the shape of the pointer changes from an arrow to an I-beam. Move the I-beam to the area you want to change and then click the mouse button.

When 1-2-3 for Windows is in Edit mode, a cursor flashes in the contents box. You use the editing keys to move the cursor. (Editing keys are listed in table 3.2.) While you edit the cell, the contents of the cell—as displayed in the worksheet—do not change; the cell's contents change only when you press Enter to complete the edit.

If you press Esc while 1-2-3 for Windows is in Edit mode, you clear the edit area and return the cell to its earlier state. If you press Enter while the edit area is blank, you do not erase the cell's contents, and you return to Edit mode.

Using the Undo Feature

When you type an entry, edit a cell, or issue a command, you change the worksheet. If you change the worksheet in error, you can press Alt+Backspace (Undo), choose the Edit Undo command, or click the Undo SmartIcon to reverse the change. If you type over an existing entry, you can undo the new entry and restore the old one. The Undo feature undoes only the last action performed, whether that action was entering data, executing a command, or running a macro.

When you use the Undo feature, 1-2-3 for Windows must remember the most recent action that changed the worksheet. This feature requires a great deal of computer memory; how much memory depends on the different actions involved. If you run low on memory, you can disable the Undo feature by using the Tools User Setup command and deselecting the Undo option from the User Setup dialog box. If you run out of memory while 1-2-3 for Windows is undoing an action, 1-2-3 suspends the undo operation.

The Undo feature is powerful. Undo also is tricky, so you must use this command carefully. To use Undo properly, you must understand what 1-2-3 for Windows considers to be a change. A change occurs between the time 1-2-3 for Windows is in Ready mode and the next time 1-2-3 for Windows is in Ready mode.

Suppose that you press F2 (Edit) to go into Edit mode to change a cell. You can make changes in the cell and then press Enter to save the changes and return to Ready mode. If you press Undo at that point, 1-2-3 for Windows returns the worksheet to the condition the worksheet was in during the last Ready mode. The cell returns to the state it was in before you performed the edit.

You can change many cells at one time or even erase everything in memory with a single command. (The commands that you may use most often are covered in Chapter 5.) If you use Undo after a command, you cancel all the effects of the command.

Some commands and actions cannot be canceled, including the Undo command. If you press Alt+Backspace (Undo) at the wrong time and cancel an entry, you cannot recover the entry. Other commands and actions that cannot be canceled include the following:

- The Chart commands
- All commands in the Control menus
- All commands that affect an outside source (that is, a linked worksheet or a remote OLE or DDE link) but have no effect on the worksheet file
- Actions that move the cell pointer or scroll the worksheet, including GoTo (F5) and Window (F6)
- Formula recalculations that result when you press F9 (Calc)

Checking Your Spelling

1-2-3 includes a handy spelling-checker utility that reviews and helps you correct spelling throughout your worksheet files. To activate the spelling checker, choose the Tools Spell Check command or click the Check Spelling SmartIcon. The Spell Check dialog box appears (see fig. 3.20).

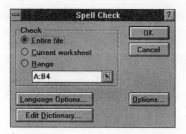

FIG. 3.20

The Spell Check
dialog box.

Select the area of the worksheet that you want to spell check—the entire file, the current worksheet, or a specific range. If desired, you can
then choose the Options button to specify your preferences. A dialog
box of options for your application appears. Options include whether
the spelling checker pays attention to upper- and lowercase letters,
checks formulas or the results of formulas, and much more. If you view
the options, choose OK to return to the Spell Check dialog box.

When you're ready, choose OK to begin checking the selection. If the
spelling checker finds an unknown word, a dialog box like the one
shown in figure 3.21 appears. Using the options in this box, you can
correct the mistake or otherwise deal with the item. If you move the
dialog box, you may be able to see the misspelled word in context.
Feel free to move the Spell Check dialog box at any time.

FIG. 3.21

The Spell Check
dialog box for
correcting words.

You can enter a replacement word in the Replace With box and then
choose Replace to continue, or you can use one of the Alternatives
provided by 1-2-3. Double-click the desired alternative in the list to use
it. You can use the Replace All command to change all occurrences of
the word throughout the worksheet; you will not encounter the word
again in this session.

The spelling checker may flag some correctly spelled words as incorrect, simply because those words are not in the spelling checker's dictionary. You can add those words to the dictionary using the Add to
Dictionary button. By adding words to the dictionary, you begin to create your own personal dictionary for repeated use. If the word is

flagged, but you don't want to add it to your dictionary, use the Skip command to skip the word or the Skip All command to skip all occurrences of the word throughout this spell check session.

When you're finished with the spell check, you can close the Spell Check dialog box by clicking the Close button or by using the Control menu's Close command.

Questions & Answers

This chapter taught you the basics of worksheets and 1-2-3. You learned the elements of the 1-2-3 screen, how to enter and edit data, and how to move around the worksheet. Following are some questions that might arise as you practice these concepts.

Worksheets and Files

Q: How do I move between two open worksheet files?

A: Press Ctrl+F6 to move to the next worksheet window, or use the Window menu to choose the worksheet name.

Q: Will I be able to access the values from one worksheet in other worksheets within the same file?

A: Access values from other worksheets in your formulas by including the worksheet name along with the cell reference. The formula +C4+C:C5, for example, adds the value in cell C4 of the current worksheet to the value of C5 in worksheet C.

Moving around the Worksheet

Q: Why didn't the cell pointer move when I pressed the arrow key?

A: The cell pointer doesn't move if you press an arrow key while 1-2-3 is in Edit mode. Pressing an arrow key in Edit mode moves the cursor inside the cell you are editing.

Entering and Editing Data

Q: Why doesn't 1-2-3 accept my entry?

A: Your numeric and text entries must adhere to specific guidelines. Numeric entries must begin with numbers and must contain no text. Other restrictions also apply.

Q: Why is 1-2-3 treating my formula like a label?

A: If you neglect to enter a plus or minus sign in front of cell references, 1-2-3 may interpret your entry as a label.

Q: Why are asterisks appearing in a cell where a value should be?

A: If a cell is too narrow to display a number in its entirety, 1-2-3 may display asterisks instead. To display the entire number, you must use the Style Column Width command to make the cell wider.

Q: Why does nothing appear in the edit line when I try to edit a cell?

A: You may be editing a blank cell. At times, a cell may appear to contain data when the data actually exists in an adjacent cell.

Q: Why is 1-2-3 truncating my text entry when nothing appears in the adjacent cells?

A: Blank spaces in cells can cause 1-2-3 to consider the cell to be non-blank. These cells are difficult to see; use the Edit Clear command to remove all data and blank spaces from cells.

Q: Why did 1-2-3 convert my date to a number?

A: You must use slash characters when you enter dates (for example, 12/24/94). Other characters may not produce a valid date. You also can spell out the date (for example, Dec. 24, 1994).

Summary

This chapter gave you the basic skills you need to use 1-2-3 for Windows. You learned about using the keyboard to move around the worksheet, including between worksheets. You also learned how to insert new worksheets into a worksheet file and how to open multiple files. You should be familiar with the 1-2-3 Help system and accessing it with the F1 function key. And, you know all about creating worksheets by entering text, numbers, and dates—and by creating formulas that reference other cells in the worksheet. To help you with mistakes, you can access the Undo command and use the spelling checker to review your worksheet labels.

In the following chapter, you learn the fundamental commands that provide tools you can wield to create and use worksheets effectively.

PART

II

OUTLINE

Building the Worksheet

Using Fundamental Commands

A lmost every task you perform in 1-2-3 for Windows involves commands. You use them to tell 1-2-3 for Windows to perform a specific task or a sequence of tasks. Commands can change the operation of the 1-2-3 for Windows program itself, or they can operate on a worksheet or on cells. You use commands to change how data appears in a cell, arrange the display of worksheets in windows on-screen, print worksheets, chart data, save and open files, copy and move cells, and perform many other tasks.

1-2-3 for Windows includes hundreds of commands. Some you use every time you use the program; others you use rarely, if ever. Some commands perform general tasks that apply to all worksheets; other specialized commands apply only to specific cells or ranges. This chapter covers the use of command menus and the most fundamental 1-2-3 for Windows commands. Later chapters cover more specific commands.

You learn not only what these fundamental 1-2-3 for Windows commands can do but also what their limitations are. Certain actions, like formatting a disk, cannot be done from 1-2-3 for Windows.

This chapter shows you how to do the following tasks:

- Use command menus and quick menus
- Move and copy data
- Use ranges and range names, including 3D ranges
- Set column widths and row heights
- Erase data from rows, columns, and worksheets
- Insert and delete rows, columns, and worksheets
- Freeze titles on-screen
- Protect and hide data
- Control recalculation
- Refer to cells with relative, absolute, and mixed addressing
- Find and replace data

Understanding the 1-2-3 for Windows Menus

The 1-2-3 for Windows main menu bar (see fig. 4.1) includes eight options or menus. The main menu bar changes from time to time, depending on your actions. For example, when you work with charts, the Range menu changes to the Chart menu to provide you with commands specific to charting.

Main menu bar ———

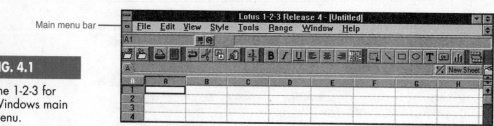

FIG. 4.1

The 1-2-3 for Windows main menu.

This chapter focuses on the following commands in the 1-2-3 for Windows main menu:

- The File commands save, open, and manage files, as well as send electronic mail and print worksheets and charts.

■ The Edit commands link cells from one worksheet to another, copy and move cells or their attributes, erase the contents of cells, undo your last action, change the arrangement of drawn objects, link to other Windows programs, and find or replace data.

■ The View commands can change the on-screen appearance of the worksheet by changing magnification, freezing the headings so that they are always visible, or splitting the worksheet window to view multiple sections of the worksheet.

■ The Style commands provide ways to change the format of values in the worksheet, including the font, color, and numeric format of data. This menu also has options for changing the height and width of cells, protecting cells from changes, hiding sections of the worksheet, inserting and deleting page breaks, and changing worksheet default settings.

■ The Tools commands provide access to various 1-2-3 features such as charting, graphics, database management, SmartIcons, and macros.

■ The Range commands provide access to the Version Manager and help you fill, manipulate, and analyze ranges of data. This includes sorting, parsing, naming, and transposing ranges.

■ The Chart commands control the 1-2-3 for Windows charting feature. (The 1-2-3 for Windows Chart menu and charting capabilities are covered in Chapter 11, "Using Charts and Graphics.")

■ The Window commands help you arrange Worksheet windows within the 1-2-3 window.

■ The Help commands give you access to on-line, context-sensitive help; you can use these commands to search for specific topics, learn 1-2-3 basics, and run a tutorial program.

Working with Command Menus

To issue a command, you use one of three methods:

■ Use the mouse to click on the command you want; 1-2-3 for Windows automatically activates the menu and chooses the command.

■ Activate the main menu by pressing the Alt key or the F10 (Menu) key. Use the arrow keys to move the menu pointer to the name of the command and then press Enter or the down-arrow key.

■ Press and hold the Alt key and type the underlined letter of the command. For example, to choose Range Name, hold Alt and type **RN**. The Alt key activates the menu, R selects the Range menu option, and N selects the Name command.

You can use lowercase letters if you prefer; for example, 1-2-3 for Windows accepts rn or RN for the Range Name command.

NOTE   The underlined letter in a command or option is called a hot key. The hot key is usually the first letter of a command or option, but not always.

T I P   The 1-2-3 Classic menu (which includes 1-2-3 for DOS Release 3.1 commands) is accessible from 1-2-3 for Windows. Just press the slash key (/) and the Classic menu appears on-screen with its original options.

Pull-Down and Cascade Menus

After you choose a menu option from the main menu, the next set of commands appears in a pull-down menu. All the main menu options lead to pull-down menus. Figure 4.2 shows the pull-down menu that appears after you select Range from the main menu. If the pull-down menu option has another level of commands, the commands appear in a cascade menu. Pull-down menu options that lead to a cascade menu are always followed by a solid triangular marker (refer to the Analyze option on the Range pull-down menu in fig. 4.2). Figure 4.3 shows the cascade menu that appears when you choose Range Analyze.

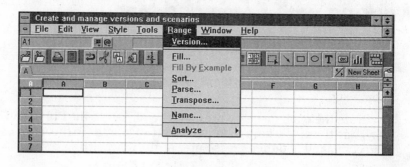

FIG. 4.2

The Range pull-down menu.

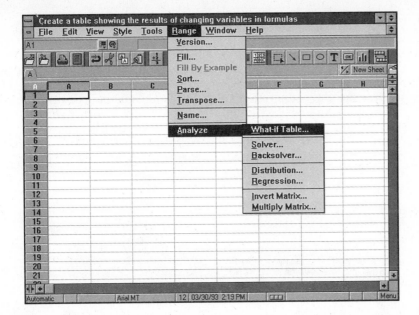

FIG. 4.3

The Range
Analyze cascade
menu.

Dialog Boxes

When 1-2-3 for Windows needs more information about a command, the selected menu option leads either to prompts on the edit line or to a dialog box. A dialog box is a window that enables you to read and enter information about a command. Menu options that lead to a dialog box are always followed by an ellipsis (...). Chapter 2, "Understanding the Graphical User Interface," explains how to move through dialog boxes and enter information in them.

You can explore command menus without actually executing the commands on them. Highlight any menu option on the main menu and read the command description in the title bar to find out more about the selected option or the next menu (refer to fig. 4.2 for an example). Then select a menu option to access the next menu. For more detailed information about a command, move the menu pointer to the command and press F1 (Help).

NOTE If you make a mistake while choosing menu commands, press Esc or Ctrl+Break to return to the preceding menu without selecting a command. For example, if you selected Range Analyze and can see the cascade menu shown in figure 4.3, you can back up to the Range pull-down menu shown in figure 4.2 by pressing Esc or Ctrl+Break. If you press Esc at the main menu level, you deactivate the menu and return to Ready mode.

Using Quick Menus

A 1-2-3 for Windows quick menu combines commands from various menus to make them available in a single location as you work in the worksheet. Quick menus provide all the commands you are likely to require for the current activity. To access a quick menu, click the right mouse button on the cell, column and row heading, or other worksheet or graphic element with which you are working. Figure 4.4 shows a quick menu for a cell; notice that the worksheet commands appropriate for a cell appear in the quick menu. Figure 4.5 shows the quick menu that appears when you right-click on a 1-2-3 for Windows chart.

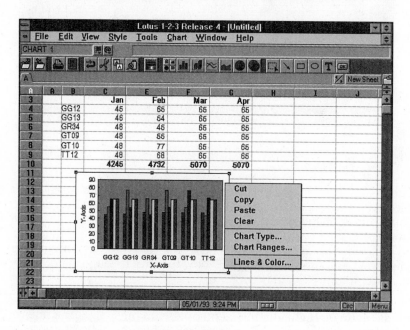

Canceling a Command

If you make a mistake while choosing menu commands, press Esc to return to the preceding menu. If you press Esc at the main menu, you deactivate the menu and return to Ready mode.

If you execute a command accidentally, you usually can undo the action of that command. For example, if you erase a range by mistake, you can press Alt+Backspace (Undo), click on the Undo SmartIcon, or use the Edit Undo command to recover the erased range.

For Related Information

◄◄ "Using the Undo Feature," p. 126.

FROM HERE...

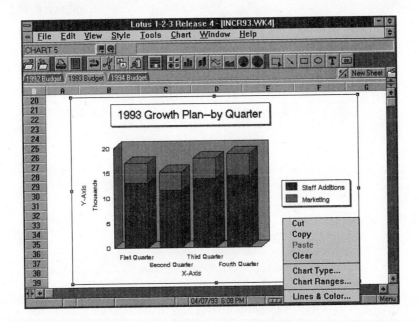

FIG. 4.5

The quick menu that appears when you right-click on a chart.

Grouping Worksheets

With 1-2-3 for Windows, you can group together all the worksheets in a worksheet file. With grouped worksheets, changes made to one worksheet affect all the other worksheets in the file. You cannot group selected worksheets; using Group mode means that all the worksheets in a file are grouped.

When you select a cell or range in one worksheet in a group, the same area is selected (even though it is not highlighted or outlined) in each worksheet in that group. When you format a cell or range in one worksheet, the corresponding area is formatted in each of the other worksheets.

To use Group mode, choose Style Worksheet Defaults and select the Group Mode option in the Worksheet Defaults dialog box. The Group indicator appears in the status bar at the bottom of the screen (see fig. 4.6). In figure 4.6, the View Split Perspective command was used to show the worksheets in perspective. When you scroll or move the cell pointer, notice that these movements are synchronized within the group so that you always see the same part of each worksheet.

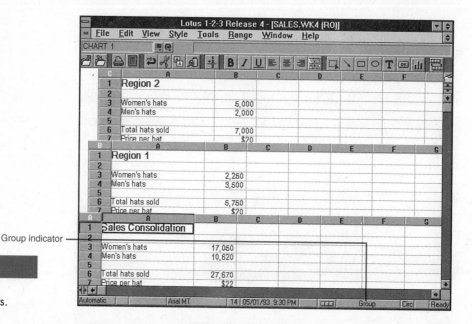

Group indicator

FIG. 4.6

Grouped worksheets.

If 1-2-3 for Windows is in Group mode, and you use commands that prompt you for a cell address, 1-2-3 for Windows does not need the address of the three-dimensional selection that spans the group—just the range in one of the worksheets. When you complete the command, the effect takes place in all worksheets in the group, even though you only referred to cells in one of the worksheets.

If you want to add one or more worksheets to an existing group, add the new worksheets with the Edit Insert Sheet command or the New Sheet button; the formatting and attributes of the active worksheet are automatically created at the same time. 1-2-3 for Windows does not copy any data, however, only cell attributes. If Group mode has not been selected before you insert the new worksheets, 1-2-3 for Windows does not copy the current worksheet's formats and settings to the new worksheets.

Working with Ranges

A range is a rectangular group of cells in a worksheet. You define a range with the cell addresses of any two diagonally opposite corners of the range. When you specify a range address, you separate the cell addresses with one or two periods when typing (but two periods always appear when 1-2-3 for Windows displays the dimensions of a range). Notice in figure 4.7 that a range can be a single cell (E1..E1), part of a row (A1..C1), part of a column (G1..G5, D13..D19, and F14..F15), or a rectangle that spans multiple rows and columns (B4..E9 and A13..B15).

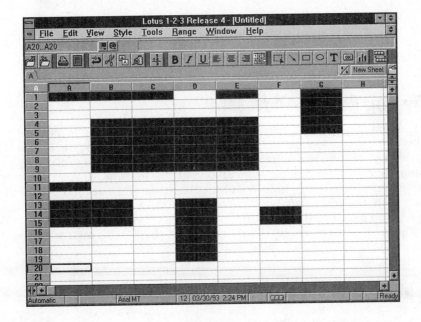

FIG. 4.7

Different types of ranges in one worksheet.

Whenever you highlight a range, the cell diagonally opposite the anchor cell is the free cell.

A range also can be three-dimensional, spanning two or more worksheets. A three-dimensional range includes the corresponding cells in each worksheet. When you use a three-dimensional range, you must include the worksheet letters with the cell addresses. For example, if cells A3 through D3 are highlighted in worksheets A, B, and C, the address of this range is A:A3..C:D3. For more information on three-dimensional ranges, see the "Using Three-Dimensional Ranges" section later in this chapter.

Specifying Ranges

Many commands act on ranges. For example, the Range Sort command prompts you for the range to be alphabetized. When 1-2-3 for Windows prompts you for a range, you can respond in one of three ways:

- Type the cell addresses of two of the opposite corners of the range or of the cells in the ranges. Separate the two references with two dots (periods). For example, the range that includes cells A1, A2, B1, and B2 can be specified as A1..B2, B2..A1, A2..B1, or B1..A2.

- Highlight the range with the keyboard or the mouse either before or after you select the command.

- Type the range name or press F3 (Name) and select the range name, if one has been assigned.

The following sections describe these options in detail.

Typing Range Addresses

The first method of specifying ranges, typing the address, is used the least because it is most prone to error. With this method, you type the addresses of any two cells in diagonally opposite corners of the range, separating the two addresses with one or two periods. (If you type only one period, 1-2-3 for Windows automatically inserts a second period to separate the addresses.) For example, to specify the range B4..E9, you can type B4..E9 or B4.E9, or E9..B4 or E9.B4. Or you can specify the other two corners: E4..B9 (E4.B9), or B9..E4 (B9.E4). No matter how you type the range, 1-2-3 for Windows stores it as B4..E9.

Highlighting a Range

You can highlight a range by clicking the mouse pointer on a cell and dragging to highlight a range. This action places you into Point mode (POINT appears as the mode indicator in the Status Bar) and is the most popular method of identifying the range. You can highlight ranges for commands and functions in the same way you point in a formula. You can highlight a range with the keyboard or the mouse either before or after you issue a command. Any special considerations for highlighting ranges in functions are covered in Chapter 7, "Using Functions."

1-2-3 for Windows enables you to highlight cells before you issue a command. When you preselect cells and then issue a command, the address automatically appears in the dialog box. You need not reenter the address. One exception exists; when you group worksheets together with Group mode, the default range is the three-dimensional range that spans the whole group, even if you have preselected a range in one worksheet only. To override the default range in this case, you must type the range address.

If you use the keyboard to preselect a range, press F4 and highlight the range by using the arrow keys. When you finish specifying the range, press Enter. Using the Shift key can make the selection process even faster (this method also works if you select the range after you issue the command). Just move to the beginning of the range, press and hold the Shift key, and press the arrow keys as necessary to highlight the rest of the range. When finished, release the Shift key.

If you have a large range of contiguous cells containing data you want to highlight, use the End key along with the Shift key. Move to the beginning of the range (that is, its upper-left cell) and press and hold the Shift key. Then press End, the right arrow, End again, and the down arrow. This technique assumes that the range contains blank cells on all sides.

T I P

To highlight a range with the mouse, just click on any corner of the range and drag to the diagonally opposite corner. All cells between the corners are highlighted. You also can click once on a corner, press and hold the Shift key, and click once on the opposite corner.

You can highlight a group of ranges, called a collection. Highlight the first range using any method you like, then press and hold the Ctrl key as you highlight other ranges. All ranges are highlighted as a collection. Figure 4.7 shows a collection of highlighted ranges.

When you press the Enter key, you move from cell to cell within the collection. Press Shift+Enter and you move backward within the collection. Also, you may click the Next Range and Previous Range icons to move between individual ranges within the existing collection. If you work with collections often, you might consider creating a SmartIcon palette that includes these two icons.

To specify a collection as a reference (such as when you type a reference into a dialog box), you must separate each distinct range reference with a semicolon. For example, you can enter A1..C1;E1;G1..G5;B4..EE9;A11;A13..B15;D13..D19;F14..F15 to specify the collection shown in figure 4.7.

It is easier and more efficient to highlight a range before you issue a command, but if you forget to select a range beforehand, you can select one after you issue the command. When the command leads to a dialog box, you can type or point to the range within the dialog box.

Pointing is faster and easier than typing range addresses. Because you can see the cells as you select them, you make fewer errors by pointing than by typing.

To highlight a range after issuing a command, simply highlight the existing reference in the text box and then click and drag on the worksheet to highlight the desired range. You can move the dialog box aside to gain better access to the worksheet; move the dialog box by dragging on its title bar. The reference of the range you highlight replaces the old reference.

Alternatively, you can click on the range selector in a dialog box that contains a range text box to specify a range (see fig. 4.8). This action removes the dialog box temporarily while you select the desired range in the worksheet. The dialog box reappears when you finish selecting the range or press Enter.

Range text box ——————

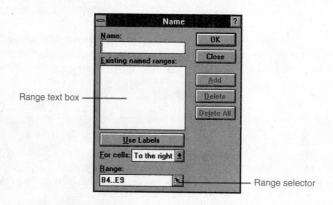

Range selector

FIG. 4.8

The range selector appears in some dialog boxes.

Using Range Names

The third way to specify a range is to refer to the range by name. Range names, which should be descriptive, can include up to 15 characters and can be used in formulas, functions, and commands. You can apply a range name with the Range Name command or the Create/Delete Range Name SmartIcon; a list of existing range names on the edit line can be viewed by using the navigator.

Using range names has a number of advantages: Range names are easier to remember than addresses. Using a range name is sometimes faster than pointing to a range in another part of the worksheet. You can, for example, remember more easily that the sales totals are in a range named TOTALS instead of in cells G5..G12.

Range names also make formulas easier to understand. For example, if you want to calculate a grand total from subtotals, you can give the range containing the subtotals a name and then use the range name in a formula that adds all the subtotals. In figure 4.9, for example, the contents box (on the edit line) shows the formula @SUM(TOTALS). Because this formula uses a range name, it is equivalent to—but easier to understand than—the formula @SUM(A:G5..A:G12).

Whenever 1-2-3 for Windows expects the address of a cell or range, you can specify a range name. Two ways to specify a range name are available. You can type the range name in the dialog box, press F3 (Name) to display existing range names, or you can click on the navigator on the edit line. The navigator lists the range names in alphabetical order (see fig. 4.10). When you edit a formula and choose a range name from the navigator's range list, the range name is inserted into the formula.

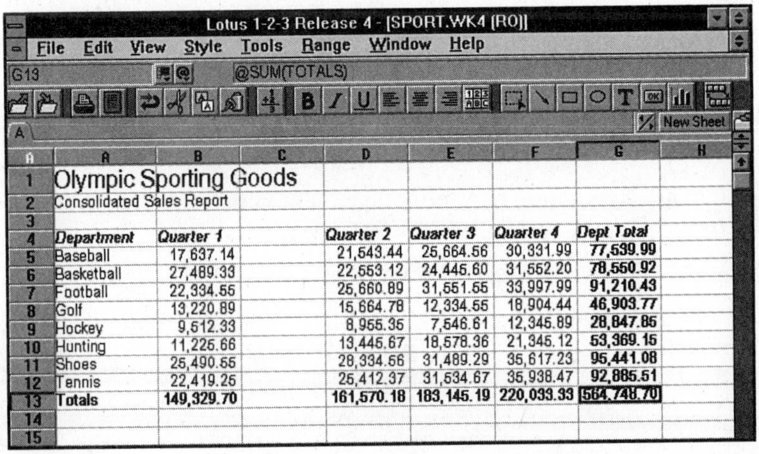

FIG. 4.9

A range name used in a formula.

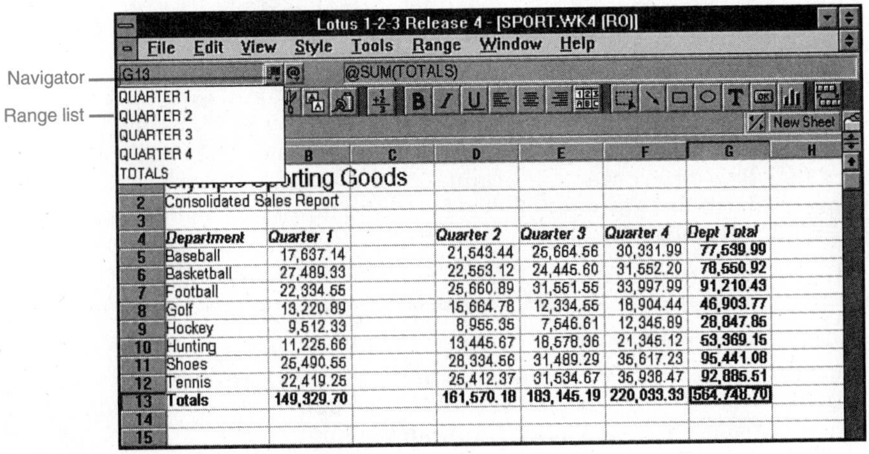

Navigator

Range list

FIG. 4.10

Displaying the navigator list.

Because a single cell is considered a valid range, you can name a single cell as a range. If a command or action, such as F5 (GoTo), calls for a single-cell address, you can specify the cell by typing its range name. If you type a range name that refers to a multiple-cell range when 1-2-3 calls for a single-cell address, 1-2-3 for Windows uses the upper-left corner of the range.

If you type a nonexistent range name, 1-2-3 for Windows displays an error message. Press Esc or Enter or choose OK to clear the error. Then try again.

Errors may occur when you use range names in formulas. These errors are covered in the section "Using Functions in the Worksheet" in Chapter 7, "Using Functions."

Naming Ranges with the Range Name Command

To create a range name, use the Range Name command to assign a name to a cell or range. Follow these steps:

1. Select the cell or range you want to name.

2. Choose Range Name or click on the Create/Delete Range Name SmartIcon. The Name dialog box appears.

3. Type the new range name and select OK or press Enter.

    If you want, you can choose the range after selecting the Range Name command: Choose the command, click on the range selector in the Range text box, and highlight the range.

> **CAUTION:** If you type an existing range name after you preselect the range, 1-2-3 for Windows changes the address of the existing range name to refer to the newly selected range—and does not warn you. If you have written formulas that contain this range name, the formulas automatically refer to the new address and may produce errors. To help prevent this problem, scan the F3 (Name) list or the navigator list before applying new range names.

A range name can include up to 15 characters. You can type or refer to the name by using any combination of uppercase and lowercase letters, but 1-2-3 for Windows stores all range names as uppercase letters. Note the following rules and precautions for naming ranges:

■ Do not use spaces, commas, semicolons, or the following characters:

+ - * / & > < @ #

■ You can use numbers in range names, but don't start the name with a number. TOTAL1 is okay, but 1TOTAL is not.

■ Do not use range names that are also cell addresses, column letters, or row numbers (such as A2, IV, or 100), names of keys (such as GoTo), function names (such as @SUM), or macro commands (such as FORM).

For Related Information

▶▶ "Using Macro Commands," p. 773.

FROM HERE...

If you have named a range but later want to change the cells that the range name refers to, you can do so easily. Follow these steps to redefine a range name's address:

1. Select Range Name or click on the Create/Delete Range Name SmartIcon.

2. Locate the range name in the Existing Named Ranges list. Click once on the name to insert it into the Name text box.

3. Click on the range selector in the Range text box at the bottom of the Name dialog box.

4. Use any method to select the new range on the worksheet.

5. Click on OK or press Enter to close the dialog box. The existing range name now refers to a new group of cells.

Creating Range Names from Labels

You can use the Range Name command to create range names from labels already typed into the worksheet. In figure 4.11, for example, you can use the labels in cells B5..B8 to name the cells with sales data in C5..C8.

By choosing the Use Labels button in the Name dialog box, you can automatically create range names using column and row labels in the highlighted range. With the For Cells drop-down list in the Name dialog box, specify whether the cells to be named appear Above, Below, To the Right, or To the Left of the labels you want to use as range names.

Because you want to name the cells to the right of the labels in figure 4.11, click on the Use Labels button in the Name dialog box and select To the Right from the For Cells list box. Specify the range B5..B8 in the Range text box and press Enter.

FIG. 4.11

Labels can be used for range names.

	A	B	C	D	E	F	G	H
1								
2		Fourth Quarter Sales						
3								
4			Oct	Nov	Dec			
5		Dept 1	6654	7565	8123			
6		Dept 2	1200	1450	1215			
7		Dept 3	3325	3680	4123			
8		Dept 4	6635	6900	7500			
9								
10		Totals	17814	19595	20961			
11								
12								
13								
14								

(Lotus 1-2-3 Release 4 - [Untitled])

When you specify cells that contain labels you want to use as range names, only cells that contain labels are used. If you specified the range B2..B10 in the preceding example (see fig. 4.11), the blank cells in B3, B4, and B9 are ignored. The first 15 characters of the label in B2 become the range name for C2 (the two words FOURTH QUARTER, the space between the words, and the space following the second word). If you specify cells that are blank, or that include numbers or formulas, 1-2-3 ignores them when it uses labels to name ranges.

To delete an unwanted range name, use Range Name or the Create/Delete Range Name SmartIcon and then select the name from the list of existing range names. Then choose the Delete button. To delete all range names in a file, use the Delete All command button.

T I P

The navigator on the edit line displays a list of all named ranges in the worksheet file.

You can use the 1-2-3 Classic command /Range Name Table to insert a table of range names and their respective range references into the worksheet at the cell-pointer location.

Using Three-Dimensional Ranges

Three-dimensional ranges are particularly useful when you build consolidation worksheets. Consolidations are worksheets that combine data from different files, each of which contains data from one department, region, product, and so on.

A three-dimensional range has the shape of a three-dimensional rectangle. The first two dimensions include the height (number of rows) and width (number of columns) in the range. The third dimension, the depth, occurs when you add worksheets to the range. A range can span multiple worksheets within a worksheet file, giving you a range that goes several levels "deep." However, you must use contiguous sheets. That is, you cannot skip sheets in your 3D references.

For example, to create the range A:C4..C:E8 shown in figure 4.12, move the cell pointer to A:C4. Press and hold the Shift key (or press F4) to anchor the range. Press the down-arrow key four times and the right-arrow key twice to highlight A:C4..A:E8; then press Ctrl+PgUp twice to move to worksheet C. release the Shift key. Alternatively, you can highlight the cells in worksheets B and C by holding the Shift key and clicking on the C page tab (you cannot click on the page tab if the worksheets are in perspective view, as is the case in fig. 4.12).

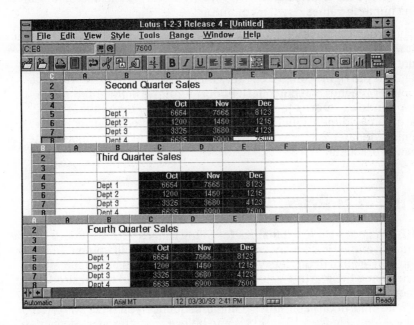

FIG. 4.12

A three-dimensional range that spans three worksheets (shown in perspective view).

You also can select three-dimensional ranges by first grouping worksheets together (see "Grouping Worksheets" earlier in this chapter). When worksheets are grouped, range selections applied to one worksheet occur in all the worksheets simultaneously. Using this feature, you can avoid moving between worksheets and can use the mouse more easily.

Highlighting a three-dimensional range is much easier than typing the corner addresses. If you do type the addresses, make sure that you use the correct worksheet letters. The corners of a three-dimensional range are diagonally opposite; usually, this means the upper-left corner cell in the first worksheet and the lower-right corner cell in the last worksheet.

Entering Data in a Range

When you highlight a range in a worksheet, the cell pointer remains within that range as you type information into the cells. When you press Enter to complete an entry, the cell pointer moves to the next cell inside the highlighted range. Until you press an arrow key or click the mouse outside the range, pressing Enter simply moves the cell pointer within the highlighted area. This arrangement can be useful for entering numeric values down a column.

The order 1-2-3 uses in moving around in a highlighted range is as follows: 1-2-3 begins in the upper-left corner cell of the range, moves down until the first column is completed, moves to the top of the next column to the right, completes that column, and so on. After the cell pointer reaches the bottom-right corner of the highlighted range, 1-2-3 for Windows returns to the upper-left corner of the range. The fill area is two-dimensional only; even if the specified range is three-dimensional, 1-2-3 for Windows fills only the specified range in the current worksheet.

Filling a Range with Values

1-2-3 includes a special feature for filling ranges with sequential values, such as numeric sequences or dates. The Range Fill command (or the Fill Range SmartIcon) lets you generate sequences automatically by specifying the starting value, the ending value, and the desired increment. The Range Fill by Example command (or the Fill Range by Example SmartIcon) continues a linear sequence you have started in a worksheet. Figure 4.13 shows some before and after sequences you can create by example. (See Chapter 13, "Creating Databases," for more details on filling ranges.)

NOTE 1-2-3 continues the sequence in any direction in which you have highlighted cells.

You can create a sequence that decreases in value by starting the two values in the negative direction.

T I P

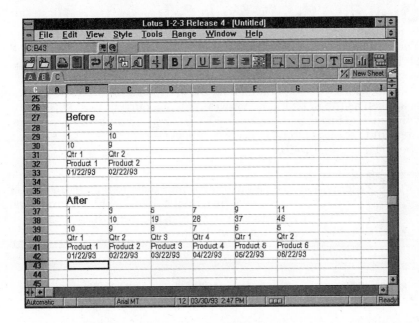

FIG. 4.13

The Fill by Example command creates sequences based on your example.

Setting Column Widths

When you start a new worksheet, the column width of all columns is nine characters. You may need to change the width of a column or the height of a row to display data properly. If columns are too narrow, asterisks appear instead of numbers in the cells, and labels are truncated if the adjacent cell to the right contains data. If columns are too wide, you may not be able to see enough data on-screen or print enough data on one page.

NOTE 1-2-3 may display more or fewer characters than you expect in a cell. The column-width number approximates the number of characters that can be displayed. The actual display depends on the typeface and point size of the cell and the individual characters in the cell's data.

You can change the width of all the columns in the worksheet or the width of individual columns.

Whether a number can fit into a cell depends on both the column width and the format of the number. Some negative numbers display with parentheses that take two extra characters. If a number displays as a row of asterisks, change the column width, the format, or both to display the number itself.

Changing the Default Column Width

You can change the column width for the entire worksheet by using the Style Worksheet Defaults command. In the Worksheet Defaults dialog box, specify the new column width, from 1 to 240 characters, in the Column Width text box and choose OK or press Enter. This new setting is applied as the default column width for the current worksheet; any columns you insert use the new width. 1-2-3 also immediately adjusts the widths of all columns in the worksheet—except those set earlier to specific individual widths.

 NOTE   Individual column-width settings override the global column width. If you change the global column width after changing the width of individual columns, the individual columns retain their adjusted widths.

Changing Individual Column Widths

You can change the width of one or more columns by using the keyboard and the Style Column Width command. Alternatively, you can use the mouse to change the width of one or more columns.

To change the width of an individual column with the keyboard, use these steps:

1. Select a cell or range in the column you want to change.

2. Choose Style Column Width. The Column Width dialog box appears.

3. Type the new column width, from 1 to 240 characters, in the Set Width To text box or use the scroll arrow to set the new value.

4. Press Enter or choose OK.

If you didn't preselect the column you want to change, you can specify the column or columns you want to change in the Column(s) text box in the Column Width dialog box.

 NOTE 1-2-3 shows the column width in the date/time/style indicator in the status bar. If the indicator shows the date and time, click on it once to display the column width and row height. The indicator displays the width of the currently selected column. If several columns are selected and contain different widths, the indicator will be blank for the width designation.

You can change the width of several columns by selecting a range that includes several columns before you issue the command. All columns represented in the range are affected when you use the Style Column Width command.

To change the width of an individual column with the mouse, use these steps:

1. Move the mouse pointer to the column border (to the right of the column letter in the worksheet frame) until the mouse pointer changes to a double-arrow pointing horizontally.

2. Press and hold the left mouse button.

3. Drag the column border to the left or right to its new position and release the mouse button.

When you use the mouse to change the width of a column, 1-2-3 for Windows displays a solid vertical line that moves with the mouse pointer to show you the position of the new column border. You can change several columns at once with the mouse by clicking on the first column's heading (for example, the letter J for column J) and dragging to highlight additional columns (see fig. 4.14). Then adjust the width of any one of the highlighted columns. All highlighted columns comply with the changes made to the single column.

Fitting the Column Width to the Data

A useful feature of 1-2-3 for Windows is its capability to set a column width to match the data contained in the column. Using this feature prevents you from guessing at the column width needed to accommodate long entries. You can adjust the column width to fit the widest entry in the column by using one of three methods:

■ Double-click on the right border of the column heading.

- Choose Style Column Width, specify Fit Widest Entry in the Column Width dialog box, specify the range in the Column text box (if you didn't preselect the range), and choose OK or press Enter.

- Place the cell pointer anywhere in the column and click on the Size Column SmartIcon.

For any of these methods, 1-2-3 for Windows immediately adjusts the column width to match the widest entry in the column.

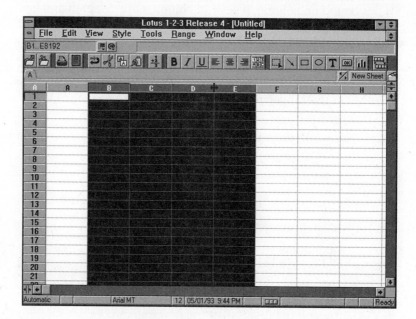

FIG. 4.14

Adjusting the width of several columns with the mouse.

Restoring the Default Width

To reset an individual column width to the worksheet default, select a cell in the column and choose Reset to Worksheet Default from the Column Width dialog box. Alternatively, you can choose the Style Column Width command and then specify the column(s) you want to reset in the Column(s) text box.

Changing Column Widths in Group Mode

Individual column widths and global column widths can apply to several worksheets if you first group them together with Group mode. In Group mode, all the worksheets change column widths at the same time based on changes made to a single worksheet's column settings.

Use Group mode when several worksheets have the same format—for example, when each worksheet contains the same data for a different department or division. When you group worksheets together, any formatting change (such as setting column widths) made to one worksheet in the group affects all the worksheets in that group.

Setting Row Heights

By adjusting row heights, you can make worksheet entries more attractive and easier to understand. The default row height, which depends on the default font, changes if you change the global font. For example, if the global font is 10-point Arial MT, the default row height is 12 points. If you change the global font to 14-point Arial MT, the default row height changes automatically to 17 points. A point is approximately 1/72 of an inch when printed; therefore, 12-point type is about one-sixth of an inch high when printed.

1-2-3 for Windows adjusts row height automatically to accommodate changes in point size. Occasionally, however, you may need to change a row's height—for example, to add more white space between rows of data. The following sections describe the process of changing row heights.

Setting the Default Row Height

You can change the row height for the entire worksheet by using the Style Row Height command. In the Row Height dialog box, enter the address A1..A8192 in the Row(s) text box. This is an address that includes all rows in the worksheet. Type the new row height (in points) in the Set Height To text box. Press Enter or choose OK.

Note that changing the default row height involves a different procedure than changing the default column width. Changing the default row height is a matter of selecting all rows and changing the height.

Setting Individual Row Heights

You can change the height of a single row by placing the cell pointer in that row, using the Style Row Height command, and typing the desired height into the Set Height To text box in the Row Height dialog box or use the scroll arrows to set the value. Press Enter or choose OK when finished.

You can change the height of several rows by selecting a range that includes all the rows you want to change before you issue the command. All rows represented in the range are affected when you use the <u>S</u>tyle <u>R</u>ow Height command.

 NOTE 1-2-3 shows the row height in the date/time/style indicator in the status bar. If the indicator shows the date and time, click on it once to display the column width and row height.

To change the height of an individual row with the mouse, use these steps:

1. Move the mouse pointer to the row border (below the row number in the worksheet frame) until the mouse pointer changes to a double-arrow pointing vertically.

2. Press and hold the left mouse button.

3. Drag the row border up or down to its new position and release the mouse button.

When you use the mouse to change the height of a row, 1-2-3 for Windows displays a solid horizontal line that moves with the mouse pointer to show the position of the new row border. You can change several rows at once with the mouse by clicking on the first row's number (for example, the number 1 for row 1) and dragging to highlight additional rows. Then adjust the height of any one of the highlighted rows. All highlighted rows comply with the changes made to the individual row.

T   I   P No command is available to hide a row (as there is to hide a column). Although you cannot change a row height to 0, you can set it to 1, which may accomplish your objective. Unless you use the Zoom feature to enlarge the display, rows with a height of 1 are barely visible.

Fitting the Row Height to the Font

You can automatically fit the row height to the largest font in the row by using the Fit Largest Font option in the Row Height dialog box. With this option selected, 1-2-3 for Windows automatically locates the largest font in the row and adjusts the row's height to fit that font. Since row heights automatically fit your font selections as you make them, the only reason you would need to select this option is when you have changed the normal row height after setting the font.

Changing Row Heights in Group Mode

Individual row heights can apply to several worksheets if you first group them together with Group mode. In Group mode, all the worksheets change row heights at the same time based on changes made to a single worksheet's row settings.

Use Group mode when several worksheets have the same format—for example, when each worksheet contains the same data for a different department or division. When you group worksheets together, any formatting change (such as setting row heights) made to one worksheet in the group affects all the worksheets in that group.

Erasing Cells and Ranges

You can clear part or all of the worksheet in several ways. Any data you clear is removed from memory—but these changes don't affect the file on disk until you save the current version of the file to disk, as explained in Chapter 6, "Managing Files." You can use either of two commands to erase a cell or range: Edit Clear or Edit Cut. Both commands have shortcut keys and SmartIcons available as alternative methods.

The Edit Clear command erases all data (label, value, formula, or function), attributes, and formats from a cell or range. (This command is not the same as the 1-2-3 Classic command /Range Erase, which erases only cell contents and not formats.) Alternatively, you can erase only the styles (formats and attributes) or the content (label, value, formula, or function) of a cell. Choose the desired option from the Clear dialog box that appears when you use the Edit Clear command.

Pressing the Del key or clicking on the Delete SmartIcon is equivalent to using the Edit Clear command, but data is erased more quickly with either of these methods than with the Edit Clear command because neither displays the Clear dialog box. The Del key and the Delete SmartIcon delete the cell contents without affecting the formatting. These two techniques are especially useful for erasing a single cell but they also can be used to erase a highlighted range.

The Edit Cut (Shift+Del) command, covered in detail later in this chapter, is designed to be followed by the Edit Paste (Shift+Ins) command.

With Edit Cut, the selected range is removed from the worksheet (including all data, attributes, and formatting) and placed on the Windows Clipboard (a holding area in memory). By using the Edit Paste command, you can paste this information in other locations. Edit Paste can be used repeatedly to paste the same data in various locations. If your intent is to remove data so that it can be pasted elsewhere, use Edit Cut, not Edit Clear.

T I P You can clear a range quickly by dragging blank cells to the filled area. Dragging cells is covered under "Moving Data," later in this chapter. Be sure to drag blank, unformatted cells to the unwanted area—otherwise, you may have changed the formatting of the old cells.

Deleting Cells, Rows, Columns, and Worksheets

When you erase cells with Edit Clear or Edit Cut, the cells still exist in the worksheet but they are empty. In contrast, when you delete a worksheet, row, or column, 1-2-3 for Windows removes the entire worksheet, row, or column and moves others to fill the gap created by the deletion. 1-2-3 for Windows also updates addresses, including those in formulas.

To delete a worksheet, row, or column, use the Edit Delete command. After you choose this command, 1-2-3 for Windows displays the Delete dialog box (see fig. 4.15). Choose Column, Row, or Sheet, depending on what you want to delete. In the Range text box, specify the range to be deleted. You can type the address, highlight cells, or preselect cells. Press Enter to confirm the dialog box and delete the specified area.

When you delete a column, 1-2-3 for Windows moves subsequent columns to the left to fill the gap caused by the deletion. When you delete a row or worksheet, 1-2-3 for Windows moves up the remaining rows and worksheets. Range references in formulas are adjusted; for example, if you delete row 4, the formula +A3+A6 becomes +A3+A5. If, however, a formula refers specifically to a deleted cell, the formulas result in ERR. (For details on how the format of addresses in formulas affects the results of deletions or insertions, see the section, "Copying Formulas," later in this chapter.)

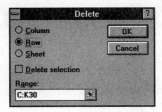

FIG. 4.15

The Delete dialog box.

To delete a block (range) of cells, simply check the box marked Delete selection in the Delete dialog box. This tells 1-2-3 that you want to re-move exactly those cells that are specified in the Range text box. In addition to checking this option, specify either Row or Column in the the dialog box. If you select Row when deleting a selection, 1-2-3 moves cells up to fill the space. If you select Column when deleting a selection, 1-2-3 moves cells to the left to fill the space.

You can also use SmartIcons to delete ranges, rows, columns, or sheets. Just select one of the icons shown below after making your selection:

—Delete Column

—Delete Row

—Delete Range

—Delete Sheet

If you delete worksheets, rows, or columns that are part of a named range, the named range becomes smaller. If these deletions involve borders of the range, the range becomes undefined. If you delete an entire named range, 1-2-3 for Windows deletes the range and its name; formulas that refer to that range name result in ERR.

> **CAUTION:** Deleting rows or columns usually affects only the cur-rent worksheet. If, however, you have grouped together several worksheets with Group mode and you delete (or add) rows or columns in one worksheet, you delete (or add) the same rows or columns in all the grouped worksheets.

Inserting Cells, Rows, Columns, and Worksheets

Just as you can delete rows, columns, and worksheets, you can insert them anywhere in the worksheet file with the Edit Insert command. When you select this command, the Insert dialog box appears (see fig. 4.16). From this dialog box, choose the dimension to insert (Column, Row, or Sheet).

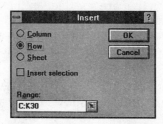

The Insert dialog box.

When you insert rows, all rows below the cell pointer move down. When you insert columns, all columns to the right of the cell pointer move to the right. When you insert worksheets, all the worksheets behind the new ones receive new worksheet letters. For example, if you insert a new worksheet after worksheet A, and worksheet B already exists, the new worksheet becomes B, the former worksheet B becomes worksheet C, and so on. All addresses and formulas are adjusted automatically.

> **CAUTION:** If Group mode is activated and you insert columns or rows in one worksheet, those changes are reflected in every worksheet in the file.

If you insert a row or column within the borders of a range, the range expands to accommodate the new rows or columns. For example, if you have the range A1..B4 referenced in a formula, and insert a row above row 3, the reference will now read A1..B5. If you insert a worksheet within a range that spans worksheets, the range expands automatically to accommodate the new worksheet. Formulas referring to that range include the new cells.

You can check the Insert selection option to insert a range of cells—the range specified in the Range text box. In addition to this check box, select either Row or Column to tell 1-2-3 whether to move existing cells down or to the right (respectively) when inserting.

You can use SmartIcons to insert ranges, rows, columns, and sheets. Use the icons below to insert quickly:

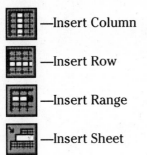

—Insert Column

—Insert Row

—Insert Range

—Insert Sheet

Changing the Display of a Worksheet File

As described in Chapter 2, "Understanding the Graphical User Interface," each 1-2-3 for Windows worksheet file appears in a Worksheet window within the 1-2-3 window. You can change the way 1-2-3 for Windows displays multiple Worksheet windows—for example, so that you can compare data in two or more worksheet files or open utility windows within a worksheet or chart.

You also can change the way you view an individual file within a Worksheet window. You can freeze titles on-screen, split the window into two horizontal or vertical panes, and view parts of up to three worksheets in a single file at the same time. You can reduce or enlarge the view of the worksheet. These options, described in the following sections, enable you to compare data within a worksheet and to see different parts of your work at the same time.

Splitting the Worksheet Window

You can split a Worksheet window either horizontally or vertically into two panes. This technique is useful if the worksheet is larger than what can be displayed on-screen and you want to see different parts of the worksheet at the same time. The technique is also useful if you want to display several windows at the same time but want to see a larger area of the window. To split a window, choose the View Split command. The Split dialog box appears (see fig. 4.17).

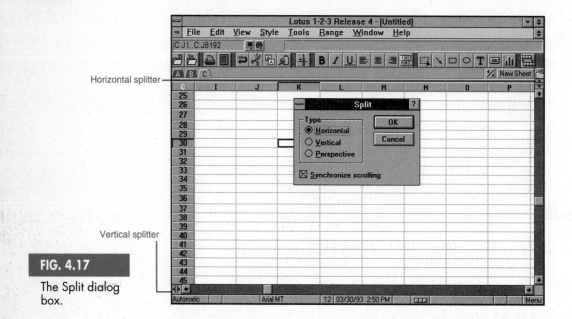

Horizontal splitter

Vertical splitter

FIG. 4.17

The Split dialog
box.

To split a window with the mouse, click on the horizontal splitter and
drag the pointer down to divide the window into two horizontal panes.
Alternatively, click on the vertical splitter and drag it to create two
vertical panes.

You can also split the window without using the mouse. Just move the
cell pointer to the desired row (for a horizontal split) or column (for a
vertical split) and choose the View Split command. Now choose Horizontal or Vertical and press OK to split the window. The position of the
cell pointer determines where the split occurs.

NOTE Because a split window displays two frames, you cannot
display quite as much data at one time as you can with a full
window. You can remove the frames by choosing View Set
View Preferences and deselecting the Worksheet Frame
option in the View Preferences dialog box, but the two
panes may be more difficult to separate visually and the
address of the current cell is less obvious.

In a split window, you can change data in one pane and see how the
change affects data in the other pane. This capability is quite useful for
what-if analysis. A split window also is useful when you write macros.
You can write the macro in one pane and see the data that the macro is
working on in the other pane.

Suppose that you want to see how a change in data affects totals, located in an area of the worksheet off-screen. You can split the window to see the data and the totals at the same time. If the worksheet is designed so that totals are in a column to the right, split the window vertically (see fig. 4.18). If the worksheet displays totals in a row at the bottom, split the window horizontally.

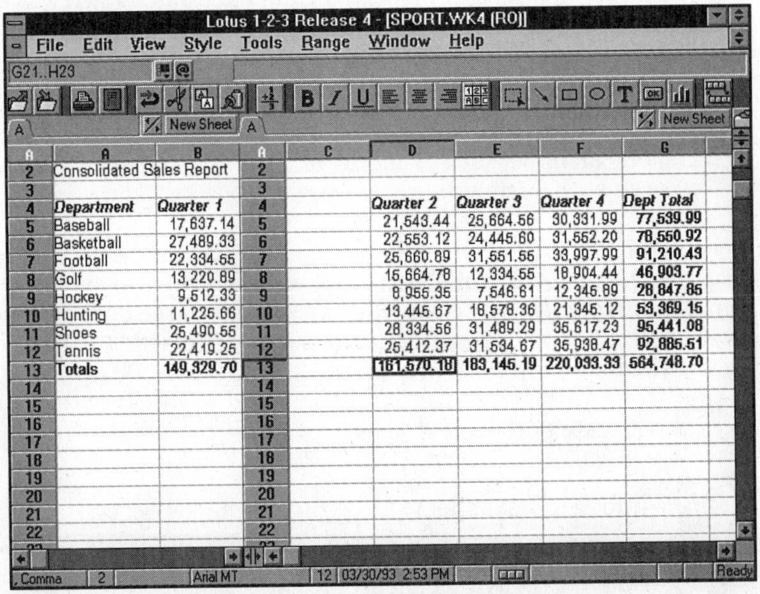

FIG. 4.18

A window split vertically.

At times, you may want to see two unrelated views of the same worksheet. For example, you may want to see data in one pane and macros in the other pane. In this case, you want the two panes to scroll separately. Use the View Split command and deselect Synchronize Scrolling in the Split dialog box to make scrolling unsynchronized; select the Synchronize Scrolling option if you want to restore synchronized scrolling. When scrolling is synchronized, both panes move together as you scroll the worksheet. To move between panes, use the F6 (Pane) key or click in the other window with the mouse.

To clear a split window and return to a single pane, use View Clear Split. No matter which pane the cell pointer is in when you choose this command, the cell pointer moves to the left pane (in a vertically split window) or to the upper pane (in a horizontally split window) when you clear a split window.

Displaying Worksheets in Perspective View

 As mentioned in Chapter 2, "Understanding the Graphical User Interface," you can display up to three worksheets in a file simultaneously in 1-2-3 for Windows; this type of display is called perspective view. To show a file in perspective view, choose View Split and select the Perspective option in the Split dialog box, or click on the Perspective View SmartIcon.

> **NOTE**   You can have a split window or a perspective view, but not both at the same time.

To move among the worksheets in a perspective view, press Ctrl+PgUp or Ctrl+PgDn. If you have more than three sheets, they will cycle through the perspective view—so you can see any three consecutive sheets at one time. You can also use the following SmartIcons to move among the sheets:

 —Create perspective view

 —Move to next sheet

 —Move to previous sheet

Freezing Titles

Most worksheets are much larger than can be displayed on-screen at one time. As you move the cell pointer, you scroll the display. New data appears at one edge of the display as the data at the other edge scrolls out of sight. Data can be hard to understand when titles at the top of the worksheet and descriptions at the left scroll off the screen. For example, you can no longer tell the departments to which data refers.

To prevent titles from scrolling off the screen, move the cell pointer to the row and/or column that marks the top-left cell of the "working area" of the sheet. In other words, everything above and/or to the left of the cell pointer will be frozen. Next, use the View Freeze Titles command to lock titles on-screen. When you select this command, the Freeze Titles dialog box appears (see fig. 4.19). You can lock the top rows of the worksheet with the Rows option, the leftmost columns with Columns, or both rows and columns with <u>B</u>oth. To unlock the titles, select View <u>C</u>lear Titles. To change the locked area, choose <u>V</u>iew Cle<u>a</u>r Titles and then specify the new titles area.

FIG. 4.19

The Freeze Titles dialog box.

To lock titles in both the top rows and the leftmost columns, follow these steps:

1. Position the worksheet so that the titles you want to lock are at the top and to the left of the display.

2. Move the cell pointer to the cell in the first row below the titles and the first column to the right of the titles.

3. Choose <u>V</u>iew Freeze <u>T</u>itles <u>B</u>oth to lock both horizontal and vertical titles.

In figure 4.19, the titles are in rows 1, 2, and 3 and column A. After these titles are locked, the data below rows 1, 2, and 3 and to the right of column A can scroll off the screen but the locked titles remain on-screen.

If you press Home when titles are locked, the cell pointer moves to the position below and to the right of the titles rather than to cell A1. In figure 4.19, the Home position is B4. When you move the mouse pointer into the titles area, you cannot select any cells. Moreover, you cannot use the direction keys to move into the titles area, although you can use F5 (GoTo). When you use GoTo to move to a cell in the titles area, the title rows and columns appear twice. Clear the duplicate display by using the direction keys (for example, pressing Tab and PgDn to put the cell pointer well beyond the titles area) and then pressing Home to return to the home position next to the locked titles.

In a split window, locking titles affects only the current pane. Unless you use Group mode, locking titles affects only the current worksheet in a file.

Zooming the Display

One of the limitations of a monitor's size is that often you cannot see very much of the worksheet on-screen. The preceding sections explained how to split a window to view data from widely separate parts of the worksheet and how to lock specific data on-screen to provide references as you scroll through a large worksheet. Sometimes, however, you want to see the layout of the worksheet, not the actual data.

By using the View Set View Preferences command and changing the Custom Zoom % setting in the Set View Preferences dialog box, you can specify a percentage (anywhere from 400 to 25) by which to enlarge or shrink the worksheet display. Select 400 to make the worksheet four times larger; select 25 to make the display shrink to one-fourth its normal size. If you reduce the display, the resulting image is barely readable, but it gives you a view of many cells. In figure 4.20, where 25-percent reduction was used, the screen shows about 80 rows and about 300 characters across a row. The readability of these settings varies from monitor to monitor.

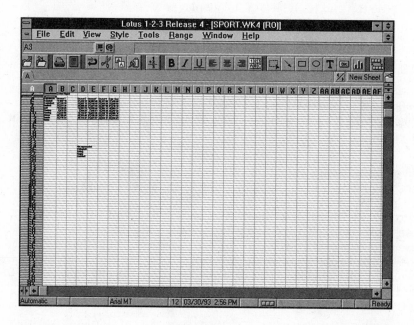

FIG. 4.20

A worksheet display reduced to 25 percent of normal size.

You can use the three commands (Zoom In, Zoom Out, and Custom) in the View menu to switch among different zoom percentages. Each time you choose Zoom In or Zoom Out, the display increases or decreases, respectively, by a factor of 10 percent—to a maximum of 400 percent or a minimum of 25 percent of the default size specified in the Set View Preferences dialog box.

You can also use the SmartIcons for these commands, they include the following:

—Zoom-In

 —Zoom-Out

 —Default Size

NOTE There is no relationship between the size of the worksheet as displayed on the screen and the size you get when printing. To enlarge or reduce the printed worksheet, use the File Page Setup command with the Size options.

For Related Information

▶▶ "Understanding 1-2-3 Printing Commands," p. 502.

FROM HERE...

Protecting and Hiding Worksheet Data

A typical 1-2-3 for Windows file contains numbers, labels, formulas, and sometimes macros. When you first build a worksheet file, especially a budget file, you may use data from an entire year. The budget model in figure 4.21 contains labels and formulas for a yearly budget. After you build this worksheet file, you do not want the labels and formulas to change. However, the detailed budget figures may change many times as different versions are submitted for approval or revision.

After the budget is approved, you may want to add actual expense data each month. Each time someone changes the detailed data, you run the risk of accidentally changing a formula or label. If a formula changes, all the totals may be wrong.

If different people add data to the file, one person may want to change a formula that seems incorrect. For example, a model may use factors for inflation, growth, or foreign-exchange rates. These factors may be decided by the Finance Department and should apply equally to all departments. Some department heads, however, may want to use their own factors. Such changes can invalidate the overall budget submitted for approval.

1-2-3 for Windows includes a number of features for situations like these. You can protect data from accidental or deliberate change, as well as hide confidential data. For example, parts of a worksheet file may contain confidential information such as salaries or cost factors. 1-2-3 for Windows provides features that enable someone to use the file without seeing certain areas of it.

You also can password-protect a file that contains confidential data when you save the file. Anyone who does not know the password is denied access to the file. No matter how well a person knows 1-2-3 for Windows, that person cannot access the file without the password.

The following sections describe 1-2-3 for Windows data-protection features.

Protecting Files

Every worksheet has areas containing formulas and labels that do not change over time. Other areas contain data that can change. You can protect the cells that should not change while still enabling changes to other cells by using two related commands. File Protect Seal File prevents changes to the entire worksheet. Style Protection overrides the sealed-file status and enables changes to specific cells and ranges. Chapter 6, "Managing Files," describes how to specifically mark cells you want to be able to change (that is, how to seal or unseal the cells) before you password-protect the entire file.

To prevent access to a file, save the file with a password. Without the password, no one can open the file, read it, or change it. However, if you lose the password, you cannot access any information in the file either. You can combine the techniques of sealing the file and saving it with a password. For example, you may want to use both techniques with a confidential personnel file. A user needs the password to open the file and then can change only unprotected cells.

FROM HERE...

For Related Information

▶▶ "Protecting Files," p. 250.

Hiding Cells and Ranges

Sometimes you want to do more than just stop someone from changing data or formulas; you want to prevent other users from even seeing the information. To hide a cell or range, use Style Number Format and select Hidden from the Format list. A hidden cell appears as a blank cell in the worksheet. To redisplay the cell contents in the worksheet, use any other number format as described in Chapter 5, "Changing the Format and Appearance of Data."

> **CAUTION:** You can hide data so that it's not easily visible, but you cannot prevent someone from seeing hidden data if that person knows how to use 1-2-3 for Windows. The only way to keep data truly confidential is to save the file with a password (see Chapter 6, "Managing Files").

You cannot use the Hidden format to hide data completely. If you move the cell pointer to that cell, you can see the contents of the cell in the edit line. And remember that all you have to do to redisplay the contents of the cell is to change the number format for that cell. If the file is sealed, however, you cannot change the format or view the contents of the cell in the edit line.

> **NOTE** When you print a range containing hidden cells, columns, or worksheets, the hidden text does not appear in the printout.

> **CAUTION:** Hidden cells appear empty; protect the cells and seal the file to prevent users from accidentally typing over the contents of hidden cells or reformatting the cells.

Hiding Worksheets, Columns, and Rows

When you hide worksheets, columns, and rows, they retain their letters and numbers but 1-2-3 for Windows skips them in the display. For example, if you hide columns B and C, 1-2-3 for Windows displays in the column border columns A, D, E, and so on. These missing letters and numbers make hiding data obvious. You can make hidden data less obvious by eliminating the frame (use the View Set View Preferences command and deselect the Worksheet Frame option).

To hide a worksheet, move the cell pointer to the worksheet you want to hide, use Style Hide, and select the Sheet option from the Hide dialog box. 1-2-3 for Windows removes the worksheet from the screen, and the cell pointer moves to the next worksheet. To display a hidden worksheet, use Style Hide, type the hidden worksheet's letter in the Range text box, along with a cell address (for example, A:A1), and click on the Show button.

Although a hidden worksheet does not appear on-screen, formulas that refer to the worksheet remain valid and intact. For example, if you hide worksheet A: and worksheet B: includes a reference to worksheet A: in a formula, the formula is not affected. The worksheet is actually still part of the file—it's just invisible. To protect data in a hidden worksheet, seal the file as described in Chapter 6, "Managing Files."

To hide a column, move the cell pointer to a cell in the column you want to hide. Then use Style Hide and select Column. If you don't preselect one or more columns, you can type a column address in the Range text box of the Hide dialog box. To redisplay hidden columns, choose Style Hide, specify a range that includes cells in the hidden columns, and click on Show.

A hidden column does not appear in the worksheet, but the column letter is retained. Formulas that refer to cells in hidden columns are calculated correctly, and 1-2-3 for Windows continues to store the full value of hidden data. Figure 4.21 shows a worksheet after columns are hidden. Notice that in the column border, column letters C through N are missing. The columns are still there, but they do not appear and you cannot move the cell pointer to them. When you print a range that contains hidden columns, the hidden columns do not print.

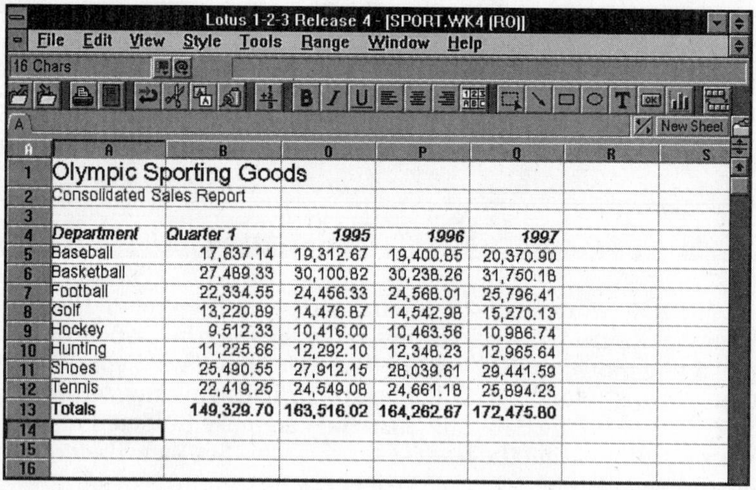

FIG. 4.21

The worksheet with hidden columns.

No specific command to hide a row is available, but you can use the Style Row Height command to set a row's height to 1, making it nearly invisible. You also can use a mouse to point to the border between the current row's number and the next row's number in the worksheet frame and then click and drag the mouse up or down to shrink or expand the height of the row. Unlike hidden columns, rows that you reduce with this procedure are not really hidden. If data appears in the reduced row, your printout may display dots and dashes where the row was located.

Use the Style Row Height command or the mouse to make the row visible again by making its height greater than 1. When you print a range that contains hidden rows, the hidden rows do not print.

Recalculating a Worksheet

When a value in a cell changes, 1-2-3 for Windows recalculates every cell that depends on the changed value. This recalculation demonstrates the power of an electronic spreadsheet. Usually, 1-2-3 recalculates a worksheet automatically when a cell changes. If you prefer, you can tell 1-2-3 for Windows you want to recalculate manually.

Unless you specify otherwise, 1-2-3 for Windows recalculates only those formulas whose values have changed since the last recalculation. If you change the data in one cell and that cell is used in one formula, 1-2-3 for Windows recalculates only that formula.

Specifying the Recalculation Method

You can tell 1-2-3 for Windows not to recalculate the worksheet automatically by choosing Tools User Setup, choosing the Recalculation button in the User Setup dialog box, and selecting Manual in the Recalculation dialog box (see fig. 4.22). (If you followed along with this example, use the Tools User Setup Recalculation command again to reset 1-2-3 for Windows to Automatic recalculation.)

After recalculation is set to manual, you must use one of the following methods to recalculate the worksheet:

- Press F9 (Calc)
- Click on the Calc button in the status bar
- Click on the Recalculate SmartIcon
- Invoke recalculation in a macro with the CALC, RECALC, or RECALCON macro command

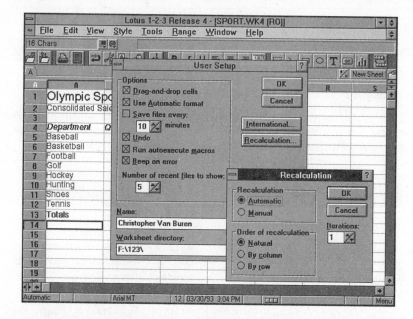

FIG. 4.22

Specifying the recalculation method.

Specifying the Recalculation Order

You can control the order in which 1-2-3 for Windows recalculates. By default, 1-2-3 for Windows recalculates in Natural order. In natural order recalculation, 1-2-3 for Windows determines which formulas depend on which cells and then sets up a recalculation order to produce the correct results.

If you prefer, you can tell 1-2-3 for Windows to recalculate By Row or By Column. Columnar recalculation starts in cell A1 and continues down the cells in column A, then column B, and so on. Row recalculation starts in cell A1 and continues across the cells in row 1, then row 2, and so on.

T I P   Generally, let 1-2-3 for Windows recalculate in natural order. When calculating by row or by column, 1-2-3 for Windows must sweep through columns and rows several times to make sure that formulas produce correct results. Natural order is faster because 1-2-3 for Windows first determines which cells have changed and then recalculates them in one sweep.

If you specify By Row or By Column, you should tell 1-2-3 for Windows the number of iterations to perform (how many times to recalculate). Specify a number from 1 (the default) to 50 in the Iterations text box. If 1-2-3 for Windows is set to recalculate in natural order and no circular references exist, 1-2-3 for Windows may stop calculating before it reaches the number of iterations indicated.

Handling Circular References

The natural order of recalculation is not always accurate if a circular reference exists. A circular reference is a formula that depends, either directly or indirectly, on its own value. Whenever 1-2-3 for Windows performs a recalculation and finds a circular reference, the Circ indicator appears on the circular-reference button in the status bar. A circular reference is almost always an error, and you should correct it immediately. Figure 4.23 shows an erroneous circular reference in which the cell containing the @SUM function includes itself.

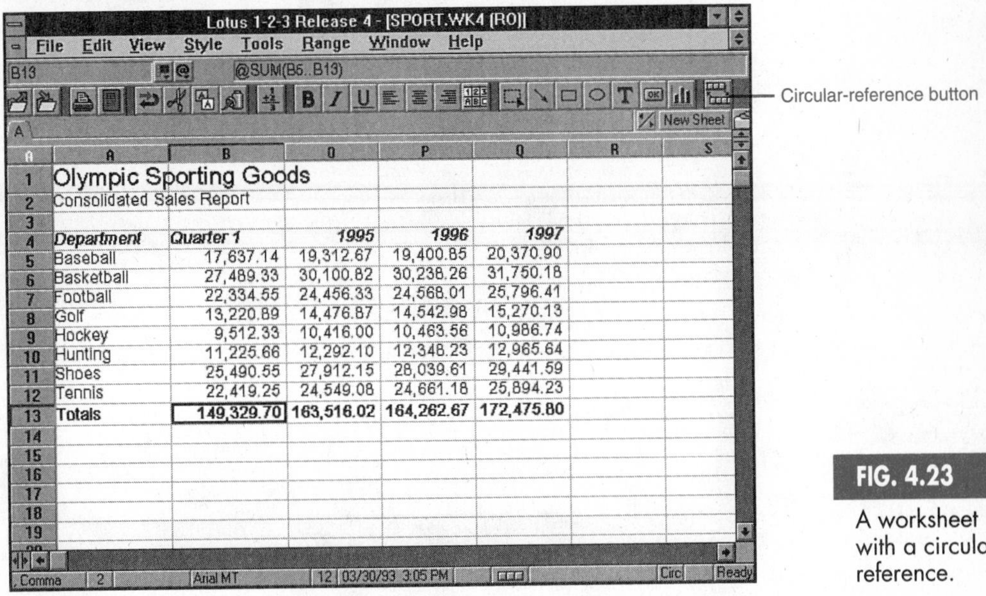

Circular-reference button

FIG. 4.23

A worksheet with a circular reference.

If the Circ indicator appears and you are not sure why, click on the circular-reference button on the status bar to go to the cell containing the circular reference. In this case, fixing the error is fairly easy. In other cases, the source of the problem may be less obvious, and you may have to check every cell referenced by the formula. You can use worksheet audit features to locate circular references more quickly.

For Related Information

▶▶ "Auditing Worksheet Formulas," p. 453.

In some cases, a circular reference is deliberate. Figure 4.24 shows a worksheet with such a reference. In this example, a company has set aside 10 percent of its net profit for employee bonuses. The bonuses themselves, however, represent an expense that reduces net profit. The formula in cell C5 shows that the amount of bonuses is net profit (in cell D5) multiplied by 0.1 (10 percent). But net profit (the formula in cell D5) is profit after bonuses (B5 minus C5). The value of employee bonuses depends on the value of net profit, and the value of net profit depends on the value of employee bonuses. In figure 4.24, C5 depends on D5, and D5 depends on C5. This situation is a classic circular reference.

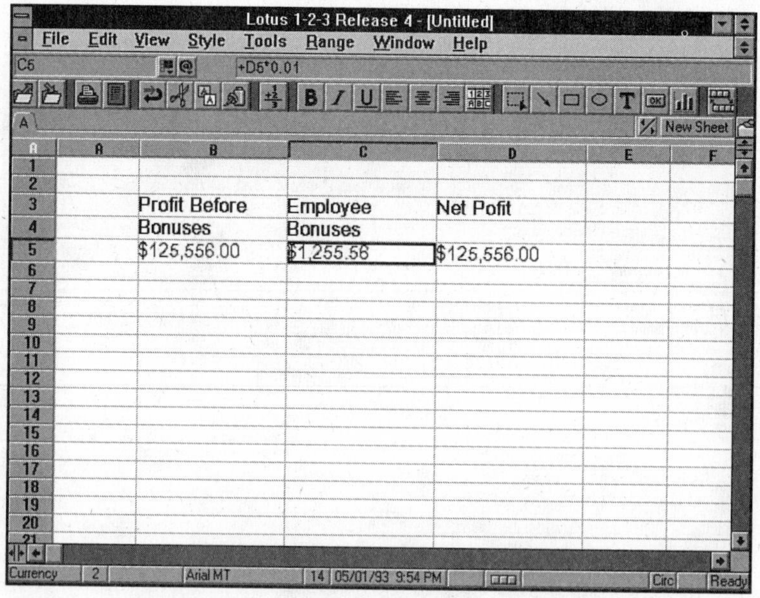

FIG. 4.24

A worksheet with a deliberate circular reference.

If a deliberate circular reference exists, each time you recalculate the worksheet, the values change by a smaller amount. Eventually, the changes become insignificant. This reduction is called convergence. Notice that the erroneous circular reference in figure 4.23 never converges, and the @SUM result is bigger every time you recalculate.

The worksheet in figure 4.24 needs five recalculations before the changes become less than one dollar. After you establish this number, you can tell 1-2-3 for Windows to recalculate the worksheet five times every time it recalculates by specifying 5 in the Iterations text box in the Recalculation dialog box. In most cases, you can calculate a converging circular reference with a macro (see Chapters 15 and 16 for details on using macros).

Moving Data

1-2-3 for Windows provides a number of ways to move data, including dragging the cell or range with the mouse, using commands or shortcut keys from the Edit menu, and using SmartIcons.

In a move operation, the data being moved or copied is called the source; the location to which you are moving the data is called the target or destination. When you move data, the source data disappears from its original location and reappears at the target location.

The following sections describe all available moving methods and discuss how 1-2-3 for Windows handles the movement of formulas or data used in formulas and the movement of formatting and style attributes.

> Remember that you can use the Edit Undo command, press Ctrl+Z (Undo), or click on the Undo SmartIcon to correct a mistake in moving a range.
>
> **T I P**

Dragging a Range to a New Location

Dragging the cell or range is the simplest way to move data. Highlight the desired range, click the mouse near one edge of the range, and drag it to another location in the same worksheet. When you move the mouse pointer to the edge of the highlighted range, the pointer changes to a hand (see fig. 4.25). You can use this technique to move a single cell or a range of cells. However, you cannot drag a collection with the mouse.

Lotus 1-2-3 Release 4 - [SPORT.WK4 [RO]]

File   Edit   View   Style   Tools   Range   Window   Help

B:C6   +$B5*1.095

	A	B	O	P	Q	R	S
1	Olympic Sporting Goods						
2	Consolidated Sales Report						
3							
4	Department	Quarter 1	1995	1996	1997		
5	Baseball	17,637.14	19,312.67	19,400.85	19,370.90		
6	Basketball	27,489.33	30,100.82	30,238.26	31,750.18		
7	Football	22,334.55	24,456.33	24,568.01	25,796.41		
8	Golf	13,220.89	14,476.87	14,542.98	15,270.13		
9	Hockey	9,512.33	10,416.00	10,463.56	10,986.74		
10	Hunting	11,225.66	12,292.10	12,348.23	12,965.64		
11	Shoes	25,490.55	27,912.15	28,039.61	29,441.59		
12	Tennis	22,419.25	24,549.08	24,661.18	25,894.23		
13	Totals	5,823,858.30	163,516.02	164,262.67	172,475.80		
14							
15							

FIG. 4.25

When moving
a range with
the mouse, the
mouse pointer
changes to a
hand.

Cutting and Pasting a Range

To move data by cutting and pasting, you cut the data from the
worksheet to the Clipboard (a Windows holding area in memory). Then
you paste the data from the Clipboard to a new location in the same
worksheet, to a different worksheet in the same file, to a different file,
or to a different Windows 3.x application. You can move entire columns, rows, or worksheets with this method, but you cannot move a
column to a row, a row to a column, or a worksheet or file to a column
or row.

You can paste data many times if you want to copy the same information to many different locations. If you want to copy data to many
different places, however, do not interrupt th pasting operation by cutting or copying other data to the Clipboard. Pasting makes a copy
of whatever is on the Clipboard; only the contents of the most recent
copy or cut operation are stored on the Clipboard.

To cut and paste data, follow these steps:

1. Highlight the range or cell you want to move.

2. Choose Edit Cut, press Shift+Del or Ctrl+X, or click on the Cut
   SmartIcon.

3. Move the cell pointer to the first cell of the destination range.

4. Choose Edit Paste, press Shift+Ins or Ctrl+V, or click on the Paste
   SmartIcon.

5. To paste the data in another location, move the cell pointer or
   select the target range and repeat step 4.

Moving a Formula

If you move one corner of a range used in a formula, the range expands or contracts and the formula is adjusted. Figure 4.26 shows a range of data that includes formulas. Figure 4.27 shows what happens after you move the range F2..H6 to G2. Notice that 1-2-3 for Windows adjusted the range in the @SUM formula (shown in the contents box of the edit line in both figures). In figure 4.26, the formula in cell G3 is @SUM(D3..F3). The move changed the formula (now in cell H3) to @SUM(D3..G3). Notice that the @SUM in both formulas starts with cell D3. Because this cell did not move, that portion of the range was not altered. But the @SUM range expanded to include D3..G3. A common use of this kind of range movement is to make room for a new row or column in the range of data.

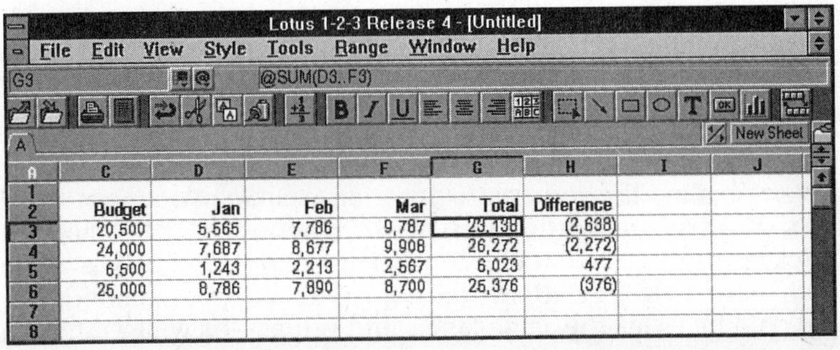

FIG. 4.26

A worksheet before cells F2..H6 move to cell G2.

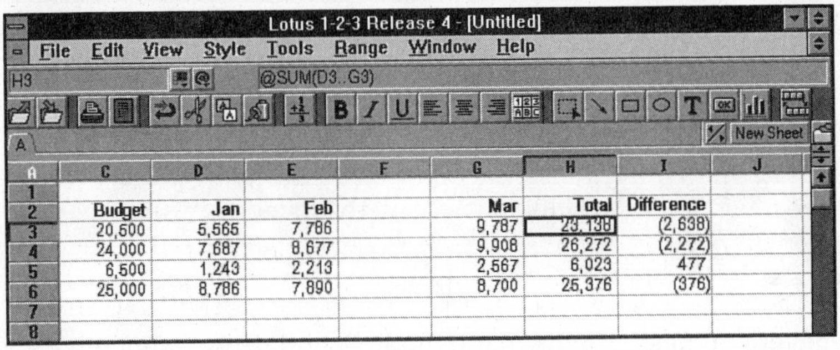

FIG. 4.27

The result after cells F2..H6 move to cell G2.

If you move the range G2..I6 in figure 4.27 back to cell F2, the formula reverts to the one shown in figure 4.26. ERR does not appear even though part of the range is eliminated. However, if you move a portion of a range without its formula, the resulting formula might not be accurate; be careful when moving cell that are referenced in formulas without also moving the formulas.

Moving Formats and Data Types

At times you may want to move the formatting and style attributes of a cell or range to another cell or range. You can do this by selecting the Edit Paste Special command instead of the Edit Paste command. In the Paste Special dialog box, you have the option of pasting only the styles from the selection (Styles only option). You can also paste the contents of the cells without the styles (Cell contents only option), or can convert formulas into values when pasting (Formulas as values option). The All option pastes normally (like the Edit Paste command).

Copying Data

The copying methods provided by 1-2-3 for Windows are very much like the moving methods described in the preceding sections. You can drag the cell or range with the mouse, use commands or shortcut keys from the Edit menu, or use SmartIcons.

In a copy operation, just as in a move operation, the data being moved or copied is called the source; the location to which you move the data is called the target or destination. When you copy data, 1-2-3 for Windows leaves the source data in its original location and places a copy of the data in the target location—the copied data appears in both places. Copied data includes the same labels and values—as well as the same formats, fonts, colors, protection status, and borders—as the original data. You do not, however, copy the column width or row height. You can use Edit Copy with Edit Paste Special to paste some of the properties or types of data that were copied.

T I P   Remember that you can use the Edit Undo command, press Ctrl+Z (Undo), or click on the Undo SmartIcon to correct a mistake in copying a range.

Whenever you need to copy data, the drag-and-drop technique is probably the right choice. The Edit Copy command is primarily for copying data to and from other applications or when you want to copy the same data to a number of different locations. The Edit Copy command is also helpful when you copy data across large areas of the worksheet and dragging would be tedious.

Copying is one of the most frequently performed actions in 1-2-3, and the copy operation can be simple or complicated. The following sections begin with simple examples of copy procedures and progress to more complex ones.

Copying with Drag-and-Drop

To copy a cell or range using the drag-and-drop technique, first high-light the cell or range you want to copy. Then move the mouse pointer to any edge of the selection (until the mouse pointer changes to a hand). Press and hold the Ctrl key as you click and drag the selection to its new location. When you reach the destination, release the mouse and the Ctrl key. The data is copied to the new location without changing the original.

Copying with Copy and Paste

You can use commands and SmartIcons to copy data. The Edit Copy command and the Copy SmartIcon use the Clipboard to copy data. No dialog box appears; 1-2-3 for Windows just copies the source data to the Clipboard. To complete the copying action, you paste the source data with the Edit Paste command or the Paste SmartIcon. You also can copy data from and to other Windows applications with these commands.

To copy data with commands or SmartIcons, follow these steps:

1. Highlight the range or cell you want to copy.

2. Choose Edit Copy, press Ctrl+Ins or Ctrl+C, or click on the Copy SmartIcon.

3. Move the cell pointer to the first cell of the destination range.

4. Choose Edit Paste, press Shift+Ins or Ctrl+V, or click on the Paste SmartIcon.

Copying Formulas

The real power of copying becomes evident when you copy formulas. When you copy a formula, 1-2-3 for Windows adjusts the new formula so that its cell references are in the same location, relative to the original formula. Relative addressing is one of the most important concepts in 1-2-3 for Windows.

The best way to understand relative addressing is to understand how 1-2-3 for Windows stores addresses in formulas. The formula @SUM(C2..C5) means to add the contents of all the cells in the range from cell C2 to cell C5. But that is not the way 1-2-3 for Windows stores this formula. If this formula is in cell C7, for example, 1-2-3 for Windows reads the formula as "add the contents of all the cells in the range from the cell five rows above this cell to the cell two rows above this cell." When you copy this formula from cell C7 to cell D7, 1-2-3 for Windows uses the same relative formula but displays it as @SUM(D2..D5).

In most cases, when you copy a formula, you want the addresses adjusted automatically. At times, however, you do not want some addresses to be adjusted, or you may want only part of an address to be adjusted. These cases are examined separately in the next sections.

Copying a Formula with Absolute Addressing

In figure 4.28, the formula in cell C9 is +C7/F7. This figure represents January's sales as a percent of the total. If you copy this formula to cell D9, the resulting formula is +D7/G7. The D7 part of the formula, which represents the sales for February, is correct. The G7 part (which refers to the difference between the budgeted amount and the actual amount), however, is incorrect. When you copy the formula from cell C9, you want the address F7 (the total sales) to copy as an absolute address. In other words, you do not want the F7 part of the formula to change when you copy the formula to cell D9.

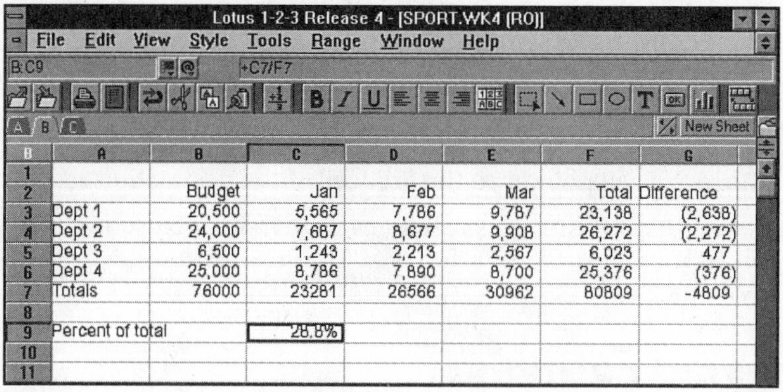

FIG. 4.28

A formula with a relative address.

	A	B	C	D	E	F	G
1							
2		Budget	Jan	Feb	Mar	Total	Difference
3	Dept 1	20,500	5,565	7,786	9,787	23,138	(2,638)
4	Dept 2	24,000	7,687	8,677	9,908	26,272	(2,272)
5	Dept 3	6,500	1,243	2,213	2,567	6,023	477
6	Dept 4	25,000	8,786	7,890	8,700	25,376	(376)
7	Totals	76000	23281	26566	30962	80809	-4809
8							
9	Percent of total		28.8%				
10							
11							

B:C9   +C7/F7

Lotus 1-2-3 Release 4 - [SPORT.WK4 (RO)]
File   Edit   View   Style   Tools   Range   Window   Help

To specify an absolute address, type a dollar sign ($) before each part of the address (worksheet, column, and row) you want to remain absolutely the same. The formula in cell C9 should be +C7/$F$7. When you copy this formula to cell D9, the formula becomes +D7/$F$7.

You can specify an absolute address without typing dollar signs. After you type the address, press F4 (Abs); the address changes to absolute. After copying the absolute formula +C7/$F$7 in cell C9 to cells D9..F9, the worksheet appears as shown in figure 4.29.

Lotus 1-2-3 Release 4 - [Untitled]							
File Edit View Style Tools Range Window Help							

C9   +C7/$F$7

	A	B	C	D	E	F	G	H
1								
2		Budget	Jan	Feb	Mar	Total	Difference	
3	Dept 1	20,500	5,565	7,786	9,787	23,138	(2,638)	
4	Dept 2	24,000	7,687	8,677	9,908	26,272	(2,272)	
5	Dept 3	6,500	1,243	2,213	2,567	6,023	477	
6	Dept 4	25,000	8,786	7,890	8,700	25,376	(376)	
7	Totals	76,000.00	23,281.00	26,566.00	30,962.00	80,809.00	(4,809.00)	
8								
9	Percent of Total		28.81%	32.88%	38.32%	100.00%		
10								
11								

FIG. 4.29

The result after copying a formula with an absolute address.

You can enter dollar signs while pointing to addresses in a formula. As you point to a cell to include it in a formula, press F4 (Abs) to make that cell's address absolute. If you make an error and forget to make an address absolute, just press F2 (Edit) to switch to Edit mode, move the cursor in the contents box to the address you want to make absolute, and press F4 (Abs).

If you want to change an absolute reference (one with dollar signs) back to a relative reference, press F2 (Edit), move the cursor to the reference, and then press F4 (Abs) as many times as necessary until the address contains no dollar signs. Press Enter to reenter the formula.

Copying a Formula with Mixed Addressing

In some cases, you must use formulas with a mix of absolute and relative references if you want the formula to copy correctly. The example presented in this section shows you how to keep a row reference absolute while letting the column reference change during the copy.

Figure 4.30 shows a price-forecasting worksheet with a different price increase percentage for each year. When you copy the formula in cell C3 down column C, you do not want the reference to cell C1 to change, but when you copy the formula across row 3, you want the reference to change for each column. The mixed reference is relative for the column and absolute for the row. The formula in cell C3 is +B3*(1+C$1). When you copy this formula down one row to cell C4, the formula becomes +B4*(1+C$1). The relative address B3 becomes B4, but the mixed address C$1 is unchanged. When you copy this formula to cell D3, the formula becomes +C3*(1+D$1). The relative address B3 becomes C3, and the mixed address C$1 becomes D$1. You can copy this mixed-address formula from cell C3 to C3..F10 for correct results throughout the worksheet.

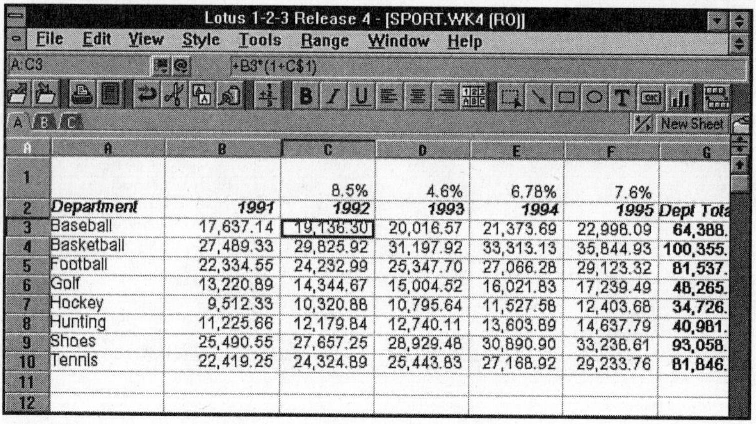

FIG. 4.30

A formula with a mixed address.

To make an address mixed without typing the dollar signs, use F4 (Abs). The first time you press F4, the address becomes absolute. If you continue to press F4, the address cycles through all the possible mixed addresses and returns to relative. The complete list of relative, absolute, and mixed addresses is found in table 4.1. To change the relative address C1 to the mixed address C$1 shown in figure 4.30, press F4 twice.

Table 4.1 Using F4 (Abs) To Change the Address Type

Address	Status
$A:$D$1	Completely absolute
$A:D$1	Absolute worksheet and row
$A:$D1	Absolute worksheet and column
$A:D1	Absolute worksheet
A:$D$1	Absolute column and row
A:D$1	Absolute row
A:$D1	Absolute column
A:D1	Relative

When you work with multiple worksheets, be careful with absolute and mixed addresses. When you first press F4, the worksheet label is made absolute. In many cases, you do not want this effect. Consider the worksheet in figure 4.30. If you changed the formula in cell C3 to $A:C$1, the absolute address of the worksheet identifier would force the C$1 reference to remain in worksheet A. If you planned to expand this model to multiple worksheets, you would want each worksheet to reference the growth range for that worksheet. You would want the worksheet letter to change relative to its new worksheet; therefore, you would want the formula to use the mixed address A:C$1 and not $A:C$1. In this case, the correct formula to place in cell C3 before copying it is +B3*(1+A:C$1).

Copying One Cell to a Range

When copying and pasting, you can copy a single cell to a range of cells by highlighting the destination range before using the Edit Paste command. (If you don't know how to select a range, see the section "Working with Ranges" earlier in this chapter.)

You also can copy a single cell to larger ranges in multiple rows and columns. In the price-forecasting model in figure 4.31, the current prices are in column B. The formula in cell C3 increases the price by the percentage in cell B1. To copy this formula through the table in worksheet A, Edit Copy cell C3 to the Clipboard, select range C3..F10, Edit Paste Clipboard contents to selected range. The result of the copy is shown in figure 4.32.

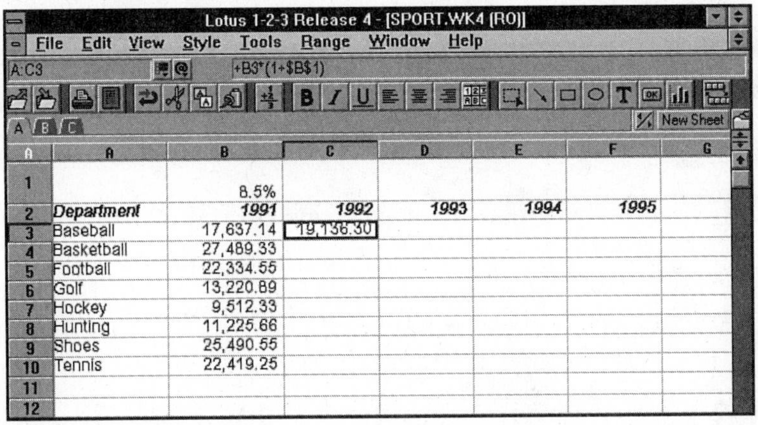

FIG. 4.31

A formula in cell C3 before being copied.

In addition, you can copy a cell to multiple rows and columns in different worksheets. For example, if the same price-forecasting model for different departments is found in different worksheets, you can fill in multiple worksheets with one three-dimensional copy. Just copy the original cell, then select a three-dimensional range as the destination for the Edit Paste command.

T I P   You can copy an entire range of cells using the mouse or the copy-and-paste procedure. Just highlight the range you want to copy first.

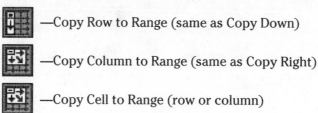

		8.5%				
	A	B	C	D	E	F
2	Department	1991	1992	1993	1994	1995
3	Baseball	17,637.14	19,136.30	20,762.88	22,527.73	24,442.58
4	Basketball	27,489.33	29,825.92	32,361.13	35,111.82	38,096.33
5	Football	22,334.55	24,232.99	26,292.79	28,527.68	30,952.53
6	Golf	13,220.89	14,344.67	15,563.96	16,886.90	18,322.29
7	Hockey	9,512.33	10,320.88	11,198.15	12,150.00	13,182.75
8	Hunting	11,225.66	12,179.84	13,215.13	14,338.41	15,557.18
9	Shoes	25,490.55	27,657.25	30,008.11	32,558.80	35,326.30
10	Tennis	22,419.25	24,324.89	26,392.50	28,635.86	31,069.91

FIG. 4.32

The results of copying cell C3 to the range C3..F10.

If you want to copy a cell across a row or down a column, you might find the Edit Copy Right and Edit Copy Down commands useful. Just highlight the original cell and any blank cells to the right or below; then use the Edit Copy Right or Edit Copy Down command respectively to copy the cell into the blank area. You can also use the SmartIcons shown below for this purpose:

—Copy Row to Range (same as Copy Down)

—Copy Column to Range (same as Copy Right)

—Copy Cell to Range (row or column)

Using Paste Special To Copy Styles

When you use the Edit Copy command, 1-2-3 for Windows copies all aspects of the cell or range—including the underlying values and the formats. If you want to paste only one aspect of the copied data, use the Edit Paste Special command instead of Edit Paste. The Paste Special command enables you to copy just the formatting of cells instead of data and formats. Formatting includes the following attributes: cell format, font, border (including lines and drop shadows), color, and shading.

You also can choose the Formulas as Values option to convert formulas into their underlying values when pasting. This can be useful when you need to reference the values elsewhere in the worksheet without the underlying formulas in place. 1-2-3 for Windows does not recalculate formulas before it converts the formulas to values. If recalculation is set to manual or if the Calc indicator appears in the status bar, press F9 (Calc), click on the Calc button in the status bar, or click on the Recalculate SmartIcon before you use the Formulas as Values option.

Transposing Ranges

The Range Transpose command and Transpose Data SmartIcon provide another way to copy data. This operation converts rows to columns or columns to rows and changes formulas to values at the same time. In figure 4.33, the range A2..D6 is to be transposed to the range E8..I11. The Transpose dialog box provides the From and To options. Figure 4.34 shows the result of transposing the range; the rows and columns are transposed, and the formulas in row 10 become numbers in column N.

The Range Transpose command copies formats, fonts, colors, and shading but does not copy shadow boxes or border lines.

> **CAUTION:** Range Transpose doesn't recalculate the worksheet before transposing data. You can freeze incorrect values if you execute the command without recalculating. Always recalculate the worksheet before you transpose a range.

Finding and Replacing Data

The Edit Find & Replace command and the Find SmartIcon can find and replace characters in a range of labels and formulas. The command works much like the search-and-replace feature in many word processing programs. When you choose Edit Find & Replace, the Find & Replace dialog box appears. You can specify what data to search for, what kind of data to search through, what characters to find or replace, and which range to search.

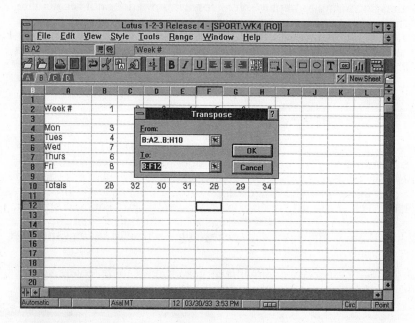

FIG. 4.33

The row and column arrangement in A2..H10 is to be transposed.

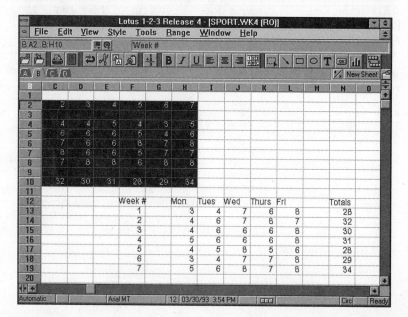

FIG. 4.34

The result of transposing A2..H10 to F12 (range F12..N19).

> **CAUTION:** An incorrect search-and-replace operation can harm a file. You should first save the file before selecting Edit Find & Replace, even though you can undo an incorrect search.

Suppose that you have a list of department names as labels and want to shorten the labels from Department to Dept. The following steps explain how to search for and replace a label:

1. Highlight the range to search. (This step is optional; you can specify the range in the Find & Replace dialog box.)

2. Choose Edit Find & Replace or click on the Find SmartIcon. The Find & Replace dialog box appears.

3. Type the search string in the Search For text box. In this example, you want to search for Department, so type Department in the Search For text box.

4. Specify the type of search: Labels, Formulas, or Both. In this example, you want to search only through label cells, so select Labels. (Formulas aren't likely to contain the text Department, so you can omit searching through formulas.)

5. Specify the action: Find or Replace With. In this example, you want to do more than just find the word Department, you want to replace it with new text. Therefore, select Replace With.

6. Enter the replacement string in the Replace With text box. In this example, you want to replace every occurrence of Department with the text Dept. Type Dept. (and remember to include the period).

7. Choose OK or press Enter. The Replace dialog box appears.

8. In the Replace dialog box, choose Replace, Replace All, Find Next, or Close.

You may want to choose Replace for the first occurrence to make sure that the change you want to make is made correctly. If it is correct, you can choose Replace All to replace all other occurrences. If the replacement isn't correct, close the dialog box and try again. If you only want to replace certain occurrences, choose Find Next and then choose Replace for each appropriate occurrence.

If you choose Find Next instead of Replace All as the search mode, the cell pointer moves to the first cell in the range. Choose Find Next to find the next occurrence; alternatively, choose Close or press Esc to cancel the search and return to Ready mode. If there are no more matching strings, 1-2-3 for Windows displays an error message and stops searching. At the end of a replace operation, the cell pointer remains at the last cell replaced.

You also can use Edit Find & Replace to modify formulas. If you have many formulas that round to two decimal places, such as @ROUND(A1*B1,2), you can change the formulas to round to four decimal places with a search string of ,2) and a replace string of ,4).

CAUTION: Be extremely careful when you replace numbers in formulas. If you try to replace 2 with 4 in this example, the formula @ROUND(A2*B2,2) becomes @ROUND(A4*B4,4).

Questions & Answers

This chapter covered the use of command menus and the most fundamental 1-2-3 for Windows commands. The following questions and answers serve to refresh your memory in these areas:

Q: The Release 4 commands are different from old 1-2-3 commands I've used. Can I use the old commands?

A: The 1-2-3 Classic menu contains commands from DOS versions of 1-2-3. Access the 1-2-3 Classic menu by pressing the slash (/) key.

Q: When I type information into one of the worksheets in a grouped worksheet file, nothing appears in the other worksheets.

A: Groups do not duplicate data you enter—only formatting and style changes.

Q: When I use a range name in a formula, 1-2-3 interprets it as a text entry.

A: When using range names as the first item in a formula, you must begin with a plus sign or equal sign, as in =JANUARY*.3. Otherwise, 1-2-3 thinks you are entering a text label.

Q: How can I get a list of all the range names in the worksheet file?

A: You can see all named ranges by clicking on the navigator in the edit line. Clicking on an item in this list causes the cell pointer to jump to that range or inserts that range into the active formula (if you are in Edit mode). You also can use the 1-2-3 Classic command /Range Name Table to place all range names and their ranges into the worksheet.

Q: I highlighted several number sequences for Range Fill by Example, but got a series of asterisks instead of the sequence.

A: You can use <u>R</u>ange Fill by <u>E</u>xample on only one value (sequence) at a time. Don't try to fill more than one row or column of values at once.

Q: I'm trying to create a sequence of values that grows geometrically, as in 1, 10, 100, 1000. How do I do this?

A: You cannot do this with the <u>R</u>ange <u>F</u>ill command. Instead, you must use a formula (such as +A1*10) to calculate the progression and then copy the formula into the range.

Q: I changed the global column width for the entire worksheet, but some columns did not change.

A: Any columns you have manually adjusted are not affected by the global column width changes. You can reset any column to the worksheet default by using the <u>S</u>tyle <u>C</u>olumn Width command and specifying <u>R</u>eset to Worksheet Default.

Q: Do I have to expand a column's width just because text entries spill over the edge of the column?

A: No. Text can spill over the edge of a column without problems. However, if the next column contains data, that data prevents the text from spilling over the edge of the column.

Q: How do I adjust the widths of several columns at once when the columns are not adjacent?

A: Select nonadjacent columns by holding the Ctrl key as you click on the column headings. Then adjust the width of any one column to affect them all.

Q: When I delete or move cells, I get errors in some formulas. Why does this happen?

A: When formulas refer to cells that are moved or deleted, those formulas cannot continue there references. In some cases, formulas will update references to reflect cells that you move. In other cases, the formulas cannot make these changes. One answer is to avoid removing data referenced in formulas. Formulas that refer to other formulas containing errors also produce errors. If you want to move cells that are referenced in formulas, be sure to move cells from the middle of a range reference—if you move the top or bottom cells, you might get errors.

Q: When I move formulas to a new location, they do not adjust to reflect their new positions in the worksheet. How do I make formulas relative while moving them?

A: You cannot adjust formulas during a move procedure. Instead, you must use the copy procedure and then remove the originals.

Summary

Learning all the commands in 1-2-3 for Windows is a formidable task. You probably will never need to know them all because many commands perform highly specialized tasks. In this chapter, you learned to use the fundamental 1-2-3 for Windows commands to build and work with worksheet files. Specifically, you learned how to use menus; how to work with groups and ranges; how to change the size of a cell or the look of the worksheet; how to insert, delete, hide, recalculate, move, and copy cells in a worksheet; how to use mixed and absolute addressing; and how to find and replace data.

In the next chapter, you learn how to change the format and appearance of cell contents so that they are clear and easily understood.

Changing the Format and Appearance of Data

U sing 1-2-3 for Windows to manipulate data is only the first step in using the worksheet. Making the results clear and easy to understand can be as important as calculating the correct answer. In this chapter, you learn how to use commands that control the way data appears on the screen—the *style*. Style includes number formats; fonts and other text attributes; lines, borders, and colors of cells and data; and the alignment of data in a cell. (Although column widths and row heights are also considered style features, these are discussed in Chapter 4, "Using Fundamental Commands.") Other advanced formatting capabilities apply only when you print reports; these features are discussed in Chapter 10, "Printing Reports."

1-2-3 allows you to set style characteristics at four different levels:

- For all new files
- For a cell or a range of cells

- For a single worksheet

- For all worksheets in a file

This chapter begins by teaching you how to change certain style settings for an individual cell or a range of cells. You then learn how to change the style *globally*—that is, for all new files you create. You also learn how to set style characteristics for an entire worksheet. 1-2-3 calls these settings *worksheet defaults*. Setting the default style for an entire worksheet saves you the time and effort of setting the style for individual cells or ranges. If you plan to create multiple worksheets in a file, you can set worksheet defaults for all worksheets in the file. Finally, you learn about named styles and the 1-2-3 Style Gallery, both designed so that you quickly can apply a set of styles to a worksheet.

The instructions and figures in this chapter refer to and explain the Formatting SmartIcons. In addition to other SmartIcons, the default Formatting palette includes SmartIcons for highlighting and aligning data, choosing fonts and attributes, and adding colors, lines, borders, and frames. With the Formatting SmartIcons, you quickly can choose certain style characteristics without making choices from menus and dialog boxes. For a complete discussion of SmartIcons, see Chapter 17, "Using SmartIcons."

Understanding Style

1-2-3 Release 4 for Windows groups all style commands under a menu called Style. The term *style* refers to virtually any type of characteristic you can apply to data in a cell, such as currency symbols; commas and decimal places; a new font or point size; bold, underline, or italics; or the alignment of data in a cell. The first four options on the Style menu allow you to change, delete, or add these types of characteristics to cell data. Figure 5.1 shows the Style menu. (The first four Style menu options are discussed in greater detail in this chapter.)

When style characteristics are applied to a cell, the entry in the cell reflects those characteristics; indicators for certain of the style characteristics appear on the status bar. For example, in figure 5.2, the entry in cell B15 displays a formula result ($10,206.75) in currency format, complete with a dollar sign, comma, and two decimal places—in an 11-point sans-serif font. The status bar displays the indicators Currency (the format), 2 (the number of decimal places), Arial (the font), and 11 (the point size).

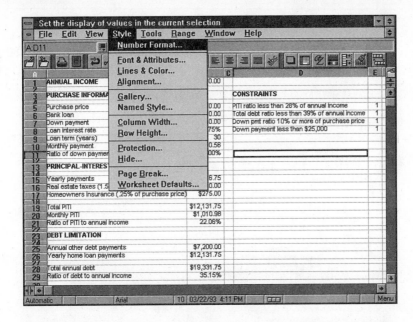

FIG. 5.1

The 1-2-3 Style menu.

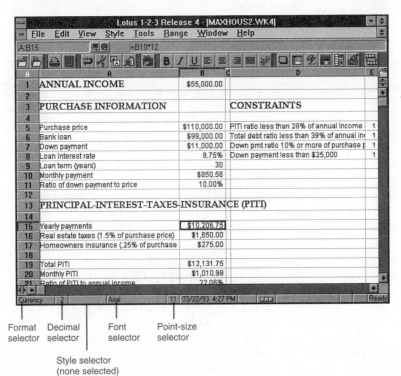

FIG. 5.2

The status bar shows style indicators for the active cell (cell B15).

Format selector   Decimal selector   Font selector   Point-size selector

Style selector (none selected)

To change the style characteristics of a cell or cell range, first select the cell or range and then choose any of the first four commands on the Style menu: Number Format, Font & Attributes, Lines & Color, or Alignment. Choose style options from the dialog box that appears.

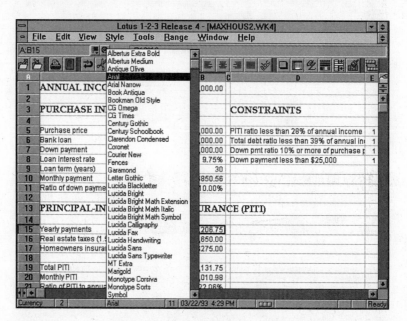

FIG. 5.3

Clicking on a button in the status bar pops up a list of other formatting choices.

You also can use the status bar to change the number format, decimal places, font, and point size of a cell or range. At first glance, you may not realize that the boxes making up the status bar are actually buttons, or *selectors*. For example, if you click on the font selector, 1-2-3 displays a pop-up list of other fonts (see fig. 5.3). The status bar selectors let you quickly change certain style characteristics for the selected cell or range without choosing menu and dialog-box options. (For a complete discussion of the status bar, see Chapter 3, "Learning Worksheet Basics.") Use the mouse or the arrow keys to choose an item from the pop-up list.

Setting Global Style Defaults

1-2-3 for Windows provides a number of default settings that determine how the program operates under most circumstances. When you choose the Tools User Setup command, you access the User Setup dialog box (see fig. 5.4). Use this dialog box to change many of the default settings that affect the display and behavior of 1-2-3 in the current session and all future sessions. Of the options in this dialog box, only two affect the formatting of data in the 1-2-3 worksheet:

- The Use Automatic Format option affects the default format of numbers in 1-2-3 cells. When you deselect this option, 1-2-3 uses the General format instead of Automatic format as the default for all new worksheets. (Number formats are described later in this chapter.)

- The International button changes the display of certain date, time, currency, and punctuation defaults.

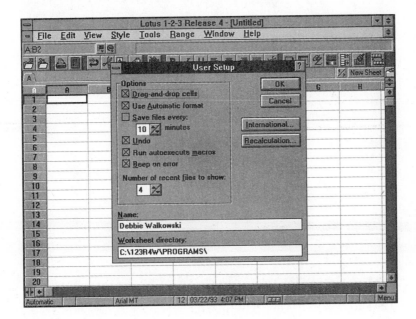

FIG. 5.4

The User Setup dialog box.

Setting International Default Values: The Date

When you install 1-2-3 for Windows, the default international values are determined by the country you choose. At times, you may want to change some or all the international settings. For example, if you work with international currency, you may want to change the currency symbol. You change international settings by clicking on the International button in the User Setup dialog box to access the International dialog box (see fig. 5.5).

The Date option specifies how 1-2-3 for Windows displays dates in cells with a date format. The Date drop-down box provides four possible formats, in which *MM*, *DD*, and *YY* stand for month, day, and year, respectively:

12/31/93 is an example of *MM/DD/YY* format

31/12/93 is an example of *DD/MM/YY* format

31.12.93 is an example of *DD.MM.YY* format

93-12-31 is an example of *YY-MM-DD* format

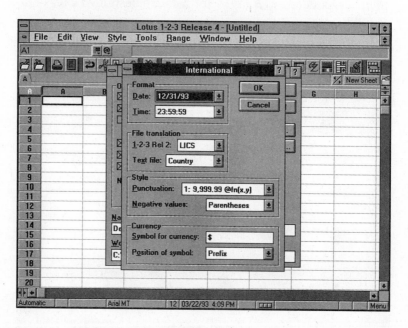

FIG. 5.5

The International
dialog box.

Setting International Default Values: The Time

The Time option in the International dialog box specifies how 1-2-3 for
Windows displays times in cells with a Time format. The Time drop-
down box provides four possible formats, in which *HH*, *MM*, and *SS*
stand for hour, minutes, and seconds, respectively:

23:59:59 is an example of: *HH:MM:SS* format

23.59.59 is an example of: *HH.MM.SS* format

23,59,59 is an example of: *HH,MM,SS* format

23h59m59s is an example of: *HHhMMmSSs* format

Setting International Default Values: Punctuation

With the Punctuation option, you control the display of numbers and
the separators used between arguments in functions. The Punctuation

drop-down box lists the possible combinations available (see fig. 5.6). The default setting uses a comma (,) as the thousands separator, the period (.) as the decimal point, and the comma (,) as the argument separator.

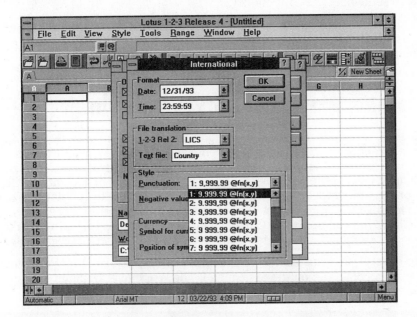

FIG. 5.6

The available Punctuation settings.

Use the Negative Values option to specify how to display a negative number in a cell formatted as Currency or , Comma. The drop-down box has two choices:

■ Parentheses: encloses a negative number in parentheses

■ Sign: places a minus sign in front of the number

Setting International Default Values: Currency

The Symbol for Currency option in the International dialog box specifies how numbers appear when you use the Currency format. (The default setting is $ for dollars.) Specify the desired symbol in the text box and indicate the position of the symbol. Choose Prefix to place the symbol in front of the cell entry; choose Suffix to place the symbol after the cell entry.

To specify a currency symbol other than $, you must type a *compose sequence* in the Symbol for Currency text box. A compose sequence consists of the key sequence Alt+F1 followed by another key sequence that represents a currency symbol. For instance, by pressing Alt+F1, then the key sequence L=, you can create the £ symbol for the British pound sterling. The compose sequence allows you to create symbols that are not represented on your keyboard. For a complete list of compose sequences, see Appendix C.

After you change the international settings, press Enter or select OK to close the International dialog box and return to the User Setup dialog box. Press Enter or click on OK to close the User Setup dialog box.

Setting Worksheet Style Defaults

In 1-2-3, you can set certain style characteristics for an entire worksheet or file before you begin entering data. Set styles for the entire worksheet when you want to specify the style characteristics used in most cells of the worksheet. For example, if you want the data in the worksheet to appear in a large typeface, you can specify a point size of 14 for the entire worksheet. If all the values in the worksheet represent dollars, you can apply the Currency number format to the entire worksheet. Later you can override the default format on a cell-by-cell basis.

To set style characteristics for the entire worksheet, use the Worksheet Defaults command on the Style menu. The Worksheet Defaults dialog box shown in figure 5.7 is displayed.

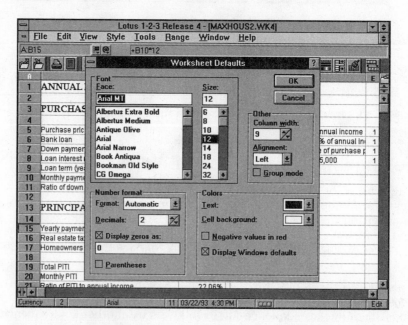

FIG. 5.7

The Worksheet Defaults dialog box.

Using the Worksheet Defaults dialog box, you can specify the font, number format, color, and other options for the entire worksheet. The options in this dialog box are the same as the options that you can specify for an individual cell or range. For detailed descriptions of these options, refer to "Changing Fonts and Attributes, Working with Number Formats," and "Formatting Cells with Color and Borders," later in this chapter. If you intend to create multiple worksheets for the current file, you can apply the style characteristics to all worksheets in the file by selecting the Group Mode check box.

After you specify the desired settings, choose OK or press Enter to close the Worksheet Defaults dialog box and save your changes.

The remainder of this chapter describes all the style characteristics you can apply to individual cells or to entire worksheets.

For Related Information

◀◀ "Grouping Worksheets," p. 139.

FROM HERE...

Understanding the Difference between Content and Format

Cell formatting changes the appearance of data—not the value of the data. For example, the number 1234 can appear as 1,234 or $1,234.00 or 1234.00%, in addition to many other ways. No matter what the number looks like, the value of the number is still the same.

NOTE In all cases, the full value of the number in a cell is used in calculations, even though the displayed value may be rounded or asterisks may appear.

Some formats display a number as a rounded value. Even when a number appears rounded in the cell, 1-2-3 for Windows still stores the exact value of the number and uses the exact value in formulas and calculations. For example, if you format 1234.5 in Fixed format with 0 decimal places, the number appears as 1235, but 1-2-3 for Windows uses the exact value 1234.5 in formulas.

In figure 5.8, the sales total in cell C11 looks like an addition error. The formula in cell C9 is +B9*1.1, resulting in 95.7. Cell C9 displays 96, however, because it is formatted as Fixed with 0 decimal places. The result of a similar formula in cell C10 is 83.6, but the cell displays 84. The result of the formula in cell C11 is 179.3, but the cell displays 179. The formula appears to add as follows: 96+84=179, when the equation should result in 180. This apparent error is produced by rounding the displayed values without rounding the actual values.

| | Lotus 1-2-3 Release 4 - [ROUNDERR.WK4] | | | | | | |

Lotus 1-2-3 Release 4 - [ROUNDERR.WK4]

File Edit View Style Tools Range Window Help

A:C9   +B9*1.1

A	A	B	C	D	E	F	G	H
1								
2			1993 Product Sales and					
3			1994 Sales Projections					
4								
5		Actual	Estimated	Actual	Estimated	Actual	Estimated	Actual
6		Qtr 1	Qtr 2	Qtr 2	Qtr 2	Qtr 3	Qtr 3	Qtr 4
7		1993	1994	1993	1994	1993	1994	1993
8								
9	Department 20	87	96	82	90			
10	Department 42	76	84	69	76			
11	Total	163	179	151	166			
12								
13								
14								
15								
16								
17								
18								

Fixed   0   Arial MT   12 03/22/93 4:55 PM   Ready

FIG. 5.8

An apparent rounding error caused by cell formatting.

To avoid rounding errors, round the *actual value* of the numbers used in formulas, not just their displayed value. To round values in a formula, use the @ROUND function. For example, to eliminate the rounding error in figure 5.8, change the formula in cell C9 to @ROUND((B9*1.1),0). Then copy the formula to cell C10. When you round the numbers in the formula with this technique, the @SUM function in cell C11 correctly results in 180. (For complete information on functions, see Chapter 7, "Using Functions.")

NOTE   1-2-3 for Windows displays numbers with up to 15 decimal places. By default, negative numbers have a minus sign and decimal values have leading zeros.

Working with Number Formats

The first option on the 1-2-3 for Windows Style menu is Number Format. You use this option to assign a specific number format to a cell or range of cells. Assigning a format to cells maintains consistency throughout the worksheet and saves you the effort of typing symbols (dollar signs, commas, parentheses, and so on) along with the cell value.

Number formats apply only to numeric data (numeric formulas and numbers). If you format a label as Fixed or Currency, for example, the number format has no effect on how a label appears. One exception to this rule is the Hidden format, which can apply to both labels and string formulas.

Table 5.1 shows samples of the available cell formats and how each one changes the appearance of data. Date formats in this table assume that the current year is 1993.

Table 5.1 Number Formats

Format	Entry	Displayed
General	1234	1234
General	1234.5	1234.5
Fixed, 2 decimal places	1234.5	1234.50
Fixed, 0 decimal places	1234.5	1235
, Comma, 2 decimal places	1234.5	1,234.50
Currency, 2 decimal places	1234.5	$1,234.50
Percent, 1 decimal place	0.364	36.4%
Scientific, 4 decimal places	1234.5	1.2345E+03
+/−	5	+++++
31-Dec-93 (date format)	2/14/93	14-Feb-93
31-Dec (date format)	2/14/93	14-Feb
Dec-93 (date format)	2/14/93	Feb-93
12/31/93 (date format)	2/14/93	02/14/93
12/31 (date format)	2/14/93	02/14
11:59:59 AM (time format)	10:15	10:15:00 AM
11:59 AM (time format)	10:15	10:15 AM
23:59:59 (time format)	10:15	10:15:00
23:59 (time format)	10:15	10:15
Text	+C6	+C6
Hidden	1234.5	No display
Label	57 Main St.	57 Main St.
Automatic	1234.5	1234.5

Automatic format is the default format that 1-2-3 uses whenever you create a new worksheet. The Automatic format
"reads" the entries you type and applies the appropriate
format. This format is discussed in detail later in this
chapter.

If a column isn't wide enough to display a formatted numeric entry,
asterisks fill the cell. If the numeric entry is unformatted and too long
to fit in the cell, 1-2-3 for Windows converts the entry to scientific notation. To display the data, you must change the format or the column
width. See Chapter 4, "Using Fundamental Commands," for instructions
on changing column width.

 If you have a color monitor, you can display negative numbers in the worksheet in red. For details, see the section
"Formatting Cells with Color and Borders" later in this
chapter.

Handling Zeros

By default, 1-2-3 displays a zero (0) in any cell that contains an entry of
zero or a formula that evaluates to zero. Using the Worksheet Defaults
dialog box (refer to fig. 5.7), you can control how 1-2-3 displays zeros in
your worksheet. You have the option of changing the Display zeros as
setting so that 1-2-3 display a blank cell or a label that you specify. (A
label is defined as any entry that begins with a letter or a label-prefix
character, such as ' for left-alignment or " for right-alignment.) To have
1-2-3 display a blank cell, delete the 0 from the Display zeros as text box
and leave the text box blank. To have 1-2-3 display a label (such as the
word "zero"), type the label in the Display zeros as text box.

Assigning Number Formats

To change the format of a cell or range use the Style Number Format
command to access the Number Format dialog box (see fig. 5.9). If you
preselected a range, that range is listed in the Range text box; if you did
not preselect a range, specify one in the dialog box. Select one of the
formats from the Format list box. You can select a format by typing the
initial character of the format (such as F for Fixed) or by using the arrow keys or the mouse.

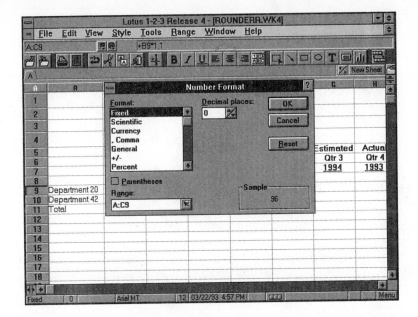

FIG. 5.9

The Number
Format dialog
box.

If you choose Fixed, Scientific, ‚ Comma, Currency, or Percent, you can
specify the number of decimal places or use the default number, 2,
shown in the Decimal Places box. To change the number of decimal
places, type another number between 0 and 15 or use the scroll arrows
to change the number. For some formats like General, the Decimal
Places text box doesn't appear in the dialog box. When all settings are
correct, select OK to close the Number Format dialog box and change
the format of the selected range.

You can use the Reset button in the Number Format dialog box to
quickly restore the default number format to the selected cell or
range.

T I P

The format selector in the status bar displays the format of the current
cell. For example, Fixed appears on the format selector when the current cell is formatted with the Fixed format. The number of decimal
places for the current cell appears on the decimal selector. In figure 5.8,
the status bar shows Fixed on the format selector and 0 on the decimal
indicator.

The following sections describe the formats available in the Number Format dialog box.

For Related Information

◄◄ "Entering Numbers," p. 116.

Fixed Format

You use *Fixed format* when you want to display numbers with a fixed number of decimal points. Table 5.2 shows several examples of Fixed format in cells that have a column width of 9 and the default font of 12-point Arial MT. In all cases, the full number in the cell is used in calculations, even though the displayed value may be rounded, or asterisks may appear.

Table 5.2 Examples of Fixed Format

Typed Entry	Number of Decimal Places	Display Result
123.46	0	123
123.46	1	123.5
–123.46	2	–123.46
123.46	4	123.4600
1234567.89	4	**************
123456789	2	**************

Scientific Format

You use *Scientific format* to display very large or very small numbers. Such numbers usually have a few significant digits and many zeros as place holders to show how large or small the number is.

A number in scientific notation has two parts; a *mantissa* and an *exponent*. The mantissa is a number from 1 to 10 that contains the significant digits. The exponent tells you how many places to move the decimal point to get the actual value of the number.

1-2-3 for Windows displays numbers in Scientific format in powers of 10, with 0 to 15 decimal places, and an exponent from –99 to +99. If a number has more significant digits than the number you specify in the format, the number is rounded on the display, although 1-2-3 for Windows uses the full value for formulas and calculations.

1230000000000 appears as 1.23E+12 in Scientific format with 2 decimal places. E+12 signifies that you must move the decimal point 12 places to the right to get the actual number. 0.000000000237 appears as 2.4E–10 in Scientific format with 1 decimal place. E-10 means that you must move the decimal point 10 places to the left to get the actual number.

NOTE A number too large to appear in a cell in General format appears in Scientific format.

Table 5.3 shows several examples of Scientific format in cells that have the default column width of 9 and the default font of 12-point Arial MT.

Table 5.3 Examples of Scientific Format

Typed Entry	Number of Decimal Places	Display Result
1632116750000	2	1.63E+12
16321167500000	2	1.63E+13
–1632116750000	1	–1.6E+12
–1632116750000	2	–1.63E+12
00000000012	2	1.20E+01
–.00000000012	0	–1E-10

Currency Format

Currency format displays numbers with a dollar sign (or other currency symbol specified in the International dialog box). Because of the dollar sign, an extra position in the column width is needed to display a number in Currency format. If you specify a currency symbol other than the dollar sign, an extra position in the column width is needed for every character in the currency symbol. Numbers formatted as Currency can have from 0 to 15 decimal places. Thousands are separated by a comma (or other specified international separator). Negative numbers appear with a minus sign or in parentheses—depending on the current setting in the International dialog box.

To change the currency symbol, thousands separator, or negative-number indicator, use the International dialog box (described earlier in this chapter). Suppose that you create a file that refers to Japanese yen. You can use Tools User Setup International Symbol for Currency to change the international currency symbol to the yen (¥). The symbol can be more than one character, such as *DM*, *FF*, or *$CAN*. Use Tools User Setup International Position of Symbol to change the currency symbol from a prefix to a suffix.

 Because Currency format with two decimal places is a common setting, 1-2-3 for Windows provides a SmartIcon to quickly select this format: select the range to format and click on the Currency 2 SmartIcon.

Table 5.4 shows several examples of Currency format in cells that have a column width of 9 and the default font of 12-point Arial MT. The examples include international currency symbols in addition to the dollar sign.

Table 5.4 Examples of Currency Format

Typed Entry	Number of Decimal Places	Display Result
123	2	$123.00
123	2	¥123.00
123	2	£123.00
−123.124	0	($123) or -$123
1234.12	0	$1,234
1234567.12	2	**************

, Comma Format

Like the Fixed format, the , *Comma format* displays data with a fixed number of decimal places (from 0 to 15). The , Comma format separates the thousands with commas (or another symbol specified with Tools User Setup International). Negative numbers appear with a minus sign or in parentheses—depending on the current setting in the International dialog box. Positive numbers less than 1,000 appear the same way in Fixed format and , Comma format.

T I P

> For large numbers, use the , Comma format instead of the Fixed format. The number 12,300,000.00 is easier to read than 12300000.00.

Table 5.5 shows several examples of , Comma format in cells that have a column width of 9 and the default font of 12-point Arial MT.

Table 5.5 Examples of , Comma Format		
Typed Entry	**Number of Decimal Places**	**Display Result**
123.46	0	123
1234.6	2	1,234.60
−1234.6	0	(1,235) or −1,235
−12345678	2	**************

To apply the comma format with zero decimal places to selected cells, click the Comma 0 SmartIcon.

General Format

Numbers in *General format* have no thousands separators and no trailing zeros to the right of the decimal point. Negative numbers are preceded by a minus sign; if the number contains decimal digits, it can contain a decimal point. If a number contains too many digits to the right of the decimal point to fit within the column width, the decimal portion is rounded. If a number has too many digits to the left of a decimal point, the number appears in Scientific format. For example, 123400000 appears as 1.2E+08.

Table 5.6 shows several examples of General format in cells that have a column width of 9 and the default font of 12-point Arial MT.

Table 5.6 Examples of General Format	
Typed Entry	**Display Result**
123.46	123.46
−123.36	−123.36
1.2345678912	1.234568

continues

Table 5.6 Continued	
Typed Entry	**Display Result**
15000000000	1.5E+10
–.000000026378	-2.6E-08

+/– Format

The *+/– format* displays numbers as a series of plus signs (+), minus signs (–), or periods (.). The number of signs displayed is equal to the entry's value, rounded to the nearest whole number. A positive number appears as a row of plus signs; a negative number appears as a row of minus signs; a number between –1 and +1 appears as a period.

This format originally was devised to create imitation bar charts in early electronic spreadsheets that had no graphing capability. The format has limited use today.

Table 5.7 shows several examples of +/– format in cells that have a column width of 9 and the default font of 12-point Arial MT.

Table 5.7 Examples of +/- Format	
Typed Entry	**Display Result**
6	++++++
.5	.
4.9	++++
–3	——
0	.
17.2	**************

Percent Format

You use *Percent format* to display percentages. A number formatted as a percentage can have from 0 to 15 decimal places. The number displayed is the value of the cell multiplied by 100, followed by a percent sign (%). Notice that the number of decimal places you specify is the number as a percent, not as a whole number: only 2 decimal places are needed to display .2456 as 24.56% in Percent format.

The number displayed is multiplied by 100, but the value of the cell is unchanged. To display 50% in a cell, type **.5** and use the Percent format. If you type **50** and use the Percent format with 0 decimal places, 5000% appears. If you simply type **50%**, 1-2-3 automatically assigns the Percent format to the cell and displays 50%.

To apply the percent format with two decimal places to selected cells, click the Percent 2 SmartIcon.

Table 5.8 shows several examples of Percent format in cells that have a column width of 9 and the default font of 12-point Arial MT.

Table 5.8 Examples of Percent Format

Typed Entry	Number of Decimal Places	Display Result
2	2	200.00%
−.3528	2	−35.28%
30	0	3000%
300	4	**************

Text Format

You use *Text format* to display numeric and string formulas instead of their results. Numbers formatted as Text appear the same way as they do in General format. If a formula is too long to appear in the column width, the formula is truncated unless the cell to the immediate right is blank. In this case, the formula spills over and is displayed in full in the cell to the right.

Text format is useful for criteria ranges (covered in Chapter 13, "Understanding Advanced Data Management"). You also can use Text format when you enter or debug complex formulas.

Hidden Format

A cell in *Hidden format* appears blank no matter what the cell contains. You use Hidden format for sensitive data or intermediate calculations you don't want to display. If a cell is unprotected, the contents of a hidden cell appear in the contents box of the edit line when you move the cell pointer to that cell. If the cell is protected, the data isn't visible in the cell or in the edit line. For more information on hiding and protecting data, see Chapter 4, "Using Fundamental Commands."

In figure 5.10, cell B1 appears to be blank but the edit line shows that the cell entry is 55000. Notice the Hidden indicator on the format selector in the status bar.

Lotus 1-2-3 Release 4 - [MAXHOUS2.WK4]					
File	Edit	View	Style	Tools	Range Window Help

A:C9   55000

	A	B	C	D	E
1	ANNUAL INCOME				
2					
3	PURCHASE INFORMATION		CONSTRAINTS		
4					
5	Purchase price	$110,000.00	PITI ratio less than 28% of annual income	1	
6	Bank loan	$99,000.00	Total debt ratio less than 39% of annual in	1	
7	Down payment	$11,000.00	Down pmt ratio 10% or more of purchase p	1	
8	Loan interest rate	9.75%	Down payment less than $25,000	1	
9	Loan term (years)	30			
10	Monthly payment	$850.56			
11	Ratio of down payment to price	10.00%			
12					
13	PRINCIPAL-INTEREST-TAXES-INSURANCE (PITI)				
14					
15	Yearly payments	$10,206.75			
16	Real estate taxes (1.5% of purchase price)	$1,650.00			
17	Homeowners insurance (.25% of purchase	$275.00			
18					
19	Total PITI	$12,131.75			
20	Monthly PITI	$1,010.98			
21	Ratio of PITI to annual income	22.06%			

Hidden   Arial   11 03/22/93 5:01 PM   Ready

FIG. 5.10

Cell B1 uses the Hidden format.

FROM HERE...

For Related Information

◄◄ "Protecting and Hiding Worksheet Data," p. 167.

Automatic Format

As mentioned earlier in this chapter, *Automatic format* is the default setting for all 1-2-3 worksheet files (unless you turn it off by using the Tools User Setup command and deselecting the Use Automatic Format option in the User Setup dialog box). When you enter data in a cell that uses Automatic format, 1-2-3 for Windows examines the entry and selects an appropriate format. For example, if you enter **$325**, 1-2-3 for Windows changes the Automatic format for that cell to Currency; if you enter **50%**, 1-2-3 changes the Automatic format to Percent. If you enter **325** or **50**, however, 1-2-3 makes no change to the format, and the cell remains formatted as Automatic.

NOTE If you turn off Automatic format as a default setting (using the User Setup dialog box mentioned earlier in this chapter) it does not affect the current worksheet. All new worksheets you create, however, will use the General format.

Table 5.9 lists examples of how entries are treated when you enter data into a cell formatted as Automatic. (The cell has a column width of 9; the default font is 12-point Arial MT.) The first column shows how the entry was typed. The second column shows the number format 1-2-3 assigns to the entry. The third column shows how the entry is stored in the worksheet; the forth column shows how the data is displayed in the worksheet. Date examples in this table assume that the current year is 1993.

Table 5.9 Examples of Automatic Format

Typed Entry	Cell Format	Data Stored	Display Result
57 Main	Automatic	57 Main	57 Main
258	Automatic	258	258
258.46	Automatic	258.46	258.46
258.00	Automatic	258	258
1,258	, Comma, 0	1258	1,258
87.00	, Comma, 2	87	87.00
$258.00	Currency, 2	258	$258.00
25%	Percent, 0	0.25	25%
2.50%	Percent, 2	0.025	2.50%
1.2e4	Scientific, 1	12000	1.2E+04
2.587e-16	Scientific, 3	2.587E-16	2.587E-16
25.87e-17	Scientific, 2	2.587E-16	2.59E-16
20-Oct-93	31-Dec-93	34262	20-Oct-93
20-Oct	31-Dec	34262*	20-Oct
Oct-93	Automatic	"Oct-93	Oct-93
10/20/93	12/31/93	34262	10/20/93
10/15	Automatic	0.66666666666666666.7	0.666667
6:23:57 AM	11:59:59 AM	0.266631944444444444	**************
6:23:57	23:59:59	0.266631944444444444	06:23:57

continues

Table 5.9 Continued

Typed Entry	Cell Format	Data Stored	Display Result
6:23:57 PM	11:59:59 AM	0.766631944444444444	**************
6:23 AM	11:59 AM	0.2659722222222222222	06:23 AM
6:23	23:59	0.2659722222222222222	06:23
6:23 PM	11:59 AM	0.7659722222222222222	06:23 PM
18:23:57	23:59:59	0.766631944444444445	18:23:57
18:23	23:59	0.765972222222222222	18:23

After you enter a number into a cell and 1-2-3 for Windows applies a format, the format stays with the cell. The format does not change if a number with a different format is entered. For example, if you type **$250.00** into a cell formatted as Automatic, 1-2-3 for Windows assigns the Currency format with 2 decimal places to the cell. If you later type **25%** into the cell, instead of formatting the cell as a percent, 1-2-3 for Windows retains the Currency format and displays the number as $0.25. To change the format after using the Automatic format, select Style Number Format.

If you type an invalid number in a cell formatted as Automatic, such as **57 Main Street**, 1-2-3 for Windows precedes the invalid entry with a label prefix and considers the entry a label.

If the number looks like one of the date or time formats, 1-2-3 for Windows uses that date or time format. However, in Automatic format, 1-2-3 for Windows does not recognize the date formats Dec-93 or 12/31; it stores Dec-93 as a label and 12/31 as a formula (12 divided by 31).

1-2-3 for Windows formats a cell automatically only when you enter a number or a label. If you enter a formula in a cell, the format remains Automatic. If you later enter a number or a label into the cell, 1-2-3 for Windows formats the cell appropriately. If the cell contains a formula and you convert the entry to a number with F2 (Edit) or F9 (Calc), 1-2-3 for Windows applies a format at that time.

Label Format

You use *Label format* on blank cells to make numbers that are labels easier to enter. In Label format, all entries are considered labels; 1-2-3 for Windows precedes the entry with the default label prefix. You can easily enter a label that looks like a number or a formula—either of which begins with a numeric character.

In a worksheet in which cells are still formatted with the default Automatic format, suppose that you type the label **57 Main Street** and press Enter. Because the entry contains letters, 1-2-3 for Windows considers the entry a label and inserts a label prefix. The format type remains Automatic. Now suppose that you type the label **10/15** and press Enter. 1-2-3 considers 10/15 a formula (10 divided by 15), converts the entry to a number, and displays 0.666667.

In both preceding examples, if you format the range as Label before you type the entry, 1-2-3 for Windows precedes the entry with a label prefix, and the entry becomes a text label.

If you format numeric entries with the Label format, they do not become labels, even though the format is changed. For example, after the Label format is applied, the entry 0.666667 remains the same until you retype the entry **10/15**. At that point, the entry appears as the label 10/15 in the cell.

For Related Information

◀◀ "Entering Labels," p. 113.

FROM HERE...

Date and Time Formats

All the formats discussed so far deal with regular numeric values. You use *date and time formats* when you work with date and time calculations or functions (see Chapter 7, "Using Functions"). For example, the Dec-93 format is used to format a date as Month-Year. 8/29/93, therefore, appears as Aug-93.

When you choose Style Number Format, the Number Format dialog box displays a Format list box. If you scroll through the list box, you can see the five date formats and four time formats. Figure 5.11 shows the five date formats and two of the time formats.

Date Formats

When you use date functions, 1-2-3 for Windows stores the date as a serial number representing the number of days since December 31, 1899. The date serial number for January 1, 1900 is 1. The date serial number for January 15, 1991 is 33253. The latest date 1-2-3 for Windows can display is December 31, 2099 (that date has the serial number 73050).

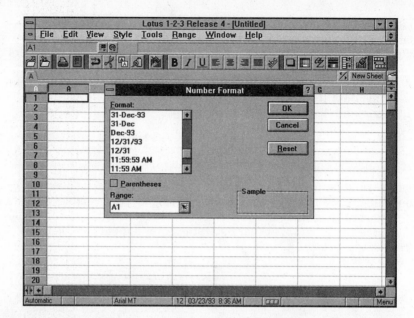

FIG. 5.11

Date and time
formats in the
Number Format
dialog box.

CAUTION: All the date serial numbers starting with March 1, 1900 are off by one day. The calendar inside 1-2-3 treats 1900 as a leap year; it isn't. A date serial number of 60 appears as 02/29/00—a date that never existed. Unless you compare dates before February 28, 1900 to dates after February 28, 1900, this error has no effect on the worksheets. Dates can be off by one day, however, if you export data to a database program.

If the number in a cell formatted with a date format is less than 1 or greater than 73050, the date appears as asterisks. Date formats ignore fractions; the value 34262.99 in a cell with the 12/31/93 date format appears as 10/20/93. The fraction represents the time—a fractional portion of a 24-hour clock.

To format a cell as a date, select Style Number Format and select one of the date formats. To quickly choose a date format, click on the format selector in the status bar and choose a format from the pop-up list.

To enter a date, you do not have to know the serial number or the date and time functions. Type what looks like a date in any of the 1-2-3 date formats that begin with a number. That is, type an entry like 10/20/93 or 20-Oct-93 or 20-Oct. (If you enter a date without the year, 1-2-3 for Windows assumes you want the current year.) 1-2-3 for Windows converts the entry to a date serial number and, if you have not yet formatted the range with a date format, 1-2-3 for Windows changes the Automatic format to the appropriate date format. The contents box in the edit line displays the serial date, and the cell displays the formatted date. If you have already formatted the range, the date appears according to the format you specified.

T I P

Don't be concerned with which serial number refers to which date. Let 1-2-3 for Windows format the date serial number to appear as a textual date.

NOTE If you type an entry such as Oct-93, 1-2-3 does not automatically apply the Dec-93 format to the cell. Instead, 1-2-3 interprets the entry as a label and retains the Automatic format because the entry begins with a letter. To use the Dec-93 format, you must enter a date in a format that begins with a number (such as 10/20/93 or 10-20-93), then apply the Dec-93 format to the cell. 1-2-3 will convert the 10 to Oct.

Table 5.10 shows several examples of dates in cells that have a column width of 9 and the default font of 12-point Arial MT. In each case, the cell format shown was applied to the cell before the entry was typed. This table assumes that the current year is 1993.

Table 5.10 Examples of Date Formats

Typed Entry	Cell Format	Data Stored	Display Result
10/20	31-Dec-93	34262	20-Oct-93
10/20	31-Dec	34262	20-Oct
10/20	Dec-93	34262	Oct-93
10/20	12/31/93	34262	10/20/93
10/20	12/31	34262	10/20
20-Oct	31-Dec-93	34262	20-Oct-93

You can quickly enter today's date in the current cell by clicking on the Insert Date icon. 1-2-3 automatically applies the 12/31/93 date format to the cell.

Time Formats

When you use a time function, such as @NOW, 1-2-3 for Windows stores the time as a *time fraction*. You can format a time fraction so that it looks like a time of day by choosing any of the time formats in the Number Format dialog box or by clicking on the format selector in the status bar and choosing a time format.

When you enter a specific time, such as **3:00 AM**, **12:00 PM**, or **6:00 PM**, 1-2-3 applies the correct time format to the entry but stores the entry as a time fraction. For example, 3:00 AM is stored as 0.125; 12:00 PM is stored as 0.5, and 6:00 PM is stored as 0.75. If you type **6:23**, **6:23:00**, **6:23AM**, or **6:23:00 AM**, 1-2-3 for Windows converts the entry to the time fraction 0.265972... (to 18 decimal places). If you type **6:23:57** or **6:23:57 AM**, 1-2-3 for Windows converts the entry to the time fraction 0.26663194... (to 18 decimal places).

1-2-3 uses a 24-hour clock system; noon is regarded as 12:00 and midnight as 24:00. Times between midnight and 1:00 A.M. are displayed as 00:01, 00:02:00, and so on. You don't have to type **AM** for times before noon. For times after noon, however, type **PM** or type the hour using the numbers 12 to 23.

 NOTE You can type the letters *AM* or *PM* in either uppercase or lowercase; it isn't necessary to type a space between the time and the AM or PM designator.

Table 5.11 shows several examples of time formats in cells that have a column width of 9 and the font of 10-point Arial MT. The Data Stored column displays only 10 of the 18 decimal places that 1-2-3 stores.

Table 5.11 Examples of Time Formats

Typed Entry	Cell Format	Data Stored	Display Result
6:23:57	11:59:59 AM	0.2666319444	6:23:57 AM
6:23:57 PM	11:59:59 AM	0.7666319444	6:23:57 PM
6:23	11:59 AM	0.2659722222	06:23 AM
6:23:57	23:59:59	0.2666319444	06:23:57
6:23:57 PM	23:59:59	0.7666319444	18:23:57
6:23	23:59	0.2659722222	06:23
6:23 PM	23:59	0.7659722222	18:23

The Parentheses Option

The parentheses option is a style characteristic that is available in the Number Format dialog box. You choose the Parentheses check box when you want 1-2-3 to enclose negative numbers in parentheses. This option adds parentheses to negative numbers that use any of 1-2-3's number formats (labels are unaffected). When you want to use parentheses for every unformatted cell in the current worksheet, select the Parentheses option in the Worksheet Defaults dialog box. (Refer to the section Setting Worksheet Style Defaults earlier in this chapter.) To use parentheses with a specific cell or range, select the Parentheses option in the Number Format dialog box and specify the range and the number format.

The Parentheses option can produce confusing results, so use it with care. For example, if you apply the Parentheses option with the Automatic format to the number 456, the number appears in the cell as (456). If you apply parentheses to a negative number, the number still appears as negative—but with varying results depending on the number format used. With the General format, –1234 appears as (-1234); with the , Comma format, –1234 appears as ((1,234)); with the Currency format, –1234 appears as (($1,234)).

Enhancing the Appearance of Data

The Style menu provides options for enhancing the appearance of data in the worksheet. These enhancements include changes to the worksheet fonts; the addition of borders, lines, shading, and colors; and changes to the alignment of data in worksheet cells. You use the Font & Attributes, Lines & Color, and Alignment options on the Style menu to change these characteristics for a cell or range of cells.

> **NOTE** You can specify a default set of worksheet styles (typeface, point size, default cell alignment, column width, default number format, and text and cell background colors) with the Worksheet Defaults dialog box. These settings apply to the current worksheet (or all the worksheets in the file if you specify Group Mode). For more details, see "Setting Worksheet Style Defaults," earlier in this chapter.

Changing Fonts and Attributes

A typeface, or *face* (as 1-2-3 calls it), is a particular style of type, such as Arial MT or TimesNewRoman PS. Typefaces can have different *attributes*, such as weight (regular, bold, italic) and underline. Most typefaces are available in a number of point sizes. The *point size* describes the height of the characters (there are 72 points in an inch). The most commonly used point sizes for "standard" print are 10 point and 12 point. Titles and headings are often set in 14-point or 18-point type.

A typeface of a given point size with a given set of attributes is called a *font*. In practice, many people use the terms *typeface* and *font* interchangeably, although they have different meanings. In 1-2-3 for Windows, a *font* is a typeface of a given size. Figure 5.12 shows a worksheet that uses a number of different fonts.

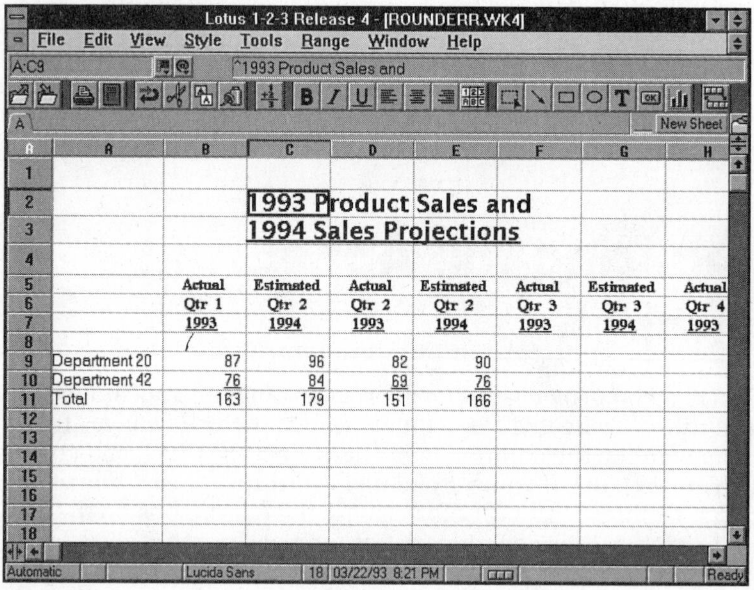

FIG. 5.12

A worksheet displaying a number of different fonts.

To change the typeface, point size, and attributes for a cell or range, use one of the following methods:

- Choose Style Font & Attributes or click on the Font & Attributes SmartIcon to open the Font & Attributes dialog box (see fig. 5.13). Change the settings as desired. If you select Underline, specify an underline style with the drop-down box. The Sample box shows how the font and other attributes you select will look in the worksheet. Select OK to close the dialog box and apply the font to the selected cell or range.

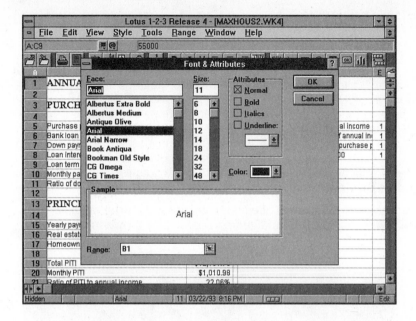

FIG. 5.13

The Font &
Attributes dialog
box.

- ◼ To apply boldfacing, italics, or underline to a selected cell or range, click on the Boldface, Italics, Single Underline, or Double Underline SmartIcon. You can apply several attributes by clicking on more than one of these formatting SmartIcons.

- ◼ Select the cell or range to change and click on the font selector or point-size selector in the status bar to reveal a pop-up list of choices. Select the font and point size from the list with the mouse or arrow keys.

If necessary, 1-2-3 for Windows enlarges the row height to fit the selected fonts. However, 1-2-3 for Windows does not adjust column widths automatically. After you change a font, numeric data may no longer fit in the columns; numeric data may display as asterisks. Change the column widths as needed to correctly display the data (see Chapter 4, "Using Fundamental Commands").

You can restore the previous font and attributes to selected cells by choosing Edit Undo immediately after applying a new font or attribute. If you have made other editing changes already, you can change the font using the Font & Attributes dialog box or by clicking on the font selector in the status bar.

To remove bold, underline, and italics all at once from selected cells, click on the Normal Format SmartIcon. To remove these characteristics individually, click on the appropriate SmartIcon.

Aligning Labels and Values

By default, 1-2-3 for Windows aligns labels to the left and values (numbers and formulas) to the right of the cell. You can change the default worksheet alignment of labels or values to the left, right, or center by choosing Style Worksheet Defaults. The Worksheet Defaults dialog box appears. Choose the desired alignment options and click on OK. If the file contains multiple worksheets, be sure to click on the Group Mode check box to change the default alignment in all the worksheets. Notice that changing the default alignment has no effect on existing worksheet entries. Any new entries you type into the worksheet, however, conform to the new default alignment style.

To change the alignment of existing entries, select the range and then use Style Alignment. The Alignment dialog box shown in figure 5.14 appears.

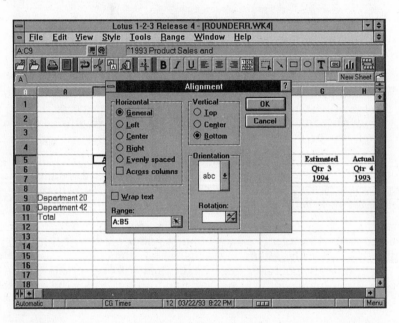

FIG. 5.14

The Alignment dialog box.

The following sections describe the options in the Alignment dialog box you can use to align text horizontally and vertically and to wrap, orient, and rotate text.

Aligning Labels Horizontally

Use the settings in the Horizontal section of the Alignment dialog box to align data. The General option left-aligns all labels and right-aligns all numbers in the selected range. The Left, Center, and Right options align data at the left of the cell, in the center of a cell, and at the right of a cell respectively. The Evenly Spaced option adds spaces, if necessary, between characters so that label entries fill the selected cell from edge to edge (like justifying text with a word processing program). The Evenly Spaced option is ignored if the label ends with a period (.), colon(:), question mark (?), or exclamation point (!). This option has no effect on numbers.

> **NOTE** Any spaces that are included at the beginning or end of an entry are considered valid characters when 1-2-3 aligns the data. For instance, if you type the entry "Sales Projections " in a right-aligned cell and the entry includes two extra spaces at the end as shown, the entry will not appear to be properly right-aligned. (The same is true if extra spaces appear at the beginning of an entry in a left-aligned cell.) When extra spaces appear in an entry that is centered, the spaces also affect where 1-2-3 centers the entry in the cell. To ensure that data is properly aligned, remove all unnecessary spaces from cell entries.

When centering a long entry, 1-2-3 will allow the label to spill over and be displayed in the cells to the immediate right and immediate left of the current cell if those cells are blank. If the adjacent cells are not blank, 1-2-3 still centers the entry but the label is truncated where data appears in an adjacent cell.

To align data quickly in a selected cell or range, click on the Left Align, Center Align, Right Align, or Even Align SmartIcon.

You can also align data automatically when you type an entry by preceding the entry with a label prefix. Type an apostrophe (') to left-align an entry, type a quotation mark (") to right-align an entry, or type a caret (^) to center an entry.

Aligning Text Vertically

Use the options in the Vertical section of the Alignment dialog box to align cell data at the top, center, or bottom of a cell. This option is most useful when the row height has been extended or when a smaller-than-normal font has been used in a particular cell in a row. In either case, the row or cell contains extra vertical space within which the entry can be moved up or down. (For an example, refer to row 1 of figure 5.17 where the worksheet title appears.) The Top option aligns data along the top boundary of the cell, the Bottom option aligns data along the lower boundary of the cell, and the Center option centers data between the top and bottom boundaries of the cell. By default, 1-2-3 uses bottom alignment in worksheet cells.

Aligning Labels across Multiple Columns

When you center or right-align a label, the alignment is relative to the column width of the cell. If you select the Across Columns option in the Alignment dialog box, the label is aligned relative to all selected columns. This option can be handy when you want to center a title over a worksheet. When you align across columns, you can specify whether the label should be aligned Left, Center, Right, or Evenly Spaced.

In figure 5.15, the title in cells B2 and B3 was centered by selecting the range B2..F3 and selecting Style Alignment Center and Across Columns. Notice that only the leftmost cell in the selected range can contain data. If any data was entered in C2..F3 in the worksheet in figure 5.15, the alignment across columns would be canceled.

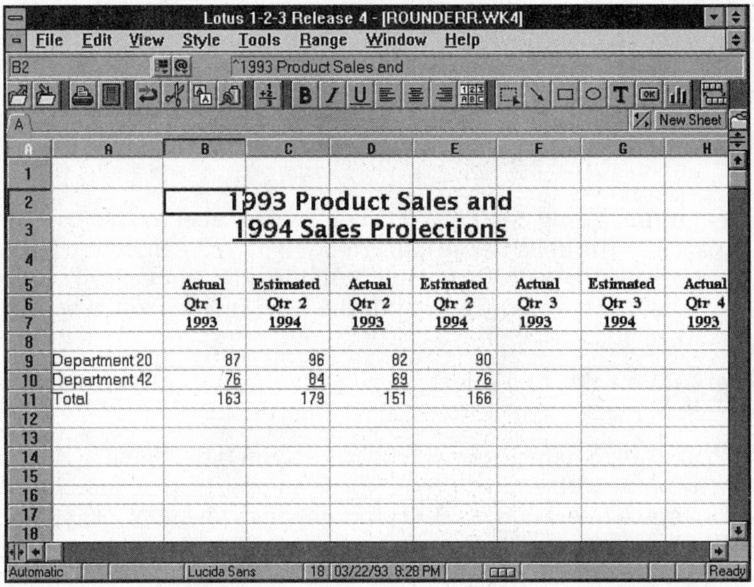

FIG. 5.15

The two-line title is centered across columns B through F.

Wrapping Text in a Cell

Sometimes you need to include a large section of text in a worksheet but you don't want it to extend across columns. Instead, you want the text to continue line by line within that cell rather than across adjacent columns. In this case, you can use the Wrap Text option in the Alignment dialog box. 1-2-3 automatically wraps text at the right edge of the column and carries it to the next line in the cell. 1-2-3 also increases the cell height automatically, if necessary. Figure 5.16 shows an example of wrapped text in cells F14 and H14.

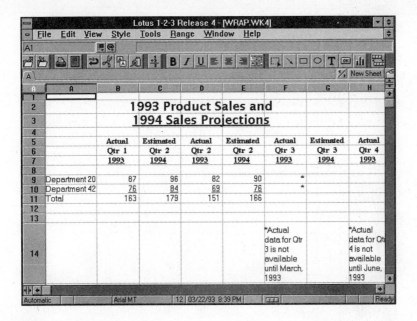

	A	B	C	D	E	F	G	H
1								
2		**1993 Product Sales and**						
3		**1994 Sales Projections**						
4								
5		Actual	Estimated	Actual	Estimated	Actual	Estimated	Actual
6		Qtr 1	Qtr 2	Qtr 2	Qtr 2	Qtr 3	Qtr 3	Qtr 4
7		1993	1994	1993	1994	1993	1994	1993
8								
9	Department 20	87	96	82	90	*		
10	Department 42	76	84	69	76	*		
11	Total	163	179	151	166			
12								
13								
14						*Actual data for Qtr 3 is not available until March, 1993		*Actual data for Qtr 4 is not available until June, 1993

FIG. 5.16

Data in cells
F14 and H14
is wrapped.

NOTE As you type an entry in a cell formatted with the <u>W</u>rap Text option, the characters appear across the adjacent columns instead of wrapping. 1-2-3 wraps the text after you press Enter to confirm the entry in the cell.

Changing the Text Orientation

You can alter the direction in which characters appear in a cell or range (the *orientation* of the text) by using the options in the Orientation section of the Alignment dialog box. This option can be useful for labeling a worksheet as shown in figure 5.17. In the figure, the labels in column A use a vertical orientation. The department labels across row 5 use a diagonal orientation of 45 degrees. Choose the 45-degree angle option in the Orientation box, then use the Rotat<u>i</u>on box to specify the exact angle in degrees.

To quickly change data in a selected cell to a 45-degree orientation, click on the Angle Text SmartIcon. Note that this SmartIcon will only set the text at 45 degrees whereas the Rotat<u>i</u>on option in the dialog box allows you to specify an exact number of degrees (between 1 and 90).

FIG. 5.17

The entries in row 5 are rotated to 45 degrees.

The screenshot shows a Lotus 1-2-3 Release 4 worksheet titled "Department Sales By Category for June, 1993" with the following data:

	Dept 21	Dept 29	Dept 31	Dept 45	Dept 48	Dept 54	Dept 69	Dept 71	Dept 73	Dept 79	Dept 8
Retail	231	335	298	928	234	309	987	502	398	239	2
Wholesale	809	807	940	942	951	899	845	750	857	445	4
Mail Order	1313	1633	1341	1635	978	1251	1841	1627	1742	1624	17
Total	$2,353	$2,775	$2,579	$3,505	$2,163	$2,459	$3,673	$2,879	$2,997	$2,308	24

(Sales by Category)

Formatting Cells with Color and Borders

The Lines & Color dialog box shown in figure 5.18 enables you to enhance and emphasize data in a worksheet by choosing colors, specifying borders, and adding frames. To access the dialog box, choose Style Lines & Color or click on the Lines & Color SmartIcon. Just under the Cancel button, the Sample box shows how the choices you make in the Lines & Color dialog box will appear in the worksheet. Refer to the Sample box as you experiment with different colors, patterns, borders, and frames before actually applying them to the selected range. When you are satisfied with the choices you have made, click on OK.

Before choosing the Lines and Color dialog box, select the cell or cell range to which you want to apply these attributes. You can apply any of the attributes to all sheets in a file by including all sheets in the Range text box. For instance, the range A:A1..D:F9 includes cells A1 through F9 in sheets A through D. (Refer to Chapter 4, "Using Fundamental Commands," for more information on specifying ranges.)

NOTE   You must have a color printer to accurately print colors chosen in the Lines & Color dialog box. However, if the colors and patterns you choose contain enough contrast, many monochrome printers can substitute shades of gray for the different colors you choose; patterns can be duplicated on the printer as closely as possible.

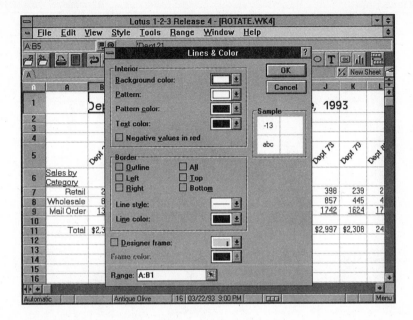

FIG. 5.18

The Lines & Color dialog box.

The settings in the Interior section of the Lines & Color dialog box enable you to specify a Background Color, Pattern, Pattern Color, and Text Color for any cells or ranges in the worksheet. The background color is the color that fills the cell (white by default). If you choose a pattern, it appears in black unless you choose a pattern color. Text appears in black as well, unless you choose a text color.

Use the settings in the Border section of the Lines & Color dialog box to draw lines above, below, on the sides of, and around cells in a range. To outline all cells in a selected range (as if they were one object), choose Outline or click on the Add Border SmartIcon. To outline individual cells in the selected range, choose All. Choose a style and color for the border from the Line Style and Line Color drop-down boxes. You can add a drop shadow to a cell or selected range by clicking on the Drop Shadow SmartIcon.

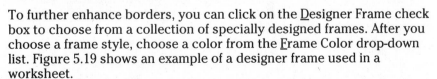

To further enhance borders, you can click on the Designer Frame check box to choose from a collection of specially designed frames. After you choose a frame style, choose a color from the Frame Color drop-down list. Figure 5.19 shows an example of a designer frame used in a worksheet.

For more details on using color, patterns, and frames in worksheets, refer to Chapter 12, "Developing Business Presentations."

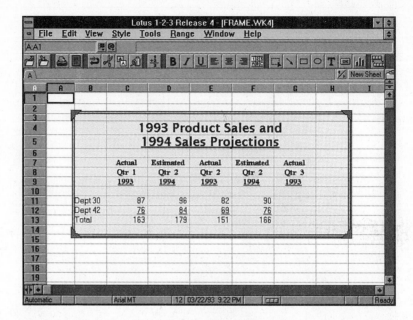

FIG. 5.19

A designer frame and background color enhance the appearance of this worksheet.

Copying a Cell's Style

With the commands on the Style menu, you can select many different characteristics to modify the appearance of data in a worksheet. Applying style attributes to cells can be time-consuming, however—especially when you use multiple styles for different areas of a worksheet. Often, you apply several styles to a cell or range and then discover you want to apply the same style characteristics to another cell or range. You can save yourself the trouble of respecifying each attribute individually by simply copying the style you want to the new range. Select the cell with the style you want to copy and choose Edit Copy. Select the cells to which you want to copy the formats and choose Edit Paste Special. In the Paste Special dialog box, choose the Styles Only option and click on OK. If the target range you copy to contains data, the style attributes are applied immediately. If the range does not contain data, the attributes are applied when you enter data.

 You can copy a cell's styles quickly by selecting the cell containing the styles you want to copy and then clicking on the Copy Styles SmartIcon. The mouse pointer changes to a paint brush. Click on the cell to which you want to copy the formats (or click-and-drag across a cell range) and release the mouse button.

Using Named Styles

Another way to assign styles (groups of formats) is to name them. Using a *named style* is especially helpful when a cell or range has several style characteristics attached to it. You can assign names to up to 16 different sets of styles with the Named Style dialog box shown in figure 5.20. Use this dialog box to define styles as well as to apply a style to a selected cell or range. You access this dialog box by choosing Style Named Style or clicking on the Named Style SmartIcon.

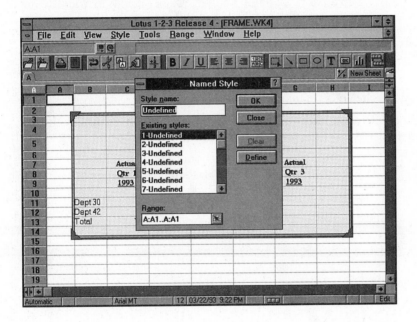

A named style includes all style characteristics (font, point size, number format, decimal places, color, border, and so on) to be assigned to the selected cell or range. To define a named style, do the following:

1. Select the cell or cell range that represents all the style characteristics you want to name.

2. Choose the Style Named Style command or click on the Named Style SmartIcon. The Named Style dialog box appears.

3. In the Existing Styles list box, choose one of the 16 existing styles. (All undefined styles are identified as #-Undefined, where # is a number between 1 and 16.)

4. In the Style <u>N</u>ame text box, enter a name for the style (up to 15 characters).

5. Click on the <u>D</u>efine button.

6. Select OK or press Enter.

When you define named styles, the third box from the left on the status bar becomes the style selector. (This selector is inactive until you create named styles.) To apply a named style, select the cell or range to which you want to apply the style, then click on the style selector. 1-2-3 pops up a list of all named styles. Click on a style from the list to apply all attributes of the style to the selected range. You can also apply a named style to a cell or range by selecting the cells, then choosing a style from the <u>E</u>xisting Styles box.

 You can quickly remove all styles from a selected range of cells by clicking on the Delete Styles SmartIcon. This removes styles only; the data in the cells remains intact.

To delete a named style from the list of named styles, follow these steps:

 1. Choose the Style Named <u>S</u>tyle command or click on the Named Style SmartIcon. The Named Style dialog box appears.

2. In the <u>E</u>xisting Styles list box, choose the style you want to delete.

3. Click on the <u>C</u>lear button.

4. Click OK.

Using the Style Gallery

 Like the named-style feature, the <u>S</u>tyle <u>G</u>allery command (or Style Gallery SmartIcon) allows you to apply styles quickly to a selected range of cells. The difference between the named-style feature and the Style Gallery is that the Style Gallery contains 14 predesigned style templates. Just choose a template from the list in the Gallery dialog box and all the style characteristics that make up the template are applied to the selected range.

 To remove a template from the selected range, choose <u>E</u>dit Cl<u>e</u>ar <u>St</u>yles Only or click on the Delete Styles SmartIcon.

The Gallery dialog box is shown in figure 5.21. Refer to the Sample area in the dialog box to preview each template before applying it to the selected range. In the figure, the Post Note template is shown in the Sample box. The worksheet underneath the dialog box is formatted with the Chisel2 template.

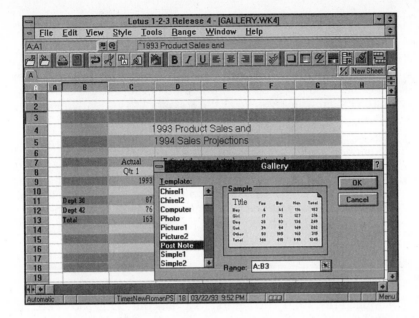

FIG. 5.21

The worksheet uses the Chisel2 template; the Gallery dialog box shows a sample of the Post Note template.

Questions & Answers

In this chapter, you learned about changing the format and appearance of data. If you have any questions about any topic covered in this chapter and cannot find the answer in any of the help windows, scan this section.

Q: If I turn off the Use Automatic Format option in the User Setup dialog box, what format does 1-2-3 use for new worksheets?

A: 1-2-3 uses the General format in all new worksheets if you turn off the Use Automatic Format default setting.

Q: How can I change the default currency symbol in the User Setup dialog box from $ to £ (British pound sterling) when I don't have a £ symbol on my keyboard?

A: You must type a *compose sequence*, which enables you to use keys on the keyboard to create the character. In the International dialog box, delete the $ in the Symbol for Currency text box, press Alt+F1 (Compose), and type the compose sequence for £: L= or L- (the *L* can be uppercase or lowercase). 1-2-3 inserts the £ symbol in the text box. Now when you assign the Currency format to a cell in the worksheet, the £ symbol appears instead of $. Use the same procedure to enter other currency symbols. For a complete list of compose sequences, refer to Appendix C.

Q: How can I enter a £ symbol in the worksheet without changing the default currency symbol in the User Setup dialog box?

A: You can compose the character as just described or you can use the @CHAR function and enter the LMBCS (Lotus Multibyte Character Set) code. The LMBCS code for £ is 156; enter **@CHAR(156)** in the cell in which you want the £ symbol to appear. Refer to Appendix C for a complete list of LMBCS codes.

Q: How do I change the alignment of data in a cell by using the edit line?

A: 1-2-3 uses label prefixes to identify the alignment of label entries. The label prefix is visible in the edit line but not in the cell itself. You can use the edit line to change the alignment of a label by erasing the old prefix and typing a new one just in front of the entry. Type an apostrophe (') for left alignment, a caret (^) for center alignment, and a quotation mark (") for right alignment. You must use a menu command or SmartIcon to evenly space an entry across a cell or range.

Q: I applied the <u>W</u>rap Text option to a cell containing a long text entry, but instead of filling the cell, the text begins near the bottom of the cell and fills the next three cells to the right. What did I do wrong?

A: Check the Alignment dialog box to make sure that the Ac<u>r</u>oss Columns option isn't selected. The Ac<u>r</u>oss Columns option causes an entry to be displayed across adjacent columns, even though the <u>W</u>rap Text option is selected.

Q: I used the Del key to delete a long text entry from a cell formatted with the <u>W</u>rap Text option. I want the new entry to display into the next column, but it wraps, too. I know I can turn off the <u>W</u>rap Text option, but isn't there a better way to solve this problem?

A: When you use the Del key to delete an entry, you delete only the contents of the cell, not the style. You can use <u>E</u>dit Cl<u>e</u>ar to display a dialog box that asks whether you want to delete the cell contents only, the style only, or both. If you select <u>B</u>oth, 1-2-3 clears the cell contents as well as the wrap-text style.

Q: When I deleted a long text entry from a cell that used the <u>W</u>rap Text option, the row height was not readjusted. Did I do something wrong?

A: No. When you use the <u>W</u>rap Text option for a long text entry, 1-2-3 adjusts the row height to accommodate the entire entry. When you delete the cell contents, style, or both, 1-2-3 doesn't assume that you want the row height readjusted. You can readjust the row height quickly by choosing the F̲it Largest Font option in the Row Height dialog box.

Q: When I enter and format a date, why does 1-2-3 display the wrong date?

A: 1-2-3 can format a date correctly only if you enter it in a format 1-2-3 recognizes. If the date you enter is in some other format, 1-2-3 interprets the entry as a label or a formula. If you enter **12-31-93**, for example, 1-2-3 recognizes the hyphens as minus signs and returns -112. However, if you enter **31-Dec-93**, 1-2-3 formats the entry correctly because 31-Dec-93 is a valid date format.

Q: When I enter time and date serial numbers, why doesn't 1-2-3 display a recognizable time or date?

A: Unless the cell is already formatted with a date or time format, 1-2-3 uses the Automatic format and interprets the number as an integer.

Q: How can I perform mathematical operations on dates and times?

A: You construct the formula just like you do for any other values in the worksheet. Remember that 1-2-3 stores dates and times as serial numbers and uses these numbers to perform the calculation you specify.

Summary

This chapter presented a number of techniques for changing the appearance of data in a worksheet. You learned how to change style characteristics (number formats, fonts and text attributes, and the alignment of cell contents) for a single cell, a range of cells, or the entire worksheet. You also learned how to change the default settings that determine the style characteristics for all new worksheets you create. In addition, you learned how to enhance worksheets by adding colors, patterns, borders, and frames to selected cells; you learned how to save style characteristics as a named style; and you learned how to apply predesigned 1-2-3 templates to worksheets. You now have the skills to build and format worksheets.

The next chapter teaches you how to manage your files with 1-2-3.

Managing Files

The File commands on the 1-2-3 for Windows main menu provide a wide range of capabilities for file management, modification, and protection. Some commands, such as File Open, File Save, and File Save As, are similar to other Windows 3 applications' commands. Other commands are related to specific 1-2-3 for Windows tasks and applications. This chapter discusses the File commands and good file management techniques in 1-2-3 for Windows.

In this chapter, you learn how to do the following:

- Create new files
- Name files
- Save files
- Change the default directory
- Open files
- Combine separate files
- Protect files
- Delete files
- Reserve a shared file

Understanding Files

Before you begin working with files, you need to understand a little about files and the terminology 1-2-3 uses in reference to files. In generic terms, a *file* is nothing more than a collection of data stored on a disk. In 1-2-3, a file consists of one worksheet or multiple worksheets that are saved together as one file (worksheet A, worksheet B, worksheet C, and so on).

An *open*, or *active*, file is a file displayed on-screen or listed on the Window menu. Many active files can be open at one time, but only one is the *current file*, which always contains the cell pointer and the highlighted title bar. (A check mark appears to the left of the current file on the Window menu.)

The File menu, shown in figure 6.1, contains the commands you use to open, save, create, and otherwise work with files. The following list provides brief descriptions of these File commands; the remainder of the chapter covers the commands in more detail.

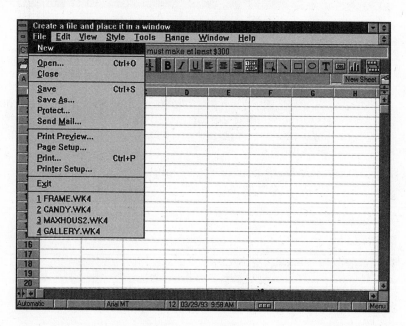

FIG. 6.1

The File pull-down menu.

- File New enables you to create a new worksheet file when one or more existing files are already open.

- File Open enables you to open an existing file on-screen and read, change, or add information to it.

- You use the File Close command when you finish working with a file and want to close it.

- File Save saves the current file, using its current file name.

- File Save As saves a worksheet file with a name you specify. Using File Save As, you have the option of saving the file in a different directory, drive, or file format.

- The File Protect command enables you to seal a file so that other users cannot make changes to the file without a valid password. You can also use this command to set file reservations for shared files on a computer network.

- If your computer has access to an electronic mail system, the File Send Mail command enables you to send the current file or a selection from the file to another mail user.

- The four File commands relating to printing—Print Preview, Page Setup, Print, and Printer Setup—are not covered in this chapter. See Chapter 10, "Printing Reports," for an explanation of these commands.

- Use File Exit when you finish working with 1-2-3 and want to close the program. Don't confuse this command with the File Close command, which only closes the current file.

Creating Files

When you start 1-2-3, a blank worksheet appears on-screen. You can use this worksheet to create one new file. If you want to create additional new files during the same work session, choose File New or click on the Create File SmartIcon, which displays a new blank worksheet in the current window. Any files that are open when you choose File New or click on the Create File SmartIcon remain open afterward. The new file becomes an open file and is listed on the Window menu. 1-2-3 assigns temporary file names to new files you create, as described in the next section.

Saving Files

When you create a new worksheet file or when you make changes to an existing file, your work exists only in the computer's memory. If you don't save a new worksheet or the changes you make before you exit 1-2-3 for Windows, you lose your work. Using a save command to save a file copies the file from memory onto the disk.

To save your work, choose File Save or File Save As, or click on the Save File SmartIcon. If you select File Save or click on the Save File

SmartIcon and the file has been saved previously, 1-2-3 saves the file under the current file name without displaying a dialog box. If you select File Save As (or if you are saving a new file for the first time and use File Save or click on the Save File SmartIcon), 1-2-3 for Windows displays the Save As dialog box, shown in figure 6.2, in which you specify the file's name, drive, directory, and file type.

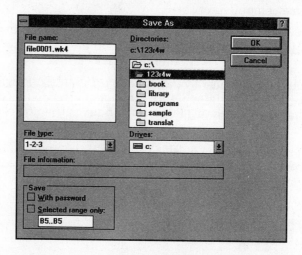

FIG. 6.2

The Save As dialog box.

After you specify the save information, choose OK or press Enter. If an existing worksheet file already uses the file name you entered in the Save As dialog box, 1-2-3 displays a message saying that the file already exists. Choose Replace to overwrite the existing file; choose Backup if you want 1-2-3 to make a backup copy of the file; or choose Cancel to cancel the save operation.

NOTE You also use the Save As dialog box to assign a password or to save only a selected range of cells in the current worksheet. These features are discussed later in this chapter.

Naming Files

When you create a new file, 1-2-3 automatically assigns the file a temporary file name, FILE*nnnn*.WK4, where *nnnn* is replaced with a number. The numbering begins with 0001 and continues sequentially. The first temporary file name is FILE0001.WK4. If you create additional new files, 1-2-3 names these files FILE0002.WK4, FILE0003.WK4, and so on, incrementing the numeric portion of the file name with each new file (see

fig. 6.3). You can save your work using the temporary file names
1-2-3 assigns, or you can choose a descriptive name.

Naming files helps you to identify your work. Identifying the content
of a file named BUDGET93.WK4 is easy, but the file name
FILE0001.WK4 doesn't tell you anything about the contents of the
file.

T I P

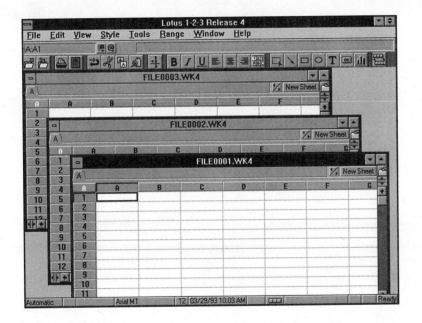

FIG. 6.3

New work-
sheets—
FILE0001.WK4,
FILE0002.WK4,
and
FILE0003.WK4—
created during
one working
session.

The maximum length of a file name is eight characters. A file name can
contain any combination of letters, numbers, hyphens, and under-
scores. However, with the exception of a single period between the file
name and the extension, you cannot use any other special characters,
such as spaces, commas, backslashes, or periods. In addition, your
computer's operating system, DOS, reserves some file names for its
use. You cannot use the following as file names:

AUX	COM1	LPT1
CLOCK$	COM2	LPT2
CON	COM3	LPT3
NUL	COM4	PRN

The standard file extension for 1-2-3 for Windows worksheet files is WK4. When you open or save a file, type only the descriptive part of the name; 1-2-3 for Windows supplies the appropriate file extension for you. 1-2-3 for Windows uses the file extensions shown in table 6.1. (You can override these standard extensions and type your own, but allowing 1-2-3 for Windows to assign file extensions is preferable so that you can easily identify the file type.)

Table 6.1 File Extensions and Descriptions

Extension	Description
AL3	A file in which named page settings are saved
BAK	A backup copy of a worksheet file
FMB	A backup version of a format file (FM3 and FMT extensions). From earlier releases of 1-2-3, a *format file* is a file that stores a worksheet's style information only.
MAC	A macro for a customized icon
NS4	A 1-2-3 shared file
TXT	A text file
WK1	1-2-3 Release 2 worksheet files
WK3	1-2-3 for Windows Release 1 and 1-2-3 for DOS Release 3 files

File extensions help identify the file type. If you use File Open to open the file BUDGET.WK1, for example, you can tell by the file extension that the file is a 1-2-3 for DOS Release 2 file. If you rename the file to BUDGET.JAN, 1-2-3 for Windows can still identify and translate the file type, but you cannot readily identify the file as a 1-2-3 worksheet file.

When you choose File Open or click on the Open File SmartIcon, 1-2-3 for Windows lists all the files with extensions beginning with WK. To open a file that has a different extension, you must type the complete file name and extension or use *wild cards* (see "Using Wild Cards To Open Files" later in this chapter).

T I P Sometimes you may want to save a file with a nonstandard extension so that the file does not automatically appear when the Open File dialog box lists files in the current directory. For example, you may want to assign a nonstandard extension to a file that is part of a macro-controlled system so that you don't accidentally open the file outside the macro. The nonstandard extension "hides" the file from the standard list of worksheet files. When you want to open the file outside the macro environment, to change the file for example, you type the entire file name and extension.

Saving a Portion of a File

The Selected Range Only option in the Save As dialog box (refer to fig. 6.2) saves data from a cell, range, or worksheet to a new or existing worksheet file. You might use this command to save part of a file before you change it, to break a large file into smaller files, to create a partial file for someone else to work on, or to send information to another file. For example, you may want to use this feature to break a large budget file into separate files, each one containing information about a single department's budget. This technique is useful when you need to work with portions of a worksheet's data in separate worksheet files.

The Selected Range Only option copies all settings associated with the copied cells, including styles, formats, protection status, range names, column widths, row heights, fonts and font characteristics.

To save a selected range, choose the File Save As option to display the Save As dialog box. In the File name box, enter a name for the file in which you want to save the range. Choose the Selected Range Only option in the Save As dialog box. When you choose OK, 1-2-3 displays the Save Range As dialog box (see fig. 6.4). Choose the Formulas and values option or the Values only option. When you save a range by using the Formulas and values option, 1-2-3 for Windows adjusts the addresses in formulas to reflect their new locations in the destination file. The Values only option, on the other hand, saves all calculated cells as values.

NOTE   If you save a range that contains a formula, be certain to include all the cells that the formula refers to; otherwise, the formula does not calculate correctly. If the cells you are saving are part of a named range, you must select the entire range; otherwise, the range name does not refer to the correct cell addresses.

FIG. 6.4

The Save Range
As dialog box.

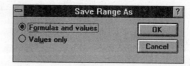

Choose OK or press Enter to return to the Save As dialog box; then
choose OK or press Enter again to complete the saving process. 1-2-3
saves the specified range in the specified file. 1-2-3 *doesn't* automatically open the file. To view the file, use the File Open command to open
the file.

Remember that 1-2-3 for Windows also enables you to copy and move
data between worksheet files with the Edit Cut, Edit Copy, Edit Paste,
and Edit Paste Special commands. In some cases, using these commands may be just as easy as saving a range of cells. See Chapters 4,
"Using Fundamental Commands," and 5, "Changing the Format and
Appearance of Data," for more details about these operations.

Saving Files in Other 1-2-3 Formats

1-2-3 Release 4 for Windows enables you to save Release 4 files in file
formats used by previous releases of 1-2-3. This feature is useful if you
need to send a file to someone who is using an earlier release of 1-2-3.
You use the Save As dialog box to specify the file type when saving the
file. You can save a 1-2-3 Release 4 worksheet file in a wk1 (1-2-3 for DOS
Release 2 format) by choosing the 1-2-3 (wk1) option in the File type
drop-down list box. You can also save a file in the WK3 (1-2-3 for Windows Release 1 or 1-2-3 for DOS Release 3) format by choosing the 1-2-3
(wk3) option (see fig. 6.5). Choosing these options adds the WK1 or
WK3 extension to the file name. If you prefer, you can simply type the
file name with the WK1 or WK3 extension in the File Name text box.

Although saving 1-2-3 for Windows files in 1-2-3 WK1 or WK3 format is
possible, you lose some of the worksheet information in the conversion
because 1-2-3 Release 4 supports features that earlier releases of 1-2-3
do not support. When you save the file, 1-2-3 warns you that you may
lose some worksheet information, such as the following:

- Any versions and scenarios created with the Version Manager

- Queries and query tables

- Drawn objects (not including charts)

- Embedded data from other Windows applications

- Worksheet settings (including tabs, range names, default text, and
  cell background colors)

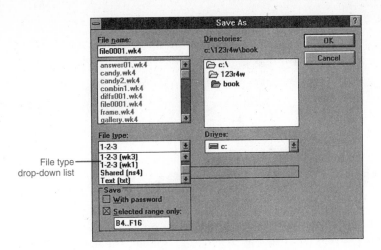

FIG. 6.5

Choosing a file format.

File type drop-down list

1-2-3 Release 4 for Windows also enables you to save files in FM3 format. This format file is used by 1-2-3 for Windows Release 1 and 1-2-3 for DOS Release 3 that saves a worksheet's style characteristics only. To save a worksheet in this format, type the file name and file extension in the File name text box of the Save As dialog box, and then click on OK.

Closing Files

Closing a file is not the same as saving a file. *Closing* a file removes the file from the screen and from memory without necessarily saving it. *Saving* a file saves the changes and keeps the file open. When you finish working with a file, choose File Close or click on the Close Window SmartIcon to remove the current file from the screen and from the list of open files on the Window menu. If you have made unsaved changes to the file when you select File Close or click on the Close Window SmartIcon, 1-2-3 displays a warning that allows you to save the recent changes. Choose Yes to save changes, No to close the file without saving changes, or Cancel to return to working on the file.

You can use the File Exit command and the End 1-2-3 Session SmartIcon to exit the 1-2-3 program; these commands don't automatically close all open files, however. If you choose File Exit or click on the End 1-2-3 Session SmartIcon while files are still open, 1-2-3 gives you the opportunity to save each open file before exiting the program.

T I P   If you are working with many open files at one time, closing a file that you are finished working with is a good idea. The more files open at a time, the less available memory you have. Closing a file frees up memory, enabling you to work more efficiently with the files that remain open.

Opening Existing Files

By using the File Open command, you can open an existing file without closing the current file. 1-2-3 displays the file you open in the current window. The file that was current before you opened the new file remains active, but the new file becomes the current file in the current window. If other worksheet files are open, they remain open and are unaffected by the file you open. (All open files are listed on the Window menu.)

 To open a file, choose File Open or click on the Open File SmartIcon to display the Open File dialog box (see fig. 6.6). The current directory name appears above the Directories box. For example, in fig. 6.6, the current directory is c:\123r4w\sample\tutorial. Tutorial is a subdirectory of sample. sample is a subdirectory of 123r4w, and 123r4w is a directory on drive c. Each directory is indented under its parent directory and under drive c:\.

In the File name text box, 1-2-3 automatically enters **.wk*** so that worksheet files are listed in the files box. Click on the name of the file you want to open, or type the file name in the File name text box.

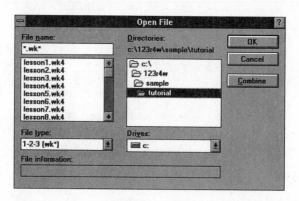

FIG. 6.6

The Open File dialog box.

Opening Files from Subdirectories and Other Drives

Often, the file you want to open is stored in a different directory, so the file name isn't currently shown in the Files list box. To list the file name in the Files list box, you must first select the correct directory name from the Directories list box.

The directory where the file is stored could be a parent directory to the current directory, or it could be a subdirectory to the current directory. To select a parent directory, click on any of the directory names listed *above* the current directory in the Directories list box. (For instance, in fig. 6.6, you could click on sample or 123r4w, or you could click on c:\ to list all directories on drive c.) To select a subdirectory, click on the directory name listed *below* the current directory in the Directories list box. (In fig. 6.6, the tutorial directory doesn't contain any subdirectories.)

When you have selected the correct directory, 1-2-3 lists all files with a .wk* extension in that directory. (If necessary, use the scroll bar or arrow keys to display all entries.) To list *all* files in the current directory, replace the .wk* entry in the File name text box with *.*. Alternatively, you can display all files of a different file type by entering the correct file extension. Select the file you want to open, then click on OK.

For more information about creating directories and subdirectories, refer to your Microsoft Windows documentation.

If the file you want to open is stored on another drive, select the appropriate drive in the Drives drop-down box. When you select a different drive, 1-2-3 displays all files with a .wk* file extension in the last directory you used on that drive. To select a different directory, follow the guidelines in the previous paragraph. Remember that you can also list all files in the current directory by typing *.* in the File name dialog box. Select a file from the files list, and then choose OK.

Using Wild Cards To Open Files

In the Open File dialog box, you can include an asterisk (*) or a question mark (?) as *wild card characters* (often just called *wild cards*) in the File name box. Wild card characters act as placeholders that match one character or any number of characters in sequence. The ? wild card matches any one character in the file name. The * matches any number of characters in sequence. When you use wild cards in a File name text box, 1-2-3 for Windows lists only the files whose names match the wild card. In fact, 1-2-3 uses the * wild card by default each time the Open File dialog box is displayed (refer to fig. 6.6).

The *.wk* in the File name box tells 1-2-3 to list all files with file extensions that begin with .WK followed by any number of other characters. Suppose that you type **????TREE.WK*** in the File Name text box shown in figure 6.6. 1-2-3 for Windows lists all the file names that start with any four characters, followed by TREE and an extension beginning with WK; examples are AUDITREE.WK4, BACKTREE.WK3, SOLVTREE.WK1, and VIEWTREE.WK. If you type **BUDGET*.***, 1-2-3 for Windows lists all the file names that start with BUDGET, such as BUDGET.WK4, BUDGET1.TXT, and BUDGET99.WK3.

Opening a File Automatically When You Start 1-2-3

When you first start 1-2-3 for Windows, a blank worksheet appears so that you can create a new file. However, if you usually begin a work session using the same worksheet file, you can tell 1-2-3 to automatically display that worksheet when the program starts. You do this by naming the file AUTO123.WK4.

Another way to open a specific worksheet in 1-2-3 is to use the Windows File Manager. Without starting 1-2-3, open the File Manager. In the File Manager window, select the 123R4W directory (or a subdirectory where the file is located) to display all the files in the directory (see fig. 6.7). Double-click on the name of the file you want to open. Because worksheet files have a WK4 file extension, the file you select is associated with the 1-2-3 for Windows program. The Windows File Manager knows to open the 1-2-3 for Windows program as well as the file you select.

Opening Recently Used Files

1-2-3 provides a convenient feature that enables you to quickly open the files you used most recently. This feature saves you the trouble of selecting a file name from the Open File dialog box when you want to open a file. To list on the File menu the files most recently used, choose the Tools User Setup command. In the User Setup dialog box, shown in figure 6.8, enter a number between 0 and 5 in the Number of recent files to show box, and then click on OK. 1-2-3 adds the names of the files (up to the number you specify) at the bottom of the File menu. You can see an example of this in figure 6.1. To open a file, simply click on the file name on the File menu.

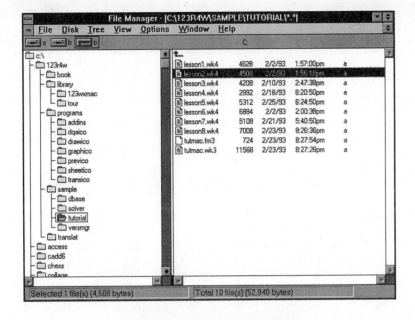

Double-click on LESSON2.WK4, highlighted in the File Manager, to open the file and 1-2-3 at one time.

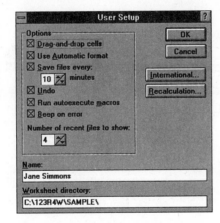

The User Setup dialog box in which you choose the number of recent files to show in the File Menu.

Opening Spreadsheet Files from Other Programs

1-2-3 Release 4 for Windows enables you to open files from previous releases of 1-2-3, from Lotus Symphony, and from Microsoft Excel. Table 6.2 lists these programs and their file extensions.

Table 6.2 Spreadsheet Programs and File Extensions

Extension	Program
WK3, FM3	1-2-3 for Windows Release 1; 1-2-3 for DOS Release 3
WKS	1-2-3 for DOS Release 1A
WK1, ALL, FMT	1-2-3 for DOS Release 2
WRK	Symphony Release 1.0 and 1.01
WR1, FMS	Symphony Release 1.1, 1.2, 2.0, 2.1, 2.2, and 3.0
XLS	Microsoft Excel version 2.1, 2.2, 3.0, and 4.0

To open any of these files, select the file from the correct directory in the Open File dialog box, and then click on OK. You can save 1-2-3 and Symphony files in their original file formats, or you can save them as 1-2-3 Release 4 (WK4) files. Keep in mind, however, that if you add features to the file that are available only in 1-2-3 Release 4, these features are lost when you save the file in its original file format. See "Saving Files in Other 1-2-3 Formats" earlier in this chapter for more information.

NOTE When you open a Microsoft Excel file, 1-2-3 opens a copy of the file in a WK4 format and leaves the original Excel file unchanged. If 1-2-3 is unable to understand any of the information in the Excel file, 1-2-3 creates a log file called DATA.LOG and saves it in the directory from which you opened the Excel file. 1-2-3 displays a dialog box saying that the file DATA.XLS contains untranslatable information from the Excel file. Choose the Explain button to view the DATA.LOG file; choose OK to see the translated worksheet file in 1-2-3. Any functions or formulas that are untranslatable must be edited in 1-2-3 before they can calculate correctly in 1-2-3.

Combining Values from Separate Files

When you work with data from several different files, being able to combine the values in one file is sometimes useful. 1-2-3 lets you use values from one file to replace values, add to values, or subtract from values in the current worksheet file, beginning at the current cell.

You generally use 1-2-3's combining feature when you are combining similar worksheets. Suppose, for example, that you have two separate worksheets containing sales figures for Department 25 and Department 26. The two departments are being merged into one—Department 30— and you want to merge the sales figures in a new worksheet. Because you want the new worksheet to reflect the sum of the sales figures from both departments, you choose to add to the values (rather than re- place or subtract from the values) in the new worksheet. The current file is the file where the values are combined. (In the example, the De- partment 30 worksheet is the current file.) The file from which values are copied is the *source file*. (In this example, the Department 25 and Department 26 worksheets are the source files.) Values in the source file remain unchanged; only the values in the current file are changed.

Combining values from separate files can be tricky, however, because 1-2-3 combines the values beginning at the current cell in the current file. For this reason, you must be careful to match up cells and ranges in both files to avoid errors. Opening both files side by side can be helpful in this situation because you can refer to both files at one time. See Chapter 2, "Understanding the Graphical User Interface," for more information about displaying multiple windows. If you are working with more than one source file, open each source file one at a time beside the current file.

To combine files, you use the Combine button in the Open File dialog box, which displays the Combine 1-2-3 File dialog box shown in figure 6.9. The From File field indicates the name of the source file. The Read box enables you to indicate whether you want to read the entire source file into the current file or read only a selected range into the current file. If you want to read a selected range only, be sure to position the cell pointer in the current file in the same cell from which you begin defining the range in the source file. An example is shown in figure 6.10.

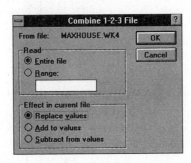

FIG. 6.9

The Combine 1-2-3 File dialog box.

Cell pointer in current file
is in cell A6

Range to read from
source file begins
at cell A6

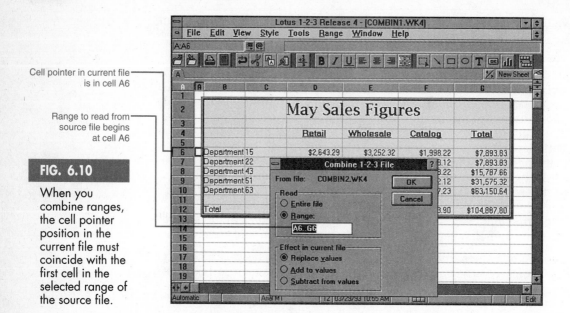

FIG. 6.10

When you
combine ranges,
the cell pointer
position in the
current file must
coincide with the
first cell in the
selected range of
the source file.

Follow these steps to open each file and combine the values:

1. Open the source file by using the File Open command.

2. Open the current file by using the File Open command.

3. Choose the Window Tile command to display the files side by side. Make sure the current file is active.

4. In the current file, place the cell pointer in the cell where you want values to be copied. (If you are combining a range in the source file with the current file, place the cell pointer in the current file at the position where you want the source cells to begin. Otherwise, place the cell pointer in cell A1.)

5. Choose File Open. In the Open File dialog box, select the source file, and then click on the Combine button. 1-2-3 displays the Combine 1-2-3 File dialog box (refer to fig. 6.10). The From File field lists the name of the source file.

6. Choose Entire file or Range. If you are copying a range from the source file, type the range in the Range text box.

7. Choose Replace values, Add to values, or Subtract from values, and then click on OK. 1-2-3 changes the values in the current worksheet file immediately, beginning at the location of the current cell.

To combine values from additional source files, repeat these steps to open and combine each additional file. In each case, you can choose to replace, add to, or subtract from the values in the current file.

In the Combine 1-2-3 File dialog box, the Add to values option adds the values of the cells in the source file to the values or blank cells in the current file. If the incoming value of a cell is combined with a value, 1-2-3 for Windows adds the two values. If the incoming value is combined with a blank cell, the cell takes the value of the number. If the incoming value is combined with a label or formula, 1-2-3 for Windows ignores the incoming value and keeps the label or formula.

The Subtract from values option subtracts the values of the cell in the source file from the value in the current file. If the incoming value of a cell is combined with a value, 1-2-3 for Windows subtracts the incoming value from the value in the current file. If the incoming value is combined with a blank cell, 1-2-3 for Windows subtracts the incoming value from zero. If the incoming value is combined with a label or formula, 1-2-3 for Windows ignores the incoming value and keeps the label or formula.

Regardless of the option you choose in the Combine 1-2-3 File dialog box, 1-2-3's combine feature changes data in the active worksheet file. To avoid accidentally losing data, be sure to save the file before you use File Open Combine. Consider saving the file under a different name.

For Related Information

◄◄ "Understanding the Graphical User Interface," p. 45.

FROM HERE...

Changing Directories

As discussed earlier in this chapter in the section "Opening Existing Files," a hard disk is divided into a number of *directories* and *subdirectories* that store related data files. The list of directories that leads from the root directory (usually c:\) to the file you want is the *path* or *path name*.

If you installed 1-2-3 for Windows according to the instructions in Appendix A, your worksheet files are stored in the path C:\123R4W\SAMPLE. This directory is called your *working directory*. Each time you choose File Save or File Save As, 1-2-3 automatically assumes you want to save files in your working directory.

To organize your work, you may have created other directories and subdirectories under 123r4w. If so, you might want 1-2-3 to save files automatically to a different directory—one that you have created. You use the Tools User Setup command to specify a new working directory. In the User Setup dialog box, shown in figure 6.11, enter a new path name in the Worksheet directory text box, and then choose OK to change the working directory for the current and all future work sessions.

Protecting Files

1-2-3 for Windows offers two methods of protecting files. You can protect confidential worksheet files by assigning a *password* when you save the file, or you can *seal* a file to prevent unauthorized changes. When you save a file with a password, no one can open, copy, or print the file without first issuing the password. When you seal a file, no one can make changes to a file's reservation status or to the data and styles in the worksheet. Sealing files is covered in the section "Sealing a File To Prevent Changes," later in this chapter.

Assigning Passwords

You assign a password to a file by using the File Save As dialog box, as explained in the following steps:

1. Choose File Save As to display the Save As dialog box (see fig. 6.12).

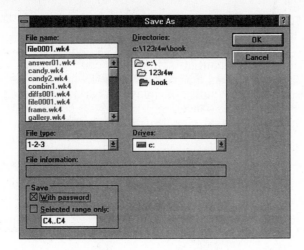

FIG. 6.12

The File Save As
dialog box.

2. Type the file name in the File name text box.

3. Select the With password check box, and then select OK. 1-2-3 for Windows displays the Set Password dialog box (see fig. 6.13).

FIG. 6.13

The Set Password
dialog box.

4. In the Password text box, type a password. For security, 1-2-3 displays an asterisk (*) for each character you type.

5. In the Verify text box, type the password again exactly as you typed it before. Again, 1-2-3 displays asterisks in place of the characters you type.

6. Select OK.

If, in the File Name box, you entered a file name that already exists, 1-2-3 for Windows asks whether you want to replace the existing file, back up the existing file, or cancel saving the file. You must select Replace or Backup to save the file with the password. If you select Cancel, 1-2-3 for Windows doesn't assign the password and returns to the worksheet window.

NOTE If the file doesn't already exist, the password is assigned automatically.

A password can contain any combination of uppercase or lowercase characters. It's best not to use obvious passwords such as your birth date, license plate number, children's or pet's names. Because longer passwords are more difficult for someone to guess, phrases with no spaces between words (such as **itrainsinapril**) work well. As you enter the password, 1-2-3 for Windows displays an asterisk for each character you type. Remember that passwords are case-sensitive; if you specify **JustForMe** as the password, typing **justforme** to open the file does not work.

> **CAUTION:** Remember your password exactly as you type it. You cannot open the file again unless you enter the password in precisely the same way.

Opening a Password-Protected File

When you try to open a password-protected file by using File Open, 1-2-3 for Windows prompts you for the password. You must enter the password exactly as you originally entered it, with the correct upper- and lowercase letters. If you make an error as you enter the password, an error message appears, saying that you entered an invalid password. Try opening the file again, using the correct password.

Changing and Deleting Passwords

You can change or delete a file's password at any time, provided you know the current password. To change a password, follow the same steps you use to assign a password: choose File Save As, but type a new password in the Password and Verify text boxes.

To remove a password from a file, open the password-protected file. Choose File Save As, and then turn off the With password check box. 1-2-3 displays a message saying that the file already exists. Choose Replace or Backup to save the file without a password.

Sealing a File To Prevent Changes

Sealing a file prevents a user from changing data, styles, or other settings used in the file. When a file is sealed, you cannot insert or delete columns; show hidden worksheets or columns; change, add, or delete range names, page breaks, frozen titles; or set new formats, column widths, row heights, or cell alignments.

You seal a file when you want other users to be able to open and read the file, but not change it—intentionally or unintentionally. A sealed file is also password-protected. Although you can open and read the file without knowing the password, you must know the password if you want to change the file in any way. The password protection on a sealed file allows you to give read access to a large group of users while giving only one or a few users the authority to change the file. (Without the password protection, only the user who creates the file can change it.)

To seal a file, you choose the File Protect command to display the Protect dialog box, shown in figure 6.14. Choose the Seal File check box, and then click on OK. 1-2-3 displays the Set Password dialog box, the same dialog box used to save a file with a password (refer to fig. 6.13). Type the password in the Password text box, and then type the password a second time in the Verify text box. Just like when you save a file with a password, you can use any combination of upper- and lowercase characters in the password. Select OK to close the Set Password dialog box. 1-2-3 returns to the Protect dialog box. Select OK.

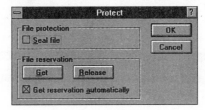

FIG. 6.14

The Protect dialog box.

Protecting Selected Cells or a Range

In some cases, you may want users to be able to change certain cells in a file, even though the file is sealed. You can leave certain cells unprotected by using the Style Protection command *before* you seal the file. First, select the cells you want unprotected, and then choose Style Protection to display the Protection dialog box, shown in figure 6.15.

FIG. 6.15

The Protection dialog box.

The Range box shows the range of cells you selected. Select the Keep data unprotected after file is sealed option, and then click on OK. Now that a range of cells has been set as unprotected, you can seal the file using the steps outlined earlier. When a sealed file contains unprotected cells, the status bar displays Pr when the cell pointer is in a protected cell, and U when the cell pointer is in an unprotected cell.

To change protected cells in a file that has been sealed, you must unseal the file first, and then change the cell protection. To unseal a file, follow these steps:

1. Choose File Protect. The Protect dialog box appears.

2. In the Protect dialog box, turn off the Seal File check box, and then click on OK. 1-2-3 displays the Set Password dialog box.

3. Type the password in the Password text box, and then click on OK.

1-2-3 displays a message saying the file is unsealed. Now you can use the Style Protection command to change the unprotected cells in the file.

Remember that sealing a file is different from protecting a file with a password. Saving a file with a password prevents *all* access to the file unless the user knows the password. When the file is open, however, a user can change it. When you seal a file, other users can open and read the file and make changes to any unprotected cells. Without a password, however, they cannot change data, styles, or other settings in protected cells.

Reserving Shared Files

If you use 1-2-3 for Windows on a network, two or more people can access or update the same file at the same time. If more than one person can change a file at the same time, the result can be inaccurate data or formulas. To avoid multiple updates of the same shared file, 1-2-3 for Windows has a *reservation* system. 1-2-3 for Windows also enables you to hide and protect confidential data in a shared file.

The File Protect command displays the Protect dialog box, which enables you to Get or Release a file reservation or change a file reservation setting to automatic or manual (refer to fig. 6.14). By default, 1-2-3 for Windows gives you the reservation when you open a shared file. If you try to open a shared file that someone else is currently working on, 1-2-3 for Windows displays a message box that asks whether you want to open the file without having the reservation. If you select Y̲es, you can read the file and change the data, but you cannot save the changes to the same file name. You can, however, save the file with another name so that your changes are preserved.

If you have the reservation for a file, you keep the reservation until you close the file, or you can release the reservation by using F̲ile P̲rotect R̲elease. The file is still open on your computer, but you cannot save the file under the same name because you no longer have the reservation.

You can change 1-2-3 for Windows' default so that a user must get the reservation manually instead of automatically. To change the default, deselect the F̲ile P̲rotect Get reservation a̲utomatically check box. Now, anyone who opens the file has read-only access until one user reserves the file using the F̲ile P̲rotect G̲et command.

You can seal a file's reservation setting after you change it so that no one else can change the setting. Select F̲ile P̲rotect and choose the S̲eal file option. When 1-2-3 displays the Set Password dialog box, enter a password in the P̲assword and V̲erify text boxes. (Passwords are case-sensitive.) Remember the password exactly as you type it. If you or someone else later tries to change the reservation setting, 1-2-3 for Windows prompts for the password.

Deleting Files

When you create and save a file, the file occupies disk space. Eventually, you run out of disk space if you do not occasionally delete old, unneeded files from the disk. Even if you have disk space left, you have more difficulty finding the files you want to open if the disk contains many obsolete files.

Before you delete old files, you may want to save them to a floppy disk in case you need them again.

T I P

1-2-3 for Windows does not have a command on the F̲ile menu for deleting unneeded files. You must use the Windows File Manager or a DOS command.

Transferring Files

1-2-3 for Windows provides a number of ways to pass data between, to, and from other programs. The simplest method is to save or print a file as a text file or an ASCII file. Most programs, including spreadsheets, word processors, and database management systems, can create and read text files. To create a text file in 1-2-3 for Windows, use File Save As and choose the Text (txt) option in the File Type drop-down box. For a complete discussion of transferring files and working with other Windows programs, see Chapter 18, "Integrating Lotus Windows Applications."

FROM HERE...

For Related Information

▶▶ "Integrating Lotus Windows Applications," p. 935.

Translating Files

You may have worksheet or database files from other programs that you would like to use in 1-2-3 Release 4. You can't open and read these files directly in Release 4, but you can use the Translate utility to convert the files to 1-2-3 Release 3 format, which lets you open the file, then save it in Release 4 format. (You can't convert a file directly to Release 4 format; you must convert a file to Release 3 format first, then save it in Release 4 format.)

If you need to use a 1-2-3 Release 3 file in another database or spreadsheet program, you can also use the Translate utility to convert files from 1-2-3 Release 3 format. The Translate utility supports the following programs when you are converting files to or from 1-2-3 Release 3 format:

Lotus 1-2-3 Release 1A

Lotus 1-2-3 Release 2

Lotus 1-2-3 Release 3

dBASE II

dBASE III and dBASE III+

DIF

Enable Version 2.0

Multiplan 4.2

SuperCalc4

Symphony 1 and 1.01

Symphony 1.1, 1.2, and 2

The Translate utility can translate files from any of these programs to 1-2-3 Release 3 format and vice versa.

The Translate utility runs outside of the 1-2-3 Release 4 for Windows program. You access it by clicking on the Translate icon in the Lotus Applications group in the Program Manager.

The Translate Utility screen shows programs to translate *from* on the left and programs to translate *to* on the right. Instructions appear at the bottom of each screen throughout the translation process. (For step-by-step instructions on using the Translate utility, press F1 at any time.) To choose items in the From and To boxes, use the up and down arrow keys, then press Enter.

Follow the instructions shown on the screen to translate a file or multiple files at once. The following steps briefly review those shown on the screen.

1. In the From list, use the up and down arrow keys to select a program or file format from which to translate, then press Enter.

2. The Translate utility highlights the To list. Choose a program or file format to which to translate, then press Enter.

   The Translate utility displays the current directory name and lists files that have the file extension for the program (or file format) you are translating from. If necessary, you can change to a different directory by editing the directory name currently shown.

3. Using the arrow keys, highlight the file you want to translate, and then press the spacebar to select the file. Repeat this step to select and translate additional files. Press Enter when all files you want to translate are selected.

4. Enter the directory name to which you want to translate the selected files. Press Enter and follow the instructions as shown on the screen.

Sending Mail

 Electronic mail systems allow you to communicate with other users of electronic mail by sending and receiving files and messages via your computer. To use electronic mail, your computer must be connected to a computer network or have access to a computer network running an electronic mail program. You can then use the Send Mail command on 1-2-3's File menu or the Send E-mail SmartIcon to send an entire file or a portion of a file (range, chart, or object) as an electronic mail message.

Files that you send via electronic mail are just like other files; you don't need to save them in a special way or with a unique file extension. You just need to know the complete file name and in which directory the file is located. For a complete discussion of this topic, refer to Chapter 18, "Integrating Lotus Windows Applications."

Questions & Answers

This section addresses some questions you may have about managing your files.

Q: How can I rename a 1-2-3 file without returning to DOS or the Windows File Manager?

A: Technically, you cannot rename the file from within 1-2-3. A command does not exist on the File menu for renaming files. However, you can save a copy of the file under a new name by using the File Save As command. The old file still exists under its original name, but 1-2-3 also creates a copy of the file under the new name you specify. If you no longer need the original file, you can return to DOS or the Windows File Manager at your convenience to delete the file.

Q: I tried to open a 1-2-3 file from the Windows File Manager and got an error message `No application is associated with this file`.

A: You tried to open a file that 1-2-3 cannot open or display. You must choose a valid worksheet file with a WK4 file extension or other format that 1-2-3 understands. Try again, using the correct file type.

Q: I tried to open a file by clicking on the file name listed at the bottom of the File menu, but 1-2-3 says `File does not exist`. What's wrong?

A: The file is no longer available from the location in which you last opened it. It has been deleted, renamed, or moved to a different directory. Open the file by using File Open, and 1-2-3 will remember its new location the next time you select it from the File menu.

Q: I tried to combine two worksheets by using the Add to values option, but 1-2-3 inserted information from the source file into blank cells in the current file. What happened?

A: You didn't position the cell pointer in the correct cell in the current file before you started the combine operation. If you are combining the entire file, place the cell pointer in cell A1 in the current file. If you are combining a range, place the cell pointer in the first cell in the current file where you want the data from the source file to be placed.

Q: I want to leave a range of cells in a sealed file unprotected, but the Protection command is unavailable (grayed) on the Style menu. How can I unprotect a cell range?

A: To leave a range of cells unprotected in a sealed file, you must use Style Protection *before* you seal the file. Unseal the file, use Style Protection, and then reseal the file.

Q: How can I seal one worksheet in a file that contains multiple worksheets?

A: 1-2-3 doesn't allow you to seal individual worksheets in a file. If you want only one worksheet sealed, copy or save that worksheet to its own file and seal that file.

Q: I can't remember the password for a spreadsheet I created some time ago. How can I display a list of all the current passwords?

A: You can't. Passwords are intended to restrict *all* access to a file and, therefore, are not recorded anywhere except with the file itself. If you forget the password, you can't reopen the file; all you can do is recreate the spreadsheet.

Q: I am trying to open an Excel file (XLS) in 1-2-3 Release 4 for Windows but can't open the file. What's wrong?

A: Check to see if the Excel file is password protected. If so, remove the password from the Excel file before opening it in 1-2-3.

Summary

In this chapter, you learned many different techniques for working with files, including creating, naming, saving, opening, and deleting files. You also learned how to combine two files, how to protect files with passwords and seals, and how to reserve shared files. In the next chapter, you learn how to expand the computation power of your worksheets by using functions.

Using Functions

In addition to building custom formulas in a worksheet, you can take advantage of the preconstructed formulas and functions provided by 1-2-3 for Windows. Over 120 new functions have been added to Release 4, along with an @function selector that provides you with easy access to all functions. If you are upgrading from earlier versions of Lotus to 1-2-3 for Windows, the following guide will point out the vast number of functions available:

If upgrading from:	No. of new functions:
1-2-3 DOS Rel. 2.x	140
1-2-3 DOS Rel. 3.x	126
1-2-3 Windows Rel. 1.x	122

This chapter describes the general steps you follow to use 1-2-3 for Windows functions and then provides discussions and examples of specific functions.

1-2-3 Release 4 for Windows provides more than 220 functions in 10 categories:

■ *Calendar functions* provide a set of conversion tools that enable you to perform date and time arithmetic. These functions are valuable for worksheets that use logic based on dates and times or for calculations showing the number of days, months, or years between specific events.

■ *Database functions* perform statistical calculations as well as queries in worksheets and external databases based on criteria you specify.

■ *Engineering functions* perform advanced mathematical operations, numeric-type conversions, as well as specific engineering calculations.

■ *Financial functions* aid you in many business spreadsheets. With these functions, you can discount cash flow, calculate depreciation, and find the interest rate necessary for an annuity to grow to a future value. This set of functions provides great flexibility with investment analysis as well as cash-planning strategies.

■ *Information functions* provide you with a quick way to find the status of cells and ranges, the system, and errors in the worksheet.

■ *Logical functions* enable you to add decision making capabilities to the worksheet. With *Logical functions* you can test whether a condition—one you have defined in a worksheet or a 1-2-3 for Windows predefined condition—is true or false. Logical tests are important for formulas that need to make decisions, and the logical functions in 1-2-3 for Windows make your job easier.

■ *Lookup functions* find and return the contents of a cell. These functions are used primarily in conjunction with logical functions in macros to determine the information contained in a cell. These functions enhance the ability to make your worksheets more efficient and valuable.

■ *Mathematical functions* are a complement to engineering functions. These tools are useful in complex and simple worksheets because they perform a variety of standard arithmetic operations such as rounding values or calculating square roots.

■ *Statistical functions* enable you to perform all the standard statistical calculations on data in the worksheet or database. You can find minimum and maximum values, calculate averages, and compute standard deviations and variances.

■ *Text functions* provide you with a means to manipulate text. Text functions, or string functions, are used to repeat characters, convert letters into uppercase, lowercase, or proper case, and change characters into numbers and numbers into text or strings. Text functions can be important when converting data for use by other programs, such as word processor mailing lists.

Understanding 1-2-3 for Windows Functions

A function is a preprogrammed set of instructions that returns a value to the user. Functions can be used as independent formulas that show results based on information in the function, such as the @NOW function which returns the value of the current date and time. Functions can also be used as a component of another formula, as the following example shows: @IF(@now < @DATE(100,01,01),"This is still the 20th Century","The 21st Century").

To successfully enter a function into the worksheet, you must have the following information in the cell:

- The @ symbol, which tells 1-2-3 for Windows that what follows is a function.

- The name of the function. There is no space between the @ symbol and the function name.

- Arguments for the function, contained in parentheses. *Arguments* are information the function needs to complete its task. If multiple arguments are required, the arguments are separated by commas.

 NOTE Some functions do not require arguments or input. Do not use parentheses for functions that do not require arguments.

Entering a 1-2-3 for Windows Function

As you type functions into the worksheet, you see them appear in the contents box as well as in the current cell. You must type the command using the correct syntax and then press Enter to enter the function into a cell. You can enter functions into the worksheet in the following three ways:

- Type the entire function, including arguments, into the cell from the keyboard. When you completely type the function and arguments into the cell line and press Enter, 1-2-3 for Windows displays the results of the function.

An example of a function is @AVG. If you type the function **@AVG(1,2,3)** and press Enter, 1-2-3 for Windows returns the calculated result in the cell in which you entered the function. The @AVG function returns the average of the arguments 1, 2, and 3 (so the result is 2).

■ Type the @ symbol and press F3 to display the @Function Names dialog box with all the functions in alphabetical order (see fig. 7.1). You can select the function you want by scrolling through the list and then clicking on the function name to highlight it. You also can start to type the function name you want; as you type the function name, the highlight bar jumps down the list to highlight the first function name that starts with the characters you have typed.

If you type the function name in the dialog box and make a mistake, press Backspace to erase mistyped characters; then retype the function. The highlight bar adjusts as you type.

When the function you want to use is highlighted, press Enter; the function is placed in the current cell. If an argument is required, an opening parenthesis is placed in the cell also. The cursor is positioned to accept the arguments required (see fig. 7.2).

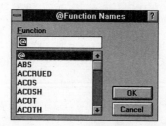

FIG. 7.1

The @Function Names dialog box.

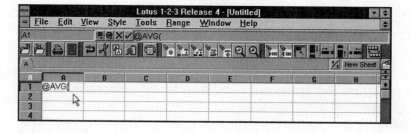

FIG. 7.2

A function in the cell waiting for arguments.

■ Click on the @function selector with the mouse. The @function selector is the second icon in the input line, just below the 1-2-3 for Windows menu (see fig. 7.3).

When you click on the @function selector, a drop-down list appears, as shown in figure 7.3. This list includes at least two sections separated by a solid line. The top selection, labeled `List All`, displays a dialog box. The remaining items in the list are commonly used functions. To use a function in this list, highlight it by pressing the down-arrow key and pressing Enter, or use the mouse to click on the function you want to use.

To see a list of all the functions, click on List All or press the Enter key. The @Function List dialog box appears (see fig. 7.4).

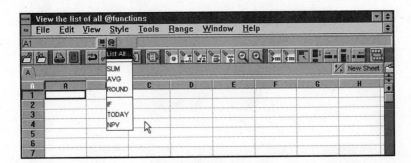

FIG. 7.3

The @function selector and a drop-down list of common functions.

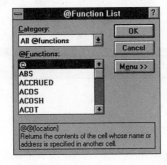

FIG. 7.4

The @Function List dialog box.

Use the Category drop-down list box to pick a category (see fig. 7.5). If you know the category from which you want to see selections, press Tab to select the Category option and type the first letter of the category you want. When you select the category you want, a list of functions for that category appears in the @Functions list box.

Use the @Functions list to pick a function from the selected category. The selection process for the @Function List dialog box is different than the selection process for the @Function Names dialog box. In the @Function List dialog box, you must first make the @Functions drop-down list the active list by pressing Tab or by clicking on a function in the list. You then can type the first letter of the function you want or scroll through the list to find the function you want. When you select the function you want to use, press Enter (or double-click on the function). The function is entered in the current cell with the correct argument syntax, as shown in figure 7.6.

FIG. 7.5

The Category drop-down list.

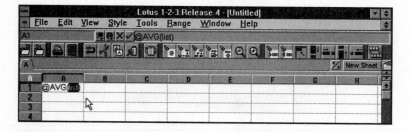

FIG. 7.6

The function and its argument list entered in the worksheet.

Scrolling through the @Function List Dialog Box

When you look for a function in the @Function List dialog box by typing its name, you cannot type the entire function name. Type only the first letter of the function name and then scroll the list until you find the function you want. If you type the second letter of the name, 1-2-3 for Windows moves the highlight to the function in the list that starts with this letter.

Suppose that you are searching for the @SUM function while the All @functions category is highlighted in the Category list box. Tab to the @Functions list box or click on a function name in the drop-down list. Type the letter S; the function name S appears in the window. Now type U; the function name UPPER appears in the window (not what you

intended). To return to the function names that start with *S*, type S.
Using the scroll bar or the down-arrow key, scroll through the list until
you find the SUM function; press Enter or double-click on the function.

The help box below the @Functions list shows the correct syntax and a
brief description of the uses for the currently selected function. When
you select a function, the information in the help box automatically
changes to reflect the selection made.

Customizing the @Function-Selector List

Use the Menu command button in the @Function List dialog box to
customize the @function-selector list (shown in fig. 7.3). You customize
the @function-selector list by adding or removing functions. When you
select the Menu command button, an Add button appears and the Current Menu drop-down list box is appended to the bottom of the @Func-
tion List dialog box (see fig. 7.7). This list shows all the functions that
currently appear when you use the @function selector.

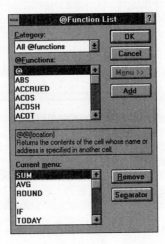

FIG. 7.7

The @Function
List dialog box
with the Current
Menu drop-down
list box.

Two new command buttons also appear to enable you to customize the
@function-selector list. The Remove button removes the highlighted
item from the list. The Separator button inserts lines in the @function-
selector list.

Because there are more than 220 functions available, you may not remember every function's name. Fortunately, 1-2-3 for Windows uses
short, 1-to-11-character abbreviations for most functions. The @Func-
tion Names dialog box and the @Function List dialog box provide you

with tools to quickly find and use the functions you are looking for. The @Function List dialog box gives you the added flexibility to customize the @function-selector list for the functions you use most.

The remainder of this chapter discusses the specific functions available in 1-2-3 Release 4 for Windows and provides examples of many of the functions. The functions are organized by the 10 categories listed earlier in this chapter.

Using Calendar Functions

The 1-2-3 for Windows calendar functions enable you to convert dates (such as November 26, 1993) and times (such as 6:00 P.M.) to serial numbers. You then can use the serial numbers in date and time arithmetic—valuable aids when dates and times affect worksheet calculations and logic.

As you review the examples showing the mechanics of the 1-2-3 for Windows date and time functions, you should develop a better appreciation of their potential contributions to your worksheets. The calendar functions available in 1-2-3 Release 4 for Windows, organized by date and time functions, are summarized in table 7.1.

As you use the calender functions, note that some of the functions use 360 days in a year and some use 365 days in a year for calculation purposes. The functions that use 360 days for the calculations are based on 12 months with 30 days and conform to the standards set by the Securities Industry Association.

Table 7.1 Calendar Functions

Date Function	Description
@D360(*date1,date2*)	Calculates the number of days between two dates based on a 360-day year. It should be noted that the @DAYS360 function will return a different answer only if the start date or end date is the first or last date of the month.
@DATE(*y,m,d*)	Calculates the serial number that represents the described date
@DATEDIF(*start-date, end-date,format*)	Returns the number of years, months, or days between two date numbers
@DATEINFO(*date,attribute*)	Returns information about a date serial number

Date Function	Description
@DATEVALUE(*date-string*)	Converts a date expressed as a quoted string into a serial number
@DAY(*date*)	Extracts the day-of-the-month number from a serial number
@DAYS(*start-date*, *end-date*,[*basis*])	Calculates the number of days between two dates using a specified day-count basis
@DAYS360(*date1*,*date2*)	Calculates the number of days between two dates based on a 360-day year. It should be noted that the @D360 function will return a different answer only if the start date or end date is the first or last date of the month.
@MONTH(*date*)	Extracts the month number from a serial number
@NOW	Calculates the serial date and time from the current system date and time
@TODAY	Calculates the serial number for the current system date
@WEEKDAY(*date-number*)	Returns the day of the week as a number
@WORKDAY(*start-date*,*days*, [*holiday-range*],[*weekends*])	Calculates the date the specified number of days before or after a specified date, excluding weekends and holidays
@YEAR(*date*)	Extracts the year number from a serial number

Time Function	Description
@HOUR(*time*)	Extracts the hour number from a serial number
@MINUTE(*time*)	Extracts the minute number from a serial number
@SECOND(*time*)	Extracts the seconds number from a serial number
@TIME(*hour*,*minute*,*second*)	Calculates the serial number representing the described time
@TIMEVALUE(*time-string*)	Converts a time expressed as a string into a serial number

@D360, @DAYS360, and @DAYS—Dealing with 360-Day Years

The @D360 function enables you to calculate the number of days between two dates, based on 30-day months and a 360-day year. Both date arguments must be expressed as valid serial numbers or the function returns the ERR value. Use the following syntax for @D360:

@D360(*date1*,*date2*)

The @D360 function proves helpful in cases where calculations are made to the number of days, using a 360-day year. The premise is there are 12 months each with 30 days.

The @DAYS360 function is a more technical version of the @D360 function. @DAYS360 has the same format as @D360; it too returns the difference between two dates based on a 360-day year. The @DAYS360 function, however, bases its calculations on the Security Industries Association's 1986 edition of the *Standard Security Calculation Methods*. This is the standard within the securities industry for calculating the difference between two dates based on a 360-day year.

The @DAYS function is a flexible version of both the @D360 and @DAYS360 functions in that the syntax includes an optional argument you can use to define the basis of the date calculation. The syntax for the @DAYS function is as follows:

@DAYS(*start-date*,*end-date*,[*basis*])

The [*basis*] component of the syntax is optional; if omitted, the @DAYS function performs exactly like the @D360 function.

[*basis*]	Days per month/Days per year	
0	30/360	Default
1	Actual	Actual
2	Actual	360
3	Actual	365

The @D360, @DAYS360, and @DAYS functions can return different results, as shown in figure 7.8. (In the figure, the function syntax is in the column to the right of the calculation.) Use @DAYS360 to calculate the number of days between two dates based on a 360-day year unless you must use calculations consistent with earlier worksheets that used the @D360 function. The @DAYS function enables you to change the basis and see the results of the different types of calculations.

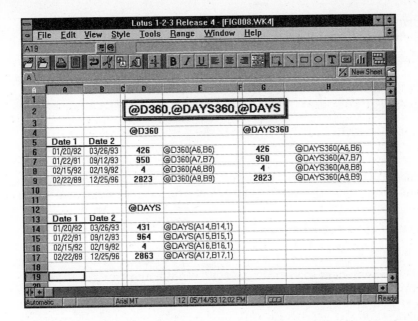

FIG. 7.8

Using @D360,
@DAYS360, and
@DAYS to calcu-
late the number
of days between
two dates based
on a 360-day
year.

@DATE—Converting Date Values to Serial Numbers

The first step in using dates in arithmetic operations is to convert the dates to date serial numbers. You then can use the serial numbers in addition, subtraction, multiplication, and division operations. 1-2-3 for Windows supports several ways of entering date information into an unformatted cell to produce a date number.

1-2-3 for Windows will allow several ways to enter date information in the correct format. The first way to enter date information into an unformatted cell and convert the date to a date serial number is to enter the date by using slashes (/). For example:

4/6/51

This produces the date serial number 18724 in the contents box; the date 04/06/51 appears in the current cell.

Another method of inputting date information into an unformatted cell and converting the date to a serial number is to place hyphens (-) between the components of the date. You must follow a proper input format when you use this method however. The day of the month *must* be first, followed by a hyphen (-), the first three letters of the month, another hyphen, and the last two numbers of the year. Use the last two digits of the year until the year 2000; for years after 2000, enter all four digits of the year. Following are some examples:

Entered Date	Serial Number
13-MAR-93	34041
13-MAR	34041
13-MAR-2000	36598

The @DATE function converts any date into a number you can use in arithmetic operations and—just as important—that 1-2-3 for Windows can display as a date.

Use the following syntax for the @DATE function:

@DATE(*year*,*month*,*day*)

You use numbers to identify the year, month, and day. For example, you enter the date April 6, 1951 into the @DATE function in one of the following ways:

@DATE(51,04,06)
@DATE(51,4,6)

1-2-3 for Windows returns the date serial number, 18724, in the current cell if the cell has not been formatted to show the number in a date format.

The numbers you enter to represent the year, month, and day must constitute a valid date or 1-2-3 for Windows returns ERR. For example, 1-2-3 for Windows "knows" that the *day* argument in February can be 29 only during leap years and that the *day* argument can never be 30 or 31 for February. However, when you specify the month as 1 (which represents January), 30 and 31 are valid *day* arguments because January has 31 days.

As you use the @DATE function, keep the following guidelines in mind:

■ The internal 1-2-3 for Windows calendar starts with the serial number 1, the first date that 1-2-3 for Windows recognizes. That date number represents January 1, 1900. A single day is represented by an increment of 1; therefore, 1-2-3 for Windows represents January 2, 1900 as 2.

■ Even though 1900 wasn't a leap year, 1-2-3 for Windows assigns the serial number 60 to the date February 29, 1900 (a date that never existed). Although this assignment should not be a problem, you may have difficulty if you transfer data between 1-2-3 for Windows and other programs. In that case, you must adjust for this error yourself.

■ Because 1-2-3 for Windows uses January 1, 1900 as the start of its counting base, the way you enter the year 2000 and beyond in the @DATE function is a little different: you use 100 to represent the year 2000, 101 for 2001, and so on. For example, the syntax for January 1, 2000 is @DATE(100,01,01); the resulting date serial number is 36526.

■ The @DATE function can be used in calculations and works with all the algebraic symbols. The syntax for adding a day to the @DATE function is @DATE(51,04,06)+1; the resulting serial number is 18725.

■ The date format only accommodates December 31, 2099, which has a serial number of 73050. The date numbers beyond 73050 work for calculating the difference between dates.

Figure 7.9 shows an example of the @DATE function being used to calculate the number of days a bill is overdue. The @DATE syntax has been added in column A to show what the results look like in column C.

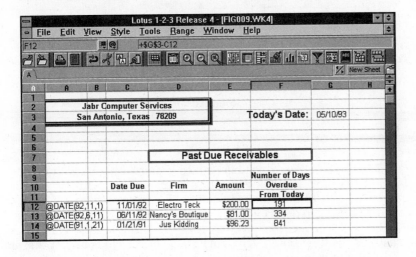

FIG. 7.9

Using @DATE to calculate the number of days a bill is overdue.

Dates created or entered with the @DATE function appear on an unformatted worksheet as a number—the number of days since the beginning of the twentieth century. To make that serial number display as a text date, format the cell by choosing Style Number Format and choosing a format from the resulting dialog box (see Chapter 5, "Changing the Format and Appearance of Data," for more information about formatting dates).

@DATEDIF—Returning the Number of Years, Months, or Days

@DATEDIF returns the number of years, months, or days between two date numbers based on a specific format you define. Use the following syntax for the @DATEDIF function:

`@DATEDIF(start-date,end-date,format)`

The *start-date* and *end-date* arguments must be date serial numbers. These values can be input directly as date serial numbers or as calculated values. The *format* argument is required; it is entered as a text value. When you enter the code for the *format* argument, you must place double quotation marks around the format code. The following chart lists the available format codes and the meaning of the number the @DATEDIF function returns when each code is used:

Format Code	Returns Number of
"y"	Years
"m"	Months
"d"	Days
"md"	Days, ignoring months and years
"ym"	Months, ignoring years
"yd"	Days, ignoring years

Figure 7.10 shows a Past Due Receivables example that uses the @DATEDIF function. (In the figure, the syntax of the function is shown in column G, next to the results in column F.) The *format* argument allows for flexibility in determining quantities of time. Notice that value in cell F12 is the overdue time given in days (because the @DATEDIF function uses "d" as the *format* argument); the value in F13 is in months; and the value in F14 is in years. Make sure that you label the output so that your audience understands the amount of time involved.

@DATEDIF is based on calendar years and includes leap-year calculations. You can use the results of a @DATE function as input for the *start-date* or *end-date* arguments. As shown in figure 7.10, the dates in column C are the result of the @DATE function; the dates in column C are used as the *start-date* arguments for the @DATEDIF functions in column F.

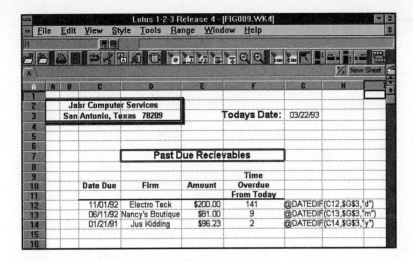

FIG. 7.10

The @DATEDIF
function.

@DATEINFO—Returning Date Serial Number Information

The @DATEINFO function returns specific information about a date serial number. The syntax for the @DATEINFO function is as follows:

@DATEINFO(*date-number*,*attribute*)

Note that an *attribute* argument is required, but because it is numeric, it does not require any special formatting. The following chart lists the valid *attribute* arguments and the results returned:

Attribute	Returns
1	Day of the week as a label, in short format (Wed)
2	Day of the week as a label, in long format (Wednesday)
3	Day of the week as an integer, where 1=Monday and 7=Sunday
4	Week of the year as an integer from 1 to 53
5	Month of the year as a label, in short format (Apr)
6	Month of the year as a label, in long format (April)

continues

Attribute	Returns
7	Number of days in the month specified by the *date-number* argument
8	Number of days left in the month specified by *date-number* argument
9	Last day of the month specified by *date-number* argument
10	The quarter that the *date-number* argument is in (an integer from 1 to 4); quarter 1 is integer 1 and Quarter 4 is integer 4
11	Leap-year designator; if the year is a leap year, a 1 is returned, if not, a 0 is returned
12	Julian Day of the year specified by the *date-number* argument (a value between 1 and 366)
13	Days remaining in the year specified by the *date-number* argument (a value between 1 and 366)

Figure 7.11 uses various *attribute* arguments with the @DATEINFO function to incorporate workweek information in cell G4 (*attribute* number 4) and specific month statistics about the remaining days in a month in cells D8..D10 (*attribute* number 8), and the total number of days in a month in cells C8..C10 (*attribute* number 7).

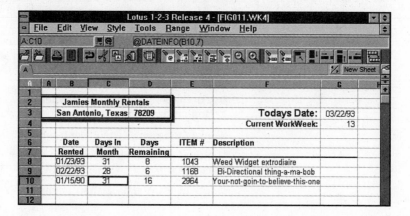

FIG. 7.11

Using @DATEINFO in a tracking worksheet.

@DATEVALUE—Changing Date Strings to Serial Numbers

@DATEVALUE computes the serial number for a date text string typed in a referenced cell. For example, if cell A1 contains the formatted date 31-Dec-2099, you can use the @DATEVALUE(A1) function to return the serial number 73050; alternatively, you can use the function @DATEVALUE("31-Dec-2099") to return the same serial number.

The text string must use one of the date formats recognized by 1-2-3 for Windows. @DATEVALUE requires the following format:

@DATEVALUE(*date-string*)

The *date-string* argument must look like one of the date formats you can select with the Style Number Format command or when you choose Range Format. If 1-2-3 for Windows cannot recognize the format, the function results in ERR. Be sure to enclose the date string in quotation marks.

If you have reset the default date format so that you can use international date formats, make sure that the *date-string* argument is in one of the date formats for the country you have selected. To change the default date format, select Tools User Setup International.

Figure 7.12 shows how @DATEVALUE converts the date strings in column C into serial numbers in column A. Use Style Number Format to format a cell containing @DATEVALUE so that the cell displays the serial date number as a text date.

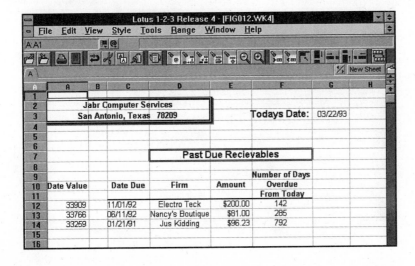

FIG. 7.12

Using @DATEVALUE to convert date strings to date serial numbers.

@DAY, @WEEKDAY, @MONTH, and @YEAR—Converting Serial Numbers to Dates

The @DAY, @WEEKDAY, @MONTH, and @YEAR functions convert serial numbers into a numeric day of the month, day of the week, month, or year, respectively. Use the following syntax for these functions:

@DAY(*date*)
@WEEKDAY(*date*)
@MONTH(*date*)
@YEAR(*date*)

The @DAY function accepts a valid date serial number as its single argument and returns the day of the month (a number from 1 to 31). The @WEEKDAY function accepts a valid date serial number and returns a numeric value for the day of the week (0 for Monday and 6 for Sunday). The @MONTH function accepts a valid date serial number as its single argument and returns the month of the year (a number from 1 to 12). The @YEAR function accepts a valid date serial number as its single argument and returns the number of the year (a number from 0 for 1900 to 199 for 2099).

Figure 7.13 shows how you can use these four date functions to extract the component of a date—year, month, day, or weekday—you want to manipulate.

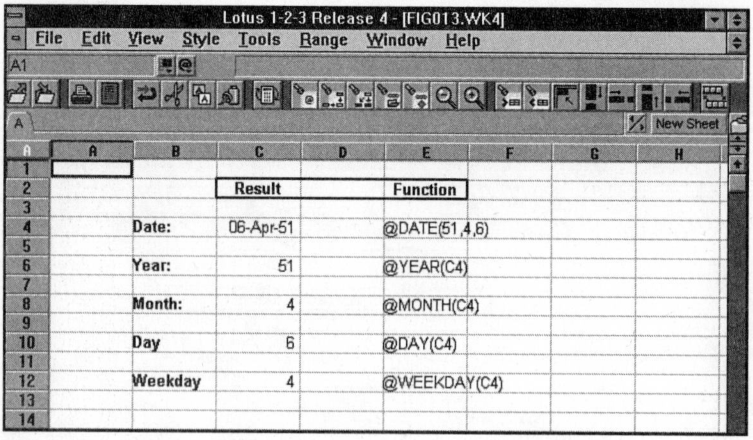

FIG. 7.13

Using @YEAR, @MONTH, @DAY, and @WEEKDAY to extract parts of a date.

@NOW and @TODAY—Finding the Current Date and Time

1-2-3 for Windows provides two functions, @NOW and @TODAY, that extract information from the system date and time. The @NOW function retrieves as a date serial number the current system date and time. The decimal places to the left of the decimal point specify the date; the decimal places to the right of the decimal point specify the time. The @TODAY function is similar to @NOW except that @TODAY retrieves only the system date (not the system time). These two functions provide convenient tools for recording the dates and times when worksheets are modified or printed. Neither function requires any arguments.

Use the @INT function to calculate the date or time portion of the @NOW function. To extract the date portion of the @NOW function, use @INT(@NOW); the result is the same as the result of @TODAY. To extract the time portion, use @NOW-@INT(@NOW); the result is the same as @NOW-@TODAY.

Figure 7.14 shows how you can use both functions. Column C shows the serial numbers that represent the system date and time. Column D shows the two serial numbers formatted as dates (with the date format selected from the Style Number format menu). Column E shows the results of the functions, formatted to show the current system time (with the time format selected from the Style Number menu). Because the @TODAY function does not include time information, the time format in cell E11 shows a time of 0, which is midnight.

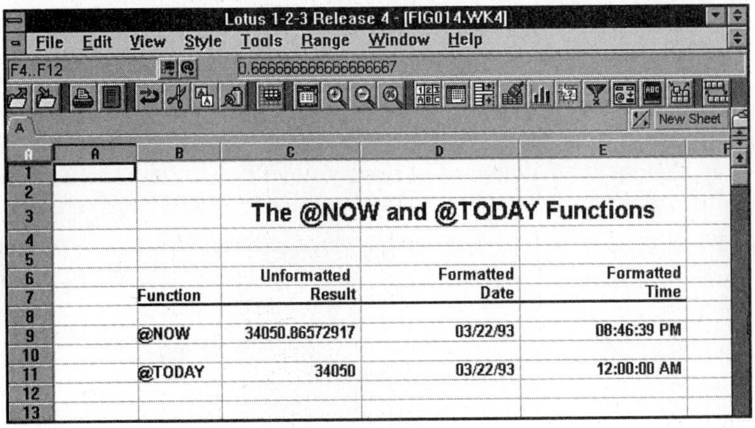

FIG. 7.14

@NOW and @TODAY return the current date and time.

@WORKDAY—Calculating the Number of Workdays

The @WORKDAY function returns the date value that corresponds to the date that is a specified number of days before or after a starting date. The syntax for this function is:

`@WORKDAY(start-date,days,[holiday-range],[weekends])`

The *start-date* is any valid date number.

Days is an integer to specifiy the number of *days* to be calculated from the *start-date*. The *days* integer can be a positive or negative number to indicate the direction for the calculation.

Holiday-range is an optional argument that specifies the holidays to exclude. Holiday range can include any of the following in any combination, remember to use argument separators (commas or semicolons) to separate the elements of *holiday range*:

```
date numbers
formulas that evaluate to date numbers
range addresses
range names that contain date numbers
```

Weekends is an optional argument.

@TIME—Converting Time Values to Serial Numbers

1-2-3 for Windows expresses time as a decimal fraction of a full day. For example, 0.5 is equal to 12 hours (or 12:00 P.M.). In addition, 1-2-3 for Windows works on international time: 10:00 P.M. in U.S. time is 22:00 in international time. Although the 1-2-3 for Windows timekeeping system may seem a little awkward at first, you will soon become used to it. Following are some guidelines to help you understand the system:

Time Increment	Serial-Number Equivalent
1 hour	0.0416666667
1 minute	0.0006944444
1 second	0.0000115741

These numeric equivalents are approximate; 1-2-3 for Windows actually calculates these numbers to 18 or 19 decimal places. The @TIME function produces a serial number for a specified time of day. Use the following format for @TIME:

@TIME(*hour-number,minute-number,second-number*)

You can use @TIME to calculate the time period between events. 1-2-3 for Windows accepts direct input of time into the worksheet and displays the input value in time format as long as the cell is formatted properly.

One way to produce a range of times is to use the Range Fill command. The following steps produce a table of times that can be used as an event calendar from 8:00 A.M. to 7:30 P.M. in 30-minute increments:

1. Specify the range in which you want the times to appear. You can do this by clicking and dragging across a selected area of the worksheet. For this example, select the range A4..A19.

2. Select Range Fill.

3. Click on the Minute option in the Interval box.

4. Select the Start text by clicking and dragging in the Start box; type **8:00**.

5. Click-and-drag to select the Increment text in the Increment box; type **30**.

6. Click-and-drag to select the Stop text in the Stop box; type **4:00pm**.

7. Click on the OK button; the range A4..A19 is filled with time-conversion numbers.

8. Format the range: The range of cells will be filled with the time format that is set as a default. To change the time format select Style Number Format and scroll the list box until you see the time format 11:59AM; double-click on this format (or select it and click on the OK command button). All the selected cells are converted to this format and the range of cells is filled in.

9. Repeat steps 1 through 8 for the range F4..F12 to fill in the time from 4:00 until 8:00 P.M.

Figure 7.15 shows the table created in the preceding steps after Event and Comment labels were added to row 3.

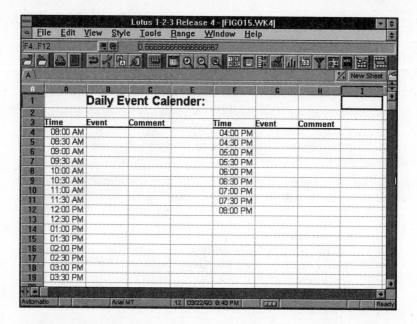

FIG. 7.15

An example of
time values
created by
Range Fill.

@TIMEVALUE—Converting Time Strings to Serial Values

Like @DATEVALUE and @DATE, the @TIMEVALUE function is a variation of @TIME. Like @TIME, @TIMEVALUE produces a serial number
from the hour, minute, and second information you supply. Unlike
@TIME, however, @TIMEVALUE uses string arguments rather than
numeric arguments.

For example, to display the time serial number for the current system
time, enter this formula: @TIMEDATE(@NOW-@TODAY). Apply an appropriate time format to the cell to display the serial number as a recognizable time.

If you type a time as text, the @TIMEVALUE function converts the entry
into a time serial number. This function requires the following format:

@TIMEVALUE(*time-string*)

The *time-string* argument must appear in one of the following time
formats:

```
HH:MM:SS      AM/PM
HH:MM  AM/PM
HH:MM:SS      (24 hour)
HH:MM  (24 hour)
```

If the string conforms to one of the time formats, 1-2-3 for Windows displays the appropriate serial number fraction. If you then format the cell, 1-2-3 for Windows displays the appropriate time of day.

@SECOND, @MINUTE, and @HOUR— Converting Date Numbers to Time Values

With the @SECOND, @MINUTE, and @HOUR functions, you can extract different units of time from the decimal portion of a date serial number. Use the following formats for these functions:

@SECOND(*time*)
@MINUTE(*time*)
@HOUR(*time*)

Figure 7.16 shows that these three functions are, in a sense, the reverse of the @TIME function—just as the @DAY, @WEEKDAY, @MONTH, and @YEAR functions are the reverse of the @DATE function.

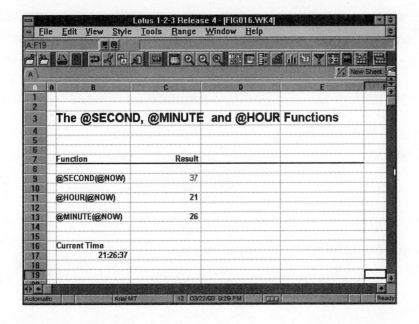

FIG. 7.16

Using @SECOND, @MINUTE, and @HOUR to extract parts of a time.

Using Database Functions

1-2-3 for Windows database functions manipulate database fields. Like the standard functions, the database functions perform—in one simple statement—calculations that would otherwise require a complex series of operations. The efficiency and ease of application make these functions excellent tools for examining database records in either worksheet databases or external database tables. The database functions are described in table 7.2.

Table 7.2 Database Functions	
Function	**Description**
@DAVG	Averages values in a field
@DCOUNT	Counts non-blank cells that contain data in a field
@DGET	Finds the contents of a cell in a field
@DMAX	Finds the largest value in a field
@DMIN	Finds the smallest value in a field
@DPURECOUNT	Counts all cells that contain data in a field
@DQUERY	Gives you access to a function of an external database and uses the result of the function in a criteria range
@DSTD	Calculates the population standard deviation of values in a field
@DSTDS	Calculates the sample standard deviation of values in a field
@DSUM	Sums values in a field
@DVAR	Calculates the population variance of values in a field
@DVARS	Calculates the sample variance of values in a field

The general syntax of database functions is as follows:

@DSUM(*input_range,field,criteria_range*)

The one exception is @DQUERY:

@DQUERY(*external_function,*[*external_arguments*])

The *input_range* argument specifies the database or part of a database to be scanned; it can be the address or name of a single-sheet range that contains a database table or the name of an external database table. You can use more than one *input_range* argument in a database function by separating the *input_range* arguments with commas. 1-2-3 for Windows reads database function arguments from right to left, so that it uses the last argument as the *criteria_range*, the next-to-last argument as the *field*, and the remaining arguments as *input_ranges*. No limit exists to the number of *input_range* arguments you can use, providing you do not exceed 512 characters in the cell that contains the function. You do not need to identify an *input_range* with the <u>T</u>ools <u>D</u>atabase <u>N</u>ew Query command before you use it as an *input_range* argument in a database function.

The *criteria_range* argument specifies which records are to be selected. The *criteria_range* argument can be a range address or a range name.

The *field* argument is the field name from the database table enclosed in quotation marks, If you use just one *input_range* argument, you can represent the *field* argument with an offset number. If you use more than one *input_range* argument, and the field name you want to use as the *field* argument appears in more than one of the input ranges, the *field* must be entered as the name of the *input_range* followed by a period and the *field* name, enclosed in quotation marks. For example, if you have two input ranges, named SALES (A1..E20) and BUDGET (A22..E42), each of which has a field called DEPARTMENT, you can refer to the DEPARTMENT field in the SALES range like this:

```
"SALES.DEPARTMENT" or "A1..E20.DEPARTMENT
```

Database functions are similar to statistical functions, but database functions process only data items that meet the criteria you specify. For example, if you have a list of employees, the departments where they work, and their annual salaries, you can use @AVG to calculate the average of all salaries. Use @DAVG to calculate the average salaries of any subgroup, such as the Sales department, without first extracting the Sales department records.

Figure 7.17 shows a list of the database functions and their syntax. In this example, a nine-record database includes employees in several departments. The database functions (except @DGET) use a criteria range that excludes the Shipping department.

Although @DGET uses the same three arguments as most other database functions, @DGET performs a different function. @DGET returns the value of the *field* argument for the record that matches the condition set in the *criteria_range* argument. Because @DGET returns ERR if either no records or more than one record matches the set conditions, @DGET often requires its own, more selective *criteria_range* argument.

In figure 7.17, the criteria range used for the @DGET function specifies the single record where the SALARY field value equals $39,100; the value returned for the NAME field is Williamson J.

Lotus 1-2-3 Release 4 - [FIG017.WK4]

File Edit View Style Tools Range Window Help

A1   "Input Range

	A	B	C	D	E
1	**Input Range**				*Criteria Range*
2	Name	Department	Salary		Department
3	Arron. R.	Shipping	16,600		<>Shipping
4	Abbott D.	Customer Support	36,600		
5	Beheler S.	Shipping	22,400		**Criteria Range for @DGET**
6	Bonkers D.	Marketing	32,500		SALARY
7	Roche D.	Administration	42,300		39,100
8	Smokey T.B.	Sales	40,250		
9	Williamson J.	Administration	39,100		
10	Williamson B.	Administration	33,300		
12	**Database @Functions**				
13	@DAVG($A$2..$C$10,"Salary",$E$2..$E$3)		37,342		
14	@DCOUNT($A$2..$C$10,"Salary",$E$2..$E$3)		6		
15	@DGET($A$2..$C$10,"Name",$E$2..$E$3)		Williamson J.		
16	@DMAX($A$2..$C$10,"Salary",$E$2..$E$3)		42,300		
17	@DMIN($A$2..$C$10,"Salary",$E$2..$E$3)		32,500		
18	@DPURECOUNT($A$2..$C$10,"Salary",$E$2..$E$3)		6		
19	@DSTD($A$2..$C$10,"Salary",$E$2..$E$3)		3,570		
20	@DSTDS($A$2..$C$10,"Salary",$E$2..$E$3)		3,911		
21	@DSUM($A$2..$C$10,"Salary",$E$2..$E$3)		224,050		
22	@DVAR($A$2..$C$10,"Salary",$E$2..$E$3)		12,743,681		
23	@DVARS($A$2..$C$10,"Salary",$E$2..$E$3)		15,292,417		

Automatic   Arial MT   14 03/23/93 7:47 PM   Ready

FIG. 7.17

A list of database functions.

The @DQUERY database function performs a function similar to Tools Database Send Command. @DQUERY sends a command to an external database management program. The syntax for @DQUERY is as follows:

@DQUERY(*external_function*,[*external_arguments*])

In this format, *external_function* is the name of a function in the external database management program; the optional *external_arguments* are the values used by the external program for that function.

To understand how @DQUERY works, suppose that the external database management program contains a function to match data phonetically. The function is called LIKE, and it has one argument: the data you are matching. For example, the database function LIKE("SMITH") matches the names *Smith*, *Smyth*, and *Smythe*.

To see how this works, assume one of the field names in the external data base is "STREET" and you are interested in finding the "STREET" associated with the people with last names like "SMITH". In the criteria range of the worksheet you are looking from, type the following:

+STREET=@DQUERY("LIKE","SMITH").

The @DQUERY function uses the LIKE function from the external database management program and the result will be the data from the external database field "STREET".

Using Engineering Functions

The engineering functions, new in 1-2-3 Release 4 for Windows, provide solutions for Bessel calculations, hex-to-decimal conversions, error-function calculations, and power-series summations. Table 7.3 contains a list of the engineering functions and a short description of each.

Table 7.3 Engineering Functions

Function	Description
@BESSELI(x,n)	Calculates the modified Bessel integer function I$n(x)$
@BESSELJ(x,n)	Calculates Bessel integer function J$n(x)$
@BESSELK(x,n)	Calculates the modified Bessel integer function K$n(x)$
@BESSELY(x,n)	Calculates the Bessel integer function Y$n(x)$
@BETA(z,w)	Calculates the Beta integer function
@BETAI(a,b,x)	Calculates the incomplete Beta integer function
@DECIMAL(*hexadecimal*)	Converts a hexadecimal string to a signed decimal value
@ERF(*lower-limit*,[*upper-limit*])	Calculates the error function
@ERFC(x)	Calculates the complementary error function
@ERFD(x)	Calculates the derivative of the error function
@GAMMA(x)	Calculates the Gamma function
@GAMMAI($a,x,$ [*complement*])	Calculates the incomplete Gamma function
@GAMMALN(x)	Calculates the natural log of the Gamma function

continues

Table 7.3 Continued	
Function	Description
@HEX(*decimal*)	Converts a signed decimal value to a hexadecimal string
@SERIESSUM(*x,n,m, coefficients*)	Calculates the sum of a power series

@BESSELI, @BESSELJ, @BESSELK, and @BESSELY—Functions Dealing with Symmetry

Bessel functions are used in calculations dealing with cylindrical symmetry. These functions are used in conjunction with diffusion, elasticity, wave propagation, and fluid motion.

The argument list in each of the functions contains two components:

x The value at which to evaluate the function (can be any value)

n The order of the function (can be any positive integer or 0)

The syntax for the @BESSEL functions is as follows:

@BESSELI(*x*,*n*)

@BESSELI calculates the modified Bessel function of integer order I$n(x)$. This function approximates to within +/-5*10^-8.

@BESSELJ(*x*,*n*)

@BESSELJ calculates the Bessel function of integer order J$n(x)$. This function approximates to within +/-5*10^-8.

@BESSELK(*x*,*n*)

@BESSELK calculates the modified Bessel function of integer order K$n(x)$. This function approximates to within +/-5*10^-8.

@BESSELY(*x*,*n*)

@BESSELY calculates the Bessel function of integer order Y$n(x)$. This is sometimes referred to as the Neumann function. This function approximates to within +/-5*10^-8.

@BETA—Calculate the Beta Function

@BETA calculates the Beta function to within at least six significant digits. The syntax for this function is as follows:

@BETA(*z*,*w*)

The arguments for this function, *z* and *w*, can be any value. Here is an example of the @BETA function:

@BETA(.5,.5) = 3.141593

@BETAI—Calculating the Incomplete Beta Function

@BETAI calculates the incomplete Beta function to within at least six significant digits. Use the following syntax for this function:

@BETAI(*a*,*b*,*x*)

The arguments for this function are as follows:

a Can be any value

b Can be any value

x A value from 0 through 1

Here is an example of the @BETA function:

@BETA(.5,.5,.668271) = 0.050012

@DECIMAL—Converting a Hex Number to a Decimal Equivalent

The @DECIMAL function converts a hexadecimal value to its signed decimal equivalent. The syntax for this function is as follows:

@DECIMAL(*hexadecimal*)

The *hexadecimal* argument can be a value from 00000000 through FFFFFFFF. The argument is entered as text, and can contain only valid hexadecimal digits and letters. The valid digits are the range 0 through 9; valid alpha characters are the range A through F. The letters are not case sensitive.

The value 0 and all positive hexadecimal numbers are in the range 00000000 through 7FFFFFFF. Negative hexadecimal numbers are in the range 80000000 through FFFFFFFF. Here is an example of the @DECIMAL function:

```
@DECIMAL("1A") = 26
```

@ERF—Calculating the Error Function

@ERF is an approximation function that calculates the error function integrated between the lower limit and the upper limit. The approximation is within +/-1.2x10^7. Use the following syntax for @ERF:

```
@ERF(lower-limit[,upper-limit])
```

The arguments are these:

lower-limit	The lower bound for integrating @ERF; not limited to any value.
upper-limit	An optional argument that specifies the upper bound for integrating @ERF; can be any value greater than or equal to *lower-limit*. If *upper-limit* is omitted, the function integrates between 0 and *lower-limit*.

Following are some examples of the @ERF function:

```
@ERF(.7) = 0.677801
```

```
@ERF(.8) = 0.742101
```

Notice that @ERF(.7,.8) = 0.0643 is the difference between the first two examples.

@ERFC—Calculating the Complementary Error Function

@ERFC calculates the complementary error function integrated between the argument and infinity. The @ERFC function is 1–@ERF(x), which approximates the complementary error function to within +/–3*10^-7. The syntax for the function is as follows:

```
@ERFC(x)
```

Where *x* can be any error function value. Following is an example of the @ERFC function:

```
@ERFC(0.7) = 0.322199
```

@ERFD—Calculating the Derivative of the Error Function

@ERFD calculates the derivative of the error function using the formula (2/@SQRT(@PI))*@EXP(–*x*^2). The syntax for @ERFD is as follows:

```
@ERFD(x)
```

Where *x* can be an error function value from approximately –106.56 to 106.56. If the argument falls outside this range, 1-2-3 for Windows returns ERR. If the argument is outside the boundaries –15.102 to 15.102, 1-2-3 can calculate and store the value for use in other calculations although it cannot display the value in the cell (a series of asterisks appears instead). Following is an example of @ERFD:

```
@ERFD(0.7) = 0.691275
```

@GAMMA—Calculating the Gamma Function

@GAMMA approximates the Gamma distribution accurately to within six significant figures. The syntax for @GAMMA is as follows:

```
@GAMMA(x)
```

Where *x* is any positive value greater than 0. Following are some examples of @GAMMA:

```
@GAMMA(.5) = 1.772454
```

```
@GAMMA(3.6) = 3.717024
```

@GAMMAI—Calculating the Incomplete Gamma Function

@GAMMAI calculates the incomplete Gamma function and is accurate to within six significant figures. The syntax is as follows:

```
@GAMMAI(a,x,[complement])
```

The arguments are these:

a	Any positive value.
x	Any positive value or 0.
[*complement*]	An optional argument that specifies how 1-2-3 calculates @GAMMAI. There are two switches that can be used in the argument:

Complement	1-2-3 Calculates
0	$P(a,x)$ (the default if [*complement*] is omitted)
1	$Q(a,x)$ or $1-P(a,x)$

For example, the value of @GAMMA(7.5,12.4497,1) is 0.050024.

@GAMMALN—Calculating the Natural Log of Gamma

The natural log of the Gamma function is calculated using the @GAMMALN function. The syntax for the @GAMMALN function is as follows:

```
@GAMMALN(x)
```

Where *x* is any value greater than 0. This function approximates the natural log of the Gamma function accurately to within six significant figures. Here is an example of the @GAMMALN function:

```
@GAMMALN(0.5) = 0.572365
```

@HEX—Converting a Decimal Value to a Hex String

The @HEX function converts a decimal value to its signed hexadecimal equivalent. The syntax for this function is as follows:

```
@HEX(decimal)
```

The *decimal* argument can be a value from –2,147,483,648 through 2,147,483,647. The argument is entered as a value; if it is not an integer,

1-2-3 for Windows truncates it to an integer. Following is an example of the @HEX function:

@HEX(162) = A2

@SERIESSUM—Calculating the Sum of a Power Series

The @SERIESSUM function calculates the sum of a power series. The syntax for the @SERIESSUM function is as follows:

@SERIESSUM(*x*,*n*,*m*,*coefficients*)

The arguments are these:

x	The power series' input value.
n	The initial power to which to raise *x* (is also a value).
m	The increment to increase *n* for each term in the series (is also a value).
coefficients	A range that contains the coefficients by which 1-2-3 for Windows multiplies each successive power of *x*. The number of terms in the series is determined by the number of cells in coefficients. For example, if *coefficients* contains eight cells, the power series contains eight terms.

Suppose that a range called INPUT contained the values 0.2, 0.7, and 1.3 for the *coefficients* argument; an example of the @SERIESSUM function is as follows:

@SERIESSUM(3.5,2,1,INPUT) = 227.5438

Using Financial Functions

1-2-3 for Windows provides a series of financial functions that calculate discounted cash flow, loan amortization, depreciation, investment analysis, and annuities. The 1-2-3 for Windows financial functions are categorized into five groups so that you can find the best type of function quickly. The groups of financial functions are Annuities, Bonds, Capital-Budgeting Tools, Depreciation, and Single-Sum Compounding. These groups are summarized in table 7.4.

Table 7.4 Financial Functions

Annuities Functions	Description
@FV(*payments,interest,term*)	Calculates the *future value* (value at the end of payments) of a stream of periodic cash flows compounded at a periodic interest rate.
@FVAL(*payments,interest,term,* [*type*],[*present-value*])	Calculates the future value of a stream of periodic cash flows compounded at a periodic interest rate. There are optional arguments for the *type* (position in the month) and *present-value*.
@IPAYMT(*principal,interest,term,* *start*,[*end*],[*type*],[*future-value*])	Calculates the cumulative interest portion of the periodic payment from an investment.
@IRATE(*term,payment,present-value*, [*type*],[*future-value*], [*guess*])	Calculates the periodic interest rate necessary for an annuity to grow to a future value.
@NPER(*payments,interest,* *future-value*, [*type*],[*present-value*])	Calculates the number of compounding payment periods of an investment.
@PAYMT(*principal,interest,term,* [*type*],[*future-value*])	Calculates the periodic payment amount needed to pay off a loan. The loan can be treated as an ordinary annuity or as an annuity due.
@PMT(*principal,interest,term*)	Calculates the loan payment amount.
@PPAYMT(*principal,interest,* *term,start*,[*end*],[*type*], [*future-value*])	Calculates the cumulative principal portion of the periodic payment for an investment.
@PV(*payments,interest,term*)	Calculates the *present value* (today's value) of a stream of periodic cash flows of even payments discounted at a periodic interest rate.
@PVAL(*payments,interest,term,* [*type*],[*future-value*])	Calculates the present value of a series of equal payments. The loan can be treated as an ordinary annuity or as an annuity due.
@TERM(*payments,interest,* *future-value*)	Calculates the number of times an equal payment must be made to accumulate the future value when payments are compounded at the periodic interest rate.

Bonds Functions	Description
@ACCRUED(*settlement, maturity,coupon,[par], [frequency],[basis]*)	Calculates the accrued interest for a bond.
@PRICE(*settlement,maturity, coupon,yield,[redemption], [frequency],[basis]*)	Calculates the price of a bond as a percentage of par.
@YIELD(*settlement,maturity, coupon,price,[redemption], [frequency],[basis]*)	Calculates the yield at maturity for a bond.

Capital-Budgeting Tools Functions	Description
@IRR(*guess,range*)	Calculates the internal rate of return on an investment.
@MIRR(*range,finance-rate, reinvest-rate*)	Calculates the modified internal rate of return for a range of cash flows.
@NPV(*interest,range*)	Calculates the present value of a stream of cash flows of uneven amounts but at evenly spaced time periods when the payments are discounted by the periodic interest rate.

Depreciation Functions	Description
@DB(*cost,salvage,life,period*)	Calculates the declining balance depreciation allowance of an asset for one period.
@DDB(*cost,salvage,life,period*)	Calculates 200-percent declining-balance depreciation.
@SLN(*cost,salvage,life*)	Calculates straight-line depreciation.

Depreciation Functions	Description
@SYD(*cost,salvage,life,period*)	Calculates sum-of-the-years'-digits depreciation.
@VDB(*cost,salvage,life, start-period,end-period, [depreciation-percent], [switch]*)	Calculates the depreciation by using the variable-rate declining-balance method.

continues

Table 7.4 Continued	
Single-Sum Compounding Functions	**Description**
@CTERM(*interest,future-value, present-value*)	Calculates the number of periods required for the present value amount to grow to a future value amount given a periodic interest rate.
@RATE(*future-value,present-value,term*)	Calculates the periodic return required to increase the present-value investment to the size of the future value in the length of time indicated (term).

Annuities Functions

Annuity functions are used as financial analysis tools. Annuity functions give you the full-range capability to calculate current payments, future values, or interest rates. You can use this information to make prudent financial decisions.

@FV and @FVAL—Calculating Future Value

The @FV function calculates the future value of an investment based on a specific interest rate and a fixed number of regular investment payments. The function is helpful for estimating the future balances of savings accounts, college funds, and investments. The @FV function uses the following syntax:

@FV(*payments,interest,term*)

The @FVAL function calculates the future value of an investment based on a specific interest rate, a fixed number of regular payments, the optional position of the period in which the payments are made, and the optional starting amount of the investment. The @FVAL function uses the following syntax:

@FVAL(*payments,interest,term*,[*type*],[*present-value*])

The arguments for each function are as follows:

payments	The amount of equal payments invested.
interest	The annual interest rate of the investment. To use a monthly interest rate, divide the annual interest rate by 12. The interest rate must be greater than –1.
term	The total number of payments to be made.
[*type*]	This optional component works with @FVAL; it determines the portion of the period in which the payments are made. The two available options are as follows:

    0   Causes the calculation to be based on payments being made at the end of the period. This value is the default value if [*term*] is omitted.

    1   Causes the calculation to be based on payments made at the beginning of the period.

[*present-value*]	This optional argument specifies the present value of the series of future payments. If the argument is omitted the value is 0.

Suppose that you want to plan for your 3-year-old's college education. Your goal is to determine the best plan for at least a good start at an education. Using the @FV or the @FVAL function, you look at future options to help you with decisions for the future. Figure 7.18 shows the result of your planning. Assume monthly contributions of $100, an annual interest rate of 6 percent, and a time period of 15 years.

If you are also trying to determine the best time of the month for the direct deposit to take effect, add additional columns to the worksheet for *type 0* (end-of-the-month deposits) and *type 1* (beginning-of-the-month deposits) future values.

You think you may be able to cough up a few grand as seed money for your toddler's college fund; the amounts in the "Initial Deposit" column, varying from 0 to $5,000, are used as the optional present-value argument in the @FVAL function.

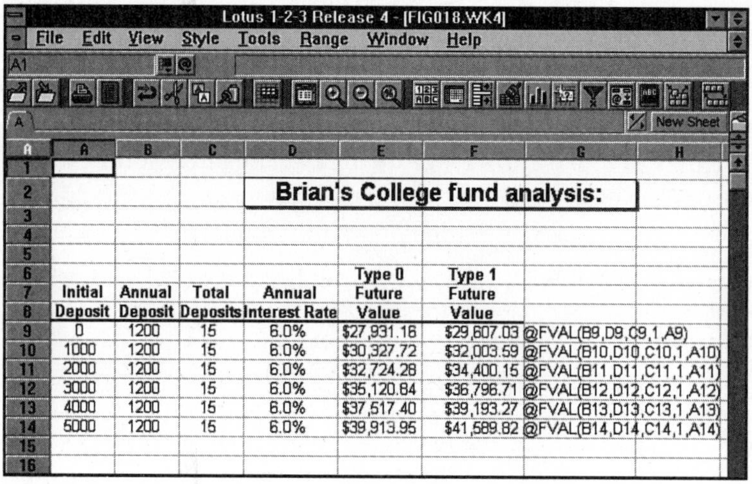

Initial Deposit	Annual Deposit	Total Deposits	Annual Interest Rate	Type 0 Future Value	Type 1 Future Value	
0	1200	15	6.0%	$27,931.16	$29,607.03	@FVAL(B9,D9,C9,1,A9)
1000	1200	15	6.0%	$30,327.72	$32,003.59	@FVAL(B10,D10,C10,1,A10)
2000	1200	15	6.0%	$32,724.28	$34,400.15	@FVAL(B11,D11,C11,1,A11)
3000	1200	15	6.0%	$35,120.84	$36,796.71	@FVAL(B12,D12,C12,1,A12)
4000	1200	15	6.0%	$37,517.40	$39,193.27	@FVAL(B13,D13,C13,1,A13)
5000	1200	15	6.0%	$39,913.95	$41,589.82	@FVAL(B14,D14,C14,1,A14)

FIG. 7.18

Using @FVAL to analyze a college fund.

@IPAYMT and @PPAYMT—Cumulative Interest of the Periodic Payment

Doing loan analysis can be very beneficial when you are looking for a loan. The @IPAYMT and @PPAYMT functions are complementary functions: @IPAYMT calculates the interest on payments you make on a loan; @PPAYMT calculates the principal contributed to the loan you are paying off. Use the following syntax for the @IPAYMT and @PPAYMT functions:

```
@IPAYMT(principal,interest,term,start,[end],[type],
  [future-value])
```

```
@PPAYMT(principal,interest,term,start,[end],[type]
  [future-value])
```

The arguments for each function are as follows:

principal	The face amount of the loan.
interest	The annual interest rate in decimal format (must be greater than a value of –1).
term	The time element or number of payment periods for the loan.
start	The period from which you want to start calculating interest or principal.
[*end*]	This optional argument brackets time periods to determine the amount of interest or principal paid during a specific time period. If you omit this argument, the *start* and [*end*] arguments are assumed to be the same.

[*type*]	This optional argument permits calculation of interest or payments made at the beginning or end of a period. The available options for this argument are as follows:

0   Tells 1-2-3 for Windows that the payment is made at the end of the period (the default [*type*] is omitted).

1   Tells 1-2-3 for Windows that the payment is made at the beginning of the period.

[*future-value*]	This optional argument specifies the future value of the series of payments. This can be any value; if omitted, [*future-value*] is assumed to be 0.

Here are some rules to keep in mind when using these functions:

- You cannot enter optional arguments without entering the ones in front of the one you want to use.

- The period for *interest* and *term* must be the same.

Figure 7.19 shows an analysis page for a $5,000 loan, to be paid back in 24 months at a 10.25-percent annual interest rate. Columns A and F represent the individual months. The amounts in the columns labeled *Interest This Term* and *Principal This Term* use the @IPAYMT and @PPAYMT functions with no optional arguments. The Total Interest-Year 2 formula (in cell H3) and Total Principal-Year 2 formula (in cell H4) use the optional [*end*] argument.

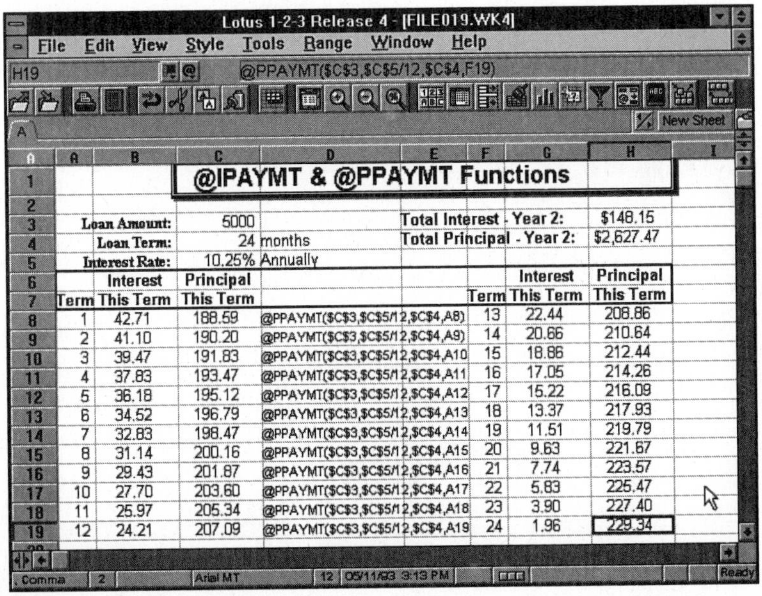

FIG. 7.19

The @IPAYMT and @PPAYMT functions.

@IRATE—Calculating Interest Rate Necessary To Obtain a Future Value

The @IRATE function calculates the rate of interest necessary for an investment to grow to a specific future value. Following is the syntax for @IRATE:

```
@IRATE(term,payment,present-value,[type],[future-
    value],[guess])
```

The arguments for the @IRATE function are as follows:

term	The number of payments.
present-value	Starting value.
[*type*]	This optional argument allows you to calculate interest or payments made at the beginning or end of a period. The options are as follows:

0   Tells 1-2-3 for Windows that the payment is made at the end of the period (the default if [*type*] is omitted).

1   Tells 1-2-3 for Windows that the payment is made at the beginning of the period.

[*future-value*]	An optional argument that specifies the future value of the series of payments. This can be any value; if omitted, the *future-value* argument is assumed to be 0.
[*guess*]	This optional argument represents your estimate of the interest rate. The [*guess*] argument is a value between 0 and 1 and is assumed to be .1 if you omit the argument.

Figure 7.20 shows an example of how the @IRATE function can be used to analyze information concerning retirement.

@NPER and @TERM—Calculating the Term of an Investment

The @TERM function calculates the number of periods required to accumulate a specified future value by making equal payments into an interest-bearing account at the end of each period. The number of periods is the *term* for an ordinary annuity.

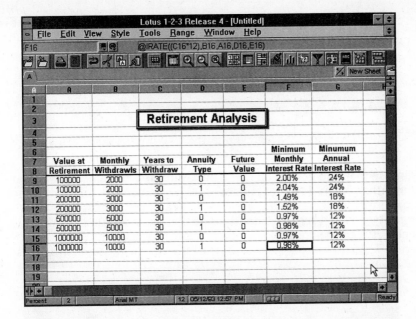

FIG. 7.20

Using @IRATE
to calculate a
necessary
interest rate for
retirement.

The @NPER function performs the same calculation with a slight twist: The @NPER function allows for optional *present-value* and *type* arguments. These arguments provide flexibility by adjusting the starting amount and the time of the period within the estimation. Use the following syntax for these functions:

@TERM(*payments*,*interest*,*future-value*)

@NPER(*payments*,*interest*,*future-value*,[*type*],[*present-value*])

@TERM is similar to @FV, with one exception. Instead of finding the future value of a stream of payments over a specified period (as @FV does), @TERM finds the number of periods required to reach the given future value. @NPER calculates from an optional starting *present-value*; you also can tell 1-2-3 what *type* of annuity period to use.

Following is a list of the arguments used by these functions:

payments	The amount of each payment.
interest	The annual interest rate.
future-value	The amount you want to have at the end of the payment schedule.
[*type*]	This optional argument tells 1-2-3 whether payments are made at the beginning or end of a period. The options are as follows:

0	Tells 1-2-3 for Windows that the payment is made at the end of the period (the default if [*type*] is omitted).
1	Tells 1-2-3 for Windows that the payment is made at the beginning of the period.
[*present-value*]	An optional argument that specifies the current value (the starting balance). This can be any value; if omitted, the *present-value* argument is assumed to be 0.

Suppose that you have $200 saved and want to determine the number of months required to accumulate $5,000 by making a monthly payment of $50 into an account that pays 8 percent annual interest compounded monthly (0.67 percent per month). You also want to know the difference between making a payment at the beginning or end of the month. Figure 7.21 shows how @TERM and @NPER can help you answer those questions.

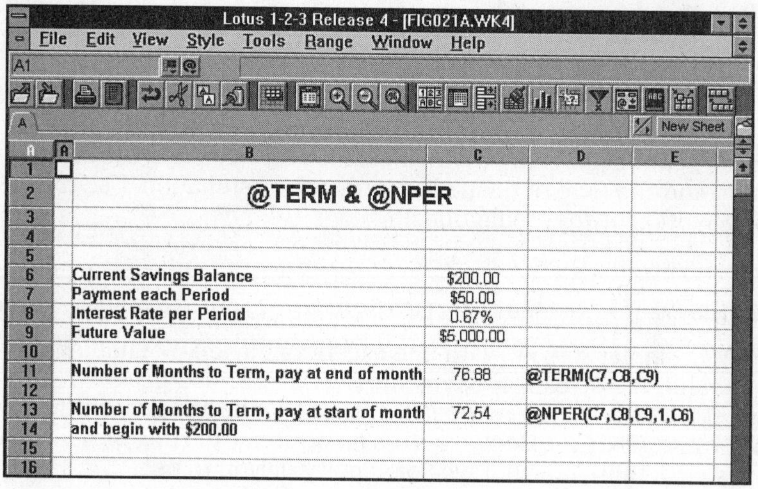

FIG. 7.21

Using @TERM and @NPER to calculate the number of months to reach a specified future value.

	B	C	D	E
2	**@TERM & @NPER**			
6	Current Savings Balance	$200.00		
7	Payment each Period	$50.00		
8	Interest Rate per Period	0.67%		
9	Future Value	$5,000.00		
11	Number of Months to Term, pay at end of month	76.88	@TERM(C7,C8,C9)	
13	Number of Months to Term, pay at start of month	72.54	@NPER(C7,C8,C9,1,C6)	
14	and begin with $200.00			

@PMT, @PAYMT, and @PMTC—Calculating Loan Payment Amounts

You use the @PMT function to calculate the periodic payments necessary to pay the entire principal on an amortizing loan. The function @PAYMT, new in 1-2-3 Release 4 for Windows, lets you optionally specify the beginning or the end of the month for payments and a future value as arguments. All you need to know is the loan amount (principal), periodic interest rate, and term.

The @PMT function requires the following three arguments:

@PMT(*principal*,*interest*,*term*)

The @PAYMT function requires the same three arguments and allows the two optional arguments [*type*] and [*future-value*]. The syntax for @PAYMT is as follows:

@PAYMT(*principal*,*interest*,*term*,[*type*],[*future-value*])

@PMT assumes that payments are made at the end of each period—an ordinary annuity. @PAYMT uses the optional [*type*] argument that has the following two available options:

0   Tells 1-2-3 for Windows that the payment is made at the end of the period (the default if [*type*] is omitted).

1   Tells 1-2-3 for Windows that the payment is made at the beginning of the period.

[*future-value*] is an optional argument that specifies the future value of the series of payments. If [future-value] is omitted 1-2-3 assumes the value to be 0.

Figure 7.22 shows how the @PMT and @PAYMT functions are used to calculate the monthly house payment on a $43,000 car loan. The loan is repaid over 120 months, and the loan rate is 1 percent—12 percent divided by 12 months. Notice the difference in payments if you pay at the beginning or end of the period.

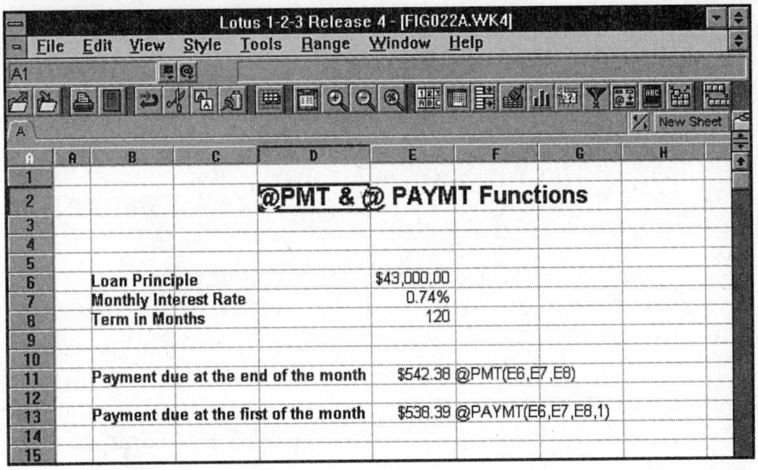

FIG. 7.22

Using @PMT and @PAYMT to calculate loan payments.

Whether you calculate ordinary annuities or annuities due, keep two important guidelines in mind:

- Calibrate the interest rate as the rate per payment period.
- Express the loan term in payment periods.

T I P If you make monthly payments, enter the interest rate as the monthly interest rate and the term as the number of months you make payments. Alternatively, if you make annual payments, enter the interest rate as the annual interest rate and the term as the number of years you make payments.

@PV and @PVAL—Calculating Present Value of an Annuity

The @PV and @PVAL functions calculate the present value of a stream of cash flows. This stream of equal cash flows is called an *ordinary annuity* or *payments in arrears*. The @PV and @PVAL functions use the following syntax:

@PV(*payments,interest,term*)

@PVAL(*payments,interest,term*,[*type*],[*future-value*])

Included in the @PVAL function are two optional arguments. [*type*] enables you to calculate for an ordinary annuity or for an annuity due. The two options are as follows:

0   Tells 1-2-3 for Windows that the payment is made at the end of the period (the default if [*type*] is omitted). If you use this option, you are making an *ordinary annuity*.

1   Tells 1-2-3 for Windows that the payment is made at the beginning of the period. If you use this option, you are making *payments in arrears*.

The optional [*future-value*] argument enables you to specify the future value of the series of payments. This argument can be any value; however, if you do not include it in the function. 1-2-3 for Windows assumes the value of 0.

Figure 7.23 shows the result of using @PV and @PVAL to calculate the present value of 24 payments of $1,000 each. Note that @PV and @PVAL both default to an ordinary annuity.

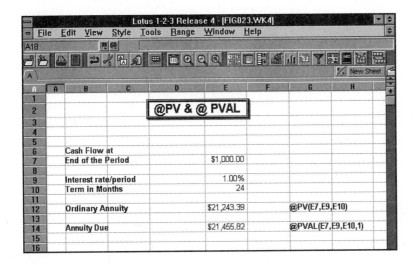

FIG. 7.23

Using @PV and @PVAL to calculate the present value of 24 payments of $1,000.

Bonds @Functions

Bond @functions provide the tools to analyze investments. With these tools you can make better investment judgements and hopefully increase your scope of investments.

@ACCRUED—Calculating Accrued Interest

The @ACCRUED function calculates the accrued interest on installments that have periodic interest payments and a maturity date. Following is the @ACCRUED function syntax:

@ACCRUED(*settlement*,*maturity*,*coupon*,[*par*],[*frequency*],[*basis*])

The arguments for the @ACCRUED function are as follows:

settlement	A date serial number that represents the settlement date for the security.
maturity	A date serial number that represents the date when the security is recovered. The maturity date must be greater than the settlement date, or @ACCRUED returns ERR.

coupon	The annual coupon rate for the coupon. The coupon rate may be any positive value or 0.
[*par*]	An optional argument that represents the value of security principal. *Security principal* is the value to be paid to the owner at the maturity of the security. 1-2-3 assumes the value of 100 if this argument is omitted. If a value is included, it must be positive.
[*frequency*]	An optional argument representing the number of coupon payments per year. There are four available options:

Frequency	Value
1	Annual
2	Semiannual (the default if omitted)
4	Quarterly
12	Monthly

[*basis*]	An optional argument specifying the *day count* (days_per_month/days_per_year) to use. There are four available options:

Basis	Days_per_Month/ Days_per_Year
0	30/360 (the default if omitted)
1	Actual/Actual
2	Actual/360
3	Actual/365

Figure 7.24 shows a bond portfolio with accrued interest.

@PRICE—Calculating Bond Price

The @PRICE function calculates the price per $100 face value on installments that have periodic interest payments and a maturity date. Following is the @PRICE function syntax:

```
@PRICE(settlement,maturity,coupon,yield,
[redemption],[frequency],[basis])
```

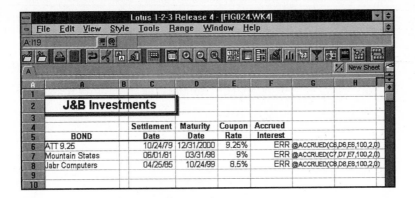

FIG. 7.24

Using the
@ACCRUED
function in a
bond portfolio.

The arguments for the @PRICE function are as follows:

settlement	A date serial number that represents the settlement date, the date of ownership, for the security.
maturity	A date serial number that represents the date when the security is recovered. The maturity date must be greater than the settlement date, or @PRICE returns ERR.
coupon	The annual coupon rate for the coupon. The coupon rate may be any positive value or 0.
yield	The annual yield on the security. The *yield* argument must be a positive value.
[*redemption*]	An optional argument that specifies the redemption value of the security per $100 face value. If used, [*redemption*] must be a positive number; if omitted from the argument list, 1-2-3 assumes the value 100.
[*frequency*]	An optional argument that represents the number of coupon payments per year. There are four available options:

Frequency	Value
1	Annual
2	Semiannual (the default if omitted)
4	Quarterly
12	Monthly

[basis]	An optional argument specifying the *day count* (days_per_month/days_per_year) to use. There are four available options:

Basis	Days_per_Month/Days_per_Year
0	30/360 (the default if omitted)
1	Actual/Actual
2	Actual/360
3	Actual/365

Figure 7.25 shows a bond portfolio with accrued interest and the price of the bond.

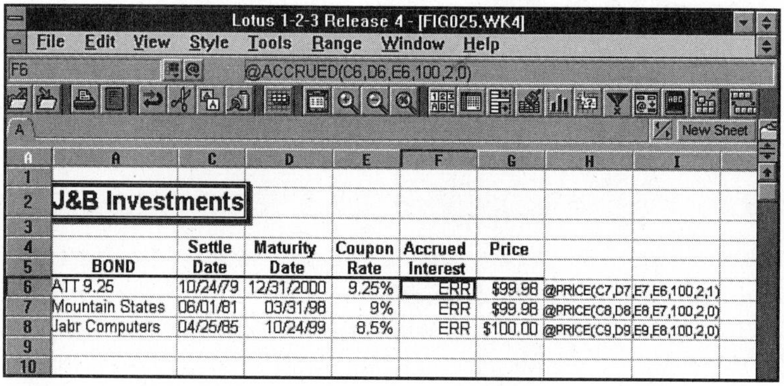

FIG. 7.25

Using the @PRICE function in a bond portfolio.

@YIELD—Calculating Maturity Yield

The @YIELD function calculates the price per $100 face value on instruments that have periodic interest payments and a maturity date. Following is the @YIELD function syntax:

@YIELD(*settlement*,*maturity*,*coupon*,*price*, [*redemption*],[*frequency*],[*basis*])

The arguments for the @YIELD function are as follows:

settlement	A date serial number that represents the settlement date, the date of ownership, for the security.
maturity	A date serial number that represents the date when the security is recovered. The maturity date must be greater than the settlement date, or @YIELD returns ERR.

coupon	The annual coupon rate for the coupon. The coupon rate may be any positive value or 0.
price	The price per $100 of face value. The *price* argument must be a positive value.
[*redemption*]	An optional argument that specifies the redemption value of the security per $100 face value. If used, [*redemption*] must be a positive number; if omitted from the argument list, 1-2-3 assumes the value 100.
[*frequency*]	An optional argument that represents the number of coupon payments per year. There are four available options:

Frequency	Value
1	Annual
2	Semiannual (the default if omitted)
4	Quarterly
12	Monthly

[*basis*]	An optional argument specifying the *day count* (days_per_month/days_per_year) to use. There are four available options:

Basis	Days_per_Month/Days_per_Year
0	30/360 (the default if omitted)
1	Actual/Actual
2	Actual/360
3	Actual/365

Figure 7.26 shows a bond portfolio with accrued interest, price, and yield.

Capital-Budgeting Tools Functions

These functions work with cash flows and rates of return.

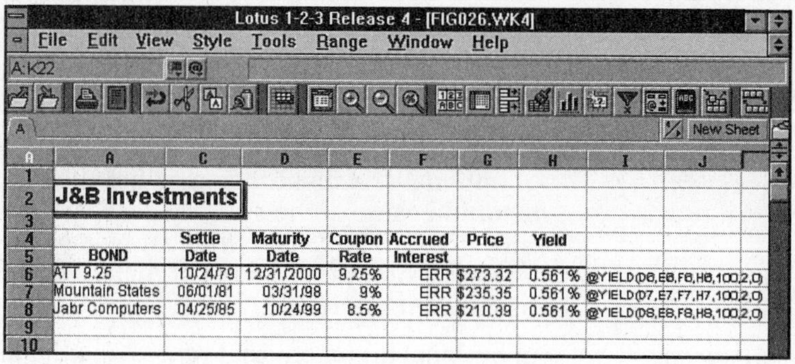

FIG. 7.26

Using the @YIELD function in a bond portfolio.

@IRR—Calculating Internal Rate of Return

The @IRR function calculates the internal rate of return on an investment. Use the following syntax for @IRR:

@IRR(*guess*,*range*)

The *guess* argument typically should be a guess at the internal rate of return which is an interest rate. Because interest rate is a percentage value it is entered as a decimal between 0 and 1.

You should start the calculation with a guessed interest rate as close as possible to the internal rate of return on your investment. From this guess, 1-2-3 for Windows attempts to converge to a correct interest rate with .0000001 precision within 30 iterations. If the program cannot do so, the @IRR function returns ERR. When that happens, try again with another *guess* argument.

The *range* argument is the address or name that contains the cash flows. Initial cash flow at time 0 is negative (because the cash flows out from you). Cash flows in the range after that may be negative (payments by you) or positive (payments to you). Cash flows occur at the end of equally spaced periods, with the initial payment by you being at time 0. 1-2-3 for Windows assigns the value of 0 to empty cells and labels in the range of cash flows (ranges can span more than one column but remember about empty cells).

Figure 7.27 shows the @IRR function calculating the internal rate of return on an investment with uneven cash flows. Notice that during some time periods, the investor injected additional cash into the investment. Notice also that multiplying the monthly amount by 12 converts the monthly internal rate of return to an annual rate.

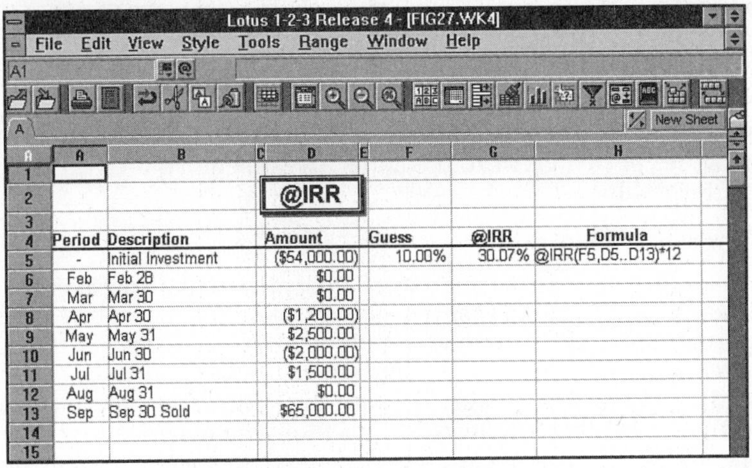

FIG. 7.27

Using @IRR to calculate the internal rate of return.

Although the internal-rate-of-return profit measure is widely used, you should be aware that the formula has multiple detriments when used to analyze investments. The problem is with the internal-rate-of-return method, not with 1-2-3's @IRR function.

One problem is evident when you use the internal-rate-of-return measure on an investment that has multiple internal rates of return. In theory, the formula for calculating the internal rate of return for an investment with cash flows over 10 years is a 10th-root polynomial equation with up to 10 correct solutions. In practice, an investment may have as many correct internal rates of return as sign changes in the cash flows.

A sign change occurs when the cash flow changes from positive to negative (or vice versa) between periods. Accordingly, even if the @IRR function returns an internal rate of return with your first guess, try other guesses to see whether another correct internal-rate-of-return answer is evident; you probably should not use the measure when it delivers multiple solutions.

A serious problem with the @IRR method is that it tends to overestimate a positive rate of return from the investment and neglects to account for additional outside investments that must be injected into the investment over its life span. The overestimate on return occurs because the @IRR method assumes that positive cash flows are reinvested at the same rate of return earned by the total investment. Actually, a small return rarely can be reinvested at the same high rate as that of a large investment. This feature is especially true when analyzing large fixed assets and land investments.

@MIRR—Calculating Profit

The @MIRR function calculates the modified internal rate of return from a range of cash-flow values in an investment. The internal rate of return is the percentage rate that equates to the present value of an expected future series of cash flows to the initial investment. Following is the syntax for @MIRR:

@MIRR(*range*,*finance-rate*,*reinvest-rate*)

The *range* argument is the address or range name that contains the cash flows. Initial cash flow at time 0 is negative (because the cash flows out from you). Cash flows in the range after that may be negative (payments by you) or positive (payments to you). Cash flows occur at the end of equally spaced periods, with the initial payment by you being at time 0. 1-2-3 for Windows assigns the value of 0 to empty cells and labels in the range of cash flows (ranges can span more than one column but remember about empty cells).

The *finance-rate* argument is the rate of interest paid on cash flows. The *reinvest-rate* argument is the interest rate you receive on cash flows as you reinvest them.

Figure 7.28 calculates the profit from a small used-car dealership, for which an initial payment of $100,000 was made. Over the next five years, the investor made a living from the sale of cars and logged the profits in a range called INCOME. The interest rate on the initial loan is 9.5 percent; because of the investor's fantastic skills, he or she has been earning 13.18 percent return on the profits.

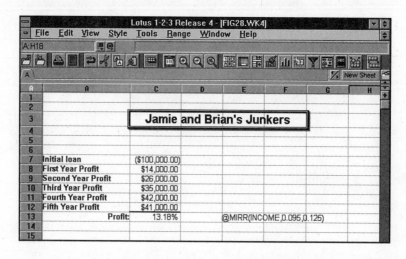

FIG. 7.28

Using @MIRR to calculate the modified internal rate of return.

@NPV—Calculating Net Present Value

The @NPV function closely resembles the @PV function except that @NPV can calculate the present value of a varying, or changing, *range* of cash flows. Use the following syntax for @NPV:

@NPV(*interest*,*range*)

The @NPV function makes the assumption that the cash outflows occur at the same intervals for each period. The assumption is that the first cash outflow occurs at the *end* of the initial period and at the same time in each subsequent period.

NOTE @NPV returns ERR if the *range* argument contains more than one row or column.

Figure 7.29 shows how you can use @NPV to calculate the present value of a stream of varying cash flows with cash outflows made at the end of the period. In the figure, the range CASH is C10..C17.

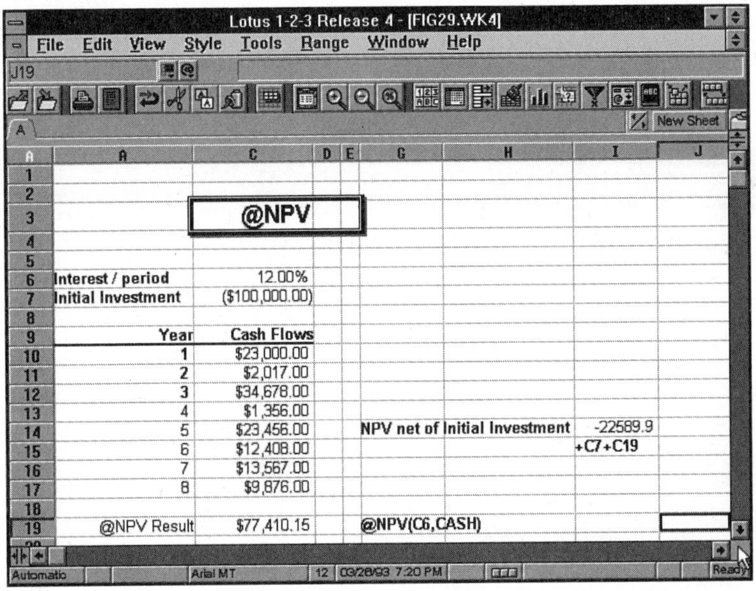

FIG. 7.29

Using @NPV to calculate the present value of varying cash flows.

Because the @NPV function assumes that the first cash flow occurs at the end of the first period, the function is actually just a flexible present-value function. If you use the @PV function, you can use the @NPV function to obtain the same result.

Accountants and financial analysts use the term *net present value* to refer to a measure of an investment's profitability by including the initial cash outlay for the investment. To calculate the actual profitability measure, or *net present value*, subtract the initial investment from the result of the @NPV function. When you construct a formula that uses the @NPV function in this way, you essentially test whether the investment meets, beats, or falls short of the interest rate specified in the @NPV function. Such a formula can be the following:

```
+INITL_AMOUNT+@NPV(interest,range)
```

The value in the cell named INITL_AMOUNT is negative because the amount is money you paid out. The formula in I14 in figure 7.29 is as follows:

```
+C7+C19
```

If the calculated result of the preceding formula is a positive amount, the investment produces an investment return that beats the interest rate specified in the @NPV function. If the calculated result equals 0, the investment produces an investment return that equals the interest rate specified in the @NPV function. If the calculated result is a negative amount, the investment produces an investment return that falls short of the interest rate specified in the @NPV function.

Depreciation Functions

Depreciation Functions allow for asset management. The following functions enable you to calculate different methods of depreciation.

@DB—Declining Balance Depreciation Allowance

@DB calculates the depreciation allowance of an asset with an initial value of *cost*, an expected useful *life*, and a final *salvage* value for a specified *period* of time. @DB uses the fixed-declining balance method. Following is the syntax for @DB:

```
@DB(cost,salvage,life,period)
```

The arguments for the @DB function are as follows:

cost	The amount paid for the asset. The *cost* argument is a positive value or 0. If the value of *cost* is 0, the value of @DB is also 0.
salvage	The estimated value of the asset at the end of its useful life. The *salvage* argument is a positive

	value. If *salvage* is larger than *cost*, the value of @DB is negative.
life	The number of periods the asset takes to depreciate to its *salvage* value.
period	The time period for which you want to find the depreciation allowance. The *period* argument is a value greater than or equal to 1.

NOTE The *life* and *period* arguments must be in the same units of time.

Figure 7.30 shows the depreciation allowance by year for a valuable widget. It is important to note that *life* and *period* must be in the same units of time if @DB is to function properly. The standard unit of time is a year.

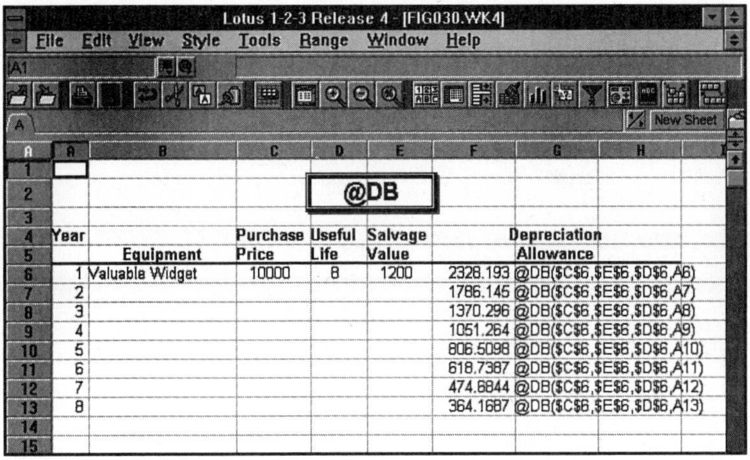

Year	Equipment	Purchase Price	Useful Life	Salvage Value	Depreciation Allowance	
1	Valuable Widget	10000	8	1200	2328.193	@DB($C$6,$E$6,$D$6,A6)
2					1786.145	@DB($C$6,$E$6,$D$6,A7)
3					1370.296	@DB($C$6,$E$6,$D$6,A8)
4					1051.264	@DB($C$6,$E$6,$D$6,A9)
5					806.5098	@DB($C$6,$E$6,$D$6,A10)
6					618.7387	@DB($C$6,$E$6,$D$6,A11)
7					474.6844	@DB($C$6,$E$6,$D$6,A12)
8					364.1687	@DB($C$6,$E$6,$D$6,A13)

FIG. 7.30 Using @DB to calculate the depreciation allowance of a widget.

@DDB—Calculating Double-Declining-Balance Depreciation

The @DDB function calculates depreciation by using the double-declining-balance method, in which depreciation ceases when the book value reaches the salvage value. The double-declining-balance method accelerates depreciation so that greater depreciation expense occurs in the earlier periods instead of in the later ones. *Book value* in any period is the purchase price less the total depreciation in all preceding periods. @DDB uses the following syntax:

@DDB(*cost*,*salvage*,*life*,*period*)

Generally, the double-declining-balance depreciation in any period is as follows:

book_value*2/n

In this formula, book_value is the book value in the period and *n* is the depreciable life of the asset. 1-2-3 for Windows, however, adjusts the result of this formula in later periods to ensure that total depreciation does not exceed the purchase price less the salvage value.

Figure 7.31 shows how the @DDB function can calculate depreciation on an asset purchased for $10,000, with a depreciable life of 8 years, and an estimated salvage value of $1,200. Compare these results with those obtained with the @DB function as shown in figure 7.30.

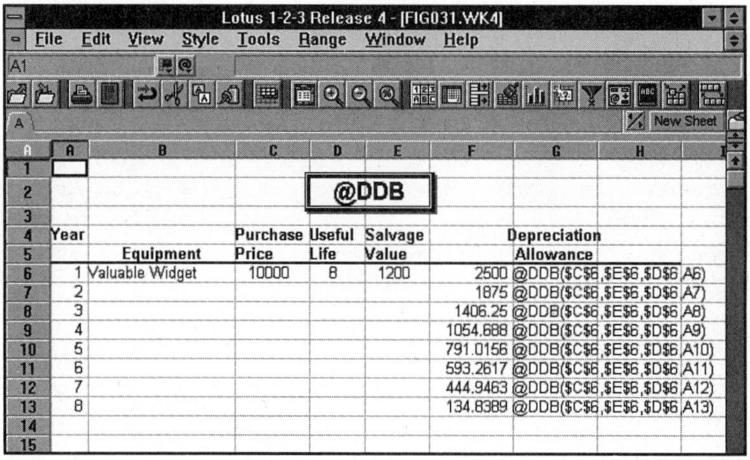

FIG. 7.31

Using @DDB to calculate double-declining-balance depreciation.

Keep in mind that when you use the double-declining-balance depreciation method for an asset with a small salvage value, the asset does not fully depreciate in the final year. If this is the case with one of your assets, use the @VDB function, discussed later in this section.

@SLN—Calculating Straight-Line Depreciation

The @SLN function calculates straight-line depreciation, given the asset's cost, salvage value, and depreciable life. @SLN uses the following syntax:

@SLN(*cost*,*salvage*,*life*)

The formula for calculating @SLN is as follows:

```
SLN = (cost-salvage_value)/life
```

@SLN conveniently calculates straight-line depreciation for an asset. Suppose that you have purchased a machine for $10,000 that has a useful life of 3 years and a salvage value estimated at 12 percent of the purchase price ($1,200) at the end of the machine's useful life. Figure 7.32 shows how to use @SLN to determine the straight-line depreciation for the machine ($1,100 per year).

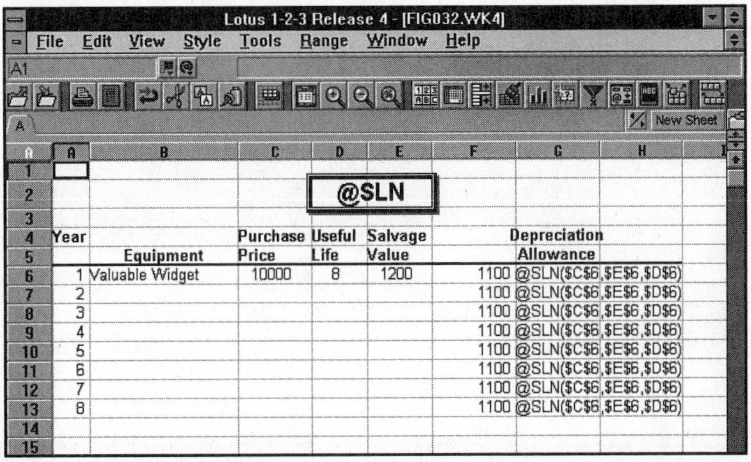

Year	Equipment	Purchase Price	Useful Life	Salvage Value	Depreciation Allowance	
1	Valuable Widget	10000	8	1200	1100	@SLN($C$6,$E$6,$D$6)
2					1100	@SLN($C$6,$E$6,$D$6)
3					1100	@SLN($C$6,$E$6,$D$6)
4					1100	@SLN($C$6,$E$6,$D$6)
5					1100	@SLN($C$6,$E$6,$D$6)
6					1100	@SLN($C$6,$E$6,$D$6)
7					1100	@SLN($C$6,$E$6,$D$6)
8					1100	@SLN($C$6,$E$6,$D$6)

FIG. 7.32

Using @SLN to calculate the straight-line depreciation.

@SYD—Calculating Sum-of-the-Years'-Digits Depreciation

The @SYD function calculates depreciation by the sum-of-the-years'-digits method. This method accelerates depreciation so that earlier periods of the item's life reflect greater depreciation than do later periods. Use the following syntax for @SYD:

@SYD(*cost*,*salvage*,*life*,*period*)

The *cost* is the purchase cost of the asset; the *salvage* is the estimated value of the asset at the end of its depreciable life. The *life* argument is the depreciable life of the asset; the *period* is the period for which depreciation is to be computed. @SYD calculates depreciation with the following formula:

$$\frac{(\text{cost}-\text{salvage})*(\text{life}-\text{period}+1)}{\text{life}*(\text{life}+1)/2}$$

The expression *(life–period+1)* in the numerator shows the life of the depreciation in the first period, decreased by 1 in each subsequent period. This expression reflects the declining pattern of depreciation over time. The expression in the denominator, *life*(life+1)/2*, is equal to the sum of the digits, as in the following expression:

$$1 + 2 +...+ \text{life}$$

From this expression, the name *sum-of-the-years'-digits* originated.

Figure 7.33 shows how the @SYD function can calculate depreciation for an asset costing $10,000 with a depreciable life of 3 years and an estimated salvage value of $1,200.

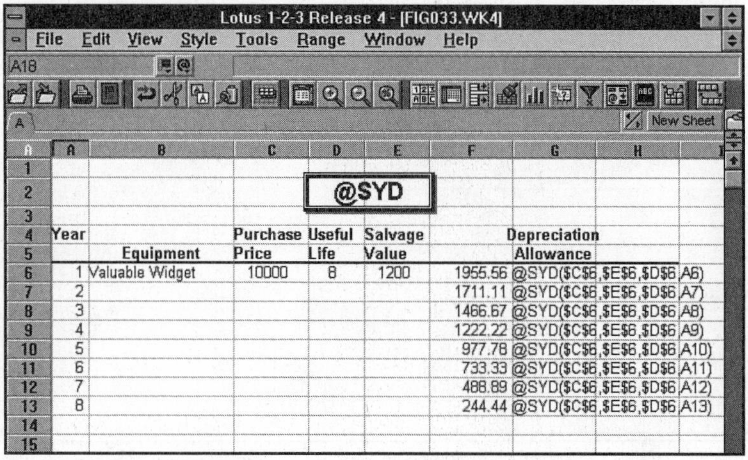

FIG. 7.33

Using @SYD to calculate the sum-of the years' digits depreciation.

@VDB—Calculating Variable Declining-Balance Depreciation

The @VDB function calculates depreciation by using a variable-rate declining-balance method. The variable-rate depreciation method provides accelerated depreciation during the early part of the term. If you do not specify a depreciation rate, 1-2-3 for Windows uses 200 percent to produce double-declining-balance depreciation. Usually, @VDB switches from accelerated depreciation to straight-line depreciation when it is most advantageous. You can set the *switch* argument if you do not want the function to automatically switch over to straight-line depreciation.

The *start-period* and *end-period* arguments correspond to the beginning and end of the asset's life, relative to the fiscal period. For example, to find the first year's depreciation of an asset purchased at the beginning of the third quarter of the fiscal year, the *start-period* is 0 and the *end-period* is .50 (half the year). The syntax of the @VDB function is as follows:

```
@VDB(cost,salvage,life,start-period,end-
period,[depreciation-percent],[switch])
```

Figure 7.34 shows how the @VDB function can calculate depreciation on an asset purchased for $10,000, with a depreciable life of 5 years, and an estimated salvage value of $1,200 when it is placed into service at the beginning of the third quarter of the fiscal year. The optional *depreciation-percent* argument is set to 150 percent.

You can include the optional [*switch*] argument if you do not want @VDB to switch to straight-line depreciation for the remaining useful life. Normally, declining-balance switches to a straight-line calculation when the straight-line calculation is greater than the declining-balance calculation.

You have two choices for the optional [*switch*] argument:

0   Automatically switches to straight-line depreciation (the default condition).

1   Never switches to straight-line depreciation.

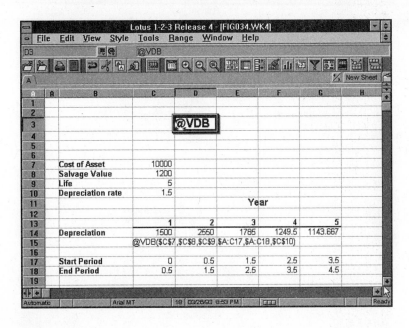

FIG. 7.34

Using @VDB to calculate 150-percent declining-balance depreciation.

Single-Sum Compounding Functions

The Single-Sum Compounding Functions deal with growing your investment. With these functions you can monitor and work with future values.

@CTERM—Calculating the Term of a Compounding Investment

The @CTERM function calculates the number of periods required for an initial investment that earns a specified interest rate to grow to a specified future value. The @TERM function calculates the number of periods needed for a series of payments to grow to a future value; the @CTERM function calculates the number of periods needed for an initial amount (its present value) to grow to a future value. Use the following format for @CTERM:

@CTERM(*interest,future-value,present-value*)

@CTERM is useful in determining the term necessary for an investment to achieve a specific future value. Suppose that you want to determine how many years it takes for $2,000 invested in an IRA at 10 percent interest to grow to $10,000. Figure 7.35 shows how to use the @CTERM function to determine the answer (just over 16 years and 10 months).

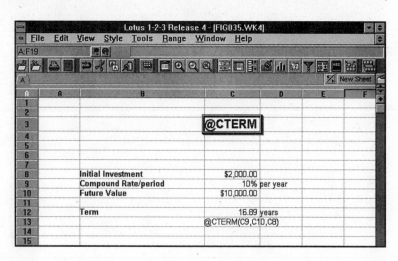

FIG. 7.35

Using @CTERM to calculate the number of years for $2,000 invested at 10 percent to grow to $10,000.

@RATE—Calculating Compound Growth Rate

The @RATE function calculates the compound growth rate for an initial investment that grows to a specified future value over a specified number of periods. The rate is the periodic interest rate; it is not necessarily an annual rate. Use the following syntax for this function:

@RATE(*future-value*,*present-value*,*term*)

For the @RATE calculation, the formula is rearranged to compute the interest rate in terms of the initial investment, the future value, and the number of periods. The actual formula for calculating the interest rate is as follows:

interest_rate = (*future_value*/*present_value*)1/term–1

You can use @RATE to determine the yield of a zero-coupon bond sold at a discount of its face value. Suppose that for $350 you can purchase a zero-coupon bond with a $1,000 face value that matures in 10 years. What is the implied annual interest rate? The answer is shown in figure 7.36 (11.07 percent).

The @RATE function is also useful in forecasting applications to calculate the compound growth rate between current and projected future revenues, earnings, and so on.

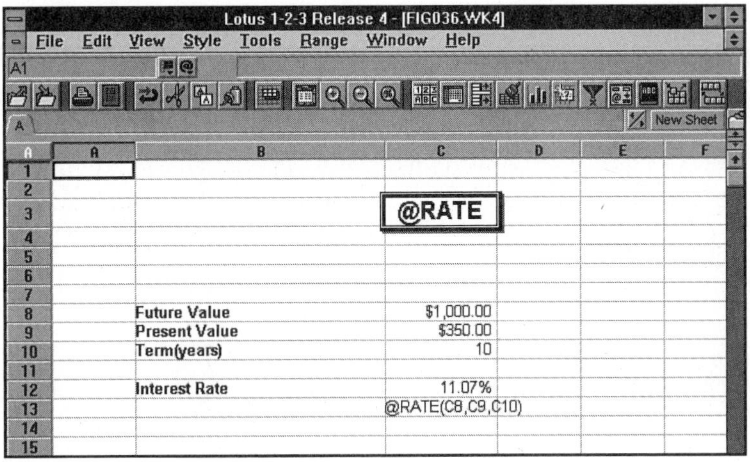

FIG. 7.36

Using @RATE to determine the interest rate for a zero-coupon bond.

Using Information Functions

The information functions return information about cells, ranges, the operating system, the Version Manager, and Solver. The information functions are broken into three major categories: Cell and Range Information, System and Session Information, and Error-Checking. The functions in these categories and a brief description of each are shown in table 7.5.

Table 7.5 Information Functions

Cell and Range Information Functions	Description
@CELL(attribute,reference)	Returns the value of the specified attribute for the cell in the upper left corner of the reference
@CELLPOINTER(attribute)	Returns the value of the specified attribute for the current cell
@COLS(range)	Computes the number of columns in the range
@COORD(worksheet,column, row,absolute)	Constructs a cell address from values corresponding to rows and columns
@RANGENAME(cell)	Returns the name of the range in which *cell* is located
@REFCONVERT(reference)	Converts the column or worksheet letters A through IV to numbers from 1-256 and the numbers 1-256 to the corresponding column and worksheet letters
@ROWS(range)	Computes the number of rows in a range
@SHEETS(range)	Computes the number of sheets in a range

System and Session Information Functions	Description
@INFO(attribute)	Retrieves system information
@SCENARIOLAST(filename)	Returns the name, if any,of the last-displayed scenario in a file.
@SOLVER(query-string)	Retrieves information about the status of the Solver utility
@USER	Returns your 1-2-3 for Windows User name.

System and Session Information Functions	Description
@VERSIONCURRENT(range)	Returns the name of the current version in range.
@VERSIONDATA(option,cell, version-range,name,[creator])	Returns the contents of a specified cell in a version.

Error-Checking Functions	Description
@ERR	Displays ERR in the cell
@NA	Displays NA in the cell

Cell and Range Information Functions

These functions return information about particular cells or ranges of cells.

@CELL and @CELLPOINTER—Checking Cell Attributes

The @CELL and @CELLPOINTER functions provide an efficient way to determine the nature of a cell; these functions return information on one of 14 cell characteristics, such as a cell's number or value, color, or width. @CELL and @CELLPOINTER are used primarily in macros and advanced macro command programs (see Chapters 15 and 16). Use the following syntax for @CELL and @CELLPOINTER:

@CELL(*attribute*,*reference*)

@CELLPOINTER(*attribute*)

Because you want to examine a cell's attributes, both functions have *attribute* as a string argument. @CELL, however, also requires the specification of a range as the *reference* argument; @CELLPOINTER works with the current cell.

The *attribute* argument is a text string and must be enclosed in quotation marks. If a range of cells is specified for the *reference* argument in the @CELL function, the returned value refers to the top-left cell in the range.

Table 7.6 lists the full set of attributes that can be examined with @CELL and @CELLPOINTER.

Table 7.6 Attributes Used with @CELL and @CELLPOINTER

Attribute	What the Function Returns
"address"	The abbreviated absolute cell address
"col"	The number of the column, from 1 (A) to 256 (IV)
"color"	1 if negative numbers are formatted in color; 0 if not
"contents"	Contents of the cell
"coord"	The full cell address (abbreviated)
"filename"	Name of the file containing the cell
"format"	F0 to F15: Fixed decimal, 0 to 15 decimal places
	S0 to S15: Scientific, 0 to 15 decimal places
	C0 to C15: Currency, 0 to 15 decimal places
	,0 to ,15: Comma, 0 to 15 decimal places
	G: General
	+: +/−
	P0 to P15: Percent, 0 to 15 decimal places
	D1 to D9: Date/Time format
	A: Automatic
	T: Text
	L: Label
	H: Hidden
	−: negative numbers displayed in color
	( ): negative numbers displayed in parentheses
"parenthesis"	1 if negative numbers are displayed in parentheses; 0 if they are displayed without parentheses
"prefix"	Same as label prefixes; blank if no label
"protect"	1 if protected; 0 if not
"row"	Row number, 1 to 8,192
"sheet"	Worksheet number, 1 (A) to 256 (IV)
"type"	b if blank; v if value; l if label
"width"	Column width

The following examples demonstrate how the @CELL function can be used to examine some cell attributes:

@CELL("*address*",SALES)

If the range named SALES is C187..E187, 1-2-3 for Windows returns the absolute address $C$187. This statement is convenient for listing the upper left corner of a range's address in the worksheet.

@CELL("*prefix*",C195..C195)

If cell C195 contains the label 'Chicago, 1-2-3 for Windows returns ' (indicating left alignment). If cell C195 is blank, however, 1-2-3 for Windows returns nothing; the current cell appears blank.

@CELL("*format*",A10)

1-2-3 for Windows returns the format of cell A10 as a text string, using the same notation as that used on the worksheet. For example, a Currency format with two decimal places appears as C2.

@CELL("*width*",B12..B12)

1-2-3 for Windows returns the width of column B.

Figure 7.37 demonstrates the use of the @CELL and @CELLPOINTER function. Note that only one attribute can be addressed at a time.

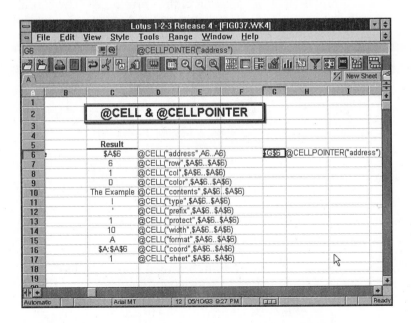

FIG. 7.37

Using @CELL to determine information about the current cell.

The @CELLPOINTER function works well in @IF statements to test whether data in a cell is numeric or text. @CELL and @CELLPOINTER frequently are used in macros to examine the current contents or format of cells. Macros that use IF then can use the results to change the worksheet accordingly.

The difference between @CELL and @CELLPOINTER is important. The @CELL function examines the string attribute of a cell you designate in a range format, such as A6..A6. If you specify a single cell, such as A6, 1-2-3 for Windows changes it to range format (A6..A6) and returns the attribute of the single-cell range. If you define a range larger than a single cell, 1-2-3 for Windows evaluates the cell in the upper left corner of the range.

The @CELLPOINTER function operates on the current cell—the cell where the cell pointer was positioned when the worksheet was last recalculated. The result remains the same as long as the current position of the cell pointer does not change and the worksheet is not recalculated by entering a value or by pressing F9 (Calc).

For example, to determine the address of the current cell, you enter **@CELLPOINTER("address")** with the cell pointer in cell G6 as shown in figure 7.37. If recalculation is set to automatic and the current cell is located at cell G6, the value displayed in that cell is displayed as the absolute address $G$6 of the position of the current cell. The result of the function will remain the same as long as the current cell does not move and the worksheet is not recalculated. If the cell pointer is repositioned to another cell and the worksheet is recalculated, the value in the cell G6 will reflect the current position of the cell pointer.

@COLS, @ROWS, and @SHEETS—Finding the Dimensions of Ranges

The @COLS, @ROWS, and @SHEETS functions describe the dimensions of ranges. Use the following formats for these functions:

@COLS(*range*)

@ROWS(*range*)

@SHEETS(*range*)

Suppose that you want to determine the number of columns in the range PRICE_TABLES, which has the cell coordinates A:D4..C:G50. You also want to display that value in the current cell. To determine the number of columns, enter **@COLS(PRICE_TABLES)**. Similarly, you can enter **@ROWS(PRICE_TABLES)** to display the number of rows in the range and **@SHEETS(PRICE_TABLES)** to display the number of sheets in the range.

@COLS, @ROWS, and @SHEETS are useful in macros to determine the size of a range. After you determine the size of a range, you can use FOR loops to step the macro through all the cells in the range.

If you specify one cell (such as C3) as the argument for the @COLS, @ROWS, or @SHEETS function, 1-2-3 for Windows changes the argument to range format (C3..C3) and the function returns the value 1.

@COORD—Creating a Cell Address

You use @COORD to create an absolute, relative, or mixed cell address. The function uses the following format:

@COORD(*worksheet,column,row,absolute*)

The *worksheet* argument corresponds to the worksheet containing the referenced cell. The *column* and *row* arguments refer to the column and row containing the cell address. The *absolute* argument refers to the exact type of reference (absolute, relative, or mixed) that you want the function to return. Enter the arguments of the @COORD function as numbers in the following manner:

Argument	Acceptable Values
worksheet	1 to 256 (enter **1** for worksheet A, **2** for worksheet B, **3** for worksheet C,...and **256** for worksheet IV)
column	1 to 256 (enter **1** for column A, **2** for column B, **3** for column C,...and **256** for column IV)
row	1 to 8192 (simply enter the row number)
absolute	1 to 8 (see table 7.7 for an explanation of these numbers)

When you use @COORD, the function returns the actual address, not a value. If you want to change the cell address A:A6 to the mixed address A:A$1, use this function: @COORD(1,1,1,6); the function returns the address A:A$1"—or whatever the function actually does return.

Table 7.7 Values of the *absolute* Argument

Value	Worksheet	Column	Row	Example
1	Absolute	Absolute	Absolute	$A:$A$1
2	Absolute	Relative	Absolute	$A:A$1

continues

Value	Worksheet	Column	Row	Example
3	Absolute	Absolute	Relative	$A:$A1
4	Absolute	Relative	Relative	$A:A1
5	Relative	Absolute	Absolute	A:$A$1
6	Relative	Relative	Absolute	A:A$1
7	Relative	Absolute	Relative	A:$A1
8	Relative	Relative	Relative	A:A1

@REFCONVERT—Convert the Column Headings

The @REFCONVERT function converts the worksheet column headings. The syntax is:

```
@REFCONVERT(reference)
```

reference is the letter or number that corresponds to the column heading you want to convert. An example of the @REFCONVERT(reference) function is:

```
@REFCONVERT(10) = J
```

```
@REFCONVERT("J") = 10
```

@INFO—Getting System Information about the Current Session

The @INFO function enables you to tap 14 types of system information for the current session. Use the following syntax for @INFO:

```
@INFO(attribute)
```

The *attribute* argument is a text string and must be enclosed in quotation marks. Table 7.8 summarizes the attributes you can check by using @INFO.

Table 7.8 Session Attributes

Attribute	Description
"dbreturncode"	Returns the most recent error code from an external database driver
"dbdrivermessage"	Returns the most recent message from an external database driver
"dbrecordcount"	Returns the number of records processed in the most recent query to an external database
"directory"	Returns the current directory path
"memavail"	Returns the amount of memory available, in bytes
"mode"	Returns a numeric code indicating one of the following modes:

0	Wait mode
1	Ready mode
2	Label mode
3	Menu mode
4	Value mode
5	Point mode
6	Edit mode
7	Error mode
8	Find mode
9	Files mode
10	Help mode
11	Stat mode
13	Names mode
99	All other modes (such as those set by the INDICATE command)

Attribute	Description
"numfile"	Returns the number of currently open files
"origin"	Returns the cell address of the first cell in the window with the cell pointer
"osreturncode"	Returns the value returned by the most recent operating system command
"osversion"	Returns the current operating system description

continues

Table 7.8 Continued

Attribute	Description
"recalc"	Returns the current recalculation setting
"release"	Returns the 1-2-3 for Windows release number
"system"	Returns the name of the operating system
"totmem"	Returns the total amount of memory, in bytes (used plus available)

Figure 7.38 demonstrates some of the system information returned.

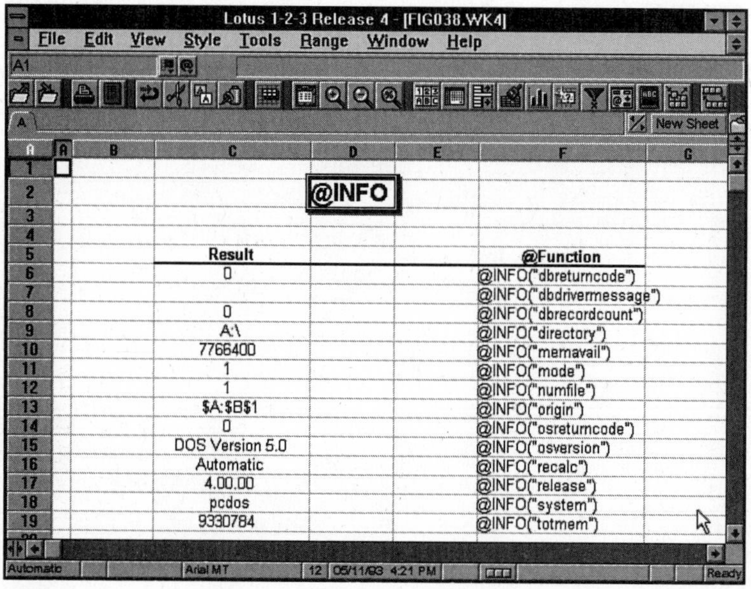

FIG. 7.38

Using @INFO to obtain information about the system.

The values returned by @INFO are useful in macros that monitor such things as application memory size, the current mode, or the current directory. After the macro obtains this information, it can warn users to make changes in their activities, upgrade their systems, and so on.

@SOLVER—Getting Information about Solver

The @SOLVER function enables you to determine the status of the Solver utility. Usually, @SOLVER is run from a macro so that the macro first can start Solver and then monitor Solver's status, making changes or requesting information if necessary. The Solver utility is discussed in Chapter 8, "Solving Formulas and Auditing Worksheets." @SOLVER uses the following syntax:

@SOLVER(*query-string*)

The *query-string* argument can be one of the eight strings listed in table 7.9. Notice that no spaces are used in the query string and that the string must be enclosed in quotation marks.

Table 7.9 String Arguments for @SOLVER

Query String	Value Returned	Description
"consistent" (Are constraints satisfied?)	1	All constraints are true (1)
	2	One or more constraints are false (0), not satisfied
	ERR	Solver not active or no answer
"done" (Is Solver done?)	1	Solver finished
	2	Still solving
	3	Solver active but not started
	ERR	Solver not active
"moreanswers" (Are there more answers?)	1	All answers found
	2	More answers may be found if you continue with Solver
"needguess" (Is a guess needed?)	1	No guess is needed
	2	Guess needed
	ERR	Solver inactive or no answer
"numanswers" (How many answers or attempts resulted?)	*n*	Number of answers found or number of Solver attempts
	ERR	Solver not active or still running

continues

Table 7.9 String Arguments for @SOLVER

Query String	Value Returned	Description
"optimal" (What type of answer was found?)	1	Optimal answer found
	2	Best answer found
	3	Problem unbounded
	4	No answer or optimization not requested
	ERR	Solver inactive or not started
"progress" (What is Solver's progress in finding an answer?)	n	Percentage complete as a decimal
	ERR	Solver inactive or not started
"result" (What is the result?)	1	One or more answers found
	2	No valid answers found
	ERR	Solver inactive or no solution found yet

The @SOLVER function does not recalculate when 1-2-3 for Windows recalculates. When you use @SOLVER in a macro, make sure that you use RECALC or RECALCCOL to recalculate the @SOLVER results.

Error-Checking Functions

These functions allow you to trap errors in your worksheet.

@ERR and @NA—Trapping Errors

When you set up templates for other people, you may want to use @NA or @ERR to screen out unacceptable values for cells. Suppose that you are developing a checkbook-balancing macro in which checks with values less than or equal to 0 are unacceptable. One way to indicate the unacceptability of such checks is to use @ERR to signal that fact. You can use the following version of the @IF function to check the value of the check and invoke @ERR if the value is less than 0:

```
@IF(B9<=0,@ERR,B9) or @IF(B9<=0,@ERR,B9)
```

In plain English, this statement says, "If the amount in cell B9 is less than or equal to 0, display ERR or NA on-screen; otherwise, use the amount." Notice that the @ERR function controls the display in almost the same way that @NA does in a preceding example. Another practice is to display a message to the operator that indicates the specific error, as in the following example:

```
@IF(B9<=0,"Enter positive amounts",B9)
```

1-2-3 for Windows also uses ERR as a signal for unacceptable numbers—for example, if you divide by 0 or mistakenly delete cells. ERR often shows up temporarily when you reorganize the cells in a worksheet. If ERR persists, you may have to do some careful analysis to figure out why.

1-2-3 for Windows displays ERR (as it does NA) in any cells that depend on a cell with an ERR value. Sometimes, the ERR cascades through other dependent cells. Use Edit Undo or Alt+Backspace to return the worksheet to the way it was before the change. See Chapter 3, "Learning Worksheet Basics," for more information about Edit Undo.

Using Logical Functions

The logical functions enable you to use Boolean logic within the worksheets. Most logical functions test whether a condition is true or false.

For most logical functions, the test—and what the function returns based on the test—are built into the function. The @ISSTRING function is a good example because this function tests whether the argument is a string and returns a 1 if the test is true or a 0 if the test is false. For one of the logical functions, @IF, you describe the test and what the function result should be, based on the test. @IF tests a condition and returns one value or label if the test is true or another value or label if the test is false.

The logical functions 1-2-3 for Windows provides are summarized in table 7.10. The following sections described the logical functions.

Table 7.10 Logical Functions

Function	Description
@FALSE	Equals 0, the logical value for false
@IF(*test*,*true-result*, *false-result*)	Tests the condition and returns one result if the condition is true and another result if the condition is false
@ISAAF(*name*)	Tests whether an add-in function is defined
@ISAPP(*name*)	Tests whether an add-in is currently in memory
@ISMACRO(*name*)	Tests name for a defined add-in macro command
@ISERR(*cell-reference*)	Tests whether the argument results in ERR
@ISFILE(*filename*)	Tests *filename* for a file on the disk
@ISNA(*cell-reference*)	Tests whether the argument results in NA
@ISNUMBER (*cell-reference*)	Tests whether the argument is a number
@ISRANGE (*cell-reference*)	Tests whether the argument is a defined range
@ISSTRING (*cell-reference*)	Tests whether the argument is a string
@TRUE	Equals 1, the logical value for true

@IF—Creating Conditional Tests

The @IF function represents a powerful tool—one you can use to manipulate text within worksheets and to affect calculations. For example, you can use the @IF function to test the condition "Is the inventory on hand below 1,000 units?" and then return one value or string if the answer to the question is true and another value or string if the answer is false. The @IF function uses the following syntax:

@IF(*test*,*true-result*,*false-result*)

Figure 7.39 shows several examples of the @IF function in action. To show clearly the functions, their arguments, and their results, the first column displays the value, the second column shows the calculated results of the function, and the third column shows the formula.

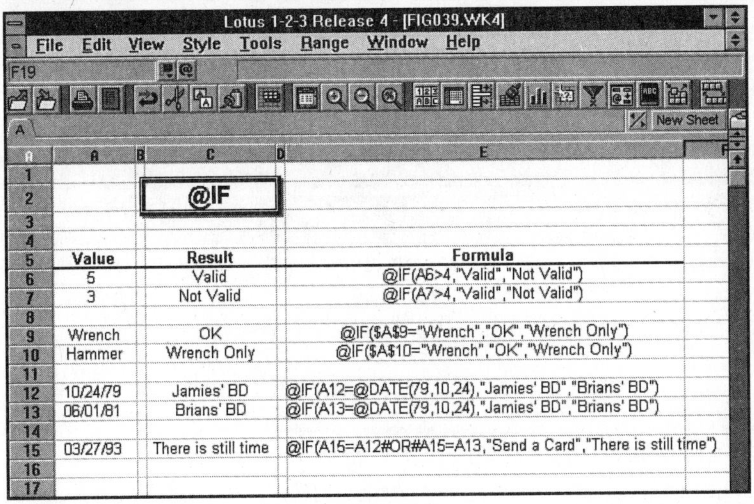

FIG. 7.39

Examples of @IF functions that use strings and numeric values.

The first two @IF functions check whether the contents of cell A6 or A7 is greater than 4. The second two @IF functions check whether a cell contains the text string *Wrench*. The next two examples check whether the dates in B12 and B13 are on or after October 24, 1979.

The @IF function can use any of six operators when testing conditions. These operators are summarized in table 7.11.

Table 7.11 Logical Test Operators

Operator	Description
<	Less than
<=	Less than or equal to
=	Equal to
>=	Greater than or equal to
>	Greater than
<>	Not equal to

As figure 7.39 shows, the @IF function is a powerful tool, enabling you to add decision-making logic to worksheets. The logical test can be based on string or numeric comparison; the function can return string or numeric values. You can further expand the power of @IF functions by using compound tests.

You also can do complex conditional tests by using @IF functions with logical operators that enable you to test multiple conditions in one @IF function. These complex operators are summarized in table 7.12.

Table 7.12 Complex Operators	
Operator	**Description**
#AND#	Used to test two conditions, both of which must be true for the entire test to be true
#NOT#	Used to test that a condition is *not* true
#OR#	Used to test two conditions; if either condition is true, the entire test condition is true.

One simple but valuable use for complex @IF functions is to test whether data entries are in the correct range of numbers. Consider the following formula:

```
@IF(A15=A12#OR#A15=A13,"Send a Card","There is Still Time")
```

This formula compares the contents of cell A15 against two other cells (A12 and A13); if A15 is the same as either A12 or A13, the string *Send a card* is inserted into the current cell; if A15 does not equal either A12 or A13, the string *There is still time* appears in the current cell.

Within an @IF function, you also can use as the *true-result* or *false-result* argument another @IF function. Putting @IF functions inside other @IF functions is a common and important logical tool. This technique, called a *nested @IF*, gives you the ability to construct sophisticated logical tests and operations in your 1-2-3 worksheets.

@ISAAF, @ISAPP, and @ISMACRO— Checking for Add-Ins

The @ISAAF function tests whether the specified add-in function is defined. The syntax is as follows:

```
@ISAAF(name)
```

If the *name* argument is a defined add-in function, the @ISAAF function returns the value 1. If the *name* argument is a built-in 1-2-3 for Windows function or is an unknown function, the @ISAAF function returns the value 0. For example, @ISAAF("orbit") returns the value 1 if @ORBIT is a defined add-in function.

The @ISAPP function tests whether the specified add-in application is currently in memory. The syntax is as follows:

@ISAPP(*name*)

If the *name* argument is the name of an add-in currently in memory, the @ISAPP function returns the value 0. For example, @ISAPP("fincalc") returns the value of 1 if FINCALC is the name of an add-in currently in memory.

The @ISMACRO function tests the *name* argument to see whether it is a defined add-in macro name. The syntax is:

@ISAMACRO(*name*)

If the result is true, a 1 is returned; otherwise a 0 (false) is returned. Suppose that you were using a macro with the defined macro command {CHECKS}, and you wanted to see whether the command was valid. Enter **@ISMACRO("checks")** (the result, by the way, would be 1).

 NOTE When you use the @ISMACRO function, do not include the curly braces ({ }) in the *name* argument. For example, you enter **@ISMACRO("checks")** and not @ISMACRO({CHECKS}). The *name* argument is not case sensitive; you can enter **checks** or **CHECKS**.

@ISAAF, @ISAPP and @ISMACRO are used primarily in macros to avoid errors if certain expected add-ins are not currently available.

@ISERR and @ISNA—Trapping Errors in Conditional Tests

The @ISERR function tests whether the argument equals ERR. If the test is true, the function returns the value 1; if the test is false, the function returns the value 0. Use the following syntax for @ISERR:

@ISERR(*cell-reference*)

This function is handy because you can use it to trap errors produced in one location that may cause more drastic results in other locations. Figure 7.40 shows how to use @ISERR to trap a possible division-by-zero error or a serious data-entry error that can cause an error to appear on-screen or in the printout.

> **NOTE**   The cell-reference argument does not have to be a simple cell reference. As in figure 7.40, the argument can do some simple arithmetic (such as divide two cells to determine whether an error exists before the actual division result is displayed in the cell).

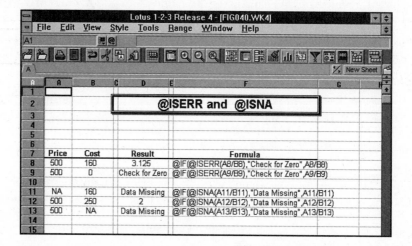

FIG. 7.40

Using @ISERR and @ISNA used to test for errors.

The @ISNA function works in a similar way. @ISNA tests whether the argument is equal to NA. If the test is true, the function returns the value 1; if the test is false, the function returns the value 0. The @ISNA function uses the following syntax:

`@ISNA(cell-reference)`

You can use the @ISNA, the @NA function represents "Not Available," function to trap NA values in worksheets in which you use the @NA function.

@TRUE and @FALSE—Checking for Errors

Use the @TRUE and @FALSE functions to check for errors. Neither function requires arguments. These functions are useful for providing documentation for formulas and advanced macro commands. The @TRUE function returns the value 1, the Boolean logical value for true. @FALSE returns the value 0, the Boolean logical value for false.

@ISRANGE—Checking for a Range Name

@ISRANGE checks whether the argument is a valid range. The range can be a valid cell address or a range name. If it is, the function returns the value 1; otherwise, the function returns the value 0. The syntax of @ISRANGE is as follows:

```
@ISRANGE(cell-reference)
```

The *cell-reference* argument can be a cell reference to a string or the string itself. The string need not be a text label; the string can be a cell reference containing a text label or a formula that returns a text label.

One of the best uses of @ISRANGE is within macro programs that test for the existence of range names. The following statement from a print macro, for example, tests for the existence of the range name PRINTAREA:

```
{IF @ISRANGE(PRINTAREA)=1}{SUBPRINT}
```

Translated, this statement says the following: If the range name PRINTAREA exists, @ISRANGE returns the value 1 (making the IF statement true); the macro then executes the subroutine to print the PRINTAREA range. If PRINTAREA does not exist, @ISRANGE returns the value 0 (making the IF statement false); the macro continues without branching to the print subroutine.

@ISSTRING and @ISNUMBER—Checking the Cell's Aspect

Two functions that help determine the type of value stored in a cell are @ISSTRING and @ISNUMBER. These functions often are used with @IF to check for data-entry errors—numbers entered in the place of text or text entered in the place of numbers. Use the following format for @ISNUMBER:

```
@ISNUMBER(cell-reference)
```

If the *cell-reference* argument is a number, the function returns 1 (true). If the *cell-reference* argument is a string, including the null string " " (nothing), the function returns 0 (false).

Suppose that you want to test whether the value entered in cell B3 is a number. If the value is a number, you want to show the label *number* in the current cell; otherwise, you want to show the label *string*. Use the following statement to accomplish this goal:

```
@IF(@ISNUMBER(B3),"number","string")
```

With this statement, you can be fairly certain that the appropriate label appears in the current cell. The @ISNUMBER function, however, returns 1 (true) after testing empty cells as well as cells containing numbers. Obviously, the function is incomplete because it assigns the label *number* to the current cell if cell B3 is empty. For complete reliability, the statement must be modified to handle empty cells.

 NOTE   Use the @CELL function to check whether a cell is empty or contains a numeric value. The @CELL function is explained earlier in this chapter in the section on information functions.

A complete test that determines whether cell B3 is blank, contains a numeric value, or contains a string value, is shown in the following example:

```
@IF(@CELL("type",B3)="b","blank",
@IF(@ISNUMBER(B3),"number","string"))
```

The first part of this formula uses @CELL to determine whether the cell type is "b" (which stands for blank). If this test is true, the formula results in the label *blank*. If this test is false, the next step is to use @ISNUMBER to test whether the cell contains a number. If the second test is true, the formula results in the label *number*. If the second test is false, the formula results in the label *string*.

Alternatively, you may want to use the @ISSTRING function. @ISSTRING works in nearly the same way as @ISNUMBER. The @ISSTRING function, however, determines whether a cell entry is a string value. Use the following syntax with this function:

```
@ISSTRING(cell-reference)
```

If the *cell-reference* argument for @ISSTRING is a string, the value of the function is 1 (true). If the *cell-reference* argument is a number or is blank, however, the value of the function is 0 (false).

Returning to the preceding example that discriminates between a number and an empty cell, you also can complete the function with the help of @ISSTRING, as follows:

```
@IF(@CELL("type",B3)="b","blank",
@IF(@ISSTRING(B3),"string","number"))
```

The first part of this formula uses @CELL to determine whether the cell type is "b" (which stands for blank). If this test is true, the formula results in the label *blank*. If this test is false, the next step is to use @ISSTRING to test whether the cell contains a string. If the second test is true, the formula results in the label *string*. If the second test is false, the formula results in the label *number*.

Using Lookup Functions

1-2-3 for Windows provides a group of functions that service the contents of a cell or a group of cells. These functions are very useful in a variety of situations, from locating the contents of a cell in a macro to matching the contents of a cell. Table 7.13 lists the lookup functions available.

Table 7.13 Lookup Functions

Function	Description
@@(*cell-address*)	Returns the contents of the cell referenced by the cell address in the argument
@CHOOSE(*offset*,*list*)	Locates in a list the entry offset a specified amount from the front of the list
@HLOOKUP(*key*,*range*, *row-offset*)	Locates the specified key in a lookup table and returns a value from that row of the range
@INDEX(*range*, *column-offset*, *row-offset*, [*worksheet-offset*])	Returns the contents of a cell specified by the intersection of a row and column within a range on a designated worksheet
@MATCH(*cell-contents*, *range*,[*type*])	Returns the position of the cell in *range* whose contents match *cell-contents*
@VLOOKUP(*key*,*range*, *column-offset*)	Locates the specified key in a lookup table and returns a value from that column of the range
@XINDEX(*range*, *column-heading*, *row-heading*, [*worksheet-heading*])	Returns the contents of a cell located at the intersection specified by *column-heading*, *row-heading*, and the optional *worksheet-heading*

@@—Referencing Cells Indirectly

The @@ function provides a way to indirectly reference one cell through the contents of another cell. Use the following format for this function:

@@(*cell-address*)

Simple examples best show how the @@ function works. If cell A1 contains the label 'A2, and cell A2 contains the number 5, then the function @@(A1) returns the value 5. If the label in cell A1 is changed to 'B10, and cell B10 contains the label 'hi there, the function @@(A1) returns the string value *hi there*.

The argument of the @@ function must be a cell reference for a cell containing an address. This address is an *indirect address*. Similarly, the cell referenced by the argument of the @@ function must contain a string value that evaluates to a cell reference. This cell can contain a label, a string formula, or a reference to another cell—as long as the resulting string value is a cell reference.

The @@ function is useful primarily in cases where several formulas have the same argument, and the argument must be changed from time to time during the course of the application. 1-2-3 for Windows enables you to specify the argument of each formula through a common indirect address, as shown in figure 7.41.

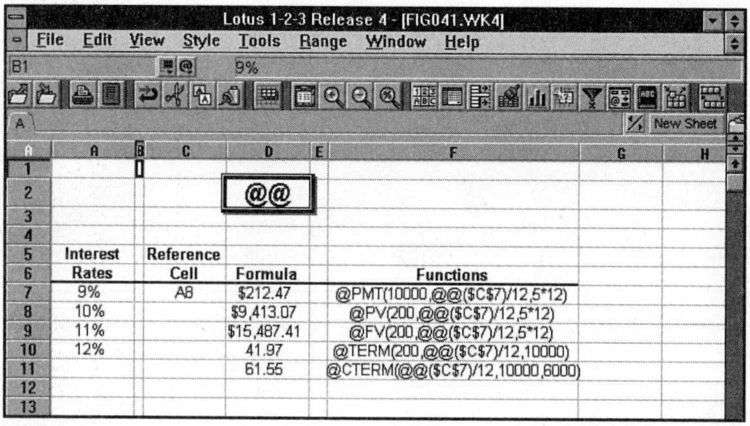

FIG. 7.41

Using @@ to reference one cell indirectly through another cell.

In figure 7.41, columns E and G contain a variety of financial functions, all of which use the @@ function to indirectly reference one of seven interest rates in column A through cell C7. When you are ready to change the cell being referenced, you change only the label in cell C7 instead of editing all five formulas in column E or G.

@CHOOSE—Selecting an Item from a List

The @CHOOSE function selects an item from a list according to the item's position in the list. The syntax of the function is as follows:

@CHOOSE(*offset*,*list*)

The function selects the item in the specified position, or *offset*, in the specified *list*. Keep in mind that positions in the list are numbered starting with 0. For example, the first position is 0; the second is 1; the third is 2; and so on.

Figure 7.42 shows examples of the @CHOOSE function. If the *offset* argument is not an integer, the decimal portion of the offset is ignored: an offset of 3.9 is treated as an offset of 3.

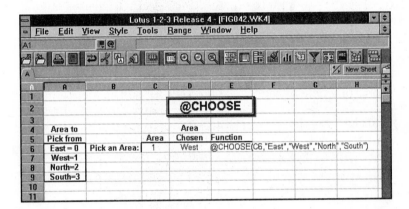

FIG. 7.42

Using @CHOOSE to select an item from a list.

@HLOOKUP and @VLOOKUP—Looking Up Entries in a Table

The @HLOOKUP and @VLOOKUP functions retrieve a string or value from a table, based on a specified key used to find the information. The operation and format of the two functions are essentially the same except that @HLOOKUP looks through *horizontal* tables (hence, the *H* in the function's name) and @VLOOKUP looks through *vertical* tables (the source of the *V* in its name). Use the following syntax for these functions:

@HLOOKUP(*key*,*range*,*row-offset*)

@VLOOKUP(*key*,*range*,*column-offset*)

When you use numeric *key* arguments, make sure that the key values in the table range are in ascending order; otherwise, you may get an incorrect value. (In contrast, if the keys are strings, they can be listed in any order.) When you use numeric keys, @HLOOKUP and @VLOOKUP actually search for the largest value less than or equal to the specified *key*. If either of these functions cannot find a value equal to *key*, the function picks the largest value less than *key*.

The *range* argument is the area that makes up the entire lookup table. The *offset* argument specifies which row or column contains the data you are looking up. This argument is always a number, in ascending order, ranging from 0 to the highest number of columns or rows in the lookup table. The offset number 0 marks the column or row containing key data. The next column or row is 1; the next is 2; and so on. When you specify an offset number, the number cannot be negative or exceed the correct number of columns or rows.

Suppose that you have taken a job as the tax accountant for Jabr Computer Services. You want to create a worksheet that figures out the state tax for all employees. This is pretty straightforward except that, for some reason, employees are constantly changing their filing status. When the filing status changes, you must change the formula that computes the tax. Figure 7.43 shows a @VLOOKUP table that solves your problem. You can see how @VLOOKUP (or @HLOOKUP) can be useful for finding any type of value you may have to look up manually in a table, such as price changes in inventory items, tax rates, shipping zones, or interest charges.

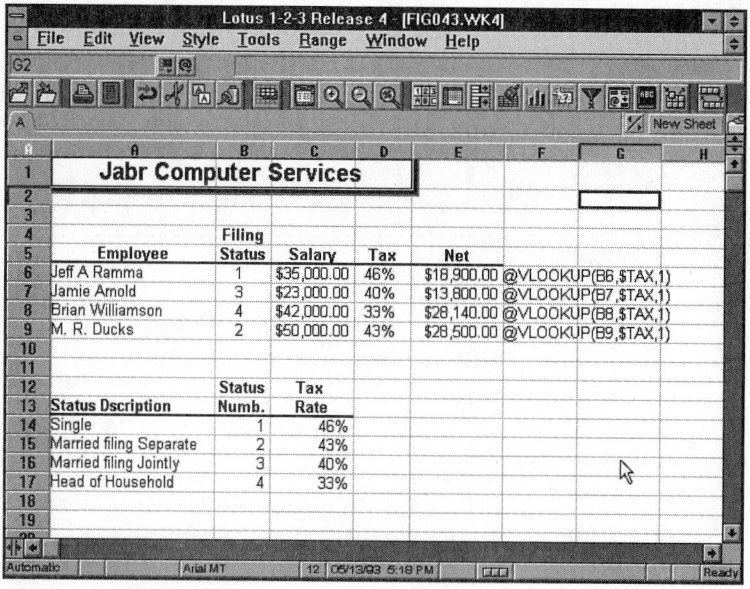

FIG. 7.43

Using @VLOOKUP to retrieve strings and values from tables.

Watch for these three common errors when you construct @HLOOKUP and @VLOOKUP functions:

- When you use a string as the *key* argument, the lookup function returns ERR if the function cannot find the string in the lookup table. If either function with a string key returns ERR, make sure that you haven't misspelled the string in the function or in the lookup table.

- If you fail to include the columns or rows that contain the key strings or values in the *range* argument for the lookup table, the result is ERR. The example in figure 7.43 uses cell addresses to define the lookup table so that you can understand the example easily. However, you will probably name your lookup tables; be aware that naming lookup tables can make spotting missing rows or columns more difficult.

- Do not place the *key* argument's strings or values in the wrong row or column. Remember that the *key* strings or values belong in the first column or row of the lookup table; column and row numbering starts at 0—at the row or column containing the key. Accordingly, the first row or column offset is 0 (the row or column containing the key); the second row or column is 1; the third is 2, and so on.

@INDEX and @XINDEX—Retrieving Data from Specified Locations

@INDEX and @XINDEX are data management functions similar to the lookup functions described in the preceding section. @INDEX and @XINDEX have some unique features. Use the following syntax for @INDEX:

`@INDEX(range,column-offset,row-offset,[worksheet-offset])`

Use the following syntax for @XINDEX:

`@XINDEX(range,column-heading,row-heading,`
`[worksheet-heading])`

Like @HLOOKUP and @VLOOKUP, @INDEX and @XINDEX find a value within a table. Unlike the lookup functions, however, @INDEX does not compare a key value against values in the first row or column of the table. Instead, @INDEX requires you to indicate the *column-offset* and *row-offset* of the *range* from which you want to retrieve data. Figure 7.44 shows an example of the @INDEX function that returns the employee's name, *M.R. Ducks*, in E13 and salary, $28,500.00, in G13.

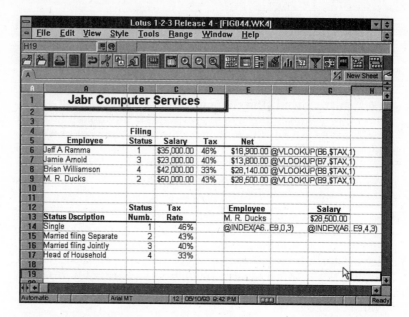

FIG. 7.44

An example of
@INDEX.

The @INDEX function uses number offsets to refer to the columns and rows. 0 corresponds to the first column; 1 corresponds to the second column; and so on. The same numbering scheme applies to rows. Using 3 for the *column-offset* argument and 2 for the *row-offset* argument indicates that you want an item from the fourth column, third row. If you use the @XINDEX function, however, you can use number offsets *or* the text of the column and row headings (see fig. 7.45).

With the @INDEX and the @XINDEX functions, you cannot use column, row, or worksheet numbers outside the specified *range*. Using negative numbers or numbers too large for the range causes 1-2-3 for Windows to return ERR.

The *worksheet-offset* number enables you to work in three-dimensional ranges. Offset numbering starts at 0: the first worksheet in a range is specified as 0; the second worksheet is specified as 1; and so on. The *worksheet-offset* argument is optional.

@MATCH—Locating the Position of a Cell Given the Contents

The @MATCH function returns the location of the cell whose contents you are searching for. The data type you are searching for can be either text or a number value. Use the following syntax for the @MATCH function:

@MATCH(*cell-contents*,*range*,[*type*])

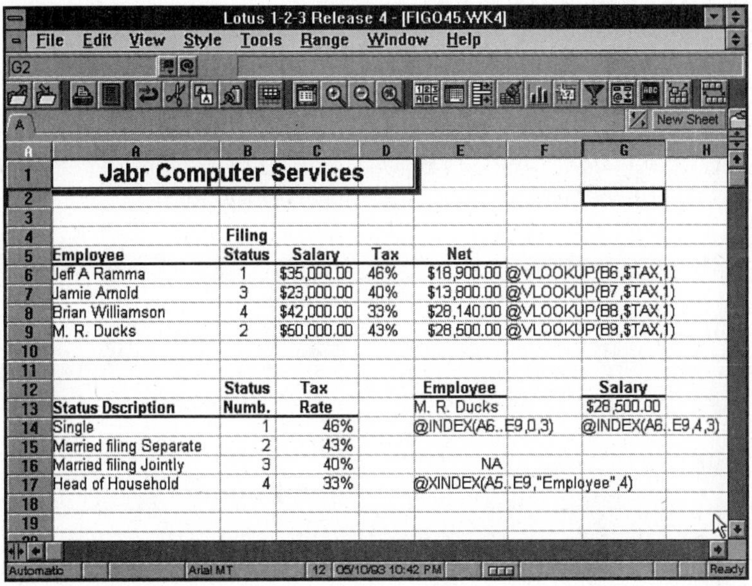

FIG. 7.45

An example of @XINDEX.

The arguments for the @MATCH function are as follows:

cell-contents	The value of the information you are searching for. The value can be text (enclosed in quotation marks) or numeric. 1-2-3 enables you to include wild cards to aid in your search.
range	The range name or address of the data you are searching from.
[*type*]	An optional argument that specifies how you want 1-2-3 to look for the data. The switches for the [*type*] argument are as follows:

Type	How @MATCH Proceeds with the Search
0	The first cell that matches the *cell-contents* argument (the default if [*type*] is omitted)

1   The first cell in which the match is less than or equal to the *cell-contents* argument

2   The first cell in which the match is greater than or equal to the *cell-contents* argument

@MATCH searches the rows of a column from top to bottom; it searches columns from left to right until it finds a match. The value returned by the function is a numerical value that indicates the offset from the upper left cell of the range you are searching. (The cells in the range are numbered down the columns and then across the rows; in the range A1..D4—a 16-cell range—an offset of 4 refers to cell B1.) Figure 7.46 shows an example of the @MATCH function.

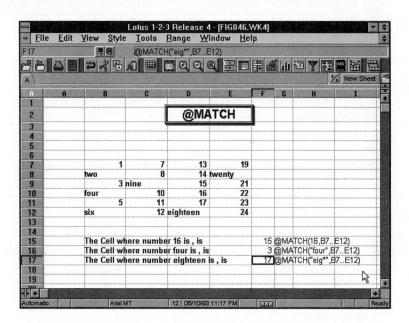

FIG. 7.46

Using @MATCH to locate values in a table.

Here are some key points to remember when you use @MATCH:

- 1-2-3 scans the range from top to bottom, left to right.

- The function returns a value that is an offset number. 1-2-3 for Windows starts counting the cells in the range with 0 and increments by 1 until the match is made.

- You can search for numbers as well as text. If you search for text, remember to place the string in quotation marks (for example, if you are searching for the text *dog*, type **"dog"** as the *cell-contents* argument).

- You can use wild cards for the search.

Using Mathematical Functions

1-2-3 for Windows provides mathematical functions that perform most of the common—and some of the more specialized—mathematical operations. 1-2-3 for Windows offers five general mathematical categories of functions to simplify calculations. The categories are Conversion, General, Hyperbolic, Rounding, and Trigonometric. Table 7.14 provides a list of the categories and the functions in each, along with brief descriptions of what these functions do.

Table 7.14 Mathematical Functions

Conversion Functions	Description
@DEGTORAD(*degrees*)	Converts degrees to radians
@RADTODEG(*radians*)	Converts radians to degrees

General Functions	Description
@ABS(*number*)	Computes the absolute value of the argument
@EXP(*number*)	Computes the number *e* raised to the power of the argument
@EXP2(*number*)	Computes the number *e* raised to the negative of a specified power squared
@FACT(*number*)	Calculates the factorial of a value
@FACTLN(*number*)	Calculates the natural log of the factorial of a value
@INT(*number*)	Computes the integer portions of a specified number
@LARGE(*range,number*)	Finds the largest specific position of a value in a range of numbers
@LN(*number*)	Calculates the natural logarithm of a specified number
@LOG(*number*)	Calculates the common, or base 10, logarithm of a specified number
@MOD(*number,divisor*)	Computes the remainder, or modulus, of a division operation
@QUOTIENT(*number,divisor*)	Calculates the integer portion of the result of a division calculation

continues

Table 7.14 Continued

Conversion Functions	Description
@RAND	Generates a random number
@SIGN(*range,number*)	Returns the sign of a value
@SMALL(*number*)	Finds the smallest specific position of a value in a range of numbers
@SQRT(*number*)	Computes the square root of a number
@SQRTPI(*number*)	Computes the square root of a number and multiplies it by pi

Hyperbolic Functions	Description
@ACOSH(*angle*)	Calculates the arc hyperbolic cosine of an angle
@ACOTH(*angle*)	Calculates the arc hyperbolic cotangent of an angle
@ACSCH(*angle*)	Calculates the arc hyperbolic cosecant of an angle
@ASECH(*angle*)	Calculates the arc hyperbolic secant of an angle
@ASINH(*angle*)	Calculates the arc hyperbolic sine of an angle
@ATANH(*angle*)	Calculates the arc hyperbolic tangent of an angle
@COSH(*angle*)	Calculates the hyperbolic cosine of an angle
@COTH(*angle*)	Calculates the hyperbolic cotangent of an angle
@CSCH(*angle*)	Calculates the hyperbolic cosecant of an angle
@SECH(*angle*)	Calculates the hyperbolic secant of an angle
@SINH(*angle*)	Calculates the hyperbolic sine of an angle
@TANH(*angle*)	Calculates the hyperbolic tangent of an angle

Rounding Functions	Descriptions
@EVEN(*number*)	Rounds a value to the nearest even integer, away from 0
@ODD(*number*)	Rounds a value to the nearest odd integer, away from 0
@ROUND(*number,precision*)	Rounds a number to a specified precision
@ROUNDDOWN(*number,* [*precision*])	Rounds a value to the nearest multiple of the power of 10, specified by the optional precision value
@ROUNDM(*number, precision,*[*direction*])	Rounds a value to a specified multiple for a given direction or power of 10
@ROUNDUP(*number,* [*precision*])	Rounds a value to the nearest multiple of the power of 10, specified by the optional precision value
@TRUNC(*number,*[*precision*])	Truncates a value to the number of decimal places specified by the optional precision value

Trigonometric Functions	Description
@ACOS(*angle*)	Calculates the arccosine, given an angle in radians
@ACOT(*angle*)	Calculates the arccotangent, given an angle in radians
@ACSC(*angle*)	Calculates the arccosecant, given an angle in radians
@ASEC(*angle*)	Calculates the arcsecant, given an angle in radians
@ASIN(*angle*)	Calculates the arcsine, given an angle in radians
@ATAN(*angle*)	Calculates the arctangent, given an angle in radians
@ATAN2(*number1,number2*)	Calculates the four-quadrant arctangent
@COS(*angle*)	Calculates the cosine, given an angle in radians

continues

Table 7.14 Continued

Trigonometric Functions	Description
@COT(*angle*)	Calculates the cotangent, given an angle in radians
@CSC(*angle*)	Calculates the cosecant, given an angle in radians
@PI	Returns the value of pi: 3.14159265358979324
@SEC(*angle*)	Calculates the secant, given an angle in radians
@SIN(*angle*)	Calculates the sine, given an angle in radians
@TAN(*angle*)	Calculates the tangent, given an angle in radians

Conversion Functions

The conversion functions deal with the angular measurements of radians and degrees.

@DEGTORAD and @RADTODEG—Changing Degrees to Radians and Radians to Degrees

The @DEGTORAD and @RADTODEG functions easily convert angular measurements. The syntax for these functions are as follows:

@DEGTORAD(*degrees*)

@RADTODEG(*radians*)

Degrees and radians are units of angular measurements, thus both are values in the arguments. Examples of conversions are shown in figure 7.47.

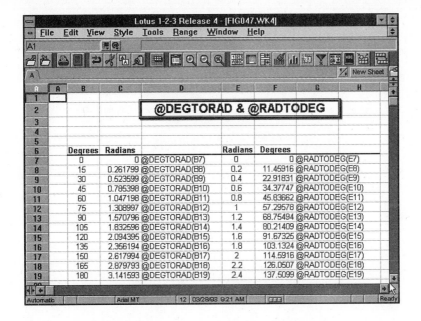

FIG. 7.47

Using
@DEGTORAD
and
@RADTODEG to
convert angular
measurements.

General Mathematical Functions

@ABS—Computing Absolute Value

The @ABS function calculates the absolute value of a number. Use the following syntax for this function:

@ABS(*number*)

The @ABS function has one argument, *number*, which can be a numeric value or the cell reference of a numeric value. The result of @ABS is the positive value of its argument. @ABS converts a negative value to its equivalent positive value. @ABS has no effect on positive values.

The @ABS function is useful for showing the difference between two values regardless of whether the difference is positive or negative. Figure 7.48 shows an example that uses @IF and @ABS to calculate the difference between two values. @ABS can be helpful if used with @IF to determine whether two numbers are within a specific range, regardless of which is greater. In data-entry macros, use @ABS to ensure that an entered number results in a positive or negative number, regardless of what the user typed. @ABS also can be helpful for some trigonometric calculations.

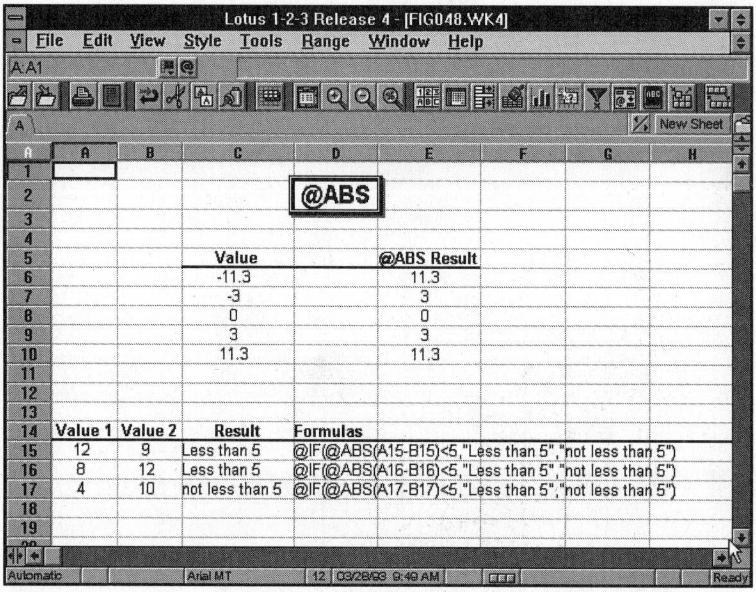

FIG. 7.48

Using @ABS and @IF to calculate the difference between two numbers.

@EXP—Finding Powers of e

The @EXP function calculates e (approximately 2.718282), raised to the power of the argument. @EXP uses the following syntax:

@EXP(*number*)

Do not use an argument larger than 709 with this function. With @EXP, you can create very large numbers quickly. If the function's resulting value is too large to be displayed, 1-2-3 for Windows displays asterisks. Figure 7.49 shows the result of the @EXP function.

@EXP2—Finding Powers of e Squared

The @EXP2 function calculates e (approximately 2.718282), raised to the power (x^2). @EXP uses the following syntax:

@EXP(*number*)

Do not use an argument larger than approximately 106.57 or one smaller than –106.57; if you do, the calculation results in ERR. Figure 7.49 shows the result of the @EXP2 function.

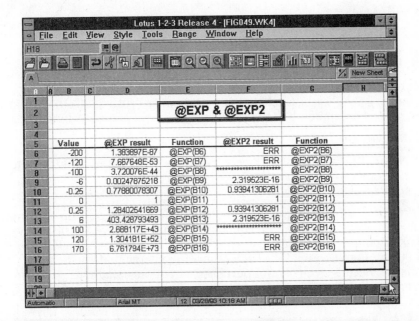

FIG. 7.49

Using @EXP and @EXP2 to calculate powers of *e*.

@FACT—Calculating the Factorial of an Integer

@FACT calculates the factorial of a number. The syntax for @FACT is as follows:

@FACT(*number*)

The factorial of a number is the product of all positive integers from 1 to *number*. The argument *number* can be any positive integer or 0. If *number* is greater than or equal to the integer 1755, the result is ERR because the result is too large for 1-2-3 for Windows to store.

@FACTLN—Calculating the Natural Log of a Factorial

@FACTLN calculates the natural log of the factorial of a number. The syntax for @FACTLN is as follows:

@FACTLN(*number*)

The argument *number* is any positive integer or 0. Following is an example of @FACTLN—the function actually calculates ln(1*2*3*4*5*6*7):

```
@FACTLN(7) = 8.525161
```

@INT—Computing the Integer

The @INT function converts a decimal number into an *integer* (a whole number). @INT creates an integer by *truncating* (cutting off) the decimal portion of a number. Use the following syntax for the @INT function:

```
@INT(number)
```

@INT has one argument, *number*, which can be a numeric value or the cell reference of a numeric value. The result of applying @INT to the values 3.1, 4.5, and 5.9 yields integer values of 3, 4, and 5.

@INT is useful for computations in which the decimal portion of a number is irrelevant or insignificant. Suppose that you have $1,000 to invest in XYZ company and that shares of XYZ sell for $17 each. You divide 1,000 by 17 to compute the total number of shares that can be purchased. Because you cannot purchase a fractional share, use @INT to truncate the decimal portion (see fig. 7.50).

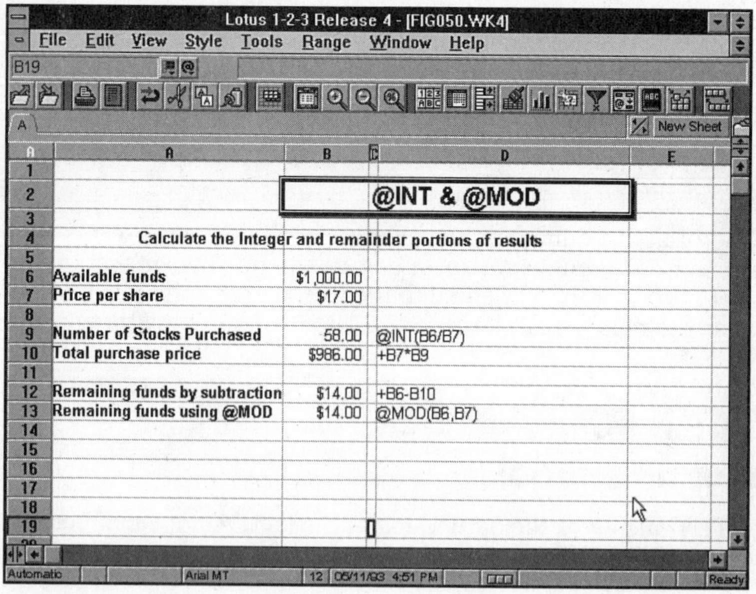

FIG. 7.50

Using @INT to calculate the number of shares and @MOD to calculate the remainder.

NOTE   Do not confuse the @INT and @ROUND functions. @ROUND rounds decimal numbers to the nearest integer; @INT cuts off the decimal portion, leaving the integer.

@LARGE—Finding the Largest Value in a Range

@LARGE finds the *n*th largest value in a *range* of values. The range of values can be a range name or an address than contains values. Use the following syntax for @LARGE:

@LARGE(*range*,*number*)

The arguments for @LARGE are as follows:

range	The range name or address that contains values
number	Any positive integer the value in that position in the ordered list you want the function to return.

If the value of *number* is larger than the number of values in the range, the function results in NA.

Suppose that you have a list of test scores, with a range name called **"SCORE"** input into a group of cells in random order. Your task is to find the top three scores. Figure 7.51 shows how you can use @LARGE to find the top scores in the range.

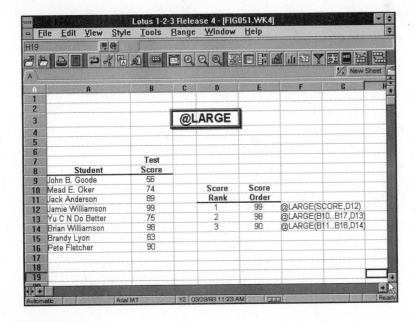

FIG. 7.51

Using @LARGE to find the largest values in a range.

@LN—Computing Natural Logarithms

The @LN function computes the natural, or base *e*, logarithm. @LN uses the following syntax:

@LN(*number*)

If you use a negative argument with @LN, 1-2-3 for Windows returns ERR.

@LOG—Computing Logarithms

The @LOG function computes the base 10 logarithm. Use the following syntax for @LOG:

@LOG(*number*)

You cannot use a negative value with this function. If you use a negative value with @LOG, 1-2-3 for Windows returns ERR.

@MOD—Finding the Modulus or Remainder

The @MOD function computes the remainder when two numbers are divided. @MOD uses two arguments that can be numeric values or cell references. The syntax of the function is as follows:

@MOD(*number,divisor*)

The *number* being divided determines the sign of the remainder, or modulus. The *divisor* cannot be 0, or @MOD returns ERR.

In an earlier example, you had $1,000 to invest in shares of XYZ stock, selling for $17 a share. You can use the @INT function to calculate the number of shares of XYZ and use @MOD, shown in figure 7.50, to determine the remainder, or the amount left over after the purchase.

@QUOTIENT—Dividing Two Values and Truncating the Result

The @QUOTIENT function computes the result, truncated to an integer, when two numbers are divided. @QUOTIENT uses two arguments that can be numeric values or cell references. The syntax of the function is as follows:

@QUOTIENT(*number,divisor*)

The *number* being divided determines the sign of the remainder, or modulus. The *divisor* cannot be 0, or @QUOTIENT returns ERR.

@RAND—Producing Random Numbers

You use the @RAND function to generate random numbers. The function uses no arguments; its syntax is as follows:

@RAND

@RAND returns a randomly generated number between 0 and 1, to 18 decimal places. If you want a random number greater than 1, multiply the @RAND function by the maximum random number you want. If you want a random number in a range of numbers, use a formula similar to the following:

+10+@RAND*20

In this example, the random numbers generated are between 10 and 30. Enclose random number calculations in an @INT function if you need random integers. The following formula returns an integer between 10 and 29:

10+@INT(@RAND*20)

Because the result of the @RAND can never be as large as 1, @INT(@RAND*20) must fall between 0 and 19.

 NOTE New random numbers are generated each time the worksheet is recalculated. To see the results from new random numbers, press F9 (Calc).

@SIGN—Determining the Sign of a Value

The @SIGN function determines whether a value in a cell (or a cell reference) is positive or negative. If the value or cell reference is positive, @SIGN returns 1; if the value is negative, @SIGN returns 0. The syntax for @SIGN is as follows:

@SIGN(number)

@SMALL—Finding the Smallest Value in a Range

@SMALL finds the nth smallest value in a *range* of values. The range of values can be a range name or an address than contains values. Use the following syntax for @SMALL:

@SMALL(range,number)

The arguments for @SMALL are as follows:

range   The name or address that contains values

number   Any positive integer the value in that position in the ordered list you want the function to return

If the value of *number* is larger than the number of values in the range, the function results in NA.

Suppose that you have a list of test scores input into a group of cells in random order. Your task is to find the top and bottom three scores. Figure 7.52 shows how you can use @LARGE and @SMALL to find the top and bottom scores in the range.

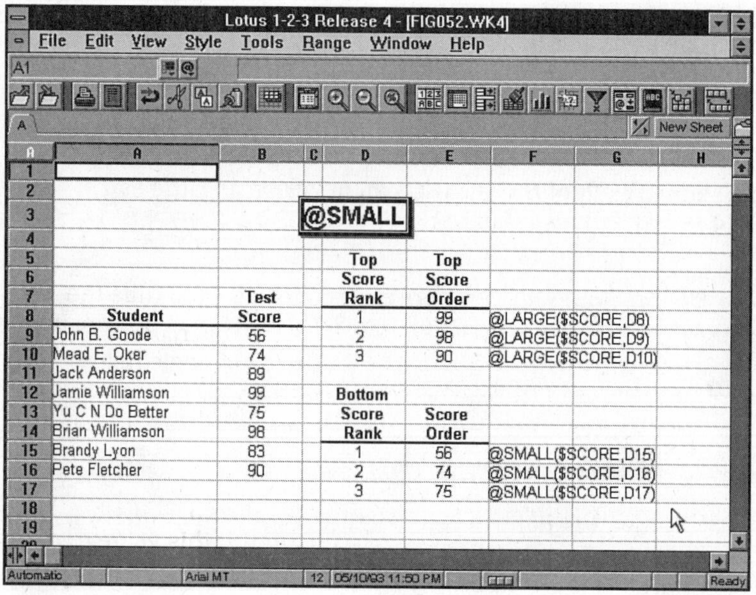

FIG. 7.52

Using @SMALL and @LARGE to find the top and bottom scores in a range.

@SQRT—Calculating the Square Root

The @SQRT function calculates the square root of a positive number. The function uses one argument, the *number* whose square root you want to find. @SQRT uses the following syntax:

@SQRT(*number*)

The *number* argument must be a nonnegative numeric value or a cell reference to such a value. If @SQRT is a negative value, the function returns ERR.

The @SQRT function is equivalent to using the ^ (exponentiation) operator with an exponent of 0.5. For example, @SQRT(25) and 25^0.5 both calculate the square root of 25 (the result of which is 5).

@SQRTPI—Calculating @SQRT Times PI

The @SQRTPI function multiplies the square root of a value times the value of pi (approximately 3.14159265358979324). The syntax of @SQRTPI is as follows:

@SQRTPI(*number*)

Refer to the descriptions of the @SQRT and @PI functions for explanations of the components of the @SQRTPI function.

Hyperbolic Functions

This section deals with the hyperbolic functions.

@ACOSH—

The @ACOSH function calculates the inverse (arc) hyperbolic cosine of an angle using the hyperbolic cosine value of the angle being calculated. The function returns a result in radians. The syntax for @ACOSH is as follows:

@ACOSH(*angle*)

If the value of the hyperbolic cosine of an angle is 3, @ACOSH(3) results in 1.762747 radians. Use @RADTODEG to convert this value to degrees.

(e)@ACOTH—

The @ACOTH function calculates the inverse (arc) hyperbolic cotangent of an angle using the hyperbolic cotangent value of the angle being calculated. The function returns a result in radians. The syntax for @ACOTH is as follows:

@ACOTH(*angle*)

If the value of the hyperbolic cotangent of an angle is 3, @ACOTH(3) results in .346574 radians. Use @RADTODEG to convert this value to degrees.

@ACSCH—

The @ACSCH function calculates the inverse (arc) hyperbolic cosecant of an angle using the hyperbolic cosecant value of the angle being calculated. The function returns a result in radians. The syntax for @ACSCH is as follows:

@ACSCH(*angle*)

If the value of the hyperbolic cosecant of an angle is 2.54, @ACSCH(2.54) results in .38418 radians. Use @RADTODEG to convert this value to degrees.

@ASECH—

The @ASECH function calculates the inverse (arc) hyperbolic secant of an angle using the hyperbolic secant value of the angle being calculated. The function returns a result in radians. The syntax for @ASECH is as follows:

@ASECH(*angle*)

If the value of the hyperbolic secant of an angle is .25, @ASECH(.25) results in 2.063437 radians. Use @RADTODEG to convert this value to degrees.

@ASINH—

The @ASINH function calculates the inverse (arc) hyperbolic sine of an angle using the hyperbolic sine value of the angle being calculated. The function returns a result in radians. The syntax for @ASINH is as follows:

@ASINH(*angle*)

If the value of the hyperbolic sine of an angle is 3, @ASINH(3) results in .247466 radians. Use @RADTODEG to convert this value to degrees.

@ATANH—

The @ATANH function calculates the inverse (arc) hyperbolic tangent of an angle using the hyperbolic tangent value of the angle being calculated. The function returns a result in radians. The syntax for @ATANH is as follows:

@ATANH(*angle*)

If the value of the hyperbolic tangent of an angle is .6223, @ATANH(.6223) results in .72875 radians. Use @RADTODEG to convert this value to degrees.

@COSH—

The @COSH function calculates the hyperbolic cosine of an angle measured in radians. The function returns a result in radians. The syntax for @COSH is as follows:

@COSH(*angle*)

The result of @COSH is a value greater than 1. The *angle* argument (the value in the cell or the value of the cell reference) must be in radians instead of an angular measurement. The value in radians can be between –11355.1371 and 11355.1371, although it cannot be the value 0. Use @DEGTORAD to convert an angle to radians before using the @COSH function. Here is an example of the @COSH of a 30-degree angle:

@COSH(@DEGTORAD(30)) = 1.140238 radians

@COTH—

The @COTH function calculates the hyperbolic cotangent of an angle. The function returns a result in radians. The syntax for @COTH is as follows:

@COTH(*angle*)

The *angle* argument (the value in the cell or the value of the cell reference) must be in radians instead of an angular measurement. The value in radians can be between –11355.1371 and 11355.1371, although it cannot be the value 0. Use the @DEGTORAD function to convert an angle to radians before using the @COTH function. Here is an example of the @COTH of a 30-degree angle:

@COTH(@DEGTORAD(30)) = 2.081283 radians

@CSCH—

The @CSCH function calculates the hyperbolic cosecant of an angle. The function returns a result in radians. The syntax for @CSCH is as follows:

@CSCH(*angle*)

The *angle* argument (the value in the cell or the value of the cell reference) must be in radians instead of an angular measurement. The value in radians can be between −11355.1371 and 11355.1371, although it cannot be the value 0. Use @DEGTORAD to convert an angle to radians before using the @CSCH function. Here is an example of the @CSCH of a 30-degree angle:

```
@CSCH(@DEGTORAD(30)) = 1.825306 radians
```

@SECH—

The @SECH function calculates the hyperbolic secant of an angle. The function returns a result in radians. The syntax for @SECH is as follows:

```
@SECH(angle)
```

The *angle* argument (the value in the cell or the value of the cell reference) must be in radians instead of an angular measurement. The value in radians can be between −11355.1371 and 11355.1371, although it cannot be the value 0. Use @DEGTORAD to convert an angle to radians before using the @SECH function. Here is an example of the @SECH of a 30-degree angle:

```
@SECH(@DEGTORAD(30)) = .87701 radians
```

@SINH—

The @SINH function calculates the hyperbolic sine of an angle. The function returns a result in radians. The syntax for @SINH is as follows:

```
@SINH(angle)
```

The *angle* argument (the value in the cell or the value of the cell reference) must be in radians instead of an angular measurement. The value in radians can be between −11355.1371 and 11355.1371, although it cannot be the value 0. Use @DEGTORAD to convert an angle to radians before using the @SINH function. Here is an example of the @SINH of a 30-degree angle:

```
@SINH(@DEGTORAD(30)) = .547853 radians
```

@TANH—

The @TANH function calculates the hyperbolic tangent of an angle. The function returns a result in radians. The syntax for @TANH is as follows:

```
@TANH(angle)
```

The *angle* argument (the value in the cell or the value of the cell reference) must be in radians instead of an angular measurement. The value in radians can be between –11355.1371 and 11355.1371, although it cannot be the value 0. Use @DEGTORAD to convert an angle to radians before using the @TANH function. Here is an example of the @TANH of a 30-degree angle:

```
@TANH(@DEGTORAD(30)) = .480473 radians
```

Rounding Functions

The rounding functions allow the user to control the scope of values. The functions do this by allowing the user to round up, round down or truncate numerical values.

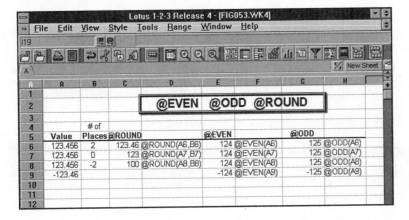

FIG. 7.53

Functions used to round values.

@ROUND—Rounding Numbers

The @ROUND function rounds values to a precision you specify. The function uses two arguments: the *number* you want to round and the *precision* you want to use in the rounding. @ROUND uses the following syntax:

```
@ROUND(number,precision)
```

The *precision* argument determines the number of decimal places to which you round *number; precision* can be a numeric value between –100 and +100. You use positive precision values to specify places to the right of the decimal place; use negative values to specify places to the left of the decimal place. A precision value of 0 rounds decimal values to the nearest integer. Figure 7.53 demonstrates the use of @ROUND to round results before totalling them.

NOTE

The @ROUND function and the <u>S</u>tyle <u>N</u>umber Format command do different things. @ROUND actually changes the contents of a cell; <u>S</u>tyle <u>N</u>umber Format changes only how the cell's contents are displayed.

In 1-2-3 for Windows, the formatted number you see on-screen or in print may not be the number used in calculations. This difference can cause errors of thousands of dollars in spreadsheets such as mortgage tables. To prevent errors, use @ROUND to round formula results or the numbers feeding into formulas so that the numbers used in calculations are the same as those in the display.

As you round numbers, keep in mind some general information about how the @ROUND function works. @ROUND rounds a number according to the old standard rule: numbers less than 0.5 are rounded down; numbers equal to or greater than 0.5 are rounded up.

The @ROUND function is most useful for rounding a value used in other formulas or functions, as shown in figure 7.53.

If want to round up to the nearest integer, you can do so by adding a number a little less than 0.5 to the number you want to round. If you work with numbers to two decimal places, add .49. If you work with numbers to four decimal places, add .4999. For example, the following formula rounds up to an integer a number that uses four decimal places:

```
@ROUND(cell-reference+.4999,0)
```

@EVEN—Rounding a Value to the Next Even Integer

The @EVEN function rounds the value in the argument to the nearest even integer value away from 0. This means that positive values are made larger and negative values are made smaller (see fig. 7.53). The syntax for @EVEN is as follows:

```
@EVEN(number)
```

@ODD—Rounding a Value to the Next Odd Integer

The @ODD function rounds the value in the argument to the nearest odd integer value away from 0. This means that positive values are made larger and negative values are made smaller (see fig. 7.53). The syntax for @ODD is as follows:

```
@ODD(number)
```

@ROUNDUP and @ROUNDDOWN—Rounding a Number to Specific Values

The @ROUNDUP and @ROUNDDOWN functions round values to an optional precision you specify. The function uses two arguments: the *number* you want to round and the optional *precision* you want to use in the rounding. The function name determines the direction you want to round. The functions use the following syntax:

@ROUNDUP(*number*,[*precision*])

@ROUNDDOWN(*number*,[*precision*])

The *precision* argument, which is optional, determines the number of decimal places to which you want to round *number; precision* can be a numeric value between –100 and +100. You use positive precision values to specify places to the right of the decimal place; use negative values to specify places to the left of the decimal place. If you omit the precision value, the default is 0, which rounds *number* to the nearest integer value.

@ROUNDM—

@ROUNDM is a derivation of @ROUND; it provides the flexibility of combining all the rounding functions into one. The syntax for @ROUNDM is as follows:

@ROUNDM(*number*,*precision*,[*direction*])

The *number* is the value that is to be rounded.

The *precision* is the number of places to round the value to.

The *direction* argument is optional; it tells 1-2-3 the direction in which to round the value. The choices available for the *direction* argument are these:

    0   round down (this is the default)

    1   round up

@TRUNC—Truncating a Value to a Specific Length

Like the rounding functions, the @TRUNC function modifies the values in the worksheet. This is done by truncating the value to the number of decimal places specified by the *precision* argument.

NOTE   @TRUNC(5849.8204)= 5849, @ROUND(5849.8204)= 5850.

The syntax for @TRUNC is as follows:

```
@TRUNC(number,[precision])
```

The *precision* argument is optional; it can be a value between −100 and +100. If the precision value is negative, the integer portion of *number* is rounded to the value of the decimal position starting from the left of the decimal point. Here are some examples of @TRUNC:

```
@TRUNC(5849.8204) = 5849
@TRUNC(5849.8204,2) = 5849.82
@TRUNC(5849.8204,-2) = 5800
@TRUNC(-5849.8204) = -5849
@TRUNC(-5849.8204,-3) = 5000
```

Trigonometric Functions

1-2-3 for Windows provides the standard trigonometric functions that will be covered in this section.

@ACOS, @ASIN, @ATAN, and @ATAN2— Computing Inverse Trigonometric Functions

The @ACOS, @ASIN, @ATAN, and @ATAN2 functions calculate the arc-cosine, the arcsine, the arctangent, and the four-quadrant arctangent, respectively. @ACOS computes the inverse of cosine. @ASIN computes the inverse of sine, returning a radians angle between −_/2 and _/2 (−90 and +90 degrees). @ATAN computes the inverse of tangent, returning a radians angle between −π_/2 and π_/2 (−90 and +90 degrees). @ATAN2 calculates the four-quadrant arctangent, using the ratio of its two arguments.

@ACOS and @ASIN each use one argument, *angle*, as shown in the following syntax:

```
@ACOS(angle)
```

```
@ASIN(angle)
```

Because all cosine and sine values lie between –1 and 1, @ACOS and @ASIN work only with values between –1 and 1. This means that the angular measurments in the argument will be in radians. Either function returns ERR if you use an argument outside this range. @ASIN returns angles between $-\pi/2$ and $+\pi/2$; @ACOS returns angles between 0 and $\pi/2$.

NOTE To convert the values from radians to degrees the @RADTODEG function is available.

Like @ACOS and @ASIN, the @ATAN function uses one argument, *angle*. @ATAN can use any number and returns a value between $-/2$ and $+/2$. @ATAN uses the following syntax:

@ATAN(*angle*)

@ATAN2 computes the angle whose tangent is specified by the ratio *number2*/*number1*—the two arguments required by the function. At least one of the arguments must be a number other than 0. @ATAN2 returns radians angles between –Pi and +Pi. Use the following syntax for @ATAN2:

@ATAN2(*number1*,*number2*)

@ACOT, @ACSC, and @ASEC—Calculating Inverse Trigonometric Functions

The @ACOT, @ACSC, and @ASEC functions calculate the arccotangent, the arccosecant, and the arcsecant, respectively, of an angle; the results of the calculations are in radians. @ACOT computes the inverse of cotangent. @ASEC computes the inverse of secant, returning a radians angle between 0 and pi (0 and +180 degrees). @ACSC computes the inverse of cosecant, returning a radians angle between $-/2$ and $/2$ (–90 and +90 degrees). The syntax for the functions are as follows:

@ACOT(*angle*)
@ACSC(*angle*)
@ASEC(*angle*)

@COT, @CSC, and @SEC—Computing Trigonometric Functions

The @COT, @CSC, and @SEC functions calculate the cotangent, cosecant, and secant, respectively, of an angle. Each function uses one argument: an *angle* measured in radians. Use the following syntax for these functions:

@COT(*angle*)
@CSC(*angle*)
@SEC(*angle*)

Be sure to convert angle measurements to radians before you use these functions. You can accomplish this quickly by using the @DEGTORAD function described earlier.

Notice that in cell E10, @TAN returns ERR. Remember that an angle's tangent equals its sine divided by its cosine. When the cosine is 0—as it is in this example—@TAN returns ERR because the function cannot divide by 0.

@COS, @SIN, and @TAN—Computing Trigonometric Functions

The @COS, @SIN, and @TAN functions calculate the cosine, sine, and tangent, respectively, of an angle. Each function uses one argument: an *angle* measured in radians. Use the following syntax for these functions:

@COS(*angle*)
@SIN(*angle*)
@TAN(*angle*)

Be sure to convert angle measurements to radians before you use these functions. You can accomplish this quickly by using the @DEGTORAD function described earlier.

Notice that in cell E10, @TAN returns ERR. Remember that an angle's tangent equals its sine divided by its cosine. When the cosine is 0—as it is in this example—@TAN returns ERR because the function cannot divide by 0.

@PI—Computing Pi

The @PI function results in the value of 3.14159265358979324. @PI uses no arguments and has the following syntax:

@PI

@PI returns the value 3.14159265358979324. Use @PI in the calculations for the area of circles and the volume of spheres. You also use @PI in the conversion of angle measurements in degrees to angle measurements in radians (if you prefer to make this calculation on your own instead of using the @DEGTORAD function).

Using Statistical Functions

1-2-3 for Windows provides five statistical function categories: Forecasting, General, Probability, Ranking, and Significance Tests. Table 7.15 lists the categories and the functions in each along with their arguments and brief descriptions.

Many statistical functions use the *list* argument. This argument can contain individually specified values, cell addresses, a range of cells, multiple ranges of cells, or range names. For example, 1-2-3 for Windows considers each of the following formats a valid *list* argument:

```
@SUM(1,2,3,4)
@SUM(B1,B2,B3,B4)
@SUM(B1..B4)
@SUM(A1..B2,B3..E10)
@SUM(NAME)
```

Labels can be used as valid items within the group of cells in a range or range name. 1-2-3 for Windows assigns a 0 to the position occupied by the label in the group.

WARNING: Blank cells imbedded within a range are ignored in calculations. However, if the blank cells in a list are referenced as specific items in the list, they are counted and used by the function. For example, the @AVG function can use either of these two *list* formats: (A1..A3) or (A1,A2,A3). In both *list* formats, assume that cell A1 is blank (that is, it has nothing in it). The @AVG(A1..A3) function does not include cell A1 as a value or position and divides by 2. In @AVG(A1,A2,A3), cell A1 is counted and @AVG divides by 3.

Table 7.15 Statistical Functions

Forecasting Function	Description
@REGRESSION(*x-range*, *y-range*, *attribute*,[*compute*])	Performs multiple linear regression analysis

General Functions	Description
@AVEDEV(*list*)	Calculates the mean deviation of the values in a list of values
@AVG(*list*)	Calculates the arithmetic mean of a list of values
@CORREL(*range1*,*range2*)	Calculates the correlation coefficient of values in two ranges
@COUNT(*list*)	Counts the number of cells that contain entries
@COV(*range1*,*range2*,[*type*])	Calculates the population or sample covariance of values in two ranges
@DEVSQ(*list*)	Calculates the sum of squared deviations of a list of values
@GEOMEAN(*list*)	Calculates the geometric mean of a list of values
@GRANDTOTAL(*list*)	Calculates the sum of all cells in a list that contain @SUBTOTAL in their formulas
@HARMEAN(*list*)	Calculates the harmonic mean of a list of values
@KURTOSIS(*range*,[*type*])	Calculates the kurtosis of a list of values
@MAX(*list*)	Returns the maximum value in a list of values
@MEDIAN(*list*)	Calculates the median of a list of values
@MIN(*list*)	Returns the minimum value in a list of values
@PRODUCT(*list*)	Calculates the product of a list of values
@PUREAVG(*list*)	Averages a list of values, ignoring text and labels
@PURECOUNT(*list*)	Counts the nonblank cells in a list of ranges, ignoring text and labels

General Functions	Description
@PUREMAX(*list*)	Finds the largest value in a list, ignoring text and labels
@PUREMIN(*list*)	Finds the smallest value in a list, ignoring text and labels
@PURSETD(*list*)	Calculates the population standard deviation of a list of values, ignoring text and labels
@PURESTDS(*list*)	Calculates the sample standard deviation of a list of values, ignoring text and labels
@PUREVAR(*list*)	Calculates the population variance of a list of values, ignoring text and labels
@PUREVARS(*list*)	Calculates the sample variance of a list of values, ignoring text and labels
@SEMEAN(*list*)	Calculates the standard error of the sample mean for the values in a list
@SKEWNESS(*range,[type]*)	Calculates the skewness of values in a list
@STD(*list*)	Calculates the population standard deviation of a list of values
@STDS(*list*)	Calculates the sample population standard deviation of a list of values
@SUBTOTAL(*list*)	Adds a list of values (use to indicate which cells @GRANDTOTAL should sum)
@SUM(*list*)	Adds a list of values
@SUMPRODUCT(*list*)	Multiplies each cell by the corresponding cell in each range in the list of ranges and sums the values
@SUMSQ(*list*)	Sums the squares of a list of values
@SUMXMY2(*range1,range2*)	Subtracts the values in corresponding cells in two ranges, squares the differences, and sums the results
@VAR(*list*)	Calculates the population variance of a list of values
@VARS(*list*)	Calculates the sample population variance of a list of values
@WEIGHTAVG(*list*)	Calculates the weighted average of a list of values

continues

Table 7.15 Continued

Probability Functions	Description
@BINOMIAL(*trials,successes, probability,*[*type*])	Calculates the cumulative binomial distribution or the binomial probability mass function
@CHIDIST(*x,degrees-of-freedom,*[*type*])	Calculates the chi-squared distribution
@COMBIN(*n,r*)	Calculates the binomial coefficient
@CRITBINOMIAL(*trials, probability,alpha*)	Returns the smallest integer for which the cumulative binomial distribution is greater than or equal to a specified value
@FDIST(*x,degrees-of-freedom1, degrees-of-freedom2,*[*type*])	Calculates the cumulative distribution function or its inverse for F-distributions
@NORMAL(*x,*[*mean*],[*std*], [*type*],[*region*])	Calculates the normal distribution
@PERMUT(*n,r*)	Calculates the number of ordered permutations of *r* objects that can be selected from a total of *n* objects
@POISSON(*x,mean,* [*cumulative*])	Calculates the Poisson distribution
@TDIST(*x,degrees-of-freedom,* [*type*],[*tails*])	Calculates the T-distribution

Ranking Functions	Description
@PERCENTILE(*x,range*)	Calculates the *x*th sample percentile among the values in a range
@PRANK(*x,range,*[*places*])	Finds the percentile of *x* among the values in a range
@RANK(*item,range,*[*order*])	Calculates the position of a value in a range relative to other values in the range, ranked in either ascending or descending order

Significance Tests Functions	Description
@CHITEST(*range1,range2,* [*type*],[*constraints*])	Performs a chi-square test on the data in two ranges
@FTEST(*range1,range2*)	Performs an F-test on the data in two ranges
@TTEST(*range1,range2,* [*type*],[*tails*])	Performs a student's T-test on the data in two ranges
@ZTEST(*range1,std1,*[*range2*], [*std2*],[*tails*])	Performs a Z-test on one or two populations

Forecasting Function

Forcasting can be done by regression analysis. The following section shows the @REGRESSION function.

The @REGRESSION function performs multiple linear regression on ranges of values and returns the statistic. Use the following syntax for the @REGRESSION function:

`@REGRESSION(x-range,y-range,attribute,[compute])`

The arguments for this function are as follows:

x-range	Also known as the *independent variable*. The independent variable can be a range name or an address that contains up to 75 columns and 8,192 rows.
y-range	Also know as the *dependant variable*. The dependant variable can be a range name or an address that has a single column and up to 8,192 rows.
attribute	Specifies which regression output value to calculate. Following is a list of the available attributes:

Attribute	Calculation Performed
1	Constant
2	Standard error of Y estimate
3	R squared
4	Number of observations
5	Degrees of freedom
01 to 175	X coefficient (slope) for the independent variable specified by *attribute*
201 to 275	Standard error of coefficient for the independent variable specified by *attribute*

[*compute*]	An optional argument that specifies the Y-intercept, compute has the following options:

compute	1-2-3
0	Uses 0 as the Y-intercept
1	Calculates the Y-intercept and is the default if omitted from the argument.

1-2-3 for Windows numbers the independent variables in the X range, starting with the number 1, from top to bottom in a column, and in columns from left to right. If the X range is A1..C10, you can find the X coefficient for the independent variable in A2 by using the attribute 102. Using the same X range, you can find the standard error of coefficient for the independent variable in A5 by using the attribute 205.

General Statistical Functions

1-2-3 for Windows provides the following general statistical functions.

@AVEDEV—Calculating the Mean Deviation

@AVEDEV calculates the average of the absolute deviations of the values in a list. The syntax for @AVEDEV is as follows:

@AVEDEV(*list*)

The *list* argument can be in any of the formats described at the beginning of the "Using Statistical Functions" section. Figure 7.58 shows an example of the @AVGDEV function using a range name PRICE.

@AVG and @PUREAVG—Computing the Arithmetic Mean

To calculate the average of a set of values, you add all the values and then divide the sum by the number of values. Essentially, the @AVG function produces the same result as if you divided @SUM(*list*) by @COUNT(*list*), two functions described later in this section. You may find the @AVG function a helpful tool for calculating the *arithmetic mean*—a commonly used measure of the average of a set of values. @AVG uses the following syntax:

@AVG(*list*)

The *list* argument can be values, cell addresses, cell names, cell ranges, range names, or a combination of all these formats. If a label is specified in *list* as a cell value, that cell is counted in the @AVG calculation.

Like @AVG, the @PUREAVG function calculates the average of a set of values. @PUREAVG, however, has the added feature of ignoring cells in *list* that are labels, **rather than converting them to zero.**

The syntax is as follows:

@PUREAVG(*list*)

@CORREL—Calculating the Correlation Coefficient

The @CORREL function calculates the correlation coefficient for two ranges of values. The syntax for @CORREL is as follows:

@CORREL(*range1,range2*)

The argument list contains two ranges of values that must be the same size and shape and must contain only values. If the ranges are not the same size and shape, @CORREL results in ERR. Blank cells in either of the ranges are ignored.

The @CORREL function matches cell pairs to calculate the correlation coefficient and orders the cell pairs. The order of the cell pairs is from top to bottom and left to right. If the ranges use multiple sheets, the sheets start at the first and progress to the last.

The result of the @CORREL function is a pure correlation value; there are no units.

@COUNT and @PURECOUNT—Counting Cell Entries

The @COUNT function totals the number of cells that contain nonblank entries of any kind, including labels, label-prefix characters, or the values ERR and NA. @COUNT uses the following syntax:

@COUNT(*list*)

The *list* argument for @COUNT can be values, cell addresses, cell names, cell ranges, range names, or a combination of these formats—including ERR and NA.

The @PURECOUNT function totals the number of cells that contain nonblank entries that are values only. @PURECOUNT uses the following syntax:

@PURECOUNT(*list*)

The *list* argument for @PURECOUNT can be values, cell addresses, cell names, cell ranges, range names, or a combination of these formats—including ERR and NA. The only cells counted, however, are the cells that contain values.

 NOTE ERR and NA are considered values. It should also be noted that different situations call for different functions to be used. The @COUNT function is used to include all cells no matter what is included in the cell. Make sure the results are accurate and are what you are trying to accomplish.

For example, you can use @COUNT and @PURECOUNT to show the number of share prices included in the @AVG calculation.

Be sure to include only ranges as the argument in the @COUNT function. If you specify an individual cell, 1-2-3 for Windows counts that cell as if it has an entry—even if the cell is empty. If you absolutely must specify a cell individually, but want that cell counted only if it actually contains an entry, use the @PURECOUNT function.

@COV—Calculating the Population or Sample Covariance

The @COV function calculates either the population covariance or a sample covariance of two ranges of numbers. *Covariance* is the average of the products of deviations of corresponding values. The syntax for @COV is as follows:

@COV(*range1*,*range2*,[*type*])

The argument list contains two ranges of values that must be the same size and shape and must only contain values. If the ranges are not the same size and shape, the function returns ERR. Also, if the ranges have blank cells, contain labels, or have text formulas, the function returns ERR.

The optional [*type*] argument specifies the covariance you are calculating. Following are the available options:

Type	Calculation
0	Population covariance is calculated (the default if [*type*] is omitted)
1	Sample covariance

The @COV function is similar to the @CORREL function in that both functions measure a relationship between two sets of values. The @COV function is dependant on the unit of measure between the ranges, which is not the case with the @CORREL function.

@DEVSQ—Calculating the Sum of Squared Deviations

The @DEVSQ function calculates the sum of squared deviations from the mean of the values in the argument. The syntax for the @DEVSQ function is as follows:

@DEVSQ(*list*)

The *list* argument accepts any of the formats described at the beginning of the "Using Statistical Functions" section. Note that a blank cell in the range of cells is not counted in the @DEVSQ calculation; a text label, however, is counted as the value 0 and can make a difference in the result. Here is an example of the @DEVSQ function:

```
@DEVSQ(2,3,9,8,15,2,1) = 159.4286
```

If you give the range containing these values the name GENERIC and insert a blank in the middle of the range, the result is the same. If you put any text or a 0 in the blank cell, however, the result changes to 188.00000. Figure 7.54 shows another example of the @DEVSQ function.

	Lotus 1-2-3 Release 4 - [FIG062.WK4]

Generic Range	@Function	Result
2	@DEVSQ(GENERIC)	159.4286
3	@GEOMEAN(GENERIC)	3.86825
	@HARMEAN(GENERIC)	2.655427
9	@KURTOSIS(GENERIC)	-0.65706
8	@KURTOSIS(GENERIC,1)	0.223055
15		
2		
1		

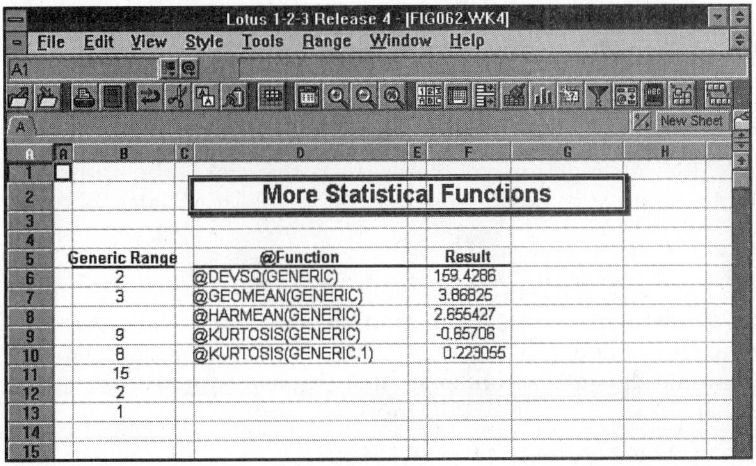

FIG. 7.54

Using @DEVSQ, @GEOMEAN, @HARMEAN, and @KURTOSIS functions.

@GEOMEAN—Calculating the Geometric Mean

@GEOMEAN calculates the geometric mean of a range of values. The syntax for @GEOMEAN is as follows:

```
@GEOMEAN(list)
```

The *list* argument must refer to cells that contain values; these cells cannot contain any elements less than or equal to 0. Blank cells are allowed but ignored in the calculation. The function returns ERR if *list* does not contain at least one positive nonzero value or values in any of the formats outlined at the beginning of the "Using Statistical Functions" section. Here is an example of the @GEOMEAN function:

```
@GEOMEAN(2,3,9,8,15,2,1) = 3.868254
```

If you give the range containing these values the name GENERIC and insert a blank cell in the middle of the range, the result is the same. If you put any text or a 0 in the blank cell, the result changes to ERR. Figure 7.54 shows an example of the @GEOMEAN function.

@GRANDTOTAL—Calculating the Sum of @SUBTOTAL Values

The @GRANDTOTAL function calculates the sum of all cells that contain the @SUBTOTAL function. The syntax for @GRANDTOTAL is as follows:

@GRANDTOTAL(*list*)

In this syntax, *list* is a group or range of @SUBTOTAL formulas. Refer to the discussion of the @SUBTOTAL function later in this chapter. Refer ahead to figure 7.58 for an example of the @GRANDTOTAL function. Notice that the range of cells for @GRANDTOTAL includes cells with @SUM formulas; the @SUM formulas are ignored.

@HARMEAN—Calculating the Harmonic Mean

The @HARMEAN function calculates the reciprocal of the arithmetic mean of a range of values. The syntax for @HARMEAN is as follows:

@HARMEAN(*list*)

The *list* argument accepts any of the list formats described at the beginning of the "Using Statistical Function" section. Note that a blank cell in the range is not counted in the @HARMEAN calculation; text labels are not allowed. The values in the list must be positive nonzero values. Here is an example of the @HARMEAN function:

@HARMEAN(2,3,9,8,15,2,1) = 2.655427

If you give the range containing these values the name GENERIC and insert a blank cell in the middle of the range, the result is the same. If you put any text or a 0 in the blank cell, the result changes to ERR. Figure 7.54 shows an example of the @HARMEAN function.

@KURTOSIS—Calculating a Distribution Concentration

@KURTOSIS measures the concentration of a distribution around the mean of a range of values. A negative kurtosis indicates a relatively flat or stable distribution; a positive kurtosis is an indication of a peaked distribution. Use the following syntax for the @KURTOSIS function:

@KURTOSIS(*range*,[*type*])

The arguments for @KURTOSIS are as follows:

range
: The name or address of a group of values. The @KURTOSIS function requires a minimum of four values or NA is returned.

[type]
: An optional argument that specifies whether to calculate for an entire population of values or a sample. The options for [type] are as follows:

Type	Calculate
0	Population (the default if [type] is omitted)
1	Sample

The *range* argument accepts any range. Note that a blank cell in a range of cells is not counted in the @KURTOSIS calculation. A text value is allowed and counted as a 0.

Suppose that you have a range named GENERIC that contains the values 2, 3, 9, 8, 15, 2, and 1; here are some examples of the @KURTOSIS function:

`@KURTOSIS(GENERIC)  =  -0.65706`

`@KURTOSIS(GENERIC,1)  =  0.223055`

If you insert a blank in the middle of the range, the result is the same. If you put any text or a 0 in the blank cell—or in any of the cells—the result calculates the kurtosis, treating the label as zero, and ignoring the blanks. e.g., @KURTOSIS(3,9,8,0 or label,15,2,1)=.51684019. Figure 7.54 shows another example of the @KURTOSIS function.

@MAX and @MIN—Finding Maximum and Minimum Values

The @MAX function finds the largest value in the *list* argument; the @MIN function finds the smallest value in the *list* argument. These functions use the following syntax:

`@MAX(list)`

`@MIN(list)`

Figure 7.55 shows information concerning prices per share of an imaginary company. Use the @MAX and @MIN functions to find the lowest and the highest prices, respectively. You can see in the input line that the argument of @MAX is the range name PRICE; the argument of @MIN is also PRICE. Notice two cells in the PRICE range: cell C9 is blank and C10 contains the label `missing`. Because the label in C10 is assigned the value 0, @MIN returns 0 as the lowest value. (The blank in cell C9 is ignored.) The @PUREMAX and @PUREMIN functions address the problem of labels being assigned the value 0.

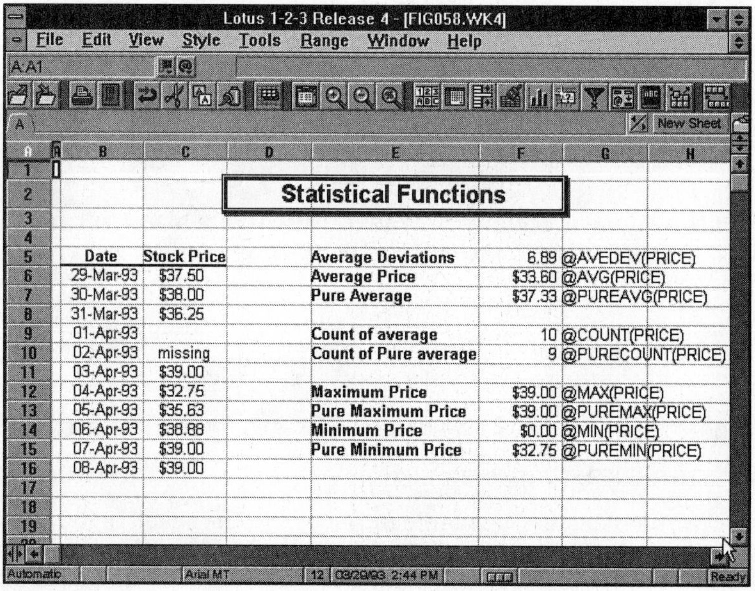

FIG. 7.55

Using @MAX and @MIN to show the highest and lowest price per share.

NOTE

If you are familiar with statistics, you may recognize that the @MAX and @MIN functions provide the two pieces of data you need to calculate a popular statistical measure: a range. A range—which is one measure of variability in a list of values—is the difference between the highest value and the lowest value in a list of values. (A *range* as a statistical measurement is not the same thing as a worksheet range—which is a rectangular block of cells.)

@PUREMAX and @PUREMIN—Finding the True Max and Min

The @MAX and @MIN functions show a sensitivity to cells in the list of values that contain labels. The @PUREMIN and @PUREMAX functions are not sensitive to labels. The functions only look at cells with values in them and return a true maximum or minimum value. The syntax for these functions is as follows:

@PUREMAX(*list*)

@PUREMIN(*list*)

Figure 7.55 shows the results of the @PUREMAX and @PUREMIN functions.

@MEDIAN—Finding the Median of a Range

@MEDIAN returns either the middle value in a list or the arithmetic average of the list. 1-2-3 for Windows looks at the number of values in a list; if the number of physical entries is odd, the result of @MEDIAN is the middle value of the list. If the number of physical entries is even, the result is the arithmetic average—the same value as @AVG—of the list. Blank cells are ignored. The syntax for @MEDIAN is as follows:

@MEDIAN(*list*)

Suppose that the GENERIC range contains the values 3, 3, a blank cell, 9, 8, 15, 2, and 1; the @MEDIAN value is 3. If you enter a 0 in the blank cell, the @MEDIAN value is 2.5.

@PRODUCT—Finding the Product of a List

The @PRODUCT function multiplies the values in the argument list. The elements in the list can be any of the valid numerical formats mentioned at the beginning of the "Using Statistical Functions" section. The syntax for this function is as follows:

@PRODUCT(*list*)

This function works exactly like a calculator. The values in the *list* argument are multiplied together to return the result. The key portion in the preceding sentence is *exactly like a calculator*. If you include a 0 or a label in the list, the result is 0. Blank cells are ignored.

@STD and @STDS—Calculating the Standard Deviation

The @STD function uses the *n*, or *population*, method of calculating standard deviation; the @STDS function uses the *n_1*, or *sample population*, method of calculating the standard deviation. Use the following syntax for these functions:

@STD(*list*)

@STDS(*list*)

Essentially, the standard deviation is a measure of how individual values vary from the mean or average of all of the values in the list. A smaller standard deviation indicates that values are grouped closely around the mean; a larger standard deviation indicates that values are widely dispersed from the mean. Perhaps not surprisingly, a standard deviation of 0 indicates no dispersion—that is, every value in the list of values is the same. Figure 7.56 shows how the @STD function is used to calculate the standard deviation of stock price values.

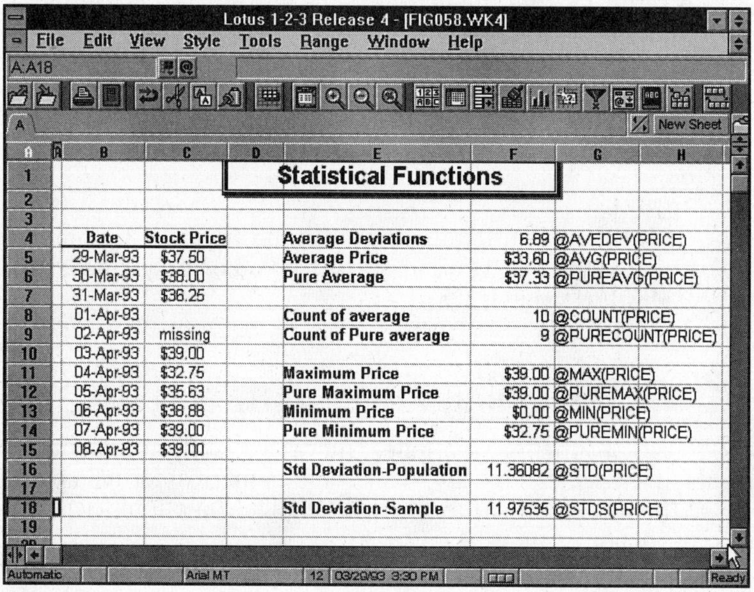

FIG. 7.56

Using @STD and @STDS to calculate standard deviation.

The precise definitions of the two standard deviation formulas are best shown by the formulas 1-2-3 for Windows uses to calculate them:

In these equations, the following abbreviations are used:

N	Number of items in *list*
X*n*	The *n*th item in *list*
avg	Arithmetic mean of *list*

To choose the correct function, you need to know whether you are dealing with the entire population or with a sample. If you are measuring, or including, every value in a calculation, you are working with a population. If you are measuring, or including, only a subset or a portion of the values in a calculation, you are working with a sample. The @STDS function uses the *n*–1, or sample population, method to calculate standard deviation for sample populations. This method adjusts the standard deviation so that it is slightly higher to compensate for possible errors because the entire population was not used.

@PURESTD and @PURESTDS—Calculating the True STD and STDS

The @PURESTD and @PURESTDS functions use the same formulas as do the @STD and @STDS functions. The difference is that @PURESTD and @PURESTDS ignore cells that contain labels. Figure 7.57 shows the difference in the results of @STD and @PURESTD and in the results of @STDS and @PURESTDS. The syntax for the functions are as follows:

@PURESTD(*list*)

@PURESTDS(*list*)

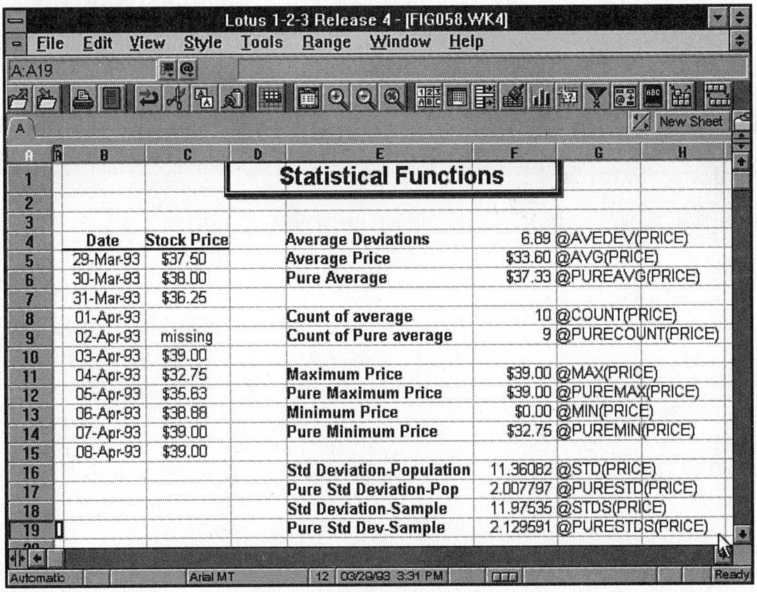

FIG. 7.57

Using @PURESTD and @PURESTDS to ignore labels.

@SEMEAN—Calculating the Standard Error of Sample Mean

The @SEMEAN function calculates the standard error of the sample mean of values. The syntax for @SEMEAN is as follows:

@SEMEAN(*list*)

Suppose that you have a range of values named GENERIC that contains the values 2, 3, a blank, another blank, 9, 8, 15, 2, and 1. Here is an example of the @SEMEAN function:

@SEMEAN(GENERIC) = 1.948312

If you fill the blank cell with text or a 0, the result is 1.832251. The @SEMEAN function ignores blanks and assigns the value 0 to text.

@SKEWNESS—Measuring the Symmetry of a Distribution

@SKEWNESS measures the symmetry of a distribution around the mean of a range of values. A negative skewness indicates a drawn-out tail to the right; a positive skewness indicates a drawn-out tail to the left. Use the following syntax for the @SKEWNESS function:

@SKEWNESS(*range*,[*type*])

The arguments for @SKEWNESS are as follows:

range	The name or address of a group of values. The @SKEWNESS function requires a minimum of three values or it returns the value NA.
[*type*]	This optional argument specifies whether to calculate for an entire population of values or a sample. The options for [*type*] are these:

Type	Calculate
0	Population (the default if [*type*] is omitted)
1	Sample

The *range* argument accepts any range. Note that a blank cell in a range of cells is not counted in the calculation. A text value is allowed and counted as a 0.

Suppose that you have a range of values named GENERIC that contains the values 2, 3, 9, 8, 15, 2, and 1. Here are some examples of the @SKEWNESS function:

@SKEWNESS(GENERIC) = .81594

@SKEWNESS(GENERIC,1) = 1.057951

If you insert a blank in the middle of the range, the result is the same. Put any text or a 0 in the blank cell (or any of the cells) and the result of the first example changes to .921696; the result of the second example changes to 1.149556.

@SUBTOTAL—Setting Up Values for @GRANDTOTAL

The @SUBTOTAL function is used to mark values for the @GRANDTOTAL function. The @SUBTOTAL function adds a list of values and returns the sum. The description of the @SUM function describes the mechanics of summing. The syntax for the @SUBTOTAL function is as follows:

@SUBTOTAL(*list*)

The @SUBTOTAL function is a tool that allows you to mark and gather specific groups of data. The most common use of this function lists range names in the argument, separated by commas, to mark larger totals for the @GRANDTOTAL function. Figure 7.58 shows the operation of the @SUBTOTAL function.

@SUM—Totaling Values

The @SUM function provides a convenient way to add a list of values. Of all the functions that 1-2-3 for Windows provides, @SUM is the one you probably use most often. @SUM uses the following syntax:

@SUM(*list*)

Column E of figure 7.58 shows the tax for each item. You can calculate a total of these taxes with the following formula:

+E5+E6+E7+E8+E9+E10+E11+E12+E13+E14

This method, however, is inefficient and prone to typing errors. A more efficient way to total the column is to use the @SUM function with the range of the taxes (see fig. 7.58).

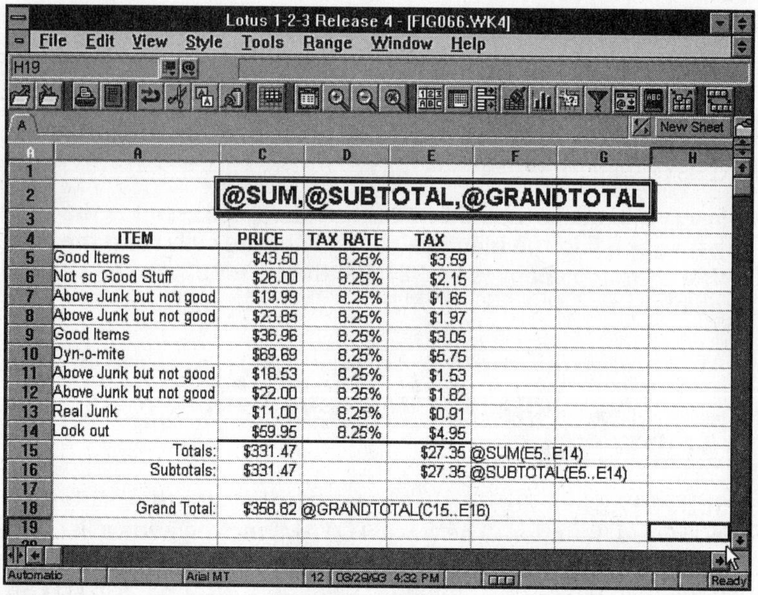

FIG. 7.58

@SUM used to
calculate the total
tax.

When you sum a range of cells and include the horizontal totaling line within the @SUM formula, you can insert or delete cells from the range and keep the formula intact and working perfectly; you never have to adjust the range. By including a placeholder (a blank or text-filled cell) at the top or bottom of the range of cells being summed, maintenance of the worksheet is easier. The placeholder cell does not affect the total because the cell is text and adds as zero.

@SUMPRODUCT—Multiplying Lists of Values

The @SUMPRODUCT function gets its name because the function sums the products of each cell in the ranges specified as its argument. @SUMPRODUCT uses the following syntax:

@SUMPRODUCT(*list*)

You can use @SUMPRODUCT to calculate, for example, the total dollars of inventory (see fig. 7.59). In effect, the @SUMPRODUCT function performs the following calculations:

@SUM(D7*F7,D8*F8,D9*F9,D10*F10,D11*F11,D12*F12,D13*F13)

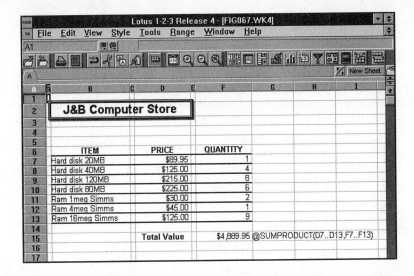

FIG. 7.59

@SUMPRODUCT
used to calculate
the total dollars
of inventory.

If you use more than two ranges, @SUMPRODUCT sums the products of each corresponding cell in each range. For example, the following two formulas are equivalent:

@SUMPRODUCT(C1..C3,D1..D3,E1..E3)

@SUM(C1*D1*E1+C2*D2*E2+C3*D3*E3)

@SUMSQ—Calculating the Sum of the Squares

The @SUMSQ function calculates the sum of the squares for the values in a list. The syntax for the function is as follows:

@SUMSQ(*list*)

The *list* argument can use any of the formats outlined at the beginning of the "Using Statistical Functions" section. Blank cells are ignored and text in any cell is assigned the value 0.

@SUMXMY2—Summing the Squared Differences

@SUMXMY2 calculates the sum of the squared differences between two ranges of values. The syntax for the @SUMXMY2 function is as follows:

@SUMXMY2(*range1*,*range2*)

The ranges must be values and must be ranges of the same size and shape. If either of these criteria are not met, @SUMXMY2 returns ERR. @SUMXMY2 can obtain a result using single-column ranges or multiple-column ranges.

If the ranges are single columns, the calculation is completed by row. If the ranges are multiple columns, the calculation is completed by column. Here is an example of two ranges and the @SUMXMY2 function that calculates them:

ColumnA	ColumnB
1	6
5	4
3	1

```
@SUMXMY2(ColumnA,ColumnB) = 30
```

@VAR and @VARS—Calculating the Variance

The variance, like the standard deviation, is a measure of how much the individual values within the measurement vary from the mean or average. The @VAR function calculates the variance by using the population, or n, method. The @VARS function calculates the variance by using the sample population, or n_1, method. Use the following syntax for these functions:

@VAR(*list*)

@VARS(*list*)

Actually, calculating a statistical variance is an intermediate step in calculating the standard deviations described in the discussion of the @STD and @STDS functions. By comparing the following two formulas, you can see that the standard deviation is the square root of the variance:

In these equations, the following abbreviations are used:

N	Number of items in *list*
Xn	The nth item in *list*
avg	Arithmetic mean of *list*

For explanations of the terms *population* and *sample*, refer to the earlier discussion of the @STD and @STDS functions.

@PUREVAR and @PUREVARS—Calculating the True Variance

The @PUREVAR and @PUREVARS functions use the same formulas as do the @VAR and @VARS functions described in the preceding section. The difference is that @PUREVAR and @PUREVARS ignore cells that contain labels. The syntax for these functions are as follows:

@PUREVAR(*list*)

@PUREVARS(*list*)

@WEIGHTAVG—Calculating the Weighted Average

@WEIGHTAVG calculates the weighted average of a list by multiplying the values in corresponding cells in multiple ranges, summing the products, and finally dividing by the number of values in the list. Use the following syntax for @WEIGHTAVG:

@WEIGHTAVG(*range1,range2*)

The ranges in the argument must be the same shape and size; if they are not, @WEIGHTAVG returns ERR. If the ranges are columns, @WEIGHTAVG multiplies by rows; otherwise @WEIGHTAVG multiplies by columns. If each list spans more than one column, @WEIGHTAVG multiplies by rows.

Suppose that you run a real estate office and want to calculate the weighted average of the sales commissions due for an agent on a month's house sales. The data obtained from the computer gives you the following information:

SOLD	COMMIS
$25,000	.04
$34,580	.04
$77,325	.05

You can use this formula to determine the agent's monthly commission amount:

@WEIGHTAVG(SOLD,COMMIS) = $4,8072.69

Probability Functions

The following section introduces you to probability functions.

@BINOMIAL—Calculates the Binomial Probability Mass Function

@BINOMIAL calculates the binomial probability mass function or the cumulative binomial distribution. It uses the following syntax:

@BINOMIAL(*trials*,*successes*,*probability*,[*type*])

The function approximates the cumulative binomial distribution to within $+/-3*10^-7$, and uses the following arguments:

trials	The number of independent trials. This value must be a positive nonzero integer. If *trials* is not entered as an integer, 1-2-3 truncates the value to an integer.
successes	The number of successes in *trials*. This value is any positive integer or 0 but must be less than or equal to *trials*. If *successes* is not entered as an integer, 1-2-3 truncates the value to an integer.
probability	The probability of success on each trial. This value must be any valid probability between 0 and 1.
[*type*]	This optional argument specifies whether 1-2-3 calculates the probability mass function or the cumulative binomial distribution. This argument has three switch options:

Type	Switch Value
0	The probability of exact successes (the default if [*type*] is omitted)
1	The probability of at most successes number of successes
2	The probability of at least successes number of successes.

Suppose that you want to know how many people prefer Cola A over Cola B in a blind taste test. You set up a polling booth at the local mall and call the local TV station. Ten random entrants appear, and you hand each two glasses containing cola. There is no difference in the glasses except for the code on the bottom that identifies which glass has which cola. Because the people showed up at random, there should be a probability of 50 percent of the participants liking either cola. Use the following formula to determine the probability that *exactly* 7 out of 10 prefer Cola A:

`@BINOMIAL(10,7,.5) = 0.117188`

Use this formula to determine the probability that *at most* 7 out of 10 prefer Cola A:

`@BINOMIAL(10,7,.5,1) = 0.945313`

Use this formula to determine the probability that *at least* 7 out of 10 prefer Cola A:

`@BINOMIAL(10,7,.5,2) = 0.171875`

@CHIDIST—Calculating the Chi-Square Distribution

@CHIDIST calculates the chi-square distribution. The chi-square distribution is a continuous, single-parameter distribution derived as a special case of the gamma distribution. The chi-square distribution is approximated to within $+/-3*10^{-7}$; if the result is not approximated to within .0000001 after 100 attempts, @CHIDIST returns ERR. Use the following syntax for @CHIDIST:

`@CHIDIST(x,degrees-of-freedom,[type])`

The arguments are as follows:

x	The value at which to evaluate the chi-squared distribution. The value for *x* depends on the optional [*type*] argument; you have two choices for *x*:
0	This value is the upper bound for the value of the chi-squared cumulative distribution random variable and is a value greater than or equal to 0 (the default if [*type*] is omitted).

1	A significance level, or probability, between 0 and 1.
degrees-of-freedom	The number of degrees of freedom for the sample; this argument is a positive integer. If the value is not entered as an integer, it is truncated to an integer.
[type]	This optional argument specifies how the @CHIDIST is calculated. There are two possible options:

Type	How Calculated
0	The significance level corresponding to *x* (the default if *[type]* is omitted)
1	The critical value that corresponds to the significance level

@COMBIN—Calculating the Binomial Coefficient for *n* and *r*

The binomial coefficient is the number of ways that *r* can be selected from *n*, without regard to order. @COMBIN approximates the binomial coefficient to within +/–3*10^–7. Use the following syntax for @COMBIN:

@COMBIN(*n*,*r*)

In this syntax, the following arguments are used:

n	The number of values; it can be any positive integer or 0
r	The number of values in each combination; it can be any positive integer less than or equal to *n* and can be 0

Suppose that a cup contains six pennies, each with a different date and mint mark. You pick two at random; as you pick a penny from the cup, you do not replace it. The number of date combinations you could have would be determined as follows:

@COMBIN(6,2) = 15

@CRITBINOMIAL—Approximating Binomial Distribution

The @CRITBINOMIAL function returns the largest integer for which the cumulative binomial distribution is less than or equal to *alpha*. @CRITBINOMIAL approximates the cumulative binomial distribution to within $+/-3*10^{-7}$ and is used with the following syntax:

@CRITBINOMIAL(*trials,probability,alpha*)

In this syntax, the following arguments are used:

trials	The number of Bernoulli trials; can be any positive integer or 0
probability	The probability of success for a single Bernoulli trial; can be a value between 0 and 1
alpha	The criterion probability; can be a value between 0 and 1

Suppose that you manage a small plant that manufactures oil filters. The filters are manufactured in lots of 100; there is an 85-percent chance that each filter is free from defects. A 100-filter lot is rejected if more than 90 percent of them are defective. Your task is to determine the greatest number of defective filters that can come off the assembly line before you have to reject the lot.

In this situation, the following facts are known; you can use them to calculate the quantity of filters:

trials = 100

probability = 85% or .85

alpha = 90% or .9

@CRITBINOMIAL(100,.85,.9) = 89

@FDIST—Calculating the F-Distribution

@FDIST is a continuous distribution obtained from the ratio of two chi-squared distributions, each divided by its number of degrees of freedom. The @FDIST function can be used to determine how much two samples vary. The @FDIST function approximates the F-distribution to within $+/-3*10^{-7}$ by comparing the result of the calculation. If the approximation cannot be accomplished to within 0.0000001 after 100 iterations, 1-2-3 for Windows returns ERR. Use the following syntax for @FDIST:

@FDIST(x,degrees-of-freedom1,degrees-of-freedom2,[type])

The arguments are as follows:

x	The value at which to evaluate the F-distribution. The value for x depends on the optional [type] argument; you have three choices for x:

0	The critical value or upper bound for the value of the F-distribution cumulative distribution random variable; can be a value greater than or equal to 0 (the default if you omit the [type] argument).
1	A probability between 0 and 1.
2	The value of the F-distribution random variable; can be a value greater than or equal to 0.

degrees-of-freedom1	The number of degrees of freedom for the first sample; must be a positive integer. If the value is not entered as an integer, it is truncated to an integer.
degrees-of-freedom2	The number of degrees of freedom for the second sample; must be a positive integer. If the value is not entered as an integer, it is truncated to an integer.
[type]	This optional argument specifies how the @FDIST is calculated. You have two options:

Type	How Calculated
0	The significance level corresponding to x (the default if [type] is omitted)
1	The critical value that corresponds to the significance level

Here are some examples of @FDIST:

@FDIST(3.07,8,10) = 0.050078

@FDIST(0.05,8,10) = 0.999865

@NORMAL—Calculating the Normal Distribution Factor for *x*

Use the following syntax for @NORMAL:

@NORMAL(*x*,[*mean*],[*std*],[*type*],[*region*])

The arguments for @NORMAL are as follows:

x	The upper bound for the value of the cumulative normal distribution. The value of *x* used in the calculation is the absolute value of the number used as the argument.
[*mean*]	This optional argument specifies the mean of the distribution. If used, [*mean*] must be a positive value; if omitted, 1-2-3 for Windows defaults to 0.
[*std*]	This optional argument specifies the standard deviation of the distribution. If used, [*std*] must be positive or 0; if omitted, 1-2-3 defaults to 1.
[*type*]	This optional argument specifies what function you want @NORMAL to calculate. You have three options:

Type	What Is Calculated
0	Cumulative distribution function (the default if [*type*] is omitted)
1	Inverse cumulative distribution function
2	Probability density function

[*region*]	This optional argument specifies which area under the cumulative normal distribution to return. There are five options:

Region	What Is Integrated
0	From – to *x* (the default if [*region*] is omitted)
1	From *x* to
2	From –*x* to *x*
3	From 0 to *x*
4	From – to *x* and from *x* to

@PERMUT—Calculating the Permutations of *r* Selected from *n*

Use the following syntax for @PERMUT:

`@PERMUT(n,r)`

The arguments *n* and *r* must be integers, or 1-2-3 for Windows truncates them to integers for the calculations. The arguments are as follows:

n Any positive integer or 0

r Any positive integer or 0; *r* cannot be greater than *n*

Suppose that meetings scheduled for 9:00, 10:00, and 11:00 are to be conducted by three of the five vice presidents of your company. To calculate the number of possible combinations (which vice president conducts which meeting), use the following formula:

`@PERMUT(5,3) = 60`

@POISSON—Calculating the Poisson Distribution

@POISSON calculates the Poisson distribution by approximation. The @POISSON function approximates the Poisson distribution to within +/- $3*10^{-7}$. Use the following syntax for this function:

`@POISSON(x,mean,[cumulative])`

The arguments used with @POISSON are as follows:

x	The number of observed events; can be a positive integer or 0
mean	The expected number of events; can be a positive integer or 0
[*cumulative*]	This optional argument specifies how @POISSON is calculated; there are two options:

Cumulative	Calculation
0	The probability of fewer than or exactly *x* events (the default if [*cumulative*] is omitted)
1	The probability of exactly *x* events

The @POISSON function is useful for predicting the number of events that occur during a specified period of time—such as the number of strollers to pass through the gates of the local amusement park. Suppose that you are expecting strollers to pass through the gates at a rate of 26 per hour. Being optimistic, you want to know the probability that at most 20 strollers will pass through the gates in an hour. Use the following formula to determine the percentage:

`@POISSON(20,26) = 4.1849`

To determine the probability that exactly 20 strollers will pass through the gates, use the following formula to determine the percentage:

`@POISSON(20,26,1) = 13.867`

@TDIST—Calculating the Students' T-Distribution

@TDIST calculates the students T-distribution. The students T-distribution is the distribution of the ratio of a standardized normal distribution to the square root of the quotient of a chi-squared distribution by the number of its degrees of freedom. The students T-distribution is approximated to within +/–3*10^–7; if the result is not approximated to within .0000001 after 100 attempts, the result is ERR. Use the following syntax for @TDIST:

`@TDIST(x,degrees-of-freedom,[type],[tails])`

The arguments are as follows:

x	The value at which to evaluate the students T-distribution. The value for *x* depends on the optional [*type*] argument; you have two choices for *x*:
	0 The upper bound for the value of the cumulative T-distribution random variable; can be a value greater than or equal to 0 (the default if [*type*] is omitted).
	1 A significance level, or probability, between 0 and 1.
degrees-of-freedom	The number of degrees of freedom for the sample; must be a positive integer. If the value is not an integer, it is truncated to an integer.
[*type*]	This optional argument specifies how the @TDIST is calculated. You have two options:

Type	How Calculated
0	The significance level corresponding to *x* (the default if [*type*] is omitted).
1	The critical value that corresponds to the significance level.

[*tails*]   This optional argument specifies the direction of the T-test. You have these options:

Tails	How Calculated
1	One-tailed T-test
2	Two-tailed T-test (the default if [*tails*] is omitted)

Ranking Functions

The following section introduces you to the ranking functions.

@PERCENTILE—Calculating the *x*th Sample

@PERCENTILE calculates the *x*th sample percentile among the values in a range. Use the following syntax for @PERCENTILE:

`@PERCENTILE(x,range)`

The arguments for @PERCENTILE are as follows:

x   The percentage, as a value from 0 to 1, that you want to find

range   The name or address of the values (*range* ignores blank cells, although cells with labels are included and assigned the value 0)

Suppose that you have given a test and gathered the scores. The scores are entered in a range named SCORES in a worksheet and have the following values: 98, 80, 59, 77, 97, 88, 69, and 89. To determine the 95th percentile, use the following formula:

`@PERCENTILE(.95,SCORES) = 97.65`

@PRANK—Finding the Percentile of *x*

@PRANK finds percentile of *x* among the values in a range. Use the following syntax for @PRANK:

@PRANK(*x*,*range*,[*places*])

The arguments for @PRANK are as follows:

x	Any value
range	The name or address of values (*range* ignores blank cells, although cells with labels are included and assigned the value 0)
[*places*]	This optional argument specifies the number of decimal places to round the result of @PRANK; can be a value from 0 to 100 (the default if [*places*] is omitted is 2)

Suppose that you have given a test and gathered the scores. The scores are entered in a range named SCORES in a worksheet and have the following values: 98, 80, 59, 77, 97, 88, 69, and 89. To determine the percentile for a score of 88, use the following formula:

@PRANK(.88,SCORES) = 57

@RANK—Calculating the Position in a Range

@RANK calculates the relative size or position of a value in a range, relative to other values in the range. 1-2-3 assigns duplicate numbers in the range the same rank, although duplicate numbers affect the rank of subsequent numbers in range. Use the following syntax for @RANK:

@RANK(*item*,*range*,[*order*])

The arguments for @RANK are as follows:

item	The value whose rank you want to determine
range	The name or address of a group of values (*item* must be included in *range*)
[*order*]	This optional argument specifies how to rank *item*; there are two options available:

Order	How To Rank *item*
0	Descending order (9 to 1) before ranking *item* (the default if [*order*] is omitted)
1	Ascending order (1 to 9) before ranking *item*

Suppose that you have given a test and gathered the scores. The scores are entered in a range named SCORES in a worksheet and have the following values: 98, 80, 59, 77, 97, 88, 69, and 89. The following formula determines that the score of 88 is the 4th highest score in the range of test scores:

`@RANK(88,SCORES) = 4`

The following formula determines that the score of 88 is the 5th lowest score in the range of test scores:

`@RANK(88,SCORES,1) = 5`

Significance Tests

The following section introduces you to significance tests.

@CHITEST—Performing a Chi-Square Test

Use the following syntax for @CHITEST:

`@CHITEST(range1,range2,[type],[constraints])`

The argument list contains two ranges of values that must be the same size and can contain only values. If the ranges are not the same size, @CHITEST returns ERR. If the ranges are blank, contain labels, or have text formulas, @CHITEST returns ERR.

The optional [*type*] argument specifies the type of chi-squared test to perform. The options are as follows:

Type	Calculation
0	A test for goodness of fit (the default if [*type*] is omitted). A chi-squared test comparing observed data in *range1* to expected data in *range2*, where *range2* can have only positive values.
1	A test for independence. A chi-squared test comparing one set of observed data in *range1* to a second set of observed data in *range2*.

@FTEST—Performing an F-Test

@FTEST performs an F-test on two ranges to determine whether two samples have different variances. The probability of @FTEST is approximated to within $+/-3*10^-7$. use the following syntax for @FTEST:

`@FTEST(range1,range2)`

The *range1* and *range2* arguments contain the values for the test. The ranges do not have to be the same size.

@TTEST—Performing a Students' T-Test

@TTEST performs a students T-test on the data in two ranges and returns the associated probability. Use the following syntax for @TTEST:

@TTEST(*range1*,*range2*,[*type*],[*tails*])

The arguments for @TTEST are as follows:

range1	Contains values; if *range1* contains labels, text formulas, or blank cells, ERR results
range2	Contains values; if *range2* contains labels, text formulas, or blank cells, ERR results
[*type*]	This optional argument specifies what type of T-test to perform; there are three options:

Type	T-Test
0	A T-test for samples drawn from populations with the same variance (*homoscedastic* populations); *range1* and *range2* do not have to contain the same number of cells (the default if [*type*] is omitted)
1	A T-test for samples drawn from populations with unequal variances (*heteroscedastic* populations); *range1* and *range2* do not have to contain the same number of cells
2	A paired T-test; *range1* and *range2* must contain the same number of cells

[*tails*]	This optional argument specifies the direction of the T-test; there are two options:

Tails	How Calculated
1	One-tailed T-test
2	Two-tailed T-test (the default if [*tails*] is omitted)

Using Text Functions

1-2-3 for Windows offers a variety of functions that give you significant power to manipulate text strings; there are also a few special functions for working with the 1-2-3 for Windows character set (the IBM PC Multi-lingual code page—code page 850). The complete character set, listed in Appendix B of this book, includes everything from the copyright sign (©) to the lowercase *e* with the grave accent (è).

Strings are labels or portions of labels. More specifically, strings are data consisting of characters (alphabetical, numeric, blank, and special) enclosed in quotation marks, such as `"total"`. The functions specifically designated as string functions are not the only 1-2-3 for Windows functions that take advantage of the power and flexibility of strings. For example, logical, error-trapping, and special functions use strings as well as values. The string functions, however, are specifically designed to manipulate strings. Table 7.16 summarizes the string functions available in 1-2-3 for Windows.

Table 7.16 String Functions

Function	Description
@CHAR(*number*)	Converts a code number (code page 850) into its corresponding character
@CLEAN(*string*)	Removes nonprintable characters from the string
@CODE(*string*)	Converts the first character in the string into a code number (code page 850)
@EXACT(*string1*,*string2*)	Returns 1 (true) if *string1* and *string2* are exact matches; otherwise, returns 0 (false)
@FIND(*search-string*,*string*, start-number*)	Locates the start position of one string within another string
@LEFT(*string*,*number*)	Extracts the leftmost specified number of characters from the string
@LENGTH(*string*)	Returns the number of characters in the string
@LOWER(*string*)	Converts all characters in the string to lowercase

Function	Description
@MID(*string,start-number, number*)	Extracts a string of a specified number of characters from the middle of another string, beginning at the starting position
@N(*range*)	Returns as a value the contents of the cell in the upper left corner of the range
@PROPER(*string*)	Converts the first character in each word in the string to uppercase and converts the remaining characters to lowercase
@REPEAT(*string,number*)	Copies the string the specified number of times in a cell
@REPLACE(*original-string, start-number,length, replacement-string*)	Replaces a number of characters in the original string with new string characters, starting at the character identified by the start position
@RIGHT(*string,number*)	Extracts the rightmost specified number of characters from the string
@S(*range*)	Returns as a label the contents of the cell in the upper left corner of the range
@STRING(*number-to-convert, decimal-places*)	Converts a value to a string, showing the specified number of decimal places
@TRIM(*string*)	Removes blank spaces from the string
@UPPER(*string*)	Converts all characters in the string to uppercase
@VALUE(*string*)	Converts a string to a value

You can link strings to other strings by using the concatenation operator (&). The discussion of the individual string functions in this section shows several examples of the use of the concatenation operator. Keep in mind that you cannot link strings to cells that contain numeric values or that are empty. If you try, 1-2-3 for Windows returns ERR.

Avoid mixing data types in string functions. For example, some functions produce strings, but other functions produce numeric results. If a function's result is not of the data type you need, use @STRING to convert a numeric value to a string; use @VALUE to convert a string to a numeric value.

The numbering scheme for positioning characters in a string begins with 0 and continues to the number corresponding to the last character in the label. The prefix (') in front of a label is not counted for numeric positioning. For example, in the label 'dog, *d* is position 0, *o* is position 1, and *g* is position 2. Negative position numbers are not allowed.

@CHAR—Displaying Multilingual Characters

The @CHAR function produces on-screen the IBM PC Multilingual code-page equivalent of a number that specifies that character. The syntax of @CHAR is as follows:

@CHAR(*number*)

Figure 7.60 shows several examples of the use of @CHAR.

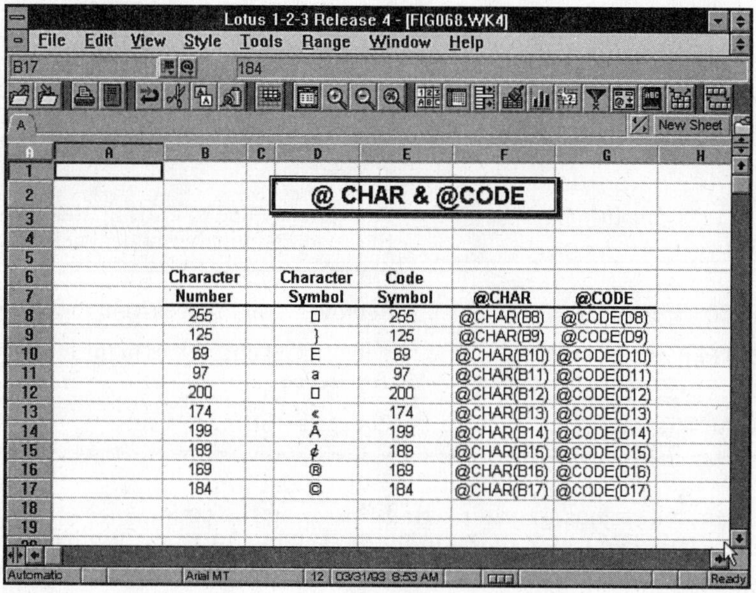

FIG. 7.60

Examples of @CHAR and @CODE.

NOTE Some numerical-equivalent characters are not supported in 1-2-3 for Windows. The characters not supported return a symbol that does not match the code-page symbol. The character numbers 255 and 200 in figure 7.60 show different characters than are presented in the code-page examples in Appendix C.

@CODE—Computing the Multilingual Code

The @CODE function does the opposite of @CHAR. @CHAR takes a number and returns an IBM multilingual character; @CODE takes as its argument an IBM multilingual character and returns a code-page number. Figure 7.60 shows how you can use the @CODE function. The syntax for @CODE is as follows:

@CODE(*string*)

Suppose that you want to find the IBM multilingual code for the letter A. Enter **@CODE("A")** in a cell, and 1-2-3 for Windows returns the number 65. If you enter **@CODE("Aardvark")**, 1-2-3 for Windows still returns 65: the code of the first character in the string. Uppercase and lowercase letters have different codes: if you enter **@CODE("a")**, 1-2-3 returns 97.

@FIND—Locating One String within Another

The @FIND function locates the starting position of one string within another string. For example, you can use @FIND to determine the position at which the blank space occurs within the string "Jim Johnson". You can use the position number of the blank space with the @LEFT and @RIGHT functions to separate "Jim" and "Johnson" into two separate cells for use in a mailing-list database. (Although this example shows a search for the single blank-space character, @FIND also finds the location of multiple character strings—such as "Calif"—within longer strings.) The @FIND function uses the following syntax:

@FIND(*search-string*,*string*,*start-number*)

The *search-string* argument is the string you want to locate. In this example, the search string is " " (a blank space enclosed in parentheses). The *string* being searched is "Jim Johnson". The *start-number* argument is the position number in *string* where you want to start the search. Remember that the first character in the string is counted as 0, not 1. To start at the first character and search through the contents of cell A6 for a blank space, use the following statement:

@FIND(" ",A6,0)

If "Jim Johnson" is the string in cell A6, the @FIND function returns the value 3. In figure 7.61, @FIND locates the last name Lange, starting at the ninth character in cell B13.

You can search for a second occurrence of *search-string* by adding 1 to the result of the first @FIND function and using that value as the *start-number* argument. This action starts the next @FIND operation at the character location after the blank space already found. The following formula searches for the character position of the second blank space:

```
@FIND(" ",A6,@FIND(" ",A6,1)+1)
```

When @FIND cannot find a match, the result is ERR.

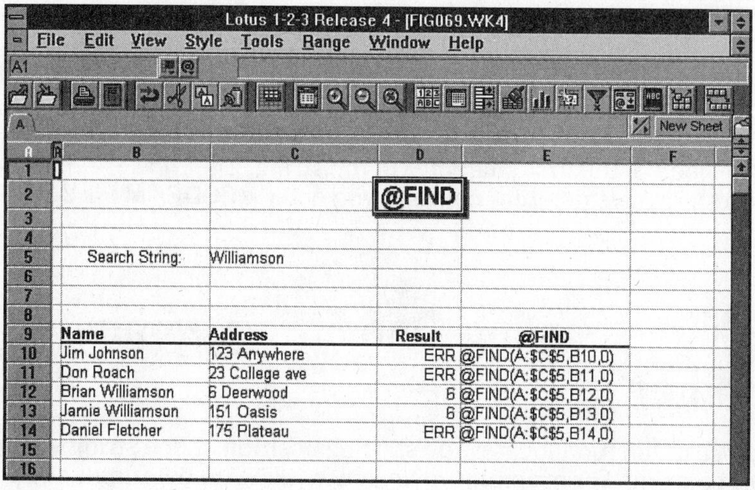

FIG. 7.61

Using @FIND to find a text string.

@MID—Extracting One String from Another

The @FIND function *locates* one string within another; the @MID function *extracts* one string from another. @MID uses the following format:

```
@MID(string,start-number,number)
```

The *start-number* argument is a number representing the character position in *string* where you want to begin extracting characters. The *number* argument indicates the length of the string to be extracted (it is the number of characters to extract). For example, to extract the first name from a label containing the full name "Mary Baggett", use the following statement:

```
@MID("Mary Baggett",0,4)
```

This function extracts the string starting in position 0 (the first character) and continuing for a length of four characters—through the string "Mary".

Suppose that you want to extract the first and last names from a column of full names, and that you want to put those two extracted names in separate columns. To accomplish both tasks, use the @MID and @FIND functions. Because you know that a blank space separates the first and last names, you can use @FIND to locate the character position of the blank space in each full name. You can use this character position to set up the functions to extract the first and last names.

If cell C9 contains the full name "Jim Johnson", as shown in figure 7.62, place the following function in cell A6:

```
@MID(C6,0,@FIND(" ",C6,0))
```

The result of this function is "Jim" because @FIND(" ",C6,0) returns a value of 6 for the *number* argument.

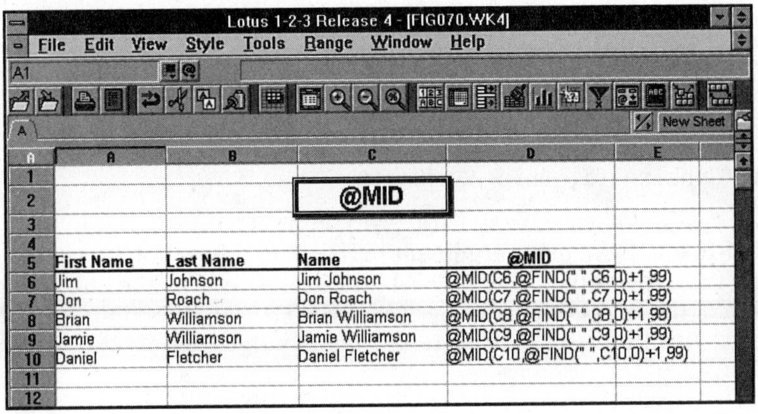

Lotus 1-2-3 Release 4 - [FIG070.WK4]
File Edit View Style Tools Range Window Help
A1

	A	B	C	D	E
1					
2			@MID		
3					
4					
5	First Name	Last Name	Name	@MID	
6	Jim	Johnson	Jim Johnson	@MID(C6,@FIND(" ",C6,0)+1,99)	
7	Don	Roach	Don Roach	@MID(C7,@FIND(" ",C7,0)+1,99)	
8	Brian	Williamson	Brian Williamson	@MID(C8,@FIND(" ",C8,0)+1,99)	
9	Jamie	Williamson	Jamie Williamson	@MID(C9,@FIND(" ",C9,0)+1,99)	
10	Daniel	Fletcher	Daniel Fletcher	@MID(C10,@FIND(" ",C10,0)+1,99)	
11					
12					

FIG. 7.62

Using @MID and @FIND to extract first and last names.

Place the following statement in cell B6, as shown in figure 7.62:

```
@MID(C9,@FIND(" ",C9,0)+1,99)
```

The @FIND function indicates that the *start-number* of the @MID function is one character beyond the blank space. The length of the string to be extracted is 99 characters (although a length of 99 is greater than you need, no ERR results from this excess). The string that 1-2-3 for Windows extracts based on the preceding formula is "Jamie Williamson".

If you use this type of formula to convert a long string in a database into shorter strings, convert the string formulas (first and last names) into values before using the database.

@LEFT and @RIGHT—Extracting Strings from Left and Right

The @LEFT and @RIGHT functions are variations of @MID; you use them to extract one string of characters from another, beginning at the leftmost and rightmost positions in the string. These functions require the following syntax:

`@LEFT(string,number)`

`@RIGHT(string,number)`

The *number* argument is the number of characters to be extracted from *string*. If you want to extract the ZIP code from the string `"Cincinnati, Ohio 45243"`, for example, use the following statement:

`@RIGHT("Cincinnati, Ohio 45243",5)`

@LEFT works the same way as @RIGHT except that @LEFT extracts from the beginning of a string. For example, use the following statement to extract the city in the preceding example:

`@LEFT("Cincinnati, Ohio 45243",10)`

In most cases, you can use @FIND(",","Cincinnati, Ohio 45243",0) instead of 10 for the *number* argument in the @LEFT function to extract the city from the address. The @FIND statement returns the character position of the first comma in the "Cincinnati, Ohio 45243" string; this character position is then used as the *number* argument by the @LEFT function.

@REPLACE—Replacing a String within a String

The @REPLACE function replaces one group of characters in a string with another group of characters. @REPLACE is a valuable tool for correcting a frequent and incorrect text entry without retyping the entry. Use the following syntax for @REPLACE:

`@REPLACE(original-string,start-number,length,`
`replacement-string)`

The *start-number* argument indicates the position where 1-2-3 for Windows begins removing characters from *original-string*. The *length* argument shows how many characters to remove; *replacement-string* contains the new characters to replace the removed ones. @REPLACE starts counting character positions in a string at 0 and continues to the end of the string (up to 511).

@LENGTH—Computing the Length of a String

The @LENGTH function calculates the length of a string. @LENGTH uses the following syntax:

@LENGTH(*string*)

@LENGTH frequently is used to calculate the length of a string being extracted from another string. This function also can be used to check for data-entry errors. The function returns ERR as the length of numeric values or formulas, empty cells, and null strings.

@EXACT—Comparing Strings

The @EXACT function compares two strings and returns 1 (true) if the strings are exactly the same or 0 (false) for strings that are different. Use the following syntax for this function:

@EXACT(*string1*,*string2*)

The @EXACT function's method of comparison is similar to the = operator in formulas (except that the = operator checks for a match regardless of uppercase and lowercase characters). @EXACT checks for an exact match that distinguishes between uppercase and lowercase characters. If cell B7 holds the string "Wrench" and cell D7 holds the string "wrench", the logical value of B7=D7 is 1 because the two strings are an approximate match. The value of @EXACT(B7,D7), however, is 0 because the two functions are not an exact match; their cases are different.

The *string1* and *string2* arguments can be text, the result of text formulas, or references to cells containing text or text formulas. The examples in figure 7.63 demonstrate the use of @EXACT and compare the results of @EXACT and = formulas. Notice that in the last three examples, @EXACT cannot compare nonstring arguments. In fact, if either argument is a nonstring value of any type (including numbers) or is blank, 1-2-3 for Windows returns ERR. (Note that you can use the @S function, explained later in this chapter, to ensure that the arguments used within @EXACT have string values.) When you use = to compare a string with a number or a blank cell, the string is treated as the number 0, as is a blank cell. This means that if you use the = formula, any string is equal to a blank cell or a cell that contains the number 0.

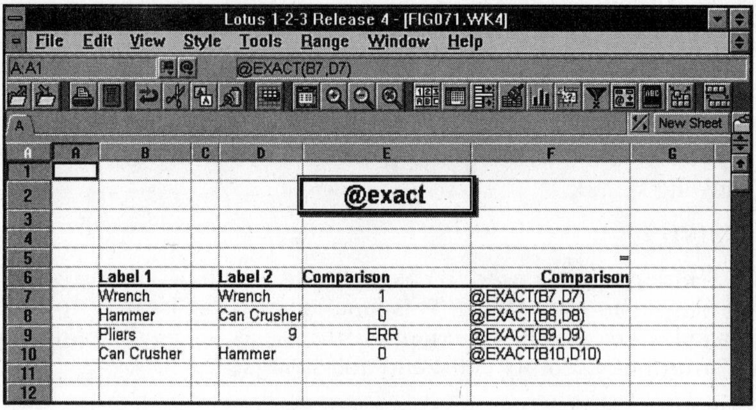

FIG. 7.63

Comparing strings with @EXACT.

@LOWER, @UPPER, and @PROPER— Converting the Case of Strings

1-2-3 for Windows offers three functions for converting the case of a string value:

@LOWER(*string*)	Converts all letters in a string to lowercase
@UPPER(*string*)	Converts all letters in a string to uppercase
@PROPER(*string*)	Capitalizes the first letter in each word of a label (words are defined as groups of characters separated by blank spaces); the remaining letters in each word are converted to lowercase

Figure 7.64 gives an example of the use of each of these functions.

These functions work with string values or references to strings. If a cell contains a number or a null string (" "), 1-2-3 for Windows returns ERR for each of these functions. (Note that you can use the @S function, explained later in this chapter, to ensure that the arguments of these functions have string values.)

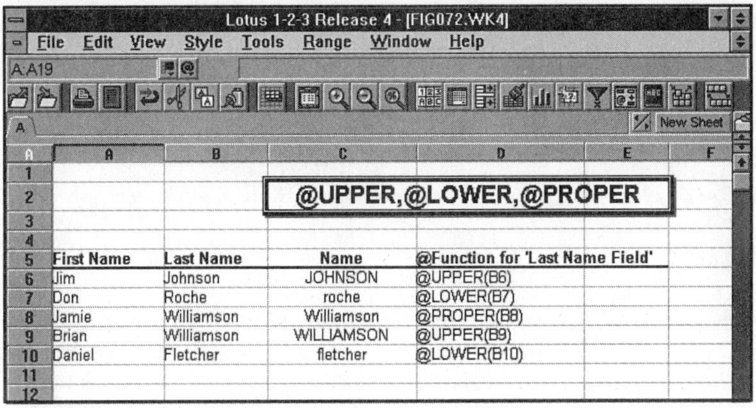

FIG. 7.64

String functions used to convert the case of alphabetic characters.

Use @LOWER, @UPPER, or @PROPER to modify the contents of a database so that all entries in a field appear with the same capitalization. This technique produces consistent reports. Capitalization also affects the sorting order: uppercase and lowercase letters do not sort together. To ensure that data with different capitalization sorts together, create a column (use one of the functions that references the data) and then sort on this new column.

@REPEAT—Repeating Strings within a Cell

The @REPEAT function repeats strings a specified number of times, much as the backslash (\) repeats strings to fill a cell. @REPEAT, however, has some distinct advantages over the backslash. With @REPEAT, you can repeat the string the precise number of times you want. If the result is wider than the cell width, the result is displayed in empty adjacent cells to the right. Use the following syntax for @REPEAT:

@REPEAT(*string*,*number*)

The *number* argument indicates the number of times you want to repeat *string* in the cell. For example, if you want to repeat the string "-**-" three times, enter **@REPEAT("-**-",3)**. The resulting string is "-**—**—**-". This string follows the 1-2-3 for Windows rule for long labels, which states that the string is displayed beyond the right boundary of the column, provided that no entry is in the cell to the right. When you use the backslash to repeat a string, however, 1-2-3 for Windows fills the column to the exact column width.

@N and @S—Testing for Strings and Values

The @N and @S functions ensure that a cell contains numeric values or string values. These functions are important when you use other functions that operate on numeric values only or on string values only. When you are in doubt about whether a cell contains a numeric or text value, use @N or @S to force the contents into becoming a number or text.

@N forces the contents of a cell to be a number. If the cell contains a numeric value, @N returns that value. If the cell is blank or contains a label, @N returns the value 0. @N always returns a numeric value.

@S forces the contents of a cell to text. If the cell contains a string or a formula that evaluates to a string, @S returns that string. If the cell contains a number or is empty, @S returns the null string (" "). @S always returns a string value.

These functions prevent formulas from resulting in ERR when data in a cell is not of the type expected. Use the following syntax for the @N and @S functions:

@N(*range*)

@S(*range*)

The *range* argument must be a range or a single-cell reference. If you use a single-cell reference, 1-2-3 for Windows adjusts the argument to range format and returns the numeric or string value of the single cell. If the *range* argument is a multicell range, @N or @S returns the numeric or string value of the upper left corner of the range.

@STRING—Converting Values to Strings

The @STRING function enables you to convert a number to its text-string equivalent so that you can work with the number as text. With @STRING, you can convert a number to text and then concatenate the result into a text sentence. As the example in cell D6 of figure 7.65 shows, the alignment of the text-string equivalent is not right justified.

The string takes on the properties of a label after conversion; if alignment is necessary, do so by using the Style Alignment command. Use the following syntax for @STRING:

@STRING(*number-to-convert,decimal-places*)

1-2-3 for Windows uses the Style Number Format Fixed Decimal format for the @STRING function. The *decimal-places* argument represents the number of decimal places to be included in the string. 1-2-3 for Windows rounds the resulting textual number to match the number of decimal places you specify. Note also that @STRING ignores all numeric formats placed on the cell and operates on just the numeric contents of the cell. Figure 7.65 shows examples of values being used as strings.

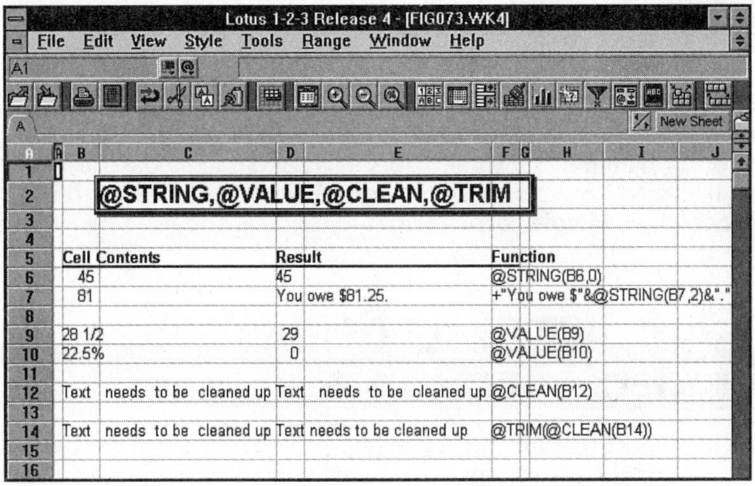

FIG. 7.65

@STRING, @VALUE, @CLEAN, and @TRIM used to convert and maintain strings and values.

@VALUE—Converting Strings to Values

The @VALUE function converts a number that is a string into a numeric value that can be used in calculations. The string must be text or a label made up only of numbers and numeric formatting characters, such as the comma, decimal point, and dollar sign. The string cannot contain other alphabetical characters or an illegal number format, such as 1,23.99. A nice feature of @VALUE is that it converts text fractions into decimal numbers (see fig. 7.65). The function is useful, therefore, in converting stock data from databases or wire services into numbers you can analyze and chart. @VALUE requires the following syntax:

@VALUE(*string*)

A few rules are important when you use @VALUE: 1-2-3 for Windows usually does not object to extra spaces left in a string. Currency signs (such as $) that precede the string are acceptable. Another point to remember is that when a numeric value is supplied as an argument for @VALUE, the original number value is returned.

@TRIM—Removing Blank Spaces from a String

The @TRIM function eliminates unwanted blank spaces from the beginning, end, or middle of a string. If multiple adjacent spaces are within a string, they are reduced to one space. Use the following syntax for @TRIM:

@TRIM(*string*)

@TRIM is useful for trimming spaces from data as it is entered into a macro or for trimming unwanted spaces from data in a database. Such spaces in a database can cause the sort order to be different than what you expect. An example of the @TRIM function is shown in figure 7.65.

@CLEAN—Removing Nonprintable Characters from Strings

When you import text files with File Import, particularly files transmitted with a modem, the strings sometimes contain nonprintable characters. The @CLEAN function removes the nonprintable characters from the strings (see fig. 7.65). Use the following syntax for @CLEAN:

@CLEAN(*string*)

The *string* argument must be a string value or a reference to a cell containing a string value. 1-2-3 for Windows cannot accept a cell entry containing @CLEAN with a range argument specified.

Summary

This chapter described the functions that 1-2-3 Release 4 for Windows provides to make formula and worksheet construction easier and, usually, error-free. 1-2-3 Release 4 for Windows includes over 120 new functions that can enhance your worksheets and provide greater flexibility in managing data. This chapter will serve as an invaluable reference tool as you become more proficient with functions.

Chapter 8 introduces you to the Solver, Backsolver, and Audit features that enable you to examine formulas and audit your worksheets.

Solving Formulas and Auditing Worksheets

N ow that you've learned how to create and use 1-2-3 for Windows worksheets, you can use the Solver and the Backsolver to help you find solutions to problems posed by the data and data relationships established in a worksheet. The Solver and the Backsolver tools let you create a variety of scenarios with the data, presenting several results found by supplying different values for one or more variables in a problem. A common way to collect a number of solutions to a problem based on different assumptions is to use scenarios. If you try to achieve the best profit margin for a product, for example, use the Solver to test several values for inventory, cost of goods, and price.

The *Solver* tool analyzes the data and relationships between data in a worksheet and determines a set of possible answers, including an optimal answer, if you request it. A powerful tool, the Solver not only finds possible answers for you, but also explains each answer and how it was found. The *Backsolver* tool uses a specified value as a solution to a problem and works backward from this solution to determine the correct value of a variable.

1-2-3 also provides a tool for auditing your worksheets. *Auditing* means identifying formulas and other cells in a worksheet and analyzing their relationships to other data in a worksheet. The audit function of 1-2-3 helps you find all formulas in a worksheet, or those formulas with special characteristics that you specify, such as those with circular references. This tool is especially useful for worksheets that are quite large, contain many formulas, or contain complex formulas. You may also find the audit feature useful for analyzing worksheets that are unfamiliar for some reason, perhaps because you did not use those worksheets for a while or because other users created those worksheets.

This chapter describes how to do the following:

- Set up scenarios to use with the Solver
- Analyze the Solver results
- Use functions with the Solver
- Use the Backsolver
- Use 1-2-3's audit feature to find and analyze formulas

Using the Solver

The Solver analyzes data and data relationships in a worksheet to determine a series of possible answers to a specific problem. You can use the Solver, for example, to find the highest price you can afford to pay for a house; determine the combination of sales items that yield the greatest profit; search for an investment strategy that yields the highest return subject to your tolerance for risk; or explore the profit potential of a new business, based on different marketing strategies.

Of course, you could find solutions to a problem by repeatedly inserting new values for the variables in a worksheet. With the proper information, however, the Solver automatically finds the solution for you. At your request, the Solver determines the optimal answer of all answers found, and shows you how each answer was derived.

After you use the Solver, you'll find that this tool makes many of the following worksheet problems easier to solve:

- Mortgage and loan determination
- Investment and stock portfolio analysis
- Budget analysis
- Scheduling and time/cost analysis

Through a series of specific examples that illustrate the range of problems the Solver can address, the following sections describe the Solver and Solver reports.

Understanding Terminology

Before you use the Solver, you need to understand a few terms.

The Solver finds answers to a problem by using the data and the data relationships contained in a worksheet. The cells that you direct Solver to look at are known as the *problem cells*. The Solver ignores data in the worksheet, such as values, formulas, labels, and so on. The Solver calculates quickly because it looks at and operates on only the problem cells.

Solver operates on three kinds of problem cells: *adjustable cells*, *constraint cells*, and *optimal cells*. The role each of these cells plays in Solver's search for answers to a problem is discussed in the following:

- **Adjustable cells.** All problems given to the Solver must contain one or more values the Solver can change to find the best solutions to a problem. In mathematical terms, these values are called *variables*. Variable values are contained in what 1-2-3 calls *adjustable cells*.

  Because the Solver changes the values in these cells, these cells can contain only numbers, not text or formulas, and the cells cannot be protected. As the Solver calculates its solutions, it may change the values in one or more adjustable cells.

- **Constraint cells.** For the Solver to find solutions within reasonable limits, each worksheet problem must also specify its limitations in *constraint cells*. If you use the Solver to determine a mortgage rate, for example, you might decide to limit the possible answers to include an interest rate between 8 percent and 12 percent. In addition, you can constrain the mortgage payment to no more than $1,100 per month. You can set more than one constraint for any worksheet problem.

  The constraint cells in a worksheet must contain logical formulas that evaluate to true (1) or false (0). Constraint cells can contain any simple logical formulas using the <, >, <=, >=, or = operators. Constraint cells cannot contain complex logical formulas, such as those that use #AND#, #NOT#, #OR#, or <>.

- **Optimal cells.** If you choose, you can also specify an *optimal cell* in a worksheet. An optimal cell contains a value that you want to maximize or minimize as part of the solution. For example, you can use the Solver to find the maximum profit in a worksheet that contains price, cost of goods, and sales figures for a product. To control costs, you can define the cell that contains the cost of goods as an optimal cell that you want to minimize while maximizing profits.

When you specify an optimal cell, the Solver looks for answers that maximize or minimize the optimal cell. The Solver presents all answers it finds, but presents the answer that satisfies the optimal cell requirement first. When an optimal cell is not specified, all answers are presented in random order.

Example #1: Finding a House You Can Afford

The house price a family can afford depends on several key factors. Of course, affordability depends on the amount of money a family earns. Next, consider the price of the house and the size of the payments relative to the family's income. The amount of other debt and the magnitude of total debt also must be reviewed—total debt includes the added burden of the new home loan. Finally, you add into the equation other constraints, such as ratios imposed by a bank to protect the value of the loan, and the size of the down payment you can deposit.

Figure 8.1 shows a sample worksheet representing these relationships. The worksheet starts by showing annual household income. The next two cells that contain values are two adjustable cells—the purchase price and the bank loan. The down payment is represented as a formula that subtracts the home loan amount from the purchase price. The loan rate and term are two constants (presumably, you shop for the best rate for a particular situation). Next, the monthly payment is an @PMT function that uses the bank loan, rate, and term as arguments (see Chapter 7, "Using Functions," for a detailed explanation of @PMT). The final entry in the Purchase Information area is the ratio of the down payment to the house price; frequently, banks have policies that specify minimum values for this ratio.

The principal, interest, taxes, and insurance (PITI) segment of the worksheet represents the monthly principal and interest value on an annual basis. The formula for the annual payment multiplies the monthly payment by 12. This section also adds estimates of the real estate tax and insurance to the principal and interest payments. Finally, the section computes PITI's share of total household income.

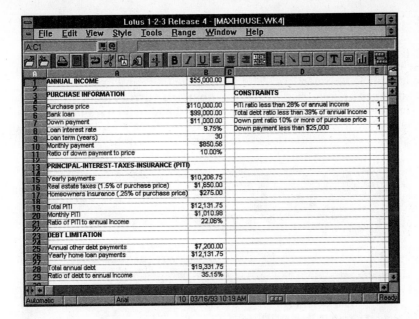

FIG. 8.1

A worksheet for computing the mortgage an applicant can afford.

To compute total household debt, the Debt Limitation section of the worksheet adds other debt to the home loan. The total value is then divided by household income to determine the share of gross income allocated for debt service after the home loan.

Defining Constraints

Column D displays a list of problem constraints. These constraints include conditions imposed by the bank or personal circumstances that limit the house price you can afford. The example shows that the bank requires PITI to be less than 28 percent and total debt to be less than 39 percent of household income. The down payment must be no less than 10 percent of the purchase price. The borrower's personal resources allow a down payment of as much as $25,000.

Constraints are written as a series of logical formulas. For example, the requirement that PITI be less than 28 percent of household income is entered in cell E5 as +B21<.28. If the quantity in cell B21 is less than 28 percent, this formula evaluates to 1; otherwise, the result is 0. Similar logical formulas represent the other constraints. For the remaining constraints, the formulas in cells E6..E8 are +B29<.39; +B11>=.1; and +B7<25,000.

Entering the Problem into Solver

Figure 8.2 shows the Solver Definition dialog box. To reach this box, select Range Analyze Solver from the 1-2-3 for Windows menu bar, or click the Solve SmartIcon. The Adjustable Cells and Constraint Cells text boxes initially display the cell pointer's current location in the worksheet. In the worksheet, you want to make the purchase price and the bank loan adjustable. To do so, enter the cell addresses in the Adjustable Cells text box (for example, specify B5..B6).

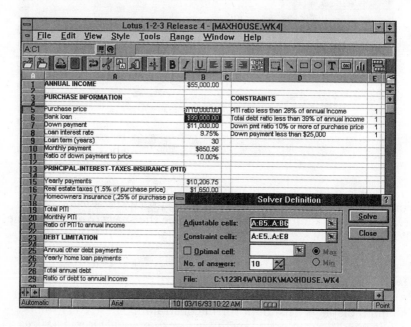

FIG. 8.2

Adjustable and constraint cell ranges shown in the Solver Definition dialog box.

To complete a problem description, you must specify a set of Constraint Cells. In this example, the constraint cells are E5 through E8. After you designate the constraint cells, click the Solve button to start the search for solutions.

T I P   To limit the number of answers you want Solver to find, select a value in the No. of Answers text box. In figure 8.2, for example, Solver finds no more than 10 answers.

Figure 8.3 shows the Solver Progress dialog box. This box displays when a solution search is in progress. In figure 8.3, Solver is seeking the third solution to the purchase price that satisfies the constraints listed in cells E5..E8. In this box, the Stop button enables you to stop a search for solutions at any time. Solver retains all solutions found before clicking the Stop button.

FIG. 8.3

The Solver Progress box shows the Solver searching for a third answer.

Interpreting Home Mortgage Solver Solutions

Figure 8.4 shows the Solver Answer dialog box. The Definition option button returns you to the Solver Definition dialog box shown in figure 8.2. The Answer option button (selected in figure 8.4), displays information about the answers found. The Reports option button enables you to choose a report type, as you learn later in this chapter.

The entry Answer (#1 of 3) indicates that the worksheet displays the first of three answers found. By successively clicking the Next button, you can cycle through all the solutions the Solver found. Each time you display a new solution, the data in the worksheet changes to reflect the new solution. Clicking the Original button at any point returns the initial worksheet values from which the search for solutions was launched. Click the First button to return to answer #1. The Save button enables you to save an answer as a scenario. (Refer to Chapter 9, Using the Version Manager, for more information about scenarios.)

> To move the Solver Definition dialog box anywhere on-screen, click the mouse on the title bar and drag the box to the desired location. You frequently may need to relocate the Definition dialog box so that you can clearly see the worksheet cells you want to see.
>
> **T I P**

In figure 8.5, the Solver Answer dialog box is moved to the right to make all the worksheet data visible. The worksheet now displays the second solution: the largest house price that still satisfies the constraints. The figure also shows that all the constraints can be satisfied if the buyer uses a $25,000 down payment on a $139,532.86 house. Cell B21 shows that PITI is less than 26 percent of income, well below the 28 percent constraint. Cell B29 shows total debt rounding to 39 percent of annual income. The cell's actual value, however, is .3899999, barely below the .39 constraint. The down payment is nearly 18 percent of the purchase price, which substantially exceeds the third constraint of at least 10 percent. Finally, the down payment is $25,000, the fourth and final constraint for the problem.

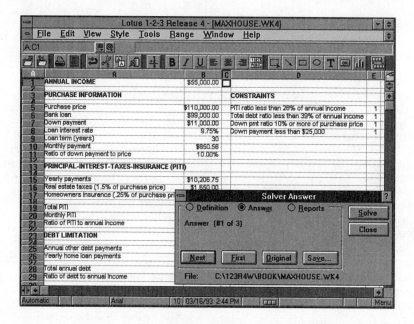

FIG. 8.4

The Solver Answer dialog box showing solution #1.

After Solver finds one or more solutions, exit from Solver by repeatedly clicking the Close button in the Solver Answer dialog box (see fig. 8.4). However, before you click the Close button, decide which solution you want to leave on the worksheet. Select a solution with the Next button, and then click the Close button. You can save the displayed solution for future reference. If you prefer to save the solution separately, create a sheet in the current worksheet file and place the selected solution in the new worksheet file.

In the home mortgage example, the third solution found by Solver designates a purchase price of $129,206.32 and a down payment of $12,920.63. This solution satisfies the 10% constraint for the down payment ratio to the purchase price and the overall debt ratio of 39%.

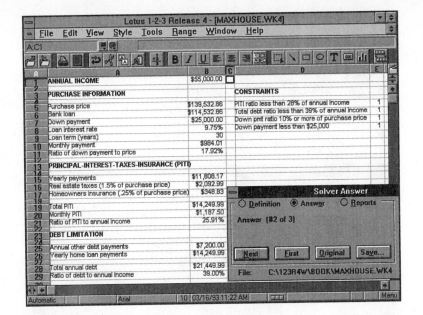

FIG. 8.5

The Solver Answer dialog box showing solution #2.

If you choose, you can alter the constraints to see other solutions Solver might find. For example, consider the case in which $2,000 of the money available for a down payment is diverted to pay off existing debt. This change drops the maximum down payment to less than $23,000. The annual other debt payment amount also is reduced to around $5,200—down from the previous value of $7,200.

Example #2: Maximizing Candy Profits

Example #1 illustrated the basic operation of Solver. For this problem, an optimal solution was not defined. In Example #2, however, you learn how to use Solver to search and rank by order the optimal solutions found. When you specify an optimal cell, you seek to maximize or minimize a particular value. Figure 8.6 shows a simple what-if problem involving school candy sales. You ask the Solver to maximize the profit.

Suppose that you want to determine the number of candy bars and gum drops to sell to make the most profit for a school. You enter the text and values shown in figure 8.6, using in the specified cells the following formulas:

E5+C5*B5

E6+C6*B6

E8 @SUM(E5..E6)

F5 +D5*B5

F6 +D6*B6

G5   +F5-E5

G6   +F6-E6

G8   @SUM(G5..G6)

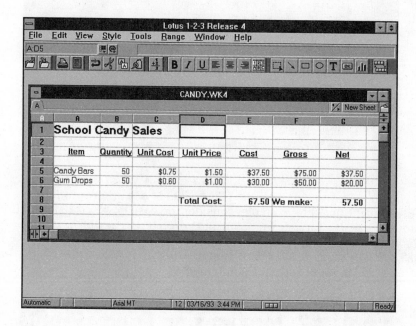

FIG. 8.6

A school candy
sales worksheet.

To find a solution to this problem without using Solver, you can enter
different values in cells C5 and C6 to see the effect these values have on
the net profit (in cell G8). Using the Solver, however, is easier and
faster.

Defining Constraints

Before you run the Solver, you first need to enter the criteria that limit
the possible answers; these criteria are the problem's constraints. For
example, the candy supplier may stipulate that you buy at least 50
units each of candy bars and gum drops. The school also may limit
your initial funds to $1,000. Finally, you may decide that selling candy is
worthwhile for the school only if you make a profit of $900 or more.

Figure 8.7 shows these criteria in the worksheet. The constraint cells are formatted as text so that you can see the logical formulas used for each constraint.

Lotus 1-2-3 Release 4 - [CANDY.WK4]

File Edit View Style Tools Range Window Help

A:D5

	A	B	C	D	E	F	G	H
1	**School Candy Sales**							
2								
3	Item	Quantity	Unit Cost	Unit Price	Cost	Gross	Net	
4								
5	Candy Bars	50	$0.75	$1.50	$37.50	$75.00	$37.50	
6	Gum Drops	50	$0.60	$1.00	$30.00	$50.00	$20.00	
7								
8				Total Cost:	67.50	We make:	57.50	
9								
10								
11								
12	Constraints							
13								
14	We must make at least $300				+G8>=300			
15	We can spend at most $1000				+E8<=1000			
16	We must by at least 50 candy bars				+B5>=50			
17	We must buy at least 50 gum drops				+B6>=50			
18								
19								

Automatic   Arial MT   12 03/16/93 3:44 PM   Ready

FIG. 8.7

The candy sales worksheet showing the logical constraint formulas for Solver.

Entering the Problem into Solver

To enter the problem in the Solver, the first step is to designate the cells for which values are adjustable. The adjustable cells (in this example, cells B5 and B6) contain the amounts of candy bars and gum drops that can be sold by the school.

You then enter the cell addresses that contain the constraints for the problem. In figure 8.7, the constraint formulas are in cells E14 through E17. When you enter the constraint cells, remember that you enter only the cells that hold the formulas; do not include any text that describes the constraints. If the constraint cells are not grouped in a range, you can enter a series of cells (or ranges), separating the cell addresses with commas. For example, to specify the cells A7 and F14 as constraint cells, enter **A7,F14**.

 NOTE The amount of memory on your computer limits Solver's ability to solve problems. To help Solver work at its best, limit the total number of adjustable, constraint, optimal, and other supporting cells to fewer than 1,000.

To optimize a value, enter the cell that contains this value as the Optimal cell. In figure 8.7, G8 was entered as the Optimal cell. When you designate an optimal cell, Solver maximizes or minimizes this cell, depending on the current selection of the Max and Min buttons in the Solver Definition dialog box. Because the amount in cell G8 is the net profit you want to make on the candy sale, maximize this value by clicking the Max button. Figure 8.8 shows the completed Solver Definition dialog box.

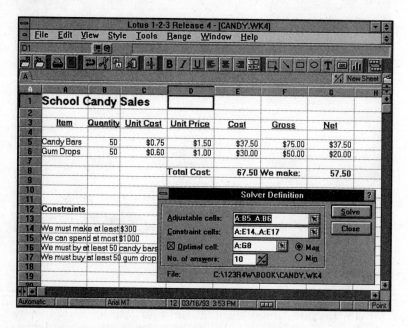

FIG. 8.8

The completed Solver Definition dialog box for the candy-selling worksheet.

Interpreting Candy Sales Solver Solutions

When you choose Solve from the Solver Definition dialog box, the Solver begins to find all the possible answers for the problem. Because you included an optimal cell, the Solver also determines which of the answers is the *best* answer. As the Solver is running, 1-2-3 for Windows displays the Solver Progress dialog box, which displays the length of time the Solver has been running and the number of answers found for the problem. When the Solver finds all the possible answers, 1-2-3 for Windows displays the Solver Answer dialog box (see fig. 8.9).

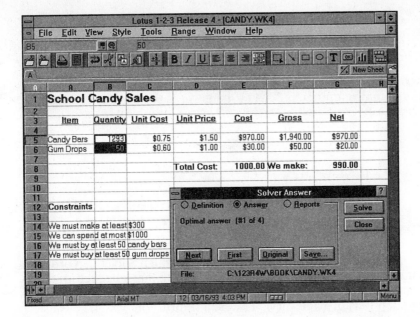

FIG. 8.9

The Solver Answer dialog box for the candy-selling worksheet, after all answers are found.

The Solver found four acceptable answers to the candy sales problem. Each time you choose Next from the Solver Answer dialog box, 1-2-3 for Windows displays one of the four solutions. As you cycle through the answers, Solver lets you know which answer is the optimal answer by labeling it Optimal answer. Notice that each time you select a new answer, 1-2-3 for Windows changes the values in the worksheet. Figure 8.9 shows the data that the Solver judged to be the optimal answer for the problem (in this example, answer #1).

To return to the optimal solution, choose First from the Solver Answer dialog box. Choose Original to view the original values in the worksheet when you cycle through the answers.

CAUTION: When you close the Solver Answer dialog box, Solver retains the data (the answer) currently shown in the worksheet. For this reason, choose the answer you want to use *before* you close the Solver Answer dialog box. If you inadvertently close the dialog box with the wrong data in the worksheet, you can choose Edit Undo to return the worksheet to the data previously shown. Or you can use a different answer in the worksheet by choosing the Range Analyze Solver command again, and then clicking the Next button to display a different answer. Worksheet data is not permanently saved until you choose File Save or File Save As after you return to the worksheet.

T I P   Solver differentiates between *best* and *optimal* answers. An *optimal* answer is determined mathematically to be the highest or lowest, depending on whether the Ma<u>x</u> or Mi<u>n</u> command button is clicked. A *best* answer is reported when Solver cannot verify precisely the mathematical optimum. This best answer is the highest or lowest found, but it may not be the highest or lowest possible answer overall.

Example #3: Maximizing Return on Investments

An investment portfolio is another area in which Solver can provide valuable insights. In the example, you seek to maximize return on investment. This section shows a situation in which alternative investment options provide varying rates of return.

The investment options with the highest rates also show the greatest volatility. For example, a passbook savings account pays 5 percent with 100 percent probability. An extremely volatile stock, in contrast, sometimes may achieve a 100 percent return on investment, but may reach this rate only 20 percent of the time; often, this volatile stock may show a loss. Assuming that you know or can estimate an investment's typical return, you can evaluate the financial rewards associated with alternative investment strategies.

These rewards must be balanced against your tolerance for uncertainty and downside potential. A conservative investor might decide to put aside $5,000 from a $15,000 nest egg for volatile investments, with the balance going to a passbook or perhaps another conservative investment vehicle. An investor willing to take more risk might place $15,000 in volatile investment vehicles and keep only $5,000 in a savings account. The objective is to maximize return in balance with your tolerance for risk.

The investment portfolio worksheet in figure 8.10 shows four investment options. The first option, Cash, is a passbook savings account, which pays 5 percent interest with 100 percent certainty. Three progressively more risky stock options also are shown. The first stock, Stock1, has a target rate of return of 20 percent but is estimated to achieve this rate only 60 percent of the time. Stock2 has a target rate that is better—50 percent—but the stock reaches the target only 30 percent of the time. Finally, Stock3 aims for 100 percent rate of return but is estimated to rise to this level of return only 20 percent of the time.

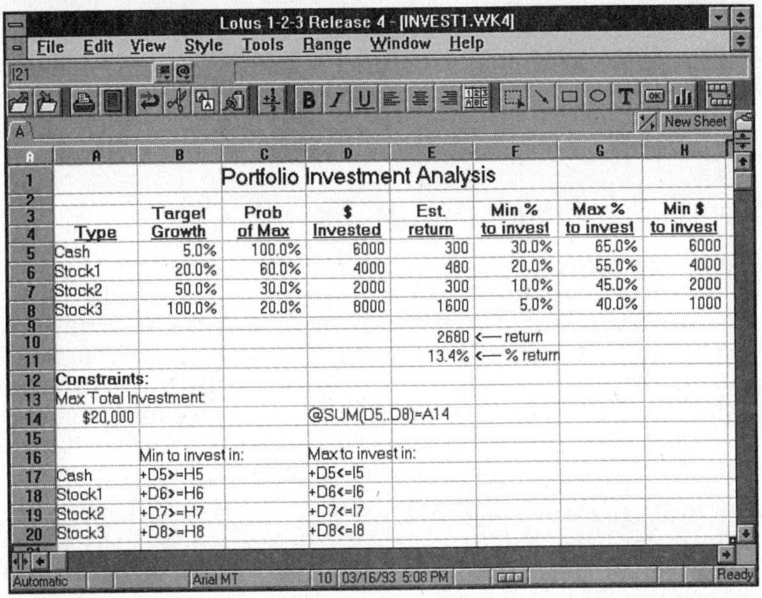

FIG. 8.10

A portfolio investment worksheet.

To compute an investment strategy's projected return, you can compute the return for individual investments, and then sum the returns for all investments in the strategy. To compute the estimated return, multiply the target growth by the percent of time the stock reaches or surpasses this growth rate. Then multiply the resulting figure by the amount invested.

Figure 8.10 uses the preceding method to compute the return for a strategy designed to invest a total of $20,000. Cells D5..D8 show that $6,000 is placed in a savings account, and allotments of $4,000, $2,000, and $8,000 are set aside for Stock1, Stock2, and Stock3, respectively. The return for cash is computed in cell E5 as B5*C5*D5; the return for the three other investments is computed by copying the formula in E5 to cells E6..E8. The total return for the investment strategy represented in cells D5..D8 is computed in cell E10 as @SUM(E5..E8). Cell E11 expresses this quantity as a percentage of the total amount invested.

Defining Constraints

The sample worksheet in figure 8.10 has nine constraints listed at the bottom. The first constraint is the total amount to be invested. In the investment portfolio worksheet, this figure is $20,000. Cell A14 contains 20000, and cell D14 contains the logical constraint formula:

@SUM(D6..D9)=A14. The other constraints specify the minimum and maximum amounts, respectively, that you are willing to place in each investment vehicle. These figures are expressed initially in cells F5..G8 as percentages of the total amount to invest.

Entering the Problem into Solver

The worksheet converts these percentages, which you must enter, to dollar amounts in cells H5..I8. The formulas in cells H5 and I5 are, respectively: +F5*$A$14 and +G5*$A$14. These formulas are copied to rows 6 through 8. After the spreadsheet computes these dollar figures, you can use the results in logical constraint formulas. An advantage of specifying the percentages in cells F5..G8 is that you can change the total amount to invest, and the worksheet computes the maximum and minimum percentages you are willing to place in each investment.

Figure 8.10 also shows in cells B17..B20 and D17..D20 the logical constraint formulas used in this example. (Notice that these cells are formatted as text so that the formulas are visible.) Cell B17 stipulates that the amount invested in cash (found in cell D5) must be greater than or equal to the minimum amount you want to keep in a savings account, entered in cell H5. This constraint is represented by the formula +D5>=H5. The amount in cash must be less than or equal to the maximum amount an investor wants in a savings account, computed in cell I5. This constraint is expressed by the formula +D5<=I5.

Figure 8.11 shows the Solver Definition dialog box for the portfolio analysis worksheet. The adjustable cells are the dollars invested in each investment option. Cells D5..D8 contain these quantities. The constraint cells are specified as cell D14, and a rectangular range that starts in cell B17 and extends to cell D20. (Notice that not every cell in the range contains a constraint formula.) Finally, you see the value to optimize in cell E10—in this example, the return from the investment strategy. To maximize the return, click the Max button.

Interpreting Portfolio Investment Solver Solutions

After you click the Solve button, Solver displays the Solver Answer dialog box (see fig. 8.12). The box shows that four answers were found and that answer #1 is the optimal answer. You see this optimal answer in the worksheet shown in figure 8.12. The maximum return for the investment strategy is shown in cell E10, stipulated by the percentages shown in cells F5..G8 and the total planned investment in cell A14. To view the other answers, you can successively click the Next button.

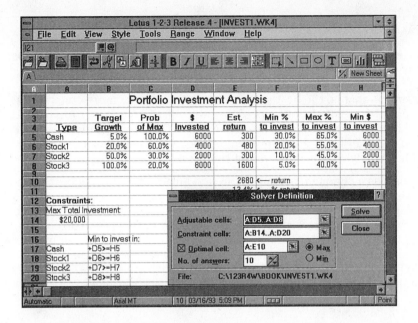

FIG. 8.11

The completed
Solver Definition
dialog box for the
portfolio invest-
ment worksheet.

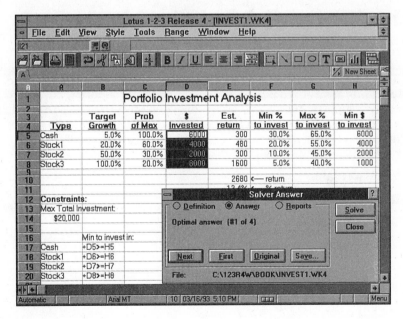

FIG. 8.12

The Solver
Answer dialog
box showing
optimal answer
#1.

Attempted Answers and Guesses

When the Solver looks for answers to a problem, it presents only those answers for which all constraints are true. When Solver can't find an answer for which all constraints are true, it presents what it calls an *attempt*—that is, the best solution given that one or more constraints cannot be satisfied. Solver presents attempts in the Solver Answer dialog box the same way it presents answers. Click the <u>N</u>ext button until you find the "best" attempt—that is, the one that seems most reasonable given what you know about the problem.

If there is a chance that Solver can find an answer, a <u>G</u>uess button appears in the Solver Answer dialog box, enabling you to supply more information to Solver about the adjustable cells in the problem. Click the <u>G</u>uess button to display the Solver Guess dialog box. You can accept the suggested value for the current adjustable cell, or enter a new value. Continue this process for all adjustable cells by clicking the Next Cell option. Then click the <u>S</u>olve button. Solver tries to find an answer to the problem based on the new information you provide.

Interpreting Solver Results

Although the Solver Answer dialog box can cycle through Solver's answers quickly and display supporting data in the worksheet, you might find it more useful to display the Solver's results in a report. After the Solver finds answers to a problem, click the <u>R</u>eports option button in the Solver Answer dialog box, which displays the Solver Reports dialog box. If you choose options in this dialog box, you can generate seven different kinds of reports on the answers found by Solver. These reports, listed in the Re<u>p</u>ort Type drop-down list, are as follows:

- Answer table
- How solved
- What-if limits
- Differences
- Nonbinding constraints
- Inconsistent constraints
- Cells used

FIG. 8.13

A Solver Reports
dialog box.

You can view most of these reports in one of two report formats: *table* or *cell*. The T<u>a</u>ble format generates a separate worksheet file that displays all the reported information. The <u>C</u>ell format uses the Solver Cell Report dialog box to display information about a new cell each time you click the <u>N</u>ext button. Examples of reports in both the table and cell formats are shown in the following sections.

NOTE Some reports are available only in T<u>a</u>ble format. For these reports (such as the Answer Table shown in fig. 8.13), the <u>C</u>ell button is available.

The Answer Table Report

The Answer table report generates a separate worksheet that displays all answers to a problem at once. To generate this worksheet, click the <u>R</u>eports option button in the Solver Answer dialog box, which then displays the Solver Reports dialog box (see fig. 8.13). In this dialog box, double-click the Answer table item in the Re<u>p</u>ort Type list box. (This report is available only in T<u>a</u>ble format—note that the <u>C</u>ell button is dimmed.) The first time you create an answer table, 1-2-3 for Windows automatically creates a worksheet file called ANSWER01.WK4. Each time you create a new answer table, the numeric part of the file name (01) is incremented by one; therefore, subsequent answer tables are named ANSWER02.WK4, ANSWER03.WK4, and so on.

Figure 8.14 shows an example of an Answer Table for the investment portfolio example. The Answer Table is divided into three key parts. The first section displays information about the optimal cell, if one is specified. The second section reveals results for the adjustable cells. The third section presents the values for supporting cells.

Column B shows the addresses for all cells in the problem; column C shows the cell names. When the cells have a range name, that name displays in all uppercase letters. When a cell has no range name, 1-2-3 assigns the column and row label closest to that cell. This practice can lead to the assignment of duplicate names for different cells. Cells A:H5 and A:I5, for example, are identified the same way because the closest row label ("Cash") and column labels ("to invest") are the same.

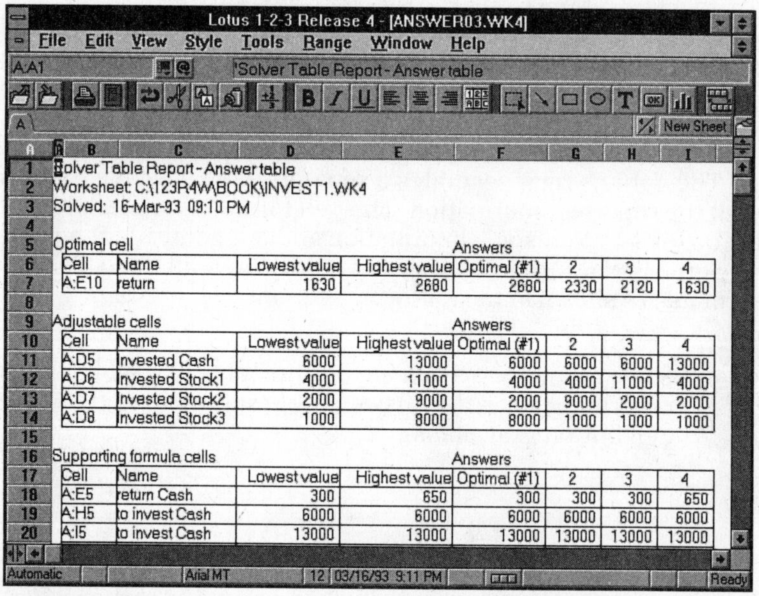

FIG. 8.14

An Answer table for the investment portfolio problem.

FIG. 8.14

An Answer table for the investment portfolio problem.

Lotus 1-2-3 Release 4 - [ANSWER03.WK4]

A:A1 'Solver Table Report - Answer table

	A	B	C	D	E	F	G	H	I
1	Solver Table Report - Answer table								
2	Worksheet: C:\123R4W\BOOK\INVEST1.WK4								
3	Solved: 16-Mar-93 09:10 PM								
4									
5	Optimal cell					Answers			
6	Cell	Name		Lowest value	Highest value	Optimal (#1)	2	3	4
7	A:E10	return		1630	2680	2680	2330	2120	1630
8									
9	Adjustable cells					Answers			
10	Cell	Name		Lowest value	Highest value	Optimal (#1)	2	3	4
11	A:D5	Invested Cash		6000	13000	6000	6000	6000	13000
12	A:D6	Invested Stock1		4000	11000	4000	4000	11000	4000
13	A:D7	Invested Stock2		2000	9000	2000	9000	2000	2000
14	A:D8	Invested Stock3		1000	8000	8000	1000	1000	1000
15									
16	Supporting formula cells					Answers			
17	Cell	Name		Lowest value	Highest value	Optimal (#1)	2	3	4
18	A:E5	return Cash		300	650	300	300	300	650
19	A:H5	to invest Cash		6000	6000	6000	6000	6000	6000
20	A:I5	to invest Cash		13000	13000	13000	13000	13000	13000

Automatic   Arial MT   12   03/16/93 9:11 PM   Ready

Columns D and E in the Answer table show the lowest and highest value found for the cells shown in column C. Subsequent columns display the value for the cell shown in column C for every answer found.

The How Solved Report

You also can choose the How Solved report from the Solver Reports dialog box. The How Solved report displays information about how the Solver found the answer currently displayed in the worksheet. To generate this report, double-click on the How Solved item in the Report Type list box. (To generate a How Solved report about a different answer found by Solver, first display the answer you want in the worksheet, click the Reports option in the Solver Answer dialog box, and then double-click on the How Solved item in the Solver Reports dialog box.)

Because this report is generated in table format, Solver creates a separate worksheet file called HOW00001.WK4. Each time you generate a new How Solved report, the numeric part of the file name (0001) is incremented by one. Subsequent reports are named HOW00002.WK4, HOW00003.WK4 and so on. Figures 8.15 and 8.16 show the complete How Solved report for the investment analysis example.

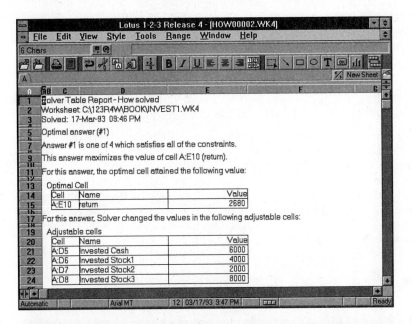

FIG. 8.15

The top portion of the How Solved report for the investment analysis worksheet.

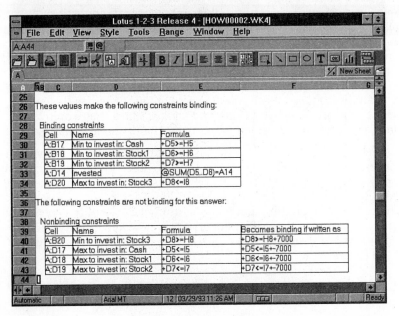

FIG. 8.16

The bottom portion of the How Solved report for the investment analysis worksheet.

This particular report shows how Solver reached the first answer, which maximizes return on investment. This information is noted in row 9 in fig. 8.15, which states `This answer maximizes the value of cell A:E10 (return)`. This note precedes row 15, which lists the final amount that the return value achieves for this optimal answer ($2,680). Rows 21 through 24 show the values Solver used in the adjustable cells to reach the answer currently displayed in the worksheet.

The next block of rows report on *binding* constraints. A binding constraint reaches at least one of its limits as Solver seeks to find an answer or an attempt. A *non-binding* constraint is one that does not reach its limit but stays within the constraint limitations.

In the Solver Definition dialog box, nine constraints were designated: the total dollar amount to be invested, the minimum percentage to be allocated to each of four investment vehicles, and the maximum percentage to be invested in the same four options. The report indicates that only five of these constraints are binding for the current answer. The four remaining constraints are listed as unused. The report also shows how you can transform these unused constraints to make the constraints binding for the current solution.

The What-If Limits Report

The What-If Limits report provides useful information if you want to change an answer. This report helps you answer the question, "What if I were to change this adjustable cell to that value?" First, the report tells you the range of values the Solver found across all answers for each adjustable cell in the problem. Second, the report lists a "what-if" range of values you can try using as the new value for the adjustable cell. The what-if range of values assumes that the final answer still meets all the constraint criteria. Because Solver provides this suggested range of values, you can avoid trying values that won't work (won't generate an answer) or won't meet the problem constraints.

To generate a What-If Limits report in a cell format, use the Solver Answer dialog box (see fig. 8.12) to display the answer you want to use in the worksheet, and then choose the Reports option button. When the Solver Reports dialog box is displayed, click on the Cell button, and then double-click on the What-If Limits item in the Report Type list box. Figure 8.17 shows a What-If Limits report for answer #1 to the school candy sales problem. The two adjustable cells, B5 and B6, are highlighted in the worksheet.

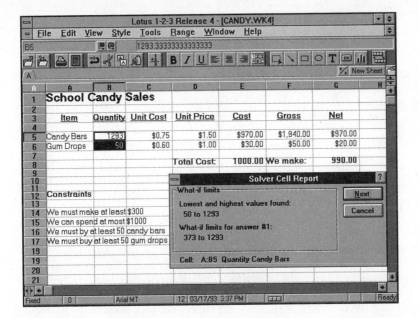

FIG. 8.17

A What-If Limits report shown in the Solver Cell Report dialog box.

The first line in the Solver Cell Report dialog box displays Lowest and highest values found: 50 to 1293. These figures represent the lowest and highest values found across all answers for cell B5 (quantity candy bars), noted near the bottom of the dialog box. The second line displays What-if limits for answer #1: 373 to 1293. This line suggests that if you want to change answer #1, you could try a value from 373 to 1293 for cell B5 (quantity candy bars). These are the values Solver suggests in order to meet all the problem constraints. Note that Solver does *not* include values between 50 and 373 in the what-if limits range, even though the Solver may have found answers using values in this range.

To change a different adjustable cell in the current problem, click the Next button. Each time you click the Next button, Solver cycles through all the adjustable cells, displaying the lowest and highest values for the current answer and the suggested range of values.

To display what-if limits for other answers to the same problem, use the Solver Answer dialog box to display the answer you want. When the answer displays in the worksheet, click the Reports option button, and then choose the What-If Limits item in the Cell Reports dialog box. Solver displays the Solver Cell Report dialog box like the one shown in figure 8.17, but for a different answer—the answer you choose.

If you choose to generate a What-If Limits report in table format, Solver creates a separate worksheet file called LIMITS01.WK4. Each time you generate a new What-If Limits report, the numeric part of the file name (01) is incremented by one. Subsequent reports are named LIMITS02.WK4, LIMITS03.WK4 and so on.

 NOTE   The values suggested in the What-If Limits report are approximate only. Using a value in the suggested what-if range may still result in a constraint that evaluates to 0.

The Differences Report

The Differences report is one of the most informative reports for comparing one answer to another. This report shows the value of each problem cell for the two answers you specify, calculates the difference between the values, and calculates the percentage of difference. The Differences report compares only two solutions per report, but you can compare different pairs of answers by repeatedly selecting the report and specifying a new pair each time.

To generate this report in cell format, choose the Reports option button in the Solver Answer dialog box. In the Solver Reports dialog box, click the Differences item in the Report Type box, and then click the Cell button. The Solver Report Differences dialog box appears (see fig. 8.18). In the Compare answers section, enter two answer numbers. In the For differences >= section, use the default value 0, or specify another number. (A 0 minimum enables you to view all differences.) Figure 8.18 uses the home mortgage problem as an example. The Solver Report Differences dialog box indicates that answers 1 and 2 will be compared, and all differences will be noted, because the value in the For Differences >= box is 0. After you review an initial difference report, you may want to set the For Differences >= value greater than 0 to screen the differences.

To view the results of this report, click the Report button. A Solver Cell Report dialog box like the one shown in figure 8.19 is displayed. Near the bottom of the box, the cell value that is being compared is noted. In this example, cell B5, purchase price, is compared. The report tells the value of this cell for both answers, the difference in the amount, and the difference percentage. Successively clicking the Next button displays the same information for other cells that were used in the problem.

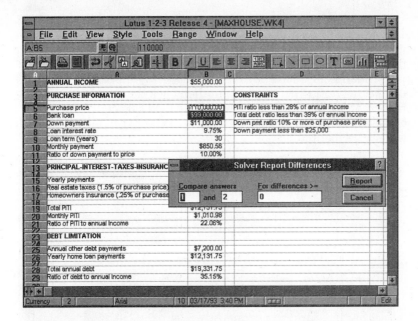

FIG. 8.18

The Solver Report Differences dialog box.

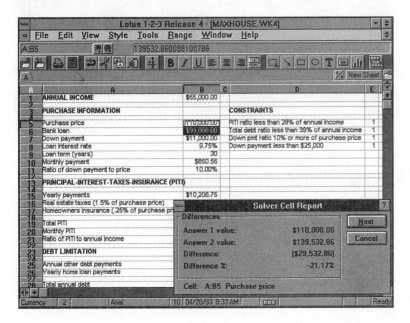

FIG. 8.19

Solver compares the purchase price between answers 1 and 2.

You can also generate this report in a table format, as shown in figure 8.20. To do so, choose the Reports option button in the Solver Answer dialog box. In the Solver Reports dialog box, click the Differences item in the Report Type box, and then click the Table button. The Solver Report Differences dialog box (refer to fig. 8.18) appears. Fill in this dialog box as described earlier, and then click the Report button. Solver creates a separate worksheet file called DIFFS001.WK4. With each new Differences report you create, the numeric portion of the file name is incremented by one.

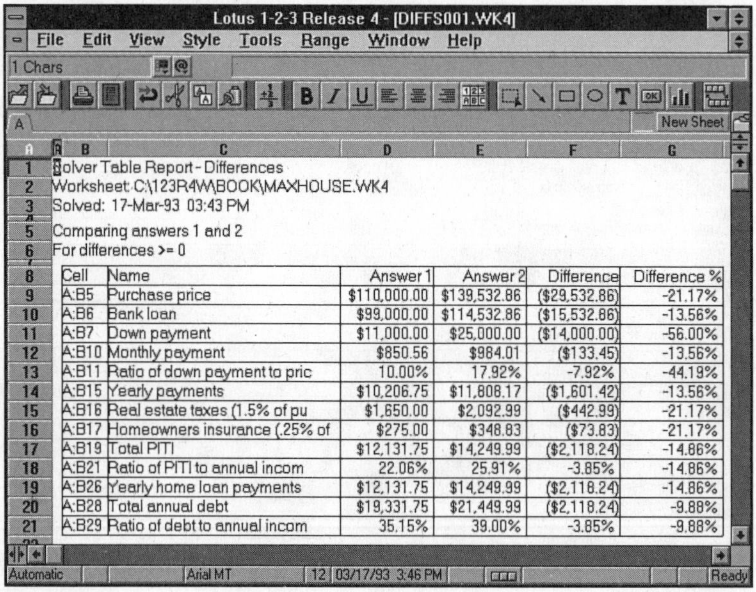

Cell	Name	Answer 1	Answer 2	Difference	Difference %
A:B5	Purchase price	$110,000.00	$139,532.86	($29,532.86)	-21.17%
A:B6	Bank loan	$99,000.00	$114,532.86	($15,532.86)	-13.56%
A:B7	Down payment	$11,000.00	$25,000.00	($14,000.00)	-56.00%
A:B10	Monthly payment	$850.56	$984.01	($133.45)	-13.56%
A:B11	Ratio of down payment to pric	10.00%	17.92%	-7.92%	-44.19%
A:B15	Yearly payments	$10,206.75	$11,808.17	($1,601.42)	-13.56%
A:B16	Real estate taxes (1.5% of pu	$1,650.00	$2,092.99	($442.99)	-21.17%
A:B17	Homeowners insurance (.25% of	$275.00	$348.83	($73.83)	-21.17%
A:B19	Total PITI	$12,131.75	$14,249.99	($2,118.24)	-14.86%
A:B21	Ratio of PITI to annual incom	22.06%	25.91%	-3.85%	-14.86%
A:B26	Yearly home loan payments	$12,131.75	$14,249.99	($2,118.24)	-14.86%
A:B28	Total annual debt	$19,331.75	$21,449.99	($2,118.24)	-9.88%
A:B29	Ratio of debt to annual incom	35.15%	39.00%	-3.85%	-9.88%

FIG. 8.20

A Differences report for the home mortgage problem displayed in table format.

The Nonbinding Constraints Report

In some situations, knowing which constraints do not bind or limit a solution may be helpful. A *nonbinding constraint* is a constraint with limits Solver did not reach as Solver searched for solutions. Constraints can be binding for some answers and nonbinding for others. To generate a Nonbinding Constraint report in a table format, click the Reports option button in the Solver Answer dialog box. When the Solver Reports dialog box appears, click the Nonbinding Constraints item in the Report Type list box, and then click the Table button. Remember that the table format generates a separate worksheet file—in this case, that file is called NBIND01.WK4. This worksheet file lists all the nonbinding constraints for the currently active answer.

Figure 8.21 presents excerpts from the candy selling worksheet showing the maximum profit answer (answer #1) and the corresponding
Nonbinding Constraint worksheet file. Row 8 in the Nonbinding Constraints worksheet reports that the $300 constraint (from cell E14) is
not binding because more than three times this amount was made in
the maximum profit answer. Column E shows how to transform this
constraint to make it binding (for example, add $690 to the amount you
must make).

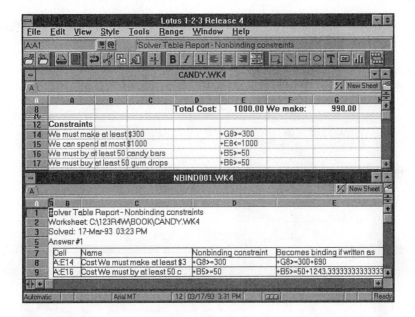

FIG. 8.21

A portion of the
candy sales
worksheet and of
the Nonbinding
Constraints report
shown on-screen
at the same time.

Similarly, the requirement that you buy at least 50 candy bars (the constraint from cell E16) is a nonbinding constraint. Because you made a
greater profit on this item, the answer says to sell all the candy bars
you can after you meet a minimum volume requirement on the gum
drops. Because the optimal answer specifies that you sell fractionally
more candy bars than 1293, the requirement to sell at least 50 is not
binding. Row 9 of the Nonbinding Constraints report specifies that you
can make the minimum amount of candy bars binding by increasing the
requirement to fractionally more than 1243.

The Inconsistent Constraints Report

Constraints are sometimes mutually inconsistent. If one constraint is true, another constraint might not be true. This situation can develop easily. Suppose that the school administration in the candy sales problem determines that they can only spend $300 on candy rather than the original $1,000.

If you enter this change into the candy selling worksheet and launch Solver, the Solver Answer dialog box reports that no answers are found, but one attempt was made (see fig. 8.22). Notice in row 14 of the worksheet that the constraint that says the school must make at least $300 now evaluates to zero (0)—in other words, this constraint is not met.

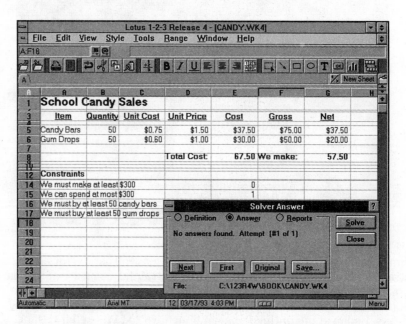

FIG. 8.22

Solver can find no answers, and cell E14 evaluates to False (0).

When Solver makes attempts instead of finding answers, you can generate an Inconsistent Constraints report to find the constraints that are not met. Choose this item in the Solver Reports dialog box. Figure 8.23 shows an example of this report in a cell format.

The Solver Cell Report dialog box confirms that the constraint in cell A:E14 is not satisfied and shows how to write the constraint in a way that satisfies the constraint (that is, reduce by $242.50 the amount that must be made).

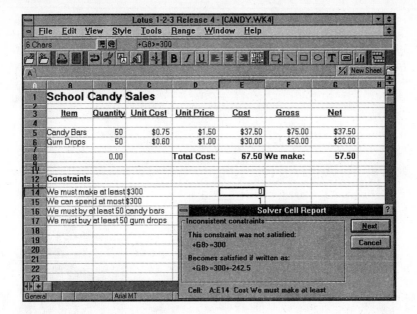

FIG. 8.23

The Inconsistent Constraints report indicates that the constraint in E14 is not met.

The Cells Used Report

The Cells Used report tells you which cells were used in a Solver problem: adjustable, constraint, and optimal cells. The report is available in cell or table format. When you generate the report in the cell format, Solver displays the address and name of the first adjustable cell in the Solver Cell Report dialog box. As you click the Next button successively, Solver cycles through all adjustable cells, and then all the constraint cells, and finally, the optimal cell, if you specified one. As the Solver cycles through these cells, each cell in the worksheet is highlighted. You may need to reposition the Solver Cell Report dialog box on-screen to make each highlighted cell visible. In figure 8.24, the second adjustable cell in the investment portfolio problem is highlighted in the worksheet. The Solver Cell Report dialog box notes the name and address of this adjustable cell.

When you generate the Cells Used report in table format, Solver lists all adjustable, constraint, and optimal cells in a separate worksheet file called CELLS001.WK4. Each time you generate a new report table, Solver increments the 001 portion of the file name; for example, CELLS002.WK4, CELLS003.WK4, and so on. You can rename the file using any name you choose.

To generate a Cells Used report as a table, choose the Reports option button in the Solver Answer dialog box. When the Solver Reports dialog box appears, click on the Cells Used item in the Report Type list box, then click the Table button. Figure 8.25 shows an example of the Cells Used report for the investment portfolio problem, as well as the Solver Reports dialog box used to generate the report. The first section of the report lists the optimal cell, the second section lists all adjustable cells, and the final section lists the constraint cells.

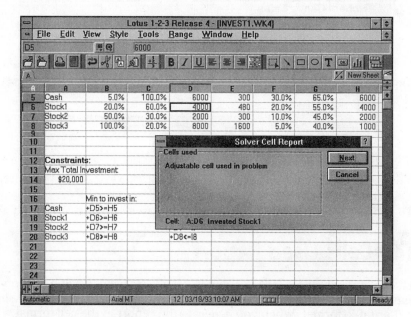

FIG. 8.24

The Cells Used report currently displays the second adjustable cell, D6, and highlights it in the worksheet.

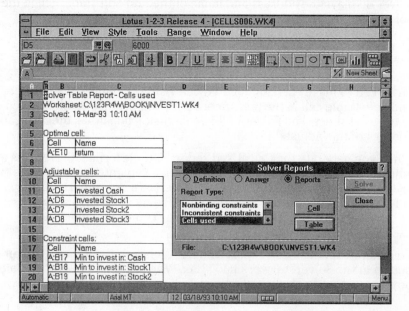

FIG. 8.25

The Cells Used report in table format generates a separate worksheet with the file name CELLS006.WK4.

Using Functions with Solver

You can include 1-2-3 for Windows functions in the formulas in all the problem cells the Solver uses to determine solutions, provided that you follow some basic rules.

Functions in problem cells must use as arguments numbers, not strings, date or time values, or values from a database. For example, you can use the function @AVG in a Solver problem cell because @AVG uses only numbers to determine a numeric average. You cannot use functions such as @TRIM or @DAVG because these functions require a string argument and a value from a database, respectively. For more information, refer to Chapter 7, "Using Functions."

Functions in problem cells must return numbers. In problem cells, you cannot use any functions that return a string (such as @STRING), a date or time value (such as @DATE), or a value from a database (such as @DQUERY). You can use functions that return Boolean values, such as @ERR and @ISNA, because 1-2-3 for Windows considers Boolean values to be regular numbers.

Remember that these rules apply only to the problem cells that contain functions. Because the Solver uses only these cells to find solutions, all other cells in the worksheet can contain any functions and formulas.

Table 9.1 lists the functions you can use in Solver problem cells. Chapter 7, "Using Functions," offers more detailed information on using these functions in formulas.

Table 9.1 Acceptable Functions in Solver Problem Cells

@ABS	@INDEX	@SHEETS
@ACOS	@INT	@SIN
@ASIN	@IRR	@SLN
@ATAN	@ISNUMBER	@SQRT
@ATAN2	@LN	@STD
@AVG	@LOG	@STDS
@CHOOSE	@MAX	@SUM
@COLS	@MIN	@SUMPRODUCT
@COS	@MOD	@SYD
@COUNT	@NPV	@TAN
@CTERM	@PAYMT	

continues

Table 9.1 Continued		
	@PI	
	@PUREAVG	
	@PURECOUNT	
	@PUREMAX	
	@PUREMIN	
	@PURESTD	
	@PURESTDS	
	@PUREVAR	
	@PUREVARS	
		@TERM
@DDB	@PMT	@TERM
@EXP	@PV	@VAR
@FALSE	@RATE	@@VARS
@FV	@ROUND	@VDB
@FVAL		
@GRANDTOTAL		
@HLOOKUP	@ROWS	@VLOOKUP
@IF		

Using the Backsolver

Often you know the result you want a formula to return, but you don't know the values the formula needs in order to achieve that return value. You can use the Backsolver, a 1-2-3 Release 4 for Windows analysis tool, to solve such a formula. When you use the Backsolver, 1-2-3 changes the value of a variable until the formula dependent on that variable returns the result you want. For example, you could use the Backsolver with the candy sales problem to find the number of candy bars you need to sell in order to reach a net profit of $2,000.

Figure 8.26 shows a revised version of the worksheet for the candy sales problem. Cell G8 indicates that the net profit yields $990, given the current values for the adjustable cells. You want the net profit to be $2,000, and you need to find out how many candy bars you must sell to reach that profit figure. Note that the constraint cells are not necessary to solve this problem, so they have been removed from the worksheet.

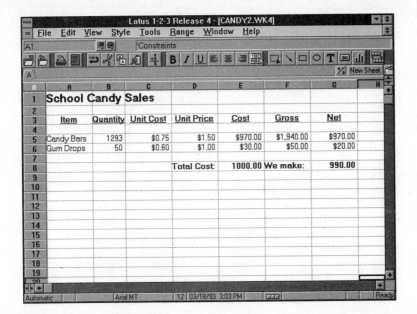

FIG. 8.26

A revised candy sales worksheet, used to illustrate the Backsolver tool.

To use the Backsolver to solve the problem, choose Range Analyze Backsolver from the menu bar. 1-2-3 for Windows displays the Backsolver dialog box (see fig. 8.26). In the Make Cell text box, specify the cell that contains the formula for which you are seeking a specific result. In the Equal to Value text box, enter the number you want the formula to return. In the By Changing Cell(s) text box, enter the cell that contains the variable you want to change to achieve this result. When all these values are entered, click the OK button.

Figure 8.27 shows the Backsolver dialog box completed for the sample problem. Cell G8 is the Make Cell because the net profit formula is found in that cell. The Equal to Value is 2000, the net profit you want to make from candy sales. The By Changing Cell(s) is B5, the number of candy bars you need to sell to achieve a net profit of $2,000.

When you choose OK from the Backsolver dialog box, 1-2-3 for Windows changes the value in the By Changing Cell(s) text box so that the formula in the Make Cell text box returns the amount for Equal to Value. Figure 8.28 shows the sample worksheet after the Backsolver finds the new variable value. 1-2-3 for Windows changes the value in cell B5 to 2640. Assuming that all the other values in the problem remain the same, you need to sell 2,640 candy bars to make a $2,000 net profit.

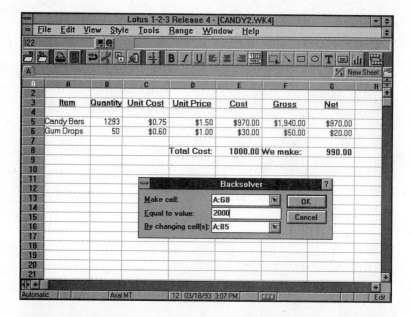

FIG. 8.27

The Backsolver dialog box for the new candy-selling example.

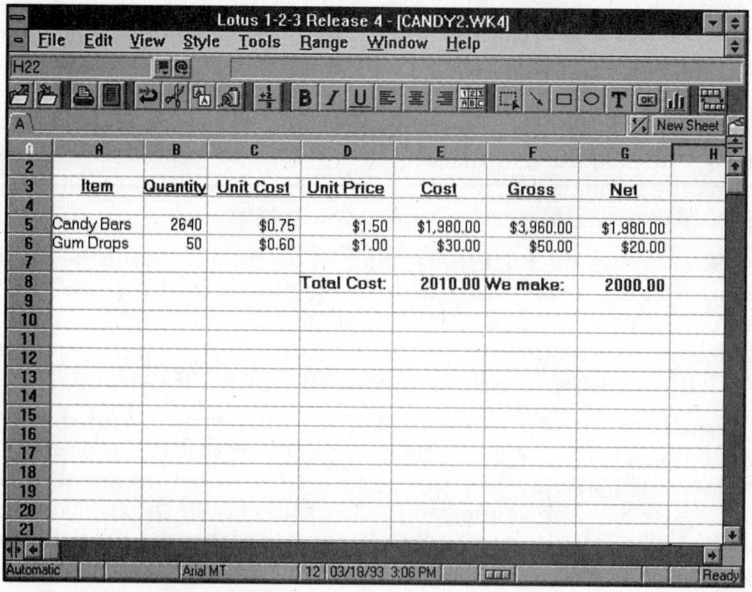

FIG. 8.28

Backsolver finds that 2,640 candy bars must be sold in order for the school to net $2,000 in candy sales.

If the Backsolver cannot find a value for By Changing Cell(s) that meets the criteria for the Make Cell formula, 1-2-3 for Windows prompts you with an error message. In this case, you may want to try running the Solver on the problem, and then generate a What-If Limits report to determine reasonable estimates for By Changing Cell(s).

CAUTION: When you use the Backsolver, remember that 1-2-3 for Windows permanently changes the value of <u>B</u>y Changing Cell(s). If you plan to use the Backsolver to try a number of different values in a what-if analysis, make sure that you save the worksheet file before you use the Backsolver so that you can return to the original worksheet that contains the starting values. If you forget to save the worksheet before you use the Backsolver, you can return to the last value in <u>B</u>y Changing Cell(s) with the <u>E</u>dit <u>U</u>ndo command. Note, however, that you return to only the preceding set of values. If you used the Backsolver a number of times, <u>E</u>dit <u>U</u>ndo cannot return you to the initial values, but returns you to the values before you last chose OK from the Backsolver dialog box.

Auditing Worksheet Formulas

When a worksheet is quite large, contains complex formulas, or formulas you're not familiar with (perhaps another user created the worksheet), you will find 1-2-3's audit feature a useful tool. You can use <u>T</u>ools <u>A</u>udit or the Audit Cells SmartIcon to identify the following:

- All formulas in a worksheet
- Formulas that refer to data in a selected range
- The cells that a formula references
- Formulas with circular references
- Formulas that refer to data in other files (file links)
- Cells that contain a link to data created with another Windows application (DDE links)

You make these choices in the upper portion of the Audit dialog box shown in figure 8.29.

T I P

1-2-3 provides a set of SmartIcons especially for sheet auditing. To display these SmartIcons, click the SmartIcons selector in the status bar and choose Sheet Auditing from the list of palettes. Among this set are tools for finding all formulas, finding formula precedents, finding cell dependents, finding file links, and finding DDE links.

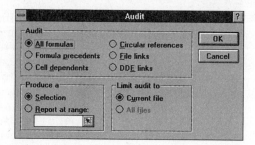

In the lower section of the dialog box, you choose how you want 1-2-3 to display the results. When you choose Selection, 1-2-3 highlights all the cells it finds in the active worksheet. Press Ctrl+Enter to move forward from one selected cell to the next; press Ctrl+Shift+Enter to move backward through the selected cells. Press any arrow key or Esc to deselect the cells. Figure 8.30 shows how the worksheet looks when you use Tools Audit to find all formulas in a worksheet.

School Candy Sales							
Item	Quantity	Unit Cost	Unit Price	Cost	Gross	Net	
Candy Bars	1293	$0.75	$1.50	$970.00	$1,940.00	$970.00	
Gum Drops	50	$0.60	$1.00	$30.00	$50.00	$20.00	
				Total Cost	1000.00	We make:	990.00

When you choose the Report at Range option in the Audit dialog box, 1-2-3 lists the address of each cell found and its formula in the range you specify—a blank area of the worksheet. If you choose a range that contains data, 1-2-3 displays an error message and closes the Audit dialog box, canceling the audit. Figure 8.31 illustrates the type of list generated in cells B10 through B19.

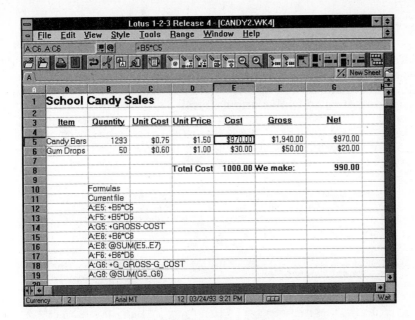

FIG. 8.31

All formulas found by the audit feature are listed in cells B10 through B19.

You can search for cells in the current worksheet only (choose the Current File option in the Audit dialog box), or in all worksheets in the active file (choose the All Files option). If you choose the All Files option, you must specify a cell range where 1-2-3 can report the results, because 1-2-3 can't display a selection of cells in multiple sheets at once.

The following sections describe each of the auditing options available in the Audit dialog box.

Finding All Formulas

Use the All Formulas option when you want to check a worksheet's formulas for accuracy or understand the formulas in a worksheet that is new or unfamiliar to you. By using the Selection option, 1-2-3 highlights in the active worksheet each formula it finds (see fig. 8.29 for an example). Using the Report at Range option, 1-2-3 lists the address of each cell it finds and displays the formula (see fig. 8.30).

If you use the Sheet Auditing SmartIcon palette, click the Find Formulas SmartIcon to instantly select all formulas in the active worksheet.

Finding Formula Precedents

Formula *precedents* are all the cells referenced by a formula, either directly or indirectly. In the candy sales worksheet, for example, the formula precedents for cell E5 are B5 and C5 because these two cells are directly referenced by the formula in cell E5. The formula precedents for cell E8, however, includes cells E5 and E6, which are referenced directly, as well as cells B5, B6, C5, and C6, which are referenced indirectly by the formula in cell E8. Figure 8.32 shows that 1-2-3 selects all these cells when the Formula <u>P</u>recedents option is selected.

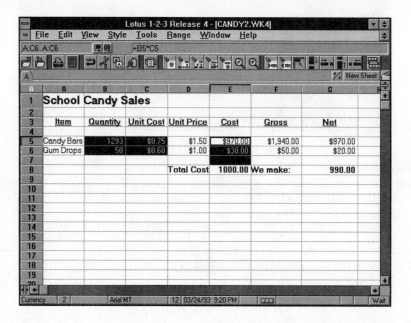

FIG. 8.32

The selected cells are formula precedents to cell E8.

 To find a formula's precedents, first select the cell in the worksheet, and then choose <u>T</u>ools <u>A</u>udit or click the Audit Cells SmartIcon. 1-2-3 finds the precedents for the currently selected cell. If the cell you select does not contain a formula, 1-2-3 displays an error message.

 To quickly find a formula's precedents, select the cell that contains the formula, and then click the Find Formula Precedents SmartIcon on the Sheet Auditing SmartIcon palette.

Finding Cell Dependents

In the Audit dialog box, the Cell Dependents option tells you which formulas depend on cells in a particular range. (This option is roughly the reverse of the Formula Precedents option.) In the candy sales worksheet, for example, if you select the two quantity figures shown in cells B5 and B6, and then choose the Cell Dependents option in the Audit dialog box, 1-2-3 finds cells E5 through G6 and cells E8 and G8 (see fig. 8.33). Cell E5..F6 refer to cells B5 or B6 directly; E8, G5, G6, and G8 refer to cells B5 or B6 indirectly.

	Lotus 1-2-3 Release 4 - [CANDY2.WK4]						
File **Edit** **View** **Style** **Tools** **Range** **Window** **Help**							
A:B5..A:B6		1293.33333333333333					
A							New Sheet
	A	**B**	**C**	**D**	**E**	**F**	**G**
1	School Candy Sales						
2							
3	Item	Quantity	Unit Cost	Unit Price	Cost	Gross	Net
4							
5	Candy Bars	1293	$0.75	$1.50	$970.00	$1,940.00	$970.00
6	Gum Drops	50	$0.60	$1.00	$30.00	$50.00	$20.00
7							
8				Total Cost	1000.00	We make:	990.00

(worksheet rows 9–20 empty; status bar: Fixed 0 Arial MT 12 03/24/93 9:18 PM Wait)

FIG. 8.33

Formulas in the selected cells are dependent on cells B5 and B6.

To quickly find a cell's dependents, select a range of cells, and then click the Find Cell Dependents SmartIcon on the Sheet Auditing SmartIcon palette.

Finding Circular References

A *circular reference* is a formula that contains a direct or indirect reference to itself. Suppose that in the candy sales worksheet you have cells named COST, GROSS, and NET. If the GROSS cell contains the formula +COST+NET, and the NET cell contains the formula +Gross-COST, you cannot calculate the NET value because the value of COST is unknown, and you cannot calculate the COST value because the value of NET is unknown. If you use Tools Audit to find circular references in the candy sales worksheet, 1-2-3 highlights cells F5 and G5, as shown in figure 8.34, or lists the cell addresses in the range you specify.

1-2-3's audit tool highlights cells F5 and G5 as circular references.

If a worksheet has more than one circular reference, 1-2-3 displays the Multiple Circular References dialog box instead of returning to the worksheet. This dialog box lists the first cell in each circular reference. In the Choose box, click on the cell you want to work with, and then click OK. In the worksheet, 1-2-3 highlights the cells in the circular reference or lists them in the range you specify. After you solve the problem with the first circular reference, you can move to the next circular reference listed in the Multiple Circular References dialog box by choosing Tools Audit again and selecting the Circular References option again.

Finding File Links and DDE Links

A *file link* is a formula that refers to data in another file. This kind of reference occurs often in "rollup" or summary worksheets. For example, you might track monthly sales figures for each department on individual worksheets and summarize the monthly figures of all departments on a separate worksheet. The summary worksheet would include file links to each of the department worksheets.

Like the File Links option, the DDE Links option in the Audit dialog box finds all cells in a worksheet that refer to data created with another Windows application. (DDE stands for Dynamic Data Exchange.)

To find file links or DDE links in a worksheet, choose Tools Audit, and then choose the File Links or DDE Links option. If you choose the Selection option for the results, 1-2-3 highlights all cells in the worksheet that contain file links or DDE links. If you choose the Report at Range option, 1-2-3 lists all cells that contain links in the range of cells you specify.

To quickly select all cells in a worksheet that contain file links or DDE links, click the Find 1-2-3 Links or Find DDE Links SmartIcon on the Sheet Auditing SmartIcon palette.

For Related Information

▶▶ "Integrating Lotus Windows Applications," p. 935.

FROM HERE...

Questions & Answers

In this chapter, you learned how to solve formulas and audit worksheets. The following questions and answers serve to refresh your memory about these areas:

Q: Solver can't locate an answer to the problem I defined. What would cause this problem and what should I do to solve it?

A: When Solver can't find an answer to a problem, it could be for a number of reasons. The problem might have too many formulas to deal with (too many adjustable cells, too many constraints), or the formulas themselves might be too complex. The problem might also contain too many functions, or invalid functions (see Table 9.1 for a list of acceptable functions in Solver problems). Try reducing the size, complexity, and the number or type of functions in the problem and run Solver again.

Q: Solver supplied several answers to my problem, but none of them seem to be correct. What should I do?

A: When the answers Solver finds don't seem correct based on everything you know about the problem, try using different values for the adjustable cells, and then run Solver again. If the answers still don't seem correct, try supplying values in the adjustable cells that you think are close to the correct answer, and then run Solver again.

Q: Solver was able to produce several answers to my problem, but could not provide an optimal answer. I defined an optimal cell—what's wrong?

A: Sometimes the optimal cell needs a constraint in order for Solver to find an optimal answer. Try adding one or two constraints that limit the value of the optimal cell, and then run Solver again.

Q: I keep getting an error message that says a constraint cell in my problem is invalid. The formulas appear to be valid, so what else can be wrong?

A: The constraint cells might contain valid formulas, but they might not be *logical* formulas. Remember that all constraint cells must evaluate to true or false. If the constraint cells are displayed in a Text format, try changing the format to Automatic. In this format, each logical formula evaluates either to 0 (false) or 1 (true).

Q: When I minimize the optimal cell, Solver returns negative numbers in some of the adjustable cells. How can I avoid this?

A: For the optimal cell and each adjustable cell you want to be positive, you must enter a constraint that specifies that the cell must be greater than (or equal to) 0. After you define the new constraint cells, be sure to include them in the Solver Definition dialog box when you define the problem and run Solver again.

Q: When I run Solver, I get an error message that says I am out of memory. Why does this happen?

A: Before Solver begins solving a problem, it scans the number of adjustable and constraint cells to see how large the problem is. If the problem appears to be too large for the amount of available memory, 1-2-3 displays an out of memory error message. When Solver is able to run and finds answers to your problem, it stores each problem in memory. If there is not enough room in memory to store your answers, Solver stores some answers on disk. If the disk doesn't have enough room to store the answers, 1-2-3 reports that it is out of memory.

To free up memory, close all Windows or other application programs you are not using. In 1-2-3, close all files that you are not using. In the current worksheet, eliminate all unnecessary rows, columns, and cells, especially those that contain unnecessary formulas. (Formulas require memory in order to calculate.) Save and close the file, and then reopen it. To free up disk space, use the Windows File Manager to delete all unnecessary or obsolete files from your hard disk.

Q: When using Backsolver, I keep getting a message that says Backsolver couldn't find a solution.

A: The Backsolver requires only three simple variables: the cell to solve for, the value, and the cells Backsolver can change in order to find a solution. Check the cell ranges defined in the Backsolver dialog box. The Make Cell box should contain a single cell reference, the Equal to Value should contain a single value, and the By Changing Cells(s) box can contain a range of cells. Make sure each refers to valid, non-blank cells.

Q: Using Tools Audit, I want to produce a selection of cells, but the Selection option isn't available when I choose All Files. Why?

A: When you choose the Selection option, 1-2-3 highlights on-screen each cell in the current worksheet. When you audit all files, 1-2-3 can't display them all on-screen at once, so the Selection option is not available. To use the Selection option, you must limit the audit to the current file.

Summary

This chapter discussed the commands and methods you use to analyze data and solve problems in worksheets. The Solver tool finds answers to problems with any number of variables and any number of constraints. The Backsolver tool quickly finds a value for a single variable, based on a given outcome for a formula. The Audit feature of 1-2-3 helps you locate and check formulas and other dependent cells in a worksheet.

The following chapter introduces you to a new feature in 1-2-3 Release 4 for Windows, the Version Manager. The Version Manager provides easy-to-use "what-if" analytical tools to enable you to create and view different sets of data for any named range.

Using the Version Manager

The Version Manager provides easy-to-use "what-if" analytical power that lets you create and view different sets of data for any named range. For example, you can create high and low projections for a range named SALES and compare their effects on other items in the application. Each different set of data you create is called a version.

To make it easier to manage versions, you also can group versions of different ranges together to create scenarios. For example, you can group the high-sales projection with the low-expenses projection so that you can easily display them together.

Keeping Track of Who, What, When, Where, and Why

Version Manager makes it easier to keep track of the changing information in your worksheets by providing audit information about the versions and scenarios you create. For example, when you create a new version of projected sales data for January or a new scenario for the first-quarter budget, you can enter comments to record the assumptions behind the numbers. Version Manager automatically keeps track of the date and time when you create or modify each version or scenario.

Version Manager makes it easy to keep track of what you entered (the data itself and the name you give it), where you entered it (the range in which the data is located), why you entered it (as recorded in the comments entered for each version or scenario), and when you entered it (because Version Manager records the date and time).

Version Manager also makes it easier for you to share data with co-workers. Different people can enter versions in the same range of a worksheet file without writing over each other's data. Version Manager keeps track of who created or modified each version or scenario and provides a powerful merge utility that combines versions and scenarios from one file into another file. If you use Lotus Notes, Version Manager lets you save your 1-2-3 worksheets as Notes databases, so that different people can enter versions into a file at the same time.

This chapter shows you how to do the following:

- Understand how to use Version Manager to manage and share data
- Create and display different versions of data in a named range
- Group versions together into scenarios
- Use the Index to display information about versions and scenarios
- Create reports about the data in the versions
- Merge versions and scenarios from one file into another file

Understanding Version Manager Basics

In the past, if you wanted to keep track of different versions of data in the same range, you could do so by saving different versions of the entire file. For example, you could save several versions of the first-quarter expense budget, naming the files Q1EXP1.WK3, Q1EXP2.WK3, and so on. Alternatively, you could save the different assumptions on separate worksheets within a single file. With Version Manager, you can store these different sets of data in a single worksheet by creating different versions of named ranges.

Version Manager provides two tools for working with versions and scenarios: the Manager and the Index. Each of these tools appears in the Version Manager window. The Manager lets you create, display, modify, and delete versions. The Index lets you do everything the Manager does plus create and manage scenarios, create reports, and merge versions and scenarios from one file into another.

Understanding Terminology

Before getting into the details of Version Manager, you should understand some terms used throughout this chapter. This section reviews some terms you may already be familiar with and introduces some new terms.

You can create different sets of data only for named ranges. A range is a single cell or a block of adjoining cells. For example, A:A1..A:A1 is a range consisting of a single cell; A:B1..A:C5 is a range consisting of a block of adjoining cells; A:C10..C:E15 is a 3D range consisting of a block of adjoining cells in adjoining worksheets.

You cannot create different sets of data for collections, or for named ranges that contain more than 2000 cells.

A named range is a range to which you have assigned a name. A range name can be up to 15 characters long. For example, you can assign the name REVENUES to the range A:B5..A:E5 and the name EXPENSES to the range A:B10..A:E10. You can use Version Manager to simultaneously assign a name to a range and create a version of that named range; alternatively, you can use Range Name Add to assign a name to a range and then use Version Manager to create a version of the range.

When you create different sets of data for a single named range, you assign each set a name, such as High Sales or Low Sales. Each named set of data for a named range is called a version of that range. When you create a version of a named range, Version Manager stores the current contents of the range as well as other information including your name, the date and time you created the version, and an optional comment.

For example, in a range named REVENUES, you can enter the values 500, 400, 300, and 200 and then use Version Manager to create a version with the name High Sales. You then can enter the values 50, 40, 30, and 20 in the same named range and create a second version with the name Low Sales. Both versions of the named range are stored in memory; you can use Version Manager to display either version. When you save the file, 1-2-3 saves both versions of the named range as part of the worksheet file.

You can create versions for any named range in a file. For example, if you want to compare different combinations of revenues and expenses, you can create several different versions of the range named EXPENSES and use Version Manager to display the different combinations.

After you create versions, you can treat selected versions of different named ranges as a group. A named group of versions is called a scenario. For example, you can group the High Sales version of the REVENUES range with the Low Expenses version of the EXPENSES range to create a scenario named Best Case. You can also create a Worst Case scenario that contains the Low Sales version of REVENUES and the High Expenses version of EXPENSES.

Using the Version Manager Window

The Version Manager appears in its own window in two different forms: the Manager and the Index. The Manager window lets you perform simple actions on one version at a time. To open the Version Manager window, choose Range Version or click on the Version Manager SmartIcon. The first time you open the Version Manager, the Manager window appears (see fig. 9.1).

FIG. 9.1

The Version Manager window.

The Index window lets you see information about many versions in one place. You can sort the information in the Index window by range name, version name, scenario name, date, or contributor name. In addition, the Index window lets you perform actions that may affect more than one version, such as creating and modifying scenarios. To use the Index window, choose the To Index button (located on the right side of the Manager window) or press Alt+T (see fig. 9.2); to return to the Manager window, choose the To Manager button (located on the right side of the Index window) or press Alt+T.

The Version Manager window is similar to a dialog box; unlike a dialog box, however, you can leave the Version Manager window open while you work so that you can move back and forth between the 1-2-3 worksheet and the Version Manager window. For example, you can use Version Manager to create a version of a range, then move to the worksheet to enter new data in the range, then return to the Version Manager window to create another version of the range. To move to the worksheet, click on the worksheet or press Alt+F6 (Zoom Pane). To move to the Version Manager window, click on the Version Manager window, press Alt+F6, or choose Range Version.

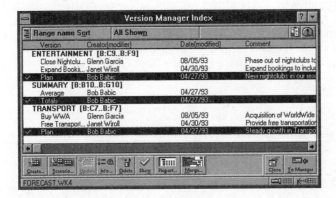

FIG. 9.2

The Version Manager Index window.

You can move, resize, and minimize the Version Manager window just as you do any other window. When you close the Version Manager window (by choosing the Close button), 1-2-3 keeps track of the window's size, position, and state (Manager or Index); the next time you choose Range Version, 1-2-3 opens the Version Manager in that size, position, and state.

> **CAUTION:** To close the Version Manager window, choose Close or press Alt+L. Don't use the Windows accelerator sequence Alt+F4; it's very easy to close 1-2-3 accidentally instead of just closing the Version Manager.

For Related Information

◄◄ "Understanding the Graphical User Interface," p. 45.

◄◄ "Using Fundamental Commands," p. 133.

FROM HERE...

Using the Manager

You use the Manager to create, display, update, modify, and delete versions. In this section, you learn how to use the Manager to create versions of named ranges in a revenue plan worksheet.

Figure 9.3 shows the 1993 Revenue Forecast worksheet for Resorts International. The chart at the bottom of the worksheet compares Lodging revenue to the total revenues from Transportation, Food, and Entertainment. Resorts International hopes to diversify its revenue sources by increasing total nonlodging revenues in 1993. You can use Version Manager to explore the results of different strategies for reaching this goal.

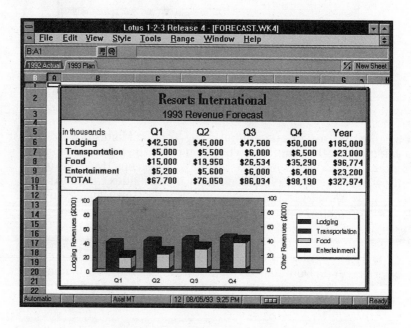

FIG. 9.3

The 1993 Revenue Forecast worksheet.

The Manager window has two drop-down boxes: Named Range and With Version(s). The Named Range drop-down box contains a list of all named ranges that have versions in the current file. The With Version(s) drop-down box contains a list of all versions for the named range selected in the Named Range drop-down box.

Below the drop-down boxes is a row of buttons labeled Create, Update, Info, Delete, Close, and To Index. The four buttons on the left let you create, modify, and delete versions. The two buttons on the right let you close the Version Manager or change its state.

At the bottom of the Manager window is another row of buttons. The button on the left displays the name of the current file; clicking on it toggles between displaying just the file name and displaying the full path. The buttons on the right control the interaction between Version Manager and the worksheet.

Click on each button with the right mouse button to see a description of what each button does. For more information about the buttons or about other parts of the Manager window, press F1 or click on the question mark in the right corner of the Manager window title bar. On the resulting help screen, click on any part of the picture of the Manager window to get more information about that part.

T I P

Creating Versions

The first step in creating a version of a range is to enter the data for the version. If the range already contains data you want to preserve, begin by creating a version that contains the data currently stored in the range. This action saves that data so that you don't lose the original data when you enter different sets of data for the range.

For example, to explore different assumptions about Lodging revenues, begin by creating a version that contains the data currently stored in the range B:C6..B:F6. If the Version Manager window is not already open, open it by choosing Range Version or by clicking on the Version Manager SmartIcon. If necessary, switch from the Index to the Manager by choosing To Manager. You're ready to create a version of the Lodging revenue data.

You can create versions only of named ranges. You can use Range Name Add to assign a name to the Lodging range and then choose Create from the Version Manager window to create a version of the range. You also can do it all in one step: the Create Version dialog box lets you name a range as you create the first version of the range.

CAUTION: Avoid using Range Name Add to assign more than one name to a range for which you already have created versions. When 1-2-3 finds more than one name for the same range, it uses the name that occurs earliest in the alphabet. This can cause problems for Version Manager, because Version Manager uses the name that existed at the time you created the first version of the range.

To create the first version of a range, begin by selecting the range (in this case, the Lodging range in B:C6..B:F6). Then choose Create from the Version Manager window. The Create Version dialog box appears as shown in figure 9.4. The Version Manager suggests names for the range name and the version name. For the Range Name, Version Manager suggests a name based on the label in the worksheet (in this example, Version manager suggests LODGING as the range name) or proposes a default name such as RANGE1. For the Version Name, Version Manager suggests a default version name such as Version1. You can accept or change either of the suggested names.

Range names can be up to 15 characters long, should not contain spaces or special characters, and are not case sensitive. Version names can be up to 32 characters long, may contain spaces or special characters, and are case sensitive.

You can create more than one version with the same name. Since Version Manager also records the date and time when you create a version, it can distinguish the Best Case version of the SALES range created by Bob Babic at 2:30 PM on April 11 from the Best Case version of the SALES range created by Bob Babic at 2:30 PM on April 12.

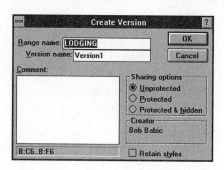

FIG. 9.4

The Create Version dialog box.

In the Create Version dialog box, you also can enter a comment for the version, select a sharing option, and choose whether to save styles as well as data with the version.

Version comments help you keep track of the assumptions behind the data in each version. In the Comment text box, enter a comment that helps you remember why you entered the data in this version. For this example, you can enter a comment identifying the data in the LODGING range as being the original revenue plan, based on actual 1992 results.

Sharing options are most useful when you use Version Manager to share data with other users. Unprotected is the default sharing option. Choose the Protected button to protect versions so that other users can't change them; choose the Protected & Hidden button to hide versions so that other users can't display them.

The Creator information box shows the creator of the new version. 1-2-3 gets this information from your E-mail name, network log-in name, or the name you entered when you installed 1-2-3. If 1-2-3 gets the name from an "authenticated" source (that is, if there is a password associated with the name, as there would be for a network log-in name), then you cannot change the name. If 1-2-3 cannot find an authenticated source, it uses the name you entered when you installed 1-2-3, and you can change the name in the Tools User Setup dialog box.

You can save styles with versions (with the Retain Styles check box) to give visual cues in the worksheet. For example, you can give all optimistic versions light-blue backgrounds. By default, 1-2-3 does not save styles with versions.

When you have completed the Create Version dialog box, choose OK to create the version and return to the Version Manager window.

Figure 9.5 shows the Create Version dialog box filled out to create the Plan version of the LODGING range.

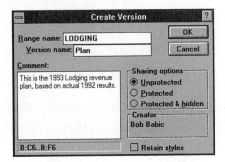

After you create a version of a range, the name of the range appears in the Named Range drop-down box of the Manager window; the name of the version appears in the With Version(s) drop-down box. A check mark appears next to the version name, indicating that this version is currently displayed in the worksheet.

To create a second version of a range, begin by entering the data for the new version into the worksheet. As soon as you enter new data in the range, the check mark next to the version name in the Manager window changes to a crossed check mark, the version name appears in italics, and the Update button becomes available (see fig. 9.6). These changes indicate that the data in the worksheet is not the data associated with the version last displayed in the range. In other words, the data in the worksheet has not been "saved" in a version.

CAUTION: Avoid creating versions for ranges that overlap. For example, the ranges A:A1..A:D2 and A:B2..A:C15 both contain the cells A:B2 and A:C2. If you do create versions for overlapping ranges, one of the ranges always appears with a crossed check mark next to its version name. If you create a scenario that includes versions in overlapping ranges, only one version's data appears in the cells that overlap. For example, if RANGE1 were A:A1..A:D2, and RANGE2 were A:B2..A:C15, and you created a scenario that included the Best case version of RANGE1 and the Worst case version of RANGE2, only the values from one of those versions could appear in cells A:B2 and A:C2.

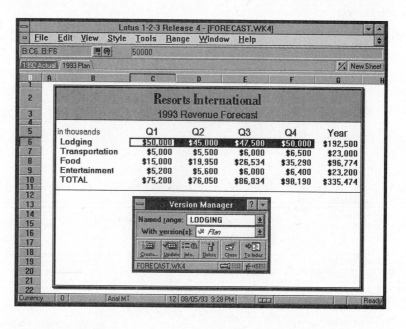

FIG. 9.6

The crossed check mark indicates that data in the LODGING range changed since you last displayed the Plan version of that range.

For example, if the Plan version of the LODGING range is currently displayed in the worksheet (that contains the value 42,500 in cell B:C6 as shown in figure 9.3), and you then enter the value 50,000 in cell B:C6 (as shown in fig. 9.6), the data in the worksheet differs from the data in the Plan version. The crossed check mark is usually an indication that you should either create a new version (if you want to preserve both values for cell B:C6) or update the current version (if you want to replace the data in the current version with the data in the worksheet).

After you enter the data for the new version, choose Create in the Version Manager window to create another version as just described.

Displaying Versions

Once you create several versions of a range, you can display the versions in the worksheet. To display a version of a range in the worksheet, select the desired range from the Named Range drop-down box and then select the version from the With Version(s) drop-down box. As soon as you select the version from the With Version(s) drop-down box, 1-2-3 places the data for that version of the range into the worksheet, replacing any data already there.

> **CAUTION:** When a crossed check mark appears next to a version name, the current data in the range has not been saved in a version. Displaying a different version in that range destroys the current data in the range. Choose Create to create a new version that includes the current data or Update to update the current version with the data in the range.

In the Resorts International example, you can create several versions of the LODGING range, the TRANSPORTATION range, the FOOD range, and the ENTERTAINMENT range. Then you can use Version Manager to display the versions in the worksheet in different combinations, and examine the effects of the revenue mix.

If you're creating a version of a range that is already named, and you want to change the range name, first display the version in the worksheet and then enter the new name in the Range Name text box in the Create Version dialog box.

> To quickly display each version of a range in the worksheet, select the range from the Named Range drop-down box, press Alt+V to move to the With Version(s) drop-down box, and then use the direction keys to cycle through the versions.
>
> **T I P**

Modifying and Updating Versions

After you create a version, you can change it in two ways: by changing the data (and styles—if you selected Retain Styles in the Create Version dialog box) for the version, or by changing the comment and other settings for the version.

To change the data in a version, first display the version in the worksheet. Then enter the new data for the version (the crossed check mark appears next to the version name in the Manager window when you enter the new data). Then choose the Update button in the Version Manager window. The Update Version dialog box appears. To confirm that you want to update the version with the new data in the worksheet, choose OK.

> **CAUTION:** When you update a version, you replace the original data stored in the version with the data currently in the worksheet.

To change a version's comment, sharing options, and style-retention setting, display the version in the worksheet and then choose Info from the Version Manager window. The Version Info dialog box appears (see fig. 9.7). Use this dialog box to edit the Comment text box and change the other settings for the version. The Version Info dialog box looks just like the Create Version dialog box, except that you can't change the version name.

FIG. 9.7

Use the Version Info dialog box to change a version's comment, sharing options, and style-retention setting.

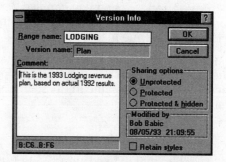

T I P   To change a version's name, create a second version with the same data, comment, and settings, but with the new name; then delete the original version.

To change a range's name without creating a new version of the range, select an existing version of that range, choose Info, enter the new name in the Range Name text box in the Version Info dialog box, and choose OK.

T I P

To change sharing options or the style-retention setting for several versions at once, move to the Index window, use Shift+click or Ctrl+click to select all the versions you want to modify, and then choose Info to display the Versions Info dialog box. This dialog box lets you change the sharing options or style-retention settings for all of the versions you selected.

Using Highlighting and Tracking

After you spend some time using Version Manager to create and manage different versions of worksheet data, you may find that some worksheets contain many named ranges with versions—and you may forget which ranges contain versions. The Highlighting and Tracking features of Version Manager can help you keep track of which ranges contain versions.

The two buttons in the lower right corner of the Version Manager window are the Tracking and Highlighting toggle buttons (see fig. 9.8). The left button, with the picture of a flashlight pointed at a worksheet grid, is the Highlighting button. Use the Highlighting feature to see which ranges in a worksheet contain versions. When Highlighting is on, 1-2-3 displays a border around each range in the worksheet that contains versions. Figure 9.8 shows the Highlighting feature active; notice that the ranges C6..F6, C7..F7, C9..F9, and B10..G10 all have a border to indicate that these ranges have associated versions. Click on the Highlighting button to turn Highlighting on and off.

The right button at the bottom of the Version Manager window, with the picture of a radar antenna pointed at a worksheet grid, is the Tracking button. Use the Tracking feature to navigate quickly to ranges that contain versions. When Tracking is on, 1-2-3 synchronizes the selection in the worksheet with the selection in the Version Manager window. For example, with Tracking on, selecting a named range in the Named Range drop-down box navigates to, and selects, that range in the worksheet. Selecting a cell in a named range in the worksheet selects that range in the Named Range drop-down box in the Version Manager window.

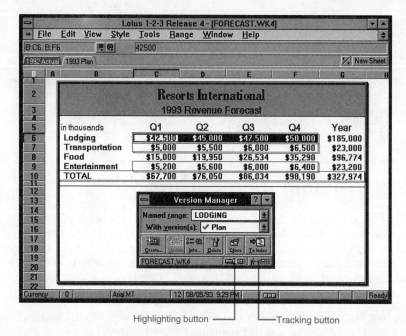

FIG. 9.8

The Highlighting button displays a border around each range that contains versions.

T I P

If you work in a large worksheet with ranges that contain versions in different parts of the worksheet, turn Tracking off to prevent 1-2-3 from navigating around the worksheet (and repainting the screen) each time you select a range in the Version Manager window.

To see the effects of different versions on a chart, turn Tracking off and then scroll to the chart. With Tracking off, you can keep the chart on-screen while you use the Manager to display different versions in the worksheet.

Displaying Version Comments in the Manager

To display the comments for the current version, drag the bottom border of the Manager window down to make the Manager window larger. The comment appears in a scrolling text box above the buttons (see fig. 9.9). This text box just displays the comments; it doesn't let you edit them. To edit a version's comments, select the version and choose Info. The Version Info dialog box appears, which lets you change the version comments, sharing options, and style retention setting.

FIG. 9.9

Expanding the
Manager
window vertically
displays version
comments.

Using the Index

The Index is more powerful and flexible than the Manager. It lets you
see information about all your versions in one place. It also lets you
group versions together into scenarios, making it easier to work with
particular groups of versions. The Index also gives you access to advanced features such as version reporting and merging. There is one
disadvantage to using the Index: it takes up more of the screen than the
Manager. However, you can minimize the Index to an icon while you
work in the worksheet and then restore it when you want to work in the
Index.

To display the Index, choose To Index from the Manager window. The
main feature of the Index is the object list that occupies the center of
the window (see fig. 9.10). This list contains information about the versions and scenarios in the current file.

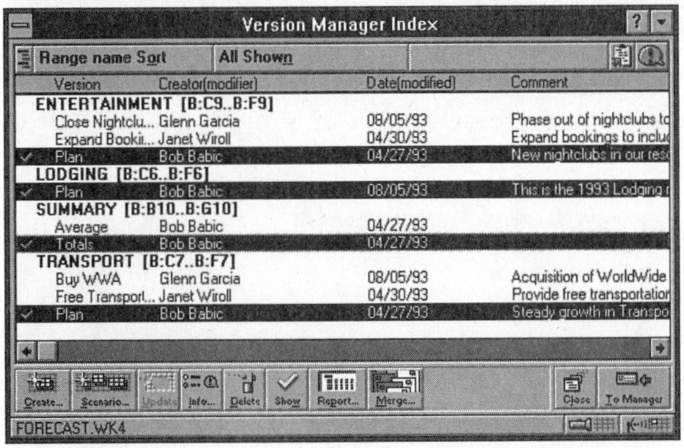

FIG. 9.10

The Index
window.

Below the object list is a row of buttons. The Create, Update, Info, Delete, Close, and To Manager buttons are the same as the corresponding
buttons in the Manager window, except that the Info and Delete buttons in the Index window also operate on scenarios. The Scenario,
Show, Report, and Merge buttons appear only in the Index window. The

three buttons at the bottom of the window (the file-name indicator and the Highlighting and Tracking buttons) are identical to the corresponding buttons in the Manager window.

Another row of buttons appears above the object list. These buttons act on the list itself, letting you change the way the list is displayed or the information it contains. The leftmost button collapses and expands the object list (see fig. 9.11). The next button, called the Sort selector, changes the way items in the object list are displayed. The Shown selector button applies filters to the object list. The button with a picture of a clipboard copies the information in the object list to the Clipboard. The last button splits the object list into two panes and displays version and scenario comments in the right pane (see fig. 9.12).

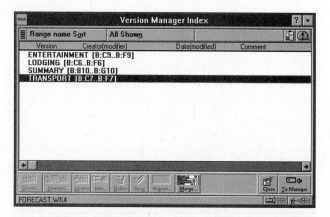

FIG. 9.11

The Index window, showing the object list collapsed.

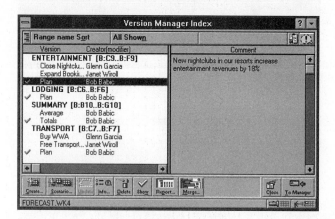

FIG. 9.12

The Index window, showing comments displayed in a second pane.

Exploring the Index

To get the most out of the Index, you must understand the object list and how to work with it. Remember that the row of buttons above the list operates on the list itself.

Using the Sort Selector Button

Two of the buttons, the Sort selector and the Shown selector, are similar to the selector buttons in the status bar at the bottom of the 1-2-3 window. Clicking on the button displays a list of options; 1-2-3 displays the option you select on the button. For example, the first time you open the Index, the text on the Sort selector button is Range Name Sort, indicating that the list is sorted by range name (refer back to fig. 9.10).

You can sort the object list by version name, scenario name, date, and user name in addition to the default range-name sort. 1-2-3 arranges the list in a hierarchy based on the sort you select. For example, in a range-name sort, the list displays each range name in boldface, followed by the versions for that range. For each version, the list displays the version name, creator, last modifier (if any), creation and modification date, and comment.

In a version-name sort, the list displays each version name in bold face, followed by the names of the ranges that contain a version with that name. In figure 9.13, there are three versions named Plan: one each for the ranges LODGING, TRANSPORT, and ENTERTAINMENT. The date sort and user-name sort are similar to the range-name and version-name sorts: they display versions sorted by date and by user, respectively. However, these two sorts display version names as range-version pairs, in the form RANGE.Version. For example, the Plan version of the TRANSPORT range appears in the date sort as TRANSPORT.Plan.

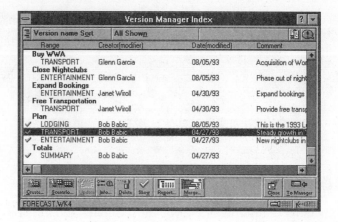

FIG. 9.13

The Index window, showing a version-name sort.

The scenario-name sort differs from the other sorts in that it is the only sort that displays scenarios. In a scenario-name sort, the list displays each scenario name in boldface, followed by the names of the versions included in the scenario. The version names are displayed as range-version pairs. Figure 9.14 shows the Index window with a scenario-name sort that has two scenarios: the Plan scenario (consisting of the Plan versions of LODGING, ENTERTAINMENT, and TRANSPORT) and the Push Entertainment scenario (consisting of the Expand Bookings version of ENTERTAINMENT and the Free Transportation version of TRANSPORT).

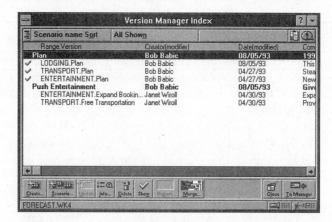

FIG. 9.14

The Index window, showing a scenario-name sort.

Using the Shown Selector Button

The Shown selector button, which contains the text All Show<u>n</u> the first time you open the Index window, lets you control which versions (and scenarios, in a scenario-name sort) 1-2-3 includes (or "shows") in the list. You can show All Current Versions (versions currently displayed in the worksheet, as shown in fig. 9.15), New Only (versions created in the current work session), Hidden Only (so that you can select hidden versions to unhide them), and Protected Only (so that you can quickly see which versions are protected).

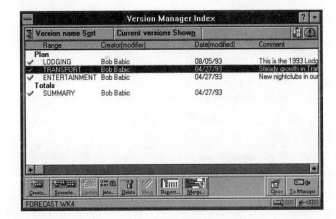

FIG. 9.15

The Index window, with the current versions shown.

Selecting and Displaying Versions in the Index Window

In the Manager window, you can select only a single version; selecting a version displays that version in the worksheet. In the Index window, you can select multiple versions; selecting a version does not display it.

Versions currently displayed in the worksheet appear in the object list in blue text with a check mark. Versions currently selected in the Index window appear in white text on a blue background. When you first open the Index window, all currently displayed versions are also selected. Figure 9.16 shows the Index window with multiple versions selected.

Being able to select multiple versions is useful because you can then perform actions on several versions at once. With multiple versions selected, you can choose any of the following buttons from the bottom of the Index window:

■ The Scenario button to group the versions together into a scenario

■ The Info button to change sharing options and style-retention settings for the versions

- The Delete button to delete the versions
- The Show button to display the versions

FIG. 9.16

The Index
window, with
multiple versions
selected.

To select multiple versions, click on the first version and then use
Ctrl+click to select additional versions. To select a group of adjacent
versions, click on the first version and drag the mouse pointer over the
other versions you want to select.

To display a single version in the worksheet when you're using the
Index window, double-click on it in the object list. To display multiple
versions, select the versions and then choose Show.

T I P   To avoid confusion, don't select more than one version for a range
and then choose Show (1-2-3 can show only one version for a range
at a time) or Scenario (1-2-3 can include only one version for each
range in a scenario).

Creating, Displaying, and Modifying Scenarios

A scenario is a named group of versions. Use scenarios when you want
to group a particular set of versions together. You may want to display
all the Plan versions in the worksheet and then display all the versions

that contain your most optimistic estimates. To do this easily, you can create a scenario named Plan that includes all the versions named Plan; create a second scenario named Optimistic that contains those versions with the most optimistic projections.

To create a scenario, choose the Scenario button in the Index window. The Create Scenario dialog box appears as shown in figure 9.17. This dialog box is similar to the Create Version dialog box: you can enter a name for the scenario, add a comment, and choose sharing options.

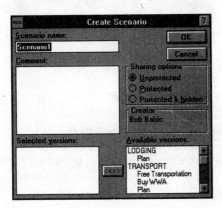

Two list boxes appear at the bottom of the dialog box: Selected Versions and Available Versions. Use these list boxes to choose the versions to include in the scenario. The Available Versions list box contains a list of all versions in the current file, sorted by range name. The Selected Versions list box lists the versions you select to include in the current scenario.

To add a version to the Selected Versions list box, select the version from the Available Versions list box and then choose ; alternatively, double-click on the version in the Available Versions list box. To remove a version from the Selected Versions list box, select the version and choose , or double-click on the version. When the Selected Versions list box contains the versions you want to include in the scenario, choose OK to create the scenario. Figure 9.18 shows the completed Create Scenario dialog box for a scenario named Big on Transportation, consisting of the Buy WWA version of TRANSPORT, the Close Nightclubs version of ENTERTAINMENT, and the Plan version of LODGING.

A scenario can contain only one version of any named range. For example, you cannot create a scenario that contains two versions of the SALES range (because you can only display one version of the range at a time).

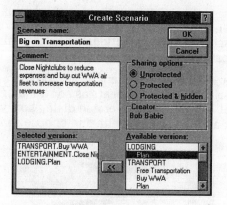

FIG. 9.18

The completed
Create Scenario
dialog box
for Big on
Transportation.

When you create a scenario, the Index window automatically changes
to the scenario-name sort (refer back to fig. 9.14).

To display a scenario in the worksheet, make sure that the Index window is in scenario-name sort. (If it is not in this sort order, choose Sort
and select Scenario name from the list of options.) From the list of scenarios in the Index window, double-click on the scenario you want to
display, or select it and choose Show.

To edit a scenario's comment, change its sharing options, or change
the versions included in the scenario, select the scenario name from
the Index-window list and choose Info. The Scenario Info dialog box
appears (see fig. 9.19). This dialog box is exactly like the Create Scenario dialog box, except that it shows the last modification date and
you cannot change the scenario name.

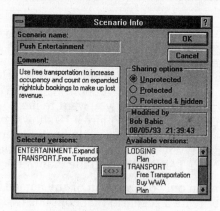

FIG. 9.19

The Scenario Info
dialog box.

To change sharing options for several scenarios at once, select all the
scenarios from the Index-window list and choose Info to display the

Scenarios Info dialog box. This dialog box lets you change the sharing options for all of the scenarios you selected.

Just as you can select multiple versions in the other sorts, you can select multiple scenarios in a scenario-name sort. However, if you select multiple scenarios and then choose Show, Version Manager can only show one version in any named range.

T I P

If your worksheet contains versions of many named ranges, you may find it easier to preselect the versions you want to include in a scenario than to select them in the Create Scenario dialog box.

One way to preselect versions for a scenario easily is to use the Manager window to display in the worksheet the versions you want to include in the scenario. Then choose To Index to move to the Index window. When you move from the Manager to the Index, the current versions (the versions currently displayed in the worksheet) are automatically selected in the Index window. Choose Scenario to display the Create Scenario dialog box. The selected versions appear in the Selected Versions list box.

To include in the object list only the versions currently in the worksheet, choose the Shown selector button and select Current Versions. Then use the mouse to select all the current versions and choose Scenario.

Another way to preselect versions for a scenario is to use a sort to collate the versions. For example, to create a Best Case scenario that includes all versions named Best Case, choose the Sort selector and select Version Name to sort the Index window by version name. Then select all the Best Case versions and choose Scenario.

Creating Reports

In addition to displaying versions and scenarios in the worksheet, you may want to create reports that show the data in different versions of a range or the effects of different versions on formulas in the worksheet.

To create a report showing the data and audit information for versions of a range—as well as the effects of the versions on formulas in the worksheet—choose the Report button from the Index window. The Version Report dialog box appears (see fig. 9.20).

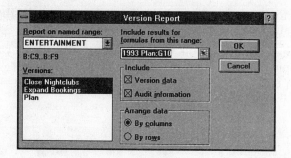

FIG. 9.20

The Version
Report dialog
box.

In the Report on Named Range list box, select the named range for
which you want to create a report. Then select one or more versions of
the range from the Versions list box.

If you want the report to include the effects of the different versions on
a range of formulas in the worksheet, specify the range in the Include
Results for Formulas From This Range text box. In the example shown
in figure 9.20, the report is to include the result of the formula located
in cell G10 of the "1993 Plan" worksheet (the total revenue for the year).
You can use point mode to select this range.

In the Include area of the dialog box, select Version Data to include in
the report the data in each version; select Audit Information to include
the name of the creator or modifier, date, and time. The default setting
selects both these options. In the Arrange Data area of the dialog box,
select By Columns or By Rows to choose the orientation of data in the
report.

When you choose OK, 1-2-3 creates the report in a new worksheet file,
makes that the active file, and minimizes the Version Manager window.
Figure 9.21 shows the report that resulted from the selections shown in
the Version Report dialog box in figure 9.20.

T I P   One way to create customized reports is to use the @VERSIONDATA,
@VERSIONINFO, and @SCENARIOINFO functions. (Functions are described in Chapter 7.) You also can create reports of the information
in the object list in the Index window by using the button near the
top-right corner of the Index window (the one that looks like a clipboard); this button copies the information in the list to the Clipboard. Paste the Clipboard contents into the worksheet and then
rearrange it or format it to suit your needs.

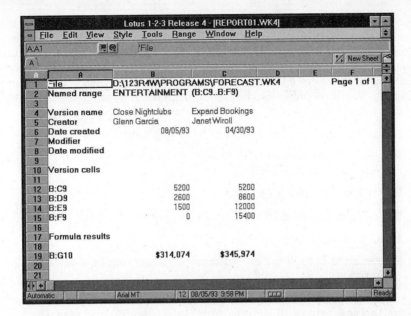

FIG. 9.21

The completed
report.

> **CAUTION:** When you use Version Report, and you specify a range in the Include Results for Formulas From This Range text box, 1-2-3 recalculates formulas in all active files once for each version you include in the report. If you have several 1-2-3 files open, or if your file takes a long time to recalculate, you may want to create reports at a time when you don't need to use the computer for something else.

Merging Versions and Scenarios

If you use Version Manager to share data with other 1-2-3 users, you may want to combine the versions and scenarios from one copy of a worksheet file into another copy of the file. The Merge Versions & Scenarios feature copies versions and scenarios from a source file into a destination file.

For example, you can give copies of the Revenue Forecast worksheet file to two members of your staff and ask them to create versions containing their projections for the different types of revenue. You can then use the Merge Versions & Scenarios dialog box to combine their versions and scenarios into your master copy of the file.

For this feature to work, both files must contain named ranges with the same names and the same dimensions. Suppose that both files contain ranges named FOOD and TRANSPORT; the FOOD range is four columns by one row in both files but the TRANSPORT range is four columns by one row in the source file and four columns by two rows in the destination file. Versions of FOOD are copied from the source file to the destination file but versions of TRANSPORT are not.

In addition, 1-2-3 does not copy the following situations:

- Versions into ranges in the destination file that contain protected cells if the file is sealed.
- Versions hidden in the source file.
- Versions identical to versions in the destination file.
- Scenarios hidden in the source file.
- Scenarios containing one or more versions that could not be merged.

To copy versions and scenarios from a source file (containing the versions and scenarios you want to copy) into a destination file (which must be the current file), begin by opening both files and making the destination file the current file. Then choose <u>M</u>erge from the Index window. The Merge Versions & Scenarios dialog box appears (see fig. 9.22). In the From File drop-down box, select the source file.

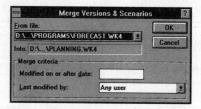

To merge only the versions and scenarios last modified on or after a particular date, enter the date in the Modified On or After Date text box (enter the date in a format 1-2-3 can recognize).

To merge only the versions and scenarios last modified by a particular person, select the person's name from the Last Modified By drop-down box.

When you choose OK, 1-2-3 begins copying the versions and scenarios from the source file to the destination file. If 1-2-3 is unable to merge any versions and scenarios from the source file that meet the criteria entered in the Merge Versions & Scenarios dialog box, the Merge

Results dialog box appears (see fig. 9.23), listing each item and the reason it could not be merged.

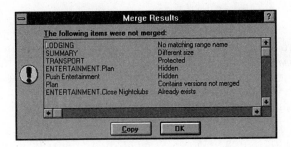

FIG. 9.23

The Merge Results dialog box.

If 1-2-3 successfully merges all versions and scenarios from the source file that meet the criteria, the Merge Versions & Scenarios dialog box closes and the Index window reappears.

> **T I P**
>
> To find out which versions were merged, remember to choose File Save to save the destination file before you do the merge. After the merge is complete, choose the Shown selector button at the top of the Index window and select New Only. 1-2-3 displays in the object list only the versions added to the file in the current session. To find out which scenarios were merged, choose the Sort selector and select Scenario Name.

> **T I P**
>
> To save information reported in the Merge Results dialog box, use the mouse to highlight the information you want to save, choose the Copy button on the Merge Results dialog box or press Ctrl+C or Ctrl+Ins to copy the information to the Clipboard, and use the Edit Paste command in the 1-2-3 menu, or press Ctrl+V or Shift+Ins to paste the information into the worksheet.

For Related Information

◀◀ "Managing Files," p.233.

◀◀ "Using Functions," p.261.

FROM HERE...

Using Version Manager To Share Data

In addition to letting you create and maintain different versions of data in your own worksheets, Version Manager makes it easier than ever to share data with other 1-2-3 users. Several users can enter versions in the same file without writing over each other's data. Version Manager provides audit information so that you always know who entered which version.

If you have a local area network, you can share data by keeping a file on a network file server. Users can add versions to the same file along with comments explaining the thinking behind each version. For example, different people can enter revenue forecasts based on their individual expertise. Co-workers can review each other's versions, use the comments section to add suggestions or ask questions, and perhaps create new versions based on someone else's ideas.

If you don't have access to a network, you can still use Version Manager to share data. One way is to pass around a single copy of a worksheet file, letting each person add versions to it. Another way is to distribute a copy of the file to each person who needs to use it. Then use the Merge Versions & Scenarios dialog box to combine all the versions and scenarios from the various copies of the file into a single master copy.

Any time you share a file, whether on a network or not, you may want to unprotect the ranges in which you want others to create versions and then seal the file with a password. This arrangement prevents other people from rearranging the file but lets them create versions in the unprotected ranges. Sealing the file also prevents other users from changing protected versions or from seeing hidden versions.

Finally, if you use Lotus Notes network communication software, you can create special files—called shared files—that are actually 1-2-3 worksheet files saved as Notes databases. Shared files let multiple users have concurrent access to a single worksheet file. Several people can create versions and scenarios in a single copy of the file, at the same time, without writing over or damaging each other's work.

FROM HERE...

For Related Information

◄◄ "Managing Files," p. 233.

Looking at Application Examples

Now that you know the mechanics of using Version Manager, you may have an application in mind that would benefit from Version Manager features. Or you may need some additional ideas for how to put Version Manager to use in your environment. The following sections give you some ideas for different ways to use Version Manager.

What-If Analysis

One of the most obvious uses for Version Manager is in what-if analysis. Suppose that your child is considering several colleges and financial aid packages; you can create named ranges for Tuition and for Financial Aid and then create versions in each range for all the options.

Another example is if you manage a cafeteria-style benefits plan where employees choose from different options in each benefit category; you can create versions for each benefit category that contain different selections of options.

Applications Requiring Frequent Updates or Iterations

Many spreadsheet applications go through several updates or iterations before being published as a finished report. For example, departmental expense budgets can go through several rounds of review and update before being approved and consolidated into the company budget. You can use Version Manager to save each round of updates without losing earlier data. You can also create customized reports to measure the effects of the changes by comparing the results of placing different versions in the worksheet.

Applications with Several Contributors

Some applications require contributions from several people. For example, a marketing forecast may require input from several product-line and marketing managers. Version Manager supports this kind of application by tracking all changes you or your co-workers make to a worksheet. You can manage this process by using a single copy of a worksheet that you pass from one person to the next, or by making a copy for each person and then merging all the contributions into a single copy.

Reporting and Presentation Applications

You can use Version Manager to help present information concisely for maximum impact in a live presentation. For example, instead of creating a chart for last year's quarterly sales and a different chart for this year's quarterly sales, you can store last year's amounts and this year's amounts as different versions of the same range and then create one chart that refers to that range. Then use Version Manager to switch versions to change the data in the chart. Instead of moving from one chart to another, you use a single chart, and change the data in the chart at the touch of a button.

Instead of storing expense totals, percent of sales, and percent change since last year in different columns of an income statement worksheet, store them as different versions of a range.

Questions & Answers

This chapter shows you how to use Version Manager to create, use, and manage versions and scenarios. If you have questions concerning situations not addressed in the examples given in the preceding sections, read through this section.

Q: Is there a limit to the size of a version?

A: Yes, you can create versions only of ranges that contain 2000 cells or fewer. If you need to track changes to larger ranges, create several ranges (each with no more than 2000 cells), create versions of the ranges, and group the versions together into scenarios.

Q: Can a version contain formulas?

A: Yes, a version can contain anything you can enter in a cell. Versions can contain values, labels, formulas, functions, or macros. You also can save styles with versions.

Q: Where can I get sample files that contain versions and scenarios?

A: The file LESSON8.WK4 in the \123R4W\SAMPLE\TUTORIAL subdirectory contains version samples. The file GLOBAL.WK4 in the \123R4W\SAMPLE subdirectory contains versions and scenarios. To practice creating versions and scenarios and using the Manager and the Index, choose Help Tutorial and then choose Lesson 8, "Using Version Manager."

Q: Where does Version Manager get my name when it creates a version or a scenario? Can I change the name it uses?

A: Version Manager looks for an authenticated name (a name that requires a password), such as a Lotus Notes or Lotus CC:Mail user name or a network logon name. If it finds an authenticated name, it uses that name; you cannot change it except to another authenticated name (for example, by logging in to the network using a different user name and password). If Version Manager does not find an authenticated name, it uses the name you specified when you installed 1-2-3. Since you can enter any name when you install 1-2-3, 1-2-3 considers this to be a non-authenticated name. A non-authenticated name is called an alias; you can change the alias that Version Manager uses by choosing Tools User Setup.

Q: After I chose Merge to merge versions and scenarios from one file into another, the Merge Results dialog box did not appear. Why not?

A: If Version Manager was able to merge all the versions and scenarios in the source file that met the criteria you specified in the Merge Versions & Scenarios dialog box, it doesn't report the results of the merge.

Q: After I chose Merge to merge versions and scenarios from one file into another, the Merge Results dialog box did not appear—but no versions or scenarios were merged. Why not?

A: There were no versions or scenarios in the source file that met your criteria. Either there were no versions or scenarios in the source file, or you specified a date in the Modified On or After Date text box in the Merge Versions & Scenarios dialog box and there were no versions or scenarios in the source file last modified on or after that date.

Q: Sometimes certain buttons in the Manager or the Index window are gray; when I try to click on them, nothing happens. Why?

A: Version Manager makes buttons unavailable by graying them to prevent you from choosing buttons that make no sense or have no effect in a particular situation. For example, the Update button is available only when a range with versions contains new data that hasn't yet been saved in a version. If you're using the Index window, the available buttons change depending on what you select in the object list. For example, if no versions are selected in the list, Update, Info, Delete, and Show are unavailable.

Q: On my computer, two buttons appear in the Index window that don't appear in the figures in this chapter. The buttons are always gray. What are these buttons?

A: The two additional buttons that appear in the Index window are for use with shared files. If 1-2-3 detects Lotus Notes on your computer during installation, it installs software that lets you work with special files called shared files. See your Notes administrator or contact Lotus Customer Support for more information about sharing files using Lotus Notes.

Q: How can I prevent other users from changing versions and scenarios that I enter in a file we share on the network?

A: When you select Protected or Protected & Hidden from the Sharing Options area of a Create or Info dialog box, you prevent accidental changes to versions and scenarios (by accidentally choosing Update, for example). However, anyone can unprotect the versions and change them. To prevent unauthorized changes to versions and scenarios, choose Style Protection to allow changes to the ranges that contain versions (so that other users can create new versions in those ranges). Then use File Protect to seal the file with a password. Other users cannot unprotect your protected versions and scenarios or see your hidden versions and scenarios.

Q: I created a version (or scenario) and selected Protected & Hidden under Sharing Options. Now I can't find the version. What happened to it?

A: The version or scenario is still in the worksheet file. To access hidden versions and scenarios, open the Index window, choose the Shown selector button at the top of the window, and select Hidden Only. 1-2-3 displays the hidden versions and scenarios in the object list (remember to select Scenario Name from the Sort selector list to display scenarios in the object list). Then you can select one or more versions or scenarios and choose Info to change the sharing options so that the versions or scenarios are no longer hidden.

Q: When I choose the Shown selector button from the Index window so that I can show my hidden versions (or scenarios), the Hidden Only option does not appear. What's wrong? How can I show my hidden versions (or scenarios)?

A: In a file sealed using File Protect, you cannot access hidden versions. Use File Protect to unseal the file and try again.

Summary

Version Manager lets you create, view, and manage different sets of data for named ranges. To work with Version Manager, open the Version Manager window by choosing Range Version. This window appears in two forms: the smaller Manager, and the larger and more powerful Index.

The Manager lets you work with one version at a time. The Index lets you see information about many versions in one place, and lets you work with more than one version at a time by grouping them together into scenarios. The Index also lets you perform more advanced tasks like creating reports and merging versions from one file into another.

To create, modify, or delete versions, use the buttons that appear in the Version Manager window in both its forms. Additional buttons that appear only in the Index give you access to more powerful features.

Version Manager makes it easier to do things that you probably already do with 1-2-3. You can use Version Manager to do what-if analysis, to share data with other 1-2-3 users, and to keep track of different versions of the same data.

The next chapter gives you some insight into printing reports.

Printing Reports and Charts

PART

III

OUTLINE

Printing Reports

1-2-3 for Windows gives you considerable control over the design of printed output—from one-page reports to longer reports that incorporate data from multiple worksheets and include sophisticated graphs.

Many features you may associate with printing are actually part of the worksheet. For example, boldface, italics, and underlining are selected from the Style menu, not through a print command. When you are ready to print, these attributes automatically print on the report. With 1-2-3 for Windows, you are always in a Wysiwyg (what-you-see-is-what-you-get) environment—what you see on-screen closely resembles the printed output on paper.

This chapter shows you how to perform the following tasks:

- Use the File Print Preview command to see how reports look before you print

- Print a one-page or multiple-page report

- Print multiple ranges

- Compress a report to fit on one page

- Hide areas within a print range

- Specify text (titles, headers, and footers) to print on every page

- Set margins

- Create and use named print settings

Enhancing Reports

Unless a report is for your eyes only, you will want to format it so that it is attractive, readable, and professional looking before you print it. 1-2-3 for Windows offers a number of features that enable you to enhance printed reports. You can use different fonts; you can also add borders, drop shadows, and shades. The Font & Attributes and the Lines & Color dialog boxes are the places to go to liven up reports. Just make sure that you don't overdo it! These formatting options are for highlighting important areas of the worksheet and for adding interest to what might otherwise be a dull report. If you use too many formatting options, your audience may be overwhelmed and you may end up with an ugly report.

To save yourself time when formatting a report, use one of the templates included with 1-2-3 Release 4. Choose Style Gallery and select one of the preformatted templates in the list. Figure 10.1 shows a printout of a worksheet formatted with the Picture 1 template.

Annual Sales Report

Annual Report	Quarter 1	Quarter 2	Quarter 3	Quarter 4	Year Total
Computers	75,000	94,500	121,258	99,205	389,963
Printers	7,456	20,378	12,090	15,468	55,392
Software	21,518	3,711	5,578	35,120	65,927
Books	16,931	18,382	9,798	22,750	67,861
Parts	11,044	12,511	5,352	12,965	41,872
Qtr totals	131,949	149,482	154,076	185,508	621,015

FIG. 10.1

This report was formatted with the Picture 1 template from the Style Gallery.

See Chapter 5, "Changing the Format and Appearance of Data," for details on the basic and enhanced formatting of 1-2-3 worksheets, such as the formatting used in the report shown in figure 10.1.

Using the Windows Default Print Settings

In 1-2-3 for Windows, you use the File Printer Setup commands to set printer defaults. Because you are using Windows, many printer settings are already in place. The Windows environment retains basic information about the printer, such as resolution, paper size, and amount of memory. This information is available to all your Windows applications, including 1-2-3 for Windows.

By using the Windows control panel in the Main program group of the Program Manager, you can change the hardware-specific printer defaults. You can add or delete printer drivers and set other printer defaults (such as the kind of paper feed, orientation, and paper size). Refer to the Windows documentation for details on changing these defaults.

Using the Printing SmartIcons

Many printing-related commands are available in the Printing SmartIcon palette, as shown in figure 10.2. These SmartIcons offer a faster way to give printing commands. Most of the SmartIcons require you to preselect a range before clicking on the SmartIcon. SmartIcons are defined and discussed throughout the chapter; in fact, the Printing palette is displayed in all the figures in this chapter. To display this palette, choose Tools SmartIcons (or click on the SmartIcons button in the status bar) and then select Printing from the list of palettes.

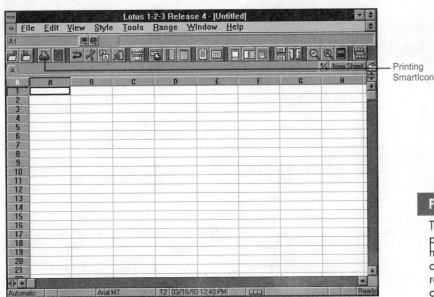

Printing SmartIcon

FIG. 10.2

The SmartIcon palette displayed here is specifically for printing-related commands.

Understanding 1-2-3 Printing Commands

The 1-2-3 for Windows commands you use to print are similar to the /Print and [:]Print commands from DOS versions of 1-2-3 (the DOS versions of these commands also are offered in the 1-2-3 Classic menu). The 1-2-3 for Windows commands, however, offer more functionality and ease of use. In 1-2-3 for Windows, printing is an easier task that involves a less complex menu structure than in DOS versions of 1-2-3.

In 1-2-3 for Windows, the File menu contains four different commands you can use to control printed output: File Print Preview, File Page Setup, File Print, and File Printer Setup. These commands are grouped together on the File menu (see fig. 10.3).

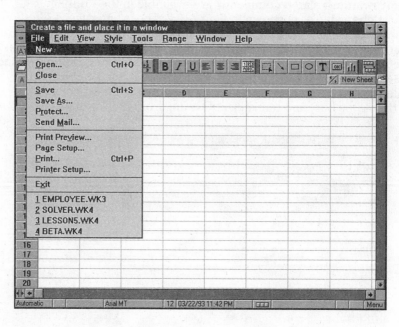

FIG. 10.3

The File menu contains the commands for printing.

The following sections provide an overview of the purpose of each printing command and the dialog box each command accesses. Later sections of this chapter explore the specific options in the dialog boxes and explain the relationship of each option to the printing process.

The File Page Setup Command

You select most printing options through the Page Setup dialog box, accessed by choosing Page Setup from the File menu or by clicking on the Page Setup SmartIcon. You also can access this dialog box from the Print and Print Preview dialog boxes (displayed by selecting the File Print and File Print Preview commands, respectively).

As shown in figure 10.4, the Page Setup dialog box includes options for specifying orientation, margins, header and footer information, size, frame, grid lines, and print titles. You also can assign a name to a particular group of settings and later use these settings from any worksheet. You can designate the current settings as the default settings, or you can restore the default settings to replace the current settings.

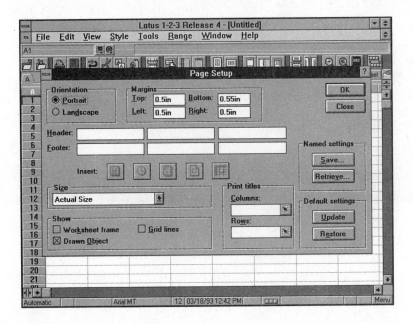

FIG. 10.4

The Page Setup dialog box.

NOTE Although no direct correlation exists between the 1-2-3 Classic commands and the standard 1-2-3 for Windows printing commands, most printing options are located in the Page Setup dialog box. Some print commands that appear in the 1-2-3 Classic menu, such as printing cell formulas, have no corresponding command in the 1-2-3 for Windows menu.

The File Print Command

The File Print command starts the printing process; you can select File Print (or press Ctrl+P) to send data directly from 1-2-3 for Windows to the printer. You also can click on the Print SmartIcon to begin printing.

When you choose File Print, 1-2-3 for Windows displays the Print dialog box (see fig. 10.5). Use this dialog box to specify the pages you want to print, the number of copies you need, the range or ranges to print, and so on. The Page Setup button accesses the Page Setup dialog box (described in the preceding section); when you close the Page Setup dialog box, you return to the Print dialog box. The Preview button display a preview of the printed output; when you are done looking at the preview, you return to the worksheet.

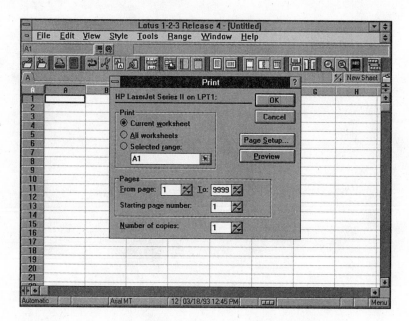

FIG. 10.5

The Print dialog box.

The File Printer Setup Command

The primary use of the File Printer Setup command is to select the printer to which you want to send the report—if you have more than one printer. You also can use Printer Setup to specify additional print settings such as the orientation of the print job on the paper (portrait or landscape), scaling, paper size, paper source, and number of copies. You set these options by clicking on the Setup button in the Printer Setup dialog box. This dialog box has additional settings you can change by clicking on its Options button. The exact options available depend on the printer you select. For example, PostScript devices offer an option for scaling but HP LaserJet printers do not.

> Use the Print Manager feature of Windows (accessible from 1-2-3 for Windows by pressing Ctrl+Esc and selecting Print Manager) to find information about print jobs in progress or in the print queue.
>
> **T I P**

The File Print Preview Command

To get an idea of what your report looks like before you print it, you can preview each page on the screen with the File Print Preview command. 1-2-3 displays the report in a special preview window so that you can determine whether the page breaks and margins are appropriate. If you like what you see, you can print the report while previewing it. Otherwise, you might want to alter your worksheet before printing.

Specifying the Print Range

Before you can print anything, you have to tell 1-2-3 what you want to print. You specify a print range in the same way you specify other ranges: you can preselect the print range before using a print command or SmartIcon, or you can specify the range from the Print or Print Preview dialog box.

Specifying a Single Print Range

To preselect a print range, you use one of two methods:

- With the mouse, click and drag to highlight the range.

- With the keyboard, press the F4 key to anchor one corner of the range and then use the arrow keys to define the extent of the range; press Enter when finished defining the range.

If you forget to preselect the range you want to print, you can specify the range in the Selected Range text box of the Print or Print Preview dialog box (see fig. 10.6). You can type the cell addresses, enter a range name, or highlight the range from this text box. To highlight the print range, first click on the range selector and then select the range in the normal fashion. With the mouse, use the click-and-drag or shift-click technique. With the keyboard, use Backspace to unanchor any previously selected range, position the cell pointer at the start of the desired range, press the period key to anchor the range, and then use the direction keys (Home, End, PgUp, PgDn, and the arrow keys) to designate the print range.

T I P To specify the entire worksheet as the print range, press Home, period, End Home.

Range selector ——

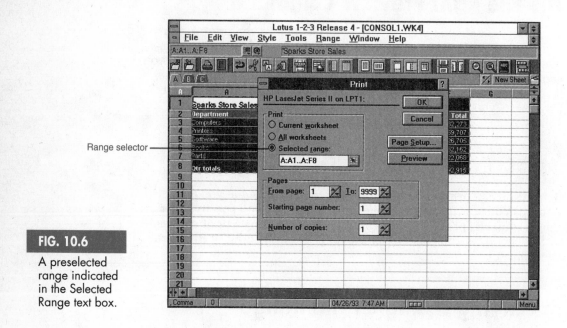

FIG. 10.6

A preselected range indicated in the Selected Range text box.

For many reports, a *two-dimensional range*—that is, a rectangular area in a worksheet—is all you need to specify. The next section describes how to specify multiple ranges for a single print job.

Printing Multiple Ranges

Most reports require only a single print range. You can, however, specify that a single print job include a *collection*—that is, several ranges in one or more worksheets.

Specifying multiple print ranges is similar to specifying a single range in a single worksheet: preselect the range or specify the range address or range name in the Print dialog box. If you are typing several print ranges in the Selected Range field, type a comma or semicolon between each range. If you want to highlight a range that spans multiple worksheets or highlight multiple ranges in the same worksheet, you *must* preselect the ranges; the Print dialog box does not permit you to highlight multiple ranges. To preselect a three-dimensional range, highlight the range in the first worksheet and then hold Shift as you click on the last worksheet tab you want to select; the same range is selected in the group of worksheets. You also can use Ctrl+PgUp and Ctrl+PgDn to move among worksheets. To preselect multiple ranges, hold Ctrl as you indicate each range (except the first) or as you click on the worksheet tab to move to other worksheets.

CAUTION: If you forget to hold Ctrl when selecting ranges, all currently selected ranges are deselected.

Figure 10.7 shows a worksheet with a three-dimensional print range selected; figure 10.8 shows the resulting report, printed on a Hewlett Packard LaserJet II. Each range was formatted using the B&W2 Style Gallery template.

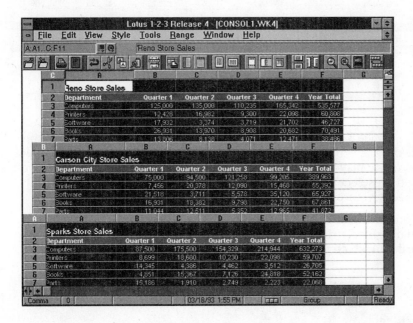

FIG. 10.7

Highlighting a 3-D range to be printed.

Sparks Store Sales

Department	Quarter 1	Quarter 2	Quarter 3	Quarter 4	Year Total
Computers	87,500	175,500	154,329	214,944	632,273
Printers	8,699	18,680	10,230	22,098	59,707
Software	14,345	4,386	4,462	3,512	26,705
Books	4,851	15,367	7,126	24,818	52,162
Parts	15,186	1,910	2,749	2,223	22,068
Qtr totals	130,581	215,843	178,896	267,595	792,915

Carson City Store Sales

Department	Quarter 1	Quarter 2	Quarter 3	Quarter 4	Year Total
Computers	75,000	94,500	121,258	99,205	389,963
Printers	7,456	20,378	12,090	15,468	55,392
Software	21,518	3,711	5,578	35,120	65,927
Books	16,931	18,382	9,798	22,750	67,861
Parts	11,044	12,511	5,352	12,965	41,872
Qtr totals	131,949	149,482	154,076	185,508	621,015

Reno Store Sales

Department	Quarter 1	Quarter 2	Quarter 3	Quarter 4	Year Total
Computers	125,000	135,000	110,235	165,342	535,577
Printers	12,428	16,982	9,300	22,098	60,808
Software	17,932	3,374	3,719	21,702	46,727
Books	26,931	13,970	8,908	20,682	70,491
Parts	13,806	8,138	4,071	12,471	38,486
Qtr totals	196,097	177,464	136,233	242,295	752,089

FIG. 10.8

The printed version of the 3-D range.

The Range To Print SmartIcon in the Printing SmartIcon palette specifies the selected range or ranges as the print range in the Print dialog box. You may find it handy to click on this SmartIcon immediately after you preselect a collection of print ranges. This icon lets you quickly specify your print ranges when you aren't ready to print yet.

You can specify any combination of two-dimensional and three-dimensional print ranges. 1-2-3 for Windows prints the ranges in the order in which you enter the range addresses.

T I P   When printing multiple ranges, always preview the report, as described in the next section.

For Related Information

◄◄ "Using Fundamental Commands," p. 133.

◄◄ "Working with Ranges," p. 140.

FROM HERE...

Previewing Reports before Printing

Previewing a worksheet on-screen before sending it to the printer can save paper, printer ink (or toner or ribbon), time, and embarrassment. Few things are as frustrating as tying up the computer for a long time with a print job or walking the length of the office to a distant printer—only to discover that the printed project doesn't look the way you want it. Perhaps you forgot to enter the data in part of the worksheet; maybe the print range is incorrect. Whatever the error, you've wasted time and resources printing an incorrect report.

You can find and fix many minor errors before printing if you use the 1-2-3 Print Preview feature. With Print Preview, you can see how 1-2-3 for Windows breaks up a large print range over several pages, how multiple ranges fit on one or more pages, whether the specified margins are appropriate, and so on.

To preview a print job, you can use any of the following methods:

■ Choose the File Print Preview command.

■ Choose the File Print command. From the resulting Print dialog box, choose the Preview button.

■ Click on the Preview SmartIcon. This SmartIcon is available in the default palette as well as the Printing palette. After you select this SmartIcon, you see a preview of the current range selection; if no current range is selected, the last range you used in a print command is depicted in the preview.

All these methods access the Print Preview dialog box (see fig. 10.9). Use the Print Preview dialog box to specify whether you want to preview the current worksheet, all worksheets, a selected range, or a range of pages. Before accessing this dialog box, you can preselect a print range (as described in the preceding section); that range is automatically entered into the Selected Range field in the dialog box.

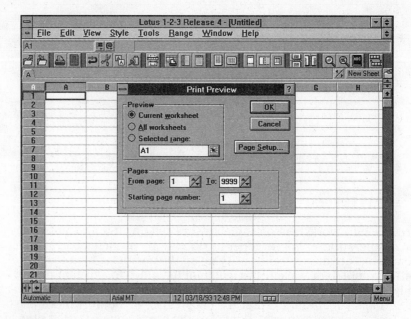

FIG. 10.9

The Print Preview
dialog box.

NOTE By choosing the Page Setup button in the Print Preview dialog box, you can access the Page Setup dialog box (refer back to fig. 10.4) and make changes to the setup before you see the preview. After making changes and choosing OK in the Page Setup dialog box, you return to the Print Preview dialog box.

After you finish specifying the options in the Print Preview dialog box, choose OK or press Enter to preview the worksheet. 1-2-3 for Windows displays the preview in a special preview window. Notice that the menu options are inactive and that the SmartIcon palette changes (see fig. 10.10). The following sections describe how to use the preview window and its associated SmartIcons.

NOTE 1-2-3 may require a few seconds to display the preview of the print job.

Browsing the Preview Report

  As you preview a report, you may want to see more than just the first page. You can use the keyboard or the mouse to browse through the report. The first two SmartIcons on the palette let you browse through the pages in a multiple-page report. Click on the Preview Next Page SmartIcon (the first SmartIcon from the left) to display the next page; click on the Preview Previous Page SmartIcon (the second SmartIcon) to display the previous page. To use the keyboard, press Enter to see the next page or PgUp to see the previous page.

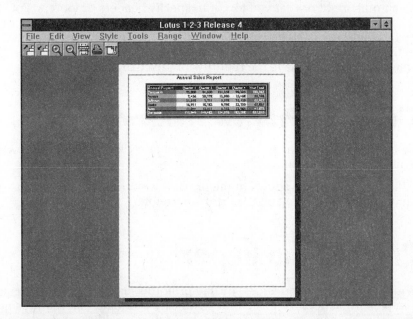

FIG. 10.10

The screen preview of an annual sales report.

Zooming the Preview Report

The two magnifying-glass SmartIcons enable you to zoom in and zoom out on the report so that you can read the worksheet text or see a miniature version of the entire worksheet. The Zoom-In SmartIcon has a plus sign; the Zoom-Out SmartIcon has a minus sign. Alternatively, you can press the gray plus key to zoom in and the gray minus key to zoom out.

You can zoom several times until you zoom to the appropriate level of magnification. Each time you zoom in or out, the screen display is magnified (when zooming in) or reduced (when zooming out) by 10 percent. Once you zoom in, use the arrow keys to move around the page. To zoom back out, click on the Zoom-Out SmartIcon or press the gray minus key to decrease the display 10 percent at a time. Alternatively, you can press the asterisk (*) key to return to the original level of magnification.

Making Setup Changes while Previewing the Report

As you preview a report, you may sometimes discover that the margins aren't quite right or that you forgot to specify headers or footers. For these types of changes, you can go directly to the Page Setup dialog box by clicking on the Page Setup SmartIcon. After you make changes to the page setup, choose OK or press Enter; 1-2-3 returns to the preview screen and displays the report with the changes you made.

Closing the Preview Window

To clear the preview at any time, press Esc or click the Close Window SmartIcon. 1-2-3 returns to the worksheet.

If the report is fine as shown in the preview window, you can print it immediately by clicking on the Print SmartIcon.

Printing the Report

With the printing commands, you can print the simplest or the most complex worksheet. To print a range quickly—for data that requires no special enhancements, such as headers, footers, or different margin settings—use the File Print command or the Print SmartIcon.

This section shows you how to print reports quickly and efficiently. First, you learn how to print a short report (one page or less of data); then you learn how to print a multiple-page report. In subsequent sections of this chapter, you learn how to include headers and footers in reports, compress a report to fit on one page, add grid lines, column letters and row numbers, and repeat certain columns or rows on each page.

Figure 10.11 shows the large cash-flow model that occupies the range A:A1..A:T130. This model, referred to throughout the chapter, is used only as an example of a complex worksheet from which you can generate reports.

CASH FLOW PROJECTOR
Copyright (c) 1993 Que Corporation

BALANCES IN WORKING CAPITAL ACCOUNTS

Assets	
Cash	$17,355
Accounts Receivable	493,151
Inventory	163,833

Liabilities	
Accounts Payable	125,000
Line of Credit	0
Net Working Capital	$549,339

SALES

	Oct	Nov	Dec	Jan	Feb	Mar	Apr	May	Jun	Jul	Aug	Sep	Oct	Nov	Dec	Total
Profit Center 1	$27,832	$25,864	$28,125	$31,336	$37,854	$43,879	$51,471	$56,953	$60,370	$65,982	$67,832	$71,902	$76,216	$80,789	$85,636	$728,330
Profit Center 2	13,489	21,444	20,140	22,572	24,888	25,167	32,588	40,140	42,548	45,101	47,807	50,678	53,716	56,939	60,356	502,489
Profit Center 3	128,811	124,382	123,618	131,685	129,044	131,273	138,221	141,879	150,382	159,415	168,960	179,119	201,258	213,334	213,334	1,935,466
Profit Center 4	94,285	92,477	89,010	95,473	98,000	96,986	95,318	103,538	106,750	116,535	123,315	130,714	138,557	148,683	155,863	1,410,340
Profit Center 5																
Total Sales	$262,417	$262,167	$258,893	$281,066	$289,894	$297,305	$316,508	$342,310	$363,061	$384,844	$407,905	$432,411	$459,356	$485,857	$515,006	$4,576,945

Percent of Collections

	Oct	Nov	Dec	Jan	Feb	Mar	Apr	May	Jun	Jul	Aug	Sep	Oct	Nov	Dec	Total
Cash	10%	10%	10%	10%	10%	10%	10%	10%	10%	10%	10%	10%	10%	10%	10%	
30 Days	20%	20%	20%	20%	20%	20%	20%	20%	20%	20%	20%	20%	20%	20%	20%	
60 Days	50%	50%	50%	50%	50%	50%	50%	50%	50%	50%	50%	50%	50%	50%	50%	
90 Days	20%	20%	20%	20%	20%	20%	20%	20%	20%	20%	20%	20%	20%	20%	20%	
Cash Collections		$282,452	$281,452	$261,096	$267,083	$280,021	$292,481	$304,602	$323,568	$346,071	$367,785	$389,882	$413,254	$438,049	$464,332	$4,150,570

PURCHASES

Cost of Goods Sold

	Oct	Nov	Dec	Jan	Feb	Mar	Apr	May	Jun	Jul	Aug	Sep	Oct	Nov	Dec	Total
Profit Center 1	33%	33%	33%	33%	33%	33%	33%	33%	33%	33%	33%	33%	33%	33%	33%	
	$9,185	$7,875	$8,621	$10,341	$12,525	$14,480	$16,985	$18,794	$19,922	$21,117	$22,385	$23,728	$25,151	$26,660	$28,260	$240,349
Profit Center 2	29%	29%	29%	29%	29%	29%	29%	29%	29%	29%	29%	29%	29%	29%	29%	
	$3,912	$6,219	$5,841	$6,546	$7,218	$7,298	$9,451	$11,641	$12,339	$13,079	$13,864	$14,696	$15,578	$16,512	$17,503	$145,725
Profit Center 3	50%	50%	50%	50%	50%	50%	50%	50%	50%	50%	50%	50%	50%	50%	50%	
	$63,446	$62,191	$61,809	$65,843	$64,522	$65,637	$69,611	$70,940	$75,198	$79,708	$84,480	$89,559	$94,933	$100,629	$106,667	$967,733
Profit Center 4	67%	67%	67%	67%	67%	67%	67%	67%	67%	67%	67%	67%	67%	67%	67%	
	$63,171	$61,960	$59,637	$63,967	$65,665	$64,981	$63,863	$69,370	$73,533	$77,945	$82,621	$87,579	$92,333	$98,403	$104,328	$945,068
Profit Center 5	30%	30%	30%	30%	30%	30%	30%	30%	30%	30%	30%	30%	30%	30%	30%	
Total Cost of Goods Sold	$138,673	$138,244	$135,908	$146,898	$149,500	$152,396	$170,743	$180,980	$191,849	$203,360	$215,562	$228,485	$242,205	$256,737	$256,737	$2,298,875

Inventory Purchasing Schedule

	Oct	Nov	Dec	Jan	Feb	Mar	Apr	May	Jun	Jul	Aug	Sep	Oct	Nov	Dec	Total
0 Days in Advance	5%	5%	5%	5%	5%	5%	5%	5%	5%	5%	5%	5%	5%	5%	5%	
30 Days in Advance	30%	30%	30%	30%	30%	30%	30%	30%	30%	30%	30%	30%	30%	30%	30%	
60 Days in Advance	50%	50%	50%	50%	50%	50%	50%	50%	50%	50%	50%	50%	50%	50%	50%	
90 Days in Advance	15%	15%	15%	15%	15%	15%	15%	15%	15%	15%	15%	15%	15%	15%	15%	
Inventory Purchases	$138,803	$141,364	$147,962	$152,005	$157,279	$165,947	$176,442	$186,316	$187,091	$210,215	$222,828	$236,198	$248,059	$256,011	$256,737	$2,467,129

Payment Schedule

	Oct	Nov	Dec	Jan	Feb	Mar	Apr	May	Jun	Jul	Aug	Sep	Oct	Nov	Dec	Total
Cash	30%	30%	30%	30%	30%	30%	30%	30%	30%	30%	30%	30%	30%	30%	30%	
30 Days	40%	40%	40%	40%	40%	40%	40%	40%	40%	40%	40%	40%	40%	40%	40%	
60 Days	30%	30%	30%	30%	30%	30%	30%	30%	30%	30%	30%	30%	30%	30%	30%	
Payment for Purchases	$0	$0	$0	$147,203	$152,380	$156,297	$166,495	$176,488	$187,264	$198,518	$210,429	$223,055	$235,743	$248,686	$255,843	$2,356,606

FIG. 10.11

The complete cash-flow model.

OPERATING EXPENSES	Oct	Nov	Dec	Jan	Feb	Mar	Apr	May	Jun	Jul	Aug	Sep	Oct	Nov	Dec	Total
Profit Center 1	$20,459	$20,667	$21,285	$21,710	$22,144	$22,587	$23,039	$23,500	$23,970	$24,449	$24,938	$25,437	$25,946	$26,465	$26,994	$291,179
Profit Center 2	14,377	14,665	14,958	15,257	15,562	15,873	16,191	16,515	16,845	17,162	17,525	17,876	18,234	18,598	18,970	204,628
Profit Center 3	25,921	26,439	26,968	27,506	28,058	28,619	29,191	29,775	30,371	30,978	31,598	32,230	32,874	33,532	34,202	368,854
Profit Center 4	13,922	14,200	14,484	14,774	15,070	15,371	15,678	15,992	16,312	16,638	16,971	17,310	17,656	18,010	18,370	194,152
Profit Center 5																0
Corporate Overhead	14,944															
Total Expenses	$89,622	$78,172	$77,685	$79,249	$80,834	$82,451	$84,100	$85,782	$87,487	$89,247	$91,032	$92,853	$94,710	$96,604	$98,536	$1,062,883
Payment Schedule																
Cash	70%	70%	70%	70%	70%	70%	70%	70%	70%	70%	70%	70%	70%	70%	70%	
30 Days	20%	20%	20%	20%	20%	20%	20%	20%	20%	20%	20%	20%	20%	20%	20%	
60 Days	10%	10%	10%	10%	10%	10%	10%	10%	10%	10%	10%	10%	10%	10%	10%	
Total Payment for Expenses			$78,503	$78,650	$80,203	$81,807	$83,443	$85,112	$86,814	$88,551	$90,322	$92,128	$93,971	$95,650	$97,787	$1,054,598
CASH-FLOW SUMMARY																
Collection of Receivables				$263,452	$267,083	$260,021	$292,481	$304,602	$323,568	$346,071	$367,795	$389,862	$413,254	$438,049	$464,332	$4,130,570
Other Cash Receipts				0	0	0	0	0	0	0	0	0	0	0	0	0
Cash Disbursements																
Payment for Purchases on Credit				147,203	152,390	158,297	168,495	176,488	187,264	198,518	210,429	223,055	238,745	246,888	253,843	2,336,606
Operating Expenses				78,630	80,203	81,807	83,443	85,112	86,814	88,551	90,322	92,128	93,971	95,650	97,787	1,054,598
Long-Term Debt Service																
Interest Payment on Line of Credit																
Interest Rate			13.50%	13.50%	13.50%	13.50%	13.50%	13.50%	13.50%	13.50%	13.50%	13.50%	13.50%	13.50%	13.50%	
Payment				5,340	5,821	6,344	6,915	7,538	8,216	8,956	9,762	10,640	11,598	12,642	13,779	107,551
Income Tax Payments																
Other																
Total Cash Disbursements				231,174	238,404	246,448	258,854	269,138	282,294	296,025	310,513	325,824	341,314	355,378	365,360	3,518,735
Net Cash Generated This Period				32,278	28,679	33,572	35,627	35,464	41,274	50,046	57,282	64,039	71,940	82,671	98,942	651,815
ANALYSIS OF CASH REQUIREMENTS		Dec	Jan	Feb	Mar	Apr	May	Jun	Jul	Aug	Sep	Oct	Nov	Dec		
Beginning Cash Balance			$17,355	$49,633	$78,312	$111,885	$147,512	$182,976	$224,249	$274,296	$331,578	$395,616	$467,557	$550,228		
Net Cash Generated This Period			32,278	28,679	33,572	35,627	35,464	41,274	50,046	57,282	64,039	71,940	82,671	98,942		
Cash Balance before Borrowings			49,633	78,312	111,885	147,512	182,976	224,249	274,296	331,578	395,616	467,557	550,228	649,170		
Minimum Acceptable Cash Balance																
Amount above(below) Minimum Acceptable Balance			49,633	78,312	111,885	147,512	182,976	224,249	274,296	331,578	395,616	467,557	550,228	649,170		
Current Short-Term Borrowings		0	0	0	0	0	0	0	0	0	0	0	0			
Total Short-Term Borrowings		0	0	0	0	0	0	0	0	0	0	0	0			
Ending Cash Balance			$49,633	$78,312	$111,885	$147,512	$182,976	$224,249	$274,296	$331,578	$395,616	$467,557	$550,228	$649,170		

FIG. 10.11

The complete cash-flow model (continued).

Printing a One-Page Report

For most one-page print jobs, once the defaults and the printer are set up, printing involves only the following steps:

1. Check that the printer is on-line and that the paper is properly positioned.

2. Select the print range.

3. Click on the Print SmartIcon, choose the File Print command, or press Ctrl+P. The Print dialog box appears (refer back to fig. 10.5).

4. Choose OK or press Enter to send the report to the printer.

Figure 10.12 shows the Cash Flow Projector worksheet with range A1..G17 highlighted for printing. Figure 10.13 shows the range printed on an HP LaserJet II.

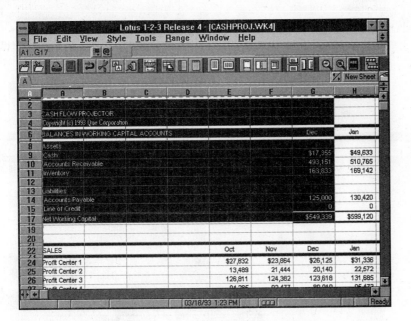

FIG. 10.12

The range A1..G17 highlighted in the cash-flow model.

Printing a Multiple-Page Report

To print a multiple-page report, follow the steps for printing a one-page report (as described in the preceding section). If the print range contains more rows or columns than can fit on a page, 1-2-3 for Windows prints the report on multiple pages. Figure 10.14 shows how 1-2-3 for

Windows indicates a split print range—the vertical and horizontal dashed lines show the page boundaries. The numbers of rows and columns that fit on a page depend on the global font, individual column widths and row heights, and whether or not you have chosen to compress the worksheet.

FIG. 10.13

The printout of the range A1..G17.

CASH FLOW PROJECTOR
Copyright (c) 1993 Que Corporation

BALANCES IN WORKING CAPITAL ACCOUNTS	Dec
Assets	
Cash	$17,355
Accounts Receivable	493,151
Inventory	163,833
Liabilities	
Accounts Payable	125,000
Line of Credit	0
Net Working Capital	$549,339

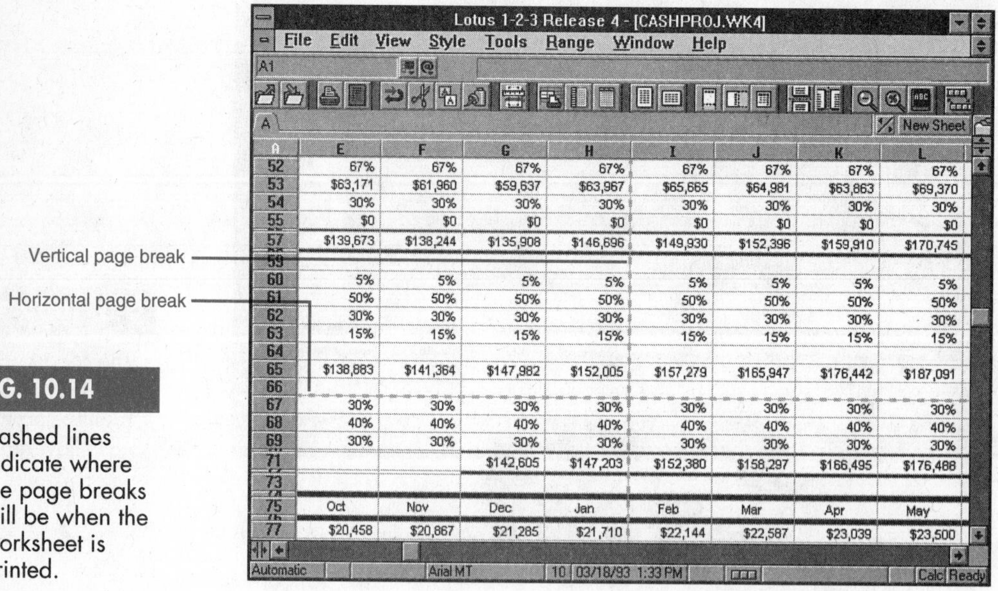

FIG. 10.14

Dashed lines indicate where the page breaks will be when the worksheet is printed.

When you print a multiple-page report, you must pay attention to where 1-2-3 for Windows splits the worksheet between pages— vertically *and* horizontally. 1-2-3 for Windows can split pages at inappropriate locations, resulting in a report that is hard to read or understand. By previewing the report as described earlier in this chapter, you can see exactly how 1-2-3 for Windows will print a large range. You can then adjust the page breaks, change the page orientation, compress the worksheet, or make other changes to improve the look of the report. The next section describes the options for changing the format of the report.

Changing the Page Contents

1-2-3 automatically sets up page breaks to fit a long worksheet onto several pages—but the page breaks may separate headings from explanatory text or columns of figures. Sometimes you may want to break the report into specific groups of data. And occasionally you may want to exclude some parts of the report from the printout, even though that text is in included in the print range. The following sections explain how to make these types of changes.

Inserting Manual Page Breaks

If you are unhappy with the way 1-2-3 splits the data in a long report, you can insert manual page breaks—both horizontal and vertical varieties. A horizontal page break controls a long worksheet; a vertical page break controls a wide worksheet. To insert a page break, move the cell pointer to where you want the page break to occur. Horizontal breaks are inserted *above* the cell pointer; vertical breaks are inserted to the *left* of the cell pointer. When you insert manual page breaks, you see dotted lines that represent the placement of these breaks.

To insert a horizontal page break just above the Purchases section of the Cash Flow Projector worksheet, for example, place the cell pointer in row 42 and choose Style Page Break or click on the Horizontal Page Break SmartIcon. If you use the SmartIcon, 1-2-3 immediately displays a dotted line indicating the page break in the worksheet. The Style Page Break command, on the other hand, displays the Page Break dialog box, from which you can choose Column (for a vertical page break) or Row (for a horizontal page break). Figure 10.15 shows the Page Break dialog box. After specifying the type of page break you want, choose OK or press Enter. A dotted line indicating the page break appears in the worksheet.

The Printing SmartIcon palette offers two page-break SmartIcons. The SmartIcon with a horizontal dotted line between two pages inserts a horizontal page break above the cell pointer. The SmartIcon with a vertical dotted line between two pages inserts a vertical page break to the left of the pointer.

To remove page breaks, choose Style Page Break and uncheck the Column or Row box.

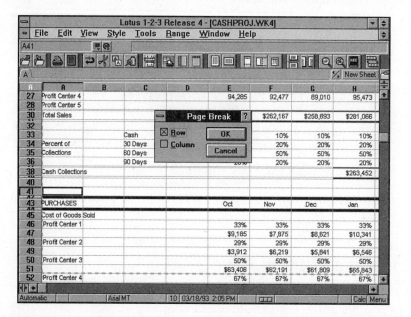

FIG. 10.15

The Page Break dialog box.

Hiding Segments in the Print Range

Sometimes data appears in a worksheet that you don't want to appear in a report. For example, you may have a column of data in the middle of the worksheet that is necessary for a calculation, but that is not important to view on a report. 1-2-3 offers different ways to exclude data from a printout, depending on whether you want to hide a cell, a row, or a column.

Excluding Rows from a Print Range

1-2-3 for Windows does not have a command to hide rows, although there is a way to exclude a row from a printout. To prevent a row from printing, type a vertical bar ($\perp$) in the row's leftmost cell within the print range. The vertical bar does not appear on-screen or on the printout; this character is a label-prefix that tells 1-2-3 for Windows not to print the contents of that row. A row marked in this way does not print, although the suppressed data remains in the worksheet and is used in all calculations.

Suppose that you want to print the Cash Flow Summary descriptions from the Cash Flow Projector worksheet. Figure 10.16 shows a printout of the range A95..D112.

CASH FLOW SUMMARY

Collection of Receivables
Other Cash Receipts

Cash Disbursements
 Payment for Purchases on Credit
 Operating Expenses
 Long-Term Debt Service
 Interest Payment on Line of Credit
  Interest Rate
  Payment
 Income Tax Payments
 Other
Total Cash Disbursements
Net Cash Generated This Period

FIG. 10.16

A printout of rows 95 to 112 of the Cash Flow worksheet.

Now suppose that you don't want the printout to show the cash-disbursements details (rows 101 through 108). Move the cell pointer to column A and insert a vertical bar in the leftmost cell of rows 101 through 108. You can avoid editing each cell if you insert a new column (column A) at the left edge of the print range and narrow this column to a width of 1. Then type the vertical bar (⊥) in cell A101 and copy this entry to cells A102..A108. Remember to include the new column in the print range, or the vertical bar (|) has no effect. Figure 10.17 shows the results of printing A95..E112 with the vertical bars in place for rows 101 through 108.

To restore the worksheet after printing, use Edit Delete Column to delete the column that contains the vertical bars. If you didn't insert the vertical bars in their own column, you'll need to edit each cell and delete this symbol.

CASH FLOW SUMMARY

Collection of Receivables
Other Cash Receipts

Cash Disbursements
Total Cash Disbursements
Net Cash Generated This Period

Excluding Columns from a Print Range

You can use the Style Hide command to indicate columns that you
don't want displayed on-screen. If you include these hidden columns in
a print range, the columns do not print.

Suppose that you are working with the Cash Flow Projector worksheet
and you want to print the Sales information for January through March
only. The January through March information is contained in the range
H22..J30; you want to hide the columns that contain the preceding
year's October, November, and December information (columns E, F,
and G). Issue the Style Hide command and specify E24..G24 to suppress
the data for October through December. Figure 10.18 shows the result
of hiding columns E, F, and G.

Another way to hide a column is to set its width to zero. To set the
column width to 0, either select Style Column Width and enter 0 in the
Set Width To field of the Column Width dialog box, or drag the right
border of the column so that it touches the left border.

To redisplay a column, use Style Hide, select the Range field, and enter
the coordinates of one cell in the column you want to redisplay. After
you click on the Show button, the column reappears. Another way to
unhide a column is to preselect the range by highlighting across the
column to be unhidden. For example, to unhide column D, drag across
columns C and E. Then click on the Show button in the Hide dialog box.

Excluding Cells and Ranges from a Print Range

A worksheet may include information you want to save on disk but
omit from a printed report. For example, you may want to omit the
copyright message in the fourth row of the Cash Flow Projector
worksheet. To hide only part of a row or column or an area that spans

one or more rows and columns, use the Style Number Format command and select Hidden from the Format list in the Number Format dialog box. For this example, select cell A4, choose Style Number Format, and highlight Hidden in the Format list; then print the range A1..G18 (see fig. 10.19).

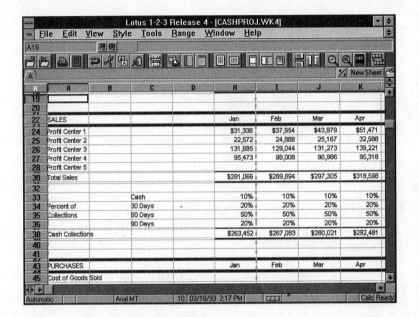

FIG. 10.18

Columns E, F, and G are hidden to prevent them from printing.

CASH FLOW PROJECTOR

BALANCES IN WORKING CAPITAL ACCOUNTS	Dec
Assets	
Cash	$17,355
Accounts Receivable	493,151
Inventory	163,833
Liabilities	
Accounts Payable	125,000
Line of Credit	0
Net Working Capital	$549,339

FIG. 10.19

The printed output does not display the data contained in cell A4 (cell A4 is formatted as hidden).

To restore the copyright message after you finish printing, select Style Number Format and click on the Reset button.

T I P If you find yourself repeating certain print operations, such as hiding the same columns or suppressing and then restoring the same documentation messages, you can save time and minimize frustration by developing and using print macros. For more information on using macros, see Chapters 15 and 16.

FROM HERE...

For Related Information

◀◀ "Using Fundamental Commands," p. 133.

◀◀ "Protecting and Hiding Worksheet Data," p. 167.

Enhancing Reports with Page Setup Options

A printed report that contains numbers without descriptive headings is difficult, if not impossible, to interpret. You can make a report easier to understand by using 1-2-3 for Windows features that help you fit an entire report on a single page by changing the orientation. You can specify that specific data ranges print on each page of a multiple-page report (these ranges are called *row* or *column titles*). You also can print the worksheet frame (the row numbers and the column letters). The sections that follow show you how to create headers and footers, repeat row and column headings on succeeding pages, and print the worksheet frame and grid lines. You also learn how to set margins and save the print settings.

Remember, to access the Page Setup dialog box, you can use any of the following techniques:

- Select File Page Setup.

- Choose the Page Setup SmartIcon.

- In the Print dialog box, choose the Page Setup button.

- In the Print Preview dialog box, choose the Page Setup button.

- In the preview window, choose the Page Setup icon.

Switching the Page Orientation

One way to get a wide report to fit on a single page is to change the *orientation* (direction) of the printing. Normally you print in *portrait orientation*; that is, the text prints vertically on the page, with the top of the printout at the narrow edge of the paper. The term *portrait orientation* makes sense if you think of a painting of someone: the person's head usually is oriented at one narrow end of the canvas; the painting is taller than it is wide. If you print horizontally on the page, you use *landscape orientation*, like that of most landscape paintings.

To switch between portrait and landscape orientation, you can click on the Portrait or Landscape SmartIcons. The SmartIcon showing a vertical page selects portrait orientation; the SmartIcon showing a horizontal page selects landscape orientation. You also can change the orientation in the Page Setup dialog box. To change the orientation with the dialog box, choose Portrait or Landscape to indicate the direction you want 1-2-3 to print.

Compressing and Expanding the Report

If your report doesn't fit on one page, you can have 1-2-3 automatically shrink the data using the Size option in the Page Setup dialog box. Five sizes are available:

- Actual Size
- Fit All to Page
- Fit Columns to Page
- Fit Rows to Page
- Manually Scale

With Actual Size (the default setting), 1-2-3 makes no attempt to alter the size of the printed output; that is, the data is not compressed at all. If you select Fit All to Page, 1-2-3 compresses the print range, in an attempt to fit the information on one page. The report can be compressed up to one-seventh of its original size. If the print range still does not fit, 1-2-3 prints the first page with the most compression possible and subsequent pages with the same compression. A new feature in Release 4 is the ability to compress just the columns (Fit Columns to Page) or just the rows (Fit Rows to Page). The report in figure 10.11 was compressed using the Fit All to Page option. Although the entire report could have fit on a single page, the type would have been too tiny to read easily. Therefore, a manual page break was inserted before the Operating Expenses section to create two pages of larger type.

You also may enter a specific percentage by choosing the Manually Scale option. If you select this option, the dialog box displays a text box in which you can enter a percentage; this number can be as low as 15 (representing 15 percent of normal size) or as high as 1000 (representing 1,000 percent, or 10 times the normal size). By manually scaling, you can compress or expand the worksheet.

The Printing SmartIcon palette offers three SmartIcons for fitting the print range on a single page: Fit Rows to Page, Fit Columns to Page, and Fit All to Page.

There are several other ways to fit more of your worksheet on a printed page. One way is to narrow the column widths as much as possible, either globally or individually. You can also print the report in landscape orientation or set smaller margins. See "Switching the Page Orientation" and "Setting Margins" for details.

FROM HERE...

For Related Information

◄◄ "Setting Column Widths," p. 151.

Creating Headers and Footers

A *header* is a single line of text that prints at the top of every page in your report; a *footer* prints at the bottom of each page. You can use headers and footers to print page numbers, the worksheet file name, the report date and time, the report title, and so on. The header text, which is printed on the first line after the top margin, is followed by two blank header lines preceding the report (for spacing). The footer text is printed above the bottom margin and below two blank footer lines (again, for spacing).

You specify a header or footer in the Page Setup dialog box. A header or footer can have three parts: left-aligned, centered, and right-aligned text. There are boxes provided for each of these three parts in the Page Setup dialog box (see fig. 10.20). Whatever is entered in the first box is aligned at the left margin; the text in the second box is centered between the left and right margins; the text in the third box is aligned at the right margin. The header and footer text is printed in the worksheet's default typeface and size.

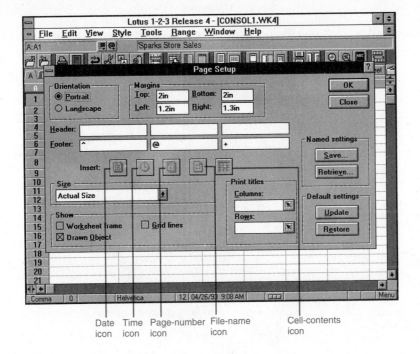

Date   Time   Page-number File-name   Cell-contents
icon   icon   icon   icon   icon

FIG. 10.20

The Page Setup
dialog box
with a footer
specified.

In addition to any text you enter, the header or footer can include codes for inserting page numbers, the date or time of printing, the file name, or the contents of a cell. First, place the cursor in the appropriate box (left-aligned, centered, or right-aligned) next to Header or Footer in the page Setup dialog box. The insert icons immediately become active. Then specify the codes you want to use from the following list:

- To number pages sequentially (starting with 1), enter a pound sign (#) or click on the page-number insert icon (the center icon).

- To print the current date, enter an at sign (@) or click on the date insert icon (the calendar).

- To print the time, enter a plus sign (+) or click on the time insert icon (the clock).

- To insert the file name, type a caret symbol (^) or click on the file-name insert icon (the one that looks like a page).

- To use the contents of a cell as a header or footer, enter a backslash (\) or click on the cell-contents insert icon (it looks like a worksheet grid). Then type the address or range name of the cell that contains the text you want to include in the header or footer. The specified cell address or range name can contain a formula. If you specify a range name, 1-2-3 for Windows uses the contents of only the first cell in the range.

Figure 10.21 shows a printout with the footer specified in figure 10.20. This footer has a left-aligned file name, a centered date, and a right-aligned time. You can see from this example how the date and time are formatted.

Sparks Store Sales

Department	Quarter 1	Quarter 2	Quarter 3	Quarter 4	Year Total
Computers	87,500	175,500	154,329	214,944	632,273
Printers	8,699	18,680	10,230	22,098	59,707
Software	14,345	4,386	4,462	3,512	26,705
Books	4,851	15,367	7,126	24,818	52,162
Parts	15,186	1,910	2,749	2,223	22,068
Qtr totals	130,581	215,843	178,896	267,595	792,915

Carson City Store Sales

Department	Quarter 1	Quarter 2	Quarter 3	Quarter 4	Year Total
Computers	75,000	94,500	121,258	99,205	389,963
Printers	7,456	20,378	12,090	15,468	55,392
Software	21,518	3,711	5,578	35,120	65,927
Books	16,931	18,382	9,798	22,750	67,861
Parts	11,044	12,511	5,352	12,965	41,872
Qtr totals	131,949	149,482	154,076	185,508	621,015

Reno Store Sales

Department	Quarter 1	Quarter 2	Quarter 3	Quarter 4	Year Total
Computers	125,000	135,000	110,235	165,342	535,577
Printers	12,428	16,982	9,300	22,098	60,808
Software	17,932	3,374	3,719	21,702	46,727
Books	26,931	13,970	8,908	20,682	70,491
Parts	13,806	8,138	4,071	12,471	38,486
Qtr totals	196,097	177,464	136,233	242,295	752,089

CONSOL1.WK4   18-Mar-93   02:32 PM

FIG. 10.21

The footer produced by entering codes in the Footer field of the Page Setup dialog box.

Printing Titles

To make a multiple-page printed report more understandable, you can add headings from row or column ranges by using the Print Titles options in the Page Setup dialog box. To specify row titles in the Ro<u>w</u>s box of the Page Setup dialog box, select one or more rows of labels to print above each print range and at the top of all pages. To specify column titles in the <u>C</u>olumns box of the Page Setup dialog box, designate one or more columns of labels to print to the left of every print range and at the left edge of all pages. Setting titles in a printout is similar to freezing titles in the worksheet. The Ro<u>w</u>s option produces a printed border similar to a frozen horizontal title display; the <u>C</u>olumns option produces a printed border similar to a frozen vertical title display. (For details on freezing titles, see the *Freezing Titles* section in Chapter 4, "Using Fundamental Commands.")

SmartIcons for these commands are also available in the Printing SmartIcon palette. To specify one or more columns to print at the left of each page, select the range of columns and then click on the Set Columns as Print Titles SmartIcon. To specify rows to print at the top of each page, select the range of rows and then click on the Set Rows as Print Titles SmartIcon.

Because the Cash Flow Projector worksheet is so wide, it is an ideal candidate for columnar print titles. Without the row headings in columns A through D printed on every page, no one can understand what the numbers on the report stand for (see fig. 10.22). However, if you specify A1..D1 in the <u>C</u>olumns text box of the Page Setup dialog box, the account names in columns A through D print on every page, allowing anyone to make sense of the numbers on any page of the printout. Figure 10.23 shows the first page of the report from figure 10.22—with print titles added.

> **CAUTION:** If you include the print titles in the print range, 1-2-3 prints these elements twice. Be careful, therefore, not to include the range containing the print titles in the print range.

To cancel a print title, highlight the entry in the <u>C</u>olumns or Ro<u>w</u>s text box in the Page Setup dialog box. Press Del to clear the contents and then press Enter.

Jan	Feb	Mar	Apr	May	Jun	Jul	Aug
$49,633	$78,312	$111,885	$147,512	$182,976	$224,249	$274,296	$331,578
510,765	533,576	550,861	576,978	614,886	654,378	693,151	733,291
169,142	176,491	190,042	206,574	222,920	240,247	258,613	278,081
130,420	135,950	144,243	154,846	166,119	177,854	190,247	203,357
0	0	0	0	0	0	0	0
$599,120	$652,430	$708,544	$776,218	$854,663	$941,021	$1,035,813	$1,139,594

Jan	Feb	Mar	Apr	May	Jun	Jul	Aug
$31,336	$37,954	$43,879	$51,471	$56,953	$60,370	$63,992	$67,832
22,572	24,888	25,167	32,588	40,140	42,548	45,101	47,807
131,685	129,044	131,273	139,221	141,879	150,392	159,415	168,980
95,473	98,008	96,986	95,318	103,538	109,750	116,335	123,315
$281,066	$289,894	$297,305	$318,598	$342,510	$363,061	$384,844	$407,935
10%	10%	10%	10%	10%	10%	10%	10%
20%	20%	20%	20%	20%	20%	20%	20%
50%	50%	50%	50%	50%	50%	50%	50%
20%	20%	20%	20%	20%	20%	20%	20%
$263,452	$267,083	$280,021	$292,481	$304,602	$323,568	$346,071	$367,795

Jan	Feb	Mar	Apr	May	Jun	Jul	Aug
33%	33%	33%	33%	33%	33%	33%	33%
$10,341	$12,525	$14,480	$16,985	$18,794	$19,922	$21,117	$22,385
29%	29%	29%	29%	29%	29%	29%	29%
$6,546	$7,218	$7,298	$9,451	$11,641	$12,339	$13,079	$13,864
50%	50%	50%	50%	50%	50%	50%	50%
$65,843	$64,522	$65,637	$69,611	$70,940	$75,196	$79,708	$84,490
67%	67%	67%	67%	67%	67%	67%	67%
$63,967	$65,665	$64,981	$63,863	$69,370	$73,533	$77,945	$82,621
30%	30%	30%	30%	30%	30%	30%	30%
$0	$0	$0	$0	$0	$0	$0	$0
$146,696	$149,930	$152,396	$159,910	$170,745	$180,990	$191,849	$203,360
5%	5%	5%	5%	5%	5%	5%	5%
50%	50%	50%	50%	50%	50%	50%	50%
30%	30%	30%	30%	30%	30%	30%	30%
15%	15%	15%	15%	15%	15%	15%	15%
$152,005	$157,279	$165,947	$176,442	$187,091	$198,316	$210,215	$222,828

FIG. 10.22

This page is difficult to interpret because it doesn't have any row headings.

Printing the Worksheet Frame and Grid Lines

Printing the worksheet frame is particularly useful during worksheet development, when you want the printouts to show the location of data in a large worksheet. In the Show section of the Page Setup dialog box, you can make two selections to print the worksheet frame. The

Worksheet Frame option prints column letters across the top of a worksheet and row numbers down the side of the worksheet. The Grid Lines option prints lines between all cells in the print range.

CASH FLOW PROJECTOR

BALANCES IN WORKING CAPITAL ACCOUNTS	Jan	Feb	Mar	Apr
Assets				
Cash	$49,633	$78,312	$111,885	$147,512
Accounts Receivable	510,765	533,576	550,861	576,978
Inventory	169,142	176,491	190,042	206,574
Liabilities				
Accounts Payable	130,420	135,950	144,243	154,846
Line of Credit	0	0	0	0
Net Working Capital	$599,120	$652,430	$708,544	$776,218

SALES			Jan	Feb	Mar	Apr
Profit Center 1			$31,336	$37,954	$43,879	$51,471
Profit Center 2			22,572	24,888	25,167	32,588
Profit Center 3			131,685	129,044	131,273	139,221
Profit Center 4			95,473	98,008	96,986	95,318
Profit Center 5						
Total Sales			$281,066	$289,894	$297,305	$318,598
	Cash		10%	10%	10%	10%
Percent of	30 Days		20%	20%	20%	20%
Collections	60 Days		50%	50%	50%	50%
	90 Days		20%	20%	20%	20%
Cash Collections			$263,452	$267,083	$280,021	$292,481

PURCHASES		Jan	Feb	Mar	Apr
Cost of Goods Sold					
Profit Center 1		33%	33%	33%	33%
		$10,341	$12,525	$14,480	$16,985
Profit Center 2		29%	29%	29%	29%
		$6,546	$7,218	$7,298	$9,451
Profit Center 3		50%	50%	50%	50%
		$65,843	$64,522	$65,637	$69,611
Profit Center 4		67%	67%	67%	67%
		$63,967	$65,665	$64,981	$63,863
Profit Center 5		30%	30%	30%	30%
		$0	$0	$0	$0
Total Cost of Goods Sold		$146,696	$149,930	$152,396	$159,910
Inventory	0 Days in Advance	5%	5%	5%	5%
Purchasing	30 Days in Advance	50%	50%	50%	50%
Schedule	60 Days in Advance	30%	30%	30%	30%
	90 Days in Advance	15%	15%	15%	15%
Inventory Purchases		$152,005	$157,279	$165,947	$176,442

FIG. 10.23

Columns A through D were selected as print titles so that the row headings appear on every page of the report.

Figure 10.24 shows an example of a report with the worksheet frame and grid lines displayed.

A	A	B	C	D	E	F
1		Darlene's Computer Warehouse				
2		1993 Annual Sales Report				
3		Reno Store Sales				
4	Department	Quarter 1	Quarter 2	Quarter 3	Quarter 4	Year Total
5	Computers	125,000	135,000	110,235	165,342	535,577
6	Printers	12,428	16,982	9,300	22,098	60,808
7	Software	17,932	3,374	3,719	21,702	46,727
8	Books	26,931	13,970	8,908	20,682	70,491
9	Parts	13,806	8,138	4,071	12,471	38,486
10	Qtr totals	196,097	177,464	136,233	242,295	752,089

FIG. 10.24

This report shows the worksheet frame and grid lines.

Setting Margins

The Page Setup dialog box enables you to change the margins of the report. Select Top, Bottom, Left, or Right, and enter the margin width in inches. The default settings are as follows:

Top	0.5
Bottom	0.55
Left	0.5
Right	0.5

If your report has a header, it will appear *after* (not within) the top margin, and footer text appears above the bottom margin. If you didn't specify a header, the report begins printing immediately after the top margin.

Naming and Saving the Current Settings

When you have several worksheet reports with a similar layout, you may want to save the page setup so that you can retrieve the settings for other files. Saving the page setup options keeps you from having to specify the same settings over and over again. The Named Settings area in the Page Setup dialog box offers buttons for saving and retrieving page settings.

To assign a name to the current print settings, select the Save button; you are prompted for a file name. The Save button creates a file, with the AL3 extension, that you can use with other worksheets. When you want to use these named settings in another worksheet file, select the

Retrieve button from the Page Setup dialog box and then select the file name from the list of settings file names.

> **TIP**
>
> The page setup file is stored in the current directory, unless you specify otherwise. For organizational purposes, you may want to store all AL3 files in the same directory.

Stopping and Suspending Printing

After starting one or more print jobs, you may realize that you made a mistake in the worksheet data or print settings and that you need to correct an error before the report finishes printing. You can halt the current print job, clear the print queue, and temporarily suspend printing by accessing the Print Manager (press Ctrl+Esc and select Print Manager). To cancel the printing of a report, click on the name of the file in the print queue and then click on the Delete button. To temporarily suspend printing, click on the Pause button. When you are ready to continue, choose the Resume button. See the Windows manual for more information on the Print Manager.

Printing a Text File to Disk

To create an ASCII text file that you can incorporate into a word processing document, you use no printing-related commands. This represents a deviation from DOS versions of 1-2-3; DOS versions of 1-2-3 use the /Print File command to print a file to disk. In 1-2-3 for Windows, you create an ASCII file by selecting the File Save As command and choosing the Text (txt) file type in the Save As dialog box. Enter a name in the File Name field; if you don't type an extension, TXT is automatically assigned.

NOTE If you want to incorporate your formatted worksheet in another Windows application, you can transfer the data via the Windows Clipboard. Select the worksheet range, and choose Edit Copy. Then switch to the application you want to copy the worksheet into, and choose Edit Paste.

FROM HERE...

For Related Information

◄◄ "Copying Data," p. 178.

◄◄ "Managing Files," p. 233.

◄◄ "Saving Files," p. 235.

Questions & Answers

This chapter introduced you to printing-related commands. If you are experiencing problems when you print, look through this section for possible solutions.

Q: I want to print my report on legal-sized paper, but the Page Setup dialog box doesn't have an option for specifying the paper size.

A: Don't worry—you can print on legal-sized paper. The option is just located in a different dialog box. Choose File Printer Setup and make sure that the printer you want to use is selected. Then click on the Setup button; from here, you can find the Paper Size option.

Q: How do I create borders—columns or rows that repeat on each page—in Release 4? There appears to be no such command.

A: In Release 4, borders are called *print titles*. The Columns and Rows print-title options are located in the Page Setup dialog box.

Q: The header is not centered over my report, even though I entered the header text in the middle Header box on the Page Setup dialog box.

A: The text in the middle Header box is centered between the report's left and right margins. If your report is not very wide and doesn't extend to the right margin, the header can look off-center. The solution is to increase the left and right margins as much as possible.

Q: When I zoom in while previewing my report, nothing shows on the screen. What's happening?

A: The zoom-in command (the gray plus key or the magnifying-glass SmartIcon that has the plus sign) magnifies the center of the page. If the report is short, you see nothing on the screen. Press the up-arrow key to see the top of the report. Use the arrow keys to see all parts of the page as you zoom.

Q: I wanted to retrieve my named print settings, but the file wasn't there. What happened to it?

A: Unless you specify otherwise, print settings are stored in the current directory—the directory in which you last saved or opened a file. You are probably in a different directory from the one in which you saved the print settings. Navigate the Directories list, changing to the different directories you use in 1-2-3, until you locate the appropriate AL3 file.

Q: I'm trying to point to multiple print ranges in the Print dialog box, but 1-2-3 won't let me. As soon as I define the first range, I return to the Print dialog box. What am I doing wrong?

A: Nothing. 1-2-3 won't let you point to multiple ranges when defining the print range from the Print dialog box. You must either type the ranges (separated by commas or semicolons) in the Selected Range field or preselect the ranges before you give the print command.

Q: I successfully hid a column I didn't want printed in my report. Now I want to display the column again but I can't get it to appear. In the Hide dialog box, I specify the column I want to unhide, but the column remains hidden.

A: After you specify a cell in the hidden column, you must click on the Show button in the Hide dialog box. If you click on OK, 1-2-3 thinks you are trying to hide the column again. The Show button is what tells 1-2-3 you want to unhide the column.

Summary

This chapter showed you how to create printed reports from worksheets and how to use settings and options to make reports more readable. Specifically, you learned how to preview ranges before printing, how to print a report immediately, how to print multiple pages and ranges, how to exclude areas from a specified print range, and how to compress printing to fit on one page. This chapter also showed you how to modify the page setup to produce better looking, more effective reports.

The following chapter shows you how to take full advantage of the powerful graphing capabilities in 1-2-3 for Windows. You learn how to create, view, and print graphs to give visual impact to worksheet data.

Using Charts and Graphics

E ven if 1-2-3 for Windows provided only worksheet capabilities, the program would be extremely powerful. Despite the importance of keeping detailed worksheets that show real or projected data, however, data that is difficult to understand can be worthless.

Drawing conclusions from countless rows of numeric data is often difficult. To make data instantly understandable, 1-2-3 for Windows offers graphics capabilities that enable you to display data graphically. The program offers several types of business charts and sophisticated options for enhancing the appearance of charts. The real strength of 1-2-3 for Windows' graphics, however, lies in the graphics' integration with the worksheet. When you create a chart in the worksheet file, the chart is linked to the worksheet file. When you change data in the graphed range, the chart is automatically updated to reflect the change.

This chapter shows you how to accomplish the following tasks:

- ■ Create charts from data in a worksheet file

- ■ Define a chart's data ranges, titles, and legends

- ■ Select an appropriate chart type

- ■ Set chart options

- ■ Change the font, color, pattern, and format of chart elements

- Print charts separately or with worksheet data
- Annotate your charts
- Preview and print charts
- Use graphics objects
- Add clip art to your worksheets and charts

Understanding Common Chart Elements

When you create a chart, 1-2-3 for Windows includes several elements. Except for pie charts, all charts have a *y-axis* (a vertical left edge) and an *x-axis* (a horizontal bottom edge). In horizontally oriented charts, the y-axis is the bottom edge, and the x-axis is the left edge. 1-2-3 for Windows also enables you to use an optional *second y-axis* along the right side of a chart.

1-2-3 for Windows divides the axes with *tick marks* and scales the numbers on the y-axis based on the minimum and maximum numbers in the associated data range. The intersection of the y-axis and the x-axis is the *origin.* Although you can plot charts with a nonzero origin, using a zero origin makes a chart easier to compare and understand.

A chart is made up of one or more *data series,* each of which reflects a category of data. The first category of data is always series A, the second is series B, and so on. Some chart types use a limited number of data ranges; for example, pie charts use one data range, and XY charts use two. Other chart types, such as lines and bars, can graph up to 23 data ranges. When a chart has more than one data series, a *legend* is necessary to describe each of the data series.

The main part of the chart is called the *plot.* The plot includes the axes and their labels and titles, and all the data plotted on the axes. A pie chart's plot is the pie and its data labels. The plot does not include the legend, titles, or footnotes.

Figure 11.1 shows the elements of a simple chart.

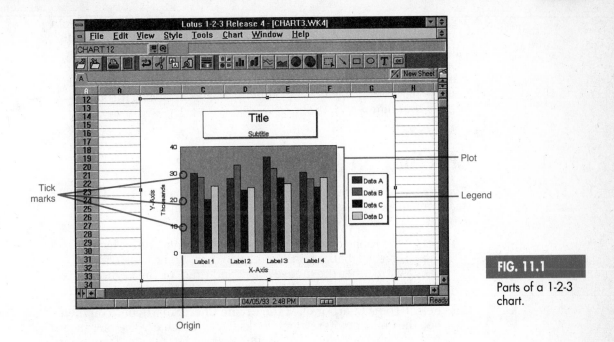

Tick marks

Plot

Legend

Origin

FIG. 11.1

Parts of a 1-2-3 chart.

Creating a Chart

To create a chart, you first must open the worksheet file that contains the data you want to plot. Many of the examples in this chapter are based on the quarterly sales report shown in figure 11.2.

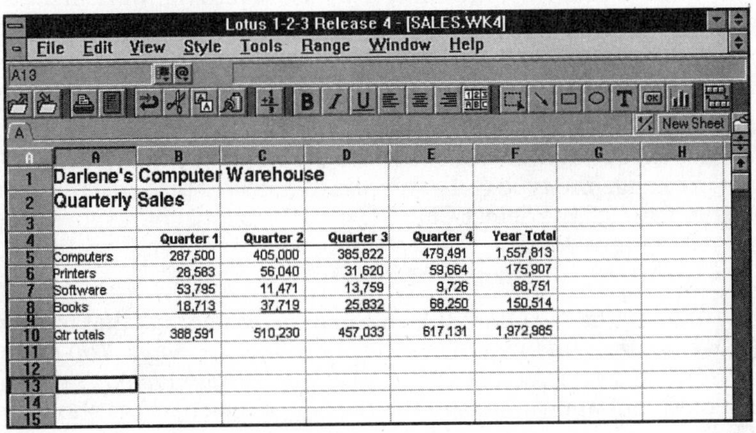

FIG. 11.2

The quarterly sales report worksheet.

To graph information from the sales report, you must know which data you want to plot and which data you want to use to label the chart. In figure 11.2, the labels in rows 1 and 2 are suitable for the chart titles. Time-period labels are listed across row 4; these labels will go on the x-axis. Category identifiers are located in column A; these labels will become part of the legend. The numeric entries in rows 5 through 8 contain four different data series.

Creating an Automatic Chart

If your worksheet is set up properly (I'll define what I mean by *properly* in a moment), creating an automatic chart is a simple, three-step process:

1. Select the range of cells to be charted, including titles, legend labels, x-axis labels, and the numeric data. You can select the range with either the mouse (click and drag) or the keyboard (press F4, use the arrow keys, then press Enter).

2. Select Tools Chart or click the Create Chart SmartIcon. You then see the chart pointer, which looks like a bar chart. The message at the top of the window tells you to click and drag where you want to display the chart.

3. Indicate where you want to place the chart in the worksheet.

There are two ways you can indicate placement of the chart. If you just click the chart pointer on the upper left corner of where you want to place the chart, it will be inserted at a default size (about 4 by 2.5 inches). Alternatively, you can click and drag a box, indicating the size of your chart. Either way, the chart is inserted into the worksheet. There is no special graph window, unlike in previous versions of the program, nor do you have to give a command to view the chart—it is always displayed in the worksheet.

Figure 11.3 shows the default automatic chart created for the worksheet range A1..E8. Notice that the default chart type is a bar chart. To change the type (for example, to a line or pie), use the Chart Type command or the Select Chart Type SmartIcon; chart types are discussed in more detail in the "Selecting the Chart Type" section, later in this chapter.

When 1-2-3 creates the chart, it is automatically *selected*; that is, you can move, resize, and manipulate the chart in other ways. You can see that the chart is selected because it displays *selection handles*—small black boxes that appear around the border of the chart (as shown in fig. 11.3).

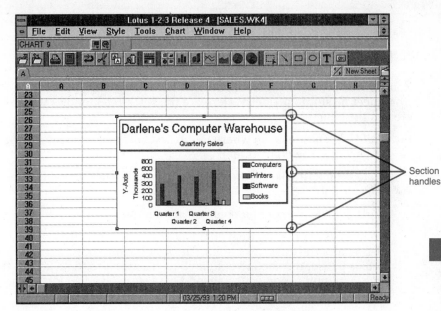

Section handles

FIG. 11.3

A bar chart created from the range A1..E8.

Here are a few other things to notice about the default chart:

- The title and subtitle are enclosed in a frame and are centered at the top of the chart.

- The framed legend is located to the right of the plot.

- The entire chart is framed.

- Default axis titles (X-Axis and Y-Axis) are inserted.

Also notice that after you create a chart, a new option, Chart, replaces Range in the menu bar. This option displays only if the chart, or an element in the chart, is selected.

CAUTION: If you click on a worksheet cell, the chart is no longer selected and the Chart menu option disappears. To access the Chart menu again, you must select an element on the chart by clicking on it; you then see selection handles around the object and the Chart menu returns.

Understanding the Rules for Automatic Charting

You learned previously that creating an automatic chart requires the worksheet be set up properly. Here are the rules 1-2-3 follows when it creates the chart:

Rule #1: If a title is anywhere in the first row of the selected range, it becomes the chart title.

Rule #2: If a title is anywhere in the second row, it becomes the chart's subtitle.

Rule #3: Blank rows and columns are completely ignored.

Rule #4: If more rows than columns are in your selected range, 1-2-3 plots the data by column. The first column becomes the x-axis labels, the second column becomes the first data series, the third column becomes the second data series, and so forth. The first row after any titles becomes the legend labels.

Rule #5: If more columns than rows are in the selected range, 1-2-3 plots the data by rows. The first row (after any titles or blank rows) becomes the x-axis labels, the second row becomes the first data series, the next row becomes the second data series, and so on. The first column becomes the legend labels.

Rule #6: If there are the same number of columns and rows in the selected range, 1-2-3 plots the data by column. (See Rule #4.)

Rule #7: If you select only numeric data when you create a chart, 1-2-3 follows Rules #4 and #5 to determine how to lay out the chart (by column or by row). 1-2-3 will create a default heading and legend, and default axis titles (see fig. 11.4); you can modify this default text by double-clicking on the appropriate chart element. You then see the appropriate dialog box (Headings, X-Axis, Y-Axis, or Legend) in which you can change the text. The next section discusses these dialog boxes.

Although it may seem that there are a lot of rules for creating automatic charts, you do have quite a bit of flexibility. 1-2-3 is smart when it looks at your selected range. It knows to ignore blank rows and columns, and can determine whether a row contains a title for the heading, labels for the x-axis or legends, or numbers to be plotted. If you don't include the legend labels or x-axis labels in your chart range, 1-2-3 Release 4 for Windows, unlike previous versions of 1-2-3, does not use the first row or column of numeric values as your labels—it leaves the row or column blank so that you can specify the range later. The labels are undefined until you specify the range.

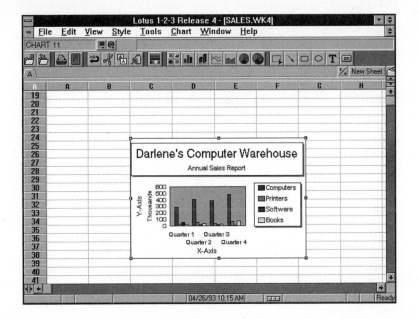

FIG. 11.4

1-2-3 creates default titles and legend labels when you have only values in the chart range.

Sometimes your selected chart range has more rows than columns, but you want the data plotted by row, not by column (as in Rule #4). In this case, your x-axis labels end up as legend labels, and vice versa. However, you can still create the automatic chart, because switching the layout is easy enough: You choose Chart Ranges and in the Assign ranges field, then choose either By row or By column. Unfortunately, this dialog box doesn't tell you what the current direction is; however, when you choose By Row or By Column, 1-2-3 does show you a sample layout. If you aren't sure which option you want (granted, it is confusing), choose one and if the chart doesn't change, go back and try the other one.

Creating Charts Manually

As you saw in the previous section, when you preselect the range, 1-2-3 uses the data in your worksheet to produce a default chart. But that isn't the only way to create a chart. 1-2-3 provides a Chart menu (see fig. 11.5) so that you can define the elements of your chart. You'll want to go to this menu if your worksheet isn't laid out in the prescribed fashion, if you must modify any of the ranges, or if you would just rather define the data series, titles, and legends yourself.

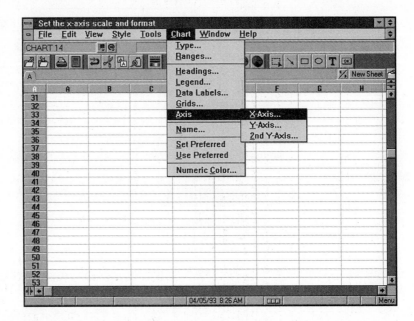

FIG. 11.5

The Chart menu.

To create a chart from scratch, go directly to the Tools Chart option or click the Create Chart SmartIcon, without preselecting a range. You then must define the chart range in the worksheet, just as with automatic charts. When you are done, you'll see an empty frame.

Your next step is to define the ranges containing your x-axis labels and your data series. The Chart Ranges command lets you define or modify your chart's x-axis labels and data series ranges. Figure 11.6 shows the Ranges dialog box. Another way to display this dialog box is to place the mouse pointer on the chart, press the right mouse button to display the Quick menu, and choose Chart Ranges.

FIG. 11.6

You can define or modify chart ranges in the Ranges dialog box.

A chart can contain up to 23 data series, represented by the letters A through W in the Series field. If you have already created a chart and specified a legend, the legend labels appear next to each series letter (as in figure 11.6). As you click on different series letters, the defined range (if any) display in the Range field. When a series range is undefined, Empty appears next to the series letter.

You can define your chart's ranges individually or as a group (choosing Individually, By row, or By column in the Assign ranges list box). Defining them as a group is clearly the easiest way. If you choose By row in the Assign ranges field, 1-2-3 displays a sample grid, showing the proper worksheet layout for this choice (x-axis labels in the first row, legend labels in the first column). If you choose By column, the sample grid displays legend labels in the first row and x-axis labels in the first column. Figure 11.7 shows the Ranges dialog box when By column is selected in the Assign ranges field.

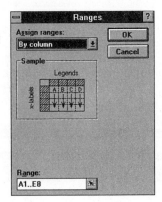

FIG. 11.7

A sample worksheet grid shows the proper layout when you choose By column for the Assign ranges field.

After you determine which layout is appropriate (By row or By column), enter the appropriate range in the Range field or use the range selector to select the range in the worksheet. When you select OK, 1-2-3 creates a chart and places it in the worksheet range you defined earlier. If you redisplay the Ranges dialog box, the legend labels appear next to each series letter, assuming you included the labels in the range you defined. If you didn't include the legend labels, the generic names (Data A, Data B, and so on) appear in the legend and in the Ranges dialog box.

Defining the ranges individually requires more work, but is sometimes the only way to define chart ranges. When you don't want to plot certain columns or rows that are in the middle of a range, you must define the series one at a time. For example, if you want to graph computer sales (as shown in row 5 of fig. 11.2) versus software sales (in row 7), you must define the series individually so that you don't plot the printer sales (in row 6).

Naming and Finding Charts

1-2-3 automatically names your charts as you create them (Chart 1, Chart 2, and so forth). The name of the selected chart (or the last one you selected) appears in the selection indicator on the edit line. To give your charts more descriptive names, use the Chart Name command. Type the new name in the Chart Name field or click on the current name in the Existing Charts list, and then click the Rename button.

To display the chart associated with a name, press F5 (GoTo) or choose Edit Go To. In the Type of Item field, choose Chart and then select the chart name from the list.

Creating Multiple Charts in a File

1-2-3 for Windows lets you create an unlimited number of charts in each worksheet file. You can define new charts and place them in different parts of the worksheet. For organizational purposes, you might want to place each chart in its own sheet; use the New Sheet button to insert a sheet after the current one.

Manipulating Chart Elements

One nice aspect of 1-2-3's charts is how malleable they are. You can move individual elements on the chart, and then move, size, delete, or format them. It's this flexibility that makes it so easy to build charts in 1-2-3 for Windows.

Resizing the Chart

The printed dimensions of a chart correspond to its size in the worksheet. However, you might discover that you didn't define the proper size, or that the default size isn't large enough. Resizing a chart is straightforward. First, click on the chart frame so that you see selection handles surrounding the chart. Next, drag one of the handles until the chart is the desired size. If you drag a corner handle, you change both the height and width of the chart. By dragging a middle handle on the right or left side of the chart, you change just the width. If you drag a middle handle on the top or bottom of the chart, you adjust the height only. If you want to size the chart proportionally, hold down the Shift key as you drag.

1-2-3 does not provide a way that you can directly define a chart's dimensions in inches. For instance, you can't go to a dialog box and specify a width of 5 and a height of 3 inches, although you can specify an option to print a full-page chart (see the "Printing a Chart" and "Previewing a Chart" sections later in this chapter).

1-2-3 offers a way to help you measure your chart size: by displaying a ruler in the chart frame. Issue the View Set View Preferences command and choose Inches for the Worksheet Frame. (You can also choose Characters, Metric, or Points/Picas.) Figure 11.8 shows the inch ruler displayed in the worksheet frame. When you finish using the ruler to measure your chart size, you'll want to go back to the standard worksheet frame (column letters and row numbers).

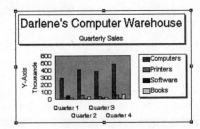

FIG. 11.8

To help you measure the size of your charts, change the worksheet frame so that it displays an inch ruler.

Selecting Chart Objects

You must select an object before you can copy, delete, rearrange, or move it, before you can adjust the object's line style or colors, and before you can make other layout changes to the object or chart. You can select one or several objects. When an object is selected, selection handles appear around the object.

To select an object, just click on the object. To select several objects with the mouse, choose the Select Objects SmartIcon, which enables you to "lasso" the objects you want to select; after selecting the icon, drag the mouse until you surround all the objects. As you drag, you see a box with a dotted outline. When you release the mouse button, all the objects that were in this box will have selection handles.

Because a chart contains so many different elements, it can be difficult sometimes to determine whether the mouse pointer is actually on the object you want to select. To help you select objects, the mouse pointer reflects what you are pointing at. For example, when you are pointing at text, the mouse pointer has a capital A underneath it. The pointer generally looks like what you are pointing at. So when you are pointing at a line, you will see a diagonal line underneath the arrow pointer, or when you are on a bar, you will see a hollow rectangle. A circle represents a data point symbol.

To deselect all selected items, position the mouse pointer anywhere on the worksheet outside the chart and click the mouse. To deselect one item when several items are selected, position the mouse pointer on the item, then press and hold down Shift while you click the mouse.

Moving Objects

The Legend dialog box has options for placing the legend to the right or below the plot, but you are not restricted to these two places: You can move the legend anywhere inside the chart frame. You can also move the plot, the titles, the footnotes, the entire chart, and any objects that you added by using the Tools Draw commands.

To move an object, first select it by clicking on it; make sure selection handles are on the desired object or you might move the wrong thing. Place the mouse pointer inside the object and begin dragging; the mouse pointer turns into a hand, and a dotted box appears around the object and is moved to the new location. (A dotted line appears on lines and arrows.) When you finish moving, the dotted box disappears and the object is moved to the new location.

> **CAUTION:** If you move the legend to the left side of the chart, the plot does not automatically move over—instead, the legend will overlay the plot. You then must move the plot to the right.

Resizing Objects

To change the size of an object, select it and then place the mouse pointer on one of the selection handles. Before dragging, make sure you see a four-headed arrow—this is the mouse pointer for sizing an object. To define the new size, drag the selection handle until the object is the desired size. Release the mouse button when you are done.

Resizing a frame works a little differently. As you drag a selection handle, both sides of the box expand or contract. For example, if you drag a right-hand handle to the right, the frame expands on the right and the left, keeping the text inside centered within the frame. This applies to title, footnote, and legend frames only.

Deleting Objects

If the chart contains an element you don't want, delete it by selecting the object and pressing the Del key. 1-2-3 lets you delete the title frame (along with its contents), the legend, axis titles, the footnote frame (and its contents), the unit indicator, individual data series, the entire chart, and any objects that you added by using the Tools Draw commands. You cannot delete the plot, x-axis labels, or the y-axis scale. Also, you cannot delete a frame's contents without deleting the entire frame.

If you accidentally delete an object, choose the Edit Undo command or press Ctrl+Z.

For Related Information

◄◄ "Developing Business Presentations," p. 597.

FROM HERE...

Modifying the Chart

Although the default chart that 1-2-3 creates may suit your needs, in most cases you must change the chart to make it more appropriate for your report or presentation. Sometimes a different type of chart can present the data more effectively; sometimes you might want to highlight specific data by exploding a pie slice (that is, to remove the slice slightly from the rest of the pie), using a special color, or adding an arrow or other device to catch the reader's attention. This section describes the many ways that 1-2-3 for Windows offers for changing and improving a chart.

Specifying the Chart Type and Style

By default, 1-2-3 for Windows displays a bar chart when you create a chart. To change the type of chart that 1-2-3 for Windows displays, select Chart Type. Another way to display the Type dialog box is with the Quick menu: select the chart, press the right mouse button, and choose Chart Type. Double-clicking on the plot will let you change the chart type, as well. If you prefer clicking on icons, you can use the Select Chart Type SmartIcon to display the Type dialog box, or click one of the other SmartIcons that directly selects a new chart type (such as the 3D Pie SmartIcon). When you choose the type of chart you want, 1-2-3 for Windows changes the display to reflect your choice.

In the Type dialog box (see fig. 11.9), you can choose from all chart types, change from vertical to horizontal orientation, and select styles such as stacked ranges. You also can include a table below the chart that shows the values used to graph each range.

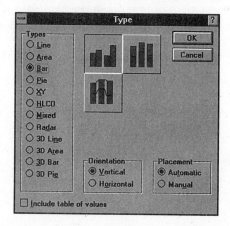

FIG. 11.9

The Type dialog box.

This section describes the many different types and styles of charts 1-2-3 offers in the Type dialog box. You can easily experiment with different chart types until you find the one just right for conveying your data. If you want to return to the default style (standard bar), use the Chart Use Preferred command.

Selecting the Chart Style

To the right of the Types field, the Type dialog box displays several large buttons showing different styles for the current type of chart. In figure 11.9, three options are displayed. The upper-left style button is used to select a standard bar chart. The button to the right produces a stacked bar chart. The button on the bottom is a variation of a stacked bar chart.

To select one of the chart style buttons, click it with the mouse. Select OK to confirm the dialog box.

Selecting the Chart Type

Choosing the best chart for a given application is often a matter of personal preference. 1-2-3 for Windows provides eight basic types of charts: line, area, bar, pie, XY, HLCO, mixed (bar and line), and radar. Four of them also are available with a three-dimensional effect: line, area, bar, and pie.

At times, however, only one chart type is appropriate. For example, selecting line, bar, or pie is appropriate if you plan to graph only one data range. HLCO charts are specialized for presenting certain types of stock market information. Table 11.1 lists and briefly explains each chart type. The next sections discuss each chart type in more detail.

Table 11.1 Chart Types

Type	Description
Line	Shows the trend of numeric data across time.
Area	Shows broad trends in data that occur over time.
Bar	Compares related data at a certain time or shows the trend of numeric data across time.
Pie	Graphs a single data range, showing what percentage of the total each data point contributes. Do not use this type of chart if the data contains negative numbers.
XY	Shows the relationship between one independent variable and one or more dependent variables.
HLCO (High-Low-Close-Open)	Shows fluctuations in data over time, such as the high, low, close, and open prices of a stock.
Mixed	Shows a bar chart for the first three ranges and a line chart for three additional ranges.
Radar	Wraps a line chart around a central point, showing the symmetry or uniformity of data.
3D Line	Shows, in a three-dimensional line chart, the trend of numeric data across time.

continues

Table 11.1 Continued

Type			Description
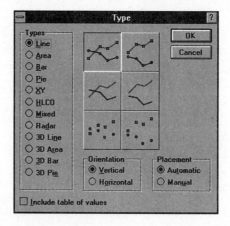		3D Area	Shows, in a three-dimensional area chart, broad trends in data that occur over time
		3D Bar	Uses a three-dimensional bar chart to compare related data at a certain time or show the trend of numeric data across time
		3D Pie	Graphs, in a three-dimensional pie chart, a data range, showing what percentage of the total each data point contributes

Line Charts

Line charts are ideal for displaying trends and changes in data over time. Figure 11.10 shows the styles available for line charts. The first style in the left column has lines with symbols at each data point, the next style down has connectors with no symbols, and the last style has symbols only (no connectors). The styles in the right-hand column are similar except that the data is *stacked*; in other words, the line closest to the x-axis is series A, the next line up is the total of series A and B, the next line up is the total of series A, B, and C, and so forth.

FIG. 11.10

Line chart styles.

The 3D Line chart type offers just two styles: standard and stacked. Because the lines are fairly thick (see fig. 11.11), you shouldn't use this type if your chart has many data series.

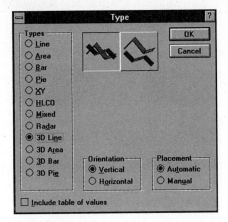

FIG. 11.11

3D Line chart
styles.

Area Charts

An Area chart, which emphasizes broad trends, is similar to a stacked
line chart except that the area between data ranges is filled with a different color or pattern. The two-dimensional Area chart has only one
basic style (see fig. 11.12). However, the 3D Area chart has two styles
(see fig. 11.13) that you can choose in the Type dialog box. In the first
style, you can see the base of each data series. In the second style, the
series are simply stacked on top of one another. If you want to show
the total of all series at each data point, use the standard area chart
or the 3D stacked area chart. To compare the individual data series,
use the 3D area chart that displays one data series behind another.

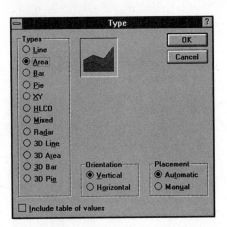

FIG. 11.12

Area charts
resemble stacked-
line charts.

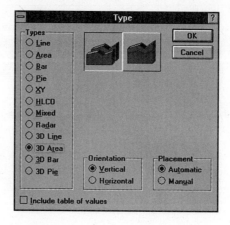

FIG. 11.13

3D Area charts
are available in
two different
styles.

Bar Charts

Although Bar is the default chart type, you might want to make a trip to the Type dialog box to choose a different style of Bar chart (for example, a stacked bar), to select a 3D Bar type, or to change the chart's orientation.

The Bar type offers three styles, as shown in figure 11.14. The standard bar chart, the default, places the bars side by side. A *stacked-bar chart* shows data as a series of bars piled on top of one another. This type of chart is useful for showing the portion that data categories contribute to a whole and for comparing totals over time. The *comparison bar chart* is also a stacked-bar chart, but has dotted lines that connect the data points, enabling you to see more easily the differences between corresponding segments in each bar.

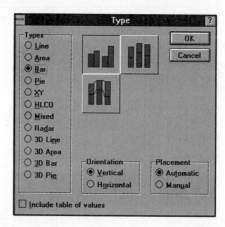

FIG. 11.14

The Bar chart
styles.

Figure 11.15 plots the same data as in figure 11.16. Both charts compare the quarterly sales of each department. However, although the two charts plot the same data, they present different messages: The chart in figure 11.15 compares the relative sales in dollars of the departments, and the chart in figure 11.16 compares each department's contribution to the combined sales.

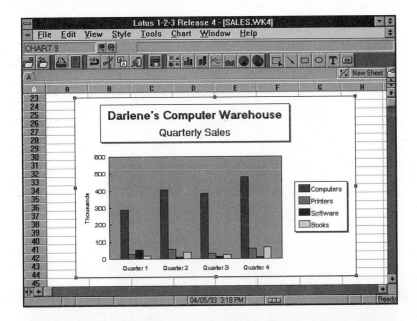

FIG. 11.15

A standard bar chart of the sales data worksheet.

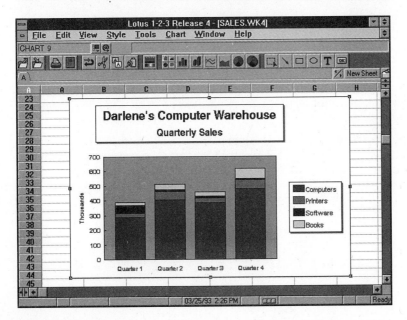

FIG. 11.16

A stacked-bar chart of the sales data worksheet.

Figure 11.17 shows the styles that the 3D Bar type offers. The first style has three-dimensional bars placed side-by-side. In the second style, the bars are placed behind one another and are slightly overlapping. With this style, you must specify the smallest series first (as series A) or the shorter bars are hidden behind the taller bars in front. Stacked bars are the third 3D Bar style.

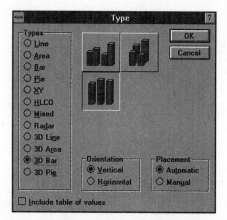

FIG. 11.17

The 3D Bar styles.

T I P   Because of the size of the bars, **3D Bar** charts work best with small amounts of data when comparing sets of data over time.

Pie Charts

In a Pie chart, each value determines the size of a pie slice and represents a percentage of the total. Unlike other chart types, Pie charts can have only one data series (the A data range). If you select an adjacent row or column of labels, 1-2-3 for Windows uses them as *pie slice labels* (the x-axis labels).

  Suppose that you want to construct a pie chart from the worksheet data shown in figure 11.2 and that you want to graph the percentage of computer equipment sales for each quarter. Use the range A4..E5 and specify Pie or 3D Pie as the chart type. (You also can use the Pie Chart or 3D Pie Chart SmartIcon to select a pie chart.) With the style buttons, you can choose to plot the data counterclockwise, starting at the 3:00 position, or clockwise, starting at 12:00. Figure 11.18 shows the standard version of the Pie chart; figure 11.19 shows the 3D Pie chart, using the clockwise style.

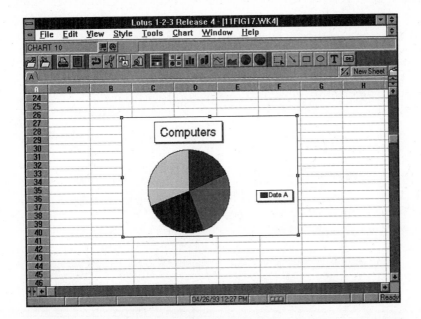

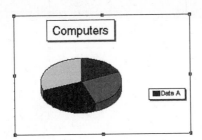

The chart in figure 11.19 shows the relative size of the quarters, represented by the four slices of the pie. ***Even though the preselected range includes the x-axis labels (B4..E4), the slices are not yet labeled. To label the slices, use the Chart Data Labels command and turn on the check box Contents of X data range.

XY Charts

The XY chart, or *scatter chart*, is a variation of a Line chart. Like a Line chart, an XY chart has values plotted as points in the chart. An XY chart, however, has its x-axis labeled with numeric values rather than labels.

XY charts show the correlation between two or more sets of data. To use XY charts effectively, you must understand two terms. One data range is the *independent variable*, which is data you can change or control. The other data ranges, the *dependent variables*, are dependent on the independent variable; you cannot control or change the dependent variables.

1-2-3 for Windows always plots the independent variable on the x-axis and the dependent variable(s) on the y-axis; the independent data should be in the first row or column of the selected range, and the dependent data should be in the second and succeeding rows or columns.

Figure 11.20 shows an XY chart based on a worksheet that plots sales as they relate to advertising expenditures. To find the correlation between sales and advertising, you can create an XY chart.

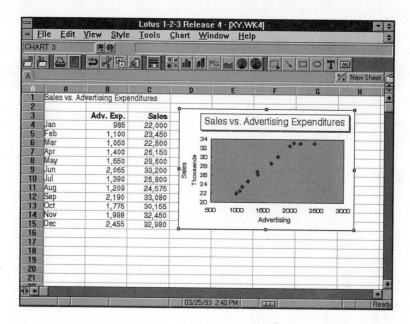

FIG. 11.20

An XY chart of sales versus advertising expenditures.

You should not use 1-2-3's automatic chart feature when creating an **XY** chart, because the worksheet data does not conform to the rules for automatic charts. Because the labels for the x-axis are values, 1-2-3 assumes that this range is a data series. Consequently, none of the ranges will be correct. You are better off creating a chart from scratch, following these basic steps:

1. Insert an empty chart frame by using the Tools Chart command or the Create Chart SmartIcon.

2. Use the Chart Ranges command to define the ranges individually. Unlike all other chart types, an XY chart uses an x-axis label range that contains values, not labels. Your series ranges (A, B, C, and so on) will also contain values.

3. Choose Chart Type or click the Select Chart Type SmartIcon and select XY. Choose the appropriate style (lines with symbols, lines with no symbols, or symbols only). Figure 11.21 shows the styles for the XY chart in the Type dialog box. The most common style for XY charts is symbols only.

4. Use the Chart Axis command to define the labels and the Chart Heading command to define the titles. (These options are described later in this chapter, in the section "Changing the Axis Titles.")

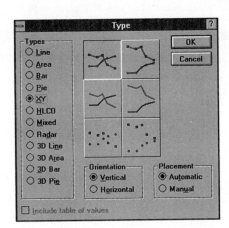

FIG. 11.21

The XY chart styles.

HLCO (High-Low-Close-Open) Charts

HLCO charts are specialized for stock market information, but you can use them to track other kinds of data that have high and low values over time, such as daily temperature or currency exchange rates.

Figure 11.22 shows the standard <u>H</u>LCO chart style, called *whisker* (referring to the tick marks on the left and right sides of the vertical lines, which resemble an animal's whiskers).

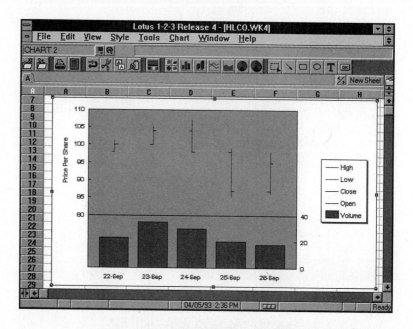

FIG. 11.22

An <u>H</u>LCO chart
using the whisker
style.

An <u>H</u>LCO chart typically has four series, representing high, low, close, and open values. This data is represented on the chart as a vertical line; the line extends from the *low value* to the *high value*. A tick mark extending to the right of the line represents the *close value*, and a tick mark extending to the left represents the *open value*. The total number of lines on the chart depends on the number of time periods included. Following are the meanings of the four values:

High   The stock's highest price in the given time period

Low   The stock's lowest price in the given time period

Close   The stock's price at the end, or close, of the time period

Open   The stock's price at the start, or open, of the time period

An <u>H</u>LCO chart can include a set of bars below the HLCO section of the chart and one or more lines across the HLCO section. In the financial world, the bars often are used to represent the daily trading volume for the stock, and the line can represent a changing stock-price average.

The first four data series (A through D) represent the high, low, close, and open values, respectively. If you specify a fifth set of data, the E range appears as bars plotted against a second y-axis on the right side of the chart's frame. Any additional ranges appear as lines plotted against the y-axis.

1-2-3 offers a second style of HLCO chart called *candlestick*. The only difference between the two styles is in the way the open and close data is illustrated. Instead of using tick marks, the candlestick style has a bar that spans the range between the open and close value. The bar is empty if the close value is lower than the open value; otherwise, it is filled in. Figure 11.23 shows an example of the candlestick style. The candlestick style places more emphasis on the open and close data—as you can see, the open/close bars in Figure 11.23 are much more prominent than the tiny tick marks of the whisker style shown in Figure 11.22. Thus, if you want to emphasize the open and close values, use the candlestick style. Otherwise, use the standard whisker style.

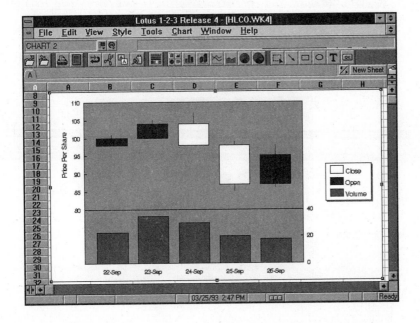

FIG. 11.23

The candlestick style of HLCO chart.

Stock market figures often are downloaded from online information services as text labels in the form '45 3/8. To change these labels to values for use in an HLCO chart, use @VALUE, as described in Chapter 7, "Using Functions."

Mixed Charts

The Mixed chart type enables you to have two or three different forms of charts on a single chart. When you choose the Mixed type in the Type dialog box, you can then assign to each data series the appropriate type (Line, Area, or Bar). Here's how it works:

1. If your worksheet data is laid out properly, create an automatic chart; otherwise, define your ranges individually.

2. Choose Chart Type or click the Select Chart Type SmartIcon and select Mixed. The dialog box will look like figure 11.24.

3. In the Type dialog box, the style buttons offer six different combinations of Line, Area, and Bar styles. Choose the appropriate style. If your Mixed chart will have lines, you can choose to have lines with or without symbols at the data points. If your Mixed chart will have bars, choose whether you want standard or stacked bars.

4. To assign types to each data series, choose Chart Ranges to display the Ranges dialog box. Click on a series letter and choose Line, Area, or Bar from the Mixed Type drop-down list; repeat for each series letter.

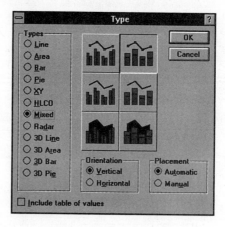

FIG. 11.24

The styles for the Mixed chart type.

One common use for a Mixed chart is to show an average or trend line on a bar chart. Suppose you are plotting temperature levels over the past three decades. First you could plot as bars the temperatures from the 1960s, 1970s, and 1980s. Then you could also plot the average temperature during the measured time span, and display this series as a line.

Radar Charts

A Radar chart plots data as a function of distance from a central point, with each spoke representing a set of data points. This chart type shows symmetry or uniformity of data. Figure 11.25 shows a Radar chart.

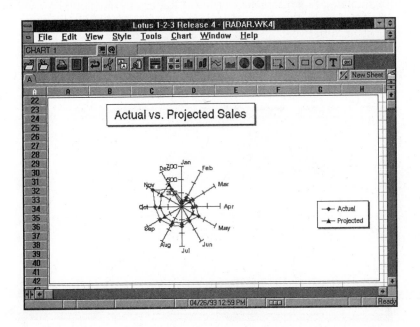

FIG. 11.25

A Radar chart.

- The central point around which each value is measured from is at 0,0 (unless you change the minimum value of the y-axis).

- Each spoke that extends from the central point is labeled with what are typically used as x-axis labels. In figure 11.25, the spokes are labeled with months.

- The data points for each series are connected, forming a spiral around the central point.

- At each major interval on the y-axis, a dotted circle is drawn around the central point. For example, in figure 11.25, there are circles at 300, 500, and 700. These circles function like gridlines, helping you to interpret the value of the data points.

You can gather two pieces of information from a Radar chart. First, you can compare the data series: The greater the distance between the data points on each spoke, the greater the difference between the series. Second, you can see how much the data fluctuates: A smooth spiral indicates a steady increase, but a jagged spiral indicates more variability. In figure 11.25, notice how smooth the spiral for the projected series is (a steady increase was predicted) and how the spiral for the actual series jumps around (sales increased some months and decreased in others).

The Type dialog box offers two styles of Radar charts. The first style is the one previously discussed. The second style stacks the series and fills in the area between spirals. Figure 11.26 shows a chart with the stacked-area style. This style is not appropriate for all types of data, because accumulating data doesn't always make sense. For example, adding together projected and actual sales makes no sense.

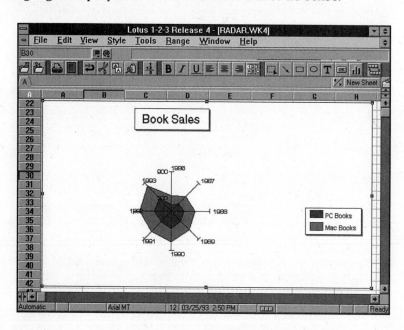

FIG. 11.26

The stacked-area style of Radar chart.

Setting the Default Chart Type and Style

As was previously mentioned, the default chart type is a standard bar. If you more commonly use a different type or style, create the desired chart style and then choose Chart Set Preferred. Thereafter, any new charts you create will have that chart type and style by default. The preferred chart setting controls only the type (such as Line or 3D Line) and style (for instance, whether the line has symbols or not). It doesn't contain other settings such as legend placement or grid lines.

Changing the Orientation of a Chart

The chart types that are plotted on an x- and y-axis (Line, Bar, Area, XY, and HLCO) offer an option in the Type dialog box for changing the orientation. Vertical is the standard orientation. If you choose Horizontal, the x- and y-axes are swapped. Figure 11.27 shows a Bar chart with Horizontal orientation.

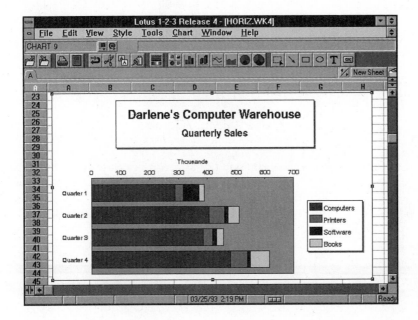

While 1-2-3 lets you select Horizontal for any chart with an x- and y-axis, this orientation is typically used in bar charts to show progress or distance. There are SmartIcons for horizontal bar charts and horizontal stacked bar charts.

Specifying a Custom Legend

When you graph a data range, 1-2-3 for Windows uses colors, symbols, or patterns to identify data ranges. The legend is the key to identifying the data ranges in a chart. By default, 1-2-3 for Windows places legend labels in a frame to the right of the chart.

The Legend dialog box enables you to specify legend labels by typing the labels directly or by specifying the cell addresses of the labels in the worksheet. To add legend labels, select Chart Legend, and the Legend dialog box shown in figure 11.28 appears. You can also display this dialog box by double-clicking on an existing legend. To choose Legend from the Quick menu, place the mouse pointer on the legend and press the right mouse button.

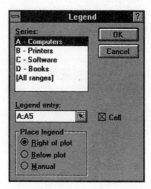

FIG. 11.28

The Legend
dialog box.

To specify a legend label, click on the appropriate data series letter and type the label in the Legend entry text box or enter the worksheet cell address that contains the label. If you enter an address, be sure to select the Cell check box. Repeat the process for each legend label.

T I P   Rather than typing the cell address, you can use the range selector to point to the cell.

If you prefer to enter legend labels for all ranges concurrently, choose [All ranges] in the Series field. Then, in the Legend entry text box, enter the worksheet range containing the legend labels or use the range selector to highlight it.

In the Legend dialog box, you can also indicate where to place the legend: Right of plot, Below plot, or Manual. Right of plot stacks the labels vertically. Below plot creates a legend with a horizontal orientation; depending on how many labels there are, the legend may wrap onto several lines. You don't have to select the Manual option—it's automatically selected after you drag the legend and move it elsewhere within the chart frame.

CAUTION: When you manually position a legend, the chart does not automatically move over to accommodate the legend. You might have to select the plot and drag it so that it doesn't overlap the legend.

Customizing the Chart Titles and Adding Notes

By using the Chart Headings command, you can create two titles and two footnotes for your chart. Figure 11.29 shows this dialog box. You use the two Title text boxes to create the title and subtitle; the titles appear centered above the chart, with the first title in larger type above the second title. You use the Note text boxes to add footnotes that appear below the chart.

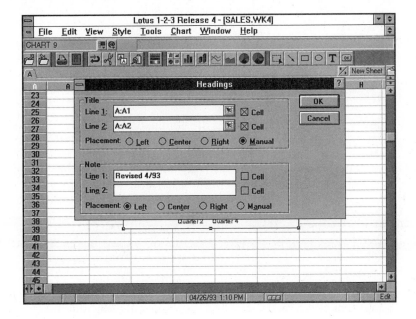

FIG. 11.29

The Headings dialog box.

To enter titles and notes, select the appropriate text box from the Headings dialog box. You can type the text directly in the text box or turn on the Cell check box and type the address of the cell that contains the label or number to be used as the title or note. Alternatively, you can click on the range selector and point to the cell in the worksheet. In figure 11.29, the cells A:A1 and A:A2 are entered as the titles.

You can edit the titles and notes by choosing the Chart Headings command and changing or editing the contents of the text boxes. If you highlight the entire text in a text box (by selecting the text box), any new text you type replaces the existing text. To delete text, press Del while the text box is highlighted. Another way to delete a title or note is to select the text on the chart and press Del.

T I P To edit a title or note, double-click on the title or note in the chart; the Headings dialog box will instantly appear. Alternatively, you can place the mouse pointer on a title or footnote, press the right mouse button to display the Quick menu, and choose Headings.

By default, titles are centered at the top and notes are left-aligned at the bottom of the chart. By using the Placement fields, you can align the titles and notes on the Left, Right, or Center. But you can move titles and notes anywhere on the chart. Simply select the text by clicking on it, and then drag the block anywhere inside the chart frame. You do not have to select the Manual option in the Placement field—this happens automatically after you manually move a title or note.

Changing the Axis Titles

You specify the axis titles by using the command Chart Axis. This command enables you to add titles for the X-Axis, Y-Axis, and 2nd Y-Axis. The placement of axis titles depends on whether the chart is horizontally or vertically oriented. In a vertical chart (the default chart orientation), the y-axis title appears left of the y-axis; the x-axis title is centered below the x-axis; and the second y-axis title appears to the right of the second y-axis. By default, 1-2-3 inserts X-Axis and Y-Axis as your axis titles. You can edit the axis titles by choosing the Chart Axis command and changing or editing the contents of the text boxes. You can also double-click on existing titles to display the appropriate Axis dialog box.

Figure 11.30 shows the standard bar chart for the revenue worksheet after the x-axis title was deleted and the y-axis title was edited.

FIG. 11.30

The bar chart after the x-axis title was deleted and the y-axis title was edited.

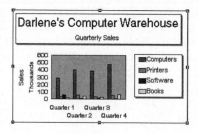

Changing the Axis Scale

When you create a chart, 1-2-3 for Windows automatically sets the
scale—the minimum to maximum range—of the y-axis based on the
smallest and largest numbers in the data range(s) plotted. This default
also applies to the second y-axis when you use it. For XY charts, 1-2-3
for Windows also establishes the x-axis scale based on values in the X
data range.

When you select Chart Axis Y-Axis, the Y-Axis dialog box appears (see
fig. 11.31). The X-Axis and 2nd Y-Axis dialog boxes offer the same settings. Another way to display these dialog boxes is to double-click on
the axis labels, or click the right mouse button on the labels and
choose X-Axis or Y-Axis.

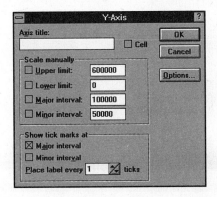

FIG. 11.31

The Y-Axis dialog
box.

You can change the scale by selecting options in the Scale manually
fields. These fields currently contain the values that 1-2-3 determined
were appropriate for your data. You can change the scale by specifying
different numbers in the Upper limit and Lower limit text boxes. Only
data that falls between the Lower and Upper limit values is graphed.
You can also use the Major interval and Minor interval text boxes to
specify the increments between tick marks. For example, the automatic
scale may have increments of 100 on the y-axis (100, 200, 300, 400, and
so on). If you want fewer increments, you can change the Major interval
setting to an increment such as 200; the major tick marks will then be
labeled 200, 400, 600, and so on. You probably shouldn't change the
Minor interval value unless your chart has tick marks displayed at
these intervals (they are turned off by default). To control the display
of tick marks, use the Show tick marks at fields; these fields include
check boxes for Major interval and Minor interval.

T I P   If your chart contains too many horizontal grid lines, increase the value in the Major interval field.

To return to automatic scaling, turn off all the check boxes in the Scale manually field—you need not clear out the values or return them to their original values.

If you choose the Options button in the X-Axis, Y-Axis, or 2nd Y-Axis dialog box, you see additional axis settings in the Options dialog box (see fig. 11.32). The Type of scale field determines whether a Standard (linear), Log (logarithmic), or 100% scale is used. On a logarithmic scale, each unit of distance represents 10 times the value of the preceding unit; the scale is labeled 1, 10, 100, 1000, and so forth.

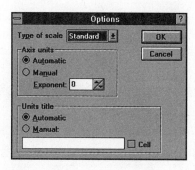

FIG. 11.32

Additional axis options.

If your chart contains widely fluctuating data, use a logarithmic scale. For example, if the minimum value you are plotting is 1,000 and the maximum value is 10,000,000, the smaller data points are virtually invisible on a standard scale (they are relatively so close to zero that they lie on the x-axis). By using a logarithmic scale, you can show all the data points. Figure 11.33 shows a chart that has a standard scale, and figure 11.34 shows the same data plotted with a logarithmic scale.

A 100% scale is similar to a pie chart in that it shows the relative portions each series is of the total; the scale is labeled from 0 to 100 percent. A 100% scale is most appropriate for stacked bar charts, as shown in figure 11.35.

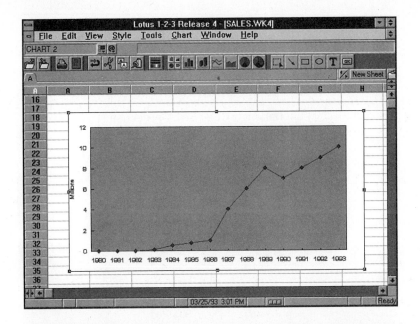

FIG. 11.33

With a standard y-axis scale, some of the values are relatively so small that the data points lie on the x-axis.

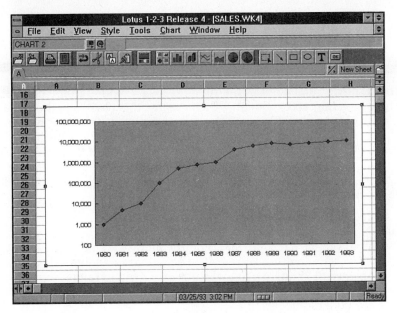

FIG. 11.34

With a logarithmic scale, you can clearly see all data points.

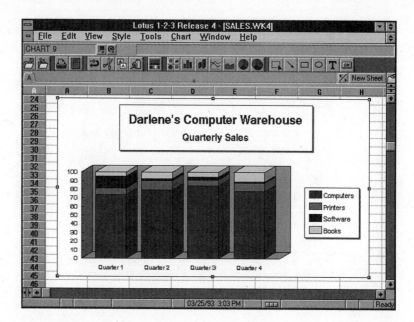

FIG. 11.35

A stacked bar chart that has a 100% scale.

In the Axis units field, you can set the order of magnitude (power of 10) used to scale the values. Usually, 1-2-3 for Windows does this automatically. If you select Ma_n_ual, you can specify a value between –95 and +95 in the Exponent text box. If you enter a positive exponent, the decimal point moves to the left that number of places. A negative exponent moves the decimal point to the right (zeros are added to the number). When you enter an exponent, 1-2-3 indicates this change in the units title next to the axis. For example, if you specify an exponent of 3, the units title will say Times 1E+03; this indicates to multiply each of the values on the scale by 10 to the third power (1,000). If this title is too cryptic, you can choose Ma_n_ual in the Units title field and type your own title (or click the Cell check box and specify a cell containing the label you want to use as your units title).

In some cases, changing the Exponent and units title can make the chart easier to interpret. For example, the automatic scale on your chart might range from 0 to 4000 and the automatic units title might read *Thousands*. In other words, 4000 actually represents 4,000,000. If you specify an Exponent value of 6, the scale would range from 0 to 4; with a Ma_n_ual units title that says *Millions*, the chart would be much easier to understand.

Sometimes 1-2-3 uses an exponent on your axis when you would rather show the exact values. For example, the scale might have the labels 1, 2, 3, 4,... with Thousands as the units title. If you would rather have the scale show 1000, 2000, 3000, 4000,... choose Ma_n_ual for the axis units and enter 0 for the Exponent.

You also can use the units title field when you want to modify the title that 1-2-3 automatically generates. For example, you could change the title from Thousands to In Thousands.

Adjusting the Placement of Axis Labels

When your axis is crowded with many labels, you can use the Place label every [__] ticks field in the Y-Axis, X-Axis, or 2nd Y-Axis dialog box to determine how many axis labels appear. For example, if the value in this field is 3, every third label appears (see fig. 11.36). You should use this field only if the axis contains values or units of time, where it's obvious what the missing labels are. However, if the axis contains labels such as product names, the chart would not make sense if every other label were missing.

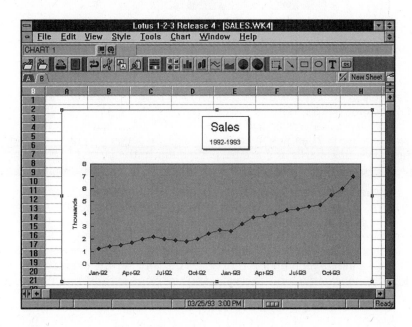

FIG. 11.36

Every third label is displayed on the x-axis.

Displaying a Background Grid

Grids often make it easier to interpret the data points in charts, especially if the data points are far from the x-axis and y-axis labels. The chart in figure 11.37, for example, uses horizontal grid lines to make the data easier to interpret.

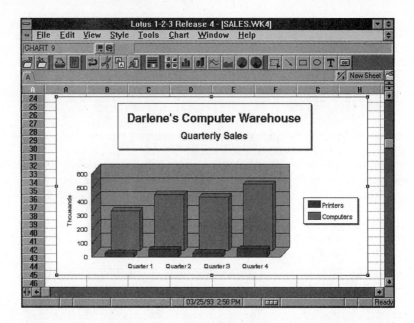

FIG. 11.37

A chart with
y-axis grid lines
added.

The Chart Grids command enables you to create horizontal and vertical grid lines for charts that have axes (Line, Bar, Area, XY, HLCO, and Mixed charts). The x-axis grid lines extend from tick marks on the x-axis and are perpendicular to the x-axis. The y-axis grid lines extend from y-axis tick marks and are perpendicular to the y-axis. The second y-axis grid lines extend from the tick marks on the second y-axis.

To turn on grid lines, choose Chart Grids and then display the drop-down list for X-Axis, Y-Axis, or 2nd Y-Axis, and choose the settings: Major interval, Minor interval, Both, or None. As described earlier, the intervals refer to the tick marks on the axis. The Major intervals are those tick marks that are labeled; the Minor intervals are the smaller tick marks in between major intervals. The Both setting draws grid lines for major *and* minor intervals, and the None setting eliminates grid lines.

T I P To create dotted or dashed grid lines, select the grid lines and choose Style Lines & Color. You can then select a different line style. You can also click the right mouse button on the grid lines and choose Lines & Color.

Adding Data Labels

Knowing the exact value of a data range in a chart is sometimes helpful. You can label data points in a chart with the corresponding value (called *data labels*) by using the Chart Data Labels command; figure 11.38 shows the resulting dialog box.

FIG. 11.38

The Data Labels
dialog box.

In the Series list box, highlight the series (A, B, C, and so on) for which you want to create data labels and then specify the range of labels in the Range of labels field. You can either type the range or use the range selector to highlight the range. Using the Placement drop-down list, you can control whether the data label appears above, centered, below, or to the left of or to the right of the data point. Repeat this process for each series. When you close the dialog box, 1-2-3 for Windows displays in the chart the exact value of each data range. Figure 11.39 shows a chart with data labels.

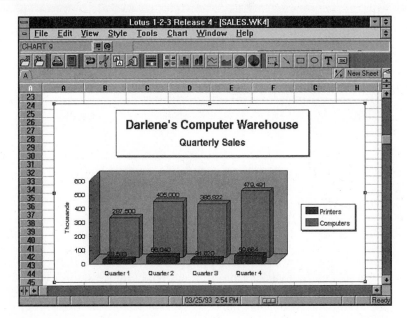

FIG. 11.39

The chart after
adding data
labels.

T I P

To specify all your data labels at once, choose [All ranges] in the
Series list and then indicate the range in the Range of labels text box
by typing or pointing.

Data labels can be difficult to read and can clutter the chart. An alternative method of displaying the data values being graphed is to select the
Include table of values check box in the Type dialog box. If you select
this option, a miniworksheet of the graphed data is displayed below the
chart (see fig. 11.40). The x-axis labels appear in the top row of the
table, and the data legend labels are placed in the left-side column. The
Include table of values option is available only with certain chart types.
Pie, XY, HLCO, Radar, and 3D pie charts do not offer this option.

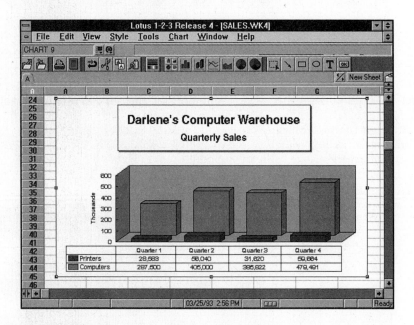

FIG. 11.40

A chart using a
table of values
rather than data
labels.

Showing the Values and Percentages of Pie Slices

If you create a pie chart, you can show the values and percentages corresponding to each pie slice by choosing Chart Data Labels to access
the Data Labels dialog box shown in figure 11.41. (Notice that this version of the dialog box varies from that shown in figure 11.38.) The pie in
figure 11.42 shows values, percentages, and the slice labels. The legend
has been removed from this chart.

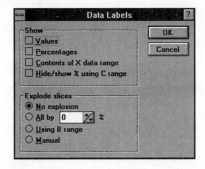

FIG. 11.41

The Data Labels
dialog box for
pie charts.

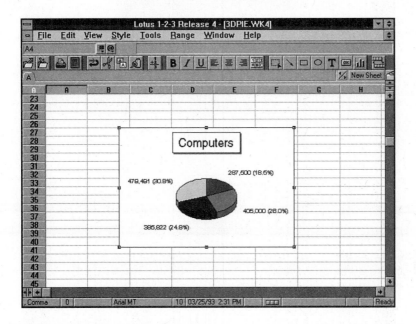

FIG. 11.42

A pie with
values, percent-
ages, and slice
labels.

Exploding a Pie Slice

To emphasize one or more portions of a pie chart, you *explode,* or pull the slice(s) out slightly from the rest of the pie. For example, the chart in figure 11.43 is the same chart shown in figure 11.42, but a slice of the pie has been exploded for emphasis. 1-2-3 offers several ways to explode slices.

Probably the fastest way to explode a single slice is to select it and drag it the desired distance. A selected pie slice has three selection handles on it. As you drag the slice, the mouse pointer is shaped like a hand (to indicate that you are moving something) and the slice has a dotted outline surrounding it. When the slice outline is where you want the slice to be, release the mouse button; the slice then moves to this position.

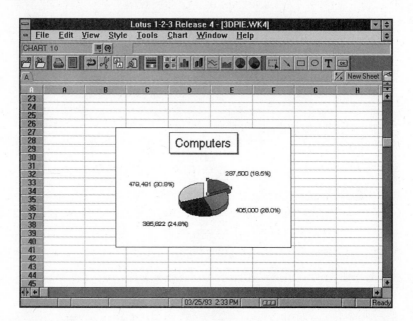

FIG. 11.43

A 3D Pie graph with an exploded slice.

CAUTION: Exploding a slice may reduce the size of the pie because of the extra space required to display the entire pie with the slice pulled out.

A second way to explode pie slices is to pull them all out by a certain percentage. To use this option, choose Chart Data Labels and enter a value in the All by [__] % field. Figure 11.44 shows a pie whose slices are exploded 10 percent.

The third way to explode slices is to create a B range and then turn on the Using B Range check box in the Data Labels dialog box. The primary use of the B data range is to control the colors of the slices (the next section discusses this in more detail), but if you add 100 to a color code, the corresponding slice explodes.

NOTE   If after exploding one or more slices you change your mind, you can eliminate this effect by choosing No Explosion in the Data Labels dialog box.

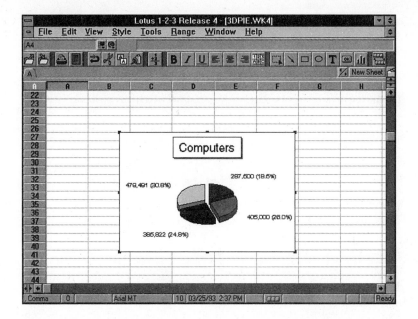

FIG. 11.44

All slices in this
pie are exploded
by 10 percent.

Changing Pie Slice Colors and Patterns

1-2-3 for Windows displays the slices of a pie chart in different colors
(or different patterns if you have a monochrome monitor). You can
control the color and patterns by specifying a B data range. The B
range enables you to determine the color of each slice and whether to
explode a section.

You can create the B range anywhere in the worksheet, but it must be
the same size as the A data range you are plotting. To specify colors,
enter a number from 1 to 14 in each cell in the B range. To explode a
slice, add 100 to the color number. To hide a slice, enter 0 or a negative
number in the cell. To define the B range, select the chart, and choose
Chart Ranges. Then click on the B series (which is titled Explosion &
colors) and specify the range of color codes in the Range field.

There are several other ways you can specify colors for your pie slices.
One way is to use the Chart Numeric Color command. This technique is
described in the "Changing Data Series Colors and Patterns" section
later in the chapter. Another way is to select each slice and use the
Style Lines & Color command, or press the right mouse button and
choose Lines & Color.

Enhancing the Chart

The Style menu offers several ways to enhance your 1-2-3 charts, including the following:

- Changing the typeface, point size, and attributes of the titles and labels
- Changing the color of any chart element
- Choosing a pattern for a data series
- Changing the style and width of the lines and outlines
- Adding designer frames to your chart

Changing the Format of Numbers

By default, 1-2-3 for Windows displays numbers in a chart in General format, which is the default format for worksheet values. You can display x-axis, y-axis, or the second y-axis labels, data labels, or pie labels in any of 1-2-3 for Windows' numeric formats. Just click on one of the numbers you want to format, and the group of numbers are selected. Then choose Style Number Format and select the desired format from the list. Some formats require that you specify a number of decimal places, and date and time formats require that you specify format types. Another way to display the Number Format dialog box is to click the right mouse button on the numbers and choose Number Format from the Quick menu.

For Related Information

◀◀ "Working with Number Formats," p. 200.

FROM HERE...

Formatting Text Attributes

You can change the typeface, point size, color, and attributes (bold-face, italics, and so on) of any text object on a chart. You also can format the chart titles, legend text, data labels, and axis labels as well as text blocks you created with the Tools Draw Text command or the Text Block SmartIcon.

Formatting text on a chart is not too different from formatting cells in your worksheet. First, select the text. If you are formatting a group of objects (such as all the data labels or the labels on the x-axis), you simply click on one of the labels and then 1-2-3 automatically selects all related labels. Next, select Style Font & Attributes or click the Font & Attributes SmartIcon. You then see the Font & Attributes dialog box, which is the same as the one you use to format text in the worksheet. (For details, see Chapter 5, "Changing the Format and Appearance of Data.") Another way to display the Font & Attributes dialog box is to click the right mouse button on the labels and choose Font & Attributes from the Quick menu.

For Related Information

◀◀ "Changing Fonts and Attributes," p. 218.

FROM HERE...

Changing Data Series Colors and Patterns

1-2-3 for Windows also enables you to select colors for each of the data series on a chart. You can change the color of lines, bars, areas, and individual pie slices. Remember that unless your printer can print in color, you may be better off using hatch patterns or symbols to differentiate data ranges.

To change the color of a series, first click on any data point of that series. For example, if you are changing the color of a line, click on one of the data points on the line. Or, if you are choosing a different color for one of the data series in a bar chart, click on one of the bars. 1-2-3 then selects all the data points in that series. Another way to change the color of a series is to click on the appropriate color box in the legend. Choose Style Lines & Color to display the Lines & Color dialog box, or click on the Lines & Color SmartIcon. Your choices in this box vary, depending on whether you selected an object that can be filled (such as a bar or pie slice) or a line. Another way to display the Lines & Color dialog box is to select a data series, click the right mouse button, and choose Lines & Color from the Quick menu.

Figure 11.45 shows the dialog box that displays when you select a line in a line chart. (The "Formatting Lines and Outlines" section covers the Style, Width, and Symbol options.) To change the line color, click on the Color field, and the color palette displays. The current color has a flashing outline around it. To select a different color, click on the desired color box.

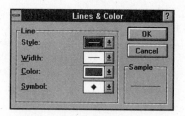

FIG. 11.45

The Lines & Color dialog box for formatting lines.

When a bar, area, pie slice, or radar spiral is selected, the Lines & Color dialog box looks like figure 11.46. Here you can change the color of the interior of the object as well as its outline. To choose a different interior color, click on the Background color field and select the new color from the palette. To change the color of the object's outline, choose Color (under the Line heading) and select the color from the palette.

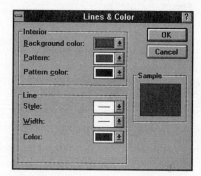

FIG. 11.46

The Lines & Color dialog box for objects that can be filled.

You can also fill the object with a pattern and choose the Background color and Pattern Color. There are 61 different patterns available (click on the Pattern field to see a pattern palette), including bricks, checkerboards, stripes, dots, basketweaves, and cross-hatches. (If you include T(ransparent) and the two solid boxes, there are 64 total boxes in the palette. However, there are only 61 actual *patterns* in the palette.) After you choose a pattern, use the Background color and Pattern color fields to select the two colors used in the pattern. To create a black-and-white pattern, choose black for the background color and white for the pattern color (or vice-versa), and then select a pattern from the palette.

> **CAUTION:** If the background color and pattern color are the same, the Pattern palette does not show any patterns. Make sure the two colors are different.

Changing Data Point Colors and Patterns

Using the Lines & Color dialog box, you can assign colors and patterns to each data *series*. If you want to assign different colors and patterns to each data *point*, use the Chart Numeric Color command. You should use this command only on bar charts that have a single data series (otherwise there is no way to distinguish one series from another) or on pie charts.

Before using this command, you must do some setup work. In the worksheet, enter a range of values between 0 and 15. Each number represents a different color or hatch pattern, except for 15, which hides the data point. The color values correspond to the colors in the top row of the color palette. (To display this palette, choose Style Lines & Color or click the Lines & Color SmartIcon, and click on any of the fields that refer to color.) With pattern codes, the values 1 through 8 represent different hatch patterns and 9 through 14 represent shades of gray. If you want both colors and hatch patterns, set up two ranges. Then select the chart and issue Chart Numeric Color. Enter the range containing your color codes in the Range of color values field, or use the range selector to point to the range. If applicable, specify the Range of pattern values.

Formatting Lines and Outlines

You can change the color, style, and width of any line on a chart, including the following:

- Lines in line, XY, HLCO, and radar charts
- Outlines of bars, areas, and pies
- Grid lines
- Objects created with the Tools Draw commands

Before you can change the style of a line or an outline, you must select the object. Then choose Style Lines & Color, choose the Lines & Color SmartIcon, or press the right mouse button and choose Lines & Color from the Quick menu. 1-2-3 offers six different line styles. From the Style drop-down list, you can choose solid lines, long dashes, short dashes, a combination of long and short dashes, two dots between each dash, large dots, and small dots. Or, if you don't want a line, choose None. The Width drop-down list offers eight different line widths.

On line and XY charts, you can choose a different symbol shape for each data series. These symbols appear at each data point and in the legend. If you select a line data series, the Symbol option appears in the Lines & Color dialog box. You can choose from a variety of symbol shapes, including boxes, squares, stars, triangles, diamonds, and circles. If you don't want any symbols at the data points, choose a line-only style in the Type dialog box.

Formatting a Frame

By default, the legend, the heading, and the chart itself are enclosed in *frames* (boxes). If you select the frame and then display the Lines & Color dialog, you see two additional options: Designer frame and Frame color. If you click on the Designer frame field, you see a palette of frame corners, shown in figure 11.47. After you select a frame, you can choose a color with the Frame color field.

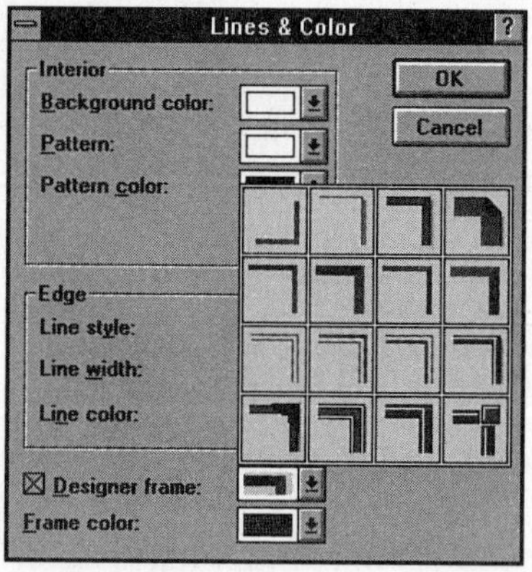

FIG. 11.47

The palette of Designer frames.

T I P   Don't overuse the Designer frames. Many are too overpowering for titles and legends.

For Related Information

◄◄ "Changing Fonts and Attributes," p. 218.

◄◄ "Formatting Cells with Color and Borders," p. 224.

FROM HERE...

Annotating a Chart

With 1-2-3 for Windows, you can add descriptive labels, lines, objects, and arrows to existing charts. For example, you might want to explain why a data point is particularly high or low, or state a conclusion illustrated by the chart. Figure 11.48 shows an example of a chart annotation. You create such an annotation by using the Tools Draw commands, as described in the section "Using Graphics" later in this chapter.

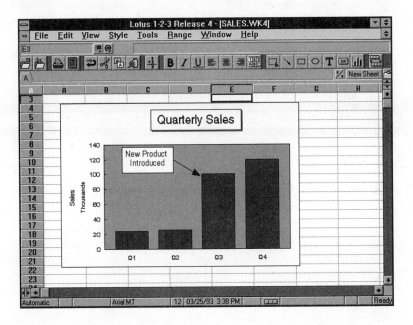

FIG. 11.48

A chart annotated with the drawing commands.

Instead of enclosing an annotation in the rectangular frame that automatically appears around a text block, you might prefer to enclose the text in an ellipse, as shown in figure 11.49. Of course, you should eliminate the text block's frame. The section "Drawing an Ellipse or Circle," later in this chapter, describes how to add an ellipse to the chart.

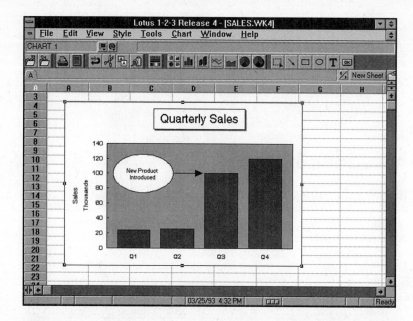

FIG. 11.49

A text block with
an ellipse drawn
around it.

For Related Information

◄◄ "Changing the Format and Appearance of Data," p. 191.

◄◄ "Aligning Labels and Values," p. 220.

Previewing and Printing Charts

Screen charts are useful for viewing by one or two people, but often
you must create printed copies. If you have used earlier versions of
1-2-3, you might notice a major change in the way charts are printed in
1-2-3 for Windows. Rather than using a separate PrintGraph program,
you now can preview and print charts by using 1-2-3 for Windows' File
Print command.

Printing a Chart

Before printing a chart, select it—any element on the chart will suffice.
Then, when you bring up the Print dialog box, the chart name is automatically entered into the Selected chart field. Figure 11.50 shows the

dialog box with the name CHART 1 as the Selected chart. When you choose OK, the chart prints at the size it appears in the worksheet.

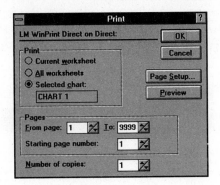

FIG. 11.50

The Print dialog box.

NOTE If you have used the Tools Draw command to add any text or objects to your chart, they will not print if you simply select the chart name in the Print dialog box. To print the chart and objects you have added to it, you must use the Select Objects SmartIcon to "lasso" the chart. Then, when you display the Print dialog box, Collection will appear in the Selected Drawn Object field.

If you want the chart to appear in the worksheet at its current size but to print in full-page size, you can use the Size option in the Page Setup dialog box (choose File Page Setup to access the dialog box). After you select a chart, the Size option has three settings: Actual Size, Fill Page, and Fill Page But Keep Proportions. If you choose Fill Page, the chart is enlarged or reduced until it fills the page. Because this stretched chart may appear somewhat distorted, a better choice is usually Fill Page But Keep Proportions. This chart is as large as possible, without any distortion. When you print a full-size chart, you usually should change the orientation to landscape since charts are usually wider than they are tall.

Previewing a Chart

Before you print a chart, you can preview it. Previewing can save you time and paper, enabling you to make all adjustments and changes before you print. You can preview a chart with two commands: the File Print Preview command and the Preview button in the Print dialog box. You can also use the Preview SmartIcon.

When you add a chart to a worksheet, you specify the size of the chart and the location at which it appears on the page. By previewing the report, you can determine how the chart fits on the printed page. You then can decide whether you should use one of the Size options described in the previous section. Figure 11.51 shows a previewed chart in Landscape orientation, with the Fill Page But Keep Proportions setting.

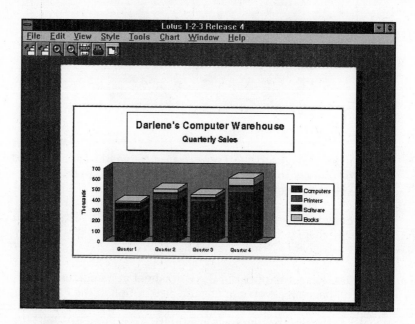

FIG. 11.51

A preview of a chart.

Printing Charts and Worksheet Data on the Same Page

You can print a chart and its supporting data on separate pages and then collate them to produce a report. However, printing a chart and its worksheet together on one page can be more effective (see fig. 11.52). How you print this type of report depends on where the chart is located in the worksheet in relation to its supporting data. If the chart and data are placed exactly where you want them in the report, you can define a single print range: select the range of cells that includes the data and the chart. If you are pointing to the range, the chart itself is not highlighted on the screen—just the cells behind the chart.

Darlene's Computer Warehouse
Quarterly Sales

	Quarter 1	Quarter 2	Quarter 3	Quarter 4	Year Total
Computers	287,500	405,000	385,822	479,491	1,557,813
Printers	28,583	56,040	31,620	59,664	175,907
Software	53,795	11,471	13,759	9,726	88,751
Books	18,713	37,719	25,832	68,250	150,514
Qtr totals	388,591	510,230	457,033	617,131	1,972,985

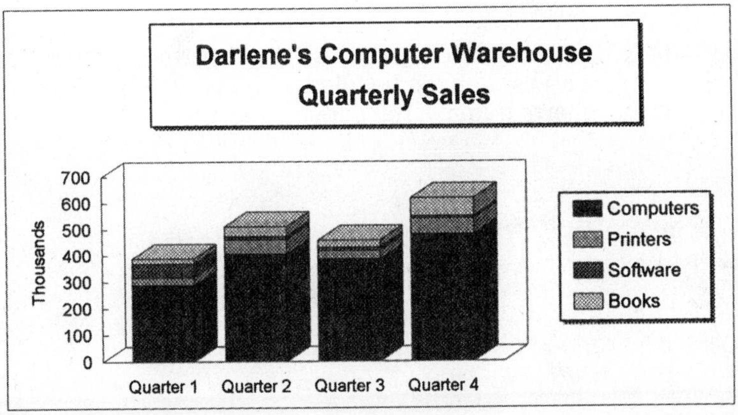

Darlene's Computer Warehouse
Quarterly Sales

FIG. 11.52

A chart printed with its supporting data.

If the data is in one part of the worksheet and the chart is in another, you must define two print ranges. To define multiple ranges, type the ranges, separated by commas or semicolons. To point to the ranges, you must preselect them; remember to hold down the Ctrl key as you select the second and subsequent ranges.

To print more than one chart on a page, you must select the worksheet cell range; you cannot preselect multiple charts by holding down Ctrl as you click on them.

Printing Color Charts on a Black-and-White Printer

If you try to use a black-and-white printer to print a color chart, here's what happens:

- Colored text prints in black
- Colored lines print in black
- The background color of the plot area is ignored
- The interior colors of objects (bars, areas, and so on) are converted to shades of gray

If you prefer, you can use black-and-white hatch patterns, rather than solid fills, in chart areas that can be filled. Also, be sure to include symbols in your line charts to make the data series easier to distinguish.

FROM HERE...

For Related Information

- ◄◄ Chapter 10, "Previewing Reports before Printing," p. 509.
- ◄◄ Chapter 10, "Printing the Report," p. 512.

Using Graphics

Included with 1-2-3 for Windows is a set of basic drawing tools that you can use to enhance your worksheets and charts. There are tools for drawing shapes (such as ellipses, rectangles, and polygons), lines, arrows, and arcs. There is also a tool that enables you to type text anywhere on the chart. These tools can help you annotate your charts, as shown earlier in figure 11.49.

All the drawing tools are listed on the Tools Draw menu.

Adding Descriptive Text to a Worksheet or Chart

When you choose Tools Draw Text or click on the Text Block SmartIcon, you are prompted to click and drag to draw a text block.

A *text block* is the container for your descriptive text. To draw the text block, place the mouse pointer on the chart or worksheet in which you want the text to go, and then click and drag to create a box the approximate height and width of the text block you are entering. (Don't worry too much about the size and placement, because it's easy enough to move and resize the text block later.) After drawing the box, type the text. To enter multiple lines of text, you can either let the text word wrap or press Enter after each line.

CAUTION: If you don't make your text block long enough, your text may scroll out of view after you type another line. If this happens, you must lengthen the block by dragging the center handle at the bottom of the selected text block.

By default, the block is surrounded by a frame with a white background. To change the interior color or to format the frame, use the Style Lines & Color command, the Lines & Color SmartIcon, or press the right mouse button and choose Lines & Color from the Quick menu. If you are adding a block of text to a chart, for example, you might want to change the interior color of the text block so that it has the same background color as the plot. To do this, select the block (you'll see selection handles around the frame), display the Lines & Color dialog box, and, in the palette for Background color, choose the same color as your plot background. To eliminate the frame from a text block, choose None for the Line style. See the "Enhancing the Chart" section earlier in this chapter for more information about changing line styles and colors.

To edit the text later, double-click on the text block. A cursor then appears at the beginning of the text. Use the mouse or arrow keys to position the cursor and make your corrections.

To change the typeface, point size, and attributes of the text block, you can use the Style Font & Attributes command, the Font & Attributes SmartIcon, or press the right mouse button and choose Font & Attributes from the Quick menu. Note that you cannot format individual characters inside the block; it's all or nothing. Before you access the Font & Attributes dialog box, select the text block (make sure selection handles are around it). For more information on making such changes, see the section "Formatting Text Attributes" earlier in this chapter.

The Style Alignment command enables you to align the text within its frame. For instance, for a multiple-line text block, you might want to center the lines inside the box. This command is for horizontal alignment only; you cannot align text vertically in a text block. Another way to display the Alignment dialog box is to select the frame, press the right mouse button, and choose Alignment.

Adding Lines and Arrows

To emphasize specific areas in a chart or worksheet, you can add lines and arrows with Tools Draw Line and Tools Draw Arrow or select the Draw Line, Draw Arrow, or Draw Double-Headed Arrow SmartIcons. (Note: Only the Draw Arrow icon is displayed in the default chart palette.) After you select the drawing tool, 1-2-3 prompts you to click and drag to draw the line or arrow. Place the cross at the location of the first data point you want to highlight, then click and drag in the direction you want to draw the line or arrow. When you reach the end of the line, simply release the mouse button. If you are creating an arrow, the final data point displays an arrowhead. (Or, if you chose the Draw Double-Headed Arrow SmartIcon, arrowheads will appear on both ends of the line.) 1-2-3 for Windows displays a line or arrow on the chart or worksheet, with handles to indicate that the line or arrow is selected. While selected, the line or arrow can be moved or changed.

To connect two or more line segments together, use the Tools Draw Polyline command or the Draw Segmented Line SmartIcon. Click at the beginning of the first line, and then click at the end of the line. The next segment will then automatically begin at the end of the first line. Each time you click, one segment ends and the next begins. When you are finished, double-click.

T I P   To draw a horizontal, vertical, or diagonal line, hold down Shift as you draw. The Shift key restricts the line to increments of 45 degrees.

To change the style, width, and color of the line, you can use the Style Lines & Color command, the Lines & Color SmartIcon, or press the right mouse button and choose Lines & Color from the Quick menu. You can use the Arrowhead option to move the arrowhead to the opposite end of the line, to place arrowheads at both ends of the line, and to add or remove the arrowhead. So, if you create a line and later decide you want it to be an arrow, use the Arrowhead option to add the arrowhead.

You can use the mouse to change the size and direction of a line or arrow. For details, see the section "Resizing Objects" earlier in this chapter.

Creating Arcs

An arc is simply a curved line and, in fact, drawing an arc is just like creating a line except you use a different tool. To create an arc, use the Tools Draw Arc command or the Draw Arc SmartIcon. Then click and drag in the direction you want the arc to curve.

Drawing Shapes

1-2-3 has four tools for drawing enclosed shapes: Ellipse, Rectangle, Rounded Rectangle, and Polygon. To draw an ellipse, select Tools Draw Ellipse (or choose the Draw Ellipse SmartIcon) and then click and drag the mouse until the ellipse is the desired size and shape. To create a perfect circle, hold down Shift as you drag.

The procedure for drawing a rectangle or rounded rectangle (a rectangle with rounded corners) is similar. First, select Tools Draw Rectangle (or Rounded Rectangle) or click on the Draw Rectangle or Draw Rounded Rectangle SmartIcon. Then you click and drag the mouse until the rectangle is the desired size. By holding down Shift as you drag, you create a square.

A polygon is a multisided object—the object can have as many connecting lines as you want. To create a polygon, choose Tools Draw Polygon or select the Draw Polygon SmartIcon. Place the mouse pointer to the first point of the polygon and click the mouse button. Move the pointer to the opposite end of the first line and click again. Continue clicking at each point of the polygon, and double-click when you are finished. You don't need to concern yourself with connecting the last point with the first because 1-2-3 automatically connects these points for you when you double-click. Holding down Shift as you move the mouse pointer restricts the angle to increments of 45 degrees.

The object's interior is white; to change the color (for example, to the color of the plot background), use the Style Lines & Color command. You can also use the Lines & Color dialog box to change the style, color, or width of the object's outline.

Drawing Freehand

When you use the Freehand tool, it's as if someone gave you a pencil and let you draw on the screen. However, unless you have some artistic ability, freehand drawing looks more like freehand scribbling. To activate this tool, choose Tools Draw Freehand or select the Freehand

Drawing tool. The mouse pointer then turns into a pencil. Place the pencil where you want to begin and click and drag to draw. Release the mouse button when you are finished drawing.

Rearranging Graphic Objects

All objects are stacked on top of one another, in the order you create them. The chart is on the bottom layer and any objects you draw or text blocks you create are layered on top of the chart. If you draw an object (such as the ellipse in figure 11.49) on top of a text block, the text will be hidden unless you change the stacking order.

1-2-3 provides commands for rearranging the stacking order of objects. On the Edit Arrange menu, choose Bring to Front or Send to Back, depending on which object is selected. These commands send an object all the way to the back or bring it all the way to the front; there is no way to move an object forward or backward one layer. For example, if you send the ellipse in figure 11.49 to the back, it ends up behind the chart. You then would have to send the chart to the back to place the ellipse in the layer between the text block and the chart. To avoid all this confusion, you could have drawn the ellipse before you created the text block. If you do this, the objects would be stacked in the desired order. Another way to change the stacking order is to select the object, press the right mouse button, and choose Bring to Front or Send to Back from the Quick menu.

Using Clip Art

You might want to further enhance your charts and worksheets by using *clip art* (simple graphic drawings). Although 1-2-3 for Windows does not have a specific command for importing graphics files, you can easily bring in clip art by using the Windows Clipboard. Simply copy the graphic to the Clipboard and use the Edit Paste command in 1-2-3. Before pasting, select a range of cells; the graphic is pasted into this range. If you don't preselect a range, the graphic is pasted into a single cell. You can then enlarge the object by dragging one of the selection handles.

 To place a piece of clip art onto a chart, you must first paste it into a worksheet range. You can then drag it onto your chart and resize it as necessary. The graphic automatically has an outline around it. To remove the frame, use the Style Lines & Color command or click the Lines & Color SmartIcon, and choose None for the Line style.

Figure 11.53 shows a chart that displays clip art—a drawing of a computer—next to the chart heading. The drawing was pasted into the worksheet and then moved onto the chart.

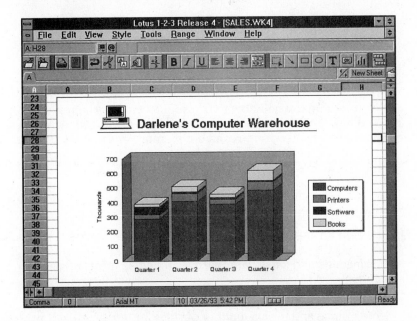

FIG. 11.53

The drawing of a computer is a graphic that was pasted into the worksheet and then moved onto the chart.

Where does clip art come from? Many drawing programs (such as CorelDRAW) come with a collection of images that you can use in other programs. You can also purchase packages of clip art from companies such as Masterclip Graphics, 3G Graphics, TMaker, and Image Club. Lotus Development offers its own clip art package, called SmartPics; figure 11.54 shows a sample graphic from the package. (The computer drawing in fig. 11.44 is also from SmartPics.) For more information on how you can obtain Lotus SmartPics for Windows, call Lotus Selects at 1-800-635-6887.

FIG. 11.54

This graphic is a sample from Lotus SmartPics for Windows.

FROM HERE...

For Related Information

▶▶ Chapter 12, "Using Clip Art," p. 626.

Questions & Answers

In this chapter you learned how to use sophisticated graphics and charts and link them together with the worksheet. The following questions and answers serve to refresh your memory in these areas:

Q: I no longer have a Chart option in my menu bar. Where did it go?

A: The Chart option displays only if a chart, or an element on a chart, is selected. Otherwise, Range displays in the menu bar. Just click anywhere on the chart, and you see the Chart option.

Q: I created an automatic chart by preselecting the range and choosing Tools Chart. However, the chart isn't set up the way I want it. The legends and x-axis labels are switched. Is there a way to fix this?

A: When 1-2-3 produces automatic charts, it looks at your preselected range and uses a number of rules for determining how to set up your chart ranges. If your worksheet doesn't follow these rules, the ranges may not be assigned properly. To switch your legends and data labels, choose Chart Ranges, and select By row or By column in the Assign ranges field. Study the sample worksheet that displays when you choose By row or By column to determine which one is appropriate for your ranges.

Q: My chart has only one data series, and 1-2-3 created a legend that I don't need. How can I get rid of it?

A: Select the legend and press Del.

Q: I have several charts in one file. How do I find out what each one is named?

A: Select the chart, and look in the selection indicator on the edit line. Repeat for each chart. The default names are Chart 1, Chart 2, and so on. To use more descriptive names, choose Chart Name.

Q: My pie slices aren't labeled, even though I indicated them as my x-axis range. How can I get them to display?

A: The Data Labels dialog box has check boxes for controlling the display of x-axis labels, values, and percentages next to each slice. To display your x-axis labels, choose Chart Data Labels and turn on Contents of X Data Range.

Q: I'm having trouble creating an XY chart. I preselected the range and created an automatic chart, but the ranges are all wrong. 1-2-3 put the x-axis values as series A and the y-axis values as series B. How do I solve this problem?

A: Because of the rules 1-2-3 follows when producing an automatic chart, you can't use this feature successfully when creating XY charts. 1-2-3 gets confused because the x-axis labels on an XY chart are actually values. Probably the best way to create an XY chart is to create a chart from scratch and define the ranges yourself.

Q: I chose the Mixed chart type, but all my data series display as bars. How can I get one of them to display as a line?

A: Choose Chart Ranges, click on the series letter (A, B, C, and so on) that you want to be a line, and choose Line from the Mixed Type drop-down list.

Q: My chart has overlapping labels on the x-axis. Is there any way to relieve this crowding?

A: Yes. Choose Chart Axis X-Axis, and then enter a skip value in the Place label every [__] ticks field.

Q: My y-axis scale shows single digit numbers (1, 2, 3,...) with a unit indicator of Thousands, but I would prefer to see the actual numbers (1000, 2000, 3000,...). How can I do this?

A: Choose Chart Axis Y-Axis and select the Options button. Then choose Manual in the Axis units field and enter 0 for the Exponent.

Q: I am using the drawing commands to annotate my chart. I created a text block and drew an ellipse around it, but then my text block disappeared. Where did it go?

A: All objects in a chart are layered, in the order you create them. Therefore, the ellipse is lying on top of your text block, hiding it. 1-2-3 provides two commands on the Edit Arrange menu for changing the stacking order of your objects: Send to Back and Bring to Front. Before issuing the command, select the appropriate object. Keep in mind that the chart is the bottom layer in the stack, and that if you send something to the back, it goes behind the chart.

Summary

In this chapter, you learned how to create and enhance various chart types, and use the Chart and Style menu commands to produce attractive and informative charts. You learned how to print charts and how to modify a chart's orientation, size, and shape, as well as how to print charts and worksheet data on the same page. Finally, you saw how to liven up your charts with drawn graphic objects and clip art. By experimenting with the techniques presented in this chapter and in Chapter 10, "Printing Reports," you can create printed reports that effectively present the data in tabular and graphical form.

In the next chapter, you learn how to use 1-2-3 for Windows to develop effective business presentations.

Developing Business Presentations

Y ou can use the graphic and printing capabilities of 1-2-3 in many creative ways in addition to charting and reporting worksheet data. This chapter discusses using 1-2-3 Release 4 for Windows to create high-quality presentation slides, overheads, and screen shows.

You can print slides and graphics, using black-and-white or color printers supported by 1-2-3 for Windows. With a color printer, you can print directly on transparent overhead projector film, resulting in colorful and persuasive overhead presentations.

You also can use your computer for a slide show by projecting the PC screen image, much as you project the image of a transparency. This technique is often called a *computer screen show*. Screen show capabilities are often found in presentation graphics packages, but 1-2-3 provides many of the same capabilities and can create a visually interesting screen show.

You can display a slide show from your computer screen directly to an audience in several ways. The method you choose depends on the size of the audience and your budget. The easiest way to make a presentation to a moderate-size group (10 to 15 people) is to use a very large computer monitor. If you are presenting to a large group (50 or more people), you may want to use a video projector. This projector is very expensive to rent, however, and often difficult to set up.

A newer device, called an *LCD projection panel*, enables you to project your PC screen with a standard overhead projector. This device fits directly on top of the overhead projector, is fairly inexpensive to buy or rent, and is easy to use. This device is often the best solution for making a presentation to a group of 20 to 100 people.

This chapter shows you how to accomplish the following:

- Set up your worksheet for presentations
- Organize the presentation layout
- Use color to emphasize main points
- Use a 3-D worksheet to organize your presentation
- Add charts and graphics to your presentation
- Print your presentation
- Use macros to make screen shows easier

This chapter also provides some guidelines for applying formats and using typefaces that can help you design persuasive presentations.

Setting Up Your Worksheet Area for Presentations

An important first step in using 1-2-3 for a presentation is setting up the work area for the presentation. The following sections describe how you can use 1-2-3 to create presentations and then provide many tips for projecting the presentation from the PC or printing it on overhead transparencies.

Using the Row-and-Column Structure To Assist with Layout

Creating a presentation in 1-2-3 is easy because of the row-and-column structure inherent in all worksheets. You can change the column widths and row heights of this row-and-column grid to customize presentations.

Creating slides in 1-2-3 is as easy as typing the text into worksheet cells. The first step is to organize your slide structure by using the rows and columns in the worksheet. Figure 12.1 shows how you can use 1-2-3 to set up a presentation template.

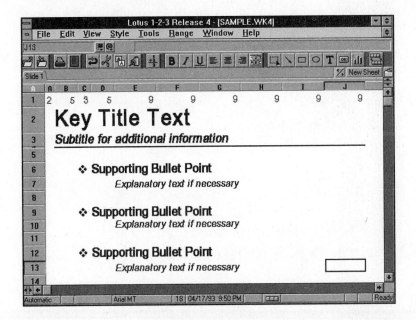

FIG. 12.1

A template for a slide layout in 1-2-3.

In this example, the column widths are shown in the first row of the worksheet. The key to creating the slide layout is setting up the appropriate column widths for text, bullets, and graphics. Organizing the columns in this manner enables you to easily indent bullets and other textual information. To add text, highlight the appropriate cell and type the new information. Long labels will appear across the adjacent columns. The following table describes how the columns are used in figure 12.1.

Column	Width	Description
A	2	Space to separate the overall slide contents from the page frame
B	5	Indentation for subtitles below the leader
C	3	Space for the bullet symbols
D	5	Indentation for text below bullet items

Because row heights automatically change to fit the largest font in each row, you usually do not need to adjust row heights when you create a layout. Just skip rows between bullet points to provide space between the lines of text.

After you add the text, you can use the Style commands, the status bar, the quick menus (displayed when you press the right mouse button), and the SmartIcons to make the text more readable. Larger typefaces and other attributes, such as bold, italics, and lines, make the information clearer for your audience.

FROM HERE...

For Related Information

◀◀ "Setting Column Widths," p. 151.

Modifying the 1-2-3 Display for On-Screen Presentations

Although the standard 1-2-3 screen looks nothing like a presentation tool, giving 1-2-3 the appearance of a presentation graphics screen show is easy. You can create an effective screen show by using the View Set View Preferences command, which provides substantial flexibility for modifying the appearance of the screen display.

In 1-2-3 for Windows, you can choose to display only the application title line and the 1-2-3 menus. However, you may also want to display the worksheet tabs, which provide an easy way to change slides during a slide show.

To change the display of the 1-2-3 screen, follow these steps:

1. Select View Set View Preferences to display the preferences dialog box.

2. Uncheck the boxes for Worksheet Frame, Grid Lines, and Scroll Bars. These settings are saved for each worksheet file.

3. Uncheck the boxes for Edit Line, SmartIcons, and Status Bar. These settings apply at the 1-2-3 level. Figure 12.2 shows the appropriate settings for the Set View Preferences dialog box.

4. Click on the OK button to apply the settings to the current worksheet.

5. Select File Save or click on the File Save SmartIcon to save the settings in the worksheet file.

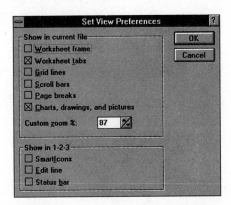

FIG. 12.2

The Set View Preferences dialog box with settings for slide shows checked.

For Related Information

◀◀ "Learning the 1-2-3 for Windows Screen," p. 91.

FROM HERE...

Although most of these settings are saved in the worksheet file, make sure that the edit line, scroll bars, and status line are turned off each time you run a screen show from 1-2-3. The following macro will choose these settings.

```
{SET "WINDOW-DISPLAY-EDIT-LINE","NO"}
{SET "WINDOW-DISPLAY-SMARTICONS","NO"}
{SET "WINDOW-DISPLAY-STATUS-BAR","NO"}
```

To run this macro each time you load the worksheet file, name the macro \0 (backslash zero). You can also add a macro button to the worksheet and attach this macro to the button.

The cell pointer can be a distraction on the screen during a screen show. However, you can make it less intrusive by moving it to the lower left corner of each slide.

T I P

T I P   To redisplay these window attributes, create a second macro replacing NO with YES. Use the Edit Copy command to duplicate the preceding macro, and then use Edit Find & Replace to change NO to YES. Name this macro \r so you can easily reset these display settings.

FROM HERE...

For Related Information

▶▶ "Naming and Running Macros," p. 741.

Developing Multiple-Page Presentations

Most presentations use more than one page or worksheet screen; 1-2-3 can accommodate presentations of almost any length. 1-2-3 Release 4 for Windows provides a three-dimensional (*multiple-page*) worksheet structure that makes organizing multiple-screen presentations easy.

With the 1-2-3 for Windows three-dimensional architecture, you can place each slide in its own worksheet. 1-2-3 Release 4 for Windows also provides tabs so that you can easily turn worksheet pages. The tabs offer an easy way to change slides, especially if you do not move sequentially through the pages. Simply click on the worksheet tab for the desired page. You can also use Ctrl+PgUp to move from page to page. Figure 12.3 shows a presentation using the worksheet tabs.

T I P   Tabs work best on shorter presentations. If you have too many tabs or tabs with long names, you cannot display all the tabs along the top of the worksheet. Use the scroll arrows to the left of the New Sheet button to display the hidden tabs or use Ctrl+PgUp to move to later slides.

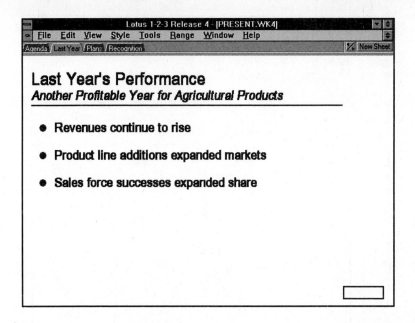

FIG. 12.3

Using the 1-2-3 worksheet tabs to organize slides on multiple pages.

T I P

1-2-3 for Windows also provides a Group mode feature, which enables you to use the format of one worksheet to format all the pages in multiple worksheets. The formats applied across the worksheets include column widths and Wysiwyg spreadsheet publishing formats. Use Style Worksheet Defaults to enable Group mode.

The easiest way to use Group mode is to set the fonts colors and other formats on one worksheet page and then enable Group mode. This will copy the format settings throughout the entire worksheet file. Disable Group mode in order to alter the format settings of individual worksheets.

For Related Information

◄◄ "Using Multiple Worksheets," p. 103.

FROM HERE...

Using 1-2-3 To Convey a Message

Although 1-2-3 provides many features to enable you to format printed pages and screen layouts, don't use all these capabilities at one time. Clear, persuasive, and successful presentations are created by following some simple rules and guidelines for style and format, and require simplicity in formatting and layout. Because an audience reads presentations from a distance, slides must be clear, in large type, and contain as few words as possible.

FROM HERE...

For Related Information

◀◀ "Understanding Style," p. 192.

Guidelines for Presenting Text

You can create persuasive slides by following some basic guidelines. 1-2-3 for Windows provides great flexibility for text size and font, colors, lines, and shading. The key to a successful presentation, however, is to use these elements in moderation. By following a few guidelines, you can create impressive and effective presentations.

Use Large Point Sizes for Text

Use fonts that can be read from a distance. For titles, use a 24-point font or larger. Never make text smaller than 14 points.

Reduce Point Size for Subtitles and Bullets

Use type size to indicate the relative importance of text in a slide. To draw attention to the slide's key message, use the largest text for titles. Choose smaller typefaces for subtitles and bullets.

Limit the Number of Fonts on a Slide

Although 1-2-3 enables you to use up to eight different fonts on a page, the best slides use only one or two typefaces in three point sizes. Too many type styles make the slide difficult to read and reduce the impact of the slide's message.

Use a Sans Serif Typeface

Format slide text in a sans serif typeface such as Arial. Serif typefaces such as Times New Roman may be appropriate with longer lines of text. However, sans serif text is easier to read, particularly if the audience is far from the projected slide.

Use Italics for Subtitles

A subtitle message usually supports or expands on the title message. Differentiate the subtitle from the title with a smaller point size and italics.

Use Boldface for Titles and Bullets

For all titles, subtitles and bullets, use boldface, which makes the text on slides much easier to read. Be sure, however, to apply the bold-facing consistently.

Emphasize the Title of the Slide

Slides convey information better when the title is easy to locate and read. You can use a solid line below the title to separate the title from the body of the slide, as shown in figure 12.4. Use the Style Lines & Color command or click on the Lines & Color SmartIcon to place a solid line under the slide title.

Dotted lines also can separate the title from the rest of the slide effectively (see fig. 12.5). Dotted lines can be less jarring than a solid line and can give a softer tone to the slide. You can create a dotted line as a series of periods separated by spaces. To create a dotted line that spans the width of the screen, you need approximately 38 periods and spaces formatted with a 24-point Arial font.

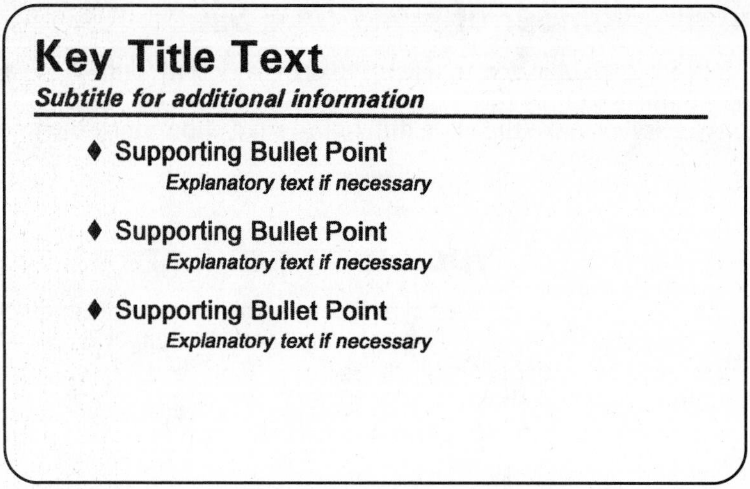

Key Title Text
Subtitle for additional information

♦ Supporting Bullet Point
   Explanatory text if necessary

♦ Supporting Bullet Point
   Explanatory text if necessary

♦ Supporting Bullet Point
   Explanatory text if necessary

FIG. 12.4

A solid line emphasizing the slide title.

Key Title Text
Subtitle for additional information

♦ Supporting Bullet Point
   Explanatory text if necessary

♦ Supporting Bullet Point
   Explanatory text if necessary

♦ Supporting Bullet Point
   Explanatory text if necessary

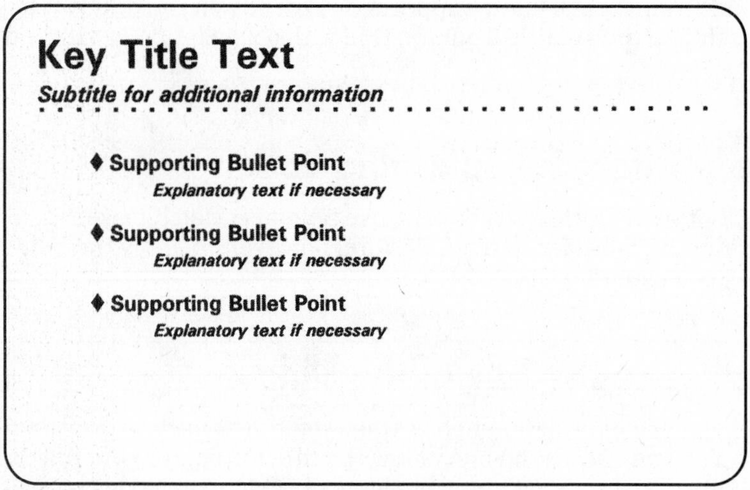

FIG. 12.5

A dotted line emphasizing the slide title.

 You also can emphasize a title by enclosing the text within a colored box. Figure 12.6 shows slide text with a shaded title box. In addition, you can use one of the designer frames to emphasize the title. Highlight the range and choose <u>S</u>tyle <u>L</u>ines & Color or click on the Lines & Color SmartIcon.

For Related Information

◄◄ "Formatting Cells with Color and Borders," p. 224.

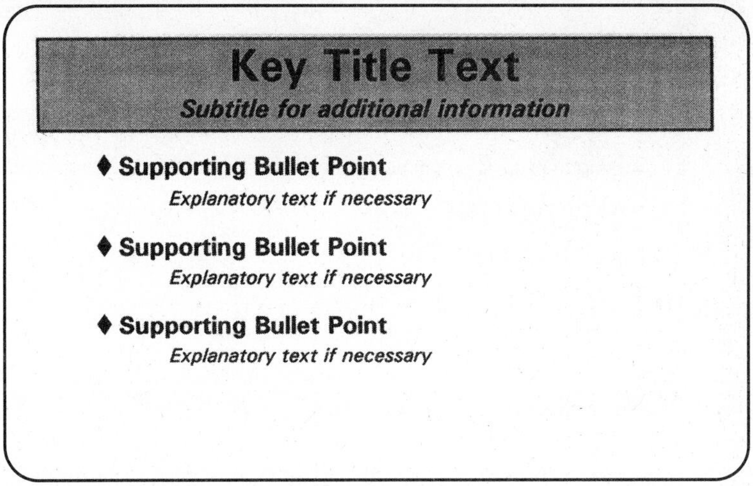

FIG. 12.6

A shaded box and designer frame emphasizing the slide title.

Keep Slide Text to a Minimum

Slides should not be narratives of the entire presentation. Use the titles, subtitles, and bullet items to present the essential points clearly. Rely on the spoken presentation to explain and elaborate on the basic information that the slides present.

Effective slides contain a title and no more than four or five bullet points. If the bullets require sub-bullets, make sure that the slide contains no more than four main bullets. Limit the sub-bullets to two or three lines.

Adding another slide is always better than crowding too much information onto a single slide.

T I P

Use Parallel Grammatical Structure

Use the same grammatical construction for all bullets on a slide. Bullets can start with a noun or a verb of any tense, but all the bullets should use the same structure. The slide shown in figure 12.7 shows bullet items that use parallel structure. Compare this slide with the one shown in figure 12.8, which does not use parallel structure. A parallel construction creates a tighter presentation and conveys information more clearly.

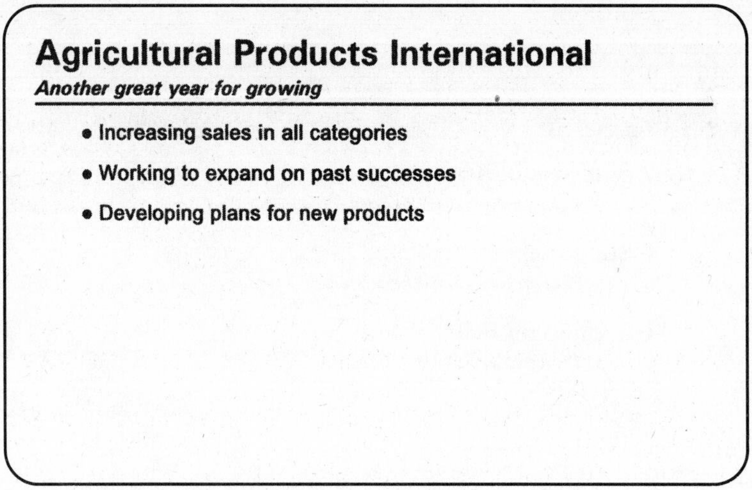

Agricultural Products International
Another great year for growing

- Increasing sales in all categories
- Working to expand on past successes
- Developing plans for new products

FIG. 12.7

Bullets that are parallel.

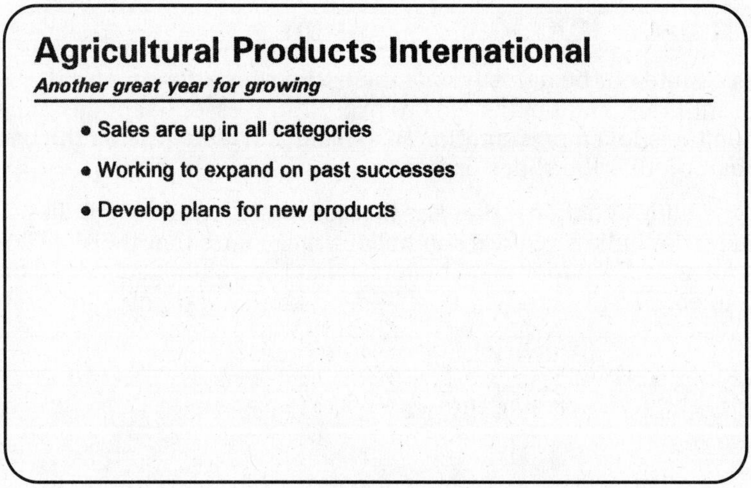

Agricultural Products International
Another great year for growing

- Sales are up in all categories
- Working to expand on past successes
- Develop plans for new products

FIG. 12.8

Bullets that aren't parallel.

Guidelines for Presenting Graphics

To make presentation slides more effective and persuasive, you can use graphics images. Like text, graphics are more effective when you follow certain guidelines.

Use Graphics To Explain the Key Point

A graphic can draw attention to the key point of the slide. You can use the Tools Chart and Tools Draw commands to add charts and drawings to a worksheet. Do not try to encompass too many concepts, however, and do not present detailed information in a single graphic. The best graphics are clear, easy-to-read presentations of a single key point.

Use Text To Introduce and Explain the Graphic

Effective graphics have a clear purpose. Use titles to introduce the key message and to establish the context for the graphic. You can use bullets in your graphics to clarify or emphasize the points made by the text; however, do not overload the page with information and make sure you balance the elements of the overall layout. In figure 12.9, the information is poorly organized and the slide is unbalanced. Figure 12.10 presents the same information clearly.

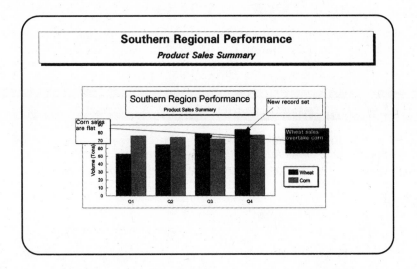

FIG. 12.9

An unbalanced presentation of graphics.

Position the Graphic To Balance the Page

Graphics add substance to a slide. You need, however, to position a graphic to balance the page. Center a graphic if the slide contains little text; otherwise, position the graphic to the right or left to offset the weight of the other slide elements (refer to fig. 12.10).

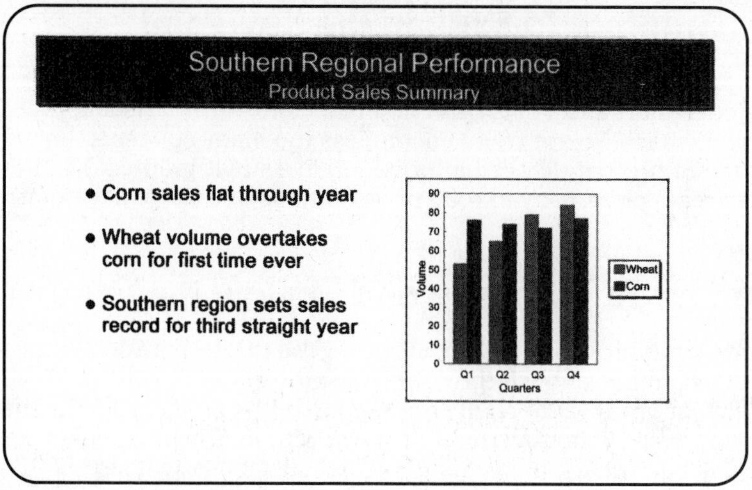

FIG. 12.10

Bullets explaining the chart and balancing it on the slide.

Use a Single Graphic Per Slide

In most cases, effective slides contain only a single graphic. The key to an effective slide presentation is to present the key points with clear, simple illustrations.

Add Visual Interest with Clip Art

You can use commercially available clip art to make the presentation more interesting. You can paste clip art in Windows metafile format directly onto the 1-2-3 for Windows worksheet. Choose images that support your presentation's theme and are appropriate to the setting (see fig. 12.11).

For Related Information

◄◄ "Using Clip Art," p. 592.

FROM HERE...

Use Graphics To Represent Concepts

Use graphics of common objects to convey new ideas. Look at your environment for metaphors that effectively communicate your message. Building blocks, for example, can show the addition of new products over time. Pie charts can show that a combination of the various parts make a whole (see fig. 12.12). A bridge can represent the joining of two separate entities.

FIG. 12.11

Clip art used to liven up a presentation.

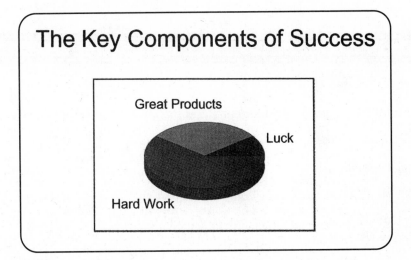

FIG. 12.12

A pie chart representing proportions.

Present Key Trends or Relationships

Use 1-2-3 charts to illustrate key trends in data or to show the relationship among items. (The chart in figure 12.10, for example, clearly shows the trends in product sales.) Keep the chart simple by limiting the amount of information.

Tables of formatted data also can make great illustrations. You can draw attention to the trends and relationships among the data by using lines and arrows added with the Tools Draw commands (see fig. 12.13). Chapter 11, "Creating and Printing Charts," describes using graphics in detail.

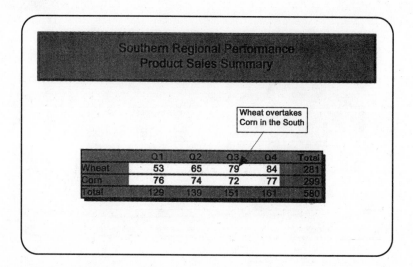

Using the Color Capabilities of 1-2-3

In addition to graphics, color enhances presentations. Color can add interest to the slides and highlight key data. Some colors, such as green and red, can add impact to the information presented.

NOTE To present color, you must be able to print to a color printer or use a computer to give the presentation as a screen show. On black-and-white printers, colors print as different shades of gray, which also can create a useful effect.

1-2-3 allows you to choose the color of cell backgrounds, text, lines, and drawing objects from 256 color choices. By using the color capabilities, you can create appropriately colorful presentations.

For Related Information

◀◀ "Formatting Cells with Colors and Borders," p. 224.

FROM HERE...

Using Color To Highlight Presentation Elements

In a presentation, you can use colors in several ways. The most obvious method of adding color is to use a different color for the main point in the presentation. Yet you can choose from several other common ways to use color.

Color can enhance the organizational structure of the presentation. Using a standard color layout makes the slides easy to understand and more interesting to read. Choose consistent colors for the different regions of the slide, such as blue text for the titles, red for the bullet symbols, and black for the bullet text. You also can use different background colors for different sections of the slide (see fig. 12.14).

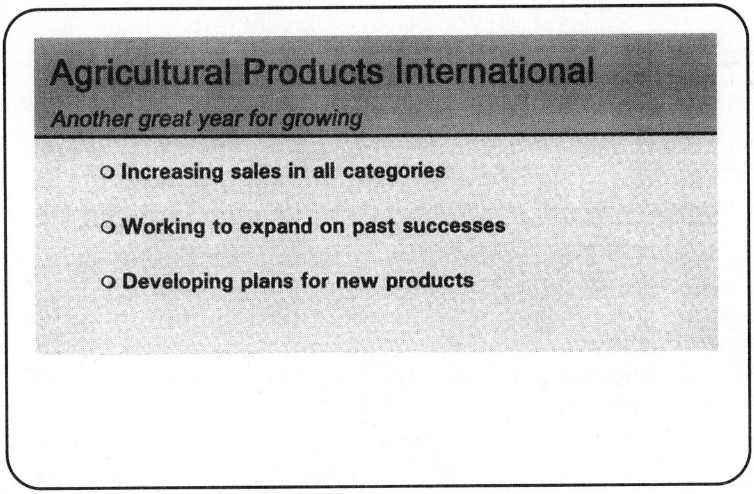

Agricultural Products International
Another great year for growing

   o Increasing sales in all categories

   o Working to expand on past successes

   o Developing plans for new products

FIG. 12.14

Using color to organize the slide layout.

Conveying Information with Selected Colors

Because many colors have common connotations, you can use color to convey meaning in a presentation. In business, for example, the color red represents a monetary loss or negative number, and black represents a profit or positive number.

Figure 12.15 shows a slide that could easily contain color. If the third bullet of the slide in figure 12.15 were red, for example, the viewer would immediately know that excessive expenses would result in a loss for the company.

Agricultural Products International
Review last year's performance

- Revenues continue to increase

- Expenses still hard to control

- Loss in Q3 a great concern!

Red also can suggest danger. Blue, generally considered a peaceful and even soothing color, can imply tranquility or coolness. Green—the color of U.S. currency and the stoplight color for GO—often implies profit or advancement. Yellow often means caution, a message that also comes from traffic lights and road signs.

Selecting Colors for Black-and-White Printing

With most printers, 1-2-3 prints different colors in different shades of gray. However, you can also directly select shades of gray from the

Styles Lines & Colors command. The color drop-down box on this dialog includes gray shades on the far right edge of the box.

Selecting Colors for Background, Text, and Graphics

With 1-2-3, you can select the color of the cell background and the cell contents. This feature enables you to emphasize text or areas of the presentation file. Use the Style Lines & Color command or the Lines & Color SmartIcon to set the background color and shading of the cells. Use the Style Font & Attributes command or the Font & Attributes SmartIcon to set the color of text.

> Set the background color before setting the text color. The Font & Attributes dialog box provides a preview of the text color against the current cell background.
>
> **T I P**

Using Color To Guide the Audience

Most presentations start with an agenda. You can tie a presentation together by repeating the agenda slide before switching to the next topic. This method is more effective if you also highlight the topic that follows. One way to highlight the topic is to use color. Figure 12.16 shows the slide you might choose to introduce the second topic (*Define plan for upcoming growing season*). In this example, the first and third bullets are shaded gray with the gray scale choices in the Font and Attributes dialog box.

For Related Information

◄◄ "Changing Fonts and Attributes," p. 218.

FROM HERE...

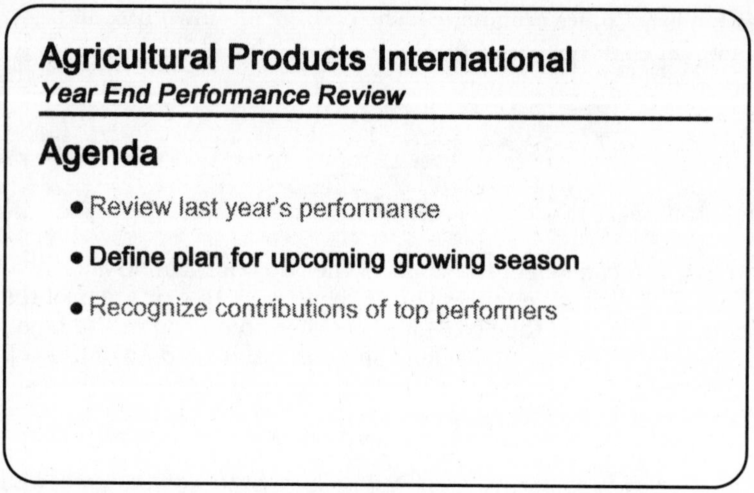

Agricultural Products International
Year End Performance Review

Agenda

- Review last year's performance

- **Define plan for upcoming growing season**

- Recognize contributions of top performers

FIG. 12.16

Introducing the
next topic by
emphasizing a
bullet item.

Emphasizing Text or Graphic Elements

1-2-3 for Windows provides extensive options for formatting worksheets. You can use these capabilities to emphasize text and charts and to make the content of the slide easier to read.

Selecting the Appropriate Font

The beginning of this chapter discusses several guidelines for choosing fonts. Although not hard and fast rules, these guidelines are important to consider as you design a slide page.

You must use point sizes that are readable from a distance and typefaces that work together and balance the images on-screen. Figure 12.17 shows a slide with effective font selections. Figure 12.18, on the other hand, contains too many typefaces and type styles. The viewer is distracted by a multitude of fonts and loses focus on the slide's message.

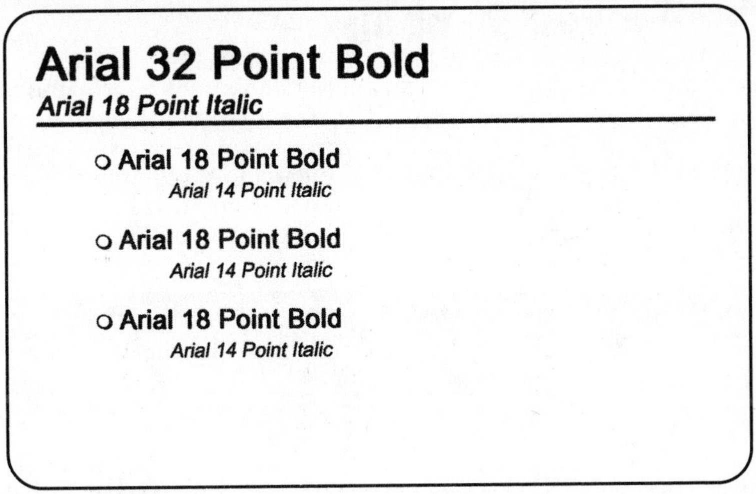

Arial 32 Point Bold
Arial 18 Point Italic

- **Arial 18 Point Bold**
  Arial 14 Point Italic

- **Arial 18 Point Bold**
  Arial 14 Point Italic

- **Arial 18 Point Bold**
  Arial 14 Point Italic

FIG. 12.17

Fonts that work together for clarity of presentation.

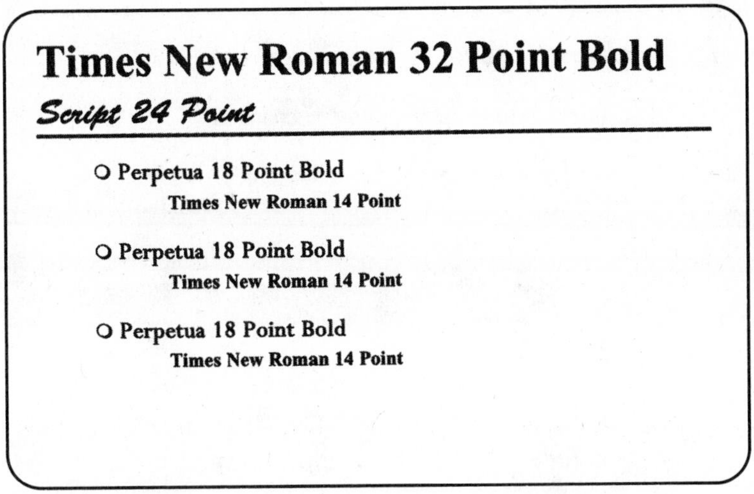

Times New Roman 32 Point Bold
Script 24 Point

- **Perpetua 18 Point Bold**
  Times New Roman 14 Point

- **Perpetua 18 Point Bold**
  Times New Roman 14 Point

- **Perpetua 18 Point Bold**
  Times New Roman 14 Point

FIG. 12.18

Fonts that make the slide hard to read and understand.

For Related Information
◄◄ "Changing Fonts and Attributes," p. 218.

FROM HERE...

Using Special Symbols

You can precede text items with special symbols such as a diamond or arrow. These symbols are available with the Windows Wingdings or Symbols typeface. You can create the arrow symbol, for example, by placing the appropriate character in a cell and formatting the character with the Wingdings font. Choose a symbol font point size that corresponds to the adjacent text. Figure 12.19 shows the bullets on-screen.

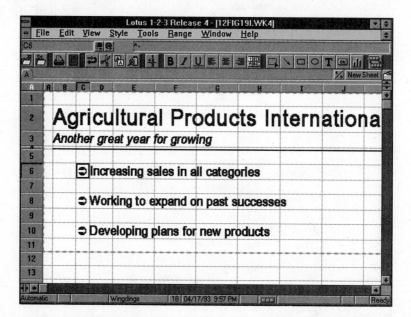

FIG. 12.19

Arrow symbols formatted with the Wingdings font.

T   I   P   The Windows accessory Character Map provides an easy way for adding special characters to Windows applications. To add special characters with the Windows Character Map, follow these steps:

1. Launch the Character Map from the Accessories group.

2. Select the Symbols or Wingdings font from the Font drop-down box. The bottom right corner of the dialog box displays the keystroke for the highlighted item.

3. Highlight the symbol you want (press the arrow keys to move to the symbol or click on the symbol). Then double-click on the symbol, press Enter, choose Select. The character appears in the Characters to Copy text box. Repeat this process until the Characters To Copy box contains all the characters you want.

4. Choose <u>C</u>opy to copy the characters to the Clipboard.

5. Switch back to 1-2-3 and place the cell pointer in the appropriate cell.

6. Set the font to Wingdings and select <u>E</u>dit <u>P</u>aste to add the character(s) to your worksheet. You can also record the keystroke for the character displayed in the character map and then type it into a cell in 1-2-3.

For Related Information

◀◀ "Understanding Microsoft Windows Basics," p. 46.

FROM HERE...

Using Boldface and Italics

Most audiences view slides from a distance. Because plain type tends to fade into the projection screen and become unreadable, use boldface for most text.

You also can use boldface to outline the structure of the slide; for example, you can reinforce the slide's structure by formatting symbols in boldface and leaving explanatory subtext plain. Figures 12.20 and 12.21 show a slide before and after adding boldface to the text.

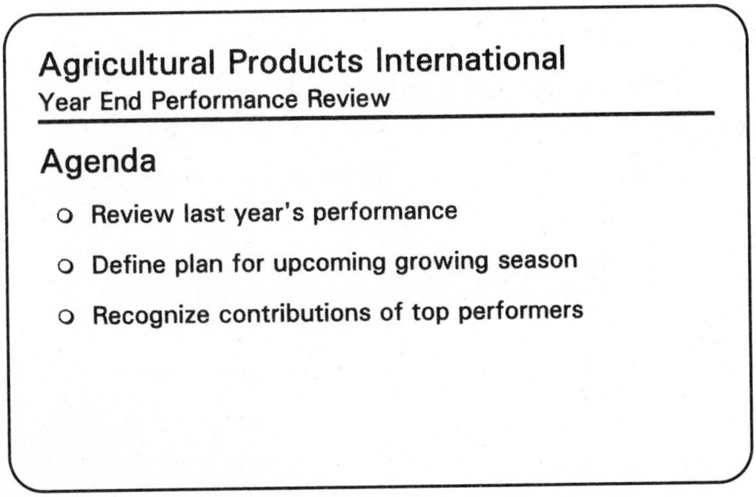

Agricultural Products International
Year End Performance Review

Agenda

○ Review last year's performance

○ Define plan for upcoming growing season

○ Recognize contributions of top performers

FIG. 12.20

An organized slide with no boldface.

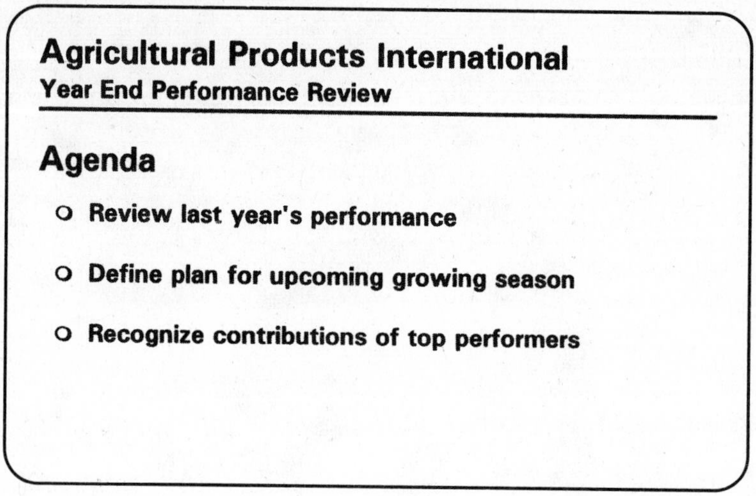

FIG. 12.21

The same slide
with the addition
of boldface.

You can also use italics to separate the parts of the slide and to show
that text has special meaning. Italics is effective for emphasizing direct
or indirect quotations, for example. If you use italic type, use boldfaced
italic because italic text tends to be lighter than plain text and disappears into the page.

Figures 12.22 and 12.23 show different ways of using bold and italics to
add emphasis and clarity to slides.

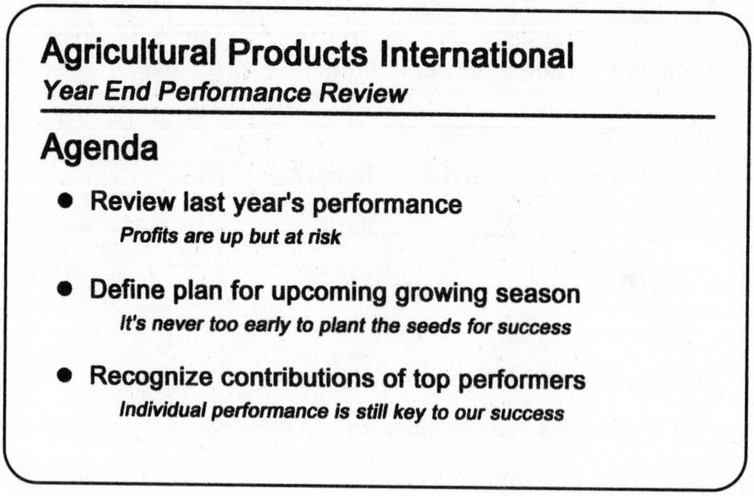

FIG. 12.22

Boldface symbols
with italic
subtext.

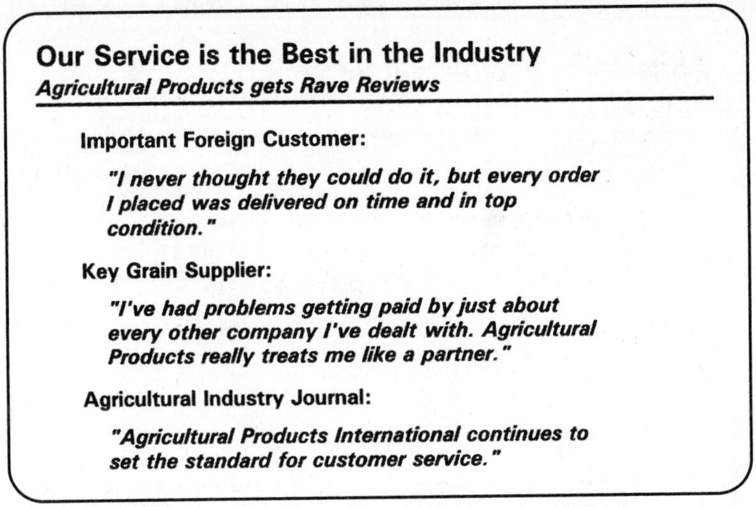

Our Service is the Best in the Industry
Agricultural Products gets Rave Reviews

Important Foreign Customer:

"I never thought they could do it, but every order I placed was delivered on time and in top condition."

Key Grain Supplier:

"I've had problems getting paid by just about every other company I've dealt with. Agricultural Products really treats me like a partner."

Agricultural Industry Journal:

"Agricultural Products International continues to set the standard for customer service."

FIG. 12.23

Using boldface italics for quotations.

Using Lines, Boxes, Frames, and Shading

By using lines, boxes, frames, and shading effectively, you can add structure and emphasis to a slide. By using these elements, you emphasize important text. You can use lines to emphasize slide titles, as described earlier, and to organize the slide.

You can use text boxes and designer frames to emphasize other text on the slide and to organize tables. Figure 12.24 shows a slide with a corporate mission statement set off from the spreadsheet by a designer frame.

The row and column structure of the 1-2-3 worksheet enables you to include tables in presentations. Simple rows and columns of numbers and labels can be very hard to read, but you can add lines, borders, and shading to a table to increase the clarity of numbers and labels. In addition to providing all the capabilities necessary to format a table, 1-2-3 also provides a gallery of 14 predefined table formats. These table formats provide a quick way to create an easy-to-read spreadsheet table. Figure 12.25 shows an example of a table with little formatting; figure 12.26 shows a table formatted with the B&W3 table format, obtained by selecting Style Gallery or clicking on the Style Gallery SmartIcon.

Agricultural Products International
Corporate Mission Statement

Our corporate mission is to provide the
best service at the best price and to
continue to lead the industry into
new and emerging markets.

Regional Performance Summary
Products Sold by Geographic Region

Region	Products			
	Wheat	Corn	Oats	Barley
U.S. North	405.1	408.8	412.4	416.1
U.S. South	405.7	409.4	NA	NA
U.S. Mid West	406.3	410.0	NA	NA
U.S. Far West	406.9	410.6	414.3	417.9
Europe	407.6	411.2	414.9	418.6
New Markets	408.2	411.8	NA	NA
Total	2439.8	2461.8	1241.6	1252.6

The use of lines, boxes, frames, and shading is essential to creating
clear, organized slides. When used judiciously, these elements greatly
enhance the effectiveness of any presentation.

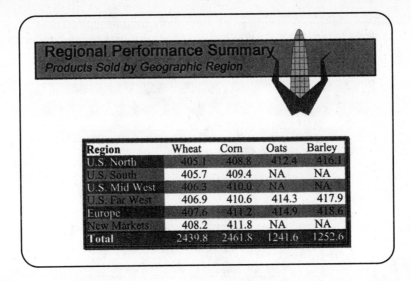

For Related Information

◀◀ "Formatting Cells with Color and Borders," p. 224.

◀◀ "Using the Style Gallery," p. 228.

FROM HERE...

Using the Tools Menu Commands To Add Impact

Graphic images can make slide presentations come alive. The Tools Chart and Draw commands provide a vast array of capabilities for adding 1-2-3 charts, clip art, and freehand drawings to presentations. Charts and graphics images can make slides easier to understand by presenting the information in pictures, relating the text to common images, or providing visually interesting breaks in the presentation.

Adding 1-2-3 Charts

Tables of data are seldom effective in slide presentations and, in most cases, should be supplemented or replaced by charts. To create an effective slide that presents worksheet data, include important conclusions drawn from the data and a chart that supports these conclusions. Figure 12.27 shows such a slide.

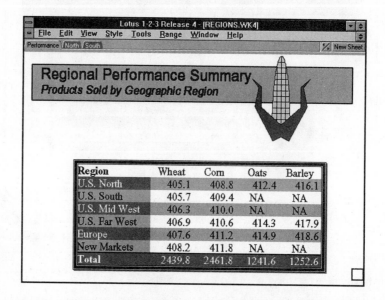

FIG. 12.27

Worksheet data
with charts
presented in a
slide.

You also can use 1-2-3 charts as the basis for diagrams and other graphic images. Figure 12.28, for example, shows the expansion of Agricultural Products' product line. The bars do not represent specific quantities, but additional products. You can draw this chart with rectangles with the Tools Draw commands. However, you also can draw the chart easily by placing equal values in a range of 1-2-3 worksheet cells. Then use this range as your chart range.

Adding Graphic Drawings to the Worksheet

You can add graphics drawings anywhere on the 1-2-3 for Windows worksheet area. Use the Tools Draw commands or the drawing SmartIcons to draw on the worksheet. You can use the draw layer to explain difficult concepts or to illustrate key points presented on the slide. Figure 12.29 shows an example of an organizational chart created by adding rectangles to the draw layer.

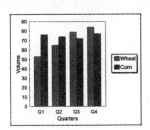

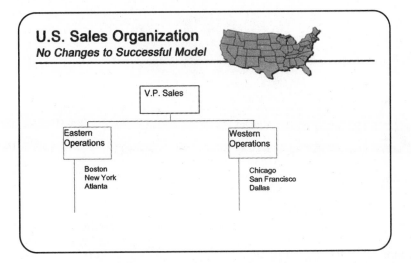

FIG. 12.28

A 1-2-3 chart.

FIG. 12.29

An organiza-
tional chart
drawn on the
worksheet draw
layer.

For Related Information

◄◄ "Creating a Chart," p. 537.

◄◄ "Using Graphics," p. 588.

FROM HERE...

Using Clip Art

Virtually any image seems to be available as clip art in the Windows Metafile format. Clip art adds interest to the slide presentation and can often communicate key concepts. After you add clip art to the worksheet, you can use the Tools Draw commands to adapt the image to the specific presentation. Figure 12.30 illustrates clip art used on slides.

FIG. 12.30

Adding clip art to a presentation.

Creating Effective Background Presentations

A distinctive background color for a slide can greatly enhance the slide's readability. You can change the default spreadsheet background colors through the Windows Control Panel. Use the following steps to change the background color:

1. Launch the Control Panel from the Main Windows applications group.

2. Double-click on the Color icon, and then click on the Color Palette button.

3. Select Window Background from the Screen Element drop down box and choose the desired background color.

4. Click on the OK button to accept the change and make this color the default window background.

Changing the background in this way has no effect on the printing of the slides.

You also can use the Style Worksheet Defaults command to select a background color for each individual worksheet page. With this method, you can have a different color for each slide. Using a different color for each slide, however, can become distracting during the presentation; yet if you use different colors judiciously, you can create a striking impression. Unlike changing the default background color, the shaded background prints with the slide. When you select the color for a background, check that the text and graphic colors offer enough contrast to be readable from a distance. Follow these steps to change the color of a worksheet:

1. Choose the Style Worksheet Defaults command.

2. Click on the Cell background Color drop down box in the colors section of the dialog box. Select a color for the background of this worksheet.

3. Click OK. Repeat these steps to change the background colors of other sheets.

Using Designer Frames for Slide Borders

You can frame a slide on a page or a printout with a border. To frame a slide with a border use the Style Lines & Color command or the Lines & Color SmartIcon to display the Lines & Color dialog box. Choose Designer Frame to display the pop-up list of frame choices. You can choose from 16 different frame styles. You can also make the frame any color with the Frame Color control. Figure 12.31 shows a designer frame used as a page border.

For Related Information

◄◄ "Formatting Cells with Color and Borders," p. 224.

FROM HERE...

Printing Slides from 1-2-3

Most presentations ultimately are printed for distribution or duplication onto overhead transparencies. You can use the 1-2-3 print commands to print slides created on-screen.

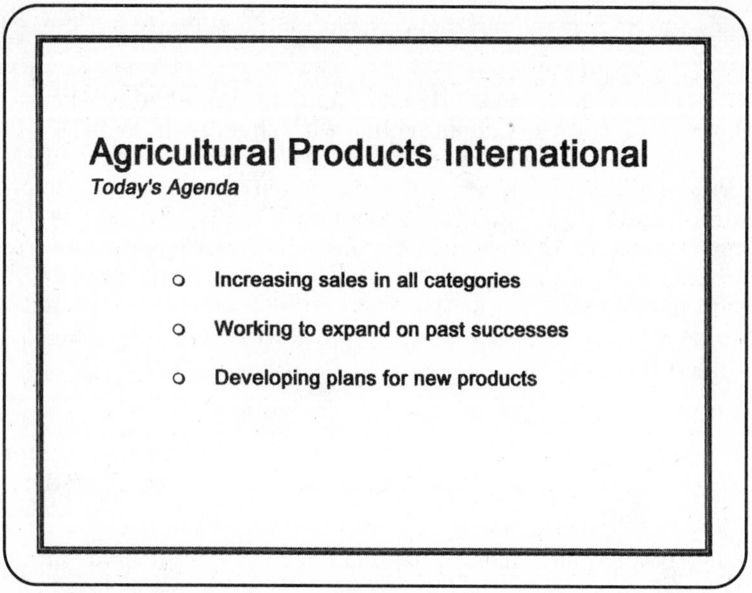

Agricultural Products International
Today's Agenda

○   **Increasing sales in all categories**

○   **Working to expand on past successes**

○   **Developing plans for new products**

FIG. 12.31

A slide framed
by a designer
frame.

 You usually design slides to fit a landscape orientation. If you have a printer capable of printing landscape, use the File Page Setup command or the Page Setup SmartIcon to select the correct orientation.

 You can use the Style Page Break command or the Page Break SmartIcons to insert page breaks between slides. Selecting Row inserts a horizontal page break in the worksheet. Place this break at the bottom of each slide. The page breaks appear on-screen.

If you have arranged your slides on multiple worksheets, you can place a page break at the bottom of each page with the following steps.

1. Place the cell pointer in the appropriate row on the first worksheet.

2. Press and hold the Shift key and then click on the last worksheet tab for the presentation.

3. Choose Style Page Break to set the page breaks in the selected range.

 A slide formatted to fit the screen does not fill a printed page. You can enlarge the slide, however, by using the File Page Setup command or the Page Setup SmartIcon. Select Size and choose Manually Scale from the drop-down box. A ratio of 125 percent enlarges the image to fit an 8 1/2-by-11-inch page. Before printing, use Print Preview to verify that the slides fit correctly on the page.

If the slides look fine in print preview, simply click on the Print SmartIcon to print the screen.	**T I P**

For Related Information

◄◄ "Using Multiple Worksheets," p. 103.

FROM HERE...

Using Macros for Computer Presentations

Although many users print presentations created in 1-2-3, more and more users are delivering presentations directly from the computer. Delivering presentations directly from the computer enables you to use color and to create a "live" presentation environment.

1-2-3 macros can make computer slide shows easier to present and more interesting to view. With macros, for example, you can move automatically from slide to slide or simulate screen animation. You can use the macros described in the following sections to automate and animate your 1-2-3 slide shows.

Using Macro Buttons for Slide Changes

1-2-3 for Windows enables you to place macro buttons in the worksheet. These buttons can provide an easy way to change between slide pages. Follow these steps to create a button:

1. Select <u>T</u>ools <u>D</u>raw <u>B</u>utton or click on the Macro Button SmartIcon and specify the desired button location. (The lower right of the screen is usually the best place for the button.)

2. The Assign to Button dialog box appears. Click on the <u>E</u>nter Macro Here box and type the macro command **{NEXTSHEET}** into the text box.

3. Click on the <u>B</u>utton text box and type **NEXT** or some other appropriate text to describe the action (see fig 12.32).

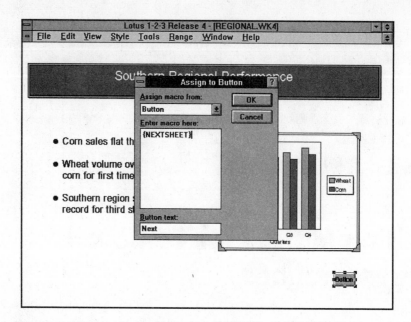

FIG. 12.32

Creating a macro
button to move
between slides.

Should you need to reverse through the slides, create another button
to move to the previous sheet. Follow the steps above, but input the
macro command **{PREVSHEET}** and appropriate text in the button
name text field. Figure 12.33 shows a slide with buttons you use to
move to the next or the previous worksheets.

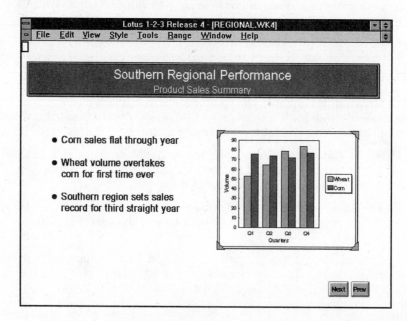

FIG. 12.33

Macro buttons
that move
between slides.

> You can use the Edit Copy and Edit Paste commands to copy these buttons to other sheets. Using the right mouse button, click on the button to select it. With the button selected, choose Edit Copy. Then move the cell pointer to the next worksheet and select Edit Paste.
>
> **T I P**

For Related Information

▶▶ "Adding Macro Buttons to a Worksheet," p. 763.

FROM HERE...

A Macro for Changing Slides with the Enter Key

The simplest screen show macro pauses until you press the Enter key and then uses the GOTO macro command to move to the next slide. To specify the worksheet letter as the range to go to, you type the worksheet letter followed by a colon for each slide. You can also specify the tab name followed by a colon (:). Figure 12.34 shows the macro in the worksheet.

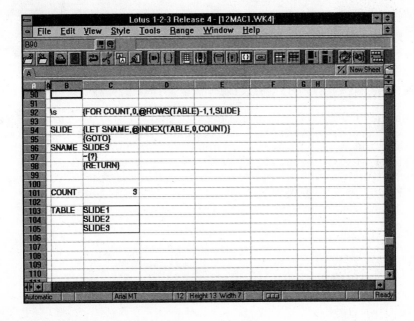

FIG. 12.34

A slide show macro.

Table 12.1 contains the macro text from the worksheet. The blank lines are intentional and must be included in the worksheet.

Table 12.1

Slide Show Macro Range Name	Macro Statement
\s	{FOR COUNT,0@ROWS(TABLE)-1,1,SLIDE}
SLIDE	{LET SNAME,@INDEX(TABLE,0,COUNT)}
	{GOTO}
SNAME	~{?}
	{RETURN}

The \s macro works for any number of slides. Build the table of slide names and use Range Name command or the Create/Delete Range Name SmartIcon to name the range TABLE.

You can use the Edit Copy and Edit Paste commands (or the Copy and Paste SmartIcons) to arrange the slides in the range TABLE without having to retype all the names.

FROM HERE...

For Related Information

▶▶ "Planning, Invoking, and Debugging Macro Command Programs," p. 778.

A Macro for Timing the Slide Changes

This macro enhances the preceding slide show macro by establishing a predetermined delay before the screen moves to the next slide. In this macro, the number of seconds of delay is entered in the column to the right of the slide name (see fig. 12.35). The range name TABLE must include both columns (columns F and G, in this example). If you press any key, the show moves to the next slide before the time elapses.

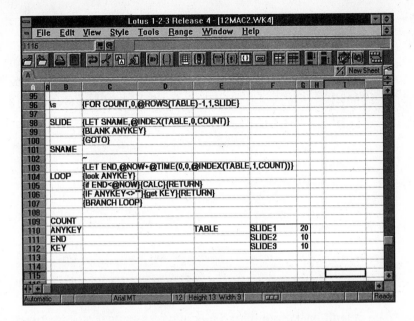

FIG. 12.35

An automatic
screen show
macro.

Table 12.2 shows the text of the timed macro screen show. Refer to
the screen shot for the layout of other named ranges. The blank rows
represent blank rows in the spreadsheet. Refer to the figure for other
essential ranges and range names.

Table 12.2 Automatic Screen Show Macro

Range Name	Macro Statement
\s	`{FOR COUNT,0,@ROWS(TABLE)-1,1,SLIDE}`

SLIDE	`{LET SNAME,@INDEX(TABLE,0,COUNT)}`
	`{BLANK ANYKEY}`
	`{GOTO}`

SNAME	`{LET END,@NOW+@TIME(0,0,@INDEX(TABLE,1,COUNT))}`

LOOP	`{LOOK ANYKEY}`
	`{IF END<@NOW}{CALC}{RETURN}`
	`{IF ANYKEY<>""}{GET KEY}{RETURN}`
	`{BRANCH LOOP}`

Questions & Answers

This chapter describes how you can use 1-2-3 Release 4 for Windows to develop business presentations. If you have questions concerning particular situations that are not addressed in the examples given, look through this section.

Q: I want almost all my presentation slides to have the same format. Do I have to apply the formats to every worksheet page individually?

A: No. Use Style Worksheet Defaults and select the Group Mode check box in the dialog box. Apply the formats to worksheet A to create the first slide. Then click on the New Sheet button to add a worksheet for each slide. Each of these slides will have the same formats as the first. Now, disable group mode by choosing Style Worksheet Defaults and unchecking the Group Mode check box.

Q: I added a clip art image to my worksheet but I want the cells under the Windows metafile to show through. How do I do this?

A: The default background for a metafile is opaque. You can choose to allow cell information to display through the clip art image. Select the clip art image, and then press the right mouse button and choose the Lines & Color command. Click on the Pattern option to display the Patterns drop down box. Choose the pattern T (for transparent) and click on the OK button.

Q: I've added some drawing objects to my slide, but when I insert columns or change widths, my drawings move around. Can I have them stay in the same place on-screen?

A: Yes. By default, the top left and lower right corners of objects are fastened to the cells behind it. However, you can fasten only the upper left of the object. Choose Edit Arrange Fasten to Cells. Check the Top Left Cell Only button to fasten the object only on the upper left.

Q: I've used a few standard text formats for my first slide. Is there an easy way to apply these to other slides in my presentation?

A: Yes. You can create named styles that contain all the style information you need. Place the cell pointer in the cell from which you want to define the named style. Choose Style Named Style, type a Style Name, and choose Define. You can now use the style with the Style Named Style command or by clicking on the style selector on the status bar.

Q: I want to change the indents on all my slides. Do I have to do this on every slide individually?

A: No. If you used the guidelines described in this chapter, you have indented your bullets by using varying column widths. You can change the column width on every slide by selecting a three-dimensional range of columns. The easiest way to do this is to place the cell pointer in the appropriate column in the first worksheet. Hold down the Shift key and click on the worksheet tab for the last worksheet you want to format. You have selected that column in every worksheet. Now choose Style Column Width, select the new column width, and click on the OK button.

Q: I want to show a general growth trend in a chart, but I don't have any real data. Do I have to draw the entire chart with the Draw tools?

A: You can draw the chart if you'd like, but you may find it easier to create dummy data from which to draw the chart. Type a starting value such as 10 in a cell. If you want 10 percent growth, type into the cell next to it a formula to multiply the first cell by 1.1. Copy the formula to the right for as many cells as you need for your chart. Then, create a chart from this range.

Q: I've been trying to put borders on my slides with the designer frames, but they turn out looking really dark and uninteresting. What am I doing wrong?

A: You are probably using black as the color for the frame. Click on the Frame Color drop down and select a gray or some other lighter color to give more contrast to your frame.

Summary

This chapter shows many ways that you can use 1-2-3 Release 4 for Windows as a powerful presentation tool. By combining 1-2-3's formatting and presentation capabilities with the three-dimensional worksheets, you can produce impressive presentations.

You learned how to combine these capabilities with 1-2-3's charting and drawing capabilities to produce high-quality, high-impact presentations. You learned how to print these presentations with color or black-and-white printers.

By using computer projection equipment, you learned how to turn 1-2-3 into a screen show system and present your slides directly from the worksheet. Multiple-page slide shows developed in the 1-2-3 worksheet can be presented on-screen one page at a time or automated with macros for easier presentation.

In the next chapter, you learn how to use 1-2-3's database capabilities.

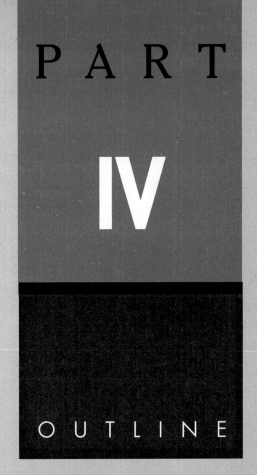

PART

IV

Managing Databases

OUTLINE

Creating Databases

I n addition to its capability to generate electronic spreadsheets and business charts, 1-2-3 for Windows has a third capability: data management. These three elements make 1-2-3 for Windows a powerful software package.

1-2-3 for Windows' database feature is fast, easy to access, and easy to use. 1-2-3 for Windows also provides many advanced database features, including some of the relational enhancements and larger databases of products such as dBASE.

The 1-2-3 for Windows database features are easy to use because they are integrated with the worksheet and chart functions. The commands you use to add, modify, and delete items in a database are the same ones you already have used to manipulate cells or groups of cells in a worksheet. Creating charts from ranges in a database is as easy as creating them in a worksheet.

This chapter covers the following topics:

■ The advantages and limitations of 1-2-3 for Windows' database

■ Creating, modifying, and maintaining data records

■ Sorting, locating, extracting, and editing data entries

■ Filling ranges with sets of values

Chapter 14 builds on the basic database commands introduced in this chapter and covers more advanced data-management techniques, including using external databases, importing text file data, and advanced data analysis. The techniques covered include crosstabs, frequency distributions, data regression, and matrix inversion and multiplication.

Defining a Database

A *database* is a collection of related information—data organized so that you can list, sort, or search it. The list of data may contain any kind of information, from addresses to tax-deductible expenditures. Telephone books, personal address books, and checkbooks are common examples of databases.

In 1-2-3 for Windows, the word *database* means a range of cells that spans at least one column and more than one row. Because a database actually is a list, the manner in which database data is organized sets it apart from data in ordinary cells. Just as a list must be organized to be useful, a database must be organized to permit access to the information that it contains.

Databases generally are organized in three ways:

■ *A single database contained in a single worksheet*. This organization method is used in most of the examples in this chapter, as well as in most real-world applications.

■ *Multiple databases in a single worksheet*. Each database occupies a different portion of the worksheet.

■ *Multiple databases in two or more worksheet levels*. Be aware, however, that a single database table cannot span different worksheet levels. As you learn in Chapter 14, "Understanding Advanced Data Management," you can relate databases that are on different worksheet levels and thus produce a more efficient overall database structure.

Remember that a 1-2-3 for Windows database is similar to any other group of cells. This knowledge may help you as you learn about the different Tools Database commands covered in this chapter. In many instances, you can use these database commands in what you may consider to be nondatabase applications.

Databases are made up of fields and records. A *field*, or single data item, is the smallest unit in a database. To develop a database of companies with which you do business, for example, you can include the following fields for each company:

Name
Address
City
State
ZIP code
Phone number

A *record* is a set of associated fields—that is, the accumulation of all data about one company forms one record. The six fields in the preceding paragraph represent one record on one company.

In 1-2-3 for Windows, a field is a single cell, and a record is a row of cells within a database.

A database must be set up so that you can access the information it contains. Retrieval of information usually involves key fields. A database *key field* is any field on which you base a list, sort, or search operation. For example, you can use ZIP as a key field to sort the data in the company database and to assign contact representatives to specific geographic areas.

Working with a 1-2-3 for Windows Database

A 1-2-3 for Windows database resides in the worksheet's row-and-column format. Figure 13.1 shows the general organization of a 1-2-3 for Windows database. Labels, or *field names*, that describe the data items appear as column headings in row 1. Information about each specific data item (field) is entered in a cell in the appropriate column. In figure 13.1, cell B5 represents data (*3500 Bacon Ct.*) for the second field (ADDRESS) in the database's fourth record, which is in row 5.

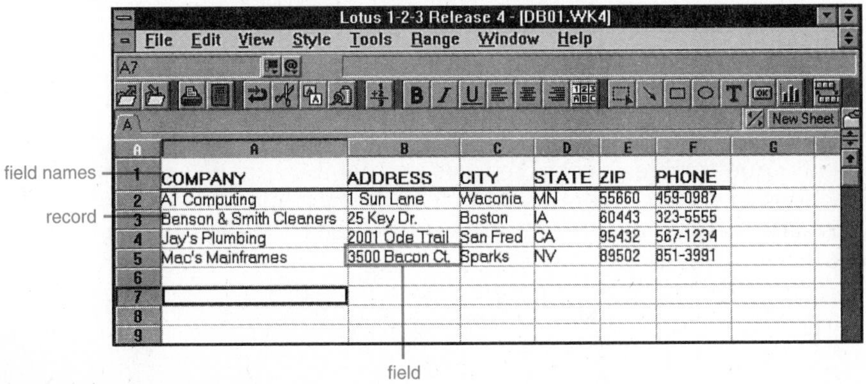

FIG. 13.1

Organization of a 1-2-3 for Windows database.

Theoretically, the maximum number of records you can have in a 1-2-3 for Windows database corresponds to the maximum number of rows in the worksheet (8,192 rows, minus 1 row for the field names). Realistically, however, the number of records in a specific database is limited by the amount of available memory: internal memory (RAM) plus disk storage for virtual memory.

When you estimate the maximum database size for your computer equipment, be sure to include enough blank rows to accommodate the maximum output you expect from extract operations. You also may be able to split a large 1-2-3 for Windows database into separate database tables on different worksheet levels if all the data does not have to be sorted or searched as a unit. You may, for example, be able to separate a telephone-list database by name (A through M in one file; N through Z in another) or area code.

> **NOTE** The size limits for 1-2-3 for Windows databases do not apply to external database files accessed with the 1-2-3 for Windows DataLens drivers (discussed in Chapter 14). External database files can hold any number of records and are limited only by available disk space.

You access the Tools Database and the Query menu commands from the 1-2-3 for Windows main menu (the Query menu appears in place of the Range menu when a *query table*—a workspace where you can manipulate database information—is selected). Because all the options in the main menu work in databases as they do in worksheets, the power of 1-2-3 for Windows is at your fingertips.

You also can use 1-2-3 for Windows' file-translation capabilities or the Tools Database Connect to External command (covered in Chapter 14) to access database files created with dBASE and with the @BASE add-in for earlier versions of 1-2-3 and for Symphony, IBM Database Manager, Informix, Paradox, and SQL Server. This feature enables you to take advantage of 1-2-3 for Windows' data and chart commands.

Figure 13.2 shows the options in the Tools Database menu. Figure 13.3 shows the options in the Query menu.

You use both the Tools Database and Query menu commands as you work with 1-2-3 for Windows databases. The Tools Database commands create new query tables, access records in a database, and control connections to external database files. The Query commands enable you to manipulate data in query tables and to update information in the database.

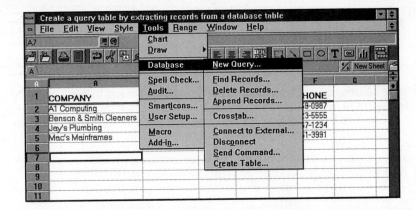

FIG. 13.2

The Tools
Database menu.

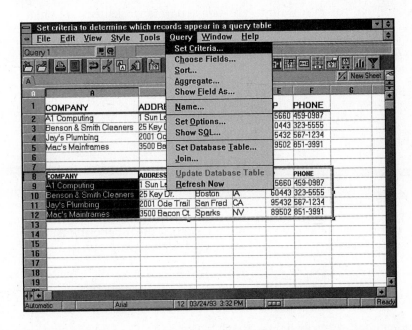

FIG. 13.3

The Query menu.

For Related Information

▶▶ "Working with External Databases," p. 682.

FROM HERE...

Creating a Database

You can create a database as a new worksheet file or as part of an existing file. If you decide to build a database in an existing worksheet, choose an area of the worksheet that you do not need for any other purpose. This area should be large enough to accommodate the number of records that you plan to enter during the current session and in the future.

A better idea, however, is to add another worksheet to the current file so that the database and the existing worksheet don't interfere with each other. To add another worksheet for the new database, click the New Sheet button or use the Edit Insert Sheet command.

In addition, you may want to create a separate worksheet to hold a query table so that the query table doesn't overwrite existing data. You may want to add names to the worksheet tabs to make it easy to remember which worksheet holds the database and which holds the query table.

T I P   Take advantage of 1-2-3 for Windows' 3-D capabilities by placing the different database elements in their own worksheets.

After you decide which area of the worksheet to use, you create a database by specifying field names across a row and entering data in cells, as you would for any other 1-2-3 for Windows application. The mechanics of entering database contents are simple; the most critical step in creating a useful database is choosing the fields properly.

Planning Your Database

In locating and retrieving database information, 1-2-3 for Windows relies on field names. You may want to write down the output you expect from the database before you create the fields; writing this information down helps you design a more useful database. You also need to consider whether any existing documents (such as order forms or customer information cards) contain information that you can use in your database (for example, names, addresses, and phone numbers).

When you are ready to set up the database, you must assign each field a name, a column width, and a data type.

A common error in setting up databases is choosing field names (and entering data) without thinking about the output you want from that field. Suppose that you established ORDERDATE as a field name to describe the last date on which a customer placed an order and then entered dates as labels, in the general form MMM-DD-YYYY (for example, JAN-01-1999). Although you can search for an ORDERDATE that matches a specific date, you cannot perform a math-based search for all ORDERDATEs within a specified period or before a certain date.

To get maximum flexibility from 1-2-3 for Windows' database commands, you should enter dates in one of the available date formats (see Chapter 5, "Changing the Format and Appearance of Data"). In addition, you probably will find it helpful to format cells with a date format (such as MM/DD/YY) before you enter dates so that 1-2-3 for Windows recognizes the entries as dates rather than numeric formulas.

You then need to choose the level of detail for each item of information, select the appropriate column width, and determine whether you will enter data as a number or a label. If you want to be able to sort by area code all records containing telephone numbers, for example, you should enter telephone numbers as two separate fields: Area Code (XXX) and Number XXX-XXXX. Because you may not want to perform math functions on telephone numbers, you can enter those numbers as labels. You probably will find it helpful to format the cells with Label format so that you do not have to type a label prefix before entering labels that start with numbers.

> **T I P**
>
> If you enter database contents from a standard source document, you can increase the speed of data entry by setting up the field names in the order in which the data items appear in the source document. Be sure to plan the database carefully before you establish field names and enter data.

Entering Data

After you plan the database, you can build it. To understand how the process works, create a Company database as a new database in a blank worksheet (in Ready mode). Enter the field names across a single row (A:A1..A:F1, as shown in fig. 13.1).

The field names must be labels, even if they are numeric labels ('1, '2, and so on). All field names must be in a single row, and field names must be unique. Do not leave any blank columns in the database. Use the Style Alignment options to adjust the appearance if the database appears to be too crowded.

After you enter field names, you can add records to the database. To enter the first record, move the cursor to the row directly below the field-name row and then enter the data across the row. To enter the first record shown in figure 13.1, for example, type the following entries in the cells shown:

A:A2: **A1 Computing**
A:B2: **'1 Sun Lane**
A:C2: **Waconia**
A:D2: **MN**
A:E2: **'55660**
A:F2: **'459-0987**

Notice that you enter the contents of the ADDRESS, PHONE, and ZIP fields by typing an apostrophe (') label character. An easier method, however, is simply formatting these fields with Label format.

The sample Company database is used periodically throughout this chapter to demonstrate the effects of various database commands. In this chapter, the fields are shown in a single screen. In real-life applications, however, you track many more data items. You can maintain 256 fields (the number of columns available) in a single 1-2-3 for Windows database.

For Related Information

◀◀ "Entering Data into the Worksheet," p. 113.

FROM HERE...

Realistically, however, the number of records in a specific database is limited by the amount of available memory: internal memory (RAM) plus disk storage for virtual memory.

Modifying a Database

After you collect the data for the database and decide which field types, widths, and formats to use, creating a database is easy. 1-2-3 for Windows also makes maintaining the accuracy of the database contents easy.

To add and delete records in a database, you use the same commands that you use to insert and delete rows. Because records correspond to rows, you can insert a record with the Edit Insert Row command or the Insert Row SmartIcon. You then can fill in the various fields in the rows with the appropriate data.

Figure 13.4 shows a row for a new record inserted into the middle of a database. Instead of inserting a record in the middle of a database, however, you probably will add new records to the end of the database and then use 1-2-3 for Windows' sorting capabilities to rearrange the order of the records.

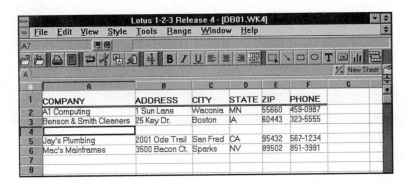

FIG. 13.4

A row inserted into a database.

To delete records, select the rows that you want to delete and then choose the Edit Delete Row command or click the Delete Row SmartIcon.

If Tools User Setup Undo is not selected, be extremely careful when you specify the records to be deleted. Edit Undo (Ctrl+Z) or the Undo SmartIcon can reverse an Edit Delete Row command if it was the last command executed. If you want to remove only inactive records, consider first using the Tools Database New Query command to store the extracted inactive records in a separate query table. (See "Deleting Specified Records" later in this chapter for information on using Tools Database Delete Records to remove database records.)

You modify fields in a database the same way that you modify the contents of cells. As you learned in Chapter 3, you change cell contents either by retyping the cell entry or by pressing the F2 (Edit) key and then editing the entry.

To add a new field to a database, place the cell pointer anywhere in the column to the right of the newly inserted column and then issue the Edit Insert Column command or click the Insert Column SmartIcon. You then can fill the field with the appropriate values for each record. To insert an AREA field between the ZIP and PHONE fields, for example, position the cell pointer on any cell in the PHONE column, issue the Edit Insert Column command, and then type the new field name (**AREA**) in cell A:F1 (see fig. 13.5).

FIG. 13.5

A column inserted for a new database field.

	A	B	C	D	E	F	G
1	COMPANY	ADDRESS	CITY	STATE	ZIP	AREA	PHONE
2	A1 Computing	1 Sun Lane	Waconia	MN	55660		459-0987
3	Benson & Smith Cleaners	25 Key Dr.	Boston	IA	60443		323-5555
4	Jay's Plumbing	2001 Ode Trail	San Fred	CA	95432		567-1234
5	Mac's Mainframes	3500 Bacon Ct.	Sparks	NV	89502		851-3991
6							
7							

Lotus 1-2-3 Release 4 - [DB02.WK4]
File Edit View Style Tools Range Window Help
F1   'AREA

To delete a field, position the cell pointer anywhere in the column that you want to remove and then choose the Edit Delete Column command.

All other commands—such as those for moving cells, formatting cells, and displaying the contents of worksheets—work the same in both database and worksheet applications.

Adding Records to a Database

Instead of inserting a new row into a database, you simply can add a new record after the last row in the database. Then, if you have named the database range, you can use the Range Name command to expand the database range name to include the new record.

Adding a record in a new row below the database, however, has certain disadvantages. If you forget to adjust the database range name, any commands or formulas that refer to the database range will not include the new records. Also, because you cannot simply add a row to an external database file, this method does not work with external databases.

The best method of adding database records works with databases in worksheet ranges and with external databases. This method involves the Tools Database Append Records command. To add a record to the database, follow these steps:

1. If you have not already assigned a range name to the database, use the Range Name command to name the database range (cells A:A1..G5 in fig. 13.5). For this exercise, use the range name **COMPANY_DB**. Although this step is optional, you will find that it makes using the database easier.

2. Double-click the worksheet tab and enter the name **Database**. This step, too, is optional, but again, it makes using the database easier.

3. Click the New Sheet button (or use the Edit Insert Sheet command) to add a new worksheet for the data-entry form. Double-click the worksheet tab and name this new worksheet **Entry Form**.

4. Copy the field names from Database:A1..G1 to Entry Form:A1.

5. Move the cell pointer to Entry Form:A2 and add the new record.

6. Make the following entries in the indicated cells:

   A2: **Ralph's Bar**
   B2: **'10 Lilac**
   C2: **Carmel**
   D2: **CA**
   E2: **'95309**
   G2: **'369-2468**

7. When you finish entering the record, highlight the entry form, A1..G2.

8. Choose Tools Database Append Records to display the Append Records dialog box (see fig. 13.6).

9. In the To Database Table text box, enter the database range name, **COMPANY_DB**. You can type the name or address, point to the database range, or press F3 (Name) to display a list of named ranges.

10. Click OK or press Enter to add the record to the database (see fig. 13.7). 1-2-3 for Windows automatically adjusts the database range name to include the new record.

For Related Information

◀◀ "Inserting Cells, Rows, Columns, and Worksheets," p. 160.

FROM HERE...

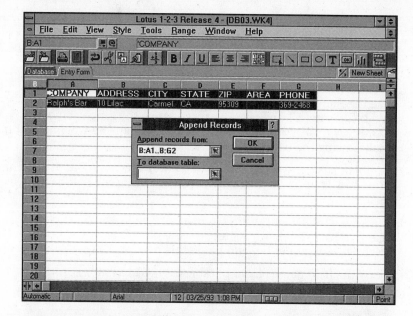

FIG. 13.6

The Append
Records dialog
box.

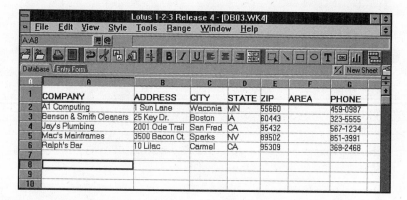

FIG. 13.7

The Tools
Database
Append Records
command adds
new records to a
database.

Using a Query Table

Although you can work with a 1-2-3 for Windows database the way you
work with any other range, 1-2-3 for Windows provides a much easier
method of working with databases: query tables. *Query tables* are special workspaces in a worksheet that simplify selecting, sorting, and
updating database records. Query tables work with any database that
1-2-3 for Windows can use—a database in a worksheet, or a database
contained in external files accessed through DataLens drivers (see
Chapter 14).

Creating a Query Table

Because query tables overwrite existing worksheet data, you should create a new worksheet for each query table you use. Add a new worksheet (and name it **Query Table**) before you create the query table.

To create a new query table, follow these steps:

1. Highlight the database range—in this case, A1..G6—and then choose <u>T</u>ools Data<u>b</u>ase <u>N</u>ew Query or click the Query Table SmartIcon. The New Query dialog box appears (see fig. 13.8).

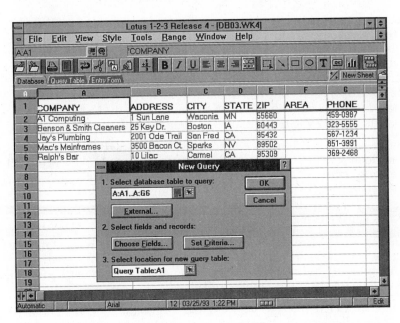

FIG. 13.8

The New Query dialog box.

2. In the Select Location for New <u>Q</u>uery Table box, select a location for the query table. For this example, select cell Query Table:A1.

 NOTE If there are more records than will fit in the query table, you can resize the query table to display more data. Click the Show All Query Table Records SmartIcon, or click the query table border and drag the handles to resize the query table.

3. Choose OK to confirm your dialog-box choices and create the query table (see fig. 13.9).

Lotus 1-2-3 Release 4 - [DB03.WK4]

	COMPANY	ADDRESS	CITY	STATE	ZIP	AREA	PHONE	
2	A1 Computing	1 Sun Lane	Waconia	MN	55660		459-0987	
3	Benson & Smith Cleaners	25 Key Dr.	Boston	IA	60443		323-5555	
4	Jay's Plumbing	2001 Ode Trail	San Fred	CA	95432		567-1234	
5	Mac's Mainframes	3500 Bacon Ct.	Sparks	NV	89502		851-3991	
6	Ralph's Bar	10 Lilac	Carmel	CA	95309		369-2468	
7								
8								

FIG. 13.9

The query table.

Using a query table offers several advantages compared with working directly with the records in a worksheet database range. You can decide whether to view all or only some of the fields; you can choose selected groups of records to include in the query table; you easily can perform summary calculations on selected records; and you can sort the records by selecting field names. In this case, however, the new query table will contain the same set of fields as the database, and the records initially will be displayed in their existing order.

Notice in figure 13.9 that both the 1-2-3 for Windows menu bar and the SmartIcon set change when a query table is selected (click a cell within the query table to select the table). The Range menu is replaced by the Query menu (refer to fig. 13.3), and several standard SmartIcons are replaced by SmartIcons that pertain specifically to query tables. These changes make using a query table even easier.

You can display a subset of the database fields in the query table by choosing Choose Fields in the New Query dialog box. Alternatively, you can issue the Query Choose Fields command or click the Choose Fields SmartIcon when a query table is displayed.

You also can use the Query Show Field As command or the Rename Field SmartIcon to change the name of a field in the query table. Finally, you can use Query Name to change the default name applied to a query table—perhaps for use with a macro command. These commands affect only the appearance of fields in a query table, not the database itself.

Setting Query Table Options

Four options enable you to control the way a query table functions. To access these options, use the Query Set Options command to display the Set Options dialog box (see fig. 13.10).

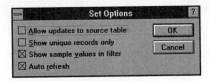

FIG. 13.10

The Set Options
dialog box.

Choose the first option, Allow Updates to Source Table, to tell 1-2-3 for
Windows to update the database after you make changes in the query
table.

Choose the second option, Show Unique Records Only, if you want to
create a set of unique values. If you create a query table that includes
only the ZIP field, for example, you can create one record for each
unique ZIP value. You might find such a list to be helpful for mailing
purposes.

Choose the third option, Show Sample Values in Filter, to make creating
criteria easier. When this option is selected, the Value box in the Set
Criteria dialog box displays a list of each unique value for a selected
field.

The fourth option, Auto Refresh, ensures that when you make changes
in any criteria, sort settings, field names, or aggregate settings, 1-2-3 for
Windows updates your query table. If your database is large, you might
find that database operations are slightly faster when this option is not
selected. If you don't choose the Auto Refresh option, you can use the
Query Refresh Now command or click the Update Query Table
SmartIcon to update the query table as necessary.

Sorting Database Records

1-2-3 for Windows enables you to change the order of records by sorting them according to the contents of the fields. Sorting a database
usually makes the database more useful. Imagine how difficult it would
be to use a database like a telephone directory if the records weren't
sorted by name! Fortunately, sorting a database is quite simple.

Although you can use the Range Sort command to sort the database
range just like any other 1-2-3 for Windows range, this command works
only in a worksheet database, not in an external database. In addition,
you easily can become confused when you use the Range Sort command to sort a database. You might sort the field names into the
records or accidentally destroy the database's integrity by neglecting
to include all the fields.

The Query Sort command solves these problems and offers additional benefits as well. When you use Query Sort, 1-2-3 for Windows displays the sorted records in the query table. You can try several different sort orders without affecting the original database. If you find a sort order that you like, you can apply the new order to the database. If you decide not to apply the changes, the database remains untouched.

Choosing Query Sort displays the Sort dialog box (see fig. 13.11).

FIG. 13.11

The Sort dialog box.

To sort the records, you must specify the keys for the sort. The field with the highest precedence is the first key, the field with the next-highest precedence is the second key, and so on. You can use up to 255 keys in a sort, but you always must set the first key.

Determining the Sort Order

When you specify numbers as labels, a problem can occur because 1-2-3 for Windows sorts from left to right, one character at a time. If you were to sort in ascending order according to ADDRESS (column B), for example, the result of the sort would resemble figure 13.12.

Although you would expect the records to be sorted in ascending order on the ADDRESS field, notice that *2001* in row 4 appears before *25* in row 5. This problem occurs because 1-2-3 for Windows sorts the numbers one character at a time when sorting labels.

Although you probably would not sort the Company database by using the ADDRESS field as a key, you sometimes may have to sort label fields that look like numbers. Possible solutions are to make all the labels that look like numbers the same length (as in the PHONE field) or to add enough leading zeros (0) to ensure that all the labels have the same format (0025 and 2001 are the same length).

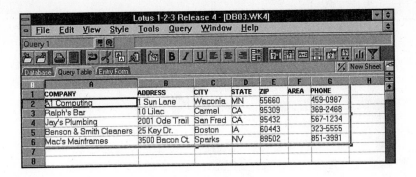

FIG. 13.12

A meaningless
ascending sort.

Restoring the Presort Order

One of the advantages of sorting the query table, as opposed to sorting the original database, is that sorting the query table does not change the original record order in the database (unless you use the Query Update Database Table command).

To ensure that you can restore the original record order after updating the database, you can add a Record Number field to the database before sorting and updating. You then can restore the original order by resorting on the Record Number field. Later in this chapter, you learn how to use the Range Fill command to enter record numbers automatically before sorting the database.

Using a One-Key Sort

An example of a database sorted according to a single key is a best selling book list. All the records are sorted in ascending numerical order, with the total of sales used as the sort key.

To specify a sort key, follow these steps:

1. Choose Query Sort to display the Sort dialog box.

2. In the drop-down Sort By list, select a field name. For this exercise, select STATE to sort the records by the values in the STATE field.

3. Choose either Ascending or Descending sort order (or click the Ascending or Descending SmartIcon), depending on how you want to sort the records. For this exercise, choose Ascending order.

4. Press Enter or click OK.

Figure 13.13 shows the query table sorted in Ascending order by state.

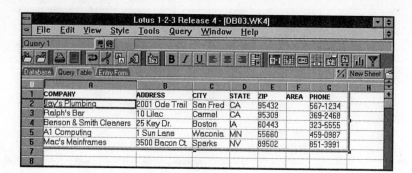

FIG. 13.13

The query table
sorted by STATE.

Using a Multiple-Key Sort

Sometimes, sorting on a single key does not sort the records in exactly the order you might need. In such a case, you can use multiple sort keys to specify additional sorting conditions.

A multiple-key sort uses more than one key to sort the records. In the telephone book's yellow pages, for example, records are sorted first according to business type (the first key) and then by business name (the second key).

To specify additional sort keys, follow these steps:

1. Use the Query Sort command to display the Sort dialog box.

2. Click the Add Key button, and specify the second key the same way that you specified the first sort key. For this example, select CITY in the Sort By drop-down list.

Figure 13.14 shows the result of the multiple-key sort. Ralph's Bar, in Carmel, California, now appears before Jay's Plumbing, in San Fred, California. Because the first key remained STATE, none of the other records moved.

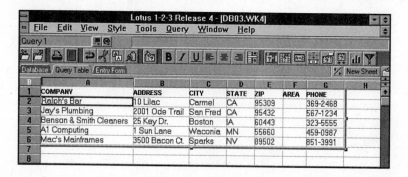

FIG. 13.14

The query table
sorted by STATE
and CITY.

Searching for Records

1-2-3 Release 4 for Windows offers a much simpler method of creating queries than other versions of 1-2-3. Instead of entering formulas in a worksheet, you select fields and matching conditions in a dialog box. This section shows you how to use this new and easy-to-use technique for selecting records.

Specifying Record-Selection Criteria

You can specify selection criteria either when you use the Tools Database New Query command to create a new query table or after an existing query table is selected. To specify selection criteria, choose Tools Database New Query Set Criteria or Query Set Criteria; alternatively, click the Set Criteria SmartIcon. The Set Criteria dialog box appears (see fig. 13.15).

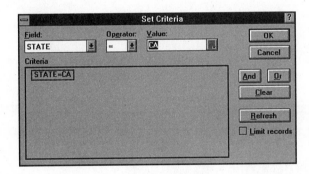

FIG. 13.15

The Set Criteria dialog box.

Looking for records that meet certain conditions is the simplest form of searching a 1-2-3 for Windows database. To determine which companies in the database are in California, for example, you can use a search operation to find any records with *CA* as the value in the STATE field.

To set the criteria for this type of record selection, select **STATE** in the Field list, = in the Operator list, and **CA** in the Value list. Click OK or press Enter to confirm your selection. The query table now contains only the records that match the selection criteria, as shown in figure 13.16.

After you locate the information that you want, you can use the query table to create a report. You also can copy or cut the information from the query table and place that information in a separate section of the worksheet—for example, to print all records with a California address.

1-2-3 for Windows also enables you to search for only the first occurrence of a specified field value to develop a unique list of field entries. You can search the STATE field to extract a list of the different states in the database. You can also delete all records in which a field contains a specified value.

FIG. 13.16

The query table, showing only records that match specified criteria.

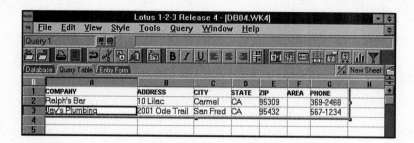

Handling More Complicated Selection Criteria

In addition to searching for an exact match of a single label field, 1-2-3 for Windows enables you to conduct a wide variety of record searches: exact matches of numeric fields; partial matches of field contents; searches for fields that meet all of several conditions; and searches for fields that meet either one condition or another. Consider first some variations of queries on single fields.

Using Wild Cards in Criteria Ranges

You can use 1-2-3 for Windows' wild cards to match labels in database operations. Two characters—the question mark (?) and the asterisk (*)—have special meaning when used in the criteria range. The ? character instructs 1-2-3 for Windows to accept any character in that specific position and can be used only to locate fields of the same length. The * character, which tells 1-2-3 for Windows to accept any and all characters that follow, can be used to locate field contents of unequal length.

Table 13.1 shows how you can use wild cards in search operations.

Table 13.1 Using Wild Cards in Search Operations

Enter	To Find
N?	Any two-character label starting with the letter *N* (NC, NJ, NY, and so on)
BO?L?	A five-character label (BOWLE) but not a shorter label (BOWL)
BO?L*	A four-or-more-character label (BOWLE, BOWL, BOLLESON, BOELING, and so on)
SAN*	A three-or-more-character label starting with SAN and followed by any number of characters (SANTA BARBARA and SAN FRANCISCO)
SAN *	A four-or-more-character label starting with SAN, followed by a space, and then followed by any number of characters (SAN FRANCISCO, but not SANTA BARBARA)

Use the ? and * wild-card characters when you are unsure of the spelling or when you need to match several slightly different records.

Using Operators in Selection Criteria

To set up criteria formulas that query numeric or label fields in the database, you can use the following relational operators (in the Operator box of the Set Criteria dialog box):

> Greater than

>= Greater than or equal to

< Less than

<= Less than or equal to

= Equal to

<> Not equal to

You create a formula that describes the values of the field entries to be selected in the Set Criteria dialog box. 1-2-3 for Windows tests the formula on each record until the program reaches the end of the database. To exclude records in which the STATE field contains *CA*, for example, you would use the following formula:

STATE<>CA

Setting Up And Conditions

You have seen how to base a selection on only one criterion. In this section, you learn how to use multiple criteria for your queries. You can set up multiple criteria as And conditions (in which *all* the criteria must be met) or as Or conditions (in which any *one* criterion must be met). For example, searching a music department's library for sheet music requiring drums And trumpets is likely to produce fewer selections than searching for music appropriate for drums Or trumpets.

You indicate two or more criteria, *all* of which must be met, by specifying the first condition, choosing the And button in the Set Criteria dialog box, and then specifying the second condition.

Suppose that you want to retrieve only those records for companies not located in California and not in cities that start with the letter *B*. To specify those conditions, follow these steps:

1. Choose either Tools Database New Query Set Criteria or Query Set Criteria to display the Set Criteria dialog box.

2. Select **STATE** in the Field list, <> in the Operator list, and **CA** in the Value list.

3. Choose the And button.

4. Select **CITY** in the Field list and <> in the Operator list, and type **B*** in the Value box.

   Figure 13.17 shows how the two conditions appear in the Criteria box. The query table also shows the results of performing this query; two records are displayed.

5. Click OK or press Enter.

Setting Up Or Conditions

To retrieve records that meet either one condition or another, you combine the conditions by using Or instead of And. 1-2-3 for Windows retrieves the records that match either condition.

Follow the same procedure you used in the preceding section, but choose the Or button instead of the And button in step 3. Figure 13.18 shows the result of the changed query.

Although this example uses the same set of criteria and simply changed the condition from And to Or to demonstrate how the two conditions compare, in most cases, you will use different criteria.

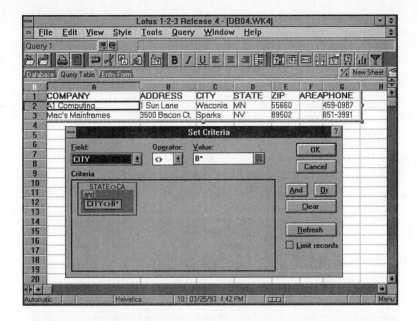

FIG. 13.17

Using And to combine two criteria.

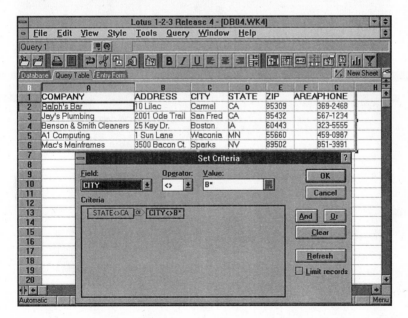

FIG. 13.18

Using Or to combine two criteria.

To set up selection criteria for records containing either *CA* or *NV* in the STATE field, follow these steps:

1. Select the criterion **STATE<>CA** by clicking on the criteria formula in the Criteria box. When you select a criterion, its description appears in the Field, Operator, and Value boxes. This enables you to modify the existing criteria.

2. Change the operator to =, because you want to match records that contain, rather than exclude, CA in the STATE field.

3. Select the criterion **CITY<>B*** by clicking on the criteria formula in the Criteria box.

4. Select **STATE** in the Field list, = in the Operator list, and **NV** in the Value list.

5. Click OK or press Enter.

Figure 13.19 shows the completed Set Criteria dialog box and the result of the new set of criteria in the query table. Only one condition or the other had to be met before the copy was made.

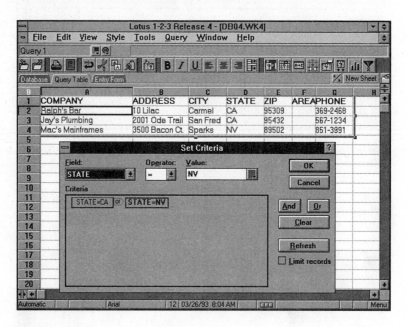

FIG. 13.19

Using Or to find two values in the same field.

Changing Condition Types

Sometimes, you may find that you combined a set of criteria incorrectly. Suppose that you created the criteria set shown in figure 13.18

but later realized that combining the criteria with Or was a mistake. You really wanted to combine the criteria with And, as shown in figure 13.17. You could choose the Clear button to remove the criteria and start over, but 1-2-3 for Windows provides an easier method.

As shown in figures 13.17 and 13.18, the Criteria box displays And conditions in a single box vertically and Or conditions in two boxes horizontally. To change condition types, you can use the mouse to drag a criteria from one position to another. To change the Or condition shown in figure 13.18 to the And condition shown in figure 13.17, for example, select the CITY<>B* criterion and drag it on top of the STATE<>CA criterion. To change an And condition to an Or condition, select one criterion and drag it to the right of the other criterion.

You can add as many And and Or criteria as necessary to select the desired set of records. You may have a little trouble determining the correct set of conditions for very complex selection requirements, but 1-2-3 for Windows enables you to correct and adjust the criteria until they are perfect.

> **T I P**
>
> If you are having difficulty narrowing down record selection to a precise set in complex situations, try extracting records in stages. First, extract a group that contains all the records you want—and also some that you don't want. Then, using the extracted records as the source, create another query table and extract a more precise set of records. If necessary, repeat the process until you have only the records that you need.

Using the Tools Database Find Records Command

When you issue the Tools Database Find Records command, each record in the database that meets the conditions specified in the Find Records dialog box is highlighted. If the criterion is STATE=CA, for example, the records for Jay's Plumbing and Ralph's Bar are highlighted (see fig. 13.20).

The highlighted records are selected, so you easily can copy, move, or delete them.

The Tools Database Find Records command has limited use, however, especially in a large database. If you want to modify information in the selected records, using a query table is easier.

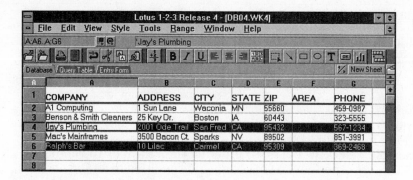

FIG. 13.20

The Tools
Database Find
Records com-
mand highlights
each record that
meets the
specified
conditions.

When you use the Tools Database Find Records command, you must
specify the database range and the selection criteria. If you select the
database range before selecting the command, however, you have to
specify only selection criteria. You use the same techniques for creating and modifying selection criteria that you used in earlier examples in
this chapter.

Deleting Specified Records

As you learned in Chapter 4, you can use the Edit Delete Row command
to remove rows from a worksheet. A fast alternative to this method is
to use the Tools Database Delete Records command to remove unwanted records from your database files.

T I P Before you issue the Tools Database Delete Records command, use
Tools Database Find Records or Tools Database New Query to make
certain that the criterion you specify selects the correct group of
records. The Tools Database Delete Records command does not
prompt for confirmation before deleting records.

Suppose that you want to remove all records with entries in the STATE
field that begin with the letter *N*. Follow these steps:

1. Select the database range (in this example, A1..G6 in the Database
   worksheet).

2. Choose Tools Database Delete Records.

   The Delete Records dialog box appears.

3. Specify the criterion as **STATE=N***.

4. Click OK or press Enter.

Figure 13.21 shows that the record for Mac's Mainframes was deleted. 1-2-3 for Windows packs the remaining records together and automatically adjusts the database range.

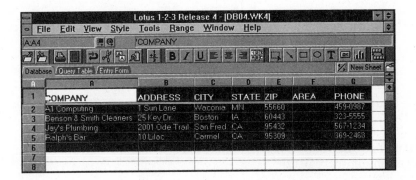

> **T I P**
>
> If you delete records in error, choose Edit Undo (Ctrl+Z) immediately to restore the records.

Modifying Records

In addition to finding and deleting database records, you probably will want to modify records. In worksheet databases, you can modify records directly in the database range, but using a query table is safer. The query-table procedure also enables you to modify records in external databases.

To use a query table to modify records, first retrieve the group of records that you want to modify. Then edit the records directly in the query table, either by making the changes manually or by using Edit Find & Replace. When you complete your changes, choose Query Update Database Table. To apply the new criteria to the query table without removing the Set Criteria dialog box, select the Refresh button.

> **NOTE**   If Query Update Database Table is dimmed, choose Query Set Options Allow Updates to Source Table.

For Related Information

▶▶ "Working with External Databases," p. 682.

Filling Ranges

Two 1-2-3 for Windows commands—Range Fill and Range Fill By Example—can be useful when you enter data. You can use these commands, for example, to fill a Record Number field in a database, add a series of dates or titles to a range, and create a series of interest-rate entries. Range Fill and Range Fill By Example fill a range of cells with a series of numbers (which can be in the form of numbers, formulas, or functions), dates, or times that increase or decrease by a specified increment or decrement.

 When you issue the Range Fill command or click the Fill Range SmartIcon, 1-2-3 for Windows displays the Fill dialog box (see fig. 13.22). You enter the starting number of the series in the Start text box, the incremental value to be added in the Increment text box, and the ending value in the Stop text box. If you did not select a range before issuing the command, or if you want to change the range to be filled, type the address in the Range text box instead.

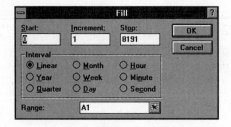

FIG. 13.22

The Fill dialog box.

Filling Ranges with Numbers

 Consider, for example, using year numbers as titles in a sales-forecast worksheet. To enter a sequence of year numbers for a five-year forecast beginning in 1995, you need to start by specifying the range of cells to be filled (after you issue the Range Fill command or click the Fill Range SmartIcon). You can select the range B2..F2, for example, and then enter the Start value **1995**. The Increment value in this example is 1. The Stop value can be left as the default (8191).

After you use <u>R</u>ange <u>F</u>ill or <u>R</u>ange <u>F</u>ill By <u>E</u>xample to fill a range of cells with a series of numbers, use the <u>S</u>tyle <u>A</u>lignment command to align the numbers.

T I P

You also can use the <u>R</u>ange <u>F</u>ill command to build a list of interest rates. After you specify the fill range, enter the starting value as a decimal fraction (**0.05** for 5 percent, for example) and another decimal fraction (**0.01** for 1 percent) for the increment value. The default ending value is 8191. The <u>R</u>ange <u>F</u>ill command fills only the specified range and doesn't fill cells beyond the end of the range.

A third use for the <u>R</u>ange <u>F</u>ill command is in combination with <u>R</u>ange <u>S</u>ort or <u>Q</u>uery <u>S</u>ort. Suppose that you are going to sort a database, and you want to be able to restore the records to their original order if you make a mistake as you are sorting. All you need to do is add a field to the database and use <u>R</u>ange <u>F</u>ill to fill the field with consecutive numbers. Then you can sort the database, including the new field of numbers. If you find that the result of the sort is unacceptable, sort the database on the new field to return the database to its original order.

Using Formulas and Functions To Fill Ranges

Instead of using regular numbers for the start, step (incremental), and stop values, you can use formulas and functions. If you want to fill a range of cells with incrementing dates after the range is set, you can use the @DATE function to set the start value–for example, @DATE(95,6,1). You also can use a cell formula, such as +E4, for the incremental value. You can enter the stop value **@DATE(95,10,1)**, for example; if the stop date is in a cell, you use that cell address as the stop value. 1-2-3 for Windows provides many different combinations of commands.

Filling Ranges with Dates or Times

<u>R</u>ange <u>F</u>ill (or the Fill Range SmartIcon) also enables you to fill a worksheet range with a sequence of dates or times without using values, formulas, or functions. You specify the starting and stopping values, the increment between values, and the interval. You can use the options listed in table 13.2 to specify intervals.

Table 13.2 Range Fill Intervals

Interval	Description
Linear	Adds the number specified by Increment to the preceding value
Year	Adds the number of years specified by Increment to the preceding value
Quarter	Adds the number of quarters specified by Increment to the preceding value
Month	Adds the number of months specified by Increment to the preceding value
Week	Adds the number of weeks specified by Increment to the preceding value
Day	Adds the number of days specified by Increment to the preceding value
Hour	Adds the number of hours specified by Increment to the preceding value
Minute	Adds the number of minutes specified by Increment to the preceding value
Second	Adds the number of seconds specified by Increment to the preceding value

When you use one of the time intervals to fill a range, 1-2-3 for Windows automatically formats the range with an appropriate date or time format. In addition, the program automatically supplies the current date or time as a default starting value (which you can change, if necessary).

Figure 13.23 shows an example of the Fill dialog box set to fill a range with monthly values, with the result already shown in the worksheet.

1-2-3 for Windows fills the range from top to bottom and left to right. The first cell is filled with the start value, and each subsequent cell is filled with the value in the preceding cell plus the increment. Filling stops when 1-2-3 for Windows reaches the stop value or the end of the fill range, whichever happens first.

NOTE   Range Fill can fill only contiguous ranges, not collections.

Notice that when you fill a range with times, 1-2-3 for Windows may put in the last cell of the fill range a time slightly different from the stop value you specified. A slight loss of accuracy sometimes occurs when

1-2-3 for Windows converts between the binary numbers that it uses internally and the decimal numbers used for times. To avoid this problem, specify a stop value less than one increment larger than the desired stop value. If the increment is 10 minutes, for example, and you want the last cell in the range to contain 10:30, specify a stop value between 10:30 and 10:40, such as 10:35.

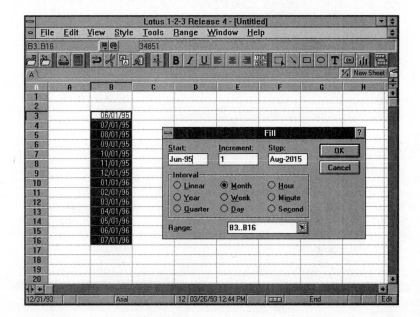

FIG. 13.23

Using Range Fill to enter dates in the worksheet.

Filling by Example

1-2-3 for Windows offers an even easier method of filling ranges with values: the Range Fill By Example command (or the Fill Range by Example SmartIcon). Instead of specifying a Start, Increment, Stop, and Interval, you simply enter one or more values in the worksheet to show 1-2-3 for Windows how to fill the range. The Range Fill By Example command then examines the values in the worksheet to determine the correct pattern and uses that pattern to fill the selected range.

The Range Fill By Example command can determine the correct fill pattern for many different types of data. You can use dates, times, month or day names, and incrementing labels (such as Qtr 1) as starting values. You even can create custom fill sequences.

Figure 13.24 shows several examples of how the Range Fill By Example command fills worksheet ranges. For each fill sequence, the value shown in column B was entered and columns B through G were highlighted.

FIG. 13.24

Examples of ranges filled by Range Fill By Example.

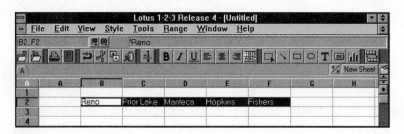

Creating Custom Fill Sequences

If you often enter the same set of labels in your worksheets, you may want to create your own custom fill sequences for use with Range Fill By Example. Row 6 in figure 13.24, for example, shows a custom fill sequence that enters planet names. Other custom fill sequences that might be useful include region names, store locations, and sales representatives' names.

Custom fill sequences are stored in a text file, FILLS.INI, which usually is located in the \123R4W\PROGRAMS directory. You can edit this file with the Windows Notepad, the DOS Edit command, or any other text editor that does not add special codes. (Most word processing programs add formatting information as special codes.)

Custom fill sequences are stored as numbered sets in FILLS.INI. Following is the custom fill sequence [SET 2], which enters planet names:

```
[SET 2]
ITEM1=Mercury
ITEM2=Venus
ITEM3=Earth
ITEM4=Mars
ITEM5=Jupiter
ITEM6=Saturn
ITEM7=Uranus
ITEM8=Neptune
ITEM9=Pluto
```

You can edit an existing custom fill sequence or create a new one, using the existing set as a model. Each custom fill sequence must follow certain rules:

■ The first line of each set must consist of [SET, the set number, and].

■ You must list the items in order in lines that begin with ITEM#= (where # is the item number).

■ To make 1-2-3 for Windows enter the data in the same combination of uppercase and lowercase letters that appear in the list, type **CASE=EXACT** on a separate line anywhere in the list. Otherwise, 1-2-3 for Windows determines case based on the label in the first cell of the range that you want to fill.

When you make all your additions or corrections, save the file. To add a special list of location names, for example, you could add the following text to FILLS.INI:

```
[SET 4]
CASE=EXACT
ITEM1=Reno
ITEM2=Prior Lake
ITEM3=Manteca
ITEM4=Hopkins
ITEM5=Fishers
```

Figure 13.25 shows how Range Fill By Example uses this custom fill sequence to enter the set of labels into the worksheet. You can create any custom fill sequence you need for values that you use in your worksheets frequently.

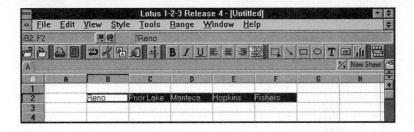

FIG. 13.25

You can create custom fill sequences for values you frequently enter in worksheets.

Questions & Answers

Q: Why don't the complete labels that I entered appear as field names in the Set Criteria dialog box?

A: Did you use two rows for your field labels? 1-2-3 for Windows uses a single row of labels at the top of the database as field names. Correct this problem by entering the complete field-name labels in a single row at the top of the database, in the row immediately above the first record row.

Q: I have too many database records to fit in one worksheet. What can I do?

A: In theory, a 1-2-3 for Windows worksheet database can hold 8,191 records, but if a database is too large, performance suffers as data is swapped in and out of memory. Very large databases are best contained in external database files, as discussed in Chapter 14.

Q: How can I find database records that fall into a range of dates?

A: First, make certain that you enter any date fields as dates that 1-2-3 for Windows can recognize. Second, when you specify selection criteria, specify an And condition so that 1-2-3 for Windows retrieves records equal to or greater than the starting date and less than or equal to the ending date.

Q: I added several new records to my database, but those records are not included when I update the query table. I'm certain that at least some of the new records match the selection criteria. What went wrong?

A: This problem usually results from adding records directly below the database range and then forgetting to expand the database range definition to include the new records. To avert this problem, create an entry form and then use Tools Database Append Records to add the new records. You can use this method, which automatically adjusts the database range, in both worksheet and external databases.

Q: When I used Tools Database New Query, existing data in my worksheet disappeared. What should I do?

A: A query table overwrites any existing data. To prevent this problem in the future, add a new worksheet for the query table. In fact, you should create several worksheets so that you can keep each major element of a 1-2-3 for Windows database separate. You may be able to recover your data using Edit Undo if you don't use any other commands which change the worksheet.

Q: I modified the records in the query table to reflect updated customer information, but I can't update the database because the Query Update Database Table command is dimmed. Why can't I use this command?

A: By default, the Allow Updates to Source Table check box in the Set Options dialog box is not selected. Use the Query Set Options command to access this dialog box, choose Allow Updates to Source Table, and then click OK or press Enter to return to the query table. You now can update the database table.

Q: I specified a set of criteria and created a query table, but too many records seem to be selected. What's wrong with my set of criteria?

A: You probably specified several criteria and joined them with an Or condition. Records have to match only one of the criteria in an Or condition, not all the criteria.

Q: I specified a set of criteria and created a query table, but my query table doesn't have any records. What's the problem?

A: In this case, you probably wanted to select records that met any of several conditions but joined the criteria with an And condition. Try changing the method of joining the criteria to Or.

Q: When I tried to use Range Fill to add numbers to a range, only part of the range was filled. Why wasn't the entire range filled, as I expected?

A: Range Fill fills the selected range until all the cells are filled or until the Stop value is reached. You may have forgotten to make the Stop value large enough to accommodate the entire range that you wanted to fill.

Q: Why did Range Fill By Example fill the entire range with the same label that I entered in the first cell of the range?

A: If Range Fill By Example cannot recognize the correct pattern to use for incrementing labels, it copies the starting label to the entire range. Make certain that the starting label is one that Range Fill By Example can recognize (for example, Qtr 1 or January), or create a custom-fill sequence so that Range Fill By Example knows how you want to fill the range.

Summary

The Tools Database and Query commands enable you to create, select, and modify database information. The commands introduced in this chapter can also be used with external databases (explored in Chapter 14).

By building on the knowledge you have already gained, Chapter 14 adds the skills that you need to take full advantage of 1-2-3 for Windows' data-management power.

Understanding Advanced Data Management

This chapter builds on the basic database commands introduced in the preceding chapter and covers more advanced data-management techniques. You learn how to join databases to take advantage of relationships between them and how to use external database files. You also learn how to use data contained in external text files. Once you enter data in a worksheet, it is important to be able to analyze the data—the balance of the chapter covers advanced data-analysis techniques.

Advanced data-management techniques show some of the real power of 1-2-3 for Windows. By mastering these techniques, you can take advantage of some of the most advanced and useful features available to computer users.

This chapter covers the following subjects:

■ Using related data contained in multiple databases

■ Using data in external database files

■ Importing data from text files

■ Analyzing data using crosstabs, frequency distributions, data regression, and matrix inversion and multiplication

Joining Multiple Databases

A powerful feature of 1-2-3 for Windows is its capability to create a query table that contains fields or calculated columns based on records contained in two or more databases. To *join* databases, you relate two or more databases that have one or more key fields in common.

You may wonder why you should keep two or more databases of related information instead of keeping all the information together in one large database. One reason is to increase efficiency. Suppose that you had several business contacts at each of the companies listed in a company database, such as the one shown in figure 14.1. You could add a NAME field to the database and place each contact in a separate record. If you had three contacts at Jay's Plumbing, for example, you could type three complete records, one for each contact person. Of course, when Jay's Plumbing moves to a larger building, you have to change the addresses for all three records. On the other hand, if you have one database with the company information and another listing the contact persons with cross-references to their companies, you only have to update one company record to update the addresses for all the contacts you have with that company.

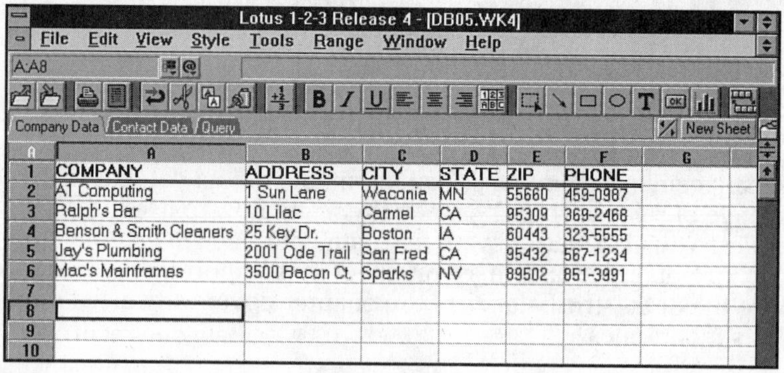

FIG. 14.1

A sample company database.

A *key field* is one whose content is unique for each record in the database. In the sample company database, for example, COMPANY is a key field because every company has a different name. STATE is not a key field because two companies may be in the same state.

The examples that follow use the sample company data, sample contact data, and a query table. To make following along with the examples easier, insert two new worksheets in the file that contains the sample company data; name the three worksheets Company Data, Contact Data, and Query as shown in figure 14.1. You can use the New Sheet button or the Edit Insert Sheet command to add the worksheets. If you do not already have the sample COMPANY database from Chapter 13, enter the data as shown in figure 14.1.

Move the cell pointer to the Contact Data worksheet and enter the information shown in figure 14.2 to create the CONTACTS database. Then use the Range Name command or click on the Create/Delete Range Name SmartIcon to name the two database ranges COMPANIES (A:A1..A:F6) and CONTACTS (B:A1..B:B10).

	Lotus 1-2-3 Release 4 - [DB05.WK4]					

File Edit View Style Tools Range Window Help

Query 1

Company Data Contact Data Query   New Sheet

	A	B	C	D	E	F	G
1	NAME	COMPANY					
2	Jones	A1 Computing					
3	MacLennan	Jay's Plumbing					
4	Mooney	Jay's Plumbing					
5	Wieber	Mac's Mainframes					
6	Anton	Benson & Smith Cleaners					
7	Brown	Ralph's Bar					
8	Smith	Jay's Plumbing					
9	Johnson	Mac's Mainframes					
10	Andersen	Benson & Smith Cleaners					
11							
12							
13							
14							

FIG. 14.2

A sample contacts database.

Understanding Database Relationships

Related database tables can have several different types of relationships. Understanding these types of relationships makes it easier to create related databases so that you can join them in a meaningful manner.

The first type of relationship is a *one-to-one* relationship. In this type of relationship, for every record in one database, only one record from another database is related to it. In a one-to-one relationship, there is no real advantage to having multiple databases.

In a *many-to-one* relationship, many records in the master database are related to one value in the second database. For example, the contacts database lists employees at each of the businesses found in the company database. Several employees can work at the same business, so many records in the contacts database point to the same value in the company database. A many-to-one relationship between databases is efficient because one record in the second database contains related information for many records in the master database.

In a *one-to-many* relationship, one record in the master database is related to many records in the second database. For example, if the company database were the master database, its relationship with the contacts database would be a one-to-many relationship. A single record in the company database can point to several records in the contacts database. A one-to-many relationship does not let you easily select unique records from the second database, and offers no real advantage in most cases.

When you join databases in 1-2-3 for Windows, you usually want to determine which method of joining databases produces a many-to-one relationship, such as that between the contacts and company databases. This kind of relationship results in the highest efficiency. If you create databases with this advantage in mind, you find that you need to enter less data, your databases require less disk space and system memory, and you have higher performance.

Performing the Join

Joining databases in 1-2-3 for Windows is quite simple. You start by creating a new query table (as explained in Chapter 13). Then you specify the name of the master database. Then you specify the related fields in the databases. Finally, you select the fields to display in the joined query table.

For example, to join the contacts and company databases (using contacts as the master database and displaying three columns of related field information), follow these steps:

1. Select the master database by highlighting its range. In this example, highlight the contacts database (cells B:A1..B10).

 2. Select Tools Database New Query or click on the Query Table SmartIcon.

3. In the Select Location for New Query Table box, specify **C:A1** (the top-left cell on the Query worksheet).

4. Click on OK or press Enter to create the query table.

5. If necessary, adjust column widths, fonts, and point sizes to display the query table as you prefer. Figure 14.3 shows the query table, which displays the information from the contacts database.

6. Select Query Set Database Table to display the Set Database Table dialog box.

7. In the Database table box, specify **CONTACTS** as the master database (see fig. 14.4).

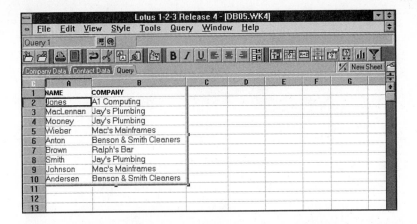

FIG. 14.3

The query table initially displays only information from the contacts database.

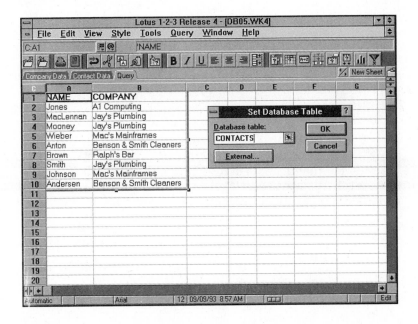

FIG. 14.4

Use the Set Database Table dialog box to specify the master database.

8. Click on OK or press Enter.

9. Select Query Join to display the Join dialog box (see fig. 14.5). This dialog box specifies the relationship between the databases.

   In this case, 1-2-3 for Windows has correctly determined that the COMPANY field in the contacts database holds the information that links it to the COMPANY field in the company database. The Join Criteria box shows the join formula:

CONTACTS.COMPANY=COMPANIES.COMPANY. If the relationship determined by 1-2-3 for Windows is incorrect, use the options in this dialog box to specify the correct relationship.

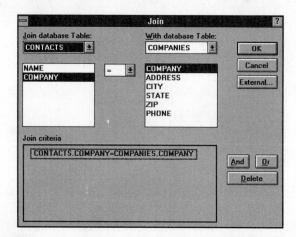

FIG. 14.5

Use the Set Join Criteria dialog box to specify the relationship between databases.

NOTE   1-2-3 specifies a field within a database using dot notation, as in COMPANIES.COMPANY. This notation specifies the COMPANY field in the COMPANIES database. Therefore, the join formula, CONTACTS.COMPANY=COMPANIES.COMPANY, means that the data in the COMPANY field of the Contacts database is related to the data in the COMPANY field of the Company database.

10. Click on OK or press Enter to display the Choose Fields dialog box (see fig. 14.6). Use this dialog box to specify the fields from the joined databases to display in the query table.

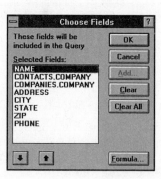

FIG. 14.6

Use the Choose Fields dialog box to specify the fields to display.

11. Select the fields you *do not* want to include in the query table. By default, the query table includes every field from both of the joined databases, including two copies of the field used to join the databases (one copy from each database). For this example, select these fields to exclude: COMPANIES.COMPANY, ADDRESS, CITY, STATE, and ZIP. To select more than one field, hold down the Ctrl key as you select additional fields.

12. Choose the Clear button to remove the selected fields.

13. Click on OK or press Enter to display the joined query table (see fig. 14.7).

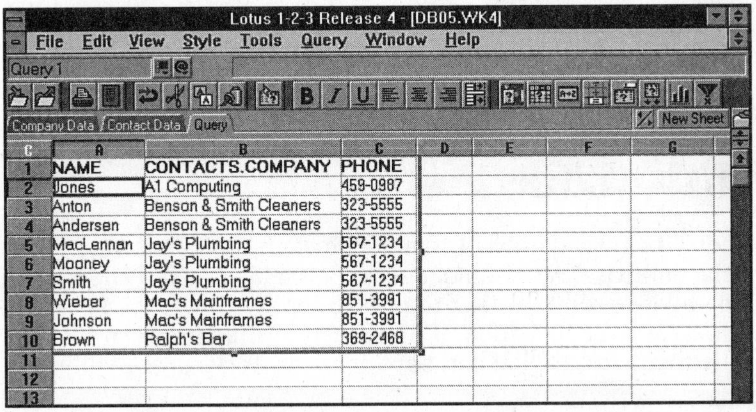

FIG. 14.7

The joined query table displays information from both databases.

If your database includes fields whose values you wish to use in calculations, you can use the Formula button to create a calculated field. For example, you might create a calculated field that budgets next month's sales as 10 percent higher than last month's sales. In addition, you can use the Clear All button to remove all database fields from the query table, and then display only any calculated fields you define.

After you have selected a field you want to display in the query table, you can click the up- or down-arrow buttons below the Selected Fields box to change the field's position in the resulting query table. Moving a field in the query table has no effect on the databases.

This example shows how you can join databases that contain related information so that you can have more complete information than is contained in either database alone. The resulting query table is similar to a single database query table, but is much more useful.

In the next section, you learn how to use external database files. The technique of joining databases is even more useful with external databases than it is with worksheet databases, because external databases often hold much larger collections of data. By applying the efficiencies gained through joining related databases, you make better use of disk space and memory.

FROM HERE...

For Related Information

◄◄ "Creating a Database," p.644.

Working with External Databases

1-2-3 for Windows' database commands can also access data within an external database. An *external database* is a file created and maintained by a database program other than 1-2-3 for Windows, such as dBASE or Paradox. After a connection or link is established between 1-2-3 for Windows and an external database, you can perform the following tasks:

- Use Tools Database New Query to find and manipulate data in the external database and then work with that data in the worksheet

- Use formulas and database functions to perform calculations based on data in the external database

- Create an external database that contains data from the worksheet or from an existing external database

When you select Tools Database New Query External or Tools Database Connect to External, the dialog box shown in figure 14.8 appears.

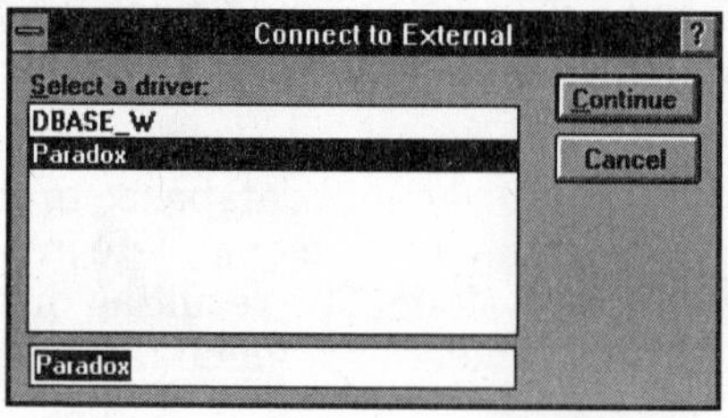

FIG. 14.8

The Connect to External dialog box specifies the type of external database.

Connect to External	?
Select a driver:	Continue
DBASE_W	Cancel
Paradox	
Paradox	

Although 1-2-3 for Windows includes several standard DataLens drivers you can use to connect to external databases, you may install only one or two, depending on the types of external databases you use. The following examples use the Paradox driver, but the procedures for using the other drivers are similar.

If more than one driver name is shown in the Select a Driver box, highlight the name of the driver you want to use and then select Continue.

If the selected DataLens driver accepts a password, the Driver Password dialog box shown in figure 14.9 appears. If a user ID and password are needed on your system, enter the information in the appropriate boxes and click on OK or press Enter. If your system does not require this information, simply click on OK or press Enter to continue.

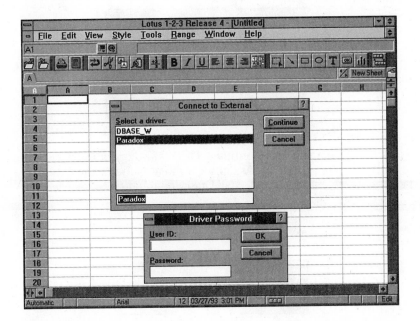

FIG. 14.9

Some drivers display the Driver Password dialog box.

NOTE Networks and database programs used on networks usually include controls to limit access to database files. These same controls apply when using 1-2-3 for Windows to access external database files. If you encounter problems, see your network administrator.

The text-box prompt in the Connect to External dialog box changes to Select a Database or Directory as shown in figure 14.10. Select the database (1-2-3 for Windows considers all database files in a directory to be a single database) and then select Continue. Once again, the text-box prompt changes—this time to Select a Table (see fig. 14.11). The *table* is the name of the database file you want to use.

FIG. 14.10

Select a directory from the second Connect to External dialog box.

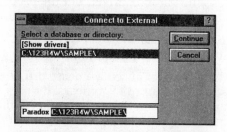

FIG. 14.11

Select an external database file from the third Connect to External dialog box.

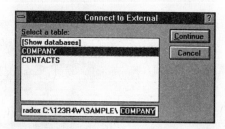

Select the table and press Continue. The text-box prompt changes to Refer To As (see fig. 14.12). Assigning a range name to the external database table enables you to use Query commands to access the external table.

FIG. 14.12

Specify a range name for the external database in the final Connect to External dialog box.

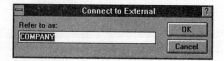

T I P   If the Refer To As text box is blank, the external database's file name is already in use as a 1-2-3 for Windows range name. Specify a different name for the range name you want to assign to the external database file.

Press Enter or select OK. If you are using the Tools Database New Query command, complete the selections in the New Query dialog box and press Enter or select OK again. Figure 14.13 shows a new query table that displays the information in the COMPANY.DB Paradox database file. The column widths were adjusted in this figure for a clearer display.

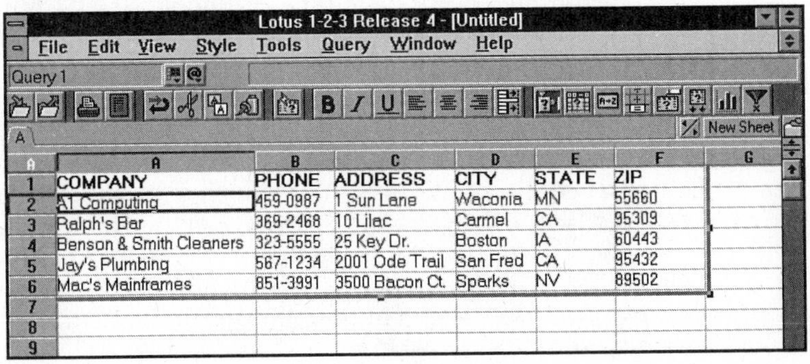

FIG. 14.13

A new query table displaying information from an external database file.

After you have established a connection with an external database table, use Tools Database Create Table to create an external table; use Tools Database Send Command to send a command to the external database; or use Tools Database Disconnect to break the connection between 1-2-3 and the external table. Use the Query commands discussed in Chapter 13 and earlier in this chapter to manipulate data in external database tables.

Understanding External Database Terms

Data management in 1-2-3 for Windows is powerful and flexible because of 1-2-3 for Windows' capability to use data from external databases. Before you begin working with this feature, however, you should be familiar with several terms.

A *DataLens driver* is a program that serves as an interface between 1-2-3 for Windows and an external database so that 1-2-3 for Windows can transfer data to and from the external database. A separate database driver is required for each external database format you use.

An *external database* is simply the path in which the external database files reside.

A *table name* identifies the external database with which you want to work. You must enter the *full* table name before you can access the database from 1-2-3 for Windows. The full table name consists of three or four parts in the following order:

- The name of the database driver

- The name of the external database (its path)

- An owner name or user ID, if required by the external database program

- The name of the database or a 1-2-3 for Windows range name assigned to the database. For example, to connect to a Paradox database named *Company* in the C:\123W\DB directory, use the following:

PARADOX C:\123W\DB COMPANY"

A *table-creation* string contains information used by a database driver to create an external database. When you create an external database from within 1-2-3 for Windows, you may have to specify a table-creation string, depending on the specific database driver in use. The Paradox driver, for example, enables you to use a table-creation string to specify a sort order for the database. When in doubt, refer to the database driver documentation.

A *table definition* is a six-column worksheet range that contains information about a new external database. Information in a table definition always includes field names, data types, and field widths, and may include column labels, table-creation strings, and field descriptions.

Using an Existing External Database

Using the data in an external database does not differ much from using a worksheet database. The major difference is that you need to establish a connection to the external database before you can use it; you also must break the connection when you are finished with the external database.

To use an existing external database, first set up the connection to the external database with the Tools Database New Query External or Tools Database Connect to External command. Figures 14.8 through 14.12 show how the Connect to External dialog box (which appears when you select either of these commands) steps through the selection of the components needed to define the full database name.

Note that when you break the connection to an external database (as described later in this chapter), the range name assigned to it is lost. Formulas and functions that reference that range name become undefined when the connection is broken. You must respecify the range name whenever you establish the connection. Be sure to use the same range name each time if the worksheet contains formulas or functions that reference the external database range.

By using the range name assigned to the database, you can treat the external database as a worksheet database and perform the following tasks:

- Use formulas and database functions in the worksheet that reference data in the external database, such as:

  @DCOUNT(COMPANY,"STATE",+STATE="CA")

- Copy some or all records from the external database to the worksheet with Tools Database New Query

- Use Tools Database Append Records to copy new records from the worksheet to the external database

- Modify records in the external database with Query Update Database Table

- Use Tools Database Send Command to perform special database functions not available in 1-2-3 for Windows

- Terminate the connection to the external table with Tools Database Disconnect

Creating a New External Table

You create an external table with the Tools Database Create Table command. When you select this command, the Create Table dialog box appears (see fig. 14.14). The first step in creating an external table is to specify the name of the external database driver.

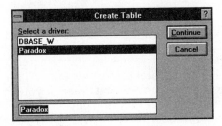

FIG. 14.14

The Create Table dialog box.

After you select the driver, you select the database (that is, its directory) and then specify a name for the new database file. You then specify the model table and, if necessary, a creation command. The *model table* is a worksheet range or the range name of an external database file you want to use as a template for the new table. You also can elect to insert records from the model table—if you want to create a duplicate of an existing database (see fig. 14.15). When you have filled out the second screen of the Create Table dialog box, press Enter or click on OK to create the new external database file. If you use an existing database as a template, the new database is either an exact copy containing all the same fields (with the same field names, field lengths, data types, and so on)but no records, or an exact copy containing all the same fields with copies of all records.

Whether or not a creation command is supported or required depends on the DataLens driver for the database you are using. See the documentation for your database manager for more information on table-creation commands.

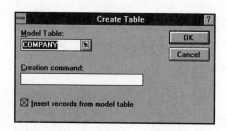

FIG. 14.15

Specify a Model Table to duplicate an existing database.

Duplicating an Existing Database

You can duplicate the structure of either a worksheet database or an external database. To use a worksheet database, it must be in an active file and must contain a row of field names and at least one data record. In the Model Table text box of the Create Table dialog box, enter the address or range name of the row of field names and the data record row. In the Model Table text box of the Create Table dialog box, enter the row of field names and the data record row.

If you duplicate the structure of a worksheet database, the data types are determined using default values for the selected DataLens driver. For example, the Paradox DataLens driver only creates alphanumeric, number, and date fields in the new database. If you want to create other types of fields, or if you want to specify index fields, you must create a *table definition range* by using the /Data External Create command (on the 1-2-3 Classic menu).

The table definition range is the area in the worksheet used to define the external table's structure. To create an external table, 1-2-3 for Windows needs to know the number, order, data types, and names of the fields in the new table. This information is provided in a table definition.

A table definition range always includes six columns, although not all DataLens drivers use every column of information. In addition, the range includes one row for each field in the database. The six columns (from left to right) specify the following information:

- Field name
- Data type
- Field width
- Column labels
- Field descriptions
- Field-creation strings

The allowable values are determined by the specified DataLens driver. Refer to the DataLens driver documentation to determine the allowable values. Figure 14.16 shows a table definition range used to create a Paradox database.

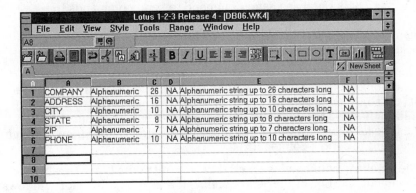

FIG. 14.16

A table definition range used to create a Paradox database.

If the new external database has a structure identical to that of an existing database, 1-2-3 for Windows can create the table definition for you automatically: use the 1-2-3 Classic menu command /Data External List Fields (if the existing database is an external database) or /Data External Create Definition Create-Definition (if the existing database is a worksheet database). Modify the table definition by adding or changing field names, changing data types or field widths, and adding field-creation strings (if used). If the database driver you are using does not require a certain piece of information, the corresponding location in the table description contains NA.

If you are using a table definition to create an external database table, you must use the /Data External Create Name command on the 1-2-3 Classic menu to create the table. At the prompts, enter the name of the

driver, the database, the new table, and the range name. Select Definition Use-Definition and enter the range that contains the modified table
definition. Select Go to create the table.

Deleting an External Table

The Tools Database and Query menus do not provide a way to delete an external database table. You must use the 1-2-3 Classic /Data
External Delete command to delete external tables from the external
database. Specify the database driver and database name and then
highlight the external table to be deleted. Select Yes to delete the
table and Quit to return to Ready mode.

Using Tools Database Send Command

You use Tools Database Send Command to send commands to a
database management program so that you can perform database
manipulations not possible with 1-2-3 for Windows alone. To use this
command, 1-2-3 for Windows must be connected to an external table.

The capabilities of the commands you issue with the Tools Database
Send Command (as well as the command syntax) depend on the external database management program—the commands have no relationship to the 1-2-3 for Windows database management commands. You
must be familiar with the commands of the database program to which
you want to send a command.

The database command is entered as a string in the Enter Database
Command text box of the Send Command dialog box. 1-2-3 for Windows
sends the command when you select OK and then returns to Ready
mode.

Using the Query Show SQL Command

If you use an external database that understands SQL (Structured
Query Language), 1-2-3 for Windows can show you the SQL command
used to create a query table. The Query Show SQL command displays
the Show SQL dialog box (see fig. 14.17). When this dialog box is displayed, you can select Copy to copy the displayed command to the
Clipboard. This command can then be pasted into the worksheet or
the Enter Database Command text box of the Send Command dialog
box.

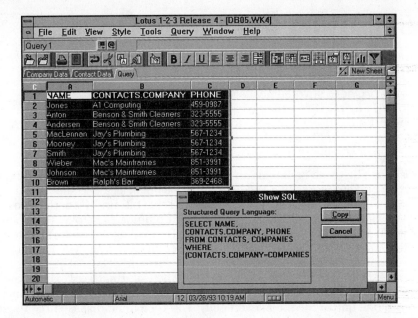

FIG. 14.17

The Query Show SQL command displays the SQL command used to create a query table.

Generate a table of SQL commands for different types of queries by using Query Show SQL. Document the purpose of each command so that you can easily select the correct command for later use.

T I P

Disconnecting 1-2-3 for Windows from the External Table

Tools Database Disconnect severs the connection between 1-2-3 for Windows and an external table. You must specify the range name of the specific table whose connection you want to break.

After you break the connection, the range name of the table becomes undefined. Any worksheet formulas or queries that use that range name may produce errors.

For Related Information

◀◀ "Creating Databases," p. 639.

FROM HERE...

Importing Data from Other Programs

Lotus provides several means of importing data from other applications. The Translate utility (described in Chapter 6) has options that convert data directly to 1-2-3 for Windows worksheets from DIF, dBASE files, and other file formats. You then can access the data by using the File Open command from the current worksheet.

Use the File Open command or click on the Open File SmartIcon to read into a current worksheet the data stored on disk as a text file. When the Open File dialog box is displayed, select Text (txt, prn) from the File Type list box (see fig. 14.18). Then select Combine to display the Combine Text File dialog box (see fig. 14.19). Depending on the format, text files can be read directly into a range or column of cells. The Formatted Text option refers to specially formatted numeric data that can be read directly into a range of worksheet cells. The Unformatted Text option refers to ASCII text that can be stored as long labels in a single column (with one line of the file in each cell). You then must disassemble these labels into the appropriate data values or fields by using functions or the Range Parse command.

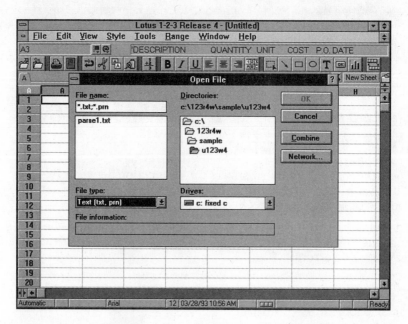

FIG. 14.18

Specify Text (txt, prn) in the File Type list box to open a text file.

Combine Text File

From file: PARSE1.TXT

Text format
- ◉ Formatted text
- ○ Unformatted text

OK

Cancel

FIG. 14.19

Specify whether
the text file
contains
formatted or
unformatted
data.

You also can use certain macro commands (as described in Chapter 16) to read and write an ASCII sequential file directly from within a 1-2-3 for Windows macro command program.

Parsing Data

The Range Parse command is a flexible and easy method of extracting numeric, string, and date data from long labels and placing it in separate columns. Suppose that you printed a report containing inventory data to a disk file, and now you want to load the ASCII file in 1-2-3 for Windows. After you load the file by using the File Open command, you must reformat the data with the Range Parse command.

NOTE Although the Range Parse command does not require, for proper operation, the use of a fixed-space font such as Courier New, the examples of the Range Parse command shown in this chapter use Courier New for clarity. 1-2-3 for Windows can create a format line and parse data properly regardless of the font used, but the examples are easier to understand when a proportional font (such as the default Arial) is not used.

The File Open command loads the inventory data into the range A1..A9 (see fig. 14.20). Although the data seems to be formatted in a typical worksheet range (A1..G9 in the example), the display is misleading. The current cell-pointer location is A3; look at the contents box to see that the entire row exists in cell A3 as a long label—and not in separate cells as you might assume.

To break the long-label columns, move the cell pointer to the first cell to be parsed (in this example, cell A3) and select Range Parse. The Parse dialog box appears.

The Format Line in the Parse dialog box specifies the pattern or patterns 1-2-3 is to use to split the long labels into numbers, labels, and dates. Use the Create command button to create a new entry in the Format Line text box (see fig. 14.21).

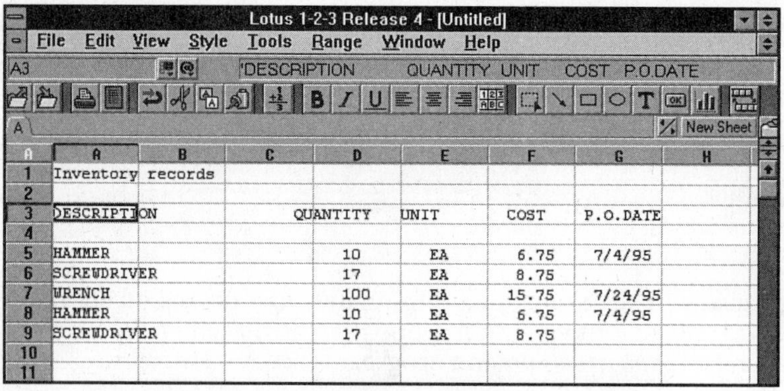

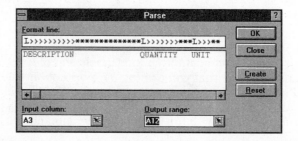

FIG. 14.20

The results of a File Open command when the source file is an unformatted text file.

FIG. 14.21

The Parse dialog box with a newly created Format Line.

Use the Input Column text box to specify the range of cells to be parsed. The input range (contained in just one column) consists of the cell containing the format line and all cells containing the long labels to be parsed.

Use the Output Range text box to specify the worksheet range where 1-2-3 for Windows is to put the parsed data. You can specify a rectangular range or the single cell at the upper-left corner of the range (make sure that there are enough empty cells to the right and below that cell to hold the newly parsed data). The output data has as many rows as there are long labels; the number of columns depends on the format line.

The Reset command button clears the previously set Input Column and Output Range text boxes. OK performs the parse based on the specified Input Column, Format Line, and Output Range.

To parse the data shown in figure 14.20, follow these steps:

1. Move the cell pointer to cell A3—the first cell in the range that has data you want to break into columns. (You do not have to parse the title in cell A1.)

2. Select Range Parse.

3. Specify the output range in the Output Range text box, making sure that the range is in an area where existing data will not be overwritten by the parsed output. For this example, specify the upper-left corner of the output range: cell A12.

4. Parse the column headings in cell A3 by using one format line; then parse the data in cells A5..A9 with another format line and output range. Different format lines are necessary because all the headings are labels, but the data is a mixture of label, numeric, and date data.

When you specify cell A3, select Range Parse Create, and then choose OK to confirm the dialog box, a suggested format line is inserted in the data at A3—moving the remaining worksheet contents down one line.

After you create a format line, you can edit it if necessary by selecting Range Parse Format Line. Use the format line to mark the column positions and the type of data in those positions. Range Parse uses the format line to break down the data and move it to its respective columns in the output range.

You use combinations of certain letters and special characters in format lines. The letters denote the beginning position and the type of data; special symbols define the length of a field and the spacing. The following letters and symbols are typically used in format lines:

Letter/Symbol	Purpose
D	Marks the beginning of a Date field.
L	Marks the beginning of a Label field.
S	Marks the beginning of a Skip position, which instructs 1-2-3 to ignore the data in this positon.
T	Marks the beginning of a Time field.
V	Marks the beginning of a Value field.
>	Defines the continuation of a field. Use one > for each position in the field (excluding the first position).
*	Defines blank spaces (in the data below the format line) that may be part of the block of data.

Add as many format lines as you need in the data you want to parse. In the inventory example, enter a second format line at cell A5 (cell A6 after you add the first format line in A3) and specify the format criteria for the data records that follow.

After setting up the first format line in the inventory example and parsing that line, select Range Parse again. In the Input Column text box of the Parse dialog box, specify **A6..A10** as the range that includes the inventory data you want to parse. In the Output Range text box, specify

A14 as the upper left corner of the blank range you want to accept the parsed data. Select Create to generate the format line. Complete the operation by selecting OK. Figure 14.22 shows the parsed inventory data.

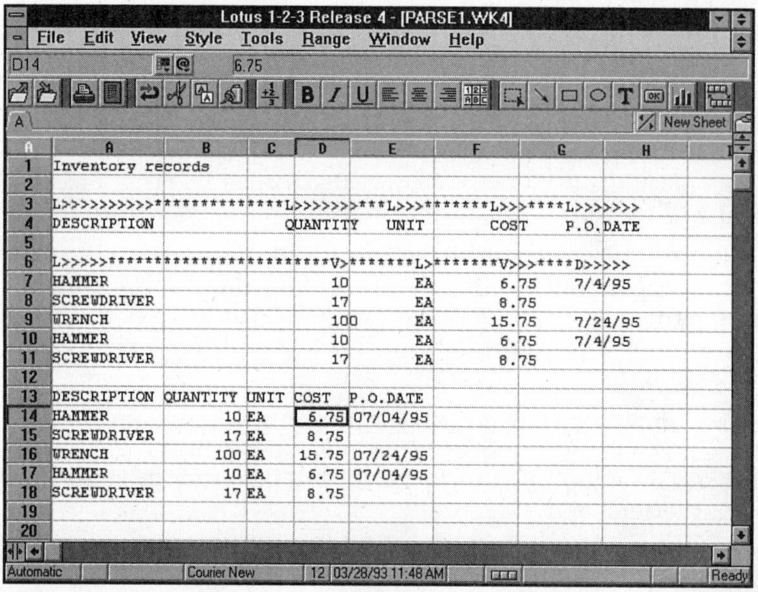

FIG. 14.22

The results of two Range Parse operations.

T I P   The data displayed in individual cells may not be exactly what you want. You can make a few changes in the format and column width, as shown in figure 14.22, and add or delete information to make the newly parsed data more usable. These enhancements are not part of the Range Parse command—but they usually are necessary after importing any parsed data.

Using Caution when Parsing Data

If you want to parse a value that continues past the end of the field, you should know that 1-2-3 parses the data until it encounters a blank or until the value runs into the next field in the format line. This means that if you parse labels, make sure that the field widths in the format line are wide enough so that you avoid losing data because of blanks. If you parse values, the field widths are less critical.

Experiment on small amounts of data until you are comfortable using the Range Parse command. After you understand how this important command works, you may find many more applications for it. Every time you develop a new application, consider whether existing data created with another software program can be imported and then changed to 1-2-3 for Windows format by using the Range Parse command.

T I P

You often can use the Edit Paste command as a shortcut to import and parse data from another Windows application. Try copying the data to the Clipboard in the other application and then using Edit Paste in 1-2-3 for Windows. You may find that this approach automatically places the data into separate worksheet cells, eliminating the need to use Range Parse.

For Related Information

◄◄ "Editing Data into the Worksheet," p. 126.

FROM HERE...

Evaluating Data with Cross Tabulations and Aggregates

One of the most useful ways to analyze data is to use a *cross-tabulation table* (or *crosstab*). Cross tabulations summarize data by showing how two factors influence a third factor. For example, the database shown in figure 14.23 tracks the amount of each sale for three different salespersons selling three different categories of products. A cross tabulation shows summary information you can use to analyze how well each salesperson is doing.

An *aggregate* is a variation of a cross tabulation. Instead of being placed in a separate cross-tabulation table, the data in an aggregate analysis is placed in a column of a query table.

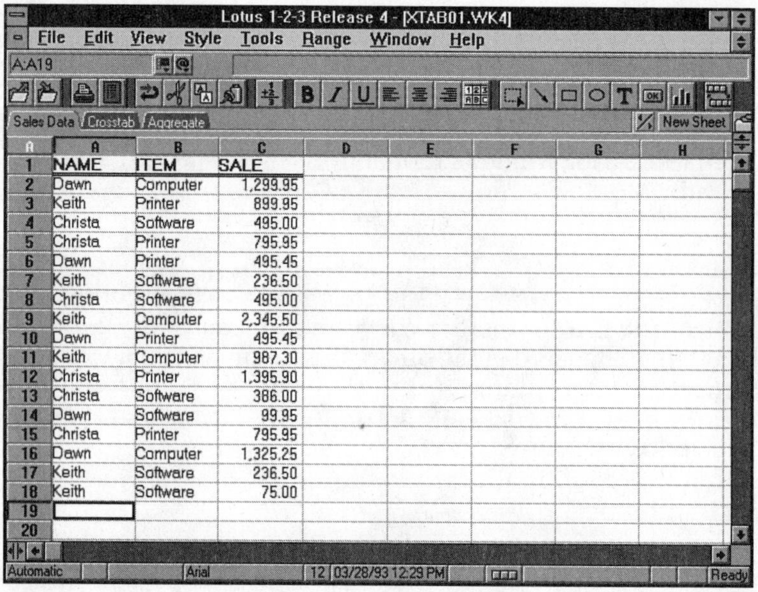

FIG. 14.23

A sales database
ready to be
analyzed using a
cross tabulation.

Creating a Cross Tabulation

To create a cross-tabulation table that summarizes the sales data
shown in figure 14.23, follow these steps:

1. Select Tools Database CrossTab or click on the Crosstab
   SmartIcon to display the Crosstab dialog box (see fig. 14.24).

2. Specify the database range you want to analyze. This range *must*
   include at least three columns and two rows. For this example,
   select A:A1..C18.

3. Select Continue to display the Crosstab Heading Options dialog
   box (see fig. 14.25). In this dialog box, specify which database field
   contains the values you want to display down the left side of the
   cross-tabulation table (these values are the row headings) and
   which database field contains the values you want to display
   across the top of the cross-tabulation table (these values are the
   column headings).

   For this example, the values in the NAME field are to be displayed
   along the left edge of the cross-tabulation table, and the values
   in the ITEM field are to be displayed along the top of the cross-
   tabulation table.

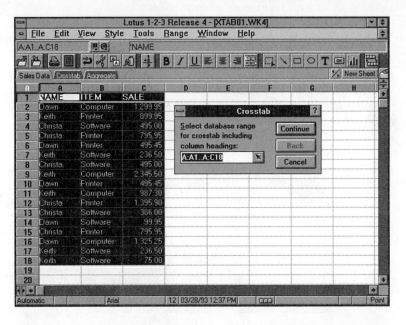

FIG. 14.24

The Crosstab
dialog box.

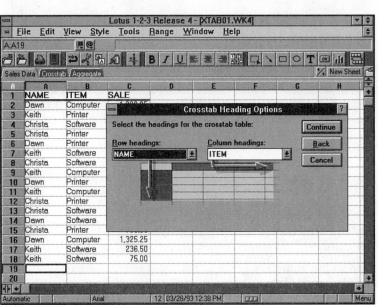

FIG. 14.25

The Crosstab
Heading Options
dialog box.

4. Select Continue to display the Crosstab Data Options dialog box (see fig. 14.26). In this dialog box, specify which database field you want to summarize as well as the type of calculation you want to perform.

   For this example, you want to summarize the values in the SALE field by showing their totals (for this example, then, select the Sum type of calculation). You can select Average, Count, Minimum, or Maximum, depending on which type of calculation provides the best analysis of your data.

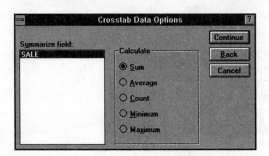

5. Select Continue. 1-2-3 for Windows calculates the cross-tabulation table and places it on a new worksheet following the current worksheet. Figure 14.27 shows the completed cross-tabulation table.

You can enhance the presentation of cross-tabulation data by using any of the Style options. You also can graph the cross-tabulated data to show the analysis graphically. Figure 14.28 shows one example of how you can quickly graph the cross-tabulated data.

Creating an Aggregate

The Tools Database Crosstab command creates a new table of cross-tabulated data; the Query Aggregate command produces a similar summary in single column of an existing query table.

To create a data summary of the sales data (shown originally in fig. 14.23) by using Query Aggregate, follow these steps:

1. If you have not already created a query table, use Tools Database New Query or click on the Query Table SmartIcon to create a query table starting at cell C:A1 (see fig. 14.29). Specify A:A1..C18 as the database range.

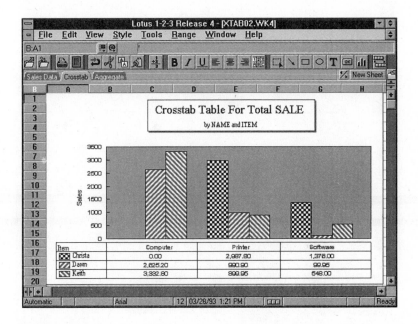

FIG. 14.27

The completed cross-tabulation table.

FIG. 14.28

You can chart cross-tabulated data quickly for graphical analysis.

2. Click on SALE to select the SALE column. This action indicates the column for which you want to produce an aggregate analysis.

3. Select Query Aggregate or click on the Query Aggregate SmartIcon to display the Aggregate dialog box. Select Sum as the analysis to perform (see fig. 14.30).

4. Click on OK or press Enter. The query table now shows the summary values in the SALE column (see fig. 14.31).

Compare the results shown in figures 14.27 and 14.31; you can see that both the Tools Database Crosstab command and the Query Aggregate command produce the same values. Choose the command that best suits your data-analysis needs.

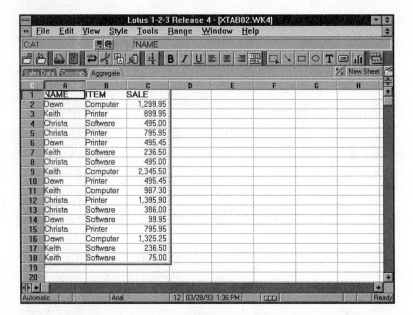

FIG. 14.29

Create a new
query table for
aggregate
analysis.

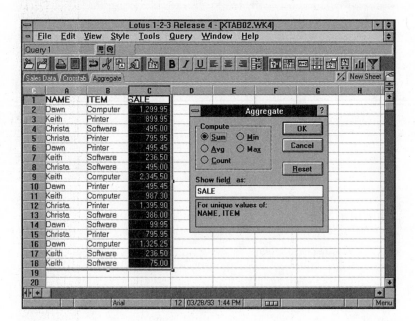

FIG. 14.30

The Aggregate
dialog box.

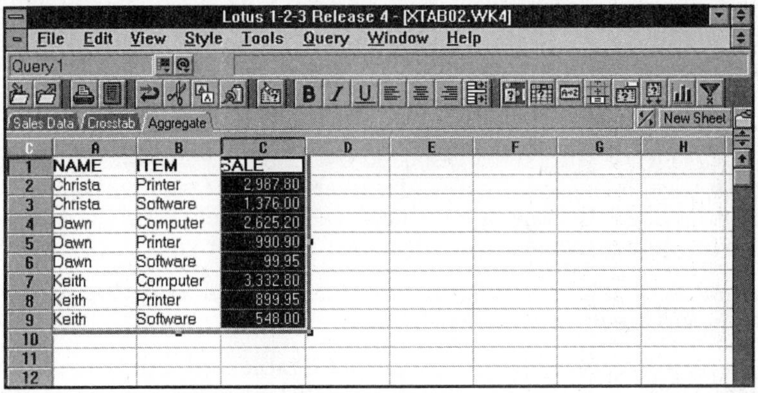

FIG. 14.31

The results of the
Query Aggregate
command.

Creating What-If Tables

In many situations, the variables used in worksheet formulas are known quantities. For example, last year's sales summary deals with variables whose exact values are known. The results of calculations performed using those values contain no uncertainties. Other situations, however, involve variables whose exact values are not known. Worksheet models for financial projections often fall into this category. For example, next year's cash-flow projection depends on prevailing interest rates. Although you can make an educated guess at what interest rates may be, you cannot predict them exactly.

What-if tables enable you to work with variables whose values are not known. With the Range Analyze What-if Table command, you can create tables that show how the results of formula calculations vary as the variables used in the formulas change.

Suppose that you decide to purchase a car that requires a $12,000 loan. Area banks offer you several combinations of loan periods and interest rates. You can use a data table to calculate the monthly payment with each combination of period and interest rate.

This section shows you how to use the Range Analyze What-if Table command to perform sensitivity or what-if analysis. First, however, you need to understand some terms and concepts.

Understanding Terms and Concepts

A *what-if table* is an on-screen view of information in column format, with the field names at the top. A what-if table contains the results of a Range Analyze What-if Table command plus some or all the information used to generate the results. A *what-if table range* is a worksheet range that contains a what-if table.

A *variable* is a formula component whose value can change.

An *input cell* is a worksheet cell used by 1-2-3 for Windows for temporary storage during calculation of a what-if table. One input cell is required for each variable in the what-if table formula. The cell addresses of the formula variables are the same as the input cells.

An *input value* is a specific value that 1-2-3 for Windows uses for a variable during the what-if table calculations.

The *results area* is the portion of a what-if table in which the calculation results are placed. One result is generated for each combination of input values. The results area of a what-if table must be unprotected, as described in Chapter 4.

The formulas used in what-if tables can contain values, strings, cell addresses, and functions. You should not use logical formulas, because this type of formula always evaluates to either 0 or 1. Although the use of a logical formula in a what-if table does not cause an error, the results generally are meaningless.

Understanding the Three Types of What-If Tables

With the Range Analyze What-if Table command, there are three types of what-if tables that 1-2-3 for Windows can generate. The three table types differ in the number of formulas and variables they can contain. Descriptions of the table types follow:

1 variable	One or more formulas with one variable
2 variables	One formula with two variables
3 variables	One formula with three variables

Creating a 1 Variable What-if Table

A what-if table created with the Range Analyze What-if Table command and specifying 1 variable shows how changing one variable affects the results of one or more formulas. Before using this command, you must set up the what-if table range and a single input cell.

The input cell can be a blank cell anywhere in the worksheet. The best practice is to identify the input cell by entering an appropriate label either above or to the left of the input cell.

The what-if table range is a rectangular worksheet area that can be placed in any empty worksheet location. The size of the what-if table range can be calculated as follows:

- The range has one more column than the number of formulas being evaluated.

- The range has one more row than the number of input values being evaluated.

The general structure of a 1 variable what-if table range is as follows:

- The top left cell in the what-if table range is empty.

- The formulas to be evaluated are entered across the first row. Each formula must refer to the input cell.

- The input values to be plugged into the formulas are entered down the first column.

- After the what-if table is calculated, each cell in the results range contains the result obtained by evaluating the formula at the top of that column with the input value at the left of that row.

Suppose that you plan to purchase a house with a 30-year mortgage in the $100,000 to $115,000 range and a 10-percent or 11-percent interest rate. For each interest rate, you want to determine the resultant monthly payment for each price.

For this example, use cell B2 as the input cell; identify it with a label in cell A2. You need one formula for each interest rate: The @PMT function can give you the payment information you want, so use it to enter the following formula for the 10-percent interest rate in cell D2:

@PMT($B$2,0.1/12,360)

In cell E2, enter the following formula for the 11-percent interest rate:

@PMT($B$2,0.11/12,360)

Because payments are monthly, each annual interest rate is divided by 12 to get the monthly interest rate. The 360 is the term of the 30-year loan in months.

Then enter the four possible prices of the house in cells C3 through C6. Select Range Analyze What-if Table to display the What-if Table dialog box. Specify 1 in the Number of Variables box; specify **C2..E6** as the Table Range; enter **B2** in the Input Cell **1** text box (see fig. 14.32).

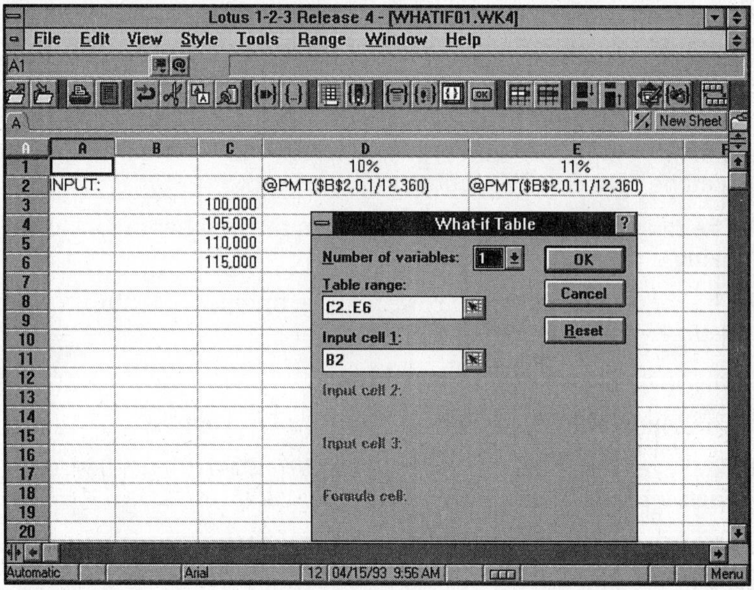

FIG. 14.32

The What-if
Table dialog
box.

Click on OK or press Enter to generate the table. The resulting table, which calculates the mortgage payments on four different amounts at two different interest rates, is shown in figure 14.33. Cells D2 and E2 have been formatted as Text so that you can see the formulas they contain. Worksheet cells containing numbers have been formatted with appropriate numeric formats, as well.

Creating a 2 Variable What-if Table

A 2 variable what-if table enables you to evaluate a single formula based on changes in two variables. To use a 2 variable what-if table, you need two blank input cells—one for each variable. They can be located anywhere in the worksheet and need not be adjacent to each other. The input cells commonly are identified with an appropriate label in a cell next to or above each input cell.

The size of the what-if table range depends on the number of values of each variable you want to evaluate. The range is one column wider than the number of values of one variable and one row longer than the number of values of the other variable.

A major difference between a 1 variable and a 2 variable what-if table is the location of the formula to be evaluated. In a 1 variable table, the formulas are placed along the top row of the table, and the upper-left corner is blank. In a 2 variable what-if table, the upper-left cell of the what-if table range contains the single formula to be evaluated. This formula *must* refer to the input cells.

Lotus 1-2-3 Release 4 - [WHATIF01.WK4]					

File   Edit   View   Style   Tools   Range   Window   Help

A1   @PMT($B$2,0.11/12,360)

New Sheet

A	A	B	C	D	E	F
1				10%	11%	
2	INPUT:			@PMT($B$2,0.1/12,360)	@PMT($B$2,0.11/12,360)	
3			100,000	877.57	952.32	
4			105,000	921.45	999.94	
5			110,000	965.33	1,047.56	
6			115,000	1,009.21	1,095.17	
7						
8						

FIG. 14.33

A 1 variable
what-if table that
calculates
mortgage
payments.

The cells below the formula contain the various input values for one variable. The cells these values occupy are what you specify in the Input Cell **1** text box in the What-if Table dialog box. The cells to the right of the formula contain the various input values for the second variable. The cells these values occupy are what you specify in the Input Cell **2** text box. Be sure that the formula refers correctly to the two input cells so that the proper input values are plugged into the correct part of the formula.

After the what-if table is calculated, each cell in the table range contains the result obtained by evaluating the formula with the input values in that cell's row and column.

Suppose that you want to create a what-if table that shows the monthly payments on a $12,000 loan at four interest rates (9, 10, 11, and 12 percent) and three loan periods (24, 36, and 48 months).

First, decide on a location for the two input cells. You can use cells B7 and B8. Put identifying labels in the adjacent cells A7 and A8.

Because you have three values of one variable and four values of the other, the what-if table range is four cells wide by five cells tall in size. Use the range C3..F7 for the table range. Enter the following @PMT formula in cell C3:

@PMT(12000,B7/12,B8)

This formula uses the @PMT function to calculate the monthly payment on a $12,000 loan. For the interest-rate argument, the formula uses the annual interest rate supplied in cell B7 and divides it by 12 to get a monthly rate. For the period argument, the formula uses the number of months supplied in cell B8.

Then enter the values in the what-if table range. Enter the four interest rates (9%, 10%, 11%, and 12%) in the range C4..C7; enter the three loan terms (24, 36, and 48) in D3..F3. Select Range Analyze What-if Table; in the What-if Table dialog box, specify **2** as the number of variables;

specify **C3..F7** as the table range; enter **B7** as input cell 1; enter **B8** as input cell 2. 1-2-3 for Windows calculates the what-if table, as shown in figure 14.34.

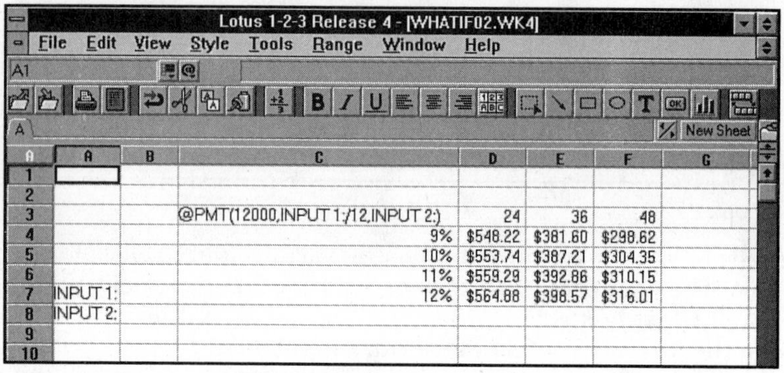

FIG. 14.34

A 2 variable what-if table.

Creating a 3 Variable What-if Table

A 3 variable what-if table shows the effects of changing three variables in a single formula. The third dimension of a 3 variable what-if table is represented by a three-dimensional worksheet range: the table spans two or more worksheets.

The structure of a 3 variable what-if table is an extension of the 2 variable what-if table structure. The different values of variables 1 and 2 are represented by different rows and columns. The new variable (the third one) is located in the upper-left corner of the what-if table range; the different values of the third variable are represented by different worksheets.

A 3 variable what-if table range spans a three-dimensional region. The size of the region is determined as follows:

Number of rows = (values of variable 1) + 1

Number of columns = (values of variable 2) + 1

Number of worksheets = (values of variable 3)

You also need three input cells. These cells can be located anywhere in any worksheet but are often grouped together for convenience. You should identify the input cells with labels in adjacent cells.

The formula evaluated in a 3 variable what-if table must correctly refer to all three input cells. When you fill out the What-if Table dialog box, the Input Cell **1** text box refers to the values in the first column of the what-if table range. Input Cell **2** refers to the values in the first row of the what-if table range. Input Cell **3** refers to the values in the upper-left corner of the what-if table range in each worksheet.

Calculating loan payments is a perfect application for a 3 variable what-if table because the relevant formula uses three variables: principal, interest rate, and term. You can create a what-if table that calculates monthly payments for three principal amounts, three interest rates, and three loan periods. To establish a 3 variable what-if table range for this application, follow these steps:

1. Insert the additional two worksheets you need for this application by selecting Edit Insert Sheet After and entering **2** in the Quantity text box. Press Enter or click on OK. Then select View Split Perspective and click on OK or press Enter to view all three active worksheets.

2. Refer to the size guidelines for a 3 variable what-if table, given earlier in this section. Use them to decide on an empty worksheet region for the what-if table.

   For this example, you need a what-if table range four rows high, four columns wide, and three worksheets deep. Use the range A:C2..C:F5 to define the table range.

3. In the top worksheet in the first column of the range, enter the values for variable 1 in the second through last cells.

   In this example, the interest rate is variable 1. Enter the three values for the interest rate (**10%, 11%,** and **12%**) in cells A:C3..A:C5 respectively.

4. In the same worksheet, enter the values for variable 2 in the second through last cells of the first row in the range.

   In this example, the term is variable 2. Enter the three values for term (**24, 36,** and **48** months) in cells A:D2..A:F2.

5. Copy the values for variables 1 and 2 to the two other worksheets in the range.

   In this example, copy **A:C2..A:F5** to **B:C2..C:C2**.

6. In the top-left cells of the what-if table range, enter the values for variable 3. Enter a different value in the corresponding cell in each worksheet.

   In this example, the principal is variable 3. Enter the three values for principal (**10000, 15000,** and **20000**) in cells A:C2, B:C2, and C:C2.

   The range for the what-if table is now established.

7. Select the input cells. Use cells A:B2..A:B4 for input cells 1, 2, and 3. Remember to put identifying labels in cells A:A2..A:A4.

8. Enter the payment formula in any cell outside the what-if table range—for example, in cell A:B6. Use the following 1-2-3 for Windows function for calculating loan payments:

@PMT(A:B4,A:B2/12,A:B3)

Because payment periods are expressed in months, you divide the annual interest rate by 12 to obtain the monthly interest rate. (Note that when you enter the @PMT function in B6, you see ERR —because there are yet no values in the input cells A:B2..A:B4. Format the cell containing the formula with the Text format to display the formula rather than ERR .) The worksheet now appears as shown in figure 14.35.

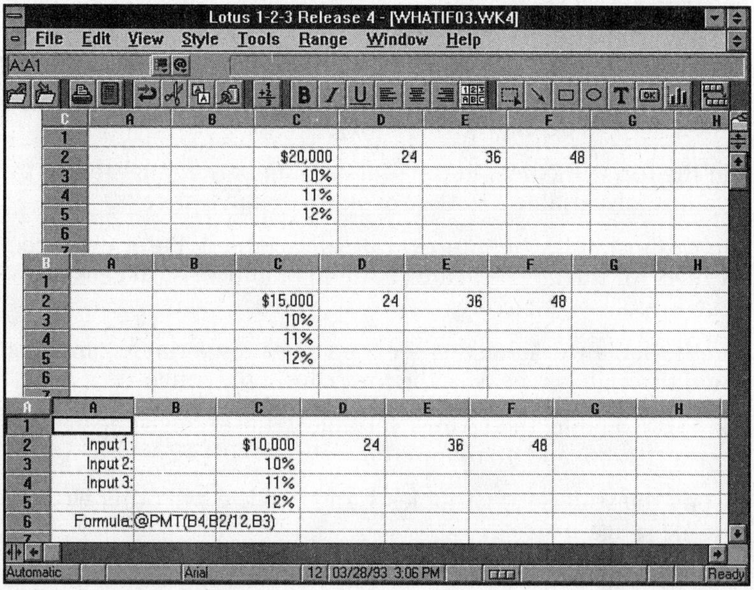

FIG. 14.35

Setting up the three-dimensional table.

9. Select Range Analyze What-if Table. In the What-if Table dialog box, specify **3** as the number of variables, **A:C2..C:F5** as the table range, **A:B6** as the formula cell, **A:B2** as input cell 1, **A:B3** as input cell 2, and **A:B4** as input cell 3. Click on OK or press Enter.

Format the resulting data table using the Currency format. The results are shown in figure 14.36.

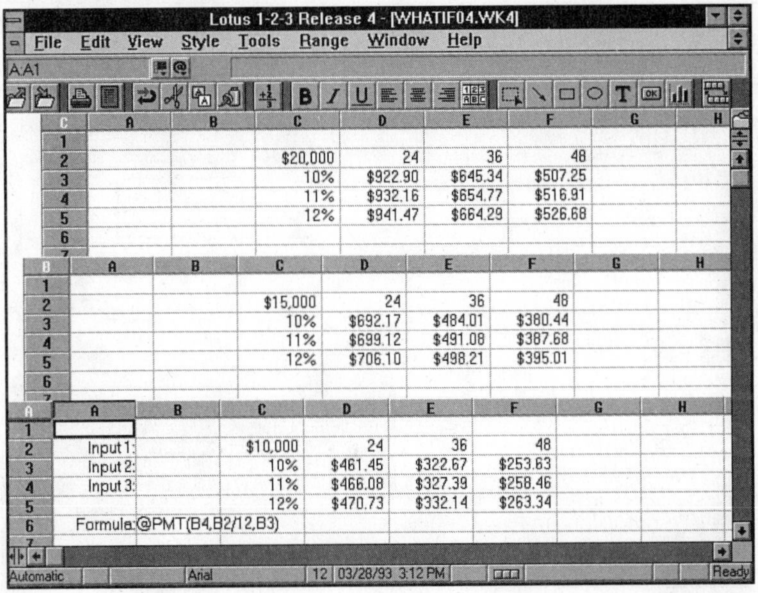

FIG. 14.36

The completed 3 variable what-if table.

Creating Frequency Distributions

The command you use to create frequency distributions in 1-2-3 for Windows is Range Analyze Distribution. A *frequency distribution* describes the relationship between a set of classes and the frequency of occurrence of members of each class. A list of consumers with their product preferences demonstrates the use of the Range Analyze Distribution command to produce a frequency distribution (see fig. 14.37).

For example, figure 14.37 shows a list of customers identified as customer A through P in column A, and their feelings about the upcoming product line expressed in a zero to ten scale in column B.

To use the Range Analyze Distribution command, you first specify a range of values (corresponding to the range of preference numbers in this example). After specifying **B3..B18** for the range of values, set up the range of intervals in D3..D7. 1-2-3 for Windows calls the range of intervals the *bin range*. If you have evenly spaced intervals, use the Range Fill command to enter the values for the bin range. If the intervals are not evenly spaced, you cannot use the Range Fill command to fill the range; you must type them in manually or copy them from some other area.

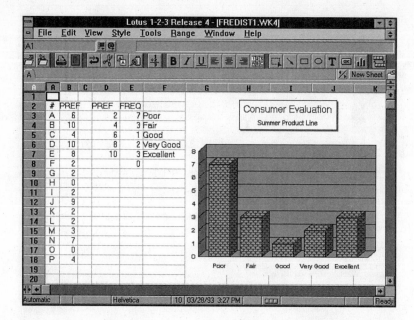

FIG. 14.37

The Range
Analyze Distribu-
tion command,
used to analyze
customer
preference data.

After you select Range Analyze Distribution and specify these ranges in the dialog box, 1-2-3 for Windows creates the results column (E3..E8) to the right of the bin range (D3..D7). The results column, which shows the frequency distribution, is always in the column to the right of the bin range and extends one row farther down than the bin range.

The values in the results column represent the frequency of distribution of the numbers in the range of values for each interval. The first interval in the bin range in this example is for values greater than 0 and less than or equal to 2; the second interval is for values greater than 2 and less than or equal to 4, and so on. The last value in the results column, in cell E8 of this example, shows the frequency of leftover numbers (the frequency of numbers that do not fit into an interval classification).

The Range Analyze Distribution command can help you create understandable results from a series of numbers. The results can be graphed easily, as shown in figure 14.37. A manufacturer looking at this graph would probably realize that this product probably won't be next summer's big seller! The labels in cells F3 through F7 were added to provide an explanation of the product ratings on a scale of 0 to 10, and were then used as X-axis labels in the chart.

Using the Range Analyze Regression Command

The Range Analyze Regression command gives you a multiple linear regression analysis package within 1-2-3 for Windows. Although most people don't have a need for this advanced feature, if you need to use it, 1-2-3 for Windows saves you the cost and inconvenience of buying a stand-alone statistical package for performing regression analysis.

Use Range Analyze Regression when you want to determine the relationship between one set of values (the *dependent variable*) and one or more other sets of values (the *independent variables*). Regression analysis has a number of uses in a business setting, including relating sales to price, promotions, and other market factors; relating stock prices to earnings and interest rates; and relating production costs to production levels.

Think of linear regression as a way of determining the best line through a series of data points. Multiple regression does this for several variables simultaneously, determining the best line relating the dependent variable to the set of independent variables. Consider, for example, a data sample showing Annual Earnings versus Age. Figure 14.38 shows the data; figure 14.39 shows the data plotted as an XY graph (using A7..A20 for the X graph range and C7..C20 for the A graph range).

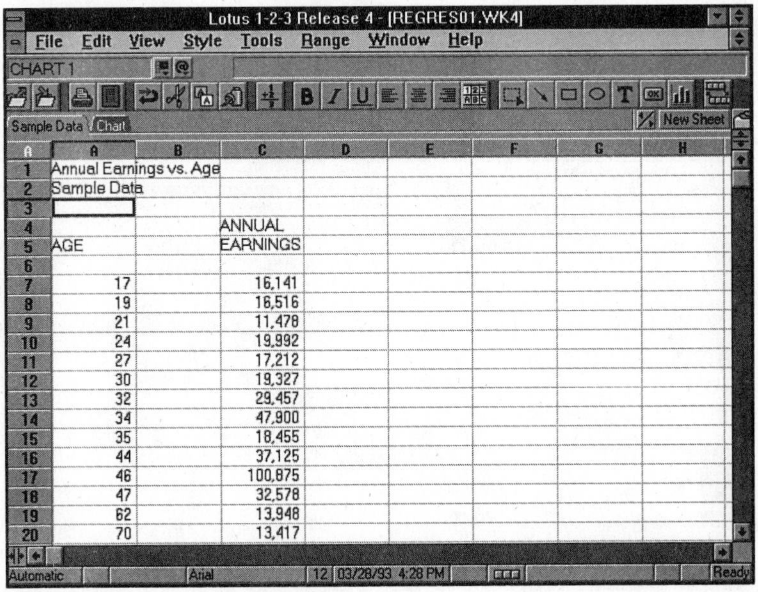

FIG. 14.38

The Annual Earnings versus Age data.

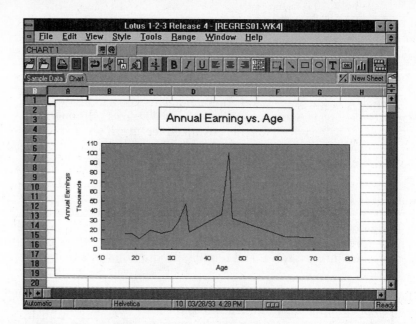

FIG. 14.39

A graph of the Annual Earnings versus Age data.

The Range Analyze Regression command can simultaneously determine how to draw a line through these data points and how well the line fits the data. When you invoke the command, the Regression dialog box shown in figure 14.40 appears.

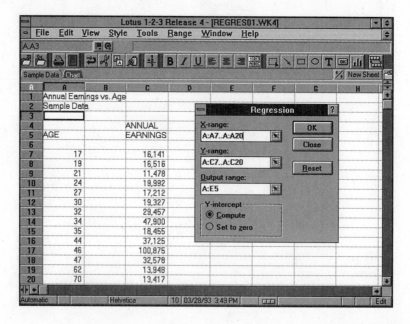

FIG. 14.40

The Regression dialog box.

Use the X-Range option to select one or more independent variables for the regression. The Range Analyze Regression command can use as many as 75 independent variables. The variables in the regression must be columns of values, meaning that any data in rows must be converted to columns with Range Transpose before you issue the Range Analyze Regression command. In this example, the X-Range is specified as **A7..A20**.

The **Y**-Range option specifies the dependent variable. The Y-Range must be a single column; in this example, **C7..C20** is the Y-Range.

The Output Range option in the Regression dialog box specifies the cell in the upper-left corner of the results range. This area should be an unused section of the worksheet because the output is written over any existing cell contents. In this example, **E5** is specified as the output range.

The Y-Intercept options enable you to specify whether or not you want the regression to calculate a constant value. Calculating the constant is the default; in some applications, however, you may need to exclude a constant.

Figure 14.41 shows the results of using the Range Analyze Regression command in the Annual Earnings versus Age example. The results (in cells E5..H13) include the value of the constant and the coefficient of the single independent variable that was specified with the X-Range option. The results also include a number of regression statistics that describe how well the regression line fits the data. In this case, the R-Squared value and the standard errors of the constant and the regression coefficient all indicate that the regression line does not explain much of the variation in the dependent variable.

The new data in column D is the computed regression line. These values consist of the constant plus the coefficient of the independent variable times its value in each row of the data. To calculate the regression line, place the formula +$H$6+$G$12*A7 in cell D7. Then use the Style Number Format , (Comma) 0 command to format the result. Finally, copy from D7..D7 to D8..D20 to copy the formula to the other cells in column D. This computed line can be plotted against the original data (as graph range B, formatted to display lines only); see figure 14.42.

When you look at the Annual Earnings versus Age plot, notice that income appears to rise with age until about age 50; then income begins to decline. You can use the Range Analyze Regression command to fit a line that describes such a relationship between Annual Earnings and Age. In figure 14.43, a column of data has been added to column B, containing the square of the age in column A. To include this new column in the regression, specify the range A7..A20 for the X-Range and adjust the formulas in column D by changing the formula in cell D7 to the following formula:

    +$H$6+$G$12*A7+$H$12*B7

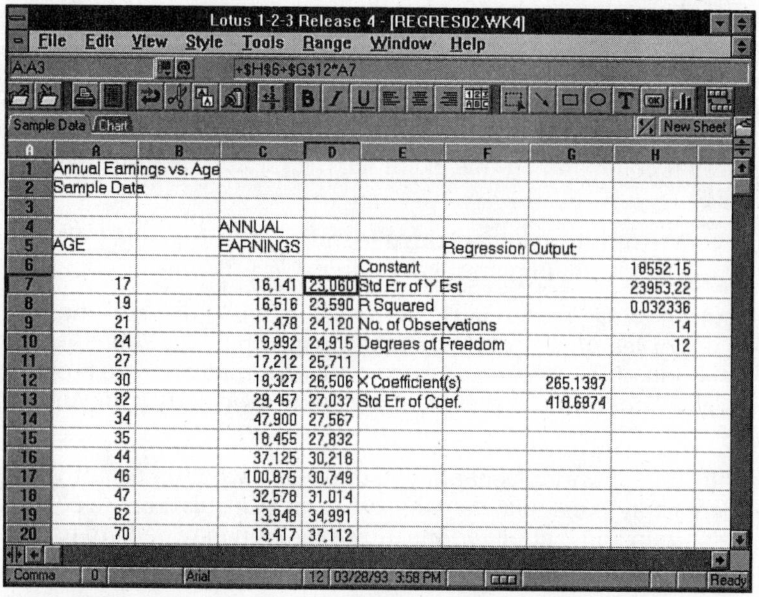

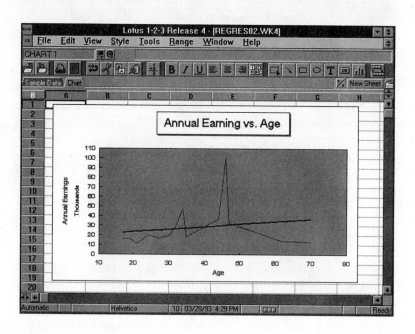

FIG. 14.41

The results of the Range Analyze Regression command on the Annual Earnings versus Age data.

FIG. 14.42

A graph of the Annual Earnings versus Age data, with a regression line.

Copy the formula in cell D7 to D8..D20 and recalculate the regression. Notice that the regression statistics are much improved over the original regression of Annual Earnings versus Age. This fact means that the new line fits the data more closely than the old one. (However, the regression statistics indicate that the regression only explains about one-third of the variation of the dependent variable.)

You must add the new regression coefficient (as mentioned earlier) to the equation that generates the regression line if you want to generate the new plot shown in figure 14.44. Note that the regression line is now a parabola that rises until age 45 and then declines. The regression line generated by a multiple regression may or may not be a straight line, depending on the independent variables used.

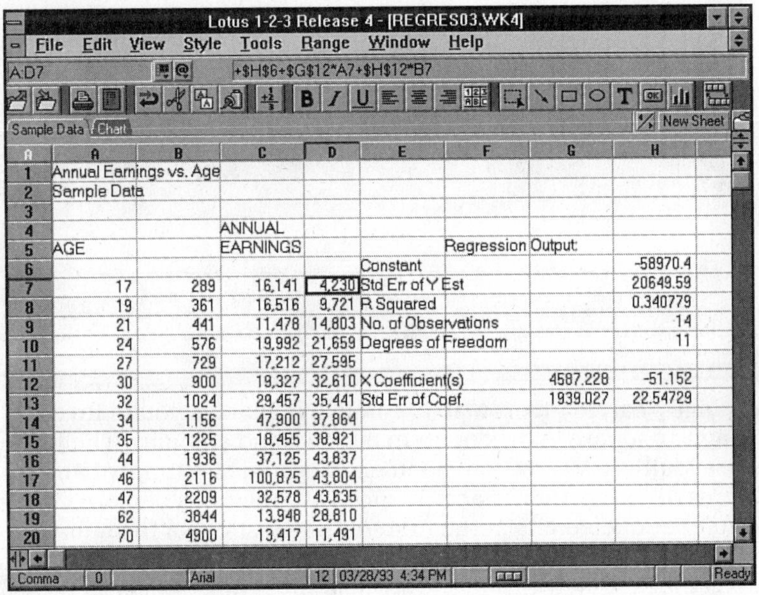

A	A	B	C	D	E	F	G	H
1	Annual Earnings vs. Age							
2	Sample Data							
3								
4			ANNUAL					
5	AGE		EARNINGS			Regression	Output:	
6					Constant			-58970.4
7	17	289	16,141	4,230	Std Err of Y Est			20649.59
8	19	361	16,516	9,721	R Squared			0.340779
9	21	441	11,478	14,803	No. of Observations			14
10	24	576	19,992	21,659	Degrees of Freedom			11
11	27	729	17,212	27,595				
12	30	900	19,327	32,610	X Coefficient(s)		4587.228	-51.152
13	32	1024	29,457	35,441	Std Err of Coef.		1939.027	22.54729
14	34	1156	47,900	37,864				
15	35	1225	18,455	38,921				
16	44	1936	37,125	43,837				
17	46	2116	100,875	43,804				
18	47	2209	32,578	43,635				
19	62	3844	13,948	28,810				
20	70	4900	13,417	11,491				

FIG. 14.43

The Annual Earnings versus Age data and the square of Age.

Using the Range Analyze Matrix Commands

The Range Analyze Invert Matrix and Range Analyze Multiply Matrix commands are specialized mathematical commands that enable you to solve systems of simultaneous linear equations and manipulate the resulting solutions. These commands are powerful but have limited applications in a business setting. If you are using 1-2-3 for Windows for certain types of economic analysis or for scientific or engineering calculations, you may find these commands valuable.

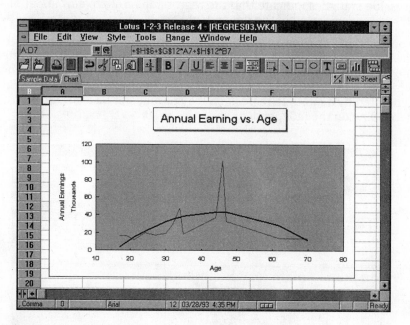

FIG. 14.44

The graph of the Annual Earnings versus Age data, with a revised regression line.

The <u>R</u>ange <u>A</u>nalyze <u>I</u>nvert Matrix command enables you to invert a nonsingular square matrix of up to 80 rows and columns. The <u>R</u>ange <u>A</u>nalyze <u>M</u>ultiply Matrix command enables you to multiply two rectangular matrices together in accordance with the rules of matrix algebra. The number of columns in the first matrix must equal the number of rows in the second matrix. The result matrix has the same number of rows as the first matrix, and the same number of columns as the second.

Figure 14.45 shows a sample problem that uses matrix inversion and multiplication to determine an airplane's air speed and the speed of the headwind or tailwind. In this problem, the distance between the two points (cell B1), the time required to travel from point 1 to point 2 (cell B2), the time required to travel from point 2 to point 1 (cell B3), and the relative wind speeds (cells B5 and B6) are known. Matrix inversion and multiplication make finding the actual air speed of the plane and the actual speed of the wind a simple task.

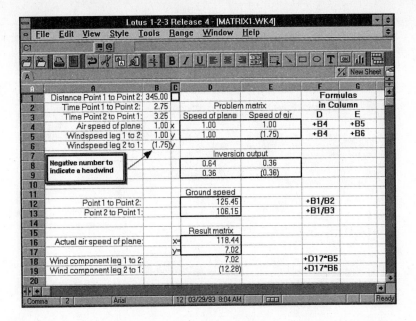

FIG. 14.45

A problem that uses matrix inversion and multiplication to calculate speeds.

To solve this problem using matrix inversion and multiplication, follow these steps:

1. Enter the labels in column A, the data shown in column B, and the formulas in columns D and E (as indicated in columns F and G). The inversion output matrix and the result matrix will be calculated, and should be left blank.

2. Select Range Analyze Invert Matrix to display the Invert Matrix dialog box (see fig. 14.46). Specify **D4..E5** as the From matrix and **D8** as the To matrix. Click on OK or press Enter.

3. Select Range Analyze Multiply Matrix to display the Multiply Matrix dialog box (see fig. 14.47). Specify **D8..E9** as the First Matrix, **D12..D13** as the Second Matrix, and **D16** as the Resulting Matrix. Click on OK or press Enter.

This problem shows an example of using matrix inversion and multiplication to solve a set of linear equations. The problem matrix (D4..E5) is used to define the equations. When you use Range Analyze Invert Matrix to display the Invert Matrix dialog box, the problem matrix is called the From matrix. When this matrix is inverted, the To matrix, (D8..E9) holds its inverse.

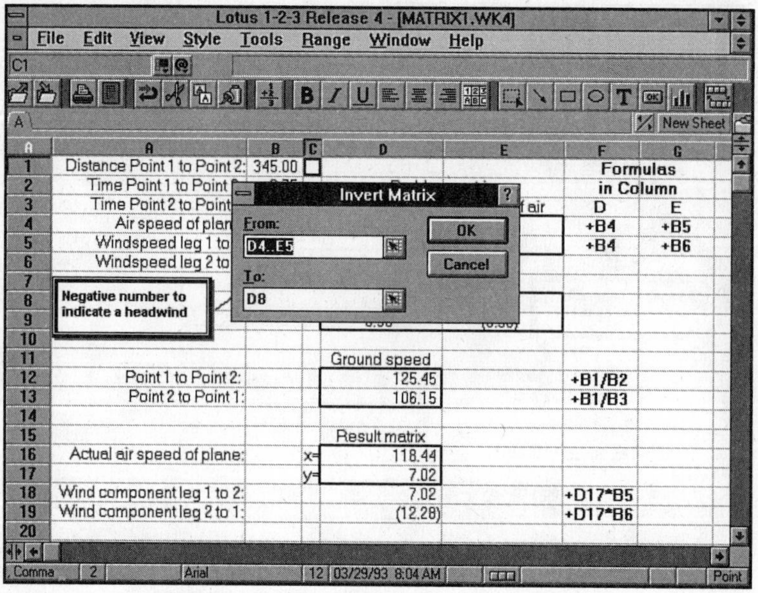

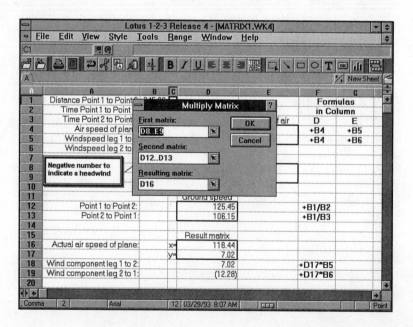

FIG. 14.46

The completed
Invert Matrix
dialog box.

After the matrix inversion is performed, the To matrix becomes the
First Matrix for the matrix multiplication, and is multiplied by the
Second Matrix (D12..D13)which contains the ground speed calculations, to produce the Resulting Matrix (D16). The Resulting Matrix
displays the results of solving for the two variables, x (air speed) and
y (wind speed).

FIG. 14.47

The completed
Multiply Matrix
dialog box.

> **T I P**
>
> When data in a problem changes, don't forget to select Range Analyze Invert Matrix and Range Analyze Multiply Matrix again to calculate updated results.

Matrix inversions and multiplications can be time consuming, especially when you are dealing with large matrices or your system lacks a numeric coprocessor. The 80486 DX processor has a built-in numeric coprocessor, but the 80486 SX, as well as all 80386 and 80286 processors, do not.

Questions & Answers

This chapter discussed advanced data management and analysis. Following are some questions you might encounter as you explore this subject further.

Q: I want to join two databases, but 1-2-3 for Windows does not find or show any records in the query table. What's wrong?

A: The most likely problem is that the databases are joined incorrectly. The fields used to join the databases must contain related information. That is, if one database refers to *Ralph's Bar* and the other to *Ralph's Cafe*, 1-2-3 for Windows cannot find a match. Make certain that the values in the join fields match.

Q: When I join two databases, the query table contains too many records. Instead of supplying unique values, the query table contains several sets of values. What can I do to correct this?

A: Make certain that a many-to-one relationship exists between the master database and the matching database.

Q: The query table correctly joined my databases, but why does it show two copies of the join field?

A: By default, a joined query table displays every field from the joined databases. Because both databases contain a copy of the field used to join the databases, the query table includes two copies of this field. Use Query Choose Fields to display a list of the fields, highlight the fields you want to remove, and select Clear. Press Enter or click on OK to return to the query table.

Q: When I try to open an external database file, why don't I see an option for my SQL server?

A: When you install 1-2-3 for Windows, you are given the option of selecting which DataLens drivers to install. You probably did not select the necessary driver. See Appendix A for more information on installing DataLens drivers.

Q: When I try to open a Paradox database, why does 1-2-3 for Windows prompt me for a password? I'm not on a network, and no one else uses my PC.

A: Some databases (including Paradox) employ user IDs and passwords. If you don't use this information on your system, simply press Enter to bypass the dialog box.

Q: Why did several formulas in my worksheet change to ERR when I disconnected from an external database file?

A: 1-2-3 for Windows uses range names to refer to external database files. If you use those range names in formulas, the formulas change to ERR because they refer to range names that are no longer defined once the external database is disconnected. To correct the problem, reconnect to the external database file and specify the same range name to refer to the file.

Q: I tried to import data from a text file, but all I get are numbers in various worksheet cells. Where is the rest of the text?

A: This is a common problem. When you select File Open and select Text as the File type, 1-2-3 for Windows displays files with TXT or PRN extensions. If you double-click on a text file, 1-2-3 for Windows imports the file using the default—Formatted Text. Instead of double-clicking on the file name, click once to select the file, and then select Combine. Choose Unformatted text and OK to correctly import the text data.

Q: Why does my cross-tabulation table only contain errors (ERR)?

A: A cross tabulation requires three columns of data. If your data only contains two columns, 1-2-3 for Windows generates a cross-tabulation table, but fills it with ERR.

Q: Why is the Query Aggregate command dimmed in my menu system?

A: You can create an aggregate column in a query table only if the column you want to analyze is selected and no other aggregate column exists in the current query table. If you want to create another aggregate column, create another query table.

Summary

This chapter addressed advanced data-management techniques. It covered how to join databases to take advantage of their related information. You also learned how to access data in external databases and text files. The balance of the chapter covered 1-2-3 for Windows' data-analysis features: cross tabulations and aggregates, what-if tables, frequency distributions, data regression, and matrix operations.

The next two chapters provide an introduction and reference to the 1-2-3 for Windows macro commands. Using these commands, you can automate simple repetitive tasks or create complete applications.

PART

V

OUTLINE

Customizing 1-2-3 for Windows

Understanding Macros

Although the basic worksheet, database, and graphics features of 1-2-3 Release 4 for Windows are very powerful, you can greatly enhance their utility by creating and using *macros*—small programs that automate 1-2-3 for Windows. Simple macros can duplicate the tasks you find yourself performing repeatedly, such as printing worksheets, changing fonts, or entering the same data in several locations.

More advanced macros, however, can provide you with even more capabilities. You can construct sophisticated business applications that function in the same way as applications written in such programming languages as BASIC, C, or FORTRAN. Fortunately, creating advanced macro programs is much easier than creating programs in most other programming languages.

This chapter covers the following topics:

- Defining a macro
- Developing and writing a macro
- Planning the layout of a macro
- Formatting a macro

- Naming and running macros

- Documenting macros

- Testing and debugging macros

- Protecting macros

- Recording macros with the Transcript window

- Adding macro buttons to a worksheet

- Translating 1-2-3 Release 1 for Windows macros

Chapter 16 introduces *macro commands*—a powerful set of programming tools that enable you to enhance macros. Chapter 16 also helps you learn the functions and applications of those commands.

Defining a Macro

The simplest type of macro is nothing more than a short collection of keystrokes that 1-2-3 for Windows enters into the worksheet for you. Because the program stores this keystroke collection as text in a cell, you can treat the text as you would any label. Consider the number of times you save and retrieve worksheet files, print reports, and set and reset worksheet formats. In each case, you perform the operation by typing a series of keystrokes—sometimes a rather long series. By running a macro, however, you can reduce any number of keystrokes to a two-keystroke abbreviation.

Consider a simple yet effective macro that enters text. Suppose that your company's name is *Darlene's Computer Warehouse*—an entry that requires quite a few keystrokes. You want to place this name at various points in worksheets. You can type the entry's many keystrokes every time you want to place the entry in the worksheet, or you can store all the keystrokes in a macro. When you want the company's name to appear in a worksheet, you can use just two keystrokes—the Ctrl key and a designated letter of the alphabet. Such a macro is called a Ctrl+*letter* macro. In a later section, you learn to create such a macro.

> **NOTE** Most macros created in earlier versions of 1-2-3 for Windows must be translated before use. Some very simple keystroke macros, such as this example, may work in 1-2-3 Release 4 for Windows, but most macros from earlier versions of 1-2-3 for Windows will not. See "Translating 1-2-3 Release 1 for Windows Macros," later in this chapter, for more information.

You name a Ctrl+*letter* macro by using the backslash key (\) and a single letter of the alphabet. DOS versions of 1-2-3 called these macros Alt+*letter* macros, and the Alt key was termed the *macro key*. Windows applications, however, usually reserve the Alt key for invoking the main menu. In 1-2-3 for Windows, therefore, Lotus changed its conventions for invoking macros named by a backslash and a single letter; you now start these macros in 1-2-3 for Windows by holding the Ctrl key and pressing the respective alphabet-letter key.

The Ctrl+*letter* method is not the only way to name a macro. You learn about other methods in later sections of this chapter.

Developing Your Own Macros

The steps for creating any macro are basic. An outline of these steps follows; later sections expand on the major steps.

Perform the following steps to create a macro:

1. **Plan what you want the macro to do.**

   Write down all the tasks you want the macro to perform; then arrange those tasks in the order in which they should be completed.

2. **Identify the keystrokes or commands the macro should use.**

   Keep in mind that macros can be as simple as labels (text) that duplicate the keystrokes you want to replay.

3. **Find an area of the worksheet in which you can enter macros.**

   When you choose the worksheet area, consider that executed macros read text from cells, starting with the top cell and working down through lower cells. Macros end when they encounter a blank cell, a cell with a numeric value, or a command that stops macro execution. Therefore, enter macros as labels in successive cells in the same column.

4. **Use the correct syntax to enter the keystrokes and macro commands into a cell or cells.**

5. **Name the macro.**

   You can give a macro a name in one of three ways:

   - Assign the macro a Ctrl+*letter* name. This type of name consists of a backslash (\) followed by an alphabetic character (for example, *a*).

■ Choose a descriptive name, such as PRINT_BUDGET, for a macro. Macro names, like other 1-2-3 range names, can contain up to 15 characters.

■ Give the name \0 (zero) to a macro if you want that macro to run automatically when the file is loaded. The User Setup dialog box enables you to disable and re-enable the auto-execute feature of macros named \0. The Run Autoexecute Macros check box in this dialog box acts like a toggle switch: when the check box is selected, a macro named \0 executes automatically when a file that contains the macro is opened.

6. **Document the macro.**

To facilitate the editing and debugging process, you can document a macro in several ways:

■ Use a descriptive macro name and consistently use range names instead of cell addresses in macros. Addresses entered in the text of a macro are not updated when changes are made to the worksheet. A macro does not work properly with incorrect addresses, which can be caused by moving, inserting, or deleting ranges. Range names in a macro *are* updated when the worksheet changes.

■ Use the /Range Name Note feature in the 1-2-3 Classic menu to attach notes to a range name.

■ Include comments as a separate column to the right of the actual macro within the worksheet.

■ Retain all the paperwork you used to design and construct the macro for later reference.

7. **Test and debug the macro.**

■ Always test your macros for proper operation before giving them to a user. Make certain the macros work correctly before you trust them to process important data.

When your macros become more complex as your expertise increases, continue to use these basic steps to create a macro. Remember that good planning and documentation are important for making macros run smoothly and efficiently.

Writing Your First Macros

The next two sections show you how to write two simple macros. The first macro enters text into a cell. The second macro enters commands specified in the macro.

Writing a Macro That Enters Text

In this section, you learn to create a macro that enters a company name, *Darlene's Computer Warehouse*, in various locations in worksheets. This simple example introduces the basic concepts required to create macros in 1-2-3 for Windows. Later, you learn to use more advanced macro programming commands and techniques to make macros execute faster and more efficiently.

Before you begin creating a macro, plan what you want the macro to do and identify the keystrokes the macro should enter. In the case of the macro that enters a company name in a worksheet, you want the macro to enter the letters, spaces, and punctuation that comprise the company's name. Then, as with any label, you want the macro to complete the entry by performing the equivalent of pressing the Enter key.

You begin building the macro by storing the keystrokes as text in a worksheet cell. After entering the letters that make up the company's name, you enter a tilde (~). In a macro, the tilde (~) represents the Enter key.

Cell B3 in figure 15.1 contains the keystrokes you want 1-2-3 for Windows to type for you as part of the macro:

`Darlene's Computer Warehouse~`

The tilde (~) is included at the end of the line. Remember that the tilde represents the press of the Enter key—an important step in ensuring that this macro executes correctly.

> You can adjust the width of column B to display all the macro's keystrokes by moving the mouse to the right edge of column B, directly above row 1, and double-clicking on the boundary between columns B and C. Then drag the column boundary to the right to widen column B. The macro works, however, no matter how wide the column containing its instructions.
>
> **T I P**

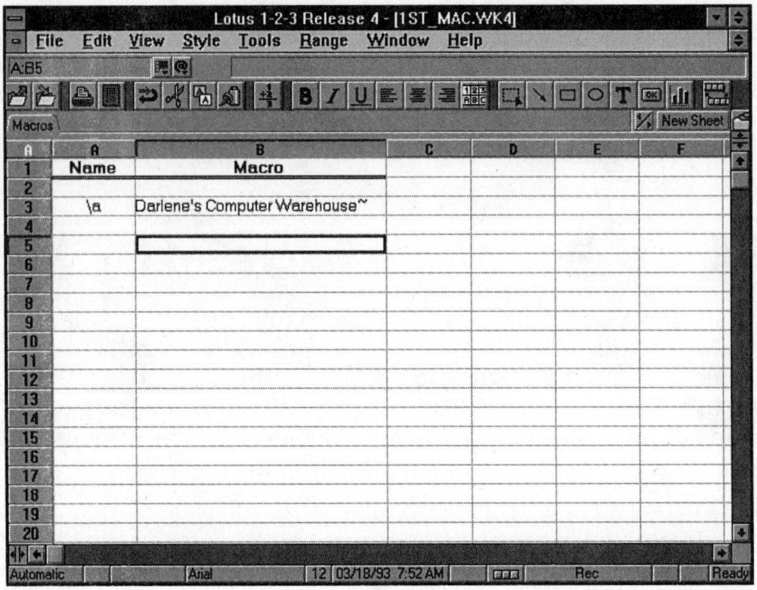

FIG. 15.1

A simple macro
for entering a
company name.

The next step in writing the macro is naming this sequence of key-strokes as a macro. This step is optional with 1-2-3 for Windows because you can run macros that have no name by using the Macro Run dialog box. Naming macros, however, has a few advantages, even in 1-2-3 for Windows. First, naming macros gives you a convenient form of self-documentation. Second, you can start named macros more quickly.

You have a few ways to name macros. One technique is described in this section; the second is described in a later section of this chapter.

The following steps are particularly convenient for naming a macro when the name is located to the left of the macro keystrokes, as is the name \a, shown in figure 15.1.

1. Move the cell pointer to cell A3.

2. From the 1-2-3 for Windows menu, select Range Name. The Name dialog box displays (see fig. 15.2).

3. From the For Cells list box, select To the right as the direction of the adjacent cell to which to apply the name.

4. Click on the Use Labels command button. This action assigns the name in cell A3, \a, to cell B3.

5. Select OK.

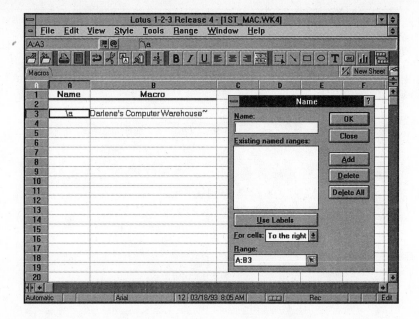

FIG. 15.2

The Name dialog
box used for
naming a macro.

By placing the macro's name one cell to the left of the first cell in the
macro, you easily can document the macro's name. This technique
helps you quickly remember the macro name for later use.

To *execute*, or run, this macro, you move the cell pointer to the cell in
which you want the company name to appear, hold the Ctrl key, and
then press A. 1-2-3 for Windows enters the sequence of characters identified as the macro \a.

Figure 15.3 shows the result of moving the cell pointer to cell B10 and
then running the \a macro. To save this macro for future use, save the
file in which the macro is located.

Writing a Simple Command Macro

In addition to writing macros that repeat text, you can write macros
that enter commands. If you follow the same procedure each time,
macro writing should become second nature to you.

1-2-3 Release 4 for Windows command macros, however, do not simply
duplicate the keystrokes you use to enter a command. Instead, command macros use a simple *command language*—a set of terms that replace keystroke representations with easy-to-read words. Macros that

use the 1-2-3 Release 4 for Windows macro command language are not only easier to read, they function more efficiently than collections of keystrokes, making macros execute more quickly. Don't worry if you don't know the 1-2-3 Release 4 for Windows macro command language; as this example shows, the macro command language is easy to learn and understand.

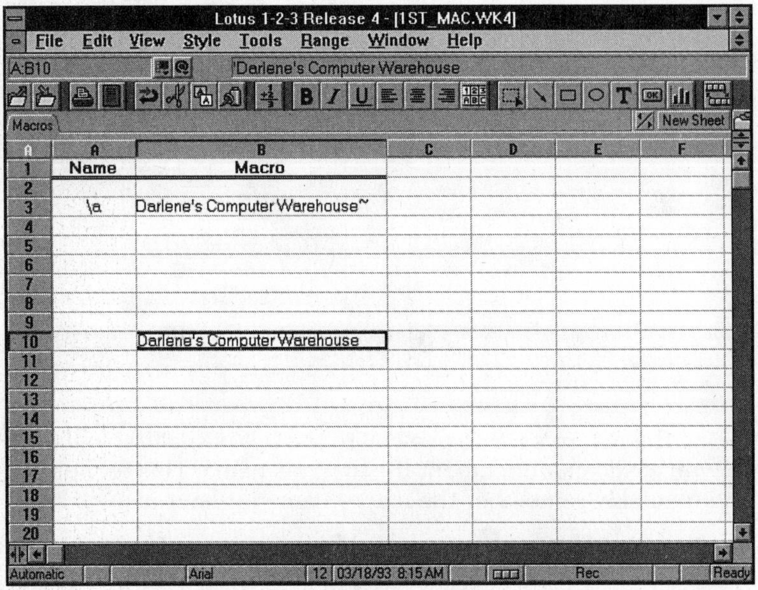

FIG. 15.3

The result of moving the cell pointer to cell B10 and running the \a macro.

As described earlier in this chapter, first plan what you want the command macro to perform. Then identify each step necessary to fully complete the task. For example, suppose that you want to create a simple macro that enters commands, such as the commands to name a macro (as you did in the preceding section). To do this task manually, you normally complete the following steps:

1. Move the cell pointer to the cell containing the label you want to use as a range name, in this case, cell A3.

2. Press the Alt key to access the 1-2-3 for Windows menu.

3. From the main menu, select the Range command; then select the Name command. 1-2-3 for Windows displays the Name dialog box.

4. Make certain that the For Cells list box displays To the right as the direction of the adjacent cell to which you want to apply the name. If this is not the case, make the proper selection in the list box.

5. Click on the Use Labels command button.

6. Select OK to confirm your selection and close the dialog box.

These steps tell 1-2-3 for Windows to use labels contained in worksheet cells to create range names for those cells to the right of the labels. You can use the 1-2-3 Release 4 for Windows command language to create a macro that performs this procedure. The equivalent macro command is as follows:

`{RANGE-NAME-LABEL-CREATE "right"}`

Cell B5 in figure 15.4 shows the macro command entered in the worksheet.

NOTE Instead of copying keystrokes, the 1-2-3 for Windows Release 4 macro command language substitutes easily read commands such as the RANGE-NAME-LABEL-CREATE command which replaces the six steps shown above. Chapter 16 includes a complete reference to the macro command language.

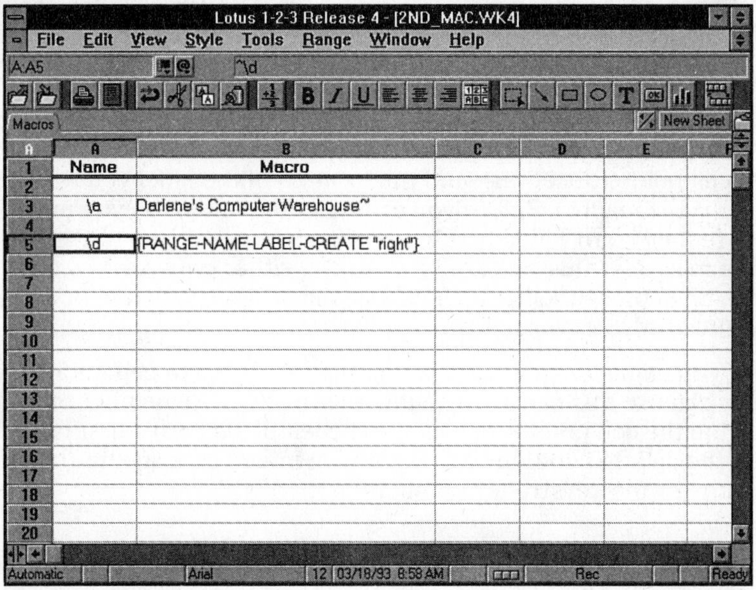

FIG. 15.4

The range-naming macro entered in cell B5.

For the purpose of this example, the intention is to name the macro \d. In this case, however, you cannot launch the macro in the typical Ctrl+*letter* fashion, because the name is not yet assigned. You can click on the Run Macro SmartIcon, press Alt+F3 (Run), or select the Tools Macro Run command to display the Macro Run dialog box and run the macro even before it is named (see fig. 15.5).

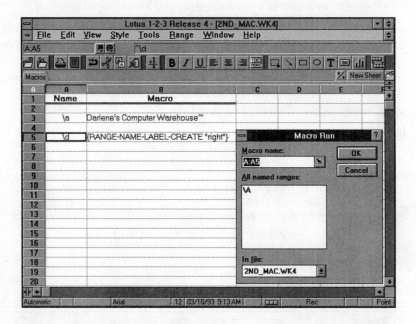

FIG. 15.5

The Macro Run dialog box, used to run an un-named macro.

In figure 15.5, the cell pointer rests in cell A:A5, one cell to the left of the macro's first line. The Macro Name text box displays A:A5 (the current cell-pointer location—and the location of the label you want to use to name the macro). Before you can execute the macro, you must change the Macro Name text box to display the address of the first cell in the macro (in this case, A:B5). You can either type **A:B5** or click on cell A:B5 in the worksheet. When you select OK, the macro in cell A:B5 executes and names itself \d.

After you name the \d macro and assign the name to cell A:B5, you easily can use this macro to name other macros. Remember to first position the cell pointer one cell to the left of a macro's first cell (that is, in the cell that contains the name you intend to assign to the macro). Then press the keystroke combination Ctrl+D.

Chapter 16, "Using Macro Commands," includes a comprehensive listing of the 1-2-3 Release 4 for Windows macro commands.

Understanding the Guidelines for Creating Macros

In the preceding sections of this chapter, you learned to write simple macros. You learned the importance of planning the macro and identifying the tasks the macro should perform. The following sections elaborate on the major elements of successful macro creation and execution. These elements include planning the layout of the macro, formatting the macro, naming and running the macro, documenting the macro, and testing and debugging the macro.

Whether your macros simply duplicate keystrokes or use the 1-2-3 Release 4 for Windows command language, you find that macros are easier to create and maintain if you follow the guidelines presented in the following sections.

Planning the Layout of Macros

Although you can enter as many as 512 characters in one cell, you should divide a long macro into smaller, more readable pieces. Break apart a macro by placing each part of the macro in consecutive cells down a column.

> An easy way to break a macro into parts is to divide it in terms of small tasks. You can limit each cell to a single task (or, at most, a few tasks). By limiting the content of each cell, you more easily can debug, modify, and document a macro. Using multiple cells to store the macro makes the macro easier to read and understand.
>
> **T I P**

Figure 15.6 shows two macros that execute an identical sequence of keystrokes. The \m macro performs the same sequence of tasks as the Print_Macros macro, but is difficult to read and understand because it is contained in a single cell (in this figure, cell B3 was selected and is being edited so that the complete text of the macro is displayed in the contents box).

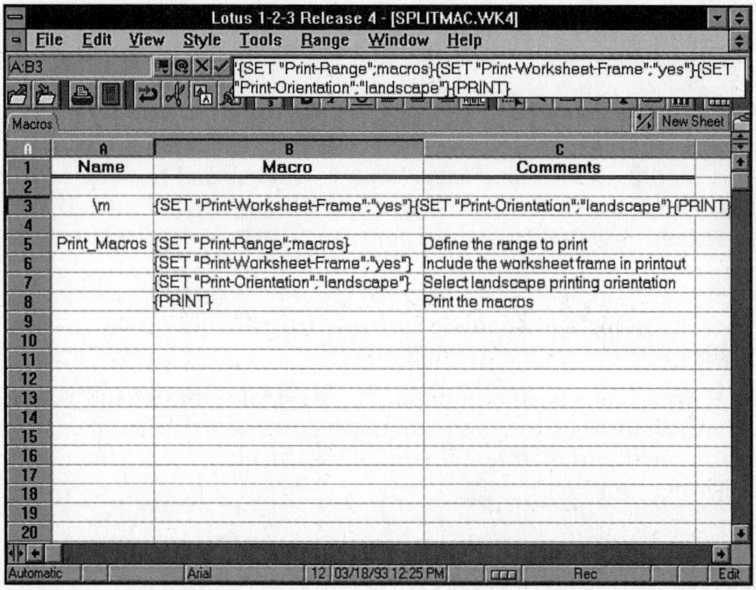

FIG. 15.6

Using multiple cells to store the macro.

Although both macros in figure 15.6 include the same set of macro commands, the Print_Macros macro has several advantages compared to the \m macro. For example, if you decide to change the range printed by the macro, the Print_Macros macro is much easier to modify. In addition, because the Print_Macros macro easily fits in a single on-screen column, you can read the macro commands it contains without moving the cell pointer to the cell containing the macro and editing the cell. Finally, the Print_Macros macro is much easier to document by using the column to the right of the macro commands.

The Print_Macros macro works whether you name the macro using just cell B5 or the entire range B5..B8. Remember that the commands execute starting at the upper left corner cell in the range. After the commands in cell B5 are executed, the macro processor moves down one cell and executes any commands in cell B6. After completing those commands, the processor again moves down one cell. The macro processor continues to move down and execute commands until it encounters one of the following situations:

■ An empty cell.

■ A cell that contains a numeric value, ERR, or NA.

■ A cell that contains a macro command that explicitly stops a macro. (These circumstances are discussed in Chapter 16.)

The macros you create will be easier to read and understand later if you logically separate macro commands into separate cells. When you use macro instructions that include braces, such as {SET} and {PRINT}, however, you must keep the entire macro command in the same cell. Splitting the macro command {PRINT} into two cells—{PR in one cell, and INT} in the cell that follows—doesn't work.

Because macro commands must be labels, the macro processor ignores the label prefix (', ", or ^) in the macro cell when the keystrokes are executed. It does not matter which of these label prefixes you use—the macros run regardless of which you choose.

1-2-3 for Windows enables you to repeat certain macro commands by including a *repetition factor*. A repetition factor tells 1-2-3 for Windows that you want a command repeated the number of times you specify. The \a and \d macros in figure 15.7 perform the same keystrokes. The \a macro uses four {DOWN} commands to move the cell pointer down four rows. The \d macro uses a repetition factor, {DOWN 4}, to repeat the {DOWN} macro command four times. Both macros accomplish the same task, but the \d macro is more efficient. When you use a repetition factor, leave a space between the macro command and the number. Refer to Chapter 16 for more information on macro commands which can use a repetition factor.

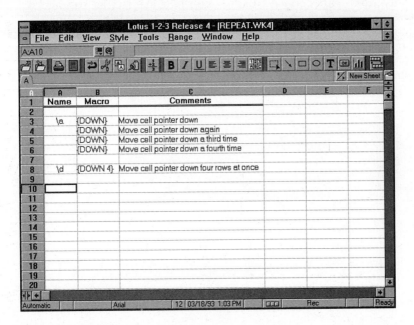

FIG. 15.7

A repetition factor used in the \d macro to repeat a macro command.

Formatting Macros

Certain formatting features are necessary to ensure the successful operation of 1-2-3 for Windows macros. Other conventions simplify the tasks of reading and analyzing macros. These tasks are particularly important when you need to debug or edit a macro by changing or adding an operation. The following sections present certain rules you should follow so that your macros run properly.

Enter Macro Cells as Text or String Formulas

When you type a macro into the worksheet, each cell of the macro must be entered as text or as a string formula. Certain keystrokes, such as numbers, cause 1-2-3 for Windows to change from Ready mode to Value mode; other keystrokes, such as the slash key (/), change 1-2-3 for Windows to Menu mode. Therefore, you must place an apostrophe (') before any of the following characters if that character is to be the first character in a macro cell:

A number from 0 to 9

/ + - @ # $. < (\

The apostrophe (') switches 1-2-3 for Windows to Label mode from Ready mode, especially if you are entering a macro that contains a number of lines which 1-2-3 does not recognize as labels. Using an apostrophe before any of the preceding characters and numbers ensures that 1-2-3 for Windows does not misinterpret your text entry. If any character *not* in this list is the first keystroke in the cell, 1-2-3 for Windows switches to Label mode and prefixes the entry with an apostrophe (') when you press Enter.

T I P   Use the Style Number Format command to apply Label format to cells where you intend to enter macro commands. 1-2-3 for Windows automatically prefixes entries in cells formatted with the Label format with an apostrophe (').

Use Braces with Macro Commands

Macro commands should be entered as described in Chapter 16. Be sure to use curly braces ({ }) to enclose macro commands.

Use Correct Syntax for Macro Commands

The syntax for macro commands must be correct. See Chapter 16 for the correct syntax for the macro commands used in 1-2-3 Release 4 for Windows. You must place each macro command within one cell; you cannot write a macro command so that the beginning brace is on one line and the closing brace is on another line.

When you use 1-2-3 for Windows macro commands, you must keep the entire macro command in the same cell. For example, you cannot split the command {BLANK} into two cells: {BL in one cell and ANK} in another does not work. You also should be careful not to mix curly braces with parentheses or square brackets; avoid such constructions as {BLANK) and [BLANK}.

Use the Tilde To Represent the Enter Key

You use the tilde (~) in a macro to represent the action of pressing the Enter key. Most 1-2-3 Release 4 for Windows command-language macros do not require a tilde, but macros that duplicate keystrokes instead of using command-language statements usually do require the tilde.

Use Repetition Factors

Use repetition factors in macros when possible. For example, instead of typing {LEFT} three times, you can type {LEFT 3} or {L 3}. When you use repetition factors, be sure to place one space between the actual macro command and the number of repetitions. Refer to Chapter 16 for more information on macro commands that can use a repetition factor.

Naming and Running Macros

You can start macros in several different ways, depending on how the macros are named. Consider the following examples:

■ Execute a macro named with the backslash (\) and a letter by holding the Ctrl key and pressing the designated letter of the alphabet. Alternatively, you can use the Macro Run dialog box. You invoke this dialog box by clicking on the Run Macro SmartIcon, pressing Alt+F3 (Run), or by selecting Tools Macro Run from the 1-2-3 for Windows menu.

- Execute a macro with a descriptive name of up to 15 characters by using the Macro Run dialog box.

- An auto-execute macro (one with the name \0) can be launched in two ways. Such a macro is started when a file containing the \0 macro is loaded, if the Run Autoexecute Macros check box is selected in the User Setup dialog box. You also can initiate auto-execute macros with the Macro Run dialog box.

- Execute any macro, even if it has no name, by using the Macro Run dialog box. Specify the macro's first cell as the address in the Macro Name text box and then select OK.

Earlier in this chapter, you learned how to name and run a macro with the Ctrl+*letter* combination. With the second method of naming and running macros, you assign a descriptive name to the first cell in the macro and then execute the macro from the Macro Run dialog box. With the third method, you create a macro named \0 that executes when you load the file. With the fourth method, you execute *any* macro by using the Macro Run dialog box. Invoking a macro in 1-2-3 for Windows with the Macro Run dialog box is a more user-friendly approach than the Alt+*letter* method available in previous versions of 1-2-3. Users of 1-2-3 for DOS versions before Release 2.2 could use only Alt+*letter* range names to start macros from the keyboard.

 When you click on the Run Macro SmartIcon, press Alt+F3 (Run), or select Tools Macro Run from the 1-2-3 for Windows menu, the Macro Run dialog box appears; the box displays a list of macro names from which you can choose. You also can type the cell address of the macro you want to run; you do not have to specify a range name.

Although you use the \0 name only if you want 1-2-3 for Windows to invoke a macro as soon as the file is retrieved, you can use the Ctrl+*letter* or descriptive name for any other macro. Both types of names have advantages. When you invoke a macro with a Ctrl+*letter* name, you use fewer keystrokes than when you invoke a macro with a descriptive name. The disadvantage of using a Ctrl+*letter* macro name, however, is that you may have difficulty remembering a macro's specific purpose, particularly when you have created many macros. Your chance of selecting the correct macro is greater when you use descriptive names.

The following sections describe all three approaches to creating, naming, and running macros. Figure 15.8 shows three macros that demonstrate the rules and conventions for naming and running macros. Although these macros are only intended to demonstrate the three ways to name and run a macro, each is a fully functioning 1-2-3 Release 4 for Windows command-language macro. The comments included in column C for each macro explain the purpose and functionality of each line in the macro.

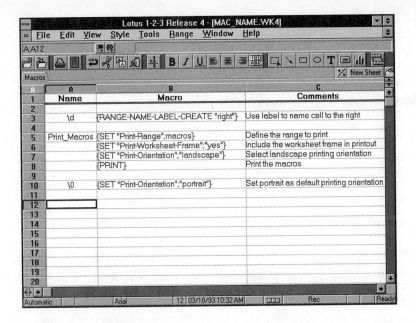

FIG. 15.8

Three macros
that show
naming
conventions.

Ctrl+*letter* Macros

You can name a macro by using the backslash key (\ ) and a letter. This method is the Ctrl+*letter* method of naming a macro. Versions of 1-2-3 before 1-2-3 for Windows called these macros Alt+*letter* macros. In 1-2-3 for Windows, however, the Alt key is reserved for invoking the 1-2-3 for Windows menu. In 1-2-3 for Windows, therefore, macros named with a backslash and a letter of the alphabet are called Ctrl+*letter* macros. You start these macros in 1-2-3 for Windows by holding the Ctrl key and pressing the appropriate alphabet-letter key.

The \d macro in figure 15.8 demonstrates the Ctrl+*letter* approach to naming a macro. The function of the \d macro is one way to automate the naming of macros. You can use uppercase or lowercase characters to name a macro; 1-2-3 for Windows does not differentiate between uppercase and lowercase letters for range names. Accordingly, \a, \A, and \m are valid names for Ctrl+*letter* macros.

1-2-3 for Windows assigns keyboard shortcuts to several Ctrl+*letter* combinations (such as Ctrl+B for changing selected text and numbers to **boldface**). If you name a macro using the same Ctrl+*letter* combination, the macro executes in place of the keyboard shortcut. To prevent conflicts with keyboard shortcuts, avoid using the letters B, C, E, I, L, N, O, P, R, S, U, V, X, or Z when naming Ctrl+*letter* macros.

T I P

To run a macro named with the backslash (\ ) and a letter, hold the Ctrl key and press the character key that identifies the macro. For example, to run the first macro in figure 15.8, press Ctrl+D.

Macros with Descriptive Names

Because you can use up to 15 characters to name a range in 1-2-3 for Windows, you can use descriptive names for macros. One way of documenting macros is to give them a longer descriptive name. Another way is to retain hard-copy documentation for macros, including printouts of the macro code. The Print_Macros macro in figure 15.8 automates the preparation of these printouts.

When naming macros with descriptive names, however, do not use range names that also are macro command names. See Chapter 16, "Using Macro Commands," for a list of command names.

You can initiate macros you have named with descriptive names from the Macro Run dialog box. Click on the Run Macro SmartIcon, press Alt+F3 (Run), or select Tools Macro Run from the 1-2-3 for Windows menu to access this dialog box. Figure 15.9 shows how the screen appears after this dialog box is invoked for the sample macros shown in figure 15.8.

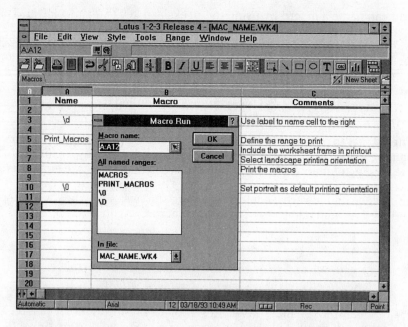

FIG. 15.9

The Macro Run dialog box displays a list of range names in the current file.

To start a macro from the current file with the Macro Name text box highlighted (see fig. 15.7), type the range name for the macro you want to run in the text box. Then select OK.

When you access the Macro Run dialog box, 1-2-3 for Windows displays all the range names in the current file, including range names that are not macro names. If you have other 1-2-3 for Windows worksheet files active in memory, 1-2-3 for Windows lists all these file names following the range names of the currently selected file.

To run a macro in a file not currently selected, select the file name by double-clicking on the desired file name in the In file list box. The Macro Run dialog box lists the range names in the selected file. Type the range name for the macro you want to run in the Macro Name text box.

You can start a macro in another file without selecting the file by preceding the macro's name in the Macro Name text box with the file name in which it is located. You enclose the file name in double angle brackets (<< >>) and then type the macro name, as in the following example:

<<BUDGET.WK4>>Print_Macro

To run a macro from the keyboard, do the following:

1. Press Alt+F3 (Run) or select Tools Macro Run from the 1-2-3 for Windows menu to access the Macro Run dialog box.

2. Press Tab to move from the Macro Name text box to the All Named Ranges list below it.

3. Use the arrow keys to highlight the desired entry and then press Enter.

You can choose from the following three ways to designate and run a macro from the Macro Run dialog box:

■ Type the name of the macro or the address of its first cell in the Macro Name text box. Then select OK. If you type the address without identifying the file, 1-2-3 for Windows assumes that you mean the current file. If you type an address that does not include the worksheet letter, 1-2-3 for Windows assumes that you mean the current worksheet. If you type a range name without identifying the file, 1-2-3 for Windows assumes that you mean a macro in the current file.

■ Highlight one of the macro range names appearing in the All Named Ranges list for the active file and then select OK. To see the range names for one of the other active files, highlight the name of that file and press Enter (alternatively, double-click on the name of the file); 1-2-3 for Windows displays the range names for that file. After the Macro Name text box displays the correct name for the macro you want to run, press Enter or click on OK.

■ Point to the first cell of the macro you want to run. With the high-light in the Macro Name text box, you can use the arrow keys or the mouse to point to the first cell of the macro you want to run. You also can click on the range selector beside the Macro Name text box to remove the dialog box and point to the first cell of the macro. Then press Enter or click on OK.

T I P   Although you can choose the method that best suits your needs, you may find the first method most useful when you want to invoke a macro located in another worksheet file, the second method generally the easiest and least error-prone, and the third method best when you want to see the actual contents of a macro before you execute it.

Auto-Execute Macros

You may want some macros to run automatically when you retrieve the worksheets that contain them. Use \0 to name the macro that you want to run as soon as the worksheet loads; such a macro is called an *auto-execute* macro. Each worksheet file can contain only a single auto-execute macro

T I P   If auto-execute macros do not run when files are retrieved, make certain that the Run Autoexecute Macros check box in the User Setup dialog box is selected.

Suppose that you print some worksheets using landscape orientation and others using portrait orientation. To ensure that the printing orientation is properly set for a worksheet requiring portrait orientation, you can include in that worksheet the \0 auto-execute macro shown in figure 15.8. By changing the argument from "portrait" to "landscape," you can create a similar auto-execute macro for worksheets that use landscape orientation.

Any task you want to perform automatically whenever a worksheet loads is a good candidate for an auto-execute macro. For example, if you create your own menus for a worksheet model, you may want to use an auto-execute macro to display the menu whenever the worksheet is loaded. You also may want to use an auto-execute macro to automatically move the cell pointer to a specific cell or to the end of a list of entries. In fact, you may have a whole series of tasks that should be performed whenever the worksheet is loaded. If so, simply include the correct commands in the auto-execute macro.

Documenting Macros

As with other parts of a 1-2-3 for Windows worksheet, you need to document the macros you write. You can document macros by using many of the same techniques you also use to document worksheets:

- Use descriptive names as macro names
- Include comments in the worksheet
- Keep any external design notes

Use Descriptive Names

You have seen how you can use the backslash and an alphabetic character to name a macro. You then can use the Ctrl+*letter* combination to execute the macro. Although a Ctrl+*letter* macro is easy to execute, its name does not describe the macro's purpose. A better naming convention is to use range names as macro names; you can execute such macros by clicking on the Run Macro SmartIcon, pressing Alt+F3 (Run), or selecting Tools Macro Run from the 1-2-3 for Windows menu.

Include Comments in the Worksheet

A description of each macro's function is found just to the right of each of the three macros shown in figure 15.10. With these simple macros, you can identify the tasks the macros perform just by reading the macro code—if you are familiar with the menu structure they reference. The addition of the documentation provides a ready reference.

With more complex and longer macros, you probably will find such internal documentation helpful. Later, when you want to make changes to the macro, these internal comments provide information about the macro's purpose and its intended action.

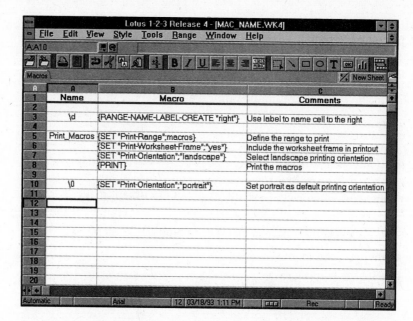

FIG. 15.10

Three macros
shown with
documentation.

You may discover that you do not need to comment on each individual
macro line, especially when you create simple macros. The following
guidelines may be helpful when you document macros:

- Document the overall purpose of a macro or subroutine.

- Document individual macro lines when specific operations are
  unclear.

- If possible, avoid spending too much time and memory documenting simple macros.

Keep External Design Notes

Be sure to retain any paperwork you created as part of designing and
constructing the macro. In addition to keeping any notes containing
keystrokes or commands you incorporated into the macro, you also
should keep printed copies of all the range names and formulas for
each worksheet.

> Use the <u>T</u>ools <u>A</u>udit command to create documentation on all
> formulas in a worksheet. See Chapter 8 for more information on
> this feature.

T I P

Don't underestimate the value of this sort of external documentation.
As with each form of macro documentation, external documentation
considerably eases the burden of trying later to understand or modify a
macro. The more people who use a macro and the more important a
macro is, the more critical external documentation becomes.

The most important piece of external documentation—which never
should be neglected—is a hard-copy printout of the macro. Examples of
other external documentation that may be particularly valuable include
notes on who requested a macro and why the macro was requested,
who created and who tested the macro, the underlying assumptions
that determined the overall design, and any diagrams or outlines of
macro operations or structure.

If you used external reference materials to help develop the worksheet,
consider including a bibliography and page references in the documentation. Any information you supply as part of external documentation
simplifies any maintenance of, or modifications to, the worksheet.

Using Single Step and Trace
To Test Macros

Macro writers soon recognize that even a well-designed macro program
can contain *bugs* (errors that prevent the macro from functioning correctly). Because 1-2-3 for Windows executes macro instructions in rapid
sequence, you often cannot determine why a macro is failing. This section introduces you to some methods that help you find and correct
errors in macros.

No matter how carefully you construct a macro, it may not run flaw-
lessly the first time. By taking a series of precautions, however, you can
minimize your efforts to get macros to work correctly.

Before you create a macro, always invest the time to design the macro
carefully. Just as a carpenter never starts construction of a house without blueprints, you should not start construction of a macro without a

carefully conceived and well-documented design. Take time to plan the detailed steps a macro is to perform, create good documentation of the macro's purpose and actions, and write descriptions of any range names used in the macro.

Even if you have a good design and thorough documentation, plan to test and debug your macros. Testing enables you to verify that a macro works precisely as you want it to. 1-2-3 for Windows provides two valuable aids to help verify the macro's operation and locate macro errors: Single Step and Trace modes. *Single Step mode* enables you to execute the macro one keystroke at a time. This mode gives you a chance to see, one instruction at a time, exactly what the macro does. *Trace mode* opens a small window that shows the macro instruction being executed and the cell location of that instruction.

Single Step and Trace are independent features, but they work well together. You can watch and analyze the macro action within the worksheet by using Single Step mode; the Macro Trace window indicates which macro instruction is being executed. Without these tools, macros often execute too rapidly for you to see the problem areas.

Suppose that you want to use the Single Step and Trace features to test a macro that you created. Follow this procedure to use these options to test that macro:

1. Choose <u>T</u>ools <u>M</u>acro <u>T</u>race or click on the Trace Mode SmartIcon. This action displays the Macro Trace window.

2. Choose <u>T</u>ools <u>M</u>acro <u>S</u>ingle Step or click on the Step Mode SmartIcon. This action causes 1-2-3 for Windows to execute macros one instruction at a time.

T I P   Press Alt+F2 (Step) or click on the Step Mode SmartIcon to toggle Single Step on or off.

Figure 15.11 shows the Macro Trace window in the worksheet; notice the Step indicator shown below the worksheet. The \a macro in this worksheet contains a deliberate spelling error in a macro command in cell B4. When the macro is executed, 1-2-3 for Windows displays an error.

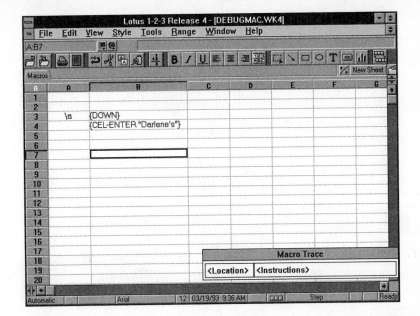

FIG. 15.11

The Macro Trace
window and the
Step indicator.

3. Start the macro you want to step through one keystroke at a time.
   After the macro starts, the <Location> and <Instructions> place
   markers in the Macro Trace window are replaced with cell addresses and macro code, respectively.

4. Start the macro by pressing any key. The first keystroke or
   macro command in the macro is executed. At the same time,
   the Macro Trace window highlights the macro instruction being
   executed and identifies the cell that contains that instruction
   (see fig. 15.12).

5. Execute each step in sequence by pressing any key after each
   subsequent step. Pressing a key tells 1-2-3 for Windows to perform
   the next step of the macro.

6. When you find an error, terminate the macro by pressing
   Ctrl+Break; then press Esc or Enter. Edit the macro to correct the
   error. Then repeat the test procedure in case other errors exist in
   the macro (as often is the case in complex macros). Figure 15.13
   shows the type of error message 1-2-3 for Windows displays when
   it encounters a macro error.

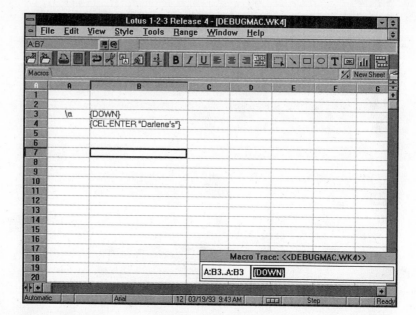

FIG. 15.12

The Macro Trace window shows each instruction as it is executed.

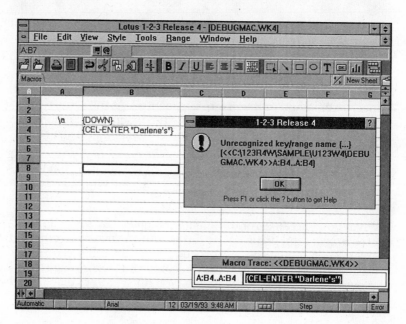

FIG. 15.13

1-2-3 for Windows displays a message when it encounters a macro error.

Edit a macro cell as you would any label. Move the cell pointer to the cell containing the label you want to edit (in this case, the macro line), press F2 (Edit) or double-click on the cell to go into Edit mode, and then make your changes to the label. If you need additional help understanding the error, press F1 or click on the ? (Help) button while the error message is displayed. Figure 15.14 shows the help text that appears when you click on the Help button for the error message displayed in figure 15.13.

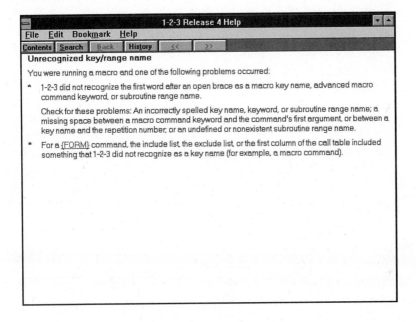

FIG. 15.14

Press F1 or click on the Help button to display a detailed message about the error.

For Related Information

◀◀ "Editing Data in the Worksheet," p. 126.

FROM HERE...

Protecting Macros

If you create worksheet applications to be used by others, secure the macros to prevent their accidental erasure or alteration. Most programs, such as database management systems, separate data and programs into individual files; 1-2-3, however, puts data and programs (macros) in the same files, making access to the macros easy—sometimes, too easy.

Even if you place all macros into separate files, the files are still 1-2-3 for Windows worksheet files; they can be changed by anyone who knows 1-2-3 for Windows well enough. You may want to consider saving macros in separate, sealed worksheet files. Macros saved in sealed worksheet files can be used by anyone who has access to the file, but they can be modified only by someone who knows the correct password to unseal the file.

Most users store macros customized for particular applications in the same files that contain the applications. In these instances, place the macros together outside the area occupied by the main model. Storing the macros together makes it easier for you to find a macro to edit and also helps you avoid accidentally overwriting or erasing part of a macro as you work with the model.

If you store macros in separate worksheets, you can avoid some common problems. Suppose that you want to use 1-2-3 for Windows commands to insert or delete columns or rows. When you use these commands—manually or within macros—the macros may become corrupted as rows are inserted or deleted (as can happen if the macros are in the same worksheet as the data being manipulated).

Inserting or deleting columns or rows also can cause problems with the cell addresses used in macros because changes in cell references that may occur as a result of an insertion or deletion are not reflected in the macros. Accordingly, use range names instead of cell addresses in macros.

T I P   Store macros on their own worksheet within a file. Name the worksheet Macros by double-clicking on the worksheet tab and typing **Macros**.

FROM HERE...

For Related Information

◀◀ Chapter 4, "Using Fundamental Commands," p. 133.

◀◀ Chapter 6, "Managing Files," p. 233.

Recording Macros with the Transcript Window

Macros can simplify your work with 1-2-3 for Windows. A powerful feature of 1-2-3 for Windows is the Transcript window. The Transcript window can record keystrokes and mouse movements as macro commands while you are in a 1-2-3 for Windows session. You can copy these recorded macros as labels into worksheet cells so that you can use or edit the macros.

Choose Tools Macro Show Transcript or click on the Transcript Window SmartIcon to display the Transcript window as it records commands (see fig. 15.15). Notice that when you display the Transcript window, 1-2-3 for Windows reduces the size of the worksheet and changes the menu bar and the SmartIcons to those appropriate for working in the Transcript window.

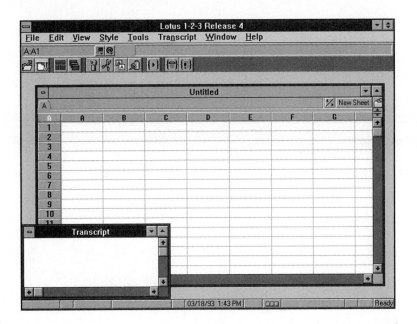

FIG. 15.15

The Transcript window records macro commands.

The Transcript window holds a fairly large number of characters. Each time you press a key or use the mouse, the action is recorded in the buffer. Some actions use one character, others can use several.

To begin recording a macro in the Transcript window, first select <u>T</u>ools <u>M</u>acro Re<u>c</u>ord or click on the Record Macro SmartIcon. Then press the keys you want to include in the macro. For example, if you press Alt+F1 and then type **y-**, the symbol for Japanese yen (¥) appears in the worksheet. When you press Enter, the Transcript window records this as the following macro command:

{CELL-ENTER "¥"}

Mouse actions are translated into their command equivalents in the Transcript window as well. This feature is particularly convenient when you work with dialog boxes, which are more mouse friendly than keyboard friendly. The recording of mouse actions also enables those upgrading from earlier versions of 1-2-3 to have 1-2-3 for Windows write detailed command instructions on how to perform basic tasks. For example, figure 15.16 shows the Transcript window after text was entered into the worksheet, the size of the type was modified, a background pattern and border was added, and a Japanese yen symbol was inserted.

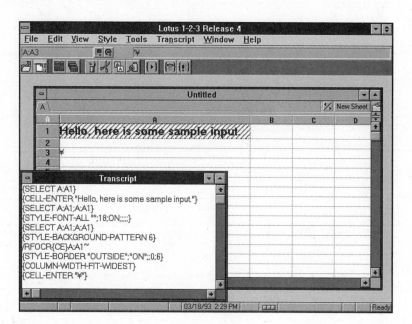

FIG. 15.16

Macro commands recorded in the Transcript window.

When the Transcript-window buffer is filled, 1-2-3 for Windows discards the oldest commands to make room for the newest ones. Save commands you do not want to lose before they are discarded from the Transcript window. You can save commands from the Transcript window at any time before they are discarded.

You can copy keystrokes from the Transcript window; you also can play back the keystrokes from the Transcript window, clear the Transcript window, and copy information into the Transcript window. The following sections describe in detail the steps for using the Transcript window to create macros and to play back recorded commands.

Creating Macros with the Transcript Window

Suppose that you want to create a macro that sets the default format for a selected range to Label. The Label format enables you to enter text that begins with numbers (or other characters that indicate numeric or formula entries) as labels without first entering a label prefix. Such a macro can be very useful for creating other macros and for entering data, such as street addresses, that 1-2-3 for Windows might otherwise interpret as incorrectly entered numbers.

You can create such a macro easily by using the steps outlined earlier in this chapter. With 1-2-3 for Windows, however, you also can create this macro with the Transcript window.

Before you begin recording the macro, clear any existing entries from the Transcript window. Although this step is not absolutely necessary, it is less confusing if the Transcript window only contains the desired macro text. To clear the Transcript window, follow these steps:

1. Select Tools Macros Show Transcript from the 1-2-3 for Windows menu or click on the Transcript Window SmartIcon.

2. Select Edit Clear All from the 1-2-3 for Windows menu (if the Edit menu does not include the Clear All command, make sure that the Transcript window is the active window).

3. Return to the worksheet (click on the worksheet or press Ctrl+F6).

You invoke the Transcript window by selecting Tools Macro Show Transcript from the 1-2-3 for Windows menu or by clicking on the Transcript Window SmartIcon. You can make the Transcript window the active window at any time after it is invoked. You can also resize the worksheet and transcript windows so both are visible. Use any of the following four ways to make the Transcript window active:

- Click on the Transcript Window SmartIcon.

- Press Ctrl+F6.

- Click the mouse anywhere inside the Transcript window.

- Use macro commands to activate the Transcript window.

All these techniques can also take you back to the worksheet from the Transcript window. For example, you can click the mouse anywhere in the worksheet to make it active again.

 To begin recording commands in the Transcript window, first select the Tools Macro Record command or click on the Record Macro SmartIcon. (If macro recording has already been started, this command changes to Tools Macro Stop Recording.)

 Now type the keystrokes you want the macro to execute. For this example, select the Style command from the 1-2-3 for Windows menu. Then select Number Format from the Style menu. Then select the Format list box and highlight Label. Click on OK. Stop recording the macro by selecting Tools Macro Stop Recording or by clicking on the Record Macro SmartIcon again. Press Ctrl+F6 to return to the Transcript window (see fig 15.17).

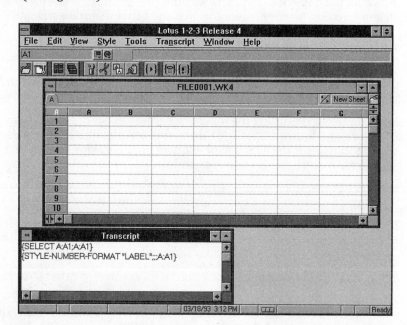

You enter recorded commands into the worksheet by copying them from the Transcript window to the Clipboard and then pasting them into the worksheet. You then can assign a range name to the cell or range containing the keystrokes as explained in the following sections. You can also attach the recorded commands to macro buttons you create in the worksheet (see "Adding Macro Buttons to a Worksheet," later in this chapter) or to custom SmartIcons (see Chapter 17, "Using SmartIcons").

Macros recorded in the Transcript window include cell addresses rather than cell-pointer movements. This makes the cell addresses easy to recognize but may not always produce the desired results. For example, the macro in figure 15.17 applies the Label format to cell A:A1, but you probably want a more general macro that applies the Label format to any selected range. Fortunately, you can easily modify the recorded macro to make it more general. The following sections explain how to make this type of modification.

Copying and Pasting the Recorded Keystrokes

To copy the keystrokes from the Transcript window into the worksheet, reactivate the Transcript window as explained in the preceding section. The commands you recorded appear in the window (refer back to fig. 15.17).

Identify the commands you want to copy by using the following process:

1. Move the cursor to the first or last character of the command sequence you want to copy to the worksheet.

2. Highlight the characters you want to copy. Drag the mouse pointer over the characters or hold the Shift key and use the arrow keys to move across the characters.

   In this example, copy the second command line (which applies the desired format) but not the first line (which selects cell A1):

   `{STYLE-NUMBER-FORMAT "LABEL";;;A1}`

   Figure 15.18 shows as highlighted the keystrokes necessary to set the desired format.

3. After highlighting the characters you want to copy, press and release the Alt key to activate the Transcript window menu; then choose Edit Copy. Or, after highlighting the characters, press Ctrl+Ins (or Ctrl+C) to copy the highlighted characters to the Clipboard. You also can click on the Copy to Clipboard SmartIcon.

4. Activate the worksheet window (press Ctrl+F6).

5. Move the cell pointer to the worksheet cell in which you want the macro to be placed (such as cell B3).

6. Use Edit Paste to paste the macro into the current cell location or use the shortcut key Shift+Ins (or Ctrl+V) to perform the paste operation (see fig. 15.19). You also can click on the Paste from Clipboard SmartIcon.

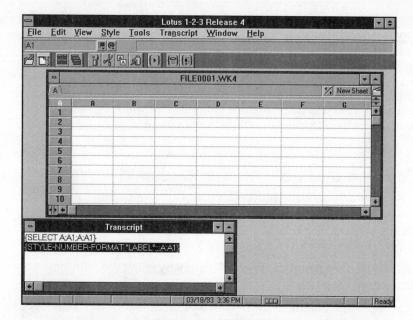

FIG. 15.18

The highlighted
keystrokes
selected in the
Transcript
window.

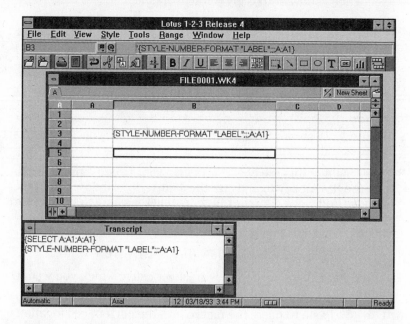

FIG. 15.19

A recorded
macro copied to
the worksheet
from the Tran-
script window
through the
Clipboard.

NOTE   After pasting the macro commands into the worksheet, the
width of column B and the cell-pointer location were adjusted in figure 15.19 for clarity.

Editing the Recorded Macro

Although the recorded macro can be run as it appears in figure 15.19, it has one distinct disadvantage: it always applies the Label format to cell A1. A simple modification, however, can convert the macro into a more general macro that applies the Label format to a selected range.

The STYLE-NUMBER-FORMAT macro command, like many 1-2-3 for Windows macro commands, has several optional arguments (these arguments are *format*, *decimals*, *parentheses*, and *range*). If you omit the optional *range* argument, the STYLE-NUMBER-FORMAT macro command applies the specified format to the currently selected range. In the example, the recorded macro includes A1 as the optional *range* argument:

`{STYLE-NUMBER-FORMAT "LABEL";;;A1}`

 NOTE   Macro command arguments must be entered in a specific order. If you omit an argument but include a later argument, you must include placeholders (semicolons) for each argument which is omitted. Chapter 16 covers macro command argument in more detail.

To convert this macro command into its more general form, edit the command to remove the optional arguments:

`{STYLE-NUMBER-FORMAT "LABEL"}`

Because no range is specified in the new version of the macro command, this generalized macro command applies the Label format to any range selected before the command is executed.

For Related Information

▶▶ "Using Macro Commands," p. 773.

FROM HERE...

Running the Recorded Macro

To run the macro in cell B3 directly from the keyboard with a Ctrl+*letter* combination, you first must name the macro. Type the label '\f in cell A3. With the cell pointer still on cell A3, select <u>R</u>ange <u>N</u>ame <u>U</u>se Labels and then select OK. The label \f is the range name assigned to the macro in cell B3. You then can press Ctrl+F to start the macro. Before running the macro, remember to highlight the range you want to format with the Label format.

Creating More Complex Macros

The macros described in the preceding sections are simple. You can use the same steps, however, to create complex and lengthy macros. When building larger or more complex macros with the Transcript window, keep the following information in mind.

Because some keys on the keyboard do not have character equivalents, you may need to use several characters to represent a keystroke. The macro command GOTO, for example, represents the F5 key.

The Transcript window does not record certain keystrokes. These keystrokes include keys that do not have character symbols or macro commands (such as Caps Lock, Num Lock, Print Screen, and Scroll Lock). The Transcript window does not record the key sequence for Compose (Alt+F1); it does, however, record the composed character.

If you execute a Ctrl+*letter* macro as you are recording a macro, the Transcript window records the name of the macro instead of the macro's individual keystrokes. For example, if you execute a macro named \f as you are recording another macro, the Transcript window shows the command as {\F}. If 1-2-3 for Windows encounters {\F} when executing a different macro, the program executes the \f macro and then continues executing the macro in which {\F} is a step.

You can specify one row or many rows for the range to which you want to copy the characters from the Transcript window. 1-2-3 for Windows uses as many rows as needed to hold the characters you select to have copied. Characters are copied down one column. Macro commands such as GOTO are not split among cells because doing so creates a macro error.

Playing Back Keystrokes

Another option available with the Transcript window is the capability to run keystrokes as a macro. This means that you can play back keystrokes without copying them into the worksheet. The steps used to play back your keystrokes, or some portion of them, parallel the steps used to create a macro. You can play back a sequence of keystrokes as many times as you want.

The playback feature is helpful when you want to repeat a sequence of keystrokes but do not want to make the extra effort to create an actual macro for those keystrokes.

Before you play back keystrokes, position the worksheet cell pointer in the specific location where you want the keystrokes to be repeated. To play back the keystrokes, follow these steps:

1. Activate the Transcript window. Click on the Transcript Window SmartIcon, press Ctrl+F6, or click the mouse anywhere inside the Transcript window.

2. Highlight the commands in the Transcript window you want 1-2-3 for Windows to perform. If you want 1-2-3 for Windows to perform all the commands in the Transcript window, highlight all the commands.

3. Choose Transcript Playback or click on the Play Back SmartIcon. 1-2-3 for Windows repeats the commands you highlighted. The highlighted commands are executed until they are completed, an error occurs, or you press the Ctrl+Break key combination. Remember that you can edit the contents of the Transcript window before highlighting and running the commands.

Adding Macro Buttons to a Worksheet

A *macro button* is a button that executes an associated macro when you click on the button. You can add a macro button to a worksheet to make it easy to perform certain tasks you have automated with macros you have recorded or written yourself.

Macro buttons always appear at the same location on a worksheet (unless you choose to move the button, as explained later in this chapter). That is, once you create a macro button, it scrolls along with the cells it covers. If you create a macro button that covers cells A:B3..C4, for example, the button scrolls off the screen when you move the cell pointer to A:C50 or to B:B3.

This characteristic makes macro buttons ideal for executing macros that depend on the user completing certain tasks. For example, you can create a macro button to run a macro that performs a set of calculations using newly entered data. Once the user finishes entering the data, he or she can click on the macro button to run the macro.

Macro buttons are an example of *event-driven programming*. That is, the macro program associated with a macro button runs when an *event*—a mouse click—is detected. When the macro button is clicked, the macro executes.

T I P Using macro buttons requires a mouse. If you create a worksheet that may be used by someone without a mouse, be sure to provide a keyboard method of performing tasks implemented as macro buttons.

Creating a Macro Button

Regardless of the type of macro you attach to a macro button, the process of creating the macro button is the same. The following example shows how to create a macro button that performs the simple task of entering a company name in the currently selected cell.

1. Create a macro button by first clicking on the Macro Button SmartIcon.

2. Point to the worksheet location where you want to place the macro button.

3. To create a button of the default size, click the left mouse button.

   To create a macro button in a different size (perhaps to allow room for more text on the button's face), drag the mouse pointer until the dotted button box is the desired size.

   The Assign to Button dialog box appears (see fig. 15.20).

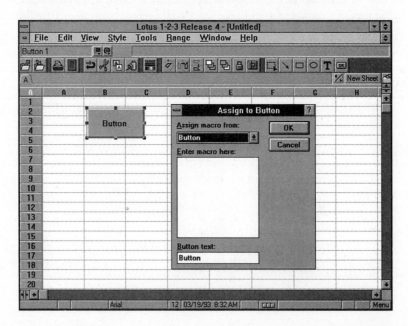

FIG. 15.20

The Assign to Button dialog box.

4. If the macro you want to assign to the button is fairly short, enter the macro text in the Enter Macro Here text box.

For example, enter the following in the Enter Macro Here text box:

{CELL-ENTER "Darlene's Computer Warehouse"}

To enter the address of a range containing a macro that already exists, select the Assign Macro From list box and choose Range. The dialog box changes as shown in figure 15.21.

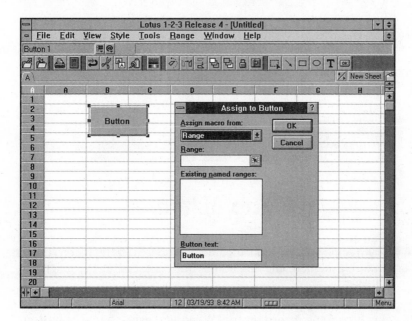

FIG. 15.21

The Assign to Button dialog box changes when you select Range.

Enter the address of the existing macro in the Range text box or select the name of the macro from the Existing Named Ranges list box.

5. Change the text on the face of the button to show the button's purpose by typing the new description in the Button Text text box. For example, type **Add Name**.

6. Click on OK or press Enter to return to the worksheet.

To test the macro button, move the cell pointer to an empty cell and then click on the macro button. Figure 15.22 shows the effect of moving the cell pointer to cell A:C9 and clicking on the Add Name macro button.

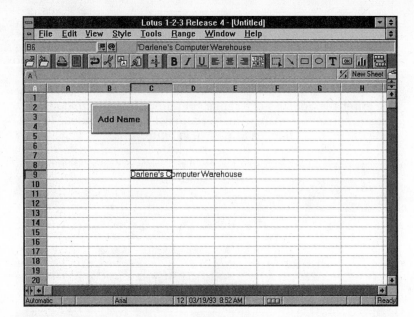

FIG. 15.22

The effect of
clicking on the
Add Name
macro button
with the cell
pointer in A:C9.

Changing a Macro Button

Once you create a macro button, it remains locked in the same location
on the worksheet unless you specifically move it. If the macro button
has a macro assigned, clicking on the button executes the macro.

To move or resize a macro button—or to modify its actions—you must
first select the macro button by holding either the Shift or Ctrl key before clicking on the macro button. When you select a macro button, it is
surrounded by eight rectangular handles. You can do the following to a
selected macro button:

■ To resize a selected button, drag one of the handles until the button is the correct size.

■ To move a selected button, drag the button to the new location.

■ To edit the button's text or to change the macro assigned to the
button, double-click on the selected button. Then use the options
in the Assign to Button dialog box to make the desired changes.

FROM HERE...

For Related Information

◀◀ "Using Graphics," p. 588.

Avoiding Common Macro Errors

When you begin building your own macros, you will discover that editing is a regular part of macro creation—particularly when macros are fairly complex. In macros, as in computer programs, errors are called *bugs. Debugging* is the process of editing or eliminating bugs or errors from macros.

If 1-2-3 for Windows cannot execute the macro as written, the program displays an error message and the cell address where the error is located. Usually, this message points you to the error. Occasionally, however, the real error—the place 1-2-3 for Windows stops executing keystrokes the way you want—precedes the error identified in the error message.

If you receive a message about an unrecognized macro command or range name that is followed by a cell address, check the macro commands and range names to be certain that they are spelled correctly. In addition, verify that you are using curly braces—{ and }—rather than parentheses—( )—or square brackets—[ ]; that arguments are correctly specified; and that no extra spaces appear in the macro—especially inside the braces.

The following list reviews some simple guidelines for preventing typical errors that can occur during the process of creating macros:

■ *Check the syntax and spelling.* Incorrect grammar and spelling are common problems in macro commands, range names, and file names used in macros. All macro syntax and spelling must be exact.

■ *List all command steps.* If your macro uses any of the 1-2-3 for Windows menu commands, the macro must include each individual step required for the menu commands to run correctly.

■ *Erase the cell below the macro.* Even if 1-2-3 for Windows works all the way through a macro without a problem, the program may end with an error message or a beep. Remember that 1-2-3 for Windows continues executing macro commands until it encounters an empty cell, a cell with a numeric value, or one of the commands that stops macros. If 1-2-3 for Windows encounters data in the cell directly below the last line of the macro, the program may interpret that cell as part of the macro. Always use the Edit Clear command or the Del key to empty the cell below the last line of the macro. If you discover that the cell is not empty, you may have identified one of the macro's problems.

■ *Use braces correctly.* Remember that macro commands must be enclosed in curly braces rather than square brackets or parentheses. Symbols and words within braces are used to represent all the special keys on the keyboard. In every case, the key's name, such as {RIGHT} for the right-arrow key or {CALC} for the function key F9, must be enclosed in curly braces—not in parentheses or square brackets. Macro commands also must be enclosed in braces within a macro.

■ *Use descriptive range names when possible.* Beginning macro users often forget that 1-2-3 for Windows macros are not like 1-2-3 for Windows formulas; cell references are *always* absolute in macros. The cell addresses in macros do not change automatically when you move data used by the macro. 1-2-3 for Windows does not update label cells; in fact, macros *are* label cells.

The absolute nature of cell references within macros is a strong argument in favor of using range names in worksheets. You should assign range names to all the cells and ranges the macros use in the worksheet. Then use these range names in your macros. If you later move the ranges or insert or delete rows and columns, 1-2-3 adjusts the range names, and the macro continues to refer to the correct cells and ranges.

■ *Use unique range names.* Do not use range names or subroutine names that duplicate macro command names. Never assign a name like CALC, LOOK, or QUIT to a range or a subroutine.

■ *Use valid cell references.* Cell references included in a macro must refer to cells that exist. Make sure that macros and formulas refer only to existing cells or ranges. Avoid incorrect cell references, such as +ZZ1..ZZ28. Remember that you can avoid such problems by using range names instead of cell addresses.

■ *Define all names.* You must define all macro names, subroutine names, and range names used in macros. For example, do not use the range name TOTAL in a macro if you have not used the Range Name command to define that range name.

■ *Use the backslash in Ctrl+letter macro names.* When using Ctrl+*letter* macros, remember that the macro's name must be exactly two characters. The first character is always a backslash (\); never use a regular slash (/). The second character is any letter from A to Z.

■ *Use file references correctly.* If a macro refers to a file, enclose the file's name in double angle brackets, such as <<FINANCE>>, if the file extension is WK4. If the extension is not WK4, also list the file extension, such as <<SCREEN.TXT>>. Remember that 1-2-3 for Windows is *not* case-sensitive. When a macro refers to a file that is not active (that is, a file not currently open), give 1-2-3 for Windows the necessary information for locating the file. This information may include the drive and path, file name, and extension (if the extension is not WK4).

If a macro refers to the file <<FINANCE>>, and the file FINANCE.WK4 is not open, 1-2-3 for Windows looks for FINANCE.WK4 in the current subdirectory of the current drive. If the file is not in the current directory, you must specify the path to the file in the following manner:

`<<C:\BUDGET\FINANCE>>`

Translating 1-2-3 Release 1 for Windows Macros

1-2-3 Release 4 for Windows macros use macro commands instead of menu-selection keystrokes. These commands result in macros that are more efficient than the older-style macro that used keystrokes. Not only do macros using macro commands execute faster, they are also easier to read and continue to function even if a menu is modified.

Before you can use 1-2-3 Release 1 for Windows macros in 1-2-3 Release 4 for Windows, the macros must be translated to the new command format. When you install 1-2-3 Release 4 for Windows, the 1-2-3 Macro Translator is installed as well. You use this tool to perform a one-time translation of the macros in existing worksheets.

The 1-2-3 Macro Translator is installed in the same Windows program group as 1-2-3 Release 4 for Windows. You run the 1-2-3 Macro Translator as a separate program. To translate the macros in your existing worksheets, double-click on the 1-2-3 Macro Translator icon in the Windows Program Manager. This action starts the 1-2-3 Macro Translator (see fig. 15.23).

Use the Directories, Drives, and Files (WK3) boxes to select the 1-2-3 Release 1 for Windows worksheet files that contain the macros you want to translate. You can select any number of files in a single directory to translate at one time.

Use the Directories box at the bottom of the dialog box to select a different destination directory for the translated files. If you do not select a new destination directory, the 1-2-3 Macro Translator places the translated files in the same directory as the original files and renames the original files with a BK3 extension.

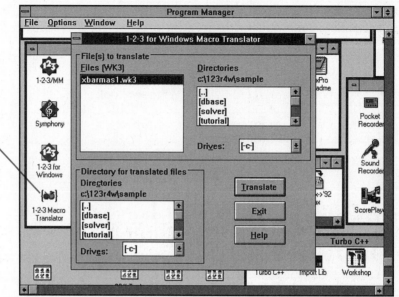

1-2-3 Macro Translator icon in the Windows Program Manager

Use the 1-2-3 Macro Translator to translate 1-2-3 Release 1 for Windows macros.

> **CAUTION:** If you use the 1-2-3 Macro Translator more than once, specify the same files to translate, and specify the same directories, the original files are overwritten.

Once you have selected the files to translate, select the Translate button. If you do not select a new destination directory, the 1-2-3 Macro Translator warns you that it will back up the originals. Select Yes to continue. After the files are translated, the 1-2-3 Macro Translator informs you of the number of files it translated. Click on OK or press Enter to return to the program. Once you have translated all the files you want to translate, select Exit to leave the Translator.

Figure 15.24 shows some typical 1-2-3 Release 1 for Windows macros and how the 1-2-3 Macro Translator changed them for Release 4. Some commands, such as those in rows 5, 6, 9, 10, 13, 14, and 15 are unchanged. Other commands, such as those in rows 7 and 8, are considerably changed.

Often, a single Release 4 command (row 8), replaces several rows of Release 1 commands. Because the 1-2-3 Macro Translator retains the same macro layout as the original macro in the translated file, it places a { — } comment line in the translated macro. When the macro executes, comment lines are ignored.

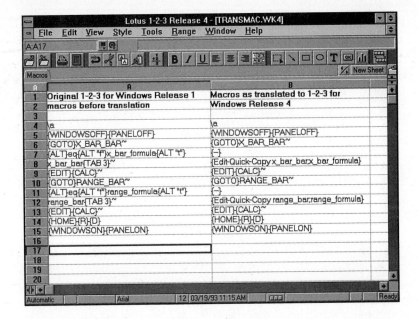

FIG. 15.24

Comparing macros before and after translation.

Questions & Answers

This chapter introduced the basic concepts of 1-2-3 for Windows macros. Following are some questions you may have about the execution of macros and the use of macro buttons.

Q: Why doesn't my auto-execute macro run when I load the worksheet?

A: Make certain that the Run Autoexecute Macros check box is selected in the User Setup dialog box. Use the Tools User Setup command to access this dialog box.

Q: I just upgraded from 1-2-3 Release 1 for Windows, and now my macro programs don't work as I expected. What's wrong?

A: Did you remember to translate the macros using the 1-2-3 Macro Translator? 1-2-3 Release 1 for Windows macros must be translated before they run correctly in Release 4.

Q: I translated my 1-2-3 Release 1 for Windows worksheet macros using the 1-2-3 Macro Translator. Why don't my macros run correctly now?

A: Are you sure that you're using the translated worksheets? If you specified a new destination directory, the source directory still contains the original, untranslated worksheet files.

Q: I want to change the macro associated with a macro button, but when I try to select the button, the macro runs. How can I select the macro button?

A: Be sure that you press and hold either the Shift or Ctrl key before you click on the macro button.

Q: I upgraded my favorite worksheet by adding macro buttons, but they weren't there when I reopened the worksheet. Where did they go?

A: Make certain that you save the worksheet in 1-2-3 Release 4 for Windows format (WK4). If you save the file as a WK3 file, the Release 4 enhancements will be lost.

Summary

The information in this chapter should give you all the confidence you need to begin creating macros—tools that save time, reduce repetition, and automate worksheet models. This chapter defined a macro and walked you through the steps required to create some simple macros.

This chapter also described the different ways you can name and run macros, reviewed techniques for documenting macros, showed you how to use the 1-2-3 for Windows Transcript window to create macros, showed you how to create macro buttons, and reviewed techniques for testing and debugging macros.

Chapter 16 presents the 1-2-3 Release 4 for Windows macro commands. You can combine the information on creating basic macros you learned in this chapter with the detailed information in Chapter 16 to create complete macro programs.

Using Macro Commands

I n addition to providing keystroke macro capabilities, 1-2-3 for Windows provides a powerful set of macro commands that offer many options available with a full-featured programming language. Although the 1-2-3 Release 4 for Windows macro command language is probably not as powerful as a dedicated programming language like C, the macro language is much easier to learn. The 1-2-3 macro language can perform high-level programming functions such as looping and transferring the flow of the macro to a separate macro routine, and testing for conditions and branching to different routines based on the results.

The preceding chapter introduced you to the process of automating 1-2-3 for Windows by using macros. By using macros to automate repetitive tasks, to perform menu keystrokes quickly, or to type a long label into a cell, you can greatly decrease the time you spend building or working with a spreadsheet. A *macro command* is a macro instruction that tells 1-2-3 for Windows to perform one of the built-in programming functions. This chapter introduces you to these commands, not by teaching programming theory and concepts but rather by describing the capabilities of programming with the macro commands. In essence, the chapter is a reference guide to the power of the macro commands.

Why Use Macro Commands?

Programs created with macro commands give you added control and flexibility in the use of 1-2-3 for Windows worksheets, especially in the Windows environment. With these commands, you can construct, customize, and control worksheet applications created in 1-2-3 for Windows. You also can use the commands to weave together data from worksheets created in 1-2-3 for Windows and other Windows applications. The macro commands enable you to prompt a user for input, create your own menus, loop a specific number of times through a series of commands, launch another Windows application, and link data between 1-2-3 for Windows and other Windows applications. After learning the concepts and the components of the macro commands discussed in this chapter, you should be ready to develop programs that perform tasks such as the following:

- Create menu-driven spreadsheet/database models

- Accept and control input from a user and make intelligent decisions based on user input

- Capture and process a user's keystrokes

- Manipulate data within 1-2-3 for Windows and between 1-2-3 for Windows and other Windows applications

- Change the contents of a cell in the middle of a program

- Execute tasks a predetermined number of times

- Control program flow

- Create a data-entry form that prompts the user for specific information, checks the responses, and enters the data in the worksheet

- Launch other Windows applications based on decisions made within a 1-2-3 for Windows worksheet

As you become more experienced with the macro commands, you can take full advantage of their power to develop a complete business system application—from order entry to inventory control to accounting.

T I P

Although macros are powerful, sometimes nonmacro approaches are better. Don't start looking for macro solutions to every new problem you face. Macros are but one spreadsheet solution; don't forget the other tools in your 1-2-3 toolbox.

Understanding the Macro Command Categories

The 1-2-3 for Windows macro commands are a rich set of commands and keystroke equivalents you use to create macro programs. This chapter examines these commands and shows you how to use them in several examples. The macro commands fit into 17 categories:

- Chart
- Data manipulation
- Database
- DDE and OLE
- Edit
- File
- Flow-of-control
- Keystroke equivalents
- Navigation
- Range
- Solver
- Style
- Text file manipulation
- Tools
- User environment
- Version manager
- Window and screen display

Each macro command category includes closely related commands. For example, the chart commands include those that control the many aspects of 1-2-3 for Windows graphs, such as data ranges, colors, and chart types. Each of the 1-2-3 Release 4 for Windows macro command categories, and the macro commands contained in each category, is detailed in later sections of this chapter.

The examples in this chapter show you how to incorporate macro commands within macros to produce complete, efficient programs that take 1-2-3 for Windows macro capability far beyond automating keystrokes. As you read through the examples, keep in mind that although the macro command descriptions are organized by category, typical macro programs may use commands from many different categories. In fact there is no limit to the number or type of macro commands you can include in a single program.

For example, you might create a 1-2-3 for Windows application that uses window and screen display commands to control what the user sees as the macro executes. The same program might use database commands to retrieve information from an external database file on a network server, and chart commands to display that information. Finally, the program might use style and file commands to prepare and print a report containing the retrieved data.

Using the Correct Syntax for Macro Commands

All 1-2-3 for Windows macro commands are enclosed in braces ({}). The braces tell 1-2-3 for Windows where a macro command begins and ends. Some macro commands are a single command enclosed in braces. For example, to quit a macro, you use the following command, without arguments:

`{QUIT}`

Many other macro commands, however, require arguments within the braces. The arguments, or parameters, that follow commands adhere to a syntax similar to that used in 1-2-3 for Windows functions. The following is the general syntax of commands that require arguments:

{COMMAND *argument1*;*argument2*;...;*argumentN*}

The *command name,* or *key word* (represented in the example by the word *COMMAND*) is the part of the command that tells 1-2-3 for Windows what action to perform. The *arguments* supply the information 1-2-3 for Windows needs to complete the command.

For example, in the following command, BLANK tells 1-2-3 for Windows to erase the contents of a cell or range (a range in this example), and the argument A:A1..A:D10 tells the command what cell or range to erase:

`{BLANK A:A1..A:D10}`

An argument can consist of numbers, strings, cell addresses, range names, formulas, or functions. Some commands, such as BLANK, only accept one argument. Other commands, such as LET or PUT, require multiple arguments. The command and the first argument always are separated by a space. For most commands, multiple arguments are separated by semicolons (;) with no spaces between the arguments.

One common type of argument is a *Boolean argument*. A Boolean argument is one that is either true or false. You can use either yes, true, or 1 for true, and no, false, or 0 for false. Boolean arguments are always enclosed in quotation marks.

> The argument separators accepted by 1-2-3 for Windows depend on your system settings. A semicolon is always acceptable, but you may also be able to use commas or periods, depending on the settings you select in the International dialog box, which you access by selecting <u>T</u>ools <u>U</u>ser Setup <u>I</u>nternational.
>
> **T I P**

For a command to execute, its syntax must be correct, so following the conventions for spacing and punctuation is vitally important. When you use the BLANK command to erase the contents from a cell or from a range, the command {BLANK} must be followed by one space and then by a cell address or a range name. If you type two spaces after the BLANK command, or if you type a bracket ([) rather than a brace, the macro produces an error when it tries to execute the BLANK command.

Use correct spelling as well as syntax. If you misspell the command or range name or if you type an invalid cell address (such as ABA12), the macro produces an error when it tries to execute the command.

The following are some basic rules of syntax to remember:

- Start the command with an open brace ({) and end the command with a close brace (}).

- Immediately after the open brace, type the command name. You can type the command name in uppercase or lowercase letters.

- If the command requires arguments, separate the command name from the first argument with one space. If the command includes two or more arguments, separate the arguments from one another with semicolons. The only space in the command syntax occurs between the command name and the first argument. Do not include any other spaces in the command unless they are part of a text argument (for example, the prompt in a GET-LABEL command can include spaces between the words in the prompt). If the command takes no arguments, the command should include no spaces.

- If the command has several optional arguments and you skip one of them but include a subsequent one, enter an argument separator as a placeholder for the skipped argument. For example, if you skip the optional *width* argument in a CONTENTS command but include the optional *format* argument, use the following format:

      {CONTENTS *target*;*source*;;*format*}

The extra semicolon between the *source* and *format* arguments is a placeholder for the missing *width* argument.

■ You can include any combination of macro commands in the same cell as long as the total number of characters does not exceed 512.

FROM HERE...

For Related Information

◀◀ "Understanding the Guidelines for Creating Macros," p. 737.

Entering a Macro Command

When you want to enter a macro command in the worksheet, you can obtain a list of all the valid macro commands by clicking on the Select Macro Command SmartIcon or by pressing F3 (Name) after you enter an open brace ({). To enter the macro command, select the desired macro command from the Macro Name list box in the Macro Keywords dialog box. You can also press the first letter of the command name to move the highlight directly to the first command name that begins with that letter. If the macro command you are looking for is not the first one, use the down-arrow key to find the command you need. For example, if you press the letter T, the highlight moves to the first command that begins with T, which is TAB.

Planning, Invoking, and Debugging Macro Command Programs

To ensure that your macro command programs are efficient and error-free, you begin by defining which actions you want the program to perform. Next, you determine the sequence of those actions. Then you develop the program, test it, debug it, and cross-check its results for all possible operations.

If you have not experimented with 1-2-3 for Windows macros, take some time to review the simple macros in Chapter 15 before you try to develop macro command programs. If you have some practice with simple macros, you will be better prepared to learn and apply the macro commands described in this chapter. Also, you might want to review Chapter 15's discussions of creating, using, and debugging macros; you also use those concepts in your more advanced macro command programs.

Planning and Documenting Macro Command Programs

You should plan macro programs carefully, not only for what they will accomplish but for where they will be positioned in the worksheet. If part of your macro is in row 10 of worksheet A and one of the instructions in the macro is to delete row 10 in worksheet A, you delete part of your macro.

Placing macro programs in a separate worksheet or file is the best practice. Take advantage of 1-2-3 for Windows multiple worksheet files and place your macros in their own worksheet. Double-click the macro worksheet tab and name the worksheet Macros so you can always easily identify which worksheet holds your macros. For example, figure 16.1 shows a macro that is stored in the worksheet named Macros; the data area and work area are in a worksheet named Data Input.

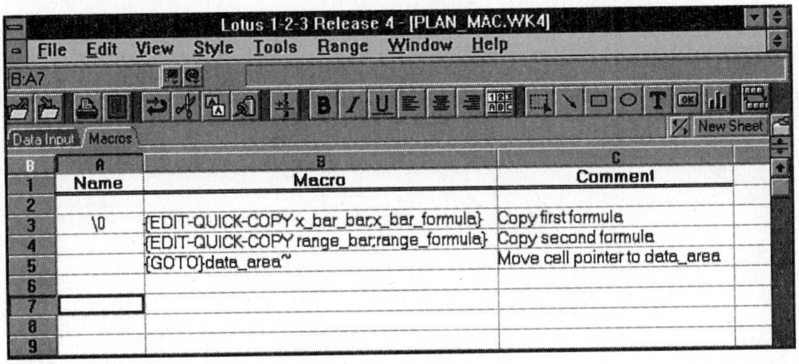

FIG. 16.1

Use a separate worksheet for your macros.

You can also place macros in a separate file that you must open in addition to any worksheet file that uses those macros. Remember, though, that 1-2-3 for Windows always searches for macros in the current file first. To run a macro in another file that has the same name as a macro in the current file, you must specify in the Macro Run dialog box the file name that contains the macro. For example:

<<MACROS.WK4>>Print_Macro

You enter macro commands as lines of text in the worksheet. Remember to use a label prefix to start any line that begins with a nontext character (such as / or <) so that the commands are entered as a line of text in your macro rather than executed by 1-2-3 for Windows. After you decide where to place the program and begin entering program lines, remember to document macro command programs. Because macro command programs may be complex, documentation is essential for debugging and modifying the macro. In figure 16.1, note that the macro is documented.

Invoking Macro Command Programs

As Chapter 15 described, you can invoke macros in several ways:

- Ctrl+*letter* macros

  To invoke macros that you name by using the backslash key and a character (Ctrl+*letter* macros), press and hold down the Ctrl key while you press the appropriate character key. For example, you invoke a macro named \a by pressing Ctrl+A.

- Alt+F3 (Run)

  To invoke Ctrl+*letter* macros or macros that you name by using descriptive range names, press Alt+F3 (Run). The Macro Run dialog box appears (see fig. 16.2). From this dialog box, you have several options for invoking a macro.

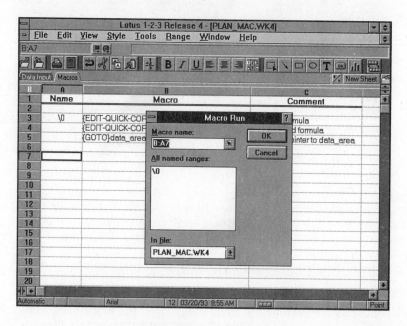

FIG. 16.2

The Macro Run dialog box.

First, you can type the macro name or select the name from the All Named Ranges list box.

Second, you can choose a macro name by using Point mode. Click the first cell of the macro, or use the direction keys to move the cell pointer to the first cell of the macro and press Enter. You also can click the range selector beside the Macro Name text box to remove the dialog box and point to the first cell of the macro. Then press Enter.

Third, you can type the cell address in the Macro Name text box.

■ The Tools Macro Run command

You can invoke any macro by selecting Tools Macro Run from the 1-2-3 for Windows menu. The Macro Run dialog box appears. This dialog box is the same one that appears when you press Alt+F3 (Run). At this point, you have the same three options for invoking a macro: type or select the macro name from the list; go into Point mode and start the macro from the worksheet; or type the cell address.

■ The Run Macro SmartIcon

You also can click on the Run Macro SmartIcon to display the Macro Run dialog box and run the macro.

■ Auto-execute macros

If you check the Run Autoexecute Macros box in the User Setup dialog box, auto-execute (\0) macros execute when you load or open a file.

Debugging Macro Command Programs

After you develop and run a macro program, you might have to debug the program. All macro programs are subject to such problems as misspelled command and range names, improper syntax, and cell address changes.

One key to eliminating such problems is the practice of using range names in place of cell addresses whenever possible. Remember that a reference to a cell location is absolute and does not change when the worksheet structure changes. Range names, however, change location when the worksheet structure changes. Suppose that cell D50 is named TOTAL. Because range names change with the worksheet, if you insert a row above cell D50, the range name TOTAL moves down a row but stays associated to the originally named cell (D51 now). If the LET statement is

```
{LET D50,@SUM(SALARIES)}
```

and you insert a row above row 50, the LET statement still places the sum of the salaries into cell D50. You can solve this problem by using range names in place of cell addresses, as in the following example:

```
{LET TOTAL,@SUM(SALARIES)}
```

Macros, however, can have problems other than absolute cell references. Debugging a macro involves finding out which macro instructions are causing the problem and editing the instructions. The easiest way to debug a macro is to use 1-2-3 for Windows Single Step and Trace debugging utilities, as discussed in Chapter 15.

FROM HERE...

For Related Information

◀◀ "Using Single Step and Trace To Test Macros," p. 749.

Using Variable Information in Macros

To be useful, macros must be flexible. For example, a macro that can apply the label format to any selected range is much more useful than one that can apply the label format only to cell A:A1.

Specifying Arguments

Many 1-2-3 for Windows macro commands accept *arguments*—variable information that helps determine how the macro functions. The three types of arguments for macro commands are numbers, text, and ranges and are used as follows:

- To enter a numeric argument, use a number, a numeric formula, or the range name or address of a cell that contains a number or numeric formula; for example, 2, +A5/2, or NUMBER_OF_DAYS.

- To enter a text argument, use any text enclosed in quotation marks, a text formula, or the range name or address of a cell that contains a label or text formula; for example, "Reno", +A5, or STORE_NAME.

■ To enter a range argument, use a range name or address, or any formula that evaluates to a range name or address; for example, STORE_NAME or @@A5.

For some text arguments, you can specify any text you want 1-2-3 for Windows to use literally—exactly as you specify it. For some other types of text arguments, you must use specific text. For example, when you use the FILE-OPEN command and you specify the type of file access, you must select R, W, M, or A (read, write, modify, or append).

One of the best ways to make your macros adaptable is to use named ranges to hold variable information and then specify the named range as the macro command argument. For example, in figure 16.3, the \a and \d macros both use the FILE-OPEN command to open a text file—in this case, FILE1.TXT. Suppose, however, you want to open a file other than FILE1.TXT. Because the \d macro uses FILE_NAME, a named range, to specify the value for the argument specifying which file to open, you simply place a different file name in cell B7, the FILE_NAME range. When you run the \d macro, the file specified in the named range is opened. Modifying the file named in the \a macro is much more difficult.

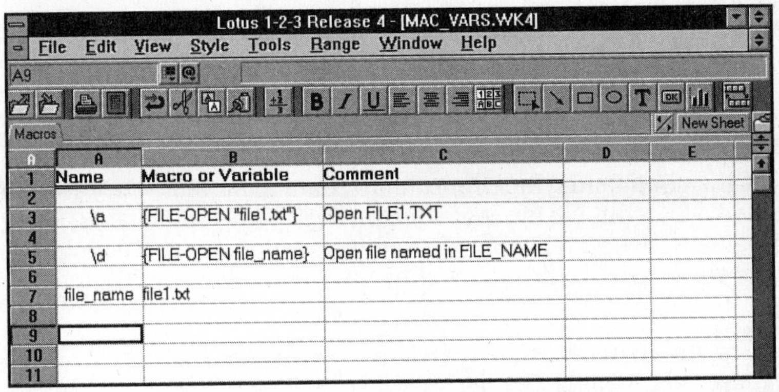

FIG. 16.3

Use named ranges to supply variable information in macros.

Avoiding Self-Modifying Macros

Because you enter macros as labels, a common technique in past versions of 1-2-3 has been to use string formulas—also called *concatenation*—to create macros that accept variable arguments. For example, another way to duplicate the functionality of the \d macro in figure 16.3 is to use the following string formula:

```
+"{FILE-OPEN "&FILE_NAME&"}"
```

If FILE_NAME contains the text file1.txt, the string formula results in a macro command identical to the \a macro.

Although this technique can be useful in limited instances, you should avoid using it in 1-2-3 Release 4 for Windows. Self-modifying macros can be difficult to understand and are often likely to result in an error. Self-modifying macros might not function quite as you expect, especially if you use macro commands that modify worksheet data but do not cause the worksheet to recalculate. Finding and correcting this type of macro program error is difficult.

Instead of using string formulas to create self-modifying macros, supply variable information to macro commands by specifying named ranges that store the variables. Not only will your macros be easier to read, they will also be less likely to result in difficult-to-find errors.

For Related Information

◄◄ "Working with Ranges," p. 140.

Categorizing the Macro Commands

The following sections group macro commands into categories that reflect the commands' functions: chart, data manipulation, database, DDE and OLE, edit, file, flow-of-control, keystroke equivalents, navigation, range, solver, style, text file manipulation, tools, user environment, version manager, and window and screen display.

 In the command syntax lines, optional arguments for macro commands are enclosed in brackets ([]). You do *not* type these brackets when entering optional arguments.

NOTE For compatibility with macros created in earlier releases, 1-2-3 Release 4 for Windows includes many macro commands that have more powerful replacements. For example, in Release 4, the GET-LABEL command replaces GETLABEL. The GET-LABEL command can accept new arguments to specify a default response and a dialog box title. If a more powerful 1-2-3 Release 4 for Windows macro command replaces an older macro command, the command tables refer you to the new command.

Commands That Manipulate Charts

The commands listed in table 16.1 create and control charts in 1-2-3 for Windows. You use these commands to graph data, to modify the settings for charts, and to control the default type of charts.

Table 16.1 Commands That Manipulate Charts

Command	Action
CHART-ASSIGN-RANGE	Assigns all data ranges for the current chart
CHART-AXIS-INTERVALS	Changes the intervals between x-axis, y-axis, or the second y-axis' tick marks in the current chart
CHART-AXIS-LIMITS	Creates a scale for the x-axis, y-axis, or the second y-axis that displays only the data that falls between an upper and lower limit
CHART-AXIS-SCALE-TYPE	Specifies the type of scale to use for an axis
CHART-AXIS-TICKS	Specifies major and minor tick marks for an axis
CHART-AXIS-TITLE	Changes an axis title
CHART-AXIS-UNITS	Changes the magnitude of the axis units and the axis-unit titles
CHART-COLOR-RANGE	Sets the color for each value in a data series by using values in the color range
CHART-DATA-LABELS	Creates labels for data points or bars by using data in the label range as the labels
CHART-FOOTNOTE	Adds footnotes to a chart
CHART-GRID	Displays or hides grid lines for an axis
CHART-LEGEND	Creates legend labels that identify the colors, symbols, or patterns of the data range
CHART-NEW	Draws a chart by using data from the currently selected range
CHART-PATTERN-RANGE	Sets the pattern for each value in a data series by using values in the pattern range

continues

Table 16.1 Continued

Command	Action
CHART-PIE-LABELS	Creates labels for a pie chart
CHART-PIE-SLICE-EXPLOSION	Explodes slices in a pie chart
CHART-RANGE	Sets the data range, series type, and the second y-axis' flag for a data series
CHART-RANGE-DELETE	Deletes a data series
CHART-RENAME	Renames a chart
CHART-SET-PREFERRED	Defines the current chart's settings as the preferred chart
CHART-TITLE	Adds chart titles
CHART-TYPE	Sets the type of chart
CHART-USE-PREFERRED	Applies the preferred chart settings to the current chart
GRAPH-NEW	Use CHART-NEW

The CHART-ASSIGN-RANGE Command

The CHART-ASSIGN-RANGE command assigns all data ranges for the current chart. Use the following syntax for CHART-ASSIGN-RANGE:

{CHART-ASSIGN-RANGE *range*;*method*;[*legend*];[*x-axis*]}

The *range* argument is the name or address of a range that contains the data ranges for the chart.

The *method* argument specifies how 1-2-3 assigns the data ranges. The method can be "by-row" to set the first row of the range as either the X data range or the legend range and each succeeding row as the A through W data ranges, or "by-column" to set the first column of the range as either the X data range or the legend range and each succeeding column as the A through W data ranges.

The *legend* argument is a Boolean (true or false) argument that specifies whether the first row or column contains legend labels. The default is to not use the first row or column for legend labels.

The *x-axis* argument is a Boolean argument that specifies whether the first row or column contains x-axis labels. The default is to not use the first row or column for x-axis labels.

The CHART-ASSIGN-RANGE command does not create a new chart. Use CHART-NEW to create a new chart before using CHART-ASSIGN-RANGE.

The CHART-AXIS-INTERVALS Command

The CHART-AXIS-INTERVALS command changes the intervals between x-axis, y-axis, or the second y-axis tick marks in the current chart. Use the following syntax for CHART-AXIS-INTERVALS:

> {CHART-AXIS-INTERVALS *axis*;[*major*];[*minor*];
> [*major-interval*];[*minor-interval*]}

The *axis* argument specifies the axis—x, y, or 2y—and is enclosed in quotation marks.

The *major* argument is a Boolean argument that specifies whether you specify the major interval.

The *minor* argument is a Boolean argument that specifies whether you specify the minor interval.

The *major-interval* argument is a value that specifies the major interval. If you choose not to specify the major interval, it is automatically calculated.

The *minor-interval* argument is a value that specifies the minor interval. If you choose not to specify the minor interval, it is automatically calculated.

 CHART-AXIS-INTERVALS changes the way tick marks are displayed on the x-axis, y-axis, or second y-axis, but does not change how the data is displayed. To change the axis scale, use CHART-AXIS-SCALE-TYPE.

The CHART-AXIS-LIMITS Command

The CHART-AXIS-LIMITS command creates a scale for the x-axis, y-axis, or second y-axis that displays only the data that falls between (and includes) upper limit and lower limit. CHART-AXIS-LIMITS changes the current chart. Use the following syntax for CHART-AXIS-LIMITS:

> {CHART-AXIS-LIMITS *axis*;[*upper*];[*lower*];[*upper-limit*];
> [*lower-limit*]}

The *axis* argument specifies the axis—x, y, or 2y—and is enclosed in quotation marks.

The *upper* argument is a Boolean argument that specifies whether you specify the upper limit.

The *lower* argument is a Boolean argument that specifies whether you specify the lower limit.

The *upper-limit* argument is a value that specifies the upper limit. If you choose not to specify the upper limit, it is automatically calculated.

The *lower-limit* argument is a value that specifies the lower limit. If you choose not to specify the lower limit, it is automatically calculated.

If you specify an upper limit that is lower than the lower limit, your data is not displayed. Data outside the upper and lower limits is also not displayed.

The CHART-AXIS-SCALE-TYPE Command

The CHART-AXIS-SCALE-TYPE command specifies the type of scale to use for an axis in the current chart. Use the following syntax for CHART-AXIS-SCALE-TYPE:

{CHART-AXIS-SCALE-TYPE *axis;type*}

The *axis* argument specifies the axis—x, y, or 2y—and is enclosed in quotation marks.

The *type* argument specifies the type of scale to use for the axis—STANDARD, LOG, or 100%—and is enclosed in quotation marks. STANDARD increases scale numbers linearly, LOG increases scale numbers logarithmically, and 100% displays scale numbers that represent percentages from 0 through 100%.

The CHART-AXIS-TICKS Command

The CHART-AXIS-TICKS command specifies whether major and minor tick marks are displayed for a specified axis in the chart. Use the following syntax for CHART-AXIS-TICKS:

{CHART-AXIS-TICKS *axis;[major];[minor];[space]*}

The *axis* argument specifies the axis—x, y, or 2y—and is enclosed in quotation marks.

The *major* argument is a Boolean argument that specifies whether 1-2-3 displays tick marks at major intervals.

The *minor* argument is a Boolean argument that specifies whether 1-2-3 displays tick marks at minor intervals.

The *space* argument is an integer that specifies how many ticks appear between labels.

NOTE   To specify the intervals between tick marks, use the CHART-AXIS-INTERVALS command.

The CHART-AXIS-TITLE Command

The CHART-AXIS-TITLE command changes an axis title in the current chart. Use the following syntax for CHART-AXIS-TITLE:

   {CHART-AXIS-TITLE *axis*;[*title*];[*title-cell*]}

The *axis* argument specifies the axis—x, y, or 2y—and is enclosed in quotation marks.

The *title* argument is text, enclosed in quotation marks, that specifies the axis title.

The *title-cell* argument is the name or address of a cell that contains a label to use as the axis title.

If a *title-cell* is specified, *title* is ignored. You can remove an existing title by using an empty string (" ") for *title*, or by specifying a blank cell for *title-cell*.

The CHART-AXIS-UNITS Command

The CHART-AXIS-UNITS command changes the size of the axis units and the axis unit titles for the current chart. Use the following syntax for CHART-AXIS-UNITS:

   {CHART-AXIS-UNITS *axis*;[*manual-calculate*];[*manual-title*];[*exponent*];[*title*];[*title-cell*]}

The *axis* argument specifies the axis—x, y, or 2y—and is enclosed in quotation marks.

The *manual-calculate* argument is a Boolean argument that specifies whether you want to specify an order of magnitude for the axis scale. If you choose not to specify the order of magnitude, it is automatically calculated.

The *manual-title* argument is a Boolean argument that specifies whether you want to create the axis units title. If you choose not to create the axis units title, it is automatically generated.

The *exponent* argument is an integer from –95 through 95 that specifies the exponent (power of 10) used to scale the units on the axis.

The *title* argument is text that specifies the units title, and is enclosed in quotation marks.

The *title-cell* argument is the name or address of a cell that contains a label to use as the units title.

If a *title-cell* is specified, *title* is ignored. You can remove an existing units title by using an empty string (" ") for *title* or by specifying a blank cell for *title-cell*.

The CHART-COLOR-RANGE Command

The CHART-COLOR-RANGE command sets the color for the values in a data series in the current chart. Use the following syntax for CHART-COLOR-RANGE:

    {CHART-COLOR-RANGE *series*;[*color-range*]}

The *series* argument specifies a data series in the current chart. The *series* is a letter from A through W, and is enclosed in quotation marks.

The *color-range* argument is the name or address of a range whose values determine the color for each value in a data range. If you do not specify *color-range*, color is not used for the specified series.

The CHART-DATA-LABELS Command

The CHART-DATA-LABELS command creates labels for data points or bars in the current chart. Data in *label-range* is used as the labels. Use the following syntax for CHART-DATA-LABELS:

    {CHART-DATA-LABELS *series*;[*label-range*];[*position*]}

The *series* argument specifies the data series in the current chart. The *series* is a letter from A through W (to specify a single data range) or the word All (to specify all data ranges), and is enclosed in quotation marks.

The *label-range* argument specifies the name or address of a range that contains the data labels. If you omit *label-range*, the data label for the *series* argument is removed from the chart.

The *position* argument specifies the location of the data labels. The *position* can be center, right, below, left, or above, and is enclosed in quotation marks. The exact location of the data labels depends on the type of chart.

The CHART-FOOTNOTE Command

The CHART-FOOTNOTE command adds footnotes to the current chart. Use the following syntax for CHART-FOOTNOTE:

> {CHART-FOOTNOTE [*line1*];[*line2*];[*position*];[*cell1*];[*cell2*]}

The *line1* argument specifies the first line of the footnote, and is enclosed in quotation marks.

The *line2* argument specifies the second line of the footnote, and is enclosed in quotation marks.

The *position* argument specifies location of the footnote—left, center, or right—and is enclosed in quotation marks.

The *cell1* argument is the name or address of a range that contains a label to use as the first line of the footnote.

The *cell2* argument is the name or address of a range that contains a label to use as the second line of the footnote.

The *cell1* argument overrides the *line1* argument, and the *cell2* argument overrides the *line2* argument. To delete existing footnote lines, specify an empty string (" ") for *line1* or *line2* or specify a blank cell for *cell1* or *cell2*.

The CHART-GRID Command

The CHART-GRID command displays or hides grid lines for an axis in the current chart. Use the following syntax for CHART-GRID:

> {CHART-GRID *axis*;[*major*];[*minor*]}

The *axis* argument specifies the axis—x, y, or 2y—and is enclosed in quotation marks.

The *major* argument is a Boolean argument that specifies whether to display or hide grid lines that originate from major-interval tick marks.

The *minor* argument is a Boolean argument that specifies whether to display or hide grid lines that originate from minor-interval tick marks.

The CHART-GRID command has no effect if the current chart is a pie chart.

The CHART-LEGEND Command

The CHART-LEGEND command creates legend labels that identify the colors, symbols, or patterns of the current chart's data range. Use the following syntax for CHART-LEGEND:

    {CHART-LEGEND series;[legend];[position];[legend-range]}

The *series* argument specifies the data series in the current chart. The *series* is a letter from A through W (to specify a single data range) or the word All (to specify all data ranges), and is enclosed in quotation marks.

The *legend* argument specifies the legend label for the *series* and is enclosed in quotation marks. If *series* is All, omit *legend* and use *legend-range* instead.

The *position* argument specifies the location of the legend label—right or below—and is enclosed in quotation marks.

The *legend-range* argument specifies the name or address of a cell or range that contains as many labels as specified by *series*.

The CHART-NEW Command

The CHART-NEW command draws a chart using data from the currently selected range. Use the following syntax for CHART-NEW:

    {CHART-NEW location;[type];[option];[name]}

The *location* argument specifies the name or address of the range for the new chart.

The *type* argument specifies a chart type—Line, Area, Bar, Pie, XY, HLCO, Mixed, Radar, 3D-Line, 3D-Area, 3D-Bar, or 3D-Pie—and is enclosed in quotation marks.

The *option* argument specifies an offset number (0 to 5) that specifies which of the optional variations to use for the specified chart type. You select the optional variations from the option panel in the Chart Type dialog box for the type of chart you specified. The upper-left selection is numbered 0, the upper-right selection is numbered 1, and so on (see fig. 16.4).

The *name* argument specifies a name for the chart, and is enclosed in quotation marks. If you omit *name*, 1-2-3 assigns a default name, such as CHART 1.

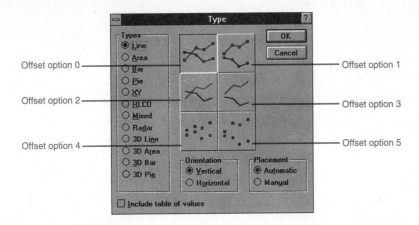

Offset option 0

Offset option 1

Offset option 2

Offset option 3

Offset option 4

Offset option 5

FIG. 16.4

Chart offset
numbers.

The CHART-PATTERN-RANGE Command

The CHART-PATTERN-RANGE command sets the fill pattern for each
value in a data series in the current chart. Use the following syntax for
CHART-PATTERN-RANGE:

> {CHART-PATTERN-RANGE *series*;[*pattern-range*]}

The *series* argument specifies a data series in the current chart. The
series is a letter from A through W, and is enclosed in quotation marks.

The *pattern-range* argument is the name or address of a range whose
values determine the pattern for each value in a data range. If you do
not specify *pattern-range*, a fill pattern is not used for the specified
series.

The CHART-PIE-LABELS Command

The CHART-PIE-LABELS command creates labels for the current pie
chart. Use the following syntax for CHART-PIE-LABELS:

> {CHART-PIE-LABELS [*values*];[*percentage*];[*x-range*];[*c-range*]}

The *values* argument is a Boolean argument that specifies whether to
display the values in the A data range.

The *percentage* argument is a Boolean argument that specifies whether
to display each value in the A data range as a percentage of the whole
rather than as a numeric value.

The *x-range* argument is a Boolean argument that specifies whether to
display the contents of the X data range.

The *c-range* argument is a Boolean argument that specifies whether 1-2-3 uses values you enter in the C data range to show or hide percentages.

The CHART-PIE-SLICE-EXPLOSION Command

The CHART-PIE-SLICE-EXPLOSION command enlarges, or *explodes*, slices in the current pie chart. Use the following syntax for CHART-PIE-SLICE-EXPLOSION:

{CHART-PIE-SLICE-EXPLOSION *explosion-type*;[*all-by-%*]}

The *explosion-type* argument specifies how to explode pie slices. Specify "none" to prevent slice explosion, "all" to explode all slices by the percent specified by *all-by-%*, or "using-b" to explode all slices based on data in the B data range.

The *all-by-%* argument is an integer from 1 through 100 that specifies a percentage by which to explode the slices if explosion-type is "all."

The CHART-RANGE Command

The CHART-RANGE command sets the data range, series type, and second y-axis flag for a data series in the current chart. Use the following syntax for CHART-RANGE:

{CHART-RANGE *series*;[*series-range*];[*series-type*];[*2Y-axis*]}

The *series* argument specifies a data series in the current chart. The *series* is a letter from A through Z, excluding Y, and is enclosed in quotation marks. If *series* is Z, the contents of *series-range* is the legend range.

The *series-range* argument specifies the name or address of the data range for *series*.

The *series-type* argument specifies the type of series—area, line, or bar—for mixed charts.

The *2Y-axis* argument is a Boolean argument that specifies whether this series should be plotted on the second y-axis.

The CHART-RANGE-DELETE Command

The CHART-RANGE-DELETE command deletes a series from the current chart. Use the following syntax for CHART-RANGE-DELETE:

{CHART-RANGE-DELETE *series*}

The *series* argument specifies a data series in the current chart. The *series* is a letter from A through Z, excluding Y, and is enclosed in quotation marks. If *series* is Z, the contents of series-range is the legend range.

The CHART-RENAME Command

The CHART-RENAME command renames a chart. Use the following syntax for CHART-RENAME:

> {CHART-RENAME *old-name;new-name*}

The *old-name* argument specifies the current name of the chart.

The *new-name* argument specifies the new name you want to give the chart.

The CHART-SET-PREFERRED Command

The CHART-SET-PREFERRED command defines the current chart's settings as the preferred chart. Use the following syntax for CHART-SET-PREFERRED:

> {CHART-SET-PREFERRED}

The CHART-SET-PREFERRED command does not use any arguments.

The CHART-TITLE Command

The CHART-TITLE command adds chart titles to the current chart. Use the following syntax for CHART-TITLE:

> {CHART-TITLE [*line1*];[*line2*];[*position*];[*cell1*];[*cell2*]}

The *line1* argument specifies the first line of the chart title, and is enclosed in quotation marks.

The *line2* argument specifies the second line of the chart title, and is enclosed in quotation marks.

The *position* argument specifies location of the title—left, center, or right—and is enclosed in quotation marks.

The *cell1* argument is the name or address of a range that contains a label to use as the first line of the chart title.

The *cell2* argument is the name or address of a range that contains a label to use as the second line of the chart title.

The *cell1* argument overrides the *line1* argument, and the *cell2* argument overrides the *line2* argument. To delete existing titles, specify an empty string (" ") for *line1* or *line2* or specify a blank cell for *cell1* or *cell2*.

The CHART-TYPE Command

The CHART-TYPE command sets the type of chart for the current chart. Use the following syntax for CHART-TYPE:

  {CHART-TYPE *type*;[*option*];[*orientation*];[*value-tables*]}

The *type* argument specifies a chart type—Line, Area, Bar, Pie, XY, HLCO, Mixed, Radar, 3D-Line, 3D-Area, 3D-Bar, or 3D-Pie—and is enclosed in quotation marks.

The *option* argument specifies an offset number (0 to 5) that specifies which of the optional variations to use for the specified chart type. You select the optional variations from the option panel in the Chart Type dialog box for the type of chart you specified. The upper-left selection is numbered 0, the upper-right selection is numbered 1, and so on (see figure 16.4).

The *orientation* argument specifies the orientation of the chart—vertical or horizontal. Vertical is the default if you do not specify *orientation*.

The *value-tables* argument is a Boolean argument that specifies whether to display data values under the chart. The default is to not display the values. If *type* is Pie, HLCO, or XY, no data values are displayed.

The CHART-USE-PREFERRED Command

The CHART-USE-PREFERRED command applies the preferred chart settings to the current chart. You define these settings by using the CHART-SET-PREFERRED command. Use the following syntax for CHART-USE-PREFERRED:

  {CHART-USE-PREFERRED}

The CHART-USE-PREFERRED command does not use any arguments.

Using Chart Macro Commands Together

Figure 16.5 shows how you can use several chart macro commands to create a new chart and modify its settings. This macro example creates a new line chart, controls the display of grid lines, adds a footnote, and sets the colors used to display the data.

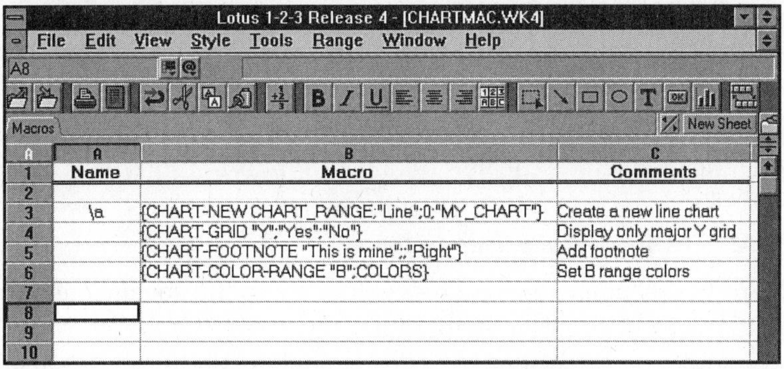

FIG. 16.5

Chart macro
commands create
a new chart and
modify its
settings.

Commands That Manipulate Data

The commands described in table 16.2 enable you to place data precisely within worksheet files, edit existing entries, erase entries, and recalculate formulas.

Table 16.2 Commands That Manipulate Data

Command	Action
APPENDBELOW	Copies the contents from a source range to the rows immediately below a target range
APPENDRIGHT	Copies the contents from a source range to the columns immediately to the right of a target range
BLANK	Erases the contents of a range
CONTENTS	Copies the contents from a source range to a target range as a label
LET	Enters a number or left-aligned label in a range
PUT	Enters a number or left-aligned label in a cell within a range
RECALC	Recalculates the values in a range, proceeding row by row
RECALCCOL	Recalculates the values in a range, proceeding column by column

The APPENDBELOW Command

The APPENDBELOW command copies the contents of one range, the *source,* to the rows immediately below another range, the *destination.* As part of the copy operation, APPENDBELOW also expands the destination range to include the new data. The syntax of APPENDBELOW is as follows:

{APPENDBELOW *destination;source*}

APPENDBELOW copies the contents of *source* to the specified *destination* and expands the destination range to include new data.

Use APPENDBELOW with the FORM command to copy data from an input form to a database range.

APPENDBELOW fails if the number of rows in the specified source exceeds the number of rows left in the worksheet below the specified destination, when the execution of the command would overwrite data in the destination range, or when the rows below the destination are protected.

When the specified *source* contains formulas, the calculated values are copied to the specified *destination.* If *destination* is a named range, the range definition is adjusted to include the new data.

APPENDBELOW is a helpful companion to the FORM command. Used together, the commands provide an easy way of copying data from an input form to a storage table or database range.

Several conditions can cause the APPENDBELOW command to fail. First, if the number of rows in the specified source exceeds the number of rows left in the worksheet below the specified destination, APPENDBELOW fails.

Second, APPENDBELOW fails when the execution of the command would overwrite—and therefore destroy—data in the destination range. Actually, this condition is a handy safety feature, because APPENDBELOW does not destroy data in the worksheet.

Third, APPENDBELOW fails when the rows below the destination are protected.

One other feature of APPENDBELOW should be mentioned. When the specified *source* contains formulas, the calculated values are copied to the specified *destination.*

The APPENDRIGHT Command

The operation of APPENDRIGHT mirrors that of APPENDBELOW, with one exception: APPENDRIGHT copies the contents of the specified source to the *right* of the specified destination. (APPENDBELOW copies the contents of the source to just *below* the destination.) The syntax of APPENDRIGHT is as follows:

{APPENDRIGHT *destination;source*}

APPENDRIGHT expands the *destination* range to include newly copied data and converts formulas in *source* to values during the copy.

APPENDRIGHT ends in an error when no room is available to copy, because data exists in the destination or because insufficient worksheet space is available.

When you use APPENDBELOW or APPENDRIGHT, specify a range name as the destination range.

The BLANK Command

The BLANK command erases a cell or a range of cells in a worksheet or in multiple worksheets. The syntax of BLANK is as follows:

{BLANK *location*}

BLANK erases the range defined by *location*.

The *location* argument also can specify a worksheet, a file, or a range name. The statement {BLANK REP_RANGE} erases the data from the range named REP_RANGE.

The CONTENTS Command

The CONTENTS command stores the contents of one cell in another cell as a label. The CONTENTS command is a hybrid version of the LET statement. The LET statement can store a number or a label in a specified cell. The purpose of the CONTENTS statement is to store a label that looks like a number. The CONTENTS command optionally assigns an individual cell width and/or cell format. Use the following syntax with CONTENTS:

{CONTENTS *destination;source;[width];[format]*}

Destination is the cell address or range name of the range where you want to store the data. Source is the cell address or range name of the range containing the existing data.

The *width* argument can be a number, a numeric formula, or a reference to a cell containing a number or a numeric formula with an absolute value from 1 to 240.

The *format* argument must be a code number from the list in table 16.3, a formula that evaluates to one of these code numbers, or a reference to a cell that contains one of these code numbers. If neither *width* nor *format* is specified, the CONTENTS command uses the column width and format of the source location to format the string.

Table 16.3 Numeric-Format Codes for the CONTENTS Command

Code	Format of the Destination String
0 to 15	Fixed, 0 to 15 decimal places
16 to 31	Scientific, 0 to 15 decimal places
32 to 47	Currency, 0 to 15 decimal places
48 to 63	Percent, 0 to 15 decimal places
64 to 79	Comma, 0 to 15 decimal places
112	+/–
113	General
114	31-Dec-93
115	31-Dec
116	Dec-93
117	Text
118	Hidden
119	11:59:59 AM
120	11:59 AM
121	12/31/93
122	12/31
123	23:59:59
124	59:59
127	Worksheet's default number format (specified with Style Worksheet Defaults Number Format)

The LET Command

The LET command stores an entry in a specified cell location. The LET command can create a label entry or a number entry. Use the following syntax for LET:

{LET *location;expression*}

The LET command places the value of *expression* in the *location* specified.

Consider the following examples:

{LET B12;A15}	Copies into cell B12 the contents of cell A15.
{LET B24;"Overextended"}	Places the label Overextended into cell B24.
{LET B21;@AVG(SALARIES)}	Places the calculated average of the range SALARIES into cell B21.

The LET command copies the displayed results of the source cell. This command does not copy functions or formulas; instead, the results of the functions or formulas are copied. For example, if the function @SUM(EXPENSES) is in cell B44 and the result is 24000, the {LET} command {LET C44,B44} places the value 24000 in cell C44.

The PUT Command

The PUT command stores an entry in a cell location. PUT is a variant of LET. Instead of stating a cell location, however, PUT determines a cell location by figuring the column and row within a stated range. Like the LET command, the PUT command can create a label entry or a number entry. Also like the LET command, the value, not the formula, is placed in the location if the entry is a formula or function. The syntax of PUT is as follows:

{PUT *range;col;row;value*}

The PUT command places *value* into a cell in a defined *range*.

The *col* argument defines the column offset within the range, and the *row* argument defines the row offset within the range.

The column offset and the range offset must be within the specified range. The *range* argument can be a range name or cell address or a formula that yields a cell address or range name. The *col, row,* and *value* arguments can be values, cell references, or formulas. The *value* argument, which represents the value to be placed in the cell location, also can be a string.

Consider the following PUT statement:

```
{PUT A1..F20;1;3;"Jo-Ann"}
```

This command places the label Jo-Ann in cell B4.

The RECALC and RECALCCOL Commands

The RECALC and RECALCCOL commands enable you to recalculate a portion of the worksheet. These commands can be useful in large worksheets in which recalculation time is long and in which you must recalculate certain values in the worksheet before you proceed to the next processing step in the macro. Use these commands only if recalculation is set to Manual recalculation (with Tools User Setup Recalculation).

The commands for partial worksheet recalculation have the following forms:

> {RECALC location;[condition];[iteration-number]}

> {RECALCCOL location;[condition];[iteration-number]}

The *location* argument is a range or range name that specifies the cells whose formulas are to be recalculated.

The *condition* and *iteration-number* arguments are optional for both commands.

If *condition* is included, the range is recalculated repeatedly until the condition has a nonzero value—*condition* evaluates to true. Remember that *condition* must be a logical expression or a reference to a cell that is within the recalculation range and that contains a logical expression. If *condition* is a reference to a cell outside the recalculation range, the value of the condition—true (nonzero) or false (0)—does not change, and the condition does not control the partial recalculation.

The *iteration-number* argument specifies the number of times that the formulas in the location range are to be recalculated.

When *condition* evaluates to true, or the recalculation has performed the number of iterations specified in *iteration-number*, the command terminates. If you want the macro to perform the full number of iterations, use zero as the *condition* argument. The value 0 makes the condition always false, forcing 1-2-3 for Windows to perform the specified number of iterations; 1-2-3 for Windows stops recalculating when the condition is true. You also can skip the *condition* argument by using two semicolons as placeholders.

RECALC or RECALCCOL always forces one recalculation, regardless of the starting value of *condition* or *iteration-number*.

The RECALCCOL command performs the calculations column by column. First, all the cells in the first column of the range are recalculated, top to bottom. Then all the cells in the second column are recalculated, then in the third column, and so on. With either command, only cells within the specified range are recalculated, even if formulas within the range refer to cells outside the recalculation range that have not been updated.

> **CAUTION:** You might have to use {CALC} if formulas in the location refer to other formulas located below and to their right or if formulas refer both to cells in rows above and to the right and to cells in columns below and to the left.

Commands That Manipulate Databases

The database commands enable you to create and use databases, both in a 1-2-3 for Windows worksheet and in separate database files. By combining these commands with the DataLens drivers, you can use data contained in almost any type of database file. Table 16.4 describes the 1-2-3 for Windows database commands.

Table 16.4 Commands That Manipulate Databases

Command	Action
COMMIT	Completes pending external database transactions
CROSSTAB	Creates a cross-tabulation table
DATA-EXTERNAL-CONNECT	Use DATABASE-CONNECT
DATA-EXTERNAL-CREATE-TABLE	Use DATABASE-CREATE-TABLE
DATA-EXTERNAL-DISCONNECT	Use DATABASE-DISCONNECT
DATA-EXTERNAL-SEND-COMMAND	Use DATABASE-SEND-COMMAND
DATABASE-APPEND	Adds new records to a database
DATABASE-CONNECT	Establishes a connection to an external database
DATABASE-CREATE-TABLE	Creates and connects to an external database table
DATABASE-DELETE	Deletes specified records from a database

continues

Table 16.4 Continued

Command	Action
DATABASE-DISCONNECT	Disconnects from an external database
DATABASE-FIND	Locates and selects records in a database
DATABASE-SEND-COMMAND	Sends a command to an external database
QUERY-ADD-FIELD	Adds a field to the currently selected query table
QUERY-AGGREGATE	Performs calculations on groups of data from a query table
QUERY-CHOOSE-FIELDS	Specifies the fields to appear in a query table
QUERY-COPY-SQL	Copies to the Clipboard the SQL command equivalent of the current query
QUERY-CRITERIA	Specifies record selection criteria to determine which records appear in a query table
QUERY-DATABASE-TABLE	Changes the database for the current query table
QUERY-JOIN	Joins multiple databases that contain a common field
QUERY-NAME	Assigns a new name to the current query table
QUERY-NEW	Creates a new query table
QUERY-OPTIONS	Specifies options for the current query table
QUERY-REFRESH	Updates records in the current query table to reflect changes made to the database, query options, criteria, aggregates, or field names
QUERY-REMOVE-FIELD	Removes a field from the current query table
QUERY-SHOW-FIELD	Specifies an alias field name for a field in the current query table

Command	Action
QUERY-SORT	Arranges data in the current query table
QUERY-SORT-KEY-DEFINE	Defines a sort key to be used in a subsequent QUERY-SORT command
QUERY-SORT-RESET	Clears all sort keys for the current query table
QUERY-UPDATE	Applies changes to records in the current query table to the corresponding database
QUERY-UPGRADE	Upgrades a query from a previous version of 1-2-3 so that it works with the Query commands in 1-2-3 Release 4
ROLLBACK	Cancels pending external database transactions
SEND-SQL	Sends an SQL command to an external database driver

The COMMIT Command

The COMMIT command, which works with the SQL Server only, finalizes pending transactions with an external database. COMMIT has the following syntax:

{COMMIT [*SQL-driver-name*];[*database-name*]}

The *SQL-driver-name* argument specifies the name of the driver.

The *database-name* argument specifies the name of the external database, and is enclosed in quotes.

You must use both arguments or no arguments. COMMIT issued with no arguments commits all pending transactions. COMMIT with arguments commits only the transaction pending for the driver and database you specify.

Consider the following command:

```
{COMMIT "SQL";"BUDGET"}
```

This command commits the transaction pending for the driver SQL and the database named BUDGET.

The **CROSSTAB** Command

The CROSSTAB command creates a cross-tabulation table in a new worksheet following the worksheet that contains the database. Use the following syntax for CROSSTAB:

> {CROSSTAB *database;row-headings;col-headings;summary-field;summary-method*}

The *database* argument specifies the range name or address of a database.

The *row-headings* argument specifies the name of the field whose entries you want to use as row headings, and is enclosed in quotation marks.

The *col-headings* argument specifies the name of the field whose entries you want to use as column headings, and is enclosed in quotation marks.

The *summary-field* argument specifies the name of the field whose values you want summarized in the cells of the crosstab table, and is enclosed in quotation marks.

The *summary-method* argument specifies the method to use to summarize in the cross tabulation—sum, avg, count, min, or max—and is enclosed in quotation marks.

Cross-tabulation tables analyze the relationships between the data in different fields of a database. For example, you can use cross-tabulation tables to compare income levels to age groups.

The **DATABASE-APPEND** Command

The DATABASE-APPEND command adds new records to a database. Use the following syntax for DATABASE-APPEND:

> {DATABASE-APPEND *source-range;database*}

The *source-range* argument is the name or address of the range or an external database that contains the records to append to *database*. The first row of *source-range* must contain field names that are the same as those in the *database* to which you are appending records.

The *database* argument is the name or address of a database.

The **DATABASE-CONNECT** Command

The DATABASE-CONNECT command establishes a connection to an external database so you can use the database with other 1-2-3 commands. Use the following syntax for DATABASE-CONNECT:

{DATABASE-CONNECT *driver-name*;[*driver-user-id*]; [*driver-password*]; [*connection-string*];*db-name*; [*db-user-id*];[*db-password*];[*owner-name*];*table-name*; [*range-name*]}

The *driver-name* argument specifies the name of the database driver associated with an external database, and is enclosed in quotation marks. This external database contains the table to which you want to connect.

The *driver-user-id* argument specifies the driver user ID, and is enclosed in quotation marks. Not all drivers require this argument. If you omit *driver-user-id*, and a user ID is required, 1-2-3 for Windows displays a dialog box to prompt for the missing information.

The *driver-password* argument specifies the driver password, and is enclosed in quotation marks. Not all drivers require this argument. If you omit *driver-password*, and a password is required, 1-2-3 for Windows displays a dialog box to prompt for the missing information.

The *connection-string* argument, which is enclosed in quotation marks, specifies additional information that may be needed to connect to a driver.

The *db-name* argument specifies the name of the external database that contains the table to which you want to connect. The argument is enclosed in quotation marks.

The *db-user-id* argument specifies the database user ID, and is enclosed in quotation marks. If you omit *db-user-id*, and a user ID is required, 1-2-3 for Windows displays a dialog box to prompt for the missing information.

The *db-password* argument specifies the database password, and is enclosed in quotation marks. If you omit *db-password*, and a password is required, 1-2-3 for Windows displays a dialog box to prompt for the missing information.

The *owner-name* argument specifies the name of the owner of the table, if one is required. The argument is enclosed in quotation marks.

The *table-name* argument specifies the name of the external table you want to create or connect to, and is enclosed in quotation marks.

The *range-name* argument specifies the range name of the table, and is enclosed in quotation marks. If you omit *range-name*, the range name is the same as *table-name*.

The DATABASE-CREATE-TABLE Command

The DATABASE-CREATE-TABLE command sets up the structure for and connects to a new table in an external database. Use the following syntax for DATABASE-CREATE-TABLE:

> {DATABASE-CREATE-TABLE *driver-name*;[*driver-user-id*];
> [*driver-password*];*db-name*;[*db-user-id*];[*db-password*];
> [*owner-name*];*table-name*;[*range-name*];[*creation-string*];
> [*table-definition*]}

The *driver-name* argument, which is enclosed in quotation marks, specifies the name of the database driver associated with an external database. This external database contains the table to which you want to connect.

The *driver-user-id* argument specifies the driver user ID, and is enclosed in quotation marks. Not all drivers require this argument. If you omit *driver-user-id* and a user ID is required, 1-2-3 for Windows displays a dialog box to prompt for the missing information.

The *driver-password* argument specifies the driver password, and is enclosed in quotation marks. Not all drivers require this argument. If you omit *driver-password* and a password is required, 1-2-3 for Windows displays a dialog box to prompt for the missing information.

The *db-name* argument, which is enclosed in quotation marks, specifies the name of the external database that contains the table to which you want to connect.

The *db-user-id* argument specifies the database user ID, and is enclosed in quotation marks. If you omit *db-user-id* and a user ID is required, 1-2-3 for Windows displays a dialog box to prompt for the missing information.

The *db-password* argument specifies the database password, and is enclosed in quotation marks. If you omit *db-password* and a password is required, 1-2-3 for Windows displays a dialog box to prompt for the missing information.

The *owner-name* argument specifies the name of the owner of the table, if one is required. The argument is enclosed in quotation marks.

The *table-name* argument specifies the name of the external table you want to create or connect to, and is enclosed in quotation marks.

The *range-name* argument specifies the range name of the table, and is enclosed in quotation marks. If you omit *range-name*, the range name is the same as *table-name*.

The *creation-string* argument specifies additional information about the table, and is enclosed in quotation marks. For example, the Paradox driver lets you use a *creation-string* to specify a sort order for the table. Not all external databases require a *creation-string*.

The *table-definition* argument specifies the name or address of a range that contains the field definitions that you want the new table to use. You must specify only the top left cell of the range containing the field information.

The DATABASE-DELETE Command

The DATABASE-DELETE command deletes records that meet specified criteria from the database. Use the following syntax for DATABASE-DELETE:

> {DATABASE-DELETE *database-table;criteria*}

The *database-table* argument specifies the name or address of a database.

The *criteria* argument specifies a criteria formula, and is enclosed in quotation marks.

The DATABASE-DISCONNECT Command

The DATABASE-DISCONNECT command disconnects an external database, ending all data exchange between 1-2-3 for Windows and the external database. Use the following syntax for DATABASE-DISCONNECT:

> {DATABASE-DISCONNECT *range-name*}

The *range name* argument specifies the range name of the database, and is enclosed in quotation marks.

After 1-2-3 for Windows executes a DATABASE-DISCONNECT command, you cannot refer to the range name of the specified database until it is reconnected with DATABASE-CONNECT. Any commands or functions that refer to the range name of a disconnected database may result in errors.

The DATABASE-FIND Command

The DATABASE-FIND command locates and selects records in a database that meet specified criteria. You cannot use DATABASE-FIND with external databases. Use the following syntax for DATABASE-FIND:

> {DATABASE-FIND *database-table;criteria*}

The *database-table* argument specifies the range name or address of a database, or the range name of a query table.

The *criteria* argument specifies a criteria formula, and is enclosed in quotation marks.

The **DATABASE-SEND-COMMAND** Command

The DATABASE-SEND-COMMAND command sends a command to an external database. Use the following syntax for DATABASE-SEND-COMMAND:

{DATABASE-SEND-COMMAND *driver-name*;[*driver-user-id*]; [*driver-password*];[*connection-string*];*db-name*; [*db-user-id*];[*db-password*];*command*}

The *driver-name* argument specifies the name of the database driver associated with an external database, and is enclosed in quotation marks. This external database contains the table to which you want to connect.

The *driver-user-id* argument specifies the driver user ID, and is enclosed in quotation marks. Not all drivers require this argument. If you omit *driver-user-id* and a user ID is required, 1-2-3 for Windows displays a dialog box to prompt for the missing information.

The *driver-password* argument specifies the driver password, and is enclosed in quotation marks. Not all drivers require this argument. If you omit *driver-password* and a password is required, 1-2-3 for Windows displays a dialog box to prompt for the missing information.

The *connection-string* argument specifies additional information that may be needed to connect to a driver. The argument is enclosed in quotation marks.

The *db-name* argument specifies the name of the external database that contains the table to which you want to connect. The argument is enclosed in quotation marks.

The *db-user-id* argument specifies the database user ID, and is enclosed in quotation marks. If you omit *db-user-id* and a user ID is required, 1-2-3 for Windows displays a dialog box to prompt for the missing information.

The *db-password* argument specifies the database password, and is enclosed in quotation marks. If you omit *db-password* and a password is required, 1-2-3 for Windows displays a dialog box to prompt for the missing information.

The *command* argument specifies the command that you want to send. The argument is enclosed in quotation marks.

The QUERY-ADD-FIELD Command

The QUERY-ADD-FIELD command adds a field to the right of the currently selected query table. Use the following syntax for QUERY-ADD-FIELD:

> {QUERY-ADD-FIELD *field*}

The *field* argument specifies the name of a valid field for the database, and is enclosed in quotation marks.

The QUERY-AGGREGATE Command

The QUERY-AGGREGATE command performs calculations on groups of data from a query table. Use the following syntax for QUERY-AGGREGATE:

> {QUERY-AGGREGATE *function;field-name*}

The *function* argument specifies the aggregate function—sum, avg, count, max, or min—and is enclosed in quotation marks.

The *field-name* argument specifies the name of a valid field for the selected query table, and is enclosed in quotation marks.

The QUERY-CHOOSE-FIELDS Command

The QUERY-CHOOSE-FIELDS command specifies the fields that you want to appear in a query table. Use the following syntax for QUERY-CHOOSE-FIELDS:

> {QUERY-CHOOSE-FIELDS [*field1*];[*field2*];...;[*field15*]}

The *field1* through *field15* arguments, which are enclosed in quotation marks, specify the field names of the fields to be displayed in the query table. The fields are displayed in the query table in the same order as they appear in the command.

If you use the QUERY-CHOOSE-FIELDS command with no arguments, all fields in the source database are displayed in the query table in the same order as they appear in the database.

The QUERY-COPY-SQL Command

The QUERY-COPY-SQL command copies to the Clipboard the SQL command equivalent to the current query. Use the following syntax for QUERY-COPY-SQL:

{QUERY-COPY-SQL}

The QUERY-COPY-SQL command does not use any arguments. This command is useful for constructing SQL (Structured Query Language) commands for use with external databases that support SQL.

The QUERY-CRITERIA Command

The QUERY-CRITERIA command specifies selection criteria to determine which records appear in a query table. Use the following syntax for QUERY-CRITERIA:

{QUERY-CRITERIA [*criteria*]}

The *criteria* argument specifies a criteria formula, and is enclosed in quotation marks. If you omit *criteria*, all records are included in the query table.

The QUERY-DATABASE-TABLE Command

The QUERY-DATABASE-TABLE command selects a different database for the currently selected query table. Use the following syntax for QUERY-DATABASE-TABLE:

{QUERY-DATABASE-TABLE *database-table*}

The *database-table* argument specifies the range name or address of a database. If the new database contains the same fields as the current database, 1-2-3 for Windows does not change the criteria, sort settings, aggregates, or the location of the query table. If the fields in the new database do not match those in the current database, 1-2-3 for Windows displays a warning and removes the criteria, sort settings, aggregates, and join criteria.

The QUERY-JOIN Command

The QUERY-JOIN command joins multiple databases that contain a common field. You can then perform queries that select related data from the different databases. Use the following syntax for QUERY-JOIN:

{QUERY-JOIN [*join-criteria*]}

The *join-criteria* argument specifies a join formula, and is enclosed in quotation marks. If you omit *join-criteria*, the connections between the databases are severed, leaving you with just the original database.

A join formula has the following format:

    +TABLE1.FIELD1=TABLE2.FIELD2

TABLE1 and TABLE2 are range names for two databases you want to query. FIELD1 and FIELD2 are the names of fields that contain similar entries in both tables, and must exactly match field names in the databases. FIELD1 and FIELD2 do not have to be identical, but the two fields must contain the same type of data. Either FIELD1 or FIELD2 should contain only unique entries—otherwise the results are unpredictable.

The QUERY-NAME Command

The QUERY-NAME command assigns a new name to the currently selected query table. Use the following syntax for QUERY-NAME:

    {QUERY-NAME *new-name*}

The *new-name* argument specifies the new name of the query table, and is enclosed in quotation marks.

The QUERY-NEW Command

The QUERY-NEW command creates a query table that contains records extracted from a database. Use the following syntax for QUERY-NEW:

    {QUERY-NEW *database-table*;*output-range*;[*criteria*];
    [*query-name*];[*field1*],[*field2*],...,[*fieldn*]}

The *database-table* argument specifies the range name or address of a database.

The *output-range* argument specifies the range name or address of the range in which you want to create the query table.

The *criteria* argument specifies a criteria formula, and is enclosed in quotation marks. If you omit *criteria*, all records are included in the query table.

The *query-name* argument specifies a name for the query table. If you omit *query-name*, 1-2-3 for Windows assigns a default name, such as QUERY 1.

The *field1* through *fieldn* arguments specify the names of fields from *database-table* that you want to display in the query table. Each of these arguments is enclosed in quotation marks. If you omit the *field* arguments, all fields are displayed in the query table.

The QUERY-OPTIONS Command

The QUERY-OPTIONS command specifies options for manipulating data in the currently selected query table. Use the following syntax for QUERY-OPTIONS:

{QUERY-OPTIONS *option;on|off;[record-limit]*}

The *option* argument specifies an option to set—allow updates, unique only, limit output, show samples, or auto refresh—and is enclosed in quotation marks.

The *option* argument values have the following meanings:

- The allow updates option allows changes made in the query table to be posted to the database.

- The unique only option excludes duplicate records from the query table.

- The limit output option limits the number of records that appear in the query table.

- The show samples option displays a list of unique values from which you can specify criteria for the query table.

- The auto refresh option updates the query table results when any criteria, sort settings, field names, or aggregates change.

The *on|off* argument is a yes or no argument that specifies whether to turn *option* on or off, and is enclosed in quotation marks.

The *record-limit* argument is a value from 1 through 8,191 that specifies how many records appear in the query table if the limit output option is turned on.

The QUERY-REFRESH Command

The QUERY-REFRESH command updates records in the currently selected query table to reflect changes made to the database, query options, criteria, aggregates, or field names. Use the following syntax for QUERY-REFRESH:

{QUERY-REFRESH}

The QUERY-REFRESH command does not use any arguments.

The QUERY-REMOVE-FIELD Command

The QUERY-REMOVE-FIELD command removes a field from the currently selected query table. Use the following syntax for QUERY-REMOVE-FIELD:

> {QUERY-REMOVE-FIELD *field*}

The *field* argument specifies the name of a valid field for the database, and is enclosed in quotation marks.

The QUERY-SHOW-FIELD Command

The QUERY-SHOW-FIELD command specifies an alias field name for a field to display in the currently selected query table. QUERY-SHOW-FIELD does not change the field name in the database, only the name used to display information in the query table. Use the following syntax for QUERY-SHOW-FIELD:

> {QUERY-SHOW-FIELD *field;field-alias*}

The *field* argument specifies the name of a valid field for the database, and is enclosed in quotation marks.

The *field-alias* argument specifies the name to use to display information in the query table, and is enclosed in quotation marks.

The QUERY-SORT Command

The QUERY-SORT command arranges data in the currently selected query table in the order you specify. Use the following syntax for QUERY-SORT:

> {QUERY-SORT [*key1*];[*order1*];[*key2*];
> [*order2*];[*key3*];[*order3*]}

The *key1*, *key2*, and *key3* arguments specify the field names to use for the first, second, and third sort keys, respectively.

The *order1*, *order2*, and *order3* arguments specify the sort order—ascending or descending—for *key1*, *key2*, and *key3*, respectively—and are enclosed in quotation marks. You must specify a sort order for each sort key.

If you do not specify any sort keys with the QUERY-SORT command, the existing defined sort keys are used. Use QUERY-SORT-KEY-DEFINE or SORT-KEY-DEFINE to sort with more than three keys.

The QUERY-SORT-KEY-DEFINE Command

The QUERY-SORT-KEY-DEFINE command defines a sort key to be used by a subsequent QUERY-SORT command. Use the following syntax for QUERY-SORT-KEY-DEFINE:

{QUERY-SORT-KEY-DEFINE *key-number;key-field; key-order*}

The *key-number* argument is an integer from 1 through 255 that specifies which sort key is being defined.

The *key-field* argument specifies the field name to be sorted for this key, and is enclosed in quotation marks.

The *key-order* argument specifies the sort order—ascending or descending—for *key-field*, and is enclosed in quotation marks.

The QUERY-SORT-RESET Command

The QUERY-SORT-RESET command clears all sort keys for the currently selected query table. Use the following syntax for QUERY-SORT-RESET:

{QUERY-SORT-RESET}

The QUERY-SORT-RESET command does not use any arguments.

The QUERY-UPDATE Command

The QUERY-UPDATE command applies any changes you make to records in the currently selected query table to the corresponding database. Use the following syntax for QUERY-UPDATE:

{QUERY-UPDATE}

The QUERY-UPDATE command does not use any arguments.

The QUERY-UPGRADE Command

The QUERY-UPGRADE command upgrades a query from a previous version of 1-2-3 so that it works with the Query commands in 1-2-3 Release 4 for Windows. Use the following syntax for QUERY-UPGRADE:

{QUERY-UPGRADE *input-range;output-range;criteria-range; [query-name]*}

The *input-range* argument specifies the range name or address of the input range that you created with /Data Query Input.

The *output-range* argument specifies the range name or address of the output range that you created with /Data Query Output. The fields in the new query table will be the same as those in *output-range*, and the new query table will occupy the same worksheet location.

The *criteria-range* argument specifies the range name or address of the criteria range you created with /Data Query Criteria.

The *query-name* argument specifies a name for the new query table, and is enclosed in quotation marks. If you omit *query-name*, 1-2-3 for Windows assigns a default name, such as QUERY 1, to the query table.

The ROLLBACK Command

The ROLLBACK command cancels pending external database transactions. Use the following syntax for ROLLBACK:

{ROLLBACK [*driver-name*];[*database-name*]}

The *driver-name* argument specifies the name of the database driver associated with an external database, and is enclosed in quotation marks.

The *database-name* argument specifies the name of the external database, and is enclosed in quotation marks.

You must use both arguments or no arguments. ROLLBACK with arguments cancels only the transaction pending for the driver and database you specify. ROLLBACK with no arguments cancels all pending transactions. ROLLBACK works with the SQL Server driver only.

The SEND-SQL Command

The SEND-SQL command sends an SQL command string to an external database driver and works only with external databases that support SQL. Use the following syntax for SEND-SQL:

{SEND-SQL *range*;*command*;[*output-range*];[*error-code-location*]}

The *range* argument specifies the range name of an external database.

The *command* argument specifies an SQL command, and is enclosed in quotation marks. If *command* is the range name or address of a range that contains labels, 1-2-3 for Windows creates the SQL command by concatenating each label in the range, from left to right in a row and from top to bottom in a column.

The *output-range* argument specifies the range name or address of a destination range for any data that might be sent from the SQL command. If you omit *output-range*, 1-2-3 for Windows uses the current cell. Any data sent from the SQL command writes over any existing data in *output-range*.

The *error-code-location* argument specifies a cell for the return code from the SQL command.

Use DATABASE-CONNECT to connect to an external database before using SEND-SQL.

Using Database Macro Commands Together

Figure 16.6 shows an example of how you can use several of the database macro commands to create a query that uses an external database file.

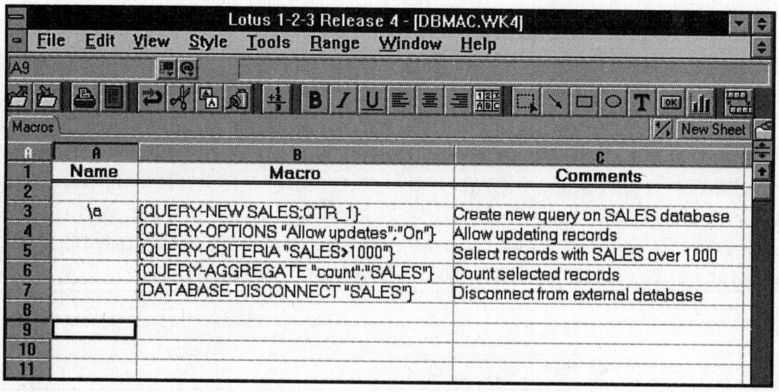

FIG. 16.6

The database macro commands manipulate databases.

Commands That Transfer Data between Windows Applications

Some of the most useful Windows features available with 1-2-3 for Windows are its Dynamic Data Exchange (DDE) and Object Linking and Embedding (OLE) capabilities. DDE and OLE enable several different Windows applications to link and share data. The 1-2-3 for Windows macro language has many DDE and OLE commands, which table 16.5 lists. The macro language DDE and OLE commands, like the LINK commands, often work with one another.

Table 16.5 Commands That Transfer Data between Windows Applications

Command	Action
DDE-ADVISE	Specifies the macro executed when data changes in the server application
DDE-CLOSE	Terminates all current conversation with a Windows application
DDE-EXECUTE	Sends a command to an application
DDE-OPEN	Initiates a conversation with a Windows application
DDE-POKE	Sends a range of data to a server application
DDE-REQUEST	Transfers data from a Windows application to 1-2-3 for Windows
DDE-TABLE	Creates a table of conversations associated with all active files that were created with {DDE} commands
DDE-UNADVISE	Ends a DDE-ADVISE command
DDE-USE	Makes a specific conversation between 1-2-3 for Windows and another Windows application the current one
EDIT-OBJECT	Executes either the primary or secondary verb for the currently selected OLE embedded object
INSERT-OBJECT	Creates and places in the worksheet an OLE embedded object
LINK-ASSIGN	Specifies a range to link to a destination range
LINK-CREATE	Creates a link between the current worksheet file or a file created with another Windows application
LINK-DEACTIVATE	Deactivates a link in the current worksheet but leaves the link intact
LINK-DELETE	Erases a link in the current worksheet but leaves the values obtained through the link in the worksheet
LINK-REMOVE	Removes the currently used destination range for a link
LINK-TABLE	Creates a table of all links associated with the current file
LINK-UPDATE	Updates a link when the link update mode is Manual
UPDATE-OBJECT	Updates a 1-2-3 OLE object embedded in another application file

The DDE-ADVISE Command

The DDE-ADVISE command specifies that the macro be executed when data changes in the server operation. This command tells 1-2-3 to branch to a range name or cell address that contains macro instructions. 1-2-3 executes the macro at the branch location each time the server application updates the item specified by *item-name*; after all updates are made, 1-2-3 then returns to the main macro.

The syntax of this command is as follows:

{DDE-ADVISE [*branch-location*];*item-name*;[*format*];[*destination*];[*acknowledge*]}

The *branch-location* argument is the address or name of a cell or range that contains the macro.

The *item-name* argument is the name of the topic item to link to, and is enclosed in quotation marks. The topic item is the item in the application file whose data you want to transfer through the link.

The *format* argument specifies one of the valid Windows Clipboard formats, and is enclosed in quotation marks. If the *format* argument is not included, 1-2-3 for Windows uses the Clipboard Text format.

The *destination* argument specifies the range name or the address of the range where you want the server application to send the data whenever it is updated.

The *acknowledge* argument is a yes or no argument that specifies whether to acknowledge data messages, and is enclosed in quotation marks. If you omit *acknowledge*, 1-2-3 for Windows acknowledges data messages.

Consider the following commands:

```
{DDE-OPEN "AMI";"JAN"}
{DDE-ADVISE "JSKI";"JAN"}
```

These commands open a conversation with Ami Pro and then tell 1-2-3 for Windows to execute the macro commands at location JSKI when the data changes to JAN in Ami Pro.

CAUTION: After successfully executing a DDE-ADVISE command, 1-2-3 for Windows goes directly to the next cell in the macro, ignoring any macro instructions after DDE-ADVISE in the same cell. DDE-EXECUTE, DDE-OPEN, DDE-REQUEST, and DDE-POKE also work in this manner.

The DDE-CLOSE Command

The DDE-CLOSE command terminates a conversation with a Windows application. If the DDE-OPEN command did not open any conversation, DDE-CLOSE does nothing.

The syntax of DDE-CLOSE is as follows:

{DDE-CLOSE [*conversation-number*]}

The *conversation-number* argument specifies which conversation to terminate. The *conversation-number* is the unique identification number Windows assigns to the conversation. If you omit *conversation-number*, the current conversation closes. To close all open conversations, specify –1 for *conversation-number*.

The DDE-EXECUTE Command

DDE-EXECUTE sends a command to an application. If the DDE-OPEN command did not open any conversation, DDE-EXECUTE returns an error.

The syntax of DDE-EXECUTE is as follows:

{DDE-EXECUTE *execute-string*}

The *execute-string* argument represents any command from the application, including macro commands.

The DDE-OPEN Command

The DDE-OPEN command opens a conversation with another Windows application. Multiple conversations can go on at the same time. For example, you can open a conversation with Ami Pro word processing program and open a second conversation with Microsoft Project for Windows. Only one conversation, however, can be the current conversation. You make a conversation current by using the DDE-USE command.

The syntax of DDE-OPEN is as follows:

{DDE-OPEN *app-name*;*topic-name*;[*location*]}

The *app-name* argument is the name of an open Windows application, and is enclosed in quotation marks.

The *topic-name* argument is the name of the file in the application to link to, and is enclosed in quotation marks.

The *location* argument specifies the address or name of a cell or range. Although the *location* argument is optional, you should include it if you plan to use more than one DDE_OPEN command in a macro.

Before using the DDE-OPEN command, you must start an application. You can start an application by using the {LAUNCH} macro command. Consider the following macro:

```
{DDE-OPEN "EXCEL","JAN",BUDGET}
{DDE-OPEN "WORD","LETTER",ADDRESS}
{DDE-OPEN "PROJECT","HOUSTON",CITIES}
{DDE-USE "WORD"}
```

This macro opens up three conversations (assuming that the Excel, Word, and Project are all opened) and then makes the conversation with Microsoft Word current.

The DDE-POKE Command

DDE-POKE sends a range of data to another application having the current conversation with 1-2-3 for Windows. The syntax of DDE-POKE is as follows:

> {DDE-POKE *range*;*item-name*;[*format*]}

The *range* argument specifies the cell address or range name that contains the data to be sent to the other application.

The *item-name* argument specifies the name of the range to send the data to.

The *format* argument specifies one of the valid Windows Clipboard formats, and is enclosed in quotation marks. If no format is specified, 1-2-3 for Windows uses the default Text format.

Consider the following macro:

```
{DDE-OPEN "EXCEL","Budget"}
{IF TOTAL>1000000}{DDE-POKE MARCH,"Budget"}
```

This macro sends to Excel the data in the range named MARCH if TOTAL is greater than 1,000,000.

The DDE-REQUEST Command

The DDE-REQUEST command transfers data from another Windows application to 1-2-3 for Windows. The syntax of DDE-REQUEST is as follows:

> {DDE-REQUEST *range*;*item-name*;[*format*]}

The *range* argument specifies the cell address or range name into which 1-2-3 for Windows enters the data.

The *item-name* argument specifies the name of the data range in the other Windows application.

The *format* argument specifies one of the valid Windows Clipboard formats, and is enclosed in quotation marks. If no format is specified, 1-2-3 for Windows uses the default Text format.

The DDE-TABLE Command

The DDE-TABLE command creates a table of conversations associated with all active files that were created with DDE commands. Use the following syntax with DDE-TABLE:

> {DDE-TABLE *location*;[*type*]}

The *location* argument specifies the address or range name of the top-left cell of the range to receive the table. The table uses two more rows than the number of conversations, and either three or seven columns, depending on whether *type* is "short" or "long." The table overwrites any existing data.

The *type* argument specifies what type of information to include in the table—short or long—and is enclosed in quotation marks. If you omit *type*, the default is long.

The DDE-UNADVISE Command

The DDE-UNADVISE command ends a DDE-ADVISE command. The syntax of DDE-UNADVISE is as follows:

> {DDE-UNADVISE *item-name*;[*format*]}

The *item-name* argument specifies the name of the topic item to link to, and is enclosed in quotation marks.

The *format* argument specifies one of the valid Clipboard formats. If the original DDE-ADVISE command uses a *format* argument, DDE-UNADVISE must use the same *format* argument.

The DDE-USE Command

DDE-USE makes current a conversation used by other macros. Because you can have multiple conversations in a macro, to make a particular one current, you use {DDE-USE}. The syntax of DDE-USE is as follows:

> {DDE-USE *conversation-number*}

DDE-USE has one required argument, *conversation-number*, which is the unique number Windows assigns to the conversation.

The EDIT-OBJECT Command

The EDIT-OBJECT command executes either the primary or secondary verb for the currently selected OLE embedded object. Use the following syntax for EDIT-OBJECT:

{EDIT-OBJECT [*verb*]}

The *verb* argument specifies the verb to be executed—primary or secondary—and is enclosed in quotation marks. If you omit the argument, the server application executes the primary verb.

The INSERT-OBJECT Command

The INSERT-OBJECT command creates and places in the worksheet an OLE embedded object. Use the following syntax for INSERT-OBJECT:

{INSERT-OBJECT *object-type*;[*location*]}

The *object-type* argument specifies the class name of a valid, registered OLE Server object, and is enclosed in quotation marks.

The *location* argument specifies the name or address of the cell in which you want to put the upper-left corner of the OLE object. If you omit *location*, the OLE object is placed in the current selection.

The LINK-ASSIGN Command

The LINK-ASSIGN command specifies the range to link data to. After you create a link with the LINK-CREATE command, you use LINK-ASSIGN to specify the range to link. You must first establish a link with the LINK-CREATE command before you can use LINK-ASSIGN. The syntax for LINK-ASSIGN is as follows:

{LINK-ASSIGN *link-name*;*range*;[*clear-styles*]}

The *link-name* argument specifies the name for the link specified in LINK-CREATE, and is enclosed in quotation marks. If *link-name* does not refer to an existing link, LINK-ASSIGN returns an error.

The *range* argument specifies the range address that specifies the destination range. If *range* is not large enough to hold the incoming data, 1-2-3 for Windows clips the incoming data that does not fit into *range* and resizes a graph that only partially fits into *range*.

The *clear-styles* argument, which is enclosed in quotation marks, is a yes or no argument that specifies whether to delete styles within the range specified by the range argument whenever the client data is updated. If you omit *clear-styles*, 1-2-3 for Windows does not delete styles. If the link is not for range data, 1-2-3 for Windows ignores *clear-styles*.

 NOTE 1-2-3 Release 4 does not support property arguments for LINK-ASSIGN. If your macros currently contain LINK-ASSIGN commands that include property arguments, remove the arguments before you run the macros.

The LINK-CREATE Command

The LINK-CREATE command creates a link between the current worksheet and another worksheet file or Windows application without using the Windows Clipboard. The syntax for LINK-CREATE is as follows:

> {LINK-CREATE *link-name;app-name;topic-name;item-name;[format];[mode];[branch-location]*}

The *link-name* argument specifies the name to identify the link, and is enclosed in quotation marks. If the specified *link-name* is already in use, the macro produces an error when it executes the LINK-CREATE command.

The *app-name* argument identifies the Windows application, and is enclosed in quotation marks.

The *topic-name* is the name of the application worksheet or file to link to, and is enclosed in quotation marks.

The *item-name* is the name of the topic item to link, and is enclosed in quotation marks. This item in the application worksheet or file is the one whose data you want transferred through the link.

The *format* argument specifies one of the valid Clipboard formats, and is enclosed in quotation marks.

The *mode* specifies when data is updated—automatic or manual. The argument is enclosed in quotation marks. Automatic updates the link each time the source item is updated, and is the default if you omit the argument. Manual only updates the link when you use LINK-UPDATE.

The *branch-location* argument specifies a location in which macro execution starts when the data from the link is updated. The argument is enclosed in quotation marks.

The LINK-DEACTIVATE Command

The LINK-DEACTIVATE command deactivates a link in the current worksheet but leaves the link intact. When a link is inactive, 1-2-3 for Windows does not update values in the destination range.

The syntax for LINK DEACTIVATE is as follows:

{LINK-DEACTIVATE *link-name*}

The *link-name* argument specifies the name for the link specified in LINK-CREATE, and is enclosed in quotation marks.

The LINK-DELETE Command

The LINK-DELETE command establishes the values from the link in the worksheet and then erases the link.

The syntax for LINK DELETE is as follows:

{LINK-DELETE *link-name*}

The *link-name* argument specifies the name for the link specified in LINK-CREATE, and is enclosed in quotation marks. If *link-name* does not refer to an existing link, LINK-DELETE returns an error.

Consider the following macro:

```
{LINK-CREATE "Budget";"EXCEL";"AN_BUDGET";"Months"}
{LINK-ASSIGN "Budget";"JAN"}
{LINK-DELETE "Budget"}
```

This macro leaves the data in the cell location JAN, but because of the LINK-DELETE command, the information is no longer dynamically linked to the Excel spreadsheet. The LINK-DELETE command effectively ends the link (which was opened by the LINK-CREATE command) to the Excel spreadsheet.

The LINK-REMOVE Command

The LINK-REMOVE command removes the currently used destination range for a link. The syntax for LINK REMOVE is as follows:

{LINK-REMOVE *link-name*}

The *link-name* argument specifies the name for the link specified in LINK-CREATE, and is enclosed in quotation marks. If *link-name* does not refer to an existing link, LINK-REMOVE returns an error.

Consider the following macro:

```
{LINK-CREATE "Budget";"EXCEL";"AN_BUDGET";"Months"}
{LINK-ASSIGN "Budget";"JAN"}
{LINK-REMOVE "Budget"}
{LINK-ASSIGN "Budget";"FEB"}
```

This macro removes the link from the original range (the cell named JAN) and reestablishes it at another location (FEB).

The LINK-TABLE Command

The LINK-TABLE command creates a table in the current worksheet of all the links associated with the current worksheet.

The syntax for LINK TABLE is as follows:

{LINK-TABLE *location*}

The *location* argument specifies the cell address or range address in which the table is created.

Consider the following command:

```
{LINK-TABLE Z1}
```

This command places in cell Z1 a list of all the links associated with the current worksheet.

The LINK-UPDATE Command

The LINK-UPDATE command updates links, or activates and updates links deactivated with LINK-DEACTIVATE. Use the following syntax with LINK-UPDATE:

{LINK-UPDATE [*link-name*]}

The *link-name* argument specifies the name for a link specified in LINK-CREATE, and is enclosed in quotation marks. If *link-name* does not refer to an existing link, LINK-UPDATE returns an error. If you omit *link-name*, all existing links are updated.

The UPDATE-OBJECT Command

The UPDATE-OBJECT command updates a 1-2-3 OLE object embedded in another application file. Use the following syntax with UPDATE-OBJECT:

{UPDATE-OBJECT}

The UPDATE-OBJECT command does not use any arguments.

Using DDE and OLE Macro Commands Together

Figure 16.7 shows an example of using DDE commands to create a link and transfer data between 1-2-3 for Windows and Word for Windows. The LINK commands function in a similar manner.

Commands That Edit Worksheets

The commands described in table 16.6 provide the worksheet editing functions found on the 1-2-3 for Windows Edit menu. These commands enable macro programs to copy and paste data as well as rearrange worksheet layout.

Table 16.6 Commands That Edit Worksheets

Command	Action
DELETE-COLUMNS	Deletes partial or complete columns in a range
DELETE-ROWS	Deletes partial or complete rows in a range
DELETE-SHEETS	Deletes each worksheet in a range
EDIT-CLEAR	Deletes data and formatting without using the Clipboard
EDIT-COPY	Copies data and formatting to the Clipboard
EDIT-COPY-FILL	Copies to a range the contents of a row, column, or worksheet
EDIT-COPY-GRAPH	Use EDIT-COPY
EDIT-CUT	Deletes data and formatting, and copies both to the Clipboard

Command	Action
EDIT-FIND	Finds specified characters in labels, formulas, or both
EDIT-FIND?	Displays the Edit Find & Replace dialog box
EDIT-PASTE	Copies data and formatting from the Clipboard
EDIT-PASTE-LINK	Creates a link between a 1-2-3 for Windows worksheet file and the file referenced on the Clipboard
EDIT-PASTE-SPECIAL	Use EDIT-PASTE
EDIT-QUICK-COPY	Copies data and formatting without using the Clipboard
EDIT-QUICK-MOVE	Moves data and formatting without using the Clipboard
EDIT-REPLACE	Finds and replaces specified characters in labels, formulas, or both
EDIT-REPLACE-ALL	Finds and replaces all instances of specified characters in labels, formulas, or both
INSERT-COLUMNS	Inserts complete or partial blank columns
INSERT-ROWS	Inserts complete or partial blank rows
INSERT-SHEETS	Inserts blank worksheets

The DELETE-COLUMNS Command

The DELETE-COLUMNS command deletes all or part of each column that includes cells in a range. Use the following syntax for DELETE-COLUMNS:

{DELETE-COLUMNS [*range*];[*delete-selection*]}

The *range* argument specifies the range name or address of a range with at least one cell in each column you want to delete. If you omit *range*, 1-2-3 for Windows deletes columns that have cells in the currently selected range or collection.

The *delete-selection* argument is a yes or no argument that specifies whether to delete only the cells in range and move existing data to the left. If you omit *delete-selection*, the entire columns are deleted.

The DELETE-ROWS Command

The DELETE-ROWS command deletes all or part of each row that includes cells in a range. Use the following syntax for DELETE-ROWS:

{DELETE-ROWS [*range*];[*delete-selection*]}

The *range* argument specifies the range name or address of a range with at least one cell in each row you want to delete. If you omit *range*, 1-2-3 for Windows deletes rows that have cells in the currently selected range or collection.

The *delete-selection* argument is a yes or no argument that specifies whether to delete only the cells in range and move existing data up. If you omit *delete-selection*, the entire rows are deleted.

The DELETE-SHEETS Command

The DELETE-SHEETS command deletes each worksheet that includes cells in a range. Use the following syntax for DELETE-SHEETS:

{DELETE-SHEETS [*range*]}

The *range* argument specifies the range name or address of a range with at least one cell in each worksheet you want to delete. If you omit *range*, 1-2-3 for Windows deletes worksheets that have cells in the currently selected range or collection.

The EDIT-CLEAR Command

The EDIT-CLEAR command deletes data and related formatting from the worksheet without moving it to the Clipboard. Use the following syntax for EDIT-CLEAR:

{EDIT-CLEAR [*selection*];[*property*]}

The *selection* argument specifies the name or address of the range whose contents you want to delete. If you omit *selection*, the contents of the current selection are deleted.

The *property* argument specifies what to delete—contents, style, or both—and is enclosed in quotation marks.

The EDIT-CLEAR command does not clear protected cells or change their format.

The EDIT-COPY Command

The EDIT-COPY command copies data and related formatting from the worksheet to the Clipboard. Use the following syntax for EDIT-COPY:

{EDIT-COPY [*selection*];[*format*]}

The *selection* argument specifies the name or address of the range whose contents you want to copy. If you omit *selection*, the contents of the current selection are copied.

The *format* argument specifies one of the Clipboard formats, and is enclosed in quotation marks. If you omit *format*, 1-2-3 for Windows includes all appropriate formats.

The EDIT-COPY-FILL Command

The EDIT-COPY-FILL command copies the contents of a row, column, or worksheet to fill a range, in a specified direction. Use the following syntax for EDIT-COPY-FILL:

{EDIT-COPY-FILL *direction*;[*range*]}

The *direction* argument specifies the direction to copy the data—down, right, up, left, back, or forward—and is enclosed in quotation marks.

The *range* argument specifies the range name or address of the range to fill. If you omit *range*, the current selection is filled.

The EDIT-CUT Command

The EDIT-CUT command cuts data and related formatting from the worksheet and copies them to the Clipboard. Use the following syntax for EDIT-CUT:

{EDIT-CUT [*selection*];[*format*]}

The *selection* argument specifies the name or address of the range whose contents you want to cut. If you omit *selection*, the contents of the current selection are cut.

The *format* argument specifies one of the Clipboard formats, and is enclosed in quotation marks. If you omit *format*, 1-2-3 for Windows includes all appropriate formats.

The EDIT-FIND Command

The EDIT-FIND command finds the first instance of specified characters in labels, formulas, or both. Use the following syntax for EDIT-FIND:

{EDIT-FIND [*search-for*];[*look-in*];[*search-through*]}

The *search-for* argument specifies the text for which you want to search, and is enclosed in quotation marks. If you omit *search-for*, 1-2-3 for Windows uses the current edit find string. EDIT-FIND does not distinguish between uppercase and lowercase letters in *search-for*. If *search-for* does not produce a match, a message box is displayed and the macro ends.

The *look-in* argument specifies in what types of cell entries to search—formulas, text, or both—and is enclosed in quotation marks. If you omit *look-in*, 1-2-3 for Windows uses the current value of edit find type.

The *search-through* argument specifies the range name or address of the range you want to search. If *search-through* is a single cell, 1-2-3 for Windows searches the entire current file. If you omit *search-through*, the current selection is searched if it is a multiple-cell range; otherwise the entire file is searched.

When searching the entire file, the search starts at cell A:A1. When searching a range, the search starts at the top-left cell in the range. The search proceeds down the leftmost column, then down the next column to the right, and so on, and from front to back by worksheet. If a match is found, the cell containing the match becomes the current cell.

The EDIT-FIND? Command

The EDIT-FIND? command displays the Edit Find & Replace dialog box. Use the following syntax for EDIT-FIND?:

{EDIT-FIND?}

The EDIT-FIND? command does not use any arguments. After the user leaves the dialog box, the macro continues.

The EDIT-PASTE Command

The EDIT-PASTE command copies data and related formatting from the Clipboard into the active worksheet file. Use the following syntax for EDIT-PASTE:

{EDIT-PASTE [*selection*];[*format*]}

The *selection* argument specifies the name or address of the range to which you want to paste. If you omit *selection*, the contents of the Clipboard are pasted to the current selection.

The *format* argument specifies one of the Clipboard formats, and is enclosed in quotation marks. If you omit *format*, 1-2-3 for Windows includes all appropriate formats.

The EDIT-PASTE-LINK Command

The EDIT-PASTE-LINK command creates a link between a 1-2-3 for Windows worksheet file and the file referenced on the Clipboard. Use the following syntax for EDIT-PASTE-LINK:

{EDIT-PASTE-LINK [*destination*];[*format*];[*reference*]}

The *destination* argument specifies the range name or address of the range to which you want the server application to send the data whenever it is updated.

The *format* argument specifies one of the Clipboard formats, and is enclosed in quotation marks. If you create a link with 1-2-3 for Windows cell data, *format* is ignored. If you omit *format*, 1-2-3 for Windows uses the Clipboard Text format.

The *reference* argument specifies the type of cell references to create—absolute or relative—when linking to 1-2-3 for Windows cell data. The argument is enclosed in quotation marks. If you are creating a link with data from another application, *reference* is ignored.

The EDIT-QUICK-COPY Command

The EDIT-QUICK-COPY command copies data and related formatting without using the Clipboard, and is equivalent to copying data with the mouse. Use the following syntax for EDIT-QUICK-COPY:

{EDIT-QUICK-COPY *destination*;[*source*]}

The *destination* argument specifies the range name or address of the range to which you are copying.

The *source* argument specifies the range name or address of the range from which you are copying. If you omit *source*, the current selection is copied.

The EDIT-QUICK-MOVE Command

The EDIT-QUICK-MOVE command moves data and related formatting without using the Clipboard, and is equivalent to moving data with the mouse. Use the following syntax for EDIT-QUICK-MOVE:

> {EDIT-QUICK-MOVE *destination*;[*source*]}

The *destination* argument specifies the range name or address of the range to which you are moving.

The *source* argument specifies the range name or address of the range from which you are moving. If you omit *source*, the current selection is moved.

The EDIT-REPLACE Command

The EDIT-REPLACE command finds the first instance of specified characters in labels, formulas, or both, and replaces the characters. Use the following syntax for EDIT-REPLACE:

> {EDIT-REPLACE [*search-for*];[*look-in*];[*replacement*]; [*search-through*]}

The *search-for* argument specifies the text for which you want to search, and is enclosed in quotation marks. If you omit *search-for*, 1-2-3 for Windows uses the current edit find string. EDIT-FIND does not distinguish between uppercase and lowercase letters in *search-for*. If *search-for* does not produce a match, a message box is displayed and the macro ends.

The *look-in* argument specifies in what types of cell entries to search— formulas, text, or both—and is enclosed in quotation marks. If you omit *look-in*, 1-2-3 for Windows uses the current value of edit find type.

The *replacement* argument specifies the text you want to use to replace existing text, and is enclosed in quotation marks. If you omit *replacement*, 1-2-3 for Windows uses the current edit replace string.

The *search-through* argument specifies the range name or address of the range you want to search. If *search-through* is a single cell, 1-2-3 for Windows searches the entire current file. If you omit *search-through*, the current selection is searched if it is a multiple-cell range; otherwise the entire file is searched.

When searching the entire file, the search starts at cell A:A1. When searching a range, the search starts at the top-left cell in the range. The search proceeds down the leftmost column, then down the next column to the right, and so on, and from front to back by worksheet. If a match is found, the cell containing the match becomes the current cell.

The EDIT-REPLACE-ALL Command

The EDIT-REPLACE-ALL command finds all instances of specified characters in labels, formulas, or both, and replaces the characters. Use the following syntax for EDIT-REPLACE-ALL:

{EDIT-REPLACE-ALL [*search-for*];[*look-in*];[*replacement*]; [*search-through*]}

The *search-for* argument specifies the text for which you want to search, and is enclosed in quotation marks. If you omit *search-for*, 1-2-3 for Windows uses the current edit find string. EDIT-FIND does not distinguish between uppercase and lowercase letters in *search-for*. If *search-for* does not produce a match, a message box is displayed and the macro ends.

The *look-in* argument specifies in what types of cell entries to search—formulas, text, or both—and is enclosed in quotation marks. If you omit *look-in*, 1-2-3 for Windows uses the current value of edit find type.

The *replacement* argument specifies the text you want to use to replace existing text, and is enclosed in quotation marks. If you omit *replacement*, 1-2-3 for Windows uses the current edit replace string.

The *search-through* argument specifies the range name or address of the range you want to search. If *search-through* is a single cell, 1-2-3 for Windows searches the entire current file. If you omit *search-through*, the current selection is searched if it is a multiple-cell range; otherwise the entire file is searched.

The INSERT-COLUMNS Command

The INSERT-COLUMNS command inserts one or more complete or partial columns. Use the following syntax for INSERT-COLUMNS:

{INSERT-COLUMNS [*range*];[*number*];[*insert-selection*]}

The *range* argument specifies the range name or address of a range that you want to move to the right when the columns are inserted. If you omit *range*, the current selection is used.

The *number* argument is an integer that specifies how many columns to insert. If you omit *number*, 1-2-3 for Windows inserts the same number of columns as are in *range*.

The *insert-selection* argument is a yes or no argument that specifies whether to insert only the cells in *range* and move existing data to the right. If you omit *insert-selection*, 1-2-3 for Windows inserts entire columns.

The INSERT-ROWS Command

The INSERT-ROWS command inserts one or more complete or partial rows. Use the following syntax for INSERT-ROWS:

{INSERT-ROWS [range];[number];[insert-selection]}

The *range* argument specifies the range name or address of a range that you want to move down when the rows are inserted. If you omit *range*, the current selection is used.

The *number* argument is an integer that specifies how many rows to insert. If you omit *number*, 1-2-3 for Windows inserts the same number of rows as are in *range*.

The *insert-selection* argument is a yes or no argument that specifies whether to insert only the cells in *range* and move existing data down. If you omit *insert-selection*, 1-2-3 for Windows inserts entire rows.

The INSERT-SHEETS Command

The INSERT-SHEETS command inserts one or more worksheets. Use the following syntax for INSERT-SHEETS:

{INSERT-SHEETS [where];[range];[insert-selection]}

The *where* argument specifies the location of the new worksheets—before or after—and is enclosed in quotation marks.

The *range* argument specifies the range name or address of a range that you want to move when the worksheets are inserted. If you omit *range*, the current selection is used.

The *number* argument is an integer that specifies how many worksheets to insert. If you omit *number*, 1-2-3 for Windows inserts the same number of worksheets as there are in *range*.

Using Edit Macro Commands Together

Figure 16.8 provides some examples of using macro commands that edit the worksheet and its data.

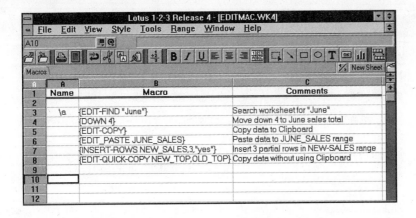

FIG. 16.8

Some examples of using macro commands that edit the worksheet and its data.

Commands That Manipulate Files

The commands described in table 16.7 provide the functions contained in the 1-2-3 for Windows File menu. These commands open and close files, print worksheets, and control network settings.

Table 16.7 Commands That Manipulate Files

Command	Action
FILE-CLOSE	Closes the current file
FILE-COMBINE	Combines data and number formats from a 1-2-3 worksheet file on disk into the current file
FILE-EXIT	Ends the 1-2-3 session
FILE-EXTRACT	Saves a range to another file
FILE-GET-RESERVATION	Gets the network reservation for the current file
FILE-IMPORT	Combines data from a text file into the current file
FILE-NEW	Creates a new blank worksheet
FILE-OPEN	Reads a file into memory
FILE-OPEN?	Displays the File Open dialog box
FILE-PRINT?	Uses PRINT?
FILE-PRINT-NAME-ADD	Uses PRINT-NAME-ADD

continues

Table 16.7 Continued

Command	Action
FILE-PRINT-NAME-USE	Uses PRINT-NAME-USE
FILE-PRINT-RESET	Uses PRINT-RESET
FILE-RELEASE-RESERVATION	Releases the network reservation for the current file
FILE-RETRIEVE	Replaces the current file in memory with a file from disk
FILE-SAVE	Saves the current file
FILE-SAVE-ALL	Saves all active files
FILE-SAVE-AS?	Displays the File Save As dialog box
FILE-SEAL	Controls the reservation for the current file and seals the file
FILE-SEAL-NETWORK-RESERVATION	Seals only the network reservation setting of the current file
FILE-UNSEAL	Unseals the current file and releases its network reservation setting
FILE-UPDATE-LINKS	Recalculates formulas in the current file that contain links to other files
PRINT	Prints the current file, using the current settings
PRINT?	Displays the File Print dialog box
PRINT-NAME-ADD	Saves the current print settings in a file
PRINT-NAME-USE	Selects a saved print-settings file
PRINT-RESET	Replaces the currently selected Margins, Print Titles, Header, Footer, Options, Compression, and Orientation settings with their defaults
SEND-MAIL	Sends a mail message by using your mail application

The FILE-CLOSE Command

The FILE-CLOSE command closes the current file. Use the following syntax for FILE-CLOSE:

{FILE-CLOSE [*discard*]}

The *discard* argument is a yes or no argument that specifies whether to discard any unsaved changes in the current file. The argument is enclosed in quotation marks. If you specify "no" and unsaved changes are in the current file, the file remains open. If you omit *discard* and unsaved changes are in the file, a dialog box appears. If you choose Cancel in the dialog box, the macro ends.

The FILE-COMBINE Command

The FILE-COMBINE command combines data and number formats from a worksheet file on disk into the current file, starting in the current cell. Use the following syntax for FILE-COMBINE:

{FILE-COMBINE [*how*];*file-name*;[*password*];[*source*]}

The *how* argument specifies how you want 1-2-3 for Windows to combine data—by adding, replacing, or subtracting—and is enclosed in quotation marks. You can include *how* only if you are combining data from 1-2-3 files.

The *file-name* argument specifies the name of the worksheet file on disk that contains the data you want to combine with data in the current file. You can use 1-2-3 files (WK*), Symphony files (WR*), and graph files (CGM and PIC).

The *password* argument specifies a password for accessing the file. If you omit *password* and a password is necessary, 1-2-3 for Windows displays a Password dialog box.

The *source* argument specifies the name or address of the range in *file-name* that contains data that you want to combine with data in the current file. The argument is enclosed in quotation marks.

The FILE-EXIT Command

The FILE-EXIT command exits 1-2-3 for Windows. Use the following syntax for FILE-EXIT:

{FILE-EXIT [*discard*]}

The *discard* argument is a yes or no argument that specifies whether to discard any unsaved changes to the current file. The argument is enclosed in quotation marks. If you specify "no" and unsaved changes are in the current file, the file remains open. If you omit *discard* and unsaved changes are in the file, a dialog box is displayed. If you choose Cancel in the dialog box, the macro ends.

The FILE-EXTRACT Command

The FILE-EXTRACT command saves a range to another file. Use the following syntax for FILE-EXTRACT:

{FILE-EXTRACT *file-name*;[*file-type*];[*password*];
[*backup*];[*extract-range*];[*properties*]}

The *file-name* argument, which specifies the name of the file you want to save, is enclosed in quotation marks. If *file-name* is a new file, 1-2-3 for Windows creates it. If *file-name* specifies an existing file and you omit *backup*, 1-2-3 for Windows displays a Backup, Replace, or Cancel dialog box.

The *file-type* argument, which specifies the format of the saved file, is enclosed in quotation marks. You can use the following values for *file-type*:

- 1-2-3   Saves the file in 1-2-3 WK4 format
- 1-2-3 (wk3)   Saves the file in 1-2-3 WK3 format
- 1-2-3 (wk1)   Saves the file in 1-2-3 WK1 format
- text (txt)   Saves the file as a text file
- shared   Saves the file as a shared file on a Lotus Notes server

The *password* argument, which specifies a password for the file, is enclosed in quotation marks. If you omit *password* and the file specified by *file-name* has a password, 1-2-3 for Windows saves the file with that password. If you specify a password for a text file, 1-2-3 ignores the password.

The *backup* argument, which specifies whether to back up or replace an existing file, is enclosed in quotation marks. If you omit *backup* and *file-name* specifies an existing file, 1-2-3 for Windows displays a Backup, Replace, or Cancel dialog box.

The *extract-range* argument specifies the range name or address of the range from which you want to extract data. If you omit *extract-range*, 1-2-3 for Windows extracts the currently selected range.

The *properties* argument specifies how to save values—as formulas or values—and is enclosed in quotation marks.

The FILE-GET-RESERVATION Command

The FILE-GET-RESERVATION command gets the network reservation for the current file. Use the following syntax for FILE-GET-RESERVATION:

{FILE-GET-RESERVATION}

The FILE-GET-RESERVATION command does not use any arguments.

Only one user can get a file's reservation. The FILE-GET-RESERVATION command fails if someone else has the reservation or has saved the file since you read it into memory.

The FILE-IMPORT Command

The FILE-IMPORT command combines data from a text file into the current file. Use the following syntax for FILE-IMPORT:

{FILE-IMPORT [*read-text-as*];*file-name*}

The *read-text-as* argument specifies how 1-2-3 should combine data from a text file—text or numbers—and is enclosed in quotation marks. Text lines longer than 512 characters are truncated. Data imported as text is added to the worksheet as long labels. Data imported as numbers is separated into columns, and non-numeric data is ignored.

The *file-name* argument specifies the name of the text file on disk that contains the data that you want to combine with data in the current file.

The FILE-NEW Command

The FILE-NEW command creates a new worksheet file on disk and in memory, and makes the new file the current one. Use the following syntax for FILE-NEW:

{FILE-NEW [*file-name*];[*where*]}

The *file-name* argument, which specifies the name of the file that you want to create, is enclosed in quotation marks. If you omit *file-name*, 1-2-3 for Windows supplies a default file name.

The *where* argument, which specifies whether to place the new file before or after the current file, is enclosed in quotation marks.

The FILE-OPEN Command

The FILE-OPEN command reads a 1-2-3 or Excel version 2.1, 3.0, or 4.0 file into memory and makes it the current file. Use the following syntax for FILE-OPEN:

> {FILE-OPEN *file-name*;[*password*];[*read-only*];[*where*];[*how*]}

The *file-name* argument, which specifies the name of the file that you want to open, is enclosed in quotation marks. If *file-name* specifies a file that already is open, or if no file with that name exists, FILE-OPEN returns an error.

The *password* argument, which specifies a password for the file, is enclosed in quotation marks. If you omit *password* and a password is necessary, 1-2-3 for Windows displays a Password dialog box.

The *read-only* argument is a yes or no argument that specifies whether 1-2-3 should open the file as read-only if another user or another application has the network reservation for the file. This argument is enclosed in quotation marks.

The *where* argument, which specifies whether to place the new file before or after the current file, is enclosed in quotation marks.

The *how* argument specifies how 1-2-3 should combine data from a text file—text or numbers—and is enclosed in quotation marks. Text lines longer than 512 characters are truncated. Data imported as text is added to the worksheet as long labels. Data imported as numbers is separated into columns, and non-numeric data is ignored.

The FILE-OPEN? Command

The FILE-OPEN? command displays the File Open dialog box. Use the following syntax for FILE-OPEN?:

> {FILE-OPEN?}

The FILE-OPEN? command does not use any arguments.

The FILE-RELEASE-RESERVATION Command

The FILE-RELEASE-RESERVATION command releases the network reservation for the current file. Use the following syntax for FILE-RELEASE-RESERVATION:

> {FILE-RELEASE-RESERVATION}

The FILE-RELEASE-RESERVATION command does not use any arguments.

The FILE-RETRIEVE Command

The FILE-RETRIEVE command replaces the current file in memory with a file from disk. Use the following syntax for FILE-RETRIEVE:

{FILE-RETRIEVE *file-name*;[*password*];[*read-only*];[*how*]}

The *file-name* argument, which specifies the name of the file that you want to retrieve, is enclosed in quotation marks.

The *password* argument, which specifies a password for the file, is enclosed in quotation marks. If you omit *password* and a password is necessary, 1-2-3 for Windows displays a Password dialog box.

The *read-only* argument is a yes or no argument that specifies whether 1-2-3 should open the file as read-only if another user or another application has the network reservation for the file. The argument is enclosed in quotation marks.

The *how* argument specifies how 1-2-3 should combine data from a text file—text or numbers—and is enclosed in quotation marks. Text lines longer than 512 characters are truncated. Data imported as text is added to the worksheet as long labels. Data imported as numbers is separated into columns, and non-numeric data is ignored.

When you use FILE-RETRIEVE, 1-2-3 removes the current file from memory without saving it and without prompting the user.

The FILE-SAVE Command

The FILE-SAVE command saves the current file. Use the following syntax for FILE-SAVE:

{FILE-SAVE [*file-name*];[*file-type*];[*password*];[*backup*]}

The *file-name* argument, which specifies the name of the file that you want to save, is enclosed in quotation marks. If *file-name* is a new file, 1-2-3 for Windows creates it. If *file-name* specifies an existing file and you omit *backup*, 1-2-3 for Windows displays a Backup, Replace, or Cancel dialog box.

The *file-type* argument, which specifies the format of the saved file, is enclosed in quotation marks. You can use the following values for *file-type*:

- 1-2-3   Saves the file in 1-2-3 WK4 format
- 1-2-3 (wk3)   Saves the file in 1-2-3 WK3 format
- 1-2-3 (wk1)   Saves the file in 1-2-3 WK1 format

■ text (txt)   Saves the file as a text file

■ shared   Saves the file as a shared file on a Lotus Notes
                      server

The *password* argument, which specifies a password for the file, is enclosed in quotation marks. If you omit *password* and the file specified by *file-name* has a password, 1-2-3 for Windows saves the file with that password. If you specify a password for a text file, 1-2-3 ignores the password.

The *backup* argument, which specifies whether to back up or replace an existing file, is enclosed in quotation marks. If you omit *backup* and *file-name* specifies an existing file, 1-2-3 for Windows displays a Backup, Replace, or Cancel dialog box.

The FILE-SAVE-ALL Command

The FILE-SAVE-ALL command saves all active files. Use the following syntax for FILE-SAVE-ALL:

    {FILE-SAVE-ALL}

The FILE-SAVE-ALL command does not use any arguments.

The FILE-SAVE-AS? Command

The FILE-SAVE-AS? command displays the File Save As dialog box. Use the following syntax for FILE-SAVE-AS?:

    {FILE-SAVE-AS?}

The FILE-SAVE-AS? command does not use any arguments.

The FILE-SEAL Command

The FILE-SEAL command controls the reservation for the current file and seals the file. Use the following syntax for FILE-SEAL:

    {FILE-SEAL [*password*]}

The *password* argument, which specifies a password for sealing the current file, is enclosed in quotation marks. If you omit *password*, 1-2-3 for Windows displays a dialog box for entering a password to seal the file.

The FILE-SEAL-NETWORK-RESERVATION Command

The FILE-SEAL-NETWORK-RESERVATION command seals only the network reservation setting of the current file. Use the following syntax for FILE-SEAL-NETWORK-RESERVATION:

{FILE-SEAL-NETWORK-RESERVATION [*password*]}

The *password* argument, which specifies a password for sealing the current file, is enclosed in quotation marks. If you omit *password*, 1-2-3 for Windows displays a dialog box for entering a password to seal the file.

The FILE-UNSEAL Command

The FILE-UNSEAL command controls the reservation for the current file and unseals the file. Use the following syntax for FILE-UNSEAL:

{FILE-UNSEAL [*password*]}

The *password* argument, which specifies a password for unsealing the current file, is enclosed in quotation marks. If you omit *password*, 1-2-3 for Windows displays a dialog box for entering a password to unseal the file.

The FILE-UPDATE-LINKS Command

The FILE-UPDATE-LINKS command recalculates formulas in the current file that contain links to other files. Use the following syntax for FILE-UPDATE-LINKS:

{FILE-UPDATE-LINKS}

The FILE-UPDATE-LINKS command does not use any arguments.

The PRINT Command

The PRINT command prints the current file according to the current page settings. Use the following syntax for PRINT:

{PRINT [*what*];[*from*];[*to*];[*start*];[*copies*]}

The *what* argument, which specifies what to print, is enclosed in quotation marks. If you omit *what*, 1-2-3 for Windows prints the current print range.

The *from* argument is a value that specifies the page number of the first page to print.

The *to* argument is a value that specifies the page number of the last page to print.

The *start* argument is a value that specifies the page number at which to start numbering pages.

The *copies* argument is a value that specifies the number of copies to print.

The PRINT? Command

The PRINT? command displays the File Print dialog box. Use the following syntax for PRINT?:

{PRINT?}

The PRINT? command does not use any arguments.

The PRINT-NAME-ADD Command

The PRINT-NAME-ADD command saves the current page settings as named page settings (print settings you can later recall and use) in a file on disk. Use the following syntax for PRINT-NAME-ADD:

{PRINT-NAME-ADD *page-setting-name*}

The *page-setting-name* argument, which specifies the name of the file, is enclosed in quotation marks. 1-2-3 for Windows automatically adds the extension AL4 to a file containing named page settings unless you enter a different extension.

The PRINT-NAME-USE Command

The PRINT-NAME-USE command makes named page settings the current page settings. Use the following syntax for PRINT-NAME-USE:

{PRINT-NAME-USE *page-setting-name*}

The *page-setting-name* argument, which specifies the name of the file, is enclosed in quotation marks.

The PRINT-RESET Command

The PRINT-RESET command replaces the currently selected Margins, Print Titles, Header, Footer, Options, Compression, and Orientation settings with the default page layout for the current file. Use the following syntax for PRINT-RESET:

{PRINT-RESET}

The PRINT-RESET command does not use any arguments.

The SEND-MAIL Command

The SEND-MAIL command sends a mail message, using your mail application, while you are working in 1-2-3 for Windows. The mail can contain text, the contents of the Clipboard, and the current file. Use the following syntax for SEND-MAIL:

{SEND-MAIL [*to*];[*cc*];[*subject*];[*body*];
[*clipboard*];[*file*]}

The *to* argument specifies the recipient of the mail. This argument can be text enclosed in quotation marks or a range that contains a single row or column of labels.

The *cc* argument specifies the recipient of copies of the mail. This argument can be text enclosed in quotation marks or a range that contains a single row or column of labels.

The *subject* argument, which specifies the subject of the mail message, is enclosed in quotation marks.

The *body* argument specifies the body of the message. If *body* is the name or address of a range that contains labels, you must enter the labels in a single row or column. If *body* is a multiple-cell range, a line feed and carriage return follows each label.

The *clipboard* argument is a Boolean argument that specifies whether to attach the contents of the Clipboard to the mail message.

The *file* argument is a Boolean argument that specifies whether to attach the current file to the mail message.

Using File Macro Commands Together

Figure 16.9 demonstrates the use of several macro commands that manipulate files. This macro first obtains the network reservation so no other user can modify the original while the macro is executing. Next it combines sales data from the R1SALES file, selects a named print setting, and prints five copies of the SALES_REPORT range. The combined file is then saved and finally, closed.

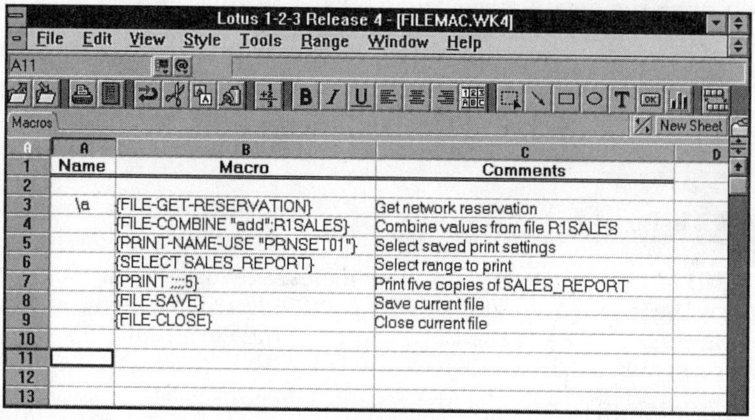

FIG. 16.9

Several macro commands that manipulate files.

Commands That Control Programs

The commands listed in table 16.8 provide varying degrees of control in 1-2-3 for Windows programs. Used alone or with decision-making commands, these commands give the macro programmer precise control of program flow.

Table 16.8 Commands That Control Programs

Command	Action
{subroutine}	Performs a call to a subroutine before continuing to the next line of a macro
BRANCH	Continues program execution at the specified location
DEFINE	Specifies cells for subroutine arguments
DISPATCH	Branches indirectly, through the specified location
FOR	Creates a FOR loop, which repeatedly performs a subroutine call to subroutine
FORBREAK	Cancels a FOR loop created by a {FOR} command
IF	Evaluates condition as true or false and branches the program

Command	Action
LAUNCH	Starts and optionally switches to a Windows application
ONERROR	Traps and handles errors that occur while a macro is running
QUIT	Ends a macro immediately
RESTART	Clears the subroutine stack, ending the macro when the current subroutine ends
RETURN	Returns macro control from a subroutine to the calling macro
SET	Sets a specified Info component to a specified value
SYSTEM	Temporarily suspends the 1-2-3 session and executes the specified operating-system command

Subroutines

A *subroutine* is an independent program that can be run from within the main macro command program. Calling a subroutine is as easy as enclosing the name or location of a macro routine in braces—for example, {GO_INVOICE}, {\S}, and {B56}. When 1-2-3 for Windows encounters a name or location in braces, the program passes control to the named routine. When the routine finishes (that is, when 1-2-3 for Windows encounters a blank cell or a {RETURN}), program control passes back to the next instruction in the macro that called the subroutine. The syntax for using a subroutine is as follows:

   {*subroutine*}

{*subroutine*} can refer to a range name or cell address. Using a range name, however, is preferable, because if you later move the entire subroutine, the subroutine command still works correctly.

> **CAUTION:** Make sure that none of your range names is the same as a macro command name or a 1-2-3 for Windows reserved word.

Using subroutines has many advantages. Subroutines enable you to isolate macro problems more easily. You also can easily enhance subroutines. If you want to add new commands, you can modify a subroutine once, and then all programs that call that subroutine reflect the new commands.

The greatest benefit of using a subroutine, however, is that any program can use the subroutine. After you create the subroutine, you can call it at any time from any program. When the subroutine finishes, program execution returns to the originating program.

The BRANCH Command

The location argument specifies the cell address or range name to which to pass program control. The program begins reading commands and statements at the cell indicated by the command. Macro control does not return to the calling macro. The syntax for the BRANCH command is as follows:

{BRANCH *location*}

The BRANCH command passes program control to the cell address or range name indicated by the *location* argument.

The BRANCH command is an unconditional statement. When the macro encounters a BRANCH statement, macro control immediately jumps to the cell specified by the *location* argument, and the macro executes the instructions in that cell. By placing a conditional statement before BRANCH, you can control the circumstances that enable BRANCH to execute. For example, you can control whether a BRANCH command is executed by preceding the command with an IF statement.

The DEFINE Command

The DEFINE command allocates storage locations and declares argument types for arguments to be passed to a subroutine. If you store arguments in range names, subroutines do not need an accompanying DEFINE statement. DEFINE is necessary if you pass arguments as part of a subroutine call. The number of arguments in the DEFINE statement must match the number in the subroutine call statement; otherwise, 1-2-3 for Windows returns an error.

The format of such a subroutine call with arguments is as follows:

{DEFINE *location1*[*:type*];*location2*[*:type*]...;
locationN[*:type*]}

The DEFINE command specifies cells for the subroutine arguments in which *location1*, *location2*, and so on are names or cell references for the cells in which to place arguments passed from the main program.

Following each *location* specifier is an optional *type* specifier that tells 1-2-3 for Windows whether to process the corresponding argument in the {*subroutine*} command as a string or value. The type specifier is :string or :value (abbreviated as :s or :v). The *type* specifier is optional; if you do not specify a type, the default is :string.

If *type* is specified as :string, the text of the corresponding argument in the subroutine call is placed in the indicated cell as a string value (label). If *type* is specified as :value, the corresponding argument in the subroutine call is treated as a formula, and its numeric or string value is placed in the argument cell.

1-2-3 for Windows returns an error if the corresponding argument in the subroutine call is not a valid number, string, or formula.

The DISPATCH Command

The DISPATCH command is a hybrid of the BRANCH command. Like the BRANCH command, DISPATCH sends the macro processor to a specified location to process instructions. The DISPATCH command, however, branches *indirectly* to that location. Following is the syntax of DISPATCH:

> {DISPATCH *location*}

DISPATCH branches to a destination specified in the *location* cell. The *location* cell contains the cell address or range name of the branch destination.

BRANCH, which tells the program where to look for the next set of instructions, is considered to be a *direct* branch. DISPATCH is an *indirect* branch. If the cell referenced by *location* does not contain a valid cell reference or range name, program execution stops, and 1-2-3 for Windows displays an error message. An ONERROR command cannot prevent macro execution from stopping, because ONERROR does not trap syntax errors.

DISPATCH often is used with IF statements. The IF statements test the conditions of cells, and the DISPATCH command decides where to go based on the results of the IF tests.

The FOR and FORBREAK Commands

The FOR command controls a program's looping process by calling a subroutine to be executed a certain number of times. FOR enables you to define the exact number of times the subroutine is executed. The FOR statement provides a loop capability (often called FOR-NEXT) similar to that provided by many other programming languages. The syntax of FOR is as follows:

> {FOR *counter,start,stop,step,routine*}

The *counter* argument is a cell that acts as the loop counter for the FOR command. 1-2-3 for Windows uses the *start*, *stop*, and *step* values to determine how many times to execute the routine. The *start* argument is the starting number for the counter, the *stop* argument is the completion number for the counter, and *step* is the incremental value for the counter. The *routine* argument is the name of the subroutine to be executed on each count.

The *start*, *stop*, and *step* arguments can be values, cell addresses, formulas, or range names. The *counter* and *routine* arguments, however, must be range names, cell addresses, or formulas that evaluate to a range name or cell address.

If you want use something other than a specified number of iterations as the basis for ending the processing of a FOR command, you can use the FORBREAK command within the FOR loop to create a conditional test. Following is the syntax of FORBREAK:

    {FORBREAK}

When 1-2-3 for Windows executes FORBREAK, the program interrupts the processing of the FOR command and continues execution with the macro instruction following the FOR statement.

FORBREAK typically is used with an IF statement. Suppose that a FOR command calls a routine to add current business expenses. You want to break the FOR command when expenses total more than $1,000,000. Consider the instructions in the following macro:

```
*MAIN           {FOR COUNT;1;@ROWS(RANGE);1;TOT_ROUT}{PRINT_RPT}
TOT_ROUT        {LET TOTAL,+CURRENT+NEXT}
                {IF TOTAL<1000000}{FORBREAK}
```

In this macro, the FOR statement runs the TOT_ROUT routine until TOTAL is greater than 1,000,000. The {FORBREAK} command breaks the FOR loop at that point and returns the macro execution to the main routine at the line below the FOR command. The PRINT_RPT routine then runs.

The IF Command

An IF statement uses IF-THEN-ELSE logic to control macro program flow or IF-THEN logic to control specific keystroke or command execution. The macro command IF enables a macro program to perform instructions based on conditions in the worksheet. The syntax of IF is as follows:

    {IF *condition*}*true*

    false

IF executes true or false statements, based on the result of the evaluated *condition*.

When the macro encounters an IF statement, it evaluates the *condition*. If *condition* evaluates to true, the macro continues to execute instructions in the same cell as the IF statement. If *condition* evaluates to false, the macro ignores any remaining instructions in the cell containing the IF command and continues to the cell directly below. In graphic terms, the process appears as follows:

{IF *condition*} Do these instructions if *condition* is true

Do these instructions if *condition* is false

The false instructions are in the cell directly below the IF command. These instructions, therefore, execute as the next line of the macro for a true condition unless you place a RETURN, a branching statement (such as BRANCH, DISPATCH, or MENUBRANCH), or a QUIT statement after the IF condition (in the same cell). If *condition* is true, the macro executes the true and the false commands unless the true command is RETURN, a branching statement, or QUIT.

You might want to use the IF statement in IF-THEN form rather IF-THEN-ELSE form. You want the keystrokes or commands on the same line as the IF statement to be performed if a certain condition is true, but you want the next line to be performed unconditionally. In such a case, do not include a BRANCH command on the same line as the IF command, so program control will always continue to the line below the IF command.

The LAUNCH Command

The LAUNCH command starts a Windows application. The syntax of LAUNCH is as follows:

{LAUNCH *command*;[*window*];[*switch-to*]}

The *command* argument, which specifies the command string that starts the Windows application, is enclosed in quotation marks.

The *window* argument is an integer (0 through 9) that controls the initial state of the application. If no *window* argument is specified, 1-2-3 for Windows assumes 7. Be aware, however, that not all Windows applications support every *window* argument. Following are the possible *window* values:

Integer	Action
0	Hides the application window and activates another window.
1	Activates and displays the application window. If the window is minimized or maximized, this argument restores the window to its original size and position.
2	Activates and minimizes the application window.
3	Activates and maximizes the application window.
4	Displays the application window in its most recent size and position. 1-2-3 remains the active application.
5	Activates the application window and displays it in its current size and position.
6	Minimizes the application window and activates the top-level window in the window manager's list.
7	Minimizes the application window. 1-2-3 remains the active application. If you do not include a *window* argument, 1-2-3 uses this value.
8	Displays the application window in its current state. 1-2-3 remains the active application.
9	Activates and displays the application window. If the window is minimized or maximized, this argument restores the window to its original size and position.

The *switch-to* argument enables you to switch to the application specified in *command* or to any Windows application that currently is running. The *switch-to* argument, which is the text that appears in the title bar of an application, can be the entire title or only the beginning of it, and is enclosed in quotes.

The ONERROR Command

If a system error (such as Invalid disk name) occurs during macro execution, the processing of macro command programs usually is interrupted. By sidestepping system errors that usually cause program termination, the ONERROR command enables programs to proceed. Use the following syntax for ONERROR:

{ONERROR *branch-location*;[*message-location*]}

The *branch-location* argument specifies the range name or address where program control branches when an error is encountered.

The *message-location* argument specifies the range name or address and where to record error messages.

The ONERROR command should be the first command (or one of the first commands) that the macro executes; you want to make sure that the ONERROR statement is executed before an error is possible. An ONERROR command remains in effect until an error occurs (each ONERROR can handle only one error) or until the ONERROR is superseded by another ONERROR. ONERROR does not trap macro syntax errors.

An ONERROR statement takes effect if the user presses Ctrl+Break unless you also have executed a BREAKOFF statement.

The QUIT Command

The QUIT command unconditionally halts program control. Even without a QUIT command, the program terminates if it encounters (within the program sequence) a cell that is empty or that contains an entry other than a string. You always should include a QUIT statement at the end of a program to indicate that you intend execution to stop. (Conversely, do not put a QUIT command at the end of a program that you intend to call as a subroutine.) Use the following syntax for QUIT:

{QUIT}

In the following example, the QUIT command forces the program sequence to terminate unconditionally:

{HOME}{QUIT}

The following macro provides an example of a conditionally executing QUIT command:

```
{GOTO}TOTAL~
{IF TOTAL>100000}{QUIT}
{NEXT_ONE}
```

This macro quits only if the number in TOTAL is greater than 100,000. If the number in TOTAL is less than 100,000, the macro runs the routine NEXT_ONE.

The RESTART Command

Just as you can call subroutines from the main program, you can call one subroutine from another. As 1-2-3 for Windows moves from one subroutine to the next, the program saves the addresses of the cells it has used. 1-2-3 for Windows uses these saved addresses to return to the calling program when the subroutine ends. This technique is called *stacking* or *saving addresses on a stack*. By saving the addresses on a stack, 1-2-3 for Windows can trace its way back through the subroutine calls to the main program. If you decide that you do not want 1-2-3 for Windows to return to the calling program by the same path, you can use the RESTART command to eliminate the return-address stack. The RESTART command prevents a subroutine from returning to the calling program when the subroutine ends.

The syntax of RESTART is as follows:

{RESTART}

RESTART continues macro execution at the next character or cell as if the character or cell were the beginning of a new macro. The result of using a RESTART statement depends on what follows the statement. If RESTART is followed by the remainder of the current subroutine, 1-2-3 for Windows finishes executing the subroutine, but when the program reaches a RETURN statement or an empty cell, the macro stops. If RESTART is followed by another subroutine call or a BRANCH statement, 1-2-3 for Windows goes to that location. If RESTART is followed by an empty cell, macro execution halts.

The RETURN Command

The RETURN command indicates the end of subroutine execution and returns program control to the macro instruction immediately below the cell that called the subroutine or immediately following the subroutine call in the same cell.

Use the following syntax for RETURN:

{RETURN}

Do not confuse RETURN with QUIT, which terminates the program.

1-2-3 for Windows also ends a subroutine and returns to the calling routine when the program encounters, while executing the subroutine, a cell that is blank or contains a number. Although this method of returning from a subroutine works, you should use the RETURN command as the last line of a subroutine because RETURN delimits a particular set of macro instructions as a subroutine.

The SET Command

The SET command sets a specified *info component*—a variable such as the current print range—to a specified value. Use the following syntax for SET:

{SET *info-id;info-value*}

The *info-id* argument, which specifies the name of the Info component whose value you want to set, is enclosed in quotation marks.

The *info-value* argument specifies the value to which you want to set the Info component. The *info-value* can be a value, text, or a location, depending on the component that you are setting.

The SYSTEM Command

The SYSTEM command temporarily suspends macro execution and executes the specified operating-system command or batch file. Use the following syntax for SYSTEM:

{SYSTEM *command*}

The *command* argument represents any DOS command, including commands that run batch files or other programs. The *command* is any text enclosed in quotation marks, a formula that results in text, or the name or address of a cell that contains a label or formula that results in a label.

When a macro executes the SYSTEM command, 1-2-3 for Windows passes control and the command string to the operating system. When the operating-system command has executed or the batch file has completed its run, control returns to the cell below the SYSTEM command.

If command sets an error level, you can test for successful completion by following the SYSTEM command with the function @INFO ("osreturncode"). Do not load memory-resident programs, because you might not be able to resume 1-2-3.

Commands That Duplicate Keystrokes

Table 16.9 describes the 1-2-3 for Windows commands that duplicate keystrokes. You can use these commands when a macro program must perform tasks that require pressing specified keys.

Table 16.9 Keystroke Equivalents

Command	Equivalent Keystrokes
{	Enters left brace
}	Enters right brace
~	Enters tilde
ABS	F4
ALT	F10
ANCHOR	F4 (in Ready mode)
APP1	Alt+F7
APP2	Alt+F8
APP3	Alt+F9
BACKSPACE or BS	Backspace
BACKTAB or BIGLEFT	Ctrl+←
BIGRIGHT	Ctrl+→
CALC	F9
DELETE or DEL	Del
DOWN or D	↓
EDIT	F2
END	End
ESCAPE or ESC	Esc
FILE	Ctrl+End
FIRSTCELL or FC	Ctrl+Home
FIRSTFILE or FF	Ctrl+End Home
GOTO	F5
HELP	F1
HOME	Home
INSERT or INS	Ins
LASTCELL or LC	End Ctrl+Home
LASTFILE or LF	Ctrl+End End
LEFT or L	←
MENU	/

Command	Equivalent Keystrokes
MENUBAR or MB	F10
NAME	F3
NEXTFILE or NF	Ctrl+End Ctrl+PgUp
NEXTSHEET or NS	Ctrl+PgUp
PGDN	PgDn
PGUP	PgUp
PREVFILE or PF	Ctrl+End Ctrl+PgDn
PREVSHEET or PS	Ctrl+PgDn
QUERY	F7
RIGHT or R	→
SELECT-BIGLEFT	Shift+Ctrl+←
SELECT-BIGRIGHT	Shift+Ctrl+→
SELECT-DOWN	Shift+↓
SELECT-FIRSTCELL	Shift+Ctrl+Home
SELECT-HOME	Shift+Home
SELECT-LASTCELL	Shift+End Ctrl+Home
SELECT-LEFT	Shift+←
SELECT-NEXTSHEET	Shift+Ctrl+PgUp
SELECT-PGDN	Shift+PgDn
SELECT-PGUP	Shift+PgUp
SELECT-PREVSHEET	Shift+Ctrl+PgDn
SELECT-RIGHT	Shift+→
SELECT-UP	Shift+↑
TAB	Tab
TABLE	F8
UP or U	↑
WINDOW	F6
ZOOM	Alt+F6

Commands That Navigate the Worksheet

The commands listed in table 16.10 move around the worksheet, select worksheet areas, and enter data in specified locations.

Table 16.10 Commands That Navigate the Worksheet

Command	Action
CELL-ENTER	Enters data in a specified location
EDIT-GOTO	Selects all or part of a range, query table, chart, or other drawn object and then scrolls to it
SCROLL-COLUMNS	Scrolls horizontally in the current worksheet
SCROLL-ROWS	Scrolls vertically in the current worksheet
SCROLL-TO-CELL	Scrolls in the current worksheet so that the first cell of a specified location is in the top left corner of the worksheet window
SCROLL-TO-COLUMN	Scrolls left or right in the current worksheet so that the leftmost column of a specified location is the leftmost column of the worksheet window
SCROLL-TO-OBJECT	Scrolls to but does not select a range, query table, chart, or other drawn object in the current worksheet
SCROLL-TO-ROW	Scrolls up or down in the current worksheet so that the top row of a specified location is the top row in the worksheet window
SELECT	Selects all or part of a range, chart, query table, or other drawn object without scrolling to it
SELECT-ALL	Selects the active area of the current worksheet, all charts or drawn objects in the current worksheet, or all worksheets in the current file
SELECT-APPEND	Selects all or part of a range, chart, or other drawn object without deselecting the current selected
SELECT-REMOVE	Removes a range, chart, or other drawn object from the currently selected collection
SELECT-REPLACE	Replaces an item in a collection or group of items

The CELL-ENTER Command

The CELL-ENTER command enters data in a specified target location. Use the following syntax for CELL-ENTER:

{CELL-ENTER *data*;[*target-location*]}

The *data* argument, which specifies the data (text, number, or formula) that you want to enter in the worksheet, is enclosed in quotation marks. If *data* is a formula, 1-2-3 for Windows enters the formula into *target-location* and displays the result of the formula in the worksheet.

The *target-location* argument specifies the range name or address of the cell in which you want to enter data. If *target-location* is a range, 1-2-3 for Windows enters the data in the first cell in the range. If you omit *target-location*, 1-2-3 enters the data in the current cell.

The EDIT-GOTO Command

The EDIT-GOTO command selects all or part of a range, query table, chart, or other drawn object and then scrolls to it. Any items in the same file that were selected become unselected. Use the following syntax for EDIT-GOTO:

{EDIT-GOTO *name*,[*part*];[*type*]}

The *name* argument, which can be in the current file or in another open file, specifies the name of the item that you want to select. For a range, *name* can also be a range address.

The *part* argument specifies a part that can be included in the item specified by *name*. If *name* specifies a range, *part* must be the name or address of a single cell. If *name* specifies a chart, *part* must be the name of a chart element, enclosed in quotation marks. If *name* specifies a query table, *part* must be a field name, enclosed in quotation marks. If you omit *part*, the entire item is selected.

The *type* argument specifies the type of item to which *name* refers— chart, draw, query, or range—and is enclosed in quotation marks.

The SCROLL-COLUMNS Command

The SCROLL-COLUMNS command scrolls horizontally in the current worksheet. Use the following syntax for SCROLL-COLUMNS:

{SCROLL-COLUMNS [*amount*]}

The *amount* argument is an integer that specifies how many columns to scroll. A positive *amount* scrolls right; a negative *amount* scrolls left. If you omit *amount*, the screen scrolls one column to the right.

The SCROLL-COLUMNS command does not change the current cell.

The SCROLL-ROWS Command

The SCROLL-ROWS command scrolls vertically in the current worksheet. Use the following syntax for SCROLL-ROWS:

> {SCROLL-ROWS [*amount*]}

The *amount* argument is an integer that specifies how many rows to scroll. A positive *amount* scrolls down; a negative *amount* scrolls up. If you omit *amount*, the screen scrolls one row down.

The SCROLL-ROWS command does not change the current cell.

The SCROLL-TO-CELL Command

The SCROLL-TO-CELL command scrolls in the current worksheet so that the first cell of *location* is in the top left corner of the worksheet window. Use the following syntax for SCROLL-TO-CELL:

> {SCROLL-TO-CELL *location*}

The *location* argument is the range name or address of the range to which you want to scroll. SCROLL-TO-CELL returns an error if *location* is not in the worksheet that contains the current cell.

The SCROLL-TO-COLUMN Command

The SCROLL-TO-COLUMN command scrolls left or right in the current worksheet so that the leftmost column of the specified location is the leftmost column of the worksheet window. Use the following syntax for SCROLL-TO-COLUMN:

> {SCROLL-TO-COLUMN *location*}

The *location* argument specifies the range name or address of the range to which you want to scroll. SCROLL-TO-COLUMN ignores worksheet letters in *location*.

The SCROLL-TO-OBJECT Command

The SCROLL-TO-OBJECT command scrolls to but does not select a range, query table, chart, or other drawn object in the current worksheet. Use the following syntax for SCROLL-TO-OBJECT:

{SCROLL-TO-OBJECT *name*;[*type*]}

The *name* argument specifies the name of the item to which you want to scroll, which must be in the current worksheet.

The *type* argument specifies the type of item to which *name* refers—chart, draw, query, or range—and is enclosed in quotation marks. If you omit *type*, 1-2-3 for Windows uses the range type.

The SCROLL-TO-OBJECT command does not change the current cell.

The SCROLL-TO-ROW Command

The SCROLL-TO-ROW command scrolls up or down in the current worksheet so that the topmost row of the specified location is the topmost row of the worksheet window. Use the following syntax for SCROLL-TO-ROW:

{SCROLL-TO-ROW *location*}

The *location* argument specifies the range name or address of the range to which you want to scroll. SCROLL-TO-ROW ignores worksheet letters in *location*.

The SELECT Command

The SELECT command selects all or part of a range, chart, query table, or other drawn object without scrolling to it. Any items in the same file that were selected become unselected. Use the following syntax for SELECT:

{SELECT *name*;[*part*];[*type*]}

The *name* argument specifies the name of the item that you want to select. The item can be in the current file or in another open file. For a range, *name* can also be a range address.

The *part* argument specifies a part that can be included in the item specified by *name*. If *name* specifies a range, *part* must be the name or address of a single cell. If *name* specifies a chart, *part* must be the name of a chart element, enclosed in quotation marks. If *name* specifies a query table, *part* must be a field name, enclosed in quotation marks. If you omit *part*, the entire item is selected.

The *type* argument specifies the type of item to which *name* refers—chart, draw, query, or range—and is enclosed in quotation marks.

The SELECT-ALL Command

The SELECT-ALL command selects the active area of the current worksheet, all charts or drawn objects in the current worksheet, or all worksheets in the current file. Use the following syntax for SELECT-ALL:

> {SELECT-ALL [*type*]}

The *type* argument specifies the type of item to select—cell, chart, draw, or sheet—and is enclosed in quotation marks.

The SELECT-APPEND Command

The SELECT-APPEND command selects all or part of a range, chart, or other drawn object without deselecting the current selection. Use the following syntax for SELECT-APPEND:

> {SELECT-APPEND *name*;[*part*]}

The *name* argument, which specifies the name of the item to be added to the currently selected collection or group of items, must be an existing name for an item of the type that currently is selected.

The *part* argument specifies a part that can be included in the item specified by *name*. If you omit *part*, 1-2-3 selects the entire item specified by *name*. If *name* specifies a range, *part* must be the name or address of a single cell. If *name* specifies a chart, *part* must be the name of a chart element, enclosed in quotation marks.

The SELECT-REMOVE Command

The SELECT-REMOVE command removes a range, chart, or other drawn object from the currently selected collection. Use the following syntax for SELECT-REMOVE:

> {SELECT-REMOVE *name*}

The *name* argument specifies the name of the item to be removed from the currently selected collection or group of items.

The SELECT-REPLACE Command

The SELECT-REPLACE command replaces an item in a collection or group of items. Use the following syntax for SELECT-REPLACE:

> {SELECT-REPLACE *old-item*;*new-item*}

The *old-item* argument specifies the name of the currently selected item that you want to replace with *new-item*.

The *new-item* argument specifies the name of the item that you want to replace *old-item*.

Both *old-item* and *new-item* must be existing names for the types of items that currently are selected.

Using Navigation Macro Commands Together

Figure 16.10 demonstrates the use of macro commands that navigate in the worksheet.

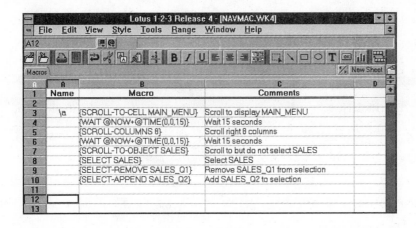

FIG. 16.10

Macro commands that navigate in the worksheet.

Commands That Manipulate Ranges

Table 16.11 describes macro commands that manipulate ranges. These commands enable macro programs to create and delete range names, create data tables, sort ranges, and perform advanced mathematics.

Table 16.11 Commands That Manipulate Ranges

Command	Action
DATA-DISTRIBUTION	Uses DISTRIBUTION
DATA-FILL	Uses FILL
DATA-MATRIX-INVERT	Uses MATRIX-INVERT
DATA-MATRIX-MULTIPLY	Uses MATRIX-MULTIPLY
DATA-PARSE	Uses PARSE
DATA-REGRESSION	Uses REGRESSION
DATA-REGRESSION-RESET	Uses REGRESSION
DATA-TABLE-1	Substitutes values for one variable in one or more formulas and enters the results in a specified output range
DATA-TABLE-2	Substitutes values for two variables in one formula and enters the results in a specified output-range
DATA-TABLE-3	Substitutes values for three variables in one formula and enters the results in a specified output range
DATA-TABLE-RESET	Clears the ranges and input-cell settings for all what-if tables in the current file
DISTRIBUTION	Creates a frequency distribution that counts how many values in a range fall within each numeric interval specified by another range
FILL	Enters a sequence of values in a specified range
FILL-BY-EXAMPLE	Fills a range with a sequence of data that is determined by the data already in the range
MATRIX-INVERT	Inverts a square matrix
MATRIX-MULTIPLY	Multiplies one matrix by another to create an output matrix
PARSE	Converts long labels from an imported text file into separate columns of data
RANGE-NAME-CREATE	Assigns a name to a range address
RANGE-NAME-DELETE	Deletes a range name

Command	Action
RANGE-NAME-DELETE-ALL	Deletes all range names in the current file
RANGE-NAME-LABEL-CREATE	Assigns an existing label as the range name for a single cell
RANGE-NAME-TABLE	Creates a two-column table of all defined ranges
RANGE-TRANSPOSE	Transposes data while copying
REGRESSION	Performs multiple-linear-regression analysis and calculates the slope of the line that best illustrates the data
SHEET-NAME	Names a 1-2-3 worksheet in the current file
SHEET-NAME-DELETE	Deletes a worksheet name in the current file
SORT	Sorts data in the order that you specify
SORT-KEY-DEFINE	Defines a sort key
SORT-RESET	Clears all sort keys and ranges

The DATA-TABLE-1, DATA-TABLE-2, and DATA-TABLE-3 Commands

The DATA-TABLE-1 command substitutes values for one variable in one or more formulas and enters the results in a specified output range.

The DATA-TABLE-2 command substitutes values for two variables in one formula and enters the result in a specified output range.

The DATA-TABLE-3 command substitutes values for three variables in one formula and enters the result in a specified output range.

Use the following syntax for these commands:

{DATA-TABLE-1 [*output-range*];[*input-cell-1*]}

{DATA-TABLE-2 [*output-range*];[*input-cell-1*];[*input-cell-2*]}

{DATA-TABLE-3 [*output-range*];[*input-cell-1*]; [*input-cell-2*];[*input-cell-3*];[*formula*]}

The *output-range* argument specifies the range name or address of the range that contains the formula, the list of input values that the formula uses in place of the variable, and the blank cells in which 1-2-3 for Windows is to place the results.

The *input-cell-1*, *input-cell-2*, and *input-cell-3* arguments specify the range names or addresses of the first, second, and third cells in which 1-2-3 for Windows temporarily enters values while performing the calculations required to create the table. These cells must be unprotected, and they should be blank or contain unimportant data.

The *formula* argument specifies the range name or address of the cell containing the formula that has the three variables you want to change.

The cells used as arguments *input-cell-1*, *input-cell-2*, *input-cell-3*, and *formula* must be outside the cells included in *output-range*.

The DATA-TABLE-RESET Command

The DATA-TABLE-RESET command clears the ranges and input-cell settings for all what-if tables in the current file. Use the following syntax for DATA-TABLE-RESET:

{DATA-TABLE-RESET}

The DATA-TABLE-RESET command does not use any arguments.

The DISTRIBUTION Command

The DISTRIBUTION command creates a frequency distribution that counts how many values fall within specified numeric intervals. Use the following syntax for DISTRIBUTION:

{DISTRIBUTION [*values-range*];[*bin-range*]}

The *values-range* argument specifies the range name or address of the range that contains the values to be analyzed. 1-2-3 for Windows ignores blank cells and cells that contain labels. If you omit *values-range*, 1-2-3 uses the last *values-range* specified in the current session.

The *bin-range* argument specifies the range name or address of a single-column range containing the values that are the upper limits of numeric intervals that define the bins of the frequency distribution. Each value must be unique and in ascending order. If you omit *bin-range*, 1-2-3 for Windows uses the last *bin-range* specified in the current session.

The frequency distribution is entered in the column to the right of *bin-range*.

The FILL Command

The FILL command enters a sequence of values in a specified range. Use the following syntax for FILL:

> {FILL [*range*];[*start*];[*step*];[*stop*];[*units*]}

The *range* argument specifies the range name or address of the range that you want to fill. Existing data in *range* is overwritten. If you omit *range*, 1-2-3 for Windows uses the currently selected range if it is a multicell range. If you omit *range* and the current selection is a single cell, 1-2-3 uses the last *range* used in FILL or Range Fill.

The *start* argument specifies the first value that 1-2-3 enters in *range*.

The *step* argument specifies the increment between each of the values in the *range*. If *step* is negative, *stop* must be less than *start*.

The *stop* argument specifies the limit of the sequence.

The *units* argument specifies whether the *step* increment is a number (numeric) or a unit of time (day, week, month, quarter, year, hour, minute, or second). The argument is enclosed in quotation marks.

The FILL-BY-EXAMPLE Command

The FILL-BY-EXAMPLE command fills a range with a sequence of data that is determined by the data already in the range. Use the following syntax for FILL-BY-EXAMPLE:

> {FILL-BY-EXAMPLE [*range*]}

The *range* argument specifies the range name or address of the range that you want to fill. If you omit *range*, 1-2-3 for Windows fills the currently selected range or collection.

The MATRIX-INVERT Command

The MATRIX-INVERT command inverts a square matrix. Use the following syntax for MATRIX-INVERT:

> {MATRIX-INVERT [*matrix-to-invert*];[*output-range*]}

The *matrix-to-invert* argument specifies the range name or address of the range containing the matrix that you want to invert.

The *output-range* argument specifies the range name or address of the range in which you want to put the results. Any existing data in *output-range* is overwritten.

You cannot invert every matrix. If MATRIX-INVERT cannot create an inverse of the matrix in *matrix-to-invert*, the macro ends with an error.

The MATRIX-MULTIPLY Command

The MATRIX-MULTIPLY command multiplies one matrix by another to create an output matrix that contains the result. Use the following syntax for MATRIX-MULTIPLY:

{MATRIX-MULTIPLY [*matrix1*];[*matrix2*];[*output-range*]}

The *matrix1* argument specifies the range name or address of the range containing the first matrix that you want to multiply.

The *matrix2* argument specifies the range name or address of the range containing the second matrix that you want to multiply.

The *output-range* argument specifies the range name or address of the range in which you want to put the results. Any existing data in *output-range* is overwritten.

The PARSE Command

The PARSE command converts labels from an imported text file into separate columns of data. Use the following syntax for PARSE:

{PARSE [*parse-range*];[*output-range*];[*format-line*]}

The *parse-range* argument specifies the range name or address of the single-column range containing the labels that you want to parse.

The *output-range* argument specifies the range name or address of a range in which the parsed data is to be placed. The *output-range* argument can specify an entire range or only the first cell. The parsed data overwrites any existing data in *output-range*.

The *format-line* argument, which specifies how to parse the data, is enclosed in quotation marks. If you omit *format-line*, the first cell in *parse-range* must be a valid format line.

The RANGE-NAME-CREATE Command

The RANGE-NAME-CREATE command assigns a name to a range address. Use the following syntax for RANGE-NAME-CREATE:

{RANGE-NAME-CREATE *range-name*;[*range-location*]}

The *range-name* argument, which specifies the name that you want to assign to the range, is enclosed in quotation marks.

The *range-location* argument specifies the address of the range that you want to name. If you omit *range-location*, 1-2-3 for Windows names the currently selected range.

The RANGE-NAME-DELETE Command

The RANGE-NAME-DELETE command deletes a range name. Use the following syntax for RANGE-NAME-DELETE:

> {RANGE-NAME-DELETE *range-name*}

The *range-name* argument, which specifies the name that you want to delete, is enclosed in quotation marks.

The RANGE-NAME-DELETE-ALL Command

The RANGE-NAME-DELETE-ALL command deletes all range names in the current file. Use the following syntax for RANGE-NAME-DELETE-ALL:

> {RANGE-NAME-DELETE-ALL}

The RANGE-NAME-DELETE-ALL command does not use any arguments.

The RANGE-NAME-LABEL-CREATE Command

The RANGE-NAME-LABEL-CREATE command assigns an existing label as the range name for a single cell. Use the following syntax for RANGE-NAME-LABEL-CREATE:

> {RANGE-NAME-LABEL-CREATE [*direction*];[*label-range*]}

The *direction* argument specifies the position—right, left, up, or down—of the single-cell range(s) relative to *label-range*. The argument is enclosed in quotation marks.

The *label-range* argument specifies the name or address of the range containing the text that you want to assign as a range name. If you omit *label-range*, 1-2-3 for Windows uses the currently selected range.

The RANGE-NAME-TABLE Command

The RANGE-NAME-TABLE command creates a table of all defined ranges in the current file. Use the following syntax for RANGE-NAME-TABLE:

{RANGE-NAME-TABLE [*table-location*]}

The *table-location* argument specifies the name or address of the range in which the table of range names and addresses is to be created. If you omit *table-location*, the table starts in the top left cell of the currently selected range.

The RANGE-TRANSPOSE Command

The RANGE-TRANSPOSE command transposes data from one location to another, replacing any copied formulas with their current values. Use the following syntax for RANGE-TRANSPOSE:

{RANGE-TRANSPOSE *destination*;[*transpose*];[*origin*]}

The *destination* argument specifies the name or address of the range to which you are copying.

The *transpose* argument specifies how to transpose the data—rows-to-columns, columns-to-sheets, or sheets-to-rows—and is enclosed in quotation marks.

The *origin* argument specifies the name or address of the range containing the data that you want to copy and transpose. If you omit *origin*, 1-2-3 uses the currently selected range.

The REGRESSION Command

The REGRESSION command performs multiple-linear-regression analysis and calculates the slope of the regression line. Use the following syntax for REGRESSION:

{REGRESSION [*X-range*];[*Y-range*];[*output-range*]; [*intercept*]}

The *X-range* argument specifies the name or address of the range that contains up to 75 columns and 8,192 rows of independent variables.

The *Y-range* argument specifies the name or address of the single-column range (with the same number of rows as *X-range*) that contains the set of values for the dependent variable.

The *output-range* argument specifies the name or address of the range in which you want to place the result of the regression analysis.

The *intercept* argument specifies whether 1-2-3 calculates the y-axis intercept (the compute option) or uses 0 as the y-axis intercept (the zero option). The argument is enclosed in quotation marks.

The SHEET-NAME Command

The SHEET-NAME command names a worksheet in the current file. Use the following syntax for SHEET-NAME:

{SHEET-NAME *new-name*;[*old-name*]}

The *new-name* argument, which specifies a new name for the worksheet, is enclosed in quotation marks.

The *old-name* argument specifies the current name or letter of the worksheet. If you omit *old-name*, 1-2-3 names the current worksheet.

The SHEET-NAME-DELETE Command

The SHEET-NAME-DELETE command deletes the name of a worksheet in the current file. Use the following syntax for SHEET-NAME-DELETE:

{SHEET-NAME-DELETE [*worksheet-name*]}

The *worksheet-name* argument specifies the worksheet name to be deleted; the name reverts to the worksheet letter. If you omit *worksheet-name*, 1-2-3 deletes the name of the current worksheet.

The SORT Command

The SORT command arranges data in a specified order. Use the following syntax for SORT:

{SORT [*key1*];[*order1*];[*key2*];[*order2*];[*key3*];[*order3*]}

The *key1*, *key2*, and *key3* arguments specify the field names to be used for the first, second, and third sort keys, respectively.

The *order1*, *order2*, and *order3* arguments specify the sort order—ascending or descending—for *key1*, *key2*, and *key3*, respectively. The arguments are enclosed in quotation marks. You must specify a sort order for each sort key.

If you do not specify any sort keys with the SORT command, 1-2-3 for Windows uses the existing defined sort keys. Use SORT-KEY-DEFINE to sort with more than three keys.

The SORT-KEY-DEFINE Command

The SORT-KEY-DEFINE command defines a sort key to be used in a subsequent SORT command. Use the following syntax for SORT-KEY-DEFINE:

  {SORT-KEY-DEFINE *key-number;key-field;key-order*}

The *key-number* argument is an integer (1 through 255) that specifies which sort key is being defined.

The *key-field* argument, which specifies the field name to be sorted for this key, is enclosed in quotation marks.

The *key-order* argument specifies the sort order—ascending or descending—for *key-field* and is enclosed in quotation marks.

The SORT-RESET Command

The SORT-RESET command clears all sort keys and ranges. Use the following syntax for SORT-RESET:

  {SORT-RESET}

The SORT-RESET command does not use any arguments.

Commands That Seek Solutions

The commands described in table 16.12 use the Solver and Backsolver tools to seek solutions to complex problems.

Table 16.12 Commands That Seek Solutions

Command	Action
BACKSOLVE	Finds values for one or more cells to produce a specified formula result
SOLVER-ANSWER	Displays Solver answers or attempts
SOLVER-ANSWER-SAVE	Saves the current answer or attempt as a scenario

Command	Action
SOLVER-DEFINE	Analyzes data in a worksheet and returns possible answers to a problem
SOLVER-DEFINE?	Displays the Solver Definition dialog box
SOLVER-REPORT	Creates a new file containing a report based on the current answer

The BACKSOLVE Command

The BACKSOLVE command finds values for one or more cells that make a formula equal to a specified value. Use the following syntax for BACKSOLVE:

> {BACKSOLVE *formula-cell*;*target-value*;*adjustable-range*}

The *formula-cell* argument specifies the name or address of the cell that contains the formula to be solved.

The *target-value* argument specifies the value that you want the formula to achieve.

The *adjustable-range* argument specifies the name or address of a range containing values that can change. The formula in *formula-cell* must depend directly or indirectly on the cells in *adjustable-range*.

The SOLVER-ANSWER Command

The SOLVER-ANSWER command displays the answers or attempts that Solver finds. Use the following syntax for SOLVER-ANSWER:

> {SOLVER-ANSWER *answer*}

The *answer* argument specifies which answer or attempt to display— next, first, original, or solve—and is enclosed in quotation marks.

After executing a SOLVER-ANSWER command, 1-2-3 returns to Ready mode.

The SOLVER-ANSWER-SAVE Command

The SOLVER-ANSWER-SAVE command saves the current answer or attempt as a scenario. Use the following syntax for SOLVER-ANSWER-SAVE:

> {SOLVER-ANSWER-SAVE *scenario*;[*comment*]}

The *scenario* argument, which specifies a name for the scenario, is enclosed in quotation marks.

The *comment* argument, which specifies a note for the scenario, is enclosed in quotation marks. If you omit *comment*, 1-2-3 uses the contents of the information box in the Solver Answer dialog box.

The SOLVER-DEFINE and SOLVER-DEFINE? Commands

The SOLVER-DEFINE command analyzes data and returns several possible solutions to a problem. Use the following syntax for SOLVER-DEFINE:

> {SOLVER-DEFINE [*adj-cells*];[*constraint-cells*];
> [*optimize*];[*opt-cell*];[*opt-type*];[*answers*]}

The SOLVER-DEFINE? command displays the Solver Definition dialog box. Use the following syntax for SOLVER-DEFINE?:

> {SOLVER-DEFINE? [*adj-cells*];[*constraint-cells*];
> [*optimize*];[*opt-cell*];[*opt-type*];[*answers*]}

The *adj-cells* argument, which specifies the names or addresses of the adjustable cells, is enclosed in quotation marks. You can use more than one range for *adj-cells* by separating the range names or addresses with argument separators.

The *constraint-cells* argument, which specifies the names or addresses of the constraint cells, is enclosed in quotation marks. You can use more than one range for *constraint-cells* by separating the range names or addresses with argument separators.

The *optimize* argument is a yes or no argument that specifies whether Solver should use *opt-cell*. The argument is enclosed in quotation marks.

The *opt-cell* argument specifies the name or address for which you want Solver to find the highest or lowest value. *Opt-cell* must depend directly or indirectly on the value of one or more cells in *adj-cells*.

The *opt-type* argument specifies the type of answer to be found: max or min, depending on whether you want the answer to obtain the largest or smallest possible value.

The *answers* argument is a value (1 through 999) that specifies the approximate number of answers you want.

After SOLVER-DEFINE? displays the Solver Definition dialog box and the user chooses OK, the Solver Progress dialog box appears while Solver analyzes the problem and looks for answers. When Solver finishes solving, the Solver Answer dialog box appears.

The **SOLVER-REPORT** Command

The SOLVER-REPORT command creates a new file that contains a report based on the current answer. Use the following syntax for SOLVER-REPORT:

{SOLVER-REPORT *type*;[*comp1*];[*comp2*];[*diff-value*]}

The *type* argument specifies the type of report to be created—answer, cells, differences, how, inconsistent, nonbinding, or what-if—and is enclosed in quotation marks (see table 16.13). You need not include *comp1*, *comp2*, or *diff-value* unless you specify differences for *type*.

Table 16.13 Report types

Type	Description
answer	Provides information about all the answers or attempts found for a problem
cells	Lists the adjustable, constraint, and optimal cells used to solve the problem
differences	Compares two answers or two attempts and reports cells used whose values differ by a specified amount
how	Lists the information used to find an answer or attempt
inconsistent	Provides information about constraint cells that were not satisfied
nonbinding	Provides information about constraint cells that were not binding
what-if	Lists the amount adjustable cells can change and still satisfy the constraints

The *comp1* argument specifies the first answer to be compared. The default is 1.

The *comp2* argument specifies the second answer to be compared. The default is 2.

The *diff-value* argument specifies a significant difference. The default is 0.

Commands That Manipulate Worksheet Styles

The commands described in table 16.14 adjust the appearance of 1-2-3 for Windows worksheets.

Table 16.14 Commands That Manipulate Worksheet Styles	
Command	**Action**
COLUMN-WIDTH	Adjusts columns to a specified width
COLUMN-WIDTH-FIT-WIDEST	Adjusts columns to fit their widest entries
COLUMN-WIDTH-RESET	Returns columns to the default width
HIDE-COLUMNS	Hides all columns in a range
HIDE-SHEETS	Hides all worksheets in a range
NAMED-STYLE-USE	Applies a named style to a range or query table
PAGE-BREAK-COLUMN	Inserts or deletes a vertical page break
PAGE-BREAK-ROW	Inserts or deletes a horizontal page break
PROTECT	Protects a range
RANGE-PROTECT	Use PROTECT
RANGE-UNPROTECT	Use UNPROTECT
ROW-HEIGHT	Adjusts rows to a specified height
ROW-HEIGHT-FIT-LARGEST	Adjusts rows to the height of the largest font
ROW-HEIGHT-RESET	Returns rows to the default height
SHOW-COLUMNS	Redisplays hidden columns
SHOW-SHEETS	Redisplays hidden worksheets
STYLE-ALIGN	Use STYLE-ALIGN-HORIZONTAL
STYLE-ALIGN-HORIZONTAL	Changes the horizontal alignment of labels and values
STYLE-ALIGN-ORIENTATION	Changes the orientation of data in a range

Command	Action
STYLE-ALIGN-VERTICAL	Aligns text within a cell whose height is greater than that of the largest typeface
STYLE-BACKGROUND-COLOR	Use STYLE-FONT
STYLE-BACKGROUND-PATTERN	Use STYLE-FONT
STYLE-BORDER	Controls borders for a range
STYLE-EDGE	Changes the color, style, and width of the edges of charts, chart elements, text blocks, drawn objects, OLE objects, and pictures created in other Windows applications
STYLE-FONT	Assigns a font to a range
STYLE-FONT-ALL	Assigns a font and adds boldface, italic, and underlining to a range
STYLE-FONT-ATTRIBUTES	Adds boldface, italic, or underlining to a range
STYLE-FONT-EMPHASIS	Use STYLE-FONT
STYLE-FONT-RESET	Restores to a range the default font, font size, attributes, and color
STYLE-FONT-SIZE	Assigns a point size to the fonts in a range
STYLE-FOREGROUND-COLOR	Use STYLE-FONT
STYLE-FRAME	Adds or removes a frame for a range
STYLE-GALLERY	Formats a range with one of 10 style templates
STYLE-INTERIOR	Adds colors and patterns to a range
STYLE-LINE	Changes the color, style, and width of the selected line for drawn lines and chart lines
STYLE-NUMBER-FORMAT	Sets the display of values
STYLE-NUMBER-FORMAT-RESET	Resets the format of a range to the default format
STYLE-TEXT-COLOR	Use STYLE-FONT
UNPROTECT	Removes protection for a range

The COLUMN-WIDTH and COLUMN-WIDTH-FIT-WIDEST Commands

The COLUMN-WIDTH command adjusts each column in a range to a specified width based on the default font and size. Use the following syntax for COLUMN-WIDTH:

{COLUMN-WIDTH *width*;[*range*]}

The COLUMN-WIDTH-FIT-WIDEST command adjusts each column in a range to the width of the widest entry in that column. Use the following syntax for COLUMN-WIDTH-FIT-WIDEST:

{COLUMN-WIDTH-FIT-WIDEST [*range*]}

The *width* argument is an integer that specifies the character width for the columns.

The *range* argument specifies the name or address of the range of columns to be adjusted. If you omit *range*, 1-2-3 uses the currently selected range, collection, or query table.

The COLUMN-WIDTH-RESET Command

The COLUMN-WIDTH-RESET command returns each column in a range to the default width. Use the following syntax for COLUMN-WIDTH-RESET:

{COLUMN-WIDTH-RESET [*range*]}

The *range* argument specifies the name or address of the range of columns to be adjusted. If you omit *range*, 1-2-3 uses the currently selected range, collection, or query table.

The HIDE-COLUMNS and HIDE-SHEETS Commands

The HIDE-COLUMNS command hides all columns in a range. Use the following syntax for HIDE-COLUMNS:

{HIDE-COLUMNS [*range*]}

The HIDE-SHEETS command hides all worksheets in a range. Use the following syntax for HIDE-SHEETS:

{HIDE-SHEETS [*range*]}

The *range* argument specifies the name or address of a range with at least one cell in each column or worksheet that you want to hide. If you omit *range*, 1-2-3 hides any column or worksheet that has cells in the currently selected range.

The NAMED-STYLE-USE Command

The NAMED-STYLE-USE command applies a named style to a range or query table. Use the following syntax for NAMED-STYLE-USE:

> {NAMED-STYLE-USE *style-name*;[*range*]}

The *style-name* argument specifies the name of the style to be applied.

The *range* argument specifies the name or address of the range to which you want to apply a named style. If you omit *range*, 1-2-3 uses the current selection.

The PAGE-BREAK-COLUMN and PAGE-BREAK-ROW Commands

The PAGE-BREAK-COLUMN command inserts or deletes a vertical page break to the left of the column containing the current cell. Use the following syntax for PAGE-BREAK-COLUMN:

> {PAGE-BREAK-COLUMN *on* | *off*}

The PAGE-BREAK-ROW command inserts or deletes a horizontal page break above the row containing the current cell. Use the following syntax for PAGE-BREAK-ROW:

> {PAGE-BREAK-ROW *on* | *off*}

The *on* | *off* argument, which specifies whether to insert (on) or delete (off) a page break, is enclosed in quotation marks.

The PROTECT Command

The PROTECT command turns on protection for an unprotected range. Use the following syntax for PROTECT:

> {PROTECT [*range*]}

The *range* argument specifies the name or address of the range that you want to protect. If you omit *range*, 1-2-3 uses the currently selected range or collection.

The ROW-HEIGHT and ROW-HEIGHT-FIT-LARGEST Commands

The ROW-HEIGHT command adjusts each row in a range to a specified height (in points). Use the following syntax for ROW-HEIGHT:

{ROW-HEIGHT *height*;[*range*]}

The ROW-HEIGHT-FIT-LARGEST command adjusts each row in a range to the height of the largest font in that row. Use the following syntax for ROW-HEIGHT-FIT-LARGEST:

{ROW-HEIGHT-FIT-LARGEST [*range*]}

The *height* argument is an integer (1 through 255) that specifies the row's height in points.

The *range* argument specifies the name or address of the range whose row height you want to adjust. If you omit *range*, 1-2-3 uses the currently selected range or query table.

The ROW-HEIGHT-RESET Command

The ROW-HEIGHT-RESET command returns each row in a range to the default height. Use the following syntax for ROW-HEIGHT-RESET:

{ROW-HEIGHT-RESET [*range*]}

The *range* argument specifies the name or address of the range of rows to be adjusted. If you omit *range*, 1-2-3 uses the currently selected range, collection, or query table.

The SHOW-COLUMNS and SHOW-SHEETS Commands

The SHOW-COLUMNS command redisplays all hidden columns in a range. Use the following syntax for SHOW-COLUMNS:

{SHOW-COLUMNS [*range*]}

The SHOW-SHEETS command redisplays all hidden worksheets in a range. Use the following syntax for SHOW-SHEETS:

{SHOW-SHEETS [*range*]}

The *range* argument specifies the name or address of a range that has at least one cell in each column or worksheet that you want to redisplay. If you omit *range*, 1-2-3 uses the currently selected range.

The STYLE-ALIGN-HORIZONTAL Command

The STYLE-ALIGN-HORIZONTAL command changes the horizontal alignment of labels and values in a range. Use the following syntax for STYLE-ALIGN-HORIZONTAL:

> {STYLE-ALIGN-HORIZONTAL *horizontal*;[*range*];
> [*over-cols*];[*wrap*]}

The *horizontal* argument specifies how to align data in a range—general, left, center, right, or evenly—and is enclosed in quotation marks.

The *range* argument specifies the name or address of the range to be adjusted. If you omit *range*, 1-2-3 uses the currently selected range.

The *over-cols* argument is a yes or no argument that specifies whether to align the text in the leftmost cell over the columns in a range. The argument is enclosed in quotation marks. If you omit *over-cols*, 1-2-3 does not align over columns.

The *wrap* argument is a yes or no argument that specifies whether labels should wrap to fit inside a single cell. The argument is enclosed in quotation marks. If you omit *wrap*, 1-2-3 does not wrap labels.

The STYLE-ALIGN-ORIENTATION Command

The STYLE-ALIGN-ORIENTATION command changes the orientation of data in a range. Use the following syntax for STYLE-ALIGN-ORIENTATION:

> {STYLE-ALIGN-ORIENTATION *orientation*;[*angle*];[*range*]}

The *orientation* argument is an offset number (0 through 4) that specifies an orientation style from the Style Alignment Orientation drop-down box.

The *angle* argument is an integer (1 through 90) that specifies the rotation angle if orientation is 4. The default is 45.

The *range* argument specifies the name or address of the range or query table in which you want to change the orientation of data. The default is the currently selected range, collection, or query table.

The STYLE-ALIGN-VERTICAL Command

The STYLE-ALIGN-VERTICAL command aligns text vertically within a cell. Use the following syntax for STYLE-ALIGN-VERTICAL:

> {STYLE-ALIGN-VERTICAL *vertical*;[*range*]}

The *vertical* argument specifies how to align data in range—top, center, or bottom—and is enclosed in quotation marks.

The *range* argument specifies the name or address of the range or query table in which you want to change the alignment of data. The default is the currently selected range, collection, or query table.

The STYLE-BORDER Command

The STYLE-BORDER command controls the borders for a range. Use the following syntax for STYLE-BORDER:

{STYLE-BORDER *border;display;[range];[color];[style]*}

The *border* argument specifies the border with which you want to work—outline, all, left, right, top, or bottom—and is enclosed in quotation marks.

The *display* argument is a yes or no argument that specifies whether to turn the display of the border on or off. The argument is enclosed in quotation marks. If *display* is off, 1-2-3 for Windows ignores *color* and *style*.

The *range* argument specifies the name or address of the range in which you want to work with borders. The default is the current selection.

The *color* argument is an offset number (0 through 15) that specifies a line color from the Style Lines & Color Line Color drop-down box.

The *style* argument is an offset number (0 through 7) that specifies a line style from the Style Lines & Color Line Style drop-down box.

The STYLE-EDGE and STYLE-LINE Commands

The STYLE-EDGE command changes the color, style, and width of the edges of charts, chart elements, text blocks, drawn objects, OLE objects, and pictures created in other Windows applications. Use the following syntax for STYLE-EDGE:

{STYLE-EDGE *[color];[style];[width];[arrowhead]*}

The STYLE-LINE command changes the color, style, and width of the selected line. Use the following syntax for STYLE-LINE:

{STYLE-LINE *[color];[style];[width];[arrowhead];*
[symbol]}

The *color* argument is an integer (0 through 255) that specifies a color in the color palette.

The *style* argument is an offset number (0 through 7) that specifies a line style from the Style Lines & Color Line Style drop-down box.

The *width* argument is an offset number (0 through 7) that specifies a line width from the Style Lines & Color Line Width drop-down box.

The *arrowhead* argument is an offset number (0 through 3) that specifies an arrowhead type from the Style Lines & Color Arrowhead drop-down box.

The *symbol* argument is an offset number (0 through 23) that specifies a data-point symbol from the Style, Lines & Color, and Symbol drop-down box.

The STYLE-FONT, STYLE-FONT-ALL, STYLE-FONT-ATTRIBUTES, STYLE-FONT-RESET, and STYLE-FONT-SIZE Commands

The STYLE-FONT command assigns a font to a range. Use the following syntax for STYLE-FONT:

> {STYLE-FONT *typeface*;[*range*];[*font-family*];
> [*character-set*]}

The STYLE-FONT-ALL command assigns a font and adds boldface, italic, and underlining to a range. Use the following syntax for STYLE-FONT-ALL:

> {STYLE-FONT-ALL [*typeface*];[*size*];[*bold*];[*italic*];
> [*underline*];[*range*];[*underline-style*];[*font-family*];
> [*character-set*]}

The STYLE-FONT-ATTRIBUTES command adds boldface, italic, or underlining to a range. Use the following syntax for STYLE-FONT-ATTRIBUTES:

> {STYLE-FONT-ATTRIBUTES *attribute*;*on-off*;[*range*];
> [*underline-style*]}

The STYLE-FONT-RESET command restores the worksheet default font, font size, attributes, and color to a range. Use the following syntax for STYLE-FONT-RESET:

> {STYLE-FONT-RESET [*range*]}

The STYLE-FONT-SIZE command assigns a point size to the fonts in a range. Use the following syntax for STYLE-FONT-SIZE:

> {STYLE-FONT-SIZE *size*;[*range*]}

The *typeface* argument, which specifies the name of the font that you want to assign, is enclosed in quotation marks.

The *range* argument specifies the name or address of the range to be changed. The default is the current selection.

The *font-family* argument specifies the font family—dontcare, decorative, modern, roman, script, or swiss—and is enclosed in quotation marks.

The *character-set* argument specifies the character set—ansi, oem, symbol, or kanji—and is enclosed in quotation marks.

The *size* argument is a value that specifies the point size that you want to assign.

The *bold*, *italic*, and *underline* arguments are yes or no arguments that add or remove boldface, italics, and underlining. These arguments are enclosed in quotation marks.

The *underline-style* argument is an offset number (0 through 2) that specifies an underline style from the Style Font & Attributes Underline drop-down box.

The *on-off* argument is a yes or no argument that specifies whether to add or remove *attribute*. The argument is enclosed in quotation marks. The attribute argument specifies the attribute that you want to add or remove—bold, italic, or underline—and is enclosed in quotes.

The STYLE-FRAME Command

The STYLE-FRAME command adds or removes a frame for a range. Use the following syntax for STYLE-FRAME:

> {STYLE-FRAME *display*;[*color*];[*style*];[*range*]}

The *display* argument is a yes or no argument that specifies whether to turn the display of the frame on or off. The argument is enclosed in quotation marks. If *display* is off, 1-2-3 for Windows ignores *color* and *style*.

The *color* argument is an integer (0 through 255) that specifies a color in the color palette. If *style* is 0 through 7, 1-2-3 for Windows ignores *color*.

The *style* argument is an offset number (0 through 15) that specifies a frame style from the Style Lines & Color Designer frame drop-down box.

The *range* argument specifies the name or address of the range to be changed. The default is the current selection.

The STYLE-GALLERY Command

The STYLE-GALLERY command formats a range with one of the 10 style templates. Use the following syntax for STYLE-GALLERY:

{STYLE-GALLERY *template*;[*range*]}

The *template* argument is an offset number (0 through 9) that specifies a template from the Style Gallery Template drop-down box.

The *range* argument specifies the name or address of the range to be changed. The default is the current selection.

The STYLE-INTERIOR Command

The STYLE-INTERIOR command adds colors and patterns to a range. Use the following syntax for STYLE-INTERIOR:

{STYLE-INTERIOR [*background-color*];[*pattern*];
[*pattern-color*];[*text-color*];[*negatives*];[*range*]}

The *background-color*, *pattern-color*, and *text-color* arguments are numbers (0 through 255) that specify colors from the color palette. The default is 0.

The *pattern* argument is an offset number (0 through 63) that specifies a pattern from the Style Lines & Color Pattern drop-down box. The default is 0.

The *negatives* argument is a yes or no argument that specifies whether to display, in red, negative values in a range or query table. The argument is enclosed in quotation marks.

The *range* argument specifies the name or address of the range to be changed. The default is the current selection.

The STYLE-NUMBER-FORMAT Command

The STYLE-NUMBER-FORMAT command sets the display of values in a range. Use the following syntax for STYLE-NUMBER-FORMAT:

{STYLE-NUMBER-FORMAT [*format*];[*decimals*];
[*parentheses*];[*range*]}

The *format* argument specifies the format to be assigned to the values in *range*: automatic, comma, currency, fixed, general, hidden, label, percent, scientific, text, +/–, dd-mmm, dd-mmm-yy, mmm-yy, date-long-international, date-short-international, hh:mm am/pm, hh:mm:ss am/pm, time-long-international, or time-short-international. The argument is enclosed in quotation marks.

The *decimals* argument is an integer (0 through 15) that specifies the number of decimal places. The default is 2.

The *parentheses* argument is a yes or no argument that specifies whether or not to enclose values in parentheses. The argument is enclosed in quotation marks.

The *range* argument specifies the name or address of the range to be formatted. The default is the current selection.

The STYLE-NUMBER-FORMAT-RESET Command

The STYLE-NUMBER-FORMAT-RESET command resets the format of a range to the current default format specified in Style Worksheet Defaults. Use the following syntax for STYLE-NUMBER-FORMAT-RESET:

{STYLE-NUMBER-FORMAT-RESET [*range*]}

The *range* specifies the name or address of the range to be reset. The default is the current selection.

The UNPROTECT Command

The UNPROTECT command turns off protection for a range. Use the following syntax for UNPROTECT:

{UNPROTECT [*range*]}

The *range* specifies the name or address of the range to be unprotected. The default is the current selection.

Commands That Manipulate Text Files

The commands described in table 16.15 enable macros to read from and write to text files.

Table 16.15 Commands That Manipulate Text Files	
Command	**Action**
CLOSE	Closes a text file and saves any changes
FILESIZE	Counts the number of bytes in an open text file
GETPOS	Reports the current byte-pointer position in the open text file

Command	Action
OPEN	Opens a text file for processing
READ	Copies bytes from the open text file to the worksheet
READLN	Copies lines from the open text file to the worksheet
SETPOS	Moves the byte pointer in an open text file
WRITE	Copies text to the open text file
WRITELN	Copies text to the open text file, and adds a carriage return and line feed

The CLOSE Command

The CLOSE command flushes the disk-write buffer and closes an open file. This command always should be the last line of a macro associated with an open file; if you are writing or modifying the file and do not close it, you can lose the last data written to the file. The syntax of CLOSE is as follows:

{CLOSE}

CLOSE does not use any arguments.

The FILESIZE Command

Another file-related command, FILESIZE, returns the length, in bytes, of the open file. The syntax of FILESIZE is as follows:

{FILESIZE *location*}

FILESIZE first records the size of the open file in the location specified by the *location* argument. The command then places the value of the open file's length (in bytes) in the cell indicated by *location*. The *location* argument can be a cell reference or range name. If *location* refers to a multicell range, 1-2-3 for Windows places the file size in the cell in the top left corner of the range.

The GETPOS Command

The GETPOS command enables you to record the current position of the file pointer. The syntax of GETPOS is as follows:

{GETPOS *location*}

GETPOS first records the position of the file pointer in the location specified by the *location* argument and then places the current position of the file pointer in the cell indicated by *location*. The *location* argument is a cell reference or a range name. If *location* points to a multicell range, 1-2-3 for Windows places the value of the file pointer in the top left corner of the range.

The OPEN Command

The OPEN command opens a text file for processing. Use the following syntax for OPEN:

{OPEN *file-name,access-type*}

The *file-name* argument specifies the full name of a text file, including the extension, or the name or address of a cell that contains a text file name. If *file-name* specifies a file name, the argument is enclosed in quotation marks.

The *access-type* argument specifies the type of access to be provided after the file is open: r (for read-only access), w (for write access), m (for modify access), or a (for append access). The argument is enclosed in quotation marks.

Only one text file can be open at a time. To work with more than one file in the application, you must open each file before using the file and then close the file again before opening and using the next file.

The OPEN command succeeds if it can open the file with the requested access mode. If the OPEN command succeeds, macro execution continues with the cell *below* OPEN. 1-2-3 for Windows ignores any commands that follow OPEN in the current cell.

The READ and READLN Commands

The READ command reads a specified number of characters from the currently open file, beginning at the current location of the file pointer. The characters read from the file are placed in the worksheet at the indicated cell location. The syntax of READ is as follows:

{READ *bytecount,location*}

The READLN command reads a line of characters from the currently open file, beginning at the current location of the file pointer. Use the following syntax for READLN:

> {READLN *location*}

READ copies from a file the number of characters indicated in *bytecount* to the *location* specified.

READLN copies from a file the next line of characters to the *location* specified, but does not copy the carriage-return and line-feed characters at the end of text lines.

The *bytecount* argument is a number (0 to 511) that specifies the number of bytes to be read, starting at the current position of the file pointer.

The *location* argument specifies the cell to be read into.

After the READ or READLN command executes, the file pointer is positioned on the character after the last character read.

The SETPOS Command

The SETPOS command moves the byte pointer in an open text file a specified number of bytes from the first byte in the file. Use the following syntax for SETPOS:

> {SETPOS *offset-number*}

The *offset-number* argument is an offset number that specifies the position in the file (relative to the first byte in the file) to which you want to move the byte pointer. The first byte is 0. SETPOS does not prevent you from placing the byte pointer past the end of a file.

The WRITE and WRITELN Commands

The WRITE command copies text to the open text file, starting at the current byte-pointer position. Use the following syntax for WRITE:

> {WRITE *text*}

The WRITELN copies text to the open text file, starting at the current byte-pointer position, and adds a carriage return and line feed. Use the following syntax for WRITELN:

> {WRITELN *text*}

The *text* argument specifies the text that you want to copy. The argument must be a string or a string formula. If *text* is a numeric value, the macro terminates with an error.

The byte-pointer position advances to the position following the last character written.

Tools Commands

Table 16.16 describes macro commands that work with add-ins, audit worksheets, spell-checking worksheets, and control SmartIcon sets.

Table 16.16 Tools Commands

Command	Action
ADDIN-INVOKE	Starts an add-in application
ADDIN-LOAD	Reads an add-in into memory
ADDIN-REMOVE	Removes an add-in from memory
ADDIN-REMOVE-ALL	Removes all add-ins from memory
AUDIT	Reports on formulas, circular references, file links, or DDE links
SMARTICONS-USE	Selects a set of SmartIcons
SPELLCHECK?	Launches spell checking

The ADDIN-INVOKE, ADDIN-LOAD, ADDIN-REMOVE, and ADDIN-REMOVE-ALL Commands

The ADDIN-INVOKE command starts an add-in application; the ADDIN-LOAD command reads an add-in into memory; the ADDIN-REMOVE command removes an add-in from memory; and the ADDIN-REMOVE-ALL command removes all add-ins from memory. Use the following syntax for these commands:

> {ADDIN-INVOKE *add-in*}
>
> {ADDIN-LOAD *add-in*}
>
> {ADDIN-REMOVE *add-in*}
>
> {ADDIN-REMOVE-ALL}

The *add-in* argument, which specifies the name of the add-in, is enclosed in quotation marks.

The AUDIT Command

The AUDIT command reports on formulas, the relationships of values and formulas, circular references, file links, or DDE links. Use the following syntax for AUDIT:

{AUDIT *audit;files;result*;[*report-range*];[*audit-range*]}

The *audit* argument specifies the object of the audit: formulas, precedents, dependents, circular, filelinks, or ddelinks. The argument is enclosed in quotation marks.

The *files* argument specifies the files to be audited—the currentfile or allopenfiles—and is enclosed in quotation marks.

The *result* argument specifies whether to highlight cells (the selection option) or produce a report (the report option). The argument is enclosed in quotation marks.

The *report-range* argument specifies the destination range for the report.

The *audit-range* argument specifies the range of cells to be audited.

The SMARTICONS-USE Command

The SMARTICONS-USE command selects a set of SmartIcons. Use the following syntax for SMARTICONS-USE:

{SMARTICONS-USE *set-name*}

The *set-name* argument, which specifies the name of the SmartIcon set to be selected, is enclosed in quotation marks.

The SPELLCHECK? Command

The SPELLCHECK? command launches spell checking. Use the following syntax for SPELLCHECK?:

{SPELLCHECK?}

The SPELLCHECK? command does not use any arguments.

Commands That Manipulate the User Environment

Table 16.17 describes commands that manipulate the user environment, display dialog boxes, accept user input, and modify menus.

Table 16.17 Commands That Manipulate the User Environment

Command	Action
?	Suspends macro execution until the user presses Enter; then enables the user to type any number of keystrokes
ALERT	Displays a message box and waits for the user to choose OK or Cancel
BREAKOFF	Disables Ctrl+Break while a macro is running
BREAKON	Restores the use of Ctrl+Break
CHOOSE-FILE	Displays a Windows common dialog box that contains a list of files and waits for the user to select one
CHOOSE-ITEM	Displays a dialog box that contains a list of data items; waits for the user to select one and then to choose OK or Cancel; and enters the index number for the user's choice in the worksheet
CHOOSE-MANY	Displays a dialog box and waits for the user to select one or more check boxes and then choose OK or Cancel
CHOOSE-ONE	Displays a dialog box and waits for the user to select an option and choose OK or Cancel; then runs the macro associated with the option
CHOOSEFILE	Uses CHOOSE-FILE
CHOOSEITEM	Uses CHOOSE-ITEM
CHOOSEMANY	Uses CHOOSE-MANY
CHOOSEONE	Uses CHOOSE-ONE
DIALOG	Displays a custom dialog box created with the Lotus Dialog Editor
DIALOG?	Displays a 1-2-3 dialog box and waits for the user to choose OK or press Enter

Command	Action
FORM	Suspends macro execution temporarily so that the user can enter and edit data in unprotected cells
FORMBREAK	Ends a FORM command
GET	Suspends macro execution until the user presses a key; then records the keystroke
GET-FORMULA	Displays a dialog box that contains a text box, and enters the data from the text box in the worksheet when the user chooses Cancel or OK
GET-LABEL	Displays a prompt and accepts any user input
GET-NUMBER	Displays a prompt and accepts numeric user input
GET-RANGE	Displays a prompt and accepts range input
GETLABEL	Use GET-LABEL
GETNUMBER	Use GET-NUMBER
LOOK	Checks the type-ahead buffer and records the first keystroke
MENU-COMMAND-ADD	Adds a command to a pull-down menu
MENU-COMMAND-DISABLE	Disables a command in a custom menu
MENU-COMMAND-ENABLE	Enables a command disabled with MENU-COMMAND-DISABLE
MENU-COMMAND-REMOVE	Removes a command from a pull-down menu
MENU-CREATE	Replaces the 1-2-3 menu bar with a customized menu bar
MENU-INSERT	Adds a custom pull-down menu to the default 1-2-3 menu bar, between the Tools and Window commands
MENU-RESET	Displays the default 1-2-3 menu bar
MENUBRANCH	Displays a dialog box that contains a list of menu commands; waits for the user to select one and then to choose OK or Cancel; and then branches to the macro instructions associated with the selected command

continues

Table 16.17 Continued

Command	Action
MENUCALL	Displays a dialog box that contains a list of menu commands; waits for the user to select one and then to choose OK or Cancel; and then performs a subroutine call to the macro instructions associated with the selected command
MENUCREATE	Uses MENU-CREATE
MENUINSERT	Uses MENU-INSERT
MENURESET	Uses MENU-RESET
PLAY	Plays a file with a WAV extension
WAIT	Suspends macro execution for a specified period
WGETFORMULA	Uses GET-FORMULA
WGETLABEL	Uses GET-LABEL
WGETNUMBER	Uses GET-NUMBER

The ? Command

The ? command pauses the program so that the user can use the keyboard or the mouse to enter any type of information or move the cell pointer around the worksheet. During the pause, no prompt appears. The macro hibernates until the user presses Enter. Program execution continues after the user presses Enter.

> **CAUTION:** Even though you press Enter after you type a ? entry, you still must include a tilde (~) for 1-2-3 for Windows to enter the information. 1-2-3 for Windows uses the press of the Enter key to continue macro execution. If the next macro command moves the cell pointer, the tilde is not necessary, because the cell-pointer movement enters the data.

Following is the syntax of ?:

    {?}

Be aware that the user can move the cell pointer while the ? command is in effect, so you never can be sure that ? will result in the correct placement of the user's information.

The ALERT Command

The ALERT command displays a message box and waits for the user to choose OK or Cancel. Use the following syntax for ALERT:

{ALERT *message*;[*buttons*];[*icon-type*];[*results-range*]}

The *message* argument, which specifies the text of the message to appear in the box, is enclosed in quotation marks.

The *buttons* argument is a number that specifies the buttons to be displayed in the dialog box: 1 for the OK button only, or 2 for both the OK and Cancel buttons.

The *icon-type* argument specifies the type of icon to be displayed in the message box—note, caution, or stop—and is enclosed in quotation marks.

The *results-range* argument specifies the name or address of a cell to store the number of the button selected by the user (1 for OK, 0 for Cancel). If you omit *results-range*, no result is saved. The number in *results-range* before an ALERT command determines which button is the default button in the message box.

The BREAKOFF and BREAKON Commands

The BREAKOFF command disables Ctrl+Break while a macro is running. The BREAKON command restores the use of Ctrl+Break. Ctrl+Break processing is restored automatically when the macro ends. Use the following syntax for BREAKOFF and BREAKON:

{BREAKOFF}

{BREAKON}

These commands do not use any arguments.

The CHOOSE-FILE, CHOOSE-ITEM, CHOOSE-MANY, and CHOOSE-ONE Commands

The CHOOSE-FILE command displays a Windows common dialog box that contains a list of files and waits for the user to make a selection.

The CHOOSE-ITEM command displays a dialog box that contains a list of data items, waits for the user to make a selection, and enters in the worksheet the index number for the user's choice.

The CHOOSE-MANY command displays a dialog box and waits for the user to select one or more check boxes.

The CHOOSE-ONE command displays a dialog box, waits for the user to select an option, and then runs the macro associated with the option.

Use the following syntax for these commands:

> {CHOOSE-FILE *file-type;results-range;title*}
>
> {CHOOSE-ITEM *list-range;results-range;prompt;title*}
>
> {CHOOSE-MANY *choices-range;results-range;prompt;title*}
>
> {CHOOSE-ONE *choices-range;results-range;prompt;title*}

The *file-type* argument specifies the type of files to be displayed in the dialog box: worksheet, all, or text. The argument is enclosed in quotation marks. The *file-type* argument also can use the wild-card characters * and ?.

The *results-range* argument specifies the name or address of a cell. For CHOOSE-FILE, if the user chooses OK, 1-2-3 stores the name of the file that the user selected. For CHOOSE-ITEM, 1-2-3 stores the index number of the item that the user selected. For CHOOSE-MANY, and CHOOSE-ONE, 1-2-3 stores 0 if the user chooses Cancel in the dialog box or 1 if the user chooses OK.

The *title* argument, which specifies the text that appears in the title bar of the dialog box, is enclosed in quotation marks.

The *list-range* argument specifies the name or address of a single-column range that contains the items displayed in the dialog box. The items must appear one per cell, in the order in which you want them to appear in the list. End the list of items in *list-range* with a blank cell or a cell that contains the value ERR or NA.

The *prompt* argument, which specifies the text that appears at the top of the dialog box, is enclosed in quotation marks.

The *choices-range* argument specifies the name or address of a range that contains descriptions of the check boxes or option buttons.

The DIALOG Command

The DIALOG command displays a custom dialog box created with the Lotus Dialog Editor. Use the following syntax for DIALOG:

> {DIALOG *range*}

The *range* argument specifies the name or address of the first cell in the dialog-description table.

The DIALOG? Command

The DIALOG? command displays a 1-2-3 for Windows dialog box and waits for the user to choose OK or press Enter. Use the following syntax for DIALOG?:

{DIALOG? *name*}

The *name* argument, which specifies the name of the dialog box to be displayed, is enclosed in quotation marks.

The *name* of a dialog box is the title that appears in the dialog-box title bar, but with hyphens substituted for spaces. To display the Freeze Titles dialog box, for example, use the command {DIALOG? "freeze-titles"}.

 NOTE To display the Sort and Name dialog boxes, you must indicate whether to display the range or query dialog box. For these dialog boxes, use one of the following as the *name* argument: Range-sort, Query-sort, Range-name, or Query-name.

The FORM Command

The FORM command suspends macro execution temporarily so that the user can enter and edit data in the unprotected cells in a specified location. Use the following syntax for FORM:

{FORM *input-location*;[*call-table*];[*include-list*];[*exclude-list*]}

The *input-location* argument specifies the range name or address of a range of any size that contains unprotected cells. This range, which cannot include any hidden columns or worksheets, is the range where the user enters data.

The *call-table* argument specifies the range name or address of a two-column range. The first column of the range contains keystroke-equivalent names; the second column contains the set of macro instructions to be performed when the specified key is pressed.

The *include-list* argument specifies the name or address of a range that contains a list of allowable keystrokes.

The *exclude-list* argument specifies the name or address of a range that contains a list of keystrokes to be ignored.

If you specify *include-list*, 1-2-3 for Windows ignores *exclude-list*.

The FORMBREAK Command

The FORMBREAK command ends a FORM command. Use the following syntax for FORMBREAK:

    {FORMBREAK}

The FORMBREAK command does not use any arguments. You should use this command only to end a FORM command.

The GET Command

The GET command suspends macro execution until the user presses a single key, and then records the keystroke as a left-aligned label in a specified location. Use the following syntax for GET:

    {GET *location*}

The *location* argument specifies the name or address of a cell or range. If *location* is a range, 1-2-3 for Windows places the keystroke in the first cell of the range.

Because GET records only a single keystroke, it cannot record user responses that require multiple key presses.

The GET-FORMULA, GET-LABEL, GET-NUMBER, and GET-RANGE Commands

The GET-FORMULA command displays a dialog box that contains a text box in which the user can enter up to 511 characters. When the user chooses OK, 1-2-3 for Windows enters enters the data in the worksheet as a label.

The GET-LABEL command displays a dialog box that contains a text box in which the user can enter up to 511 characters. When the user chooses OK, 1-2-3 for Windows enters the data in the worksheet as a label.

The GET-NUMBER command displays a dialog box that contains a text box in which the user can enter a number or numeric formula. When the user chooses OK, 1-2-3 for Windows enters the data in the worksheet as a number.

The GET-RANGE command displays a dialog box that contains a text box in which the user can enter a range name or address. When the user chooses OK, 1-2-3 for Windows enters the data in the worksheet as a label.

Use the following syntax for these commands:

{GET-FORMULA [*prompt*];*result*;[*default*];[*title*]}

{GET-LABEL [*prompt*];*result*;[*default*];[*title*]}

{GET-NUMBER [*prompt*];*result*;[*default*];[*title*]}

{GET-RANGE [*prompt*];*result*;[*default*];[*title*]}

The *prompt* argument, which specifies the text that appears at the top of the dialog box, is enclosed in quotation marks.

The *result* argument specifies the name or address of the range in which you want to store the user entry.

The *default* argument, which specifies the default entry in the text box, is enclosed in quotation marks. If you omit *default*, the text box is blank.

The *title* argument, which specifies the text that appears in the title bar of the dialog box, is enclosed in quotation marks. If you omit *title*, the title bar is blank.

The LOOK Command

The LOOK command checks the type-ahead buffer for keystrokes and records the first keystroke as a left-aligned label in a specified location. If the buffer is empty, 1-2-3 for Windows records an empty string. Use the following syntax for LOOK:

{LOOK *location*}

The *location* argument specifies the name or address of the cell or range in which you want to store the label.

The LOOK command does not pause a macro and is used to check for user input without removing the keystroke from the type-ahead buffer. If the user presses a key, use GET to remove the keystroke from the type-ahead buffer.

The MENU-COMMAND-ADD and MENU-COMMAND-REMOVE Commands

The MENU-COMMAND-ADD command adds a command to a pull-down menu, and the MENU-COMMAND-REMOVE command removes a command from a pull-down menu.

Use the following syntax for these commands:

{MENU-COMMAND-ADD *menu-description-range*; *menu-index*;*command-index*}

{MENU-COMMAND-REMOVE *menu-index*;*command-index*}

The *menu-description-range* argument specifies the name or address of the range that contains a description of the command to be added. The rows of *menu-description-range* must include the following:

Row 1	The name of the command
Row 2	A description of the command
Row 3	NA, 1, or a blank, to make the command appear dimmed, checked, or neither, respectively
Row 4	A blank cell
Row 5	Macro commands executed by the command

The *menu-index* argument is an integer that specifies which menu to add the command to or remove the command from, starting with 1 for the first menu.

The *command-index* argument is an integer that specifies where in the pull-down menu to add or remove the command. The integer corresponds to the position of a command in the pull-down menu, starting with 1 for the first menu item.

The MENU-COMMAND-DISABLE and MENU-COMMAND-ENABLE Commands

The MENU-COMMAND-DISABLE command disables (dims) a command in a custom menu, and the MENU-COMMAND-ENABLE command enables a command disabled with MENU-COMMAND-DISABLE.

Use the following syntax for these commands:

{MENU-COMMAND-DISABLE *menu-index*;*command-index*}

{MENU-COMMAND-ENABLE *menu-index*;*command-index*}

The *menu-index* argument is an integer that specifies which menu to add the command to or remove the command from, starting with 1 for the first menu.

The *command-index* argument is an integer that specifies where in the pull-down menu to add or remove the command. The integer corresponds to the position of a command in the pull-down menu, starting with 1 for the first menu item.

MENU-COMMAND-ENABLE and MENU-COMMAND-DISABLE work only with custom menus created with MENU-CREATE; you cannot disable commands in the default menu bar.

The MENU-CREATE Command

The MENU-CREATE command replaces the current 1-2-3 menu bar with a customized menu bar. Use the following syntax for MENU-CREATE:

{MENU-CREATE *menu-description-range*}

The *menu-description-range* argument specifies the name or address of the range that contains a description of each command name in the menu bar and points to a description of each command in the corresponding pull-down menu. The *menu-description-range* requires 4 rows and can be up to 10 columns wide (9 commands and a blank cell to end the list). The rows contain the following:

Row 1   The names of the commands in the menu bar. The row of commands ends with a blank cell or a cell that contains the value ERR or NA.

Row 2   A description of the commands.

Row 3   A blank cell to make a pull-down menu available, or NA to dim the pull-down menu.

Row 4   The range name or address of a *pulldown-menu-description* range for the corresponding command.

The *pulldown-menu-description* range contains a description of each command in a pull-down menu, requires five or more rows, and can be up to 25 columns wide (24 commands and a blank cell to end the list). The rows contain the following:

Row 1   The name of a command in the pull-down menu. End the list of menu commands with a blank cell or a cell that contains the value ERR or NA.

Row 2   A description of the commands.

Row 3   A value of NA if the command is to be dimmed; 1 if the command is to be checked; or a blank cell if the command is to be neither dimmed nor checked.

Row 4   Nothing; this row is blank.

Row 5   The macro commands to be executed when the user chooses the command.

The MENU-INSERT Command

The MENU-INSERT command adds a custom pull-down menu to the default 1-2-3 for Windows menu bar, between the Tools and Window commands. Use the following syntax for MENU-INSERT:

{MENU-INSERT *menu-description-range*}

The *menu-description-range* argument specifies the name or address of a range that contains a description of the command name to be inserted into the default 1-2-3 menu bar and points to a description of each command in the corresponding pull-down menu. The *menu-description-range* requires four rows and one column. The rows contain the following:

Row 1   The name of the pull-down menu.

Row 2   A description of the pull-down menu.

Row 3   A blank cell to make the pull-down menu available, or NA to dim the pull-down menu.

Row 4   The range name or address of a *pulldown-menu-description* range for the pull-down menu.

The *pulldown-menu-description* range contains a description of each command in a pull-down menu, requires five or more rows, and can be up to 25 columns wide (24 commands and a blank cell to end the list). The rows contain the following:

Row 1   The name of a command in the pull-down menu. End the list of menu commands with a blank cell or a cell that contains the value ERR or NA.

Row 2   A description of the commands.

Row 3   A value of NA if the command is to be dimmed; 1 if the command is to be checked; or a blank cell if the command is to be neither dimmed nor checked.

Row 4   Nothing; this row is blank.

Row 5   The macro commands to be executed when the user chooses the command.

The MENU-RESET Command

The MENU-RESET command restores the default 1-2-3 for Windows menu bar. Use the following syntax for MENU-RESET:

> {MENU-RESET}

The MENU-RESET command does not use any arguments.

The MENUBRANCH and MENUCALL Commands

The MENUBRANCH command displays a dialog box that contains a list of menu commands, waits for the user to select a command and then to choose OK or Cancel, and then branches to the selected macro.

The MENUCALL command displays a dialog box that contains a list of menu commands, waits for the user to select a command and then to choose OK or Cancel, and then performs a subroutine call to the selected macro.

Use the following syntax for these commands:

> {MENUBRANCH *location*}

> {MENUCALL *location*}

The *location* argument specifies the range name or address of the macro commands to be executed.

The PLAY Command

The PLAY command plays WAV (sound) files on systems equipped with soundboards or speaker drivers. Use the following syntax for PLAY:

> {PLAY *filename*}

The *filename* argument, which specifies the name of the .WAV file to be played (including the path and extension), is enclosed in quotation marks.

The WAIT Command

The WAIT command suspends macro execution for a specified period. Use the following syntax for WAIT:

> {WAIT *time-number*}

The *time-number* argument is a serial number specifying the time at which macro execution is to resume. Usually, *time-number* specifies a time serial number by adding a delay factor to the current time. To add the delay, the argument uses the formula @NOW+@TIME(*h,m,s*), where *h*, *m*, and *s* represent the hours, minutes, and seconds to delay.

Commands That Manage Scenarios

The commands described in table 16.18 use the 1-2-3 for Windows Version Manager to manage scenarios. These macro commands provide strong what-if capabilities.

Table 16.18 Commands That Manage Scenarios

Command	Action
RANGE-VERSION?	Provides access to Version Manager
SCENARIO-ADD-VERSION	Adds a version to a scenario
SCENARIO-CREATE	Creates a scenario
SCENARIO-DELETE	Deletes a scenario
SCENARIO-SHOW	Displays a selected scenario
VERSION-CREATE	Creates a new version
VERSION-DELETE	Deletes a specified version
VERSION-INDEX-MERGE	Copies versions and scenarios from another file
VERSION-INFO	Modifies style retention and sharing options for a version
VERSION-SHOW	Displays a selected version
VERSION-UPDATE	Updates an existing version with new data

The RANGE-VERSION? Command

The RANGE-VERSION? command provides access to Version Manager. Use the following syntax for RANGE-VERSION?:

{RANGE-VERSION? [*option*]}

The *option* argument, which specifies whether to close the Version Manager window or open it in either Manager or Index form, is enclosed in quotation marks. The options available in the window are on, off, manager, and index.

The SCENARIO-ADD-VERSION Command

The SCENARIO-ADD-VERSION command adds a version to a scenario. Use the following syntax for SCENARIO-ADD-VERSION:

> {SCENARIO-ADD-VERSION *scenario-name*;[*scenario-creator*];
> *version-range*;*version-name*;[*version-creator*]}

The *scenario-name* argument, which specifies the name of the scenario, is enclosed in quotation marks.

The *scenario-creator* argument, which specifies the name of the user who created the scenario, is enclosed in quotation marks.

The *version-range* argument specifies the name of the existing named range that contains the version to be added.

The *version-name* argument, which specifies an existing version of *version-range*, is enclosed in quotation marks.

The *version-creator* argument, which specifies the name of the user who created the version, is enclosed in quotation marks.

The SCENARIO-CREATE, SCENARIO-DELETE, and SCENARIO-SHOW Commands

The SCENARIO-CREATE command creates a new scenario.

The SCENARIO-DELETE command deletes a scenario.

The SCENARIO-SHOW command displays a selected scenario.

Use the following syntax for these commands:

> {SCENARIO-CREATE *name*;[*share*];[*comment*]}

> {SCENARIO-DELETE *name*;[*creator*]}

> {SCENARIO-SHOW *name*;[*creator*]}

The *name* argument specifies the name of the scenario. If *name* already exists, 1-2-3 for Windows creates a new scenario with the same name and a different date/time stamp.

The *share* argument specifies the sharing option for the version—unprotected, protected, or hidden—and is enclosed in quotation marks.

The *comment* argument, which specifies a comment about the scenario, is enclosed in quotation marks.

The *creator* argument specifies the name of the user who created the scenario and is used to determine which scenario to use or delete. The argument is enclosed in quotation marks. If you omit *creator*, 1-2-3 for Windows uses the most recently created scenario specified by *name*.

The VERSION-CREATE, VERSION-DELETE, VERSION-SHOW, and VERSION-UPDATE Commands

The VERSION-CREATE command creates a new version.

The VERSION-DELETE command deletes a specified version.

The VERSION-SHOW command displays a selected version.

The VERSION-UPDATE command updates an existing version with new data.

Use the following syntax for these commands:

{VERSION-CREATE *version-range*;*name*;[*share*];
[*retain-styles*];[*comment*]}

{VERSION-DELETE *version-range*;*name*;[*creator*]}

{VERSION-SHOW *version-range*;*name*;[*creator*];[*goto*]}

{VERSION-UPDATE *version-range*;*name*;[*creator*]}

The *version-range* argument specifies the name of the existing named range that contains the version.

The *name* argument, which specifies the name of the version, is enclosed in quotation marks. If you are creating a version and *name* already exists, 1-2-3 for Windows creates a new version with the same *name* and a different date/time stamp.

The *share* argument specifies the sharing option for the version—unprotected, protected, or hidden—and is enclosed in quotation marks.

The *retain-styles* argument is a yes or no argument that specifies whether to save style information with the version. The default is to save the style information. The argument is enclosed in quotation marks.

The *comment* argument, which specifies a comment about the version, is enclosed in quotation marks.

The *creator* argument specifies the name of the user who created the version and is used to determine which version to use or delete. The default is the most recently created version for the *version-range* specified by *name*. The argument is enclosed in quotation marks.

The *goto* argument is a yes or no argument that specifies whether to scroll to *version-range*. The argument is enclosed in quotation marks.

The VERSION-INDEX-MERGE Command

The VERSION-INDEX-MERGE command copies versions and scenarios into the current file. Use the following syntax for VERSION-INDEX-MERGE:

> {VERSION-INDEX-MERGE *source-file*;[*date-filter*];
> [*user-filter*]}

The *source-file* argument specifies the name of the file containing the versions and scenarios that you want to merge.

The *date-filter* argument specifies merging only those versions and scenarios created on or after a particular date. The *date-filter* is a date number or text that specifies the date in day-month-year, day-month, or Long International Date format.

The *user-filter* argument, which specifies merging only those versions and scenarios created or last modified by a particular user, is enclosed in quotation marks.

The VERSION-INFO Command

The VERSION-INFO command modifies style retention and sharing options for a version. Use the following syntax for VERSION-INFO:

> {VERSION-INFO *version-range*;*name*;[*creator*];
> [*share*];[*retain-styles*]}

The *version-range* argument specifies the name of a range that contains the version.

The *name* argument, which specifies the name of the version, is enclosed in quotation marks.

The *creator* argument specifies the name of the user who created the version and is used to determine which version to use. The default is the most recently created version for the *version-range* specified by *name*.

The *share* argument specifies the sharing option for the version—unprotected, protected, or hidden—and is enclosed in quotation marks.

The *retain-styles* argument is a yes or no argument that specifies whether to save style information with the version. The default is to save the style information. The argument is enclosed in quotation marks.

Commands That Enhance Programs

The commands described in table 16.19 can "dress up" a program by creating a better visual presentation or by speeding program execution.

Table 16.19 Commands That Enhance Programs

Command	Action
APP-ADJUST	Moves and sizes the 1-2-3 window
APP-STATE	Minimizes, maximizes, or restores the 1-2-3 window
BEEP	Sounds one of four tones
BREAK	Clears the edit line and returns to Ready mode
INDICATE	Displays text in the title bar
PANELOFF	Freezes the control panel
PANELON	Unfreezes the control panel and the status line
VIEW-ZOOM	Decreases or increases the display size of cells
WINDOW-ACTIVATE	Makes a specified window the active window
WINDOW-ADJUST	Moves and sizes the active window
WINDOW-ARRANGE	Sizes and arranges open windows
WINDOW-STATE	Minimizes, maximizes, or restores the active window
WINDOWSOFF	Suppresses screen updates while a macro is running
WINDOWSON	Restores normal screen updates
WORKSHEET-TITLES	Freezes or unfreezes columns along the top of the worksheet, rows along the left edge of the worksheet, or both

The APP-ADJUST Command

The APP-ADJUST command moves and sizes the 1-2-3 window. Use the following syntax for APP-ADJUST:

{APP-ADJUST *x;y;width;height*}

The *x* argument specifies the horizontal position, in pixels, measured from the left side of the screen to the left side of the 1-2-3 window.

The *y* argument specifies the vertical position, in pixels, measured from the top of the screen to the top of the 1-2-3 window.

The *width* argument specifies the window width, in pixels, from the left border to the right border.

The *height* argument specifies the window height, in pixels, from the top border to the bottom border.

You should set *x*, *y*, *width*, and *height* to prevent the window from moving partly or completely out of view. The correct settings depend on the current display mode. Standard VGA mode is 640 by 480 pixels.

The APP-STATE Command

The APP-STATE command minimizes, maximizes, or restores the 1-2-3 window. Use the following syntax for APP-STATE:

{APP-STATE *state*}

The *state* argument specifies the action to be taken—maximize, minimize, or restore—and is enclosed in quotation marks.

The BEEP Command

The BEEP command sounds one of four tones through the system speaker. Use the following syntax for BEEP:

{BEEP [*tone-number*]}

The *tone-number* argument is a value (1 through 4) that tells 1-2-3 which tone to sound.

The BREAK Command

The BREAK command clears the edit line or leaves the current dialog box, and returns to Ready mode. In any other situation, BREAK has no effect. Use the following syntax for BREAK:

{BREAK}

The BREAK command does not use any arguments.

The INDICATE Command

The INDICATE command displays text in the title bar. Use the following syntax for INDICATE:

{INDICATE [*text*]}

The *text* argument, which specifies the text to be displayed, is enclosed in quotation marks. To return the title bar to normal display, do not specify *text*.

The PANELOFF and PANELON Commands

The PANELOFF command freezes the control panel until 1-2-3 encounters a PANELON command or until the macro ends.

The PANELON command unfreezes the control panel and the status line.

Use the following syntax for these commands:

{PANELOFF}

{PANELON}

These commands do not use any arguments.

The VIEW-ZOOM Command

The VIEW-ZOOM command controls the display size of cells. Use the following syntax for VIEW-ZOOM:

{VIEW-ZOOM *how*}

The *how* argument, which specifies how to zoom, is enclosed in quotation marks. "In" increases the display by 10 percent to as large as 400 percent of normal size. "Out" decreases by 10 percent to as small as 25 percent of normal size. "Custom" restores the default display size.

The WINDOW-ACTIVATE Command

The WINDOW-ACTIVATE command makes a window the active window. Use the following syntax for WINDOW-ACTIVATE:

{WINDOW-ACTIVATE [*window-name*];[*reserved*];[*pane*]}

The *window-name* argument specifies the name of an open window as that name appears in the title bar. You do not have to include the file extension or path as part of *window-name* unless files with the same name but different extensions are open.

The *reserved* argument is a placeholder for compatibility with 1-2-3 for the Macintosh. You can omit *reserved* by including an extra argument separator.

The *pane* argument is an offset number (starting with 0) that specifies the pane you want to make current. The default is the current pane.

The WINDOW-ADJUST Command

The WINDOW-ADJUST command moves and sizes the active window. Use the following syntax for WINDOW-ADJUST:

{WINDOW-ADJUST *x;y;width;height*}

The *x* argument specifies the horizontal position, in pixels, measured from the left side of the 1-2-3 window to the left side of the window that you want to move.

The *y* argument specifies the vertical position, in pixels, measured from the top of the 1-2-3 window to the top of the window that you want to move.

The *width* argument specifies the window width, in pixels, from the left border to the right border.

The *height* argument specifies the window height, in pixels, from the top border to the bottom border.

You should set *x*, *y*, *width*, and *height* to prevent the window from moving partly or completely out of view. The correct settings depend on the current display mode. Standard VGA mode is 640 by 480 pixels.

The WINDOW-ARRANGE Command

The WINDOW-ARRANGE command sizes and arranges open windows. Use the following syntax for WINDOW-ARRANGE:

{WINDOW-ARRANGE *how*}

The *how* argument specifies how to arrange the open windows—stack or vertical-tile—and is enclosed in quotation marks.

The WINDOW-STATE Command

The WINDOW-STATE command minimizes, maximizes, or restores the active window. Use the following syntax for WINDOW-STATE:

{WINDOW-STATE *state*}

The *state* argument specifies what to do with the active window—maximize, minimize, or restore—and is enclosed in quotation marks.

The WINDOWSOFF and WINDOWSON Commands

The WINDOWSOFF command suppresses screen updates while a macro is running.

The WINDOWSON command restores normal worksheet display.

Use the following syntax for these commands:

{WINDOWSOFF}

{WINDOWSON}

The WINDOWSOFF and WINDOWSON commands do not use any arguments.

The WORKSHEET-TITLES Command

The WORKSHEET-TITLES command freezes or unfreezes columns along the top of the worksheet, rows along the left edge of the worksheet, or both. Use the following syntax for WORKSHEET-TITLES:

{WORKSHEET-TITLES *direction*}

The *direction* argument specifies which titles to freeze—horizontal, vertical, both, or none—and is enclosed in quotation marks.

Questions & Answers

This chapter has provided a reference to the macro command language contained in 1-2-3 for Windows. As you use these commands to build your applications, you may encounter some of the following questions.

Q: I already have a macro command program I developed in an earlier version of 1-2-3. What do I have to do to use that program in 1-2-3 Release 4 for Windows?

A: Because the macro command language has been greatly updated, you must use the 1-2-3 Macro Translator to convert your older version macros before using them in 1-2-3 Release 4 for Windows. While a few simple macros may still work without translation, it only takes a few minutes to translate your macros. Then you can be certain your macros will function correctly. See Chapter 15 for more information on the 1-2-3 Macro Translator.

Q: In the past I've always used commas as argument separators, but when I upgraded to 1-2-3 Release 4 for Windows, my macros generate syntax errors. What's wrong?

A: 1-2-3 Release 4 for Windows can use commas and semicolons, or periods and semicolons as argument separators. You may have your system configured to use periods and semicolons as argument separators. Use the Tools User Setup International Punctuation command to select your choice. Incidentally, you may want to make it a habit to always use semicolons as macro command argument separators—that way your macros can be used regardless of the Tools User Setup International Punctuation setting.

Q: Some of my macros don't work correctly. Instead of using the literal argument I specified, they seem to be using information from the worksheet as arguments. Why is this?

A: Literal arguments should be enclosed in quotes. If you forget to enclose a literal argument in quotes, 1-2-3 first tries to use the argument as the name of a range in the worksheet, and then uses the contents of that range as the argument.

Q: I just upgraded from 1-2-3 for DOS, but none of my Alt+*letter* macros will work. How do I use my macros?

A: Don't forget that 1-2-3 Release 4 for Windows uses the Ctrl key, not the Alt key to start macros. Just press Ctrl and the *letter* to run your macros.

Q: I created a complex macro, tested it, and it seemed to work just fine. When someone else started using my worksheet, my macros suddenly went wild, entering data in the wrong cells, and generally causing problems. What did they do to my masterpiece?

A: That's a tough question, but let's look at this carefully. Did you use range names exclusively, or did your macros ever refer to specific cell addresses? One of the most difficult problems to overcome is a macro which uses cell addresses does not correctly adjust when the worksheet is rearranged. Make certain your macros always use range names—never cell addresses.

If your macros use range names exclusively, but are still having problems, did you remember to create a separate worksheet for your macros? If your macros are on the same worksheet as the data, they can be destroyed or modified inadvertently when rows or columns are inserted or deleted. Other common operations, such as database queries, can also overwrite macros in the current worksheet.

Q: Someone gave me a 1-2-3 worksheet application which works pretty well, but I need to make a few changes to the macros. Unfortunately, every time I look at the macros, some of them are different. What's wrong with my eyes?

A: There's probably nothing wrong with your eyes, but there may be something wrong with the macros. In the past, some macro programmers used string formulas to create "self-modifying" macros that changed depending on values stored in worksheet cells. These types of macros are not only difficult to read, they can be deceptive, because they may change while a macro is running. If you need to create macros which use variable information, store the variable information in named ranges, and use those named ranges as macro command arguments.

Summary

In this chapter, you learned about the powerful macro command language contained in 1-2-3 for Windows. The commands described in this chapter enable you to create sophisticated applications that automate every aspect of 1-2-3 for Windows and make your worksheets much easier to use.

Chapter 17, "Using SmartIcons," shows you how to manipulate SmartIcons. You can use any of the commands introduced in this chapter to create and modify macros that you attach to custom SmartIcons.

Using SmartIcons

SmartIcons are on-screen buttons that you can use to make many 1-2-3 for Windows tasks easier and more automatic. Instead of moving through several layers of menus to choose commands, you can click a SmartIcon to initiate the action. You need a mouse to use SmartIcons; they cannot be accessed from the keyboard.

1-2-3 for Windows provides nearly 200 SmartIcons, which duplicate common menu commands or perform tasks for which no menu command exists. SmartIcons are grouped together into palettes that you can display on-screen. The standard palette (the one that appears at the top of the screen when you start 1-2-3) includes SmartIcons that perform a broad range of common tasks. You aren't limited, however, to the SmartIcons displayed in the standard palette; you can create custom SmartIcons to execute the macros that you create.

This chapter shows you how to use and customize 1-2-3's SmartIcons. Specifically, the chapter covers the following topics:

- Switching SmartIcon palettes

- Identifying the purpose of a SmartIcon

- Hiding and displaying SmartIcons

- Moving and rearranging SmartIcons

- Creating custom SmartIcons

- Creating custom SmartIcon palettes

Understanding SmartIcon Basics

To use a SmartIcon, place the mouse pointer on the SmartIcon and click the left mouse button once. This click invokes the SmartIcon's action. Depending on the purpose of the SmartIcon, you may want to select data or otherwise prepare the worksheet before clicking the SmartIcon.

If you are not sure what action is associated with a SmartIcon, use the right mouse button to click the SmartIcon; a description appears at the top of the screen, in the program's title bar. To see the description of another SmartIcon, hold down the right mouse button and move the mouse pointer to that SmartIcon.

T I P   The inside front and back covers of this book show the SmartIcons in the standard palettes.

Figure 17.1 shows the default Worksheet window SmartIcon palette that appears when you first install 1-2-3 for Windows.

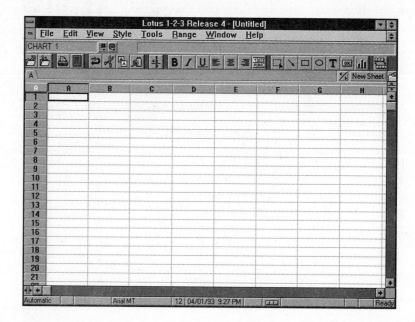

FIG. 17.1

The default worksheet window SmartIcon palette.

If you click on the first SmartIcon from the left in any of the standard palettes, you activate the Open File dialog box, in which you can select a worksheet file to open. To save your work, click the second SmartIcon in any of the standard palettes; this SmartIcon executes the File Save command.

Using the Standard SmartIcon Palettes

As you work in 1-2-3, you will notice that the SmartIcon palette changes from time to time, depending on your actions. Actually, 1-2-3 switches among four SmartIcon palettes. When you are working with ranges, the Default Sheet palette appears (see fig. 17.2). When you are working with a chart, the Default Chart palette appears (see fig. 17.3). When you are working with drawn objects in the worksheet, the Default Arrange palette appears (see fig. 17.4). When you are working with a query table, the Default Table palette appears (see fig. 17.5).

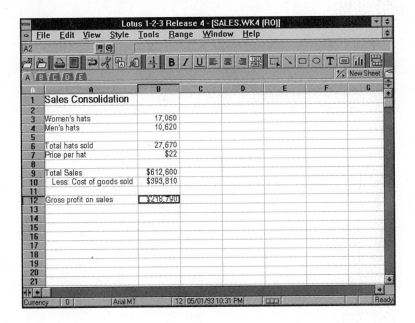

FIG. 17.2

The Default Sheet SmartIcon palette.

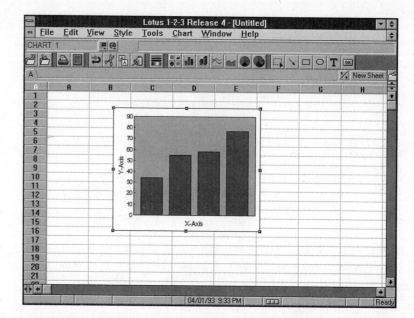

FIG. 17.3

The Default Chart
SmartIcon
palette.

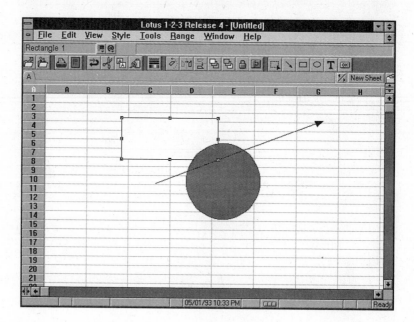

FIG. 17.4

The Default
Arrange
SmartIcon
palette.

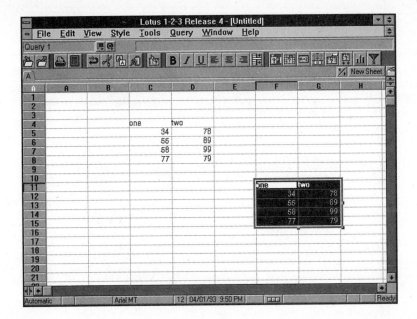

FIG. 17.5

The Default Table
SmartIcon
palette.

1-2-3 automatically switches among these SmartIcon palettes when the appropriate object is selected in the worksheet. As soon as you select a chart, for example, the Default Chart palette replaces the current palette. When you select a range or cell, the Default Sheet palette appears again.

Customizing the SmartIcons

Because 1-2-3 for Windows includes a large collection of standard and optional SmartIcons, you may find that the SmartIcon you want already exists but isn't in the default palette. Or you might want to combine several SmartIcons from different palettes into a single palette for convenience. 1-2-3 for Windows gives you several options for customizing the SmartIcon palette. You can add or remove SmartIcons, create your own named palettes, and even create your own SmartIcons.

The following sections describe the many ways in which you can customize the 1-2-3 for Windows SmartIcons to meet your needs.

Switching SmartIcon Palettes

Besides the default palettes, 1-2-3 provides optional SmartIcon palettes. You can switch among the optional palettes in several ways. First, you can click the SmartIcons selector in the status bar at the bottom of the screen. When you click this button, a list of optional palettes appears (including any custom palettes that you have created). Figure 17.6 shows this list.

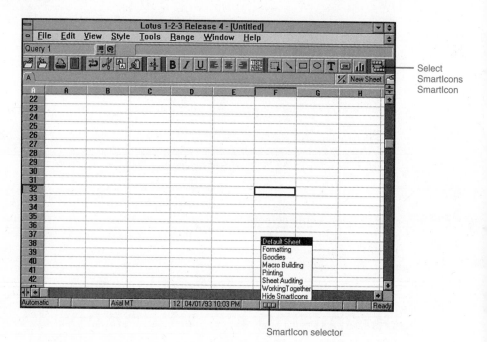

Select
SmartIcons
SmartIcon

SmartIcon selector

FIG. 17.6

The SmartIcon
list.

Select the desired palette from this list, and 1-2-3 immediately replaces the current palette with the one you selected. You can switch among these palettes at any time.

NOTE   You cannot access the default palettes (other than the current one) from the palette list.

 The second way to switch among SmartIcon palettes is to click on the Select SmartIcons SmartIcon, which appears at the far right end of some palettes (shown in fig. 17.6). Clicking this SmartIcon cycles through the SmartIcon sets in the palette list.

The third way to switch among SmartIcon palettes is to use the Tools SmartIcons command. Follow these steps:

1. Choose Tools SmartIcons to access the SmartIcons dialog box (see fig. 17.7).

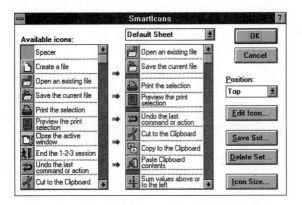

FIG. 17.7

The SmartIcons
dialog box.

2. Click the drop-down list at the top of the dialog box. This list contains the names of all SmartIcon palettes.

3. Select the desired palette.

4. Click OK or press Enter.

Changing the Position of the Palette

You can move the SmartIcon palette around the screen if you don't like its position. You can position the palette on any side of the screen or make it "float" within the program window. To move the palette, follow these steps:

1. Choose Tools SmartIcons to access the SmartIcons dialog box.

2. Click the Position drop-down list to display a list of positions (Floating, Left, Top, Right, and Bottom).

3. Select the desired position.

4. Click OK or press Enter.

If you choose the Floating option, you can click any area of the palette and then drag the palette around the screen. You also can change the size and shape of the palette by dragging its borders. If you want to close a floating palette, simply click on its control menu (the upper-left corner of the palette window) and the palette disappears. Figure 17.8 shows a floating SmartIcon palette.

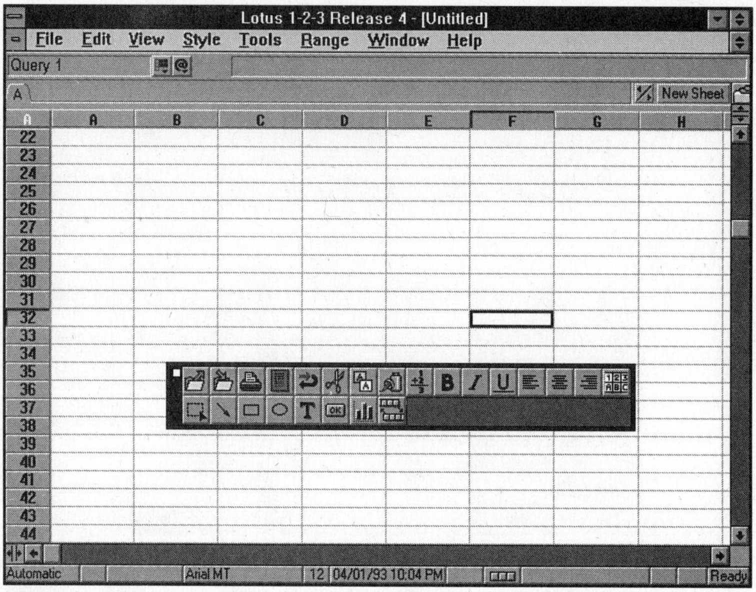

FIG. 17.8

A floating
SmartIcon
palette.

Even with the Worksheet window expanded to maximum size, the floating SmartIcon palette overlays the window and hides some data. One great advantage of using a floating palette, however, is that you can expand it to accommodate any number of SmartIcons—more than the default palette.

The Left and Right options provide less space for SmartIcons. Even the default SmartIcon palette is too large, and some SmartIcons at the end of the palette are not displayed.

Hiding the Palette

One of the options in the palette list (the list that appears when you click the SmartIcon selector in the status bar) is Hide SmartIcons. This option removes the SmartIcon palette from the screen. You may want to hide the palette when you require maximum screen space for a worksheet.

After hiding the palette, you can show it again by choosing the Show SmartIcons option from the same list. You also can hide the SmartIcon palette by using the View Set View Preferences SmartIcons command.

Rearranging SmartIcons in a Palette

If you don't like the arrangement of SmartIcons in a palette, you can rearrange them to suit your needs. Rearranging SmartIcons is simple: hold down the Ctrl key as you click a SmartIcon in the palette, drag the SmartIcon to a new position, and then release both the mouse button and the Ctrl key. Figure 17.9 shows a SmartIcon being moved in the palette at the top of the Worksheet window.

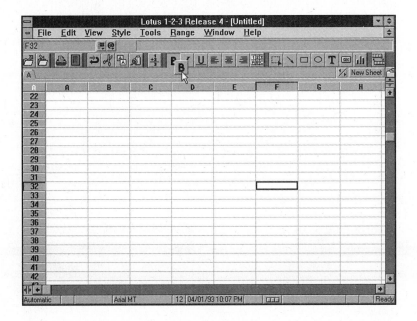

Moving a
SmartIcon with
Ctrl+click and
drag.

> If you Ctrl+click and drag the SmartIcon off the palette, 1-2-3 moves the SmartIcon to the end of the palette.
>
> **T I P**

Another way to move SmartIcons is to click the Rearrange SmartIcons SmartIcon and begin dragging icons around the screen. When finished, press the Escape key to return to normal.

Adding and Removing SmartIcons

To add or remove a SmartIcon in a SmartIcon palette, follow these steps:

1. Choose Tools SmartIcons to access the SmartIcons dialog box (refer to fig. 17.7).

2. In the drop-down list at the top of the dialog box, select the SmartIcon palette that you want to modify. The SmartIcons in the selected palette appear below the name of the palette.

3. In the Available Icons list, locate the SmartIcon that you want to add.

4. Click the SmartIcon, drag it across to the palette list, and then release the mouse button. The SmartIcon appears in the palette where you dropped it.

   To remove a SmartIcon from a palette, drag it out of the palette list.

Figure 17.10 shows a SmartIcon being moved into the list for the Default Sheet palette. (You can change the order of the SmartIcons by dragging them in the palette list.)

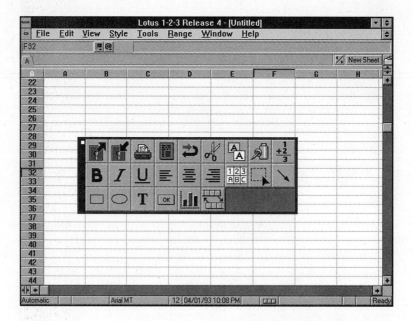

FIG. 17.10

Moving a SmartIcon to the current palette.

Use the Spacer SmartIcon (at the top of the Available Icons list) to separate SmartIcons into groups within a palette. You can use as many spacers as you want.

T I P

If you want to save the changes you made in a set of SmartIcons, follow these steps:

1. Click <u>S</u>ave Set in the SmartIcons dialog box. 1-2-3 for Windows displays the Save Set of SmartIcons dialog box.

2. If you want to change the name of the SmartIcon set, type a new name in the <u>N</u>ame of Set text box.

3. If you want to change the file name, type a new file name in the <u>F</u>ile Name text box. (Each SmartIcon set is stored on disk under a file name with the extension SMI.)

4. Click OK to close the Save Set of SmartIcons dialog box. You return to the SmartIcons dialog box.

5. Click OK to close the SmartIcons dialog box and return to the worksheet.

If you save your changes, the new version of the palette will be available the next time you use 1-2-3 for Windows. You can change the palettes provided by 1-2-3 or create new ones, depending on whether you keep the same set and file names or enter new ones.

Creating a New Palette

Creating a new SmartIcon palette is a simple variation on the procedure described in the preceding section. Use the SmartIcons dialog box to group the desired SmartIcons into the current set (you can start with any set). Add and remove SmartIcons from that set as desired. Then use the <u>S</u>ave Set option to provide a new set name and file name for the palette. The new palette appears in the palette list along with the others.

 NOTE You can delete SmartIcon palettes by using the <u>D</u>elete Set button in the SmartIcons dialog box. This button deletes the set that currently is selected in the list.

Changing the Size of SmartIcons

You can display SmartIcons in two sizes: medium and large. By default, 1-2-3 for Windows displays medium SmartIcons. To display large SmartIcons, follow these steps:

1. Choose Tools SmartIcons to access the SmartIcons dialog box.

2. Click the Icon Size button to access the Icon Size dialog box.

3. Click Large.

4. Click OK to close the Icon Size dialog box. You return to the SmartIcons dialog box.

5. Click OK to close the dialog box and return to the worksheet.

NOTE   To return to medium size, repeat the preceding steps, but click on Medium in step 3.

Figure 17.11 shows the Default Sheet SmartIcons in a large floating palette. Notice that some SmartIcons change when you display them in a larger size; the pictures become more detailed. Large SmartIcons are usually best on super VGA monitors, but can be useful in other situations.

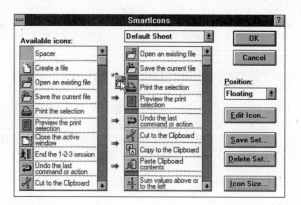

FIG. 17.11

The Default Sheet SmartIcon palette displayed large.

Creating SmartIcons

Although nearly 200 SmartIcons are supplied with 1-2-3 for Windows, the most interesting feature of SmartIcons is your capability to create custom SmartIcons. You can assign to a SmartIcon any 1-2-3 for Windows task that can be performed by a macro—for example, placing your name and address in a worksheet. Another SmartIcon could perform a more complex task, such as combining data from several files and printing a report that includes the latest sales figures and a chart. The possibilities are endless.

One good use for custom SmartIcons is to automate a worksheet application that you create and distribute to other users in your company. Instead of a standard SmartIcon, such as one that prints a range, your application can have a SmartIcon that prints all the ranges of a standard company report. You can create another SmartIcon that uses the FORM macro command to automate data input.

Understanding Custom SmartIcons

Unlike the standard and optional SmartIcons provided with 1-2-3 for Windows, custom SmartIcons can be modified. You can control their appearance and actions.

Custom SmartIcons are made up of two parts: a Windows 3.x bitmap file, which contains the image you see on the button; and a text file, which contains the macro actions to be performed when the custom SmartIcon is selected. Both files have the same name, but the bitmap file uses a BMP extension and the text file uses a MAC extension.

When you install 1-2-3 for Windows, special directories are created under the \123R4W\PROGRAMS directory. Many of these directories contain the various SmartIcon files required for SmartIcon palettes, including the MAC files, the BMP files, and the SMI files.

Because the various SmartIcons are stored in different directories, based on their palettes, you can use the same names for different SmartIcons, provided that those SmartIcons appear in different palettes (i.e., in different directories). If you want to add the same custom SmartIcon to two or more SmartIcon palettes, you must place copies of the corresponding macro and bitmap file in both directories. Details for adding SmartIcon files are covered in the next few sections.

Creating SmartIcon Images

A Windows 3.x bitmap file is a special type of image file used by many Windows 3.x programs. Windows Paintbrush (a standard accessory provided with Windows 3.x) uses the Windows 3.x bitmap image format by default. You can use Paintbrush or any other Windows bitmap paint package to create or edit SmartIcon files, but in this section, you learn how to use 1-2-3's icon editor.

To create the SmartIcon image file, follow these steps:

1. Choose Tools SmartIcons to display the SmartIcons dialog box.

2. Choose Edit Icon. The Edit Icon dialog box appears.

3. Choose the New Icon button to start a new icon from scratch. You are presented with a Save dialog box where you can enter a name for the new icon.

4. Type a name (including a directory path if desired) for the new icon. Remember to specify the desired directory inside the 123R4W\PROGRAMS directory for the image. After you specify the name, a blank edit screen appears along with a blank icon in the Available Icons list (see fig. 17.12).

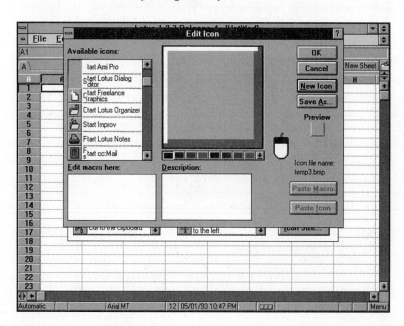

FIG. 17.12

Creating a new SmartIcon in the icon editor.

5. Click on the arrow beside the color palette to view more colors for your drawing. Click on any color to select it. The selected color appears in the mouse icon to the right of the color palette to confirm your selection.

6. Use the mouse to draw in the edit area using the color you selected. You can erase parts of your image by selecting the background color and drawing over existing colors.

When you finish editing the image, you're ready to add a description and macro to the SmartIcon. The following section explains this procedure. If you are following along in 1-2-3, keep the Edit Icon dialog box open for the next procedure.

You can create new icons by using existing icon images as a starting point. Just select the image in the Available Icons list box (on the left side of the Edit Icon dialog box), enter a name for the new image, and then use the edit area to change the original.

T I P

Creating the Macro for Your Custom SmartIcon

Before you assign a macro to a custom SmartIcon, create and test the macro in a 1-2-3 for Windows worksheet. When your macro is complete, ensure that it runs properly by using the Tools Macro Run command. When you edit the SmartIcon image, you can apply the macro to the icon using one of three methods.

First, you can simply type the macro commands directly into the Edit Macro Here text box in the Edit Icon dialog box. Type the macro exactly as it appears in the worksheet when you tested it. Be sure to type a description into the Description text box before you return to the worksheet.

Another way to attach macros to your icons is to refer to macros in your worksheets. This is useful when your macros are long or complex. Simply enter the macro command {BRANCH *macroname*} into the Edit Macro Here text box, where *macroname* is a reference to the macro in the worksheet. The worksheet containing the macro you reference must be active when you click this icon in the future.

A final way to attach a macro to your custom icon is to copy it from the worksheet. Follow these steps to complete this procedure:

1. Highlight the entire macro, then choose the Edit Copy command.

2. Select Tools SmartIcons and choose Edit Icon to return to the Edit Icon dialog box.

3. Select the new icon from the Available Icons list. Any icon you created will appear in this list.

4. Place the mouse pointer (cursor) into the Edit Macro Here text box and click once.

5. Press Ctrl+V or choose <u>E</u>dit <u>P</u>aste to paste the macro into place.

6. Type a description for the macro into the <u>D</u>escription text box.

Figure 17.13 shows a sample macro that enters a name and address in the worksheet, formats the new text as bold, and moves the cell pointer. Although this macro is relatively simple, the macros that you assign to custom SmartIcons do not have to be simple.

NOTE You are limited to 512 characters in the Edit Macro Here text box. If your macro requires more space, use the {BRANCH *macroname*} command to access a macro stored on a worksheet.

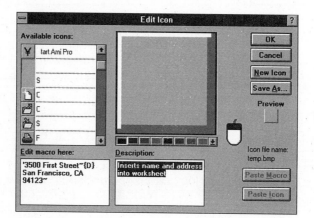

FIG. 17.13

A sample macro to be assigned to a custom SmartIcon.

NOTE When you enter a macro, remember that 1-2-3 requires numbers to have a label prefix if those numbers are part of a label. In cell A:A2 of the sample macro, for example, two apostrophes appear in front of the address. 1-2-3 treats the first ' as a label prefix in the worksheet and stores the second ' in the macro. The macro enters the second ' when it runs, to make the address a label. If you use only one ' when you enter the macro in the worksheet, the macro fails to complete its task because it does not enter a label prefix before the address.

When you finish editing the image and entering the macro and description, choose the Save <u>A</u>s button and enter a name for the SmartIcon. You now can return to the SmartIcons dialog box and add the custom SmartIcon to any palette, as described previously.

> You can view the macro associated with any existing SmartIcon (and
> even copy the macro) by selecting the SmartIcon in the Edit Icon
> dialog box. The macro attached to the SmartIcon appears in the Edit
> Macro Here text box.

T I P

Distributing Custom Icon Files

SmartIcons are stored in palettes; each palette is stored as a file on
disk with the SMI extension. Application developers can distribute copies of these files with their applications to control which SmartIcons
are displayed.

If you distribute copies of SMI files, be certain to copy them into the
C:\123R4W\PROGRAMS\SHEETICO directory of the destination com-
puter. The copy of 1-2-3 running on that computer will use the
SmartIcons that you distributed.

Questions & Answers

This chapter showed you how to use and customize 1-2-3's SmartIcons.
Specifically, the chapter covered switching SmartIcon palettes, identifying the purpose of a SmartIcon, hiding and displaying SmartIcons,
moving and rearranging SmartIcons, creating custom SmartIcons, and
creating custom SmartIcon palettes.

Q: Some of the SmartIcons I added to the palette are not appearing
on-screen. What should I do?

A: If you added more SmartIcons than the palette can display across
the top of the screen (or along the side), 1-2-3 truncates the palette. To display all your SmartIcons, choose Tools SmartIcons
Position Floating.

Q: The macro I assigned to the icon is not running when I click the
icon. What's wrong?

A: You may have used the {BRANCH *macroname*} command incorrectly. Check that your macro is properly reference by name, including the worksheet name if the macro appears on a different
sheet. Also, if the macro appears on a different sheet, that
worksheet must be active when you click the icon. For this reason, it's best to branch to macros that exist on the worksheet that
will be using the icon you developed.

Q: Can I use existing artwork for my icon images?

A: Yes. The best way is to open one of the BMP icon files into a paint program (such as PrintBrush), then copy existing artwork into the existing image. This gives you the proper size and proportions for your image. You can save the new BMP file directly into one of the SmartIcon directories inside the 123R4W\PROGRAMS directory to specify on which palette it belongs.

Summary

SmartIcons make 1-2-3 for Windows easy to use, providing shortcuts to commonly used commands and options so that you need not remember how to access a particular command. You can create your own SmartIcons and SmartIcon palettes.

In the next chapter, you learn how to integrate the following Lotus Windows applications: 1-2-3 for Windows, Freelance Graphics for Windows, and Ami Pro for Windows.

Integrating Lotus Windows Applications

B ack when most programs ran on DOS without the benefit of Windows, getting work from one program to another was difficult, if not impossible. Even when a transfer was conceivable, you often had to export work to a file, convert the file with a second program, and then import the converted work into the final destination software. To use a simple spreadsheet of numbers in a report created in a word processor, for example, you had to export the numbers as an ASCII print file, convert the space-separated columns into tab-separated columns, and then import the ASCII file into a document.

Among all the other benefits that Windows provides, easy communications among applications makes it possible to create work in one application and then freely use it in another. You can create a logo in a graphics program and quickly transfer it to a word processor or spreadsheet. You also can use the numbers in a spreadsheet to create a graph you then can incorporate in a printed report.

Passing work among applications easily is only the beginning. Windows makes it possible to set up and maintain active links between the work in the original application and the copies you transfer to other applications. These links communicate any changes you make to the work, so the work is updated automatically in every application to which it has been copied. The result is an integrated system that lets you stay within the domain of each application, but still combines the output of several applications to accomplish a task. You can use the data-analysis powers of a spreadsheet, the visual-representation capabilities of a graphics program, and the presentation powers of a word processor—all to create a monthly report.

The ability to link applications provides several other benefits. First, you can revise work in the application in which it originally was made and know that the revision will appear in every other instance of the work. You need not find the work in every place it appears and make the same update over and over. Second, you can be confident that the original and its copies remain synchronized. Third, you virtually eliminate any chance of inadvertent human error that can cause discrepancies from one set of data to another. Nobody needs to retype the numbers from a spreadsheet into a word processor, for example.

This chapter describes how you can combine the best features of 1-2-3 Release 4 for Windows with strengths of the other Lotus Windows applications in the SmartSuite bundle that contains 1-2-3 for Windows, the presentation graphics program Freelance Graphics for Windows, and the Windows word processor Ami Pro. The chapter describes the technical features of Windows that make such tight integration possible and offers real-world examples of how you can use the Lotus SmartSuite applications together. The general techniques you will learn also work for other Lotus Windows applications such as Lotus Improv and Windows applications from other software makers.

This chapter covers how you can integrate the following Lotus applications with 1-2-3 for Windows:

- Lotus Freelance Graphics for Windows 2.0.

- Ami Pro for Windows 3.0

Only these releases of the software are capable of the object linking and embedding techniques described in this chapter.

Understanding the Techniques

To transfer data from one Windows application to another, you can perform a simple copy and paste, or you can use the more sophisticated commands of Object Linking and Embedding (OLE). These techniques are described in the following sections.

Using the Clipboard for Basic Copying and Pasting

All Windows applications share a common Clipboard that can transfer virtually anything from one Windows application to another. In this book, you have already learned how to use the Windows Clipboard to copy and paste 1-2-3 data between cells or between worksheets. The same principle lets you copy and paste information between different applications. You can copy a range of cells from 1-2-3 into an Ami Pro document, for example. Or you can copy a corporate logo created in Freelance Graphics for Windows to a 1-2-3 worksheet so that the logo appears on a worksheet printout.

When you use the Clipboard to copy and paste work from one application to another, you end up with two unrelated objects: the original in the application in which it was made and the duplicate, in another application, with no ties that link it to the original. If you modify the original, the duplicate remains unchanged. Often, this arrangement is perfectly satisfactory. Your corporate logo has not changed in years, for example, and no changes are anticipated for years more. After you create the logo in Freelance Graphics for Windows, you copy and paste it to a worksheet to be printed, examined one time, and then filed. In this case, setting up a link between the original in Freelance and the copy in 1-2-3 would be wasted effort. You have no need to ensure that any changes to the corporate logo are updated in the worksheet.

To perform such a simple copy and paste, you select the item to be copied in the first application and use the Edit Copy command to copy the item to the Windows Clipboard. Then you switch to the second application and use the Edit Paste command to retrieve the item from the Windows Clipboard.

To copy a table of numbers from a 1-2-3 worksheet to an Ami Pro letter, for example, follow these steps:

1. In 1-2-3, select the range of cells to copy to the document you have open in an Ami Pro window (see fig. 18.1).

2. From the 1-2-3 menu, select Edit Copy, press Ctrl+C or Ctrl+Ins, or click on the Copy SmartIcon.

3. Switch to Ami Pro by using Alt+Tab or Ctrl+Esc, or by clicking on the Ami Pro SmartIcon.

4. Click in the Ami Pro document where you want the table to appear.

5. From the Ami Pro menu, select Edit Paste, press Ctrl+V or Shift+Ins, or click on the Paste SmartIcon. The range of numbers appears in an Ami Pro table, as shown in figure 18.2.

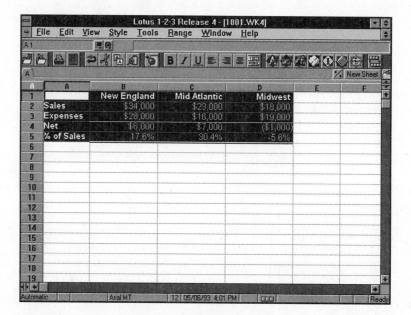

FIG. 18.1

Selecting a range of cells to copy in 1-2-3.

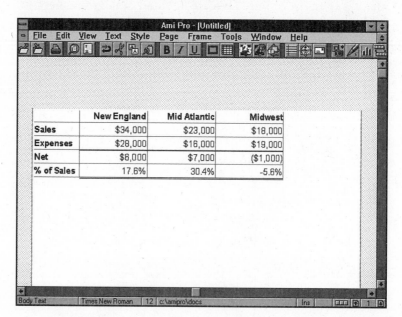

FIG. 18.2

The table of numbers pasted into Ami Pro.

Here's another example of a simple copy and paste. In this example, you copy a logo created in Freelance Graphics for Windows to a 1-2-3 worksheet. After the logo is created in Freelance, follow these steps:

1. In Freelance, select the logo you want to copy to a worksheet that is open in a 1-2-3 window (see fig. 18.3). If the logo is composed of a number of objects, you may want to group the objects before selecting the group by selecting them and then selecting Arrange Group.

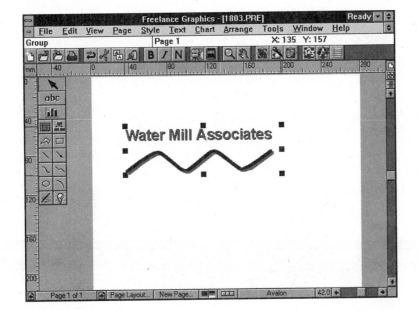

FIG. 18.3

The logo selected in Freelance Graphics for Windows.

2. From the Freelance menu, select Edit Copy, press Ctrl+C or Ctrl+Ins, or click on the Copy SmartIcon.

3. Switch to 1-2-3 for Windows by using Alt+Tab or Ctrl+Esc, or by clicking on the 1-2-3 SmartIcon.

4. Click on a cell that marks the upper-left corner of the location for the logo.

5. From the 1-2-3 menu, select Edit Paste, press Ctrl+V or Shift+Ins, or click on the Paste SmartIcon. The logo appears in the selected cell in the 1-2-3 worksheet, as shown in figure 18.4.

6. Position the pointer on a corner handle of the logo and drag diagonally out from the center to increase the size of the logo. Figure 18.5 shows how to increase the size of the logo to fit properly on the page.

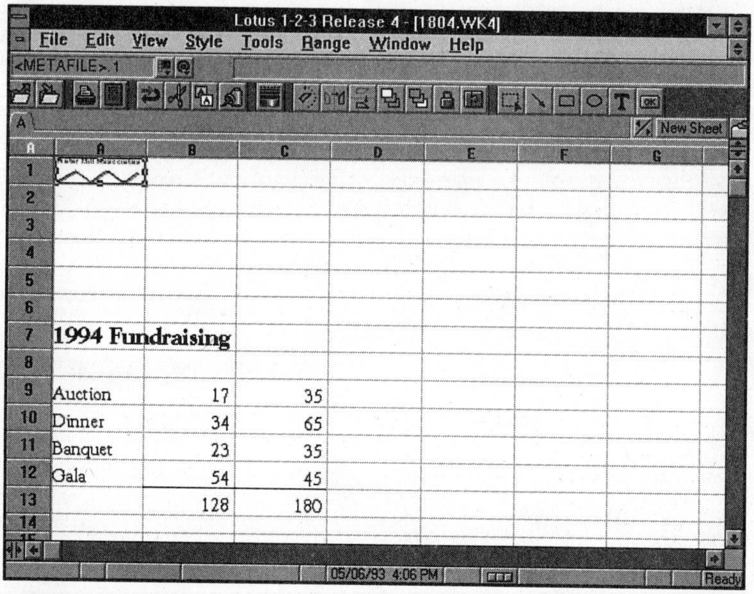

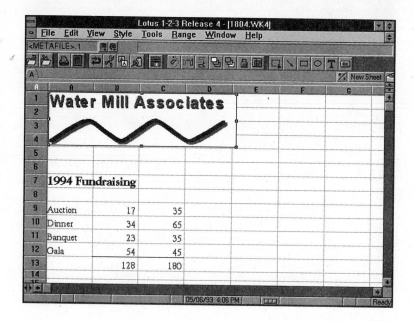

FIG. 18.4

The Freelance logo pasted into a 1-2-3 worksheet.

FIG. 18.5

Dragging a corner handle of the logo to size it properly.

Using Object Linking and Embedding (OLE)

Using Edit Copy and Edit Paste to transfer data from one Windows application to another does not set up a link between the original and the copy. Without a link, you can change either version without affecting the other. To establish a link, you must use a special capability of Windows applications called Object Linking and Embedding (OLE). The entire suite of Lotus Windows applications can take full advantage of OLE.

> **CAUTION:** Lotus recommends that you include in the PATH statement of your computer's AUTOEXEC.BAT file the full paths to the applications you use when linking and embedding data. If you have 1-2-3 for Windows, Ami Pro, and Freelance Graphics for Windows, for example, consider adding the following to the end of the existing PATH statement:
>
>   C:\123R4W\PROGRAMS;C:\AMIPRO;C:\FLW

Understanding the Difference between Linking and Embedding

Object linking and object embedding are two related techniques that seem to accomplish similar goals. The difference between the two can be confusing. Both techniques enable you to create work in one application and use a copy of the work in another application. You can create a graphic in Freelance Graphics and use it in Ami Pro and 1-2-3, for example.

When you copy an object by using object linking, the object appears in the second application, but the data for the object resides in the file in which it was originally created. If you use object linking to copy a table of numbers from 1-2-3 to Ami Pro, for example, the data remains in 1-2-3 but the table appears in Ami Pro also. To change the table in Ami Pro, you return to 1-2-3 and change the original numbers. Because a Dynamic Data Exchange (DDE) link has been set up between the two applications, any changes to the data in 1-2-3 will change the table in Ami Pro.

Windows makes switching between applications easy: to return to the application in which an object originally was created, simply double-click on the object. To return to 1-2-3 after linking the 1-2-3 data to Ami

Pro, you double-click on the 1-2-3 data in Ami Pro. If 1-2-3 is not running, it will be started for you. After you have changed the data in the original application, the change flows through to the other application through the DDE link.

When you copy an object by using object embedding, the data for the object is copied to the destination application. Because it resides there rather than only in the original application, you can move the file with the embedded data to another computer. When you take a file with embedded data to a different computer, you don't have to take all the files in which the original data is stored (as you would with object linking). As long as the computer to which you move the file has a copy of the same application you used to create the embedded data, you can use that application's facilities to edit the embedded data.

When an object is embedded in another application, any edits you make to the object in the original application are not reflected in the embedded copy.

With object embedding, you can create an object in an application and then embed it in another application. You also can temporarily switch to another application to create an object you need. When you return to the first application, the object you created is embedded in the first application's work area: You switched to the second application only long enough to create an object before returning to the first application. The object appears in the application you started in—and its data is stored in the starting application, too.

As you type an Ami Pro report, for example, you may realize you need a 1-2-3 table of numbers and a Freelance graph. Using Ami Pro's Insert Object command, you visit Freelance only long enough to create the graph you need and then return to Ami Pro. The graph appears in Ami Pro—and its data is stored in the Ami Pro document. Using the Insert Object command again, you next dip into 1-2-3 long enough to create a 1-2-3 table of numbers and then return to Ami Pro, where the table is stored and used.

Whether you use object linking or object embedding depends on several factors. If you have to give to someone else a document that contains objects from several applications, embed the objects. Only if the objects are embedded is their data stored in the file you give. For example, if you create an Ami Pro report that includes 1-2-3 numbers and a Freelance graph, and you intend to distribute the report to other offices, use object embedding. The 1-2-3 numbers and Freelance graph are stored within the Ami Pro file. The result is a larger file than if you had used object linking, but having the data available in the file is well worth the cost in disk space. However, if the document is to remain on your PC, and your concern is setting up a system that automatically updates the copies of objects if you update the originals, object linking does that job.

Linking Data

There are several ways to link an object from one application to another, but the easiest is to follow these steps:

1. Create the object.

2. Copy it to the Windows Clipboard.

3. Switch to the second application.

4. Use Paste Link to copy the object into the second application.

Here is the procedure in detail: First, create the object you need. In Freelance Graphics, create a design or a graph. In Ami Pro, create a block of text. In 1-2-3, create a range of numbers. Be sure to save the file before continuing. An object to be linked must be stored in a saved file in its original application. Even if you modify the object after you save the file, the modified object will be linked properly.

Select the object to be linked by clicking on it. If the object is a range of numbers in 1-2-3, for example, select the range. From the application's Edit menu, select Copy or click on the Copy SmartIcon. This action places a copy of the object on the Windows Clipboard. To see the object on the Clipboard, open a Windows accessory called Clipboard Viewer. (It's in the Accessories group of the Windows Program Manager.)

To carry out the second half of object linking, switch to the second application. Position the pointer where the linked object should appear in that application. In 1-2-3, move the cell pointer to the cell the object should fill. In Ami Pro, move the typing cursor to the point in the document where the object should appear. In Freelance, turn to the presentation page on which the object should appear.

From the Edit menu of the second application, select Paste Link. Figure 18.6 shows the Paste Link command on the Edit menu of Ami Pro.

> **NOTE** In Freelance Graphics for Windows, you choose Paste Special, choose the Clipboard format you need, and then click on Link.

> **CAUTION:** While still in the application you use to create an object, you must save the object in a file before you can link it to another application. Otherwise, the Paste Link command is not available when you switch to the second application.

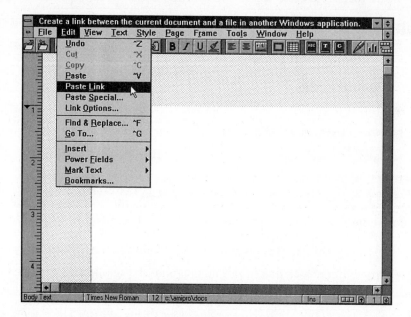

FIG. 18.6

The Paste Link
command in
Ami Pro.

After you link an object, you can switch to the original application, make a change to the object, and see the revision appear in the second application, too.

To edit an object that has been linked, you do not need to manually switch to the application that created the object and then load and edit the object. You can simply double-click on the object in the application to which it has been linked. If you linked a table of numbers from 1-2-3 to an Ami Pro file, for example, you can double-click on the table in Ami Pro.

When you double-click on a linked object, Windows automatically opens the application used to create the object and loads the file with the data for the object. Because Windows tracks the origin of each linked object, you do not have to worry about where an object came from when it needs revision. You can simply double-click on the object and let Windows retrieve the object in its original application for you. If the creator application is not installed, you cannot edit the object.

Embedding an Object

You have several ways to embed an object from one application into another. One way is to use the Insert Object command from within an application.

To use the Insert <u>O</u>bject command, follow these steps:

1. Position the pointer in the application where the object should appear.

2. Choose <u>I</u>nsert Object from the <u>E</u>dit menu or click on the Embed Data SmartIcon.

> **NOTE** In Ami Pro, select <u>I</u>nsert from the <u>E</u>dit menu and then choose New <u>O</u>bject.

A dialog box appears, listing all the available object types (see fig. 18.7). The types listed are determined by the applications in your system that can provide objects for embedding. The more applications you have, the more object types you see on the list.

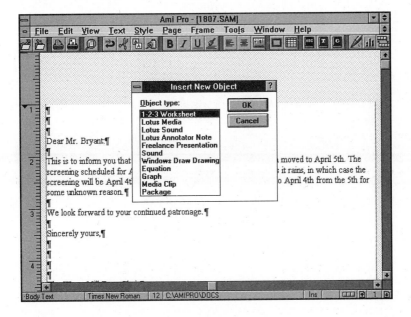

3. From the list of object types, select a type. The application that creates objects of that type opens so that you can make the object you need.

4. Create the object using the tools of the second application.

5. When finished, select File E<u>x</u>it & Return. The second application closes and you return to the original application—with the newly created object in place.

With this method of embedding, you visit a second application just long enough to create an object expressly for use in the first application. The data for the object is stored in the first application along with information about which application created the object.

To edit the object, you can double-click on it just as you double-click on a linked object. The application used to create the object reopens, with the object on-screen and ready for editing.

You can use a second method to embed an object by following these steps:

1. Create the object in an application.

2. Save the file.

3. Select the object.

4. Copy it to the Windows Clipboard.

5. Switch to a second application.

6. Select Edit Paste Special. The Paste Special dialog box appears, as shown in figure 18.8.

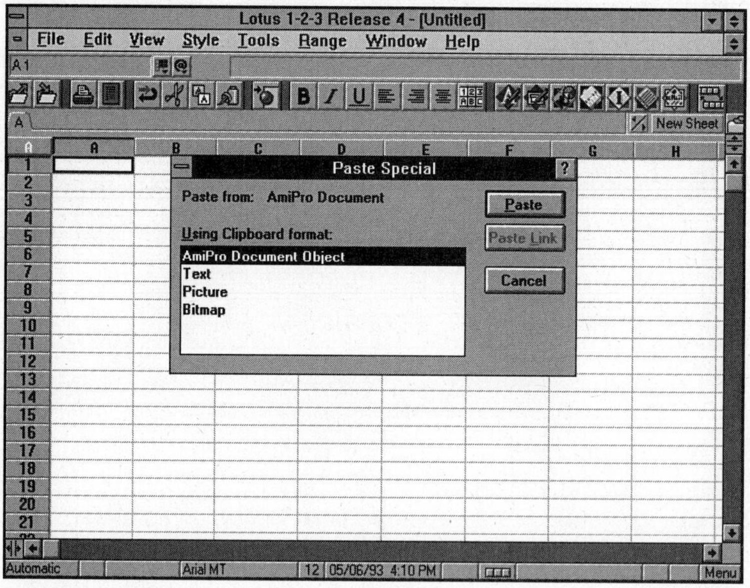

FIG. 18.8

The Paste Special dialog box.

7. Select the object you just created from the list of available formats on the Clipboard. (When you copy something to the Clipboard, it is stored there in several different representations so the destination application can automatically select the format it needs.) In

this case, you must specify the format manually by selecting the item referred to as an "object."

8. Click on the P̲aste button.

This second method is the method to use when you want to embed an object already created in another application. The end result of both methods is the same, however.

> **CAUTION:** While still in the application you used to create an object, you must save the object in a file before you can embed it in another application.

The remainder of this chapter describes the specific steps you use to copy and paste, link, or embed work between particular pairs of Lotus Windows applications.

For Related Information

◄◄ "Copying Data," p. 178.

FROM HERE...

Using a Table of Data from 1-2-3 in an Ami Pro Document

Ami Pro's table features are sophisticated and easy to use. They let you enter text and numbers and format a table quickly. But if you already have entered and calculated a set of data in the cells of a 1-2-3 worksheet, there's no need to manually reproduce that work in Ami Pro. You can easily transfer a range of cells from a 1-2-3 worksheet to an Ami Pro document.

The fastest way to copy a range of data from 1-2-3 is to select the range, copy the data to the Clipboard, switch to Ami Pro, and paste the data there. The labels and values in the 1-2-3 range appear in a neatly formatted Ami Pro table. You can use all the table-formatting commands on the Ami Pro Table menu to change the appearance of the table. If you have formatted the range in 1-2-3, that formatting is transferred to Ami Pro along with the data. Even formatting applied with a Style menu Gallery template transfers properly to Ami Pro.

Using Edit Copy and Edit Paste to transfer a range from 1-2-3 to Ami Pro copies only the results of any formulas in the range. The formulas themselves are not copied to Ami Pro. Therefore, you cannot recalculate any of the data in the Ami Pro table unless you use Ami Pro formulas.

To create a table in Ami Pro that you can update if you revise any of the numbers in 1-2-3, you must either link or embed the data.

Linking the Data

Using object linking to copy a range from 1-2-3 to Ami Pro sets up a connection between the original range in the worksheet and the data in Ami Pro. Changes to the range in 1-2-3 update the Ami Pro data, too.

You have several options for object linking, though. The option you choose depends on how you want the data to appear in Ami Pro. To have the data appear with Ami Pro formatting in an Ami Pro table that is linked to the original data, you can set up a standard Paste Link. To have the 1-2-3 range appear in Ami Pro as it is formatted in 1-2-3, set up an OLE Link.

Setting Up a Standard Paste Link

The easiest way to set up a standard Paste Link is to select the data in 1-2-3, copy it to the Windows Clipboard, switch to Ami Pro, and then use the Edit Paste Link command or the Paste Link SmartIcon to paste the data into Ami Pro. To use this procedure, follow these steps:

1. Enter the data and formulas needed in a 1-2-3 worksheet.

2. In 1-2-3, select the range you want to link to Ami Pro. Figure 18.9 shows a sample selected range in 1-2-3.

3. From the 1-2-3 menu, select Edit Copy or click on the Copy SmartIcon.

4. Switch to Ami Pro by using Alt+Tab or Ctrl+Esc, or by clicking on the Ami Pro SmartIcon.

5. Position the cursor in the Ami Pro document where you want the table of numbers to appear.

6. From the Edit menu, select Paste Link. The range appears as an Ami Pro table

The text and numbers in the range take on the default formatting characteristics of the Ami Pro table. If you formatted the range in 1-2-3, the 1-2-3 styling is transferred to Ami Pro along with the data. Figure 18.10

shows a range formatted in 1-2-3 with the B&W3 template; figure 18.11 shows the same range as it appears in an Ami Pro table. Notice that the title, which spills into adjacent cells in 1-2-3, is word-wrapped within a cell of the Ami Pro table. You may want to pull the title from the cell and center it outside and above the table.

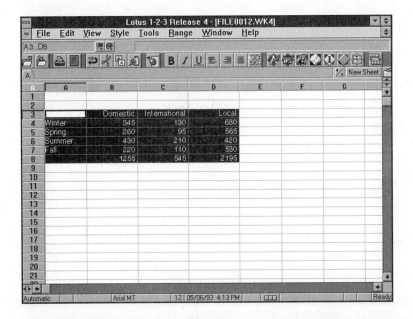

FIG. 18.9

A selected range in 1-2-3.

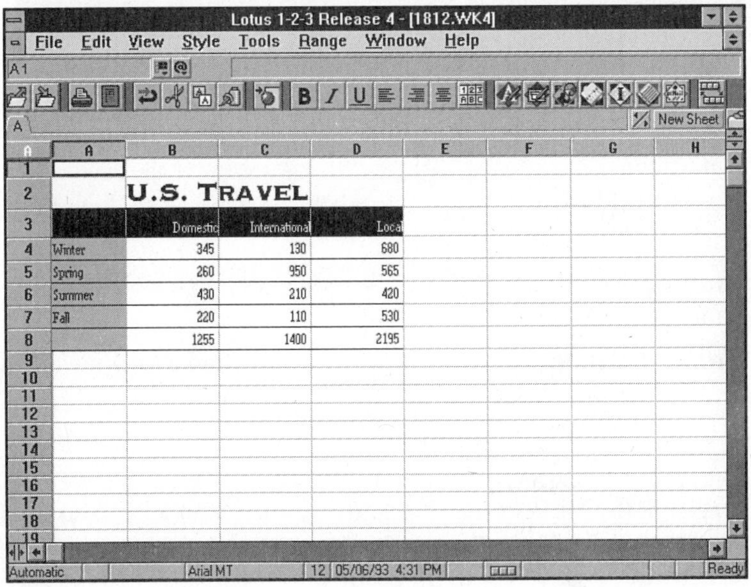

FIG. 18.10

A formatted 1-2-3 range.

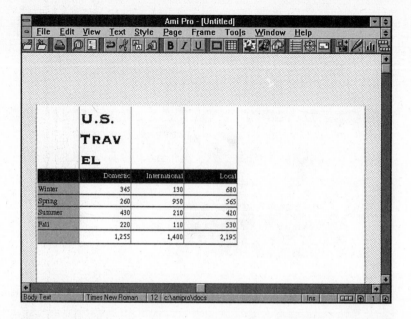

FIG. 18.11

The same formatted 1-2-3 range as it appears in Ami Pro.

Another method you can use to create the same kind of link between 1-2-3 data and an Ami Pro document is to use the Paste Special command in Ami Pro and then select a DDE Link. A DDE Link is the kind of link that is set up when you use the Paste Link command. The result is the same as that for the preceding method—only the procedure is different. To use the Paste Special command to create a standard link, follow these steps:

1. Enter the data and formulas needed in a 1-2-3 worksheet.

2. In 1-2-3, select the range you want to link to Ami Pro.

3. From the 1-2-3 menu, select Edit Copy or click on the Copy SmartIcon.

4. Switch to Ami Pro by using Alt+Tab or Ctrl+Esc, or by clicking on the Ami Pro SmartIcon.

5. Position the cursor in the Ami Pro document where you want the table of numbers to appear.

6. From the Edit menu, select Paste Special. The Paste Special dialog box appears (see fig. 18.12).

7. From the list of formats, select DDE Link.

After you link a 1-2-3 range with an Ami Pro table, you can select individual cells of the table in Ami Pro and edit them just as you could if you had created the table in Ami Pro. You even can edit the text and numbers in the table. But if you make any changes to the original data in 1-2-3, the changes in Ami Pro are overwritten when the link is updated.

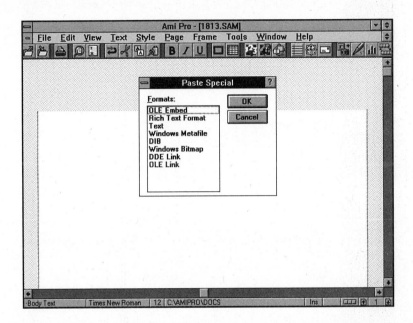

FIG. 18.12

The Paste Special dialog box.

Every time you open a saved Ami Pro file that contains a DDE link to a table of 1-2-3 data, Ami Pro opens a message box that asks whether to update the DDE links in the document. If you click on Yes, Ami Pro reads the 1-2-3 worksheet file and reflects any changes in the data it finds. If you select No, Ami Pro opens the document and displays the version of the 1-2-3 data it had when the document was last saved.

Linking a Snapshot of the Data in Ami Pro

Another approach to linking 1-2-3 and Ami Pro data is to create an OLE link between 1-2-3 and Ami Pro. This method copies a snapshot of the 1-2-3 data and its formatting to Ami Pro. The method you learned about earlier, creating a DDE Link, copies the data into Ami Pro where it takes on Ami Pro formatting. When you set up an OLE link, the result is a tabular arrangement of data in Ami Pro that looks just as the data did in 1-2-3. The picture fits in an Ami Pro frame you have created that can have standard frame formatting (such as a line surrounding the frame, a shadow, and rounded or square corners). Figure 18.13 shows how the same range of data used in an earlier example appears in an Ami Pro document when it is linked with an OLE link. Notice the shadow frame with rounded edges.

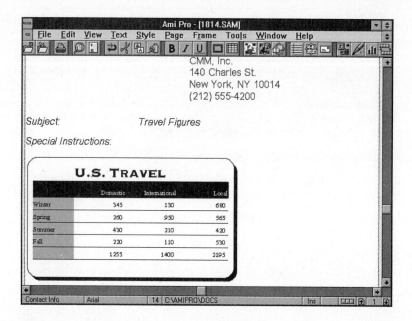

FIG. 18.13

1-2-3 data
copied to Ami
Pro with an OLE
link.

To copy data from 1-2-3 to Ami Pro with an OLE link, follow the same
procedure described above to create a DDE link, except create an Ami
Pro frame with the Frame Create Frame command first. Then, select
Edit Paste Special and select OLE link from the Paste Special dialog box
rather than DDE Link.

You cannot directly edit data copied to Ami Pro with an OLE link. Instead, you must double-click on the picture of the data to reopen a 1-2-3
window and see the original range of data. Any changes made to the
1-2-3 range are reflected immediately in the Ami Pro document. In fact,
if you arrange the 1-2-3 and Ami Pro windows side-by-side, you can see
the data update in the Ami Pro window as soon as you change it in the
1-2-3 window.

Updating the Data in 1-2-3

To update data that has been copied to Ami Pro and linked, you should
return to the original data in 1-2-3 and make edits there. If you created a
DDE link, any edits you make to the data in Ami Pro will be overwritten
when the link is updated. Therefore, you should edit the data in 1-2-3. If
you created an OLE link, you must return to 1-2-3 to edit the data.

If you used Paste Link to copy a range of 1-2-3 data into an Ami Pro
table, you must switch to 1-2-3 manually (use Alt+Tab or Ctrl+Esc). If
you used Paste Special and then chose OLE Link to copy 1-2-3 data into

Ami Pro, you can double-click on the picture of the data (or single-click and then press Enter). This action opens the 1-2-3 window for you.

If the file containing the range is not open in 1-2-3, you must open the file, make changes to the data, and then switch back to Ami Pro. The changes do not appear in Ami Pro until you either manually update the link or save the file and then reopen it later. When you reopen the file, Ami Pro recognizes that the document contains links and asks whether you want to update them. Select Yes to update the links.

To manually update a link in Ami Pro, follow these steps:

1. From the Ami Pro menu, select Edit Link Options. The Link Options dialog box appears (see fig. 18.14). The dialog box lists all the links in the document.

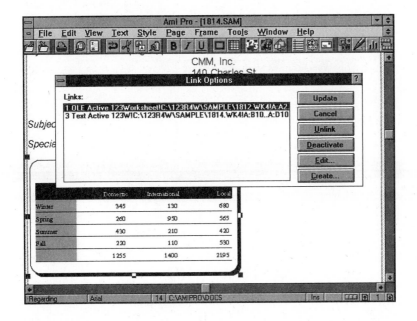

FIG. 18.14

The Link Options dialog box.

2. Click on the link in the list that you want to update and then click on Update.

Each row of the list in the Link Options dialog box contains a complete set of information about a link. The items within the rows are separated by exclamation marks. The first item identifies the link as Text (a standard link) or OLE (an OLE link). The next item identifies whether the link is active or inactive. (An active link automatically updates whenever the 1-2-3 data changes.) The next item identifies the application that provided the data (123W or 123Worksheet, in this case, represents 1-2-3 for Windows). The last two items identify the file name of the worksheet and the range address of the data in 1-2-3. To see the application name, file name, and range address of a link more clearly, click on the link and then click on Edit. The Application, Topic (path and file name), and Item (range address) appear in text boxes in a Link dialog box. Figure 18.15 shows a Link dialog box.

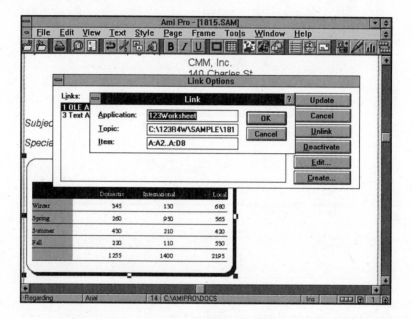

FIG. 18.15

A Link dialog box.

Editing the Link

Selecting a link from the Link Options dialog box and then clicking on Edit is also the way to redirect the link. You can have the link point to different data in a different part of the 1-2-3 worksheet or even to a different range in a different worksheet. After you click on Edit, modify the entries in the Topic and Item text boxes in the Link dialog box to link a different range to the Ami Pro document. Be sure to include the full path and file name in the Topic text box.

Removing the Link

To stop a link, select the link from the Link Options dialog box and then click on Unlink. This action removes the link between the original data in 1-2-3 and the copy in Ami Pro. Any changes you make to the 1-2-3 data are no longer reflected in Ami Pro, but the data still remains in

Ami Pro so you can have just the data without the complications of the link. After you remove a link, you cannot update the link but you can re-create the link.

Deactivating the Link

To temporarily deactivate a link, select the link from the Link Options dialog box and then click on Deactivate. This action stops Ami Pro from updating the link every time the data changes in 1-2-3. You might want to do this if a document should contain a historical picture of the data as it existed at a point in time rather than continually updated data. To reactivate the link, select the link and then click on Update. A deacti-vated link preserves memory in Windows and can make your work in Ami Pro faster.

Embedding the Data

The alternative to pasting a link into Ami Pro is to embed 1-2-3 data in an Ami Pro file. In Ami Pro, the embedded 1-2-3 data appears as a pic-ture of the data just the way it looked in 1-2-3. The embedded data auto-matically goes into an Ami Pro frame.

The advantage to embedded 1-2-3 data is that the data is contained in the Ami Pro file rather than in the original 1-2-3 worksheet. You can transport the Ami Pro file to another computer without also having to transport the 1-2-3 worksheet file. When you need to edit the 1-2-3 data, double-click on it and Ami Pro uses the facilities of 1-2-3 on the current computer to edit the data.

You can embed 1-2-3 data in an Ami Pro file two ways:

- You can select Edit Insert New Object in Ami Pro to temporarily visit 1-2-3 and create the object you need. This procedure works best when you need to create a new 1-2-3 table while working in Ami Pro.

- You can select Edit Paste Special in Ami Pro and then select OLE Embed to paste the 1-2-3 data into Ami Pro. This procedure works best when you need to embed preexisting 1-2-3 data into an Ami Pro document.

Creating an Embedded Object While Working in Ami Pro

To create a 1-2-3 table and embed it in an Ami Pro document, follow these steps:

1. Position the cursor in the Ami Pro document where you want the table to appear.

2. From the Ami Pro menu, select Edit Insert.

3. From the Insert menu, select New Object. The New Object dialog box appears (see fig. 18.16).

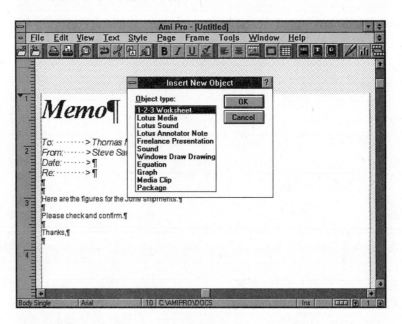

4. Select 1-2-3 Worksheet from the list of object types. A frame for the embedded worksheet appears in the Ami Pro document and the 1-2-3 window opens. If necessary, the 1-2-3 application is started. The 1-2-3 range will be resized to fit the frame.

5. Create the worksheet. Figure 18.17 shows a sample worksheet created in 1-2-3, ready to be embedded in Ami Pro.

6. From the 1-2-3 menu, select File Update. You can skip this step and proceed to step 7. After step 7, 1-2-3 will ask whether you want to update the link. Click on Yes to proceed.

7. From the 1-2-3 menu, select File Exit & Return.

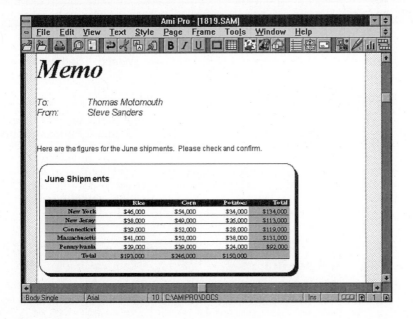

The worksheet appears in the frame in the Ami Pro document. You can stretch the frame by dragging the right, bottom, or lower right-corner handle. Figure 18.18 shows the frame sized properly on an Ami Pro page.

To edit the worksheet in 1-2-3, double-click on the frame or select the frame and then press Enter. The 1-2-3 window reopens, showing the 1-2-3 worksheet. After you edit the 1-2-3 worksheet, select File Update and then select File Exit & Return.

T I P   While in 1-2-3, you can select Save Copy As from the File menu to save the worksheet you created as a separate file so that you can use it outside of Ami Pro later.

Embedding a Preexisting Object in an Ami Pro Document

If the 1-2-3 worksheet you want to embed in Ami Pro already exists, follow these steps:

1. Open the worksheet in 1-2-3.

2. Select the range you want to embed in the Ami Pro document.

3. From the 1-2-3 menu, select Edit Copy or click on the Copy SmartIcon.

4. Switch to Ami Pro by using Alt+Tab or Ctrl+Esc, or by clicking on the Ami Pro SmartIcon.

5. Position the cursor in the Ami Pro document where you want the embedded copy of the worksheet data.

6. From the Ami Pro menu, select Edit Paste Special. The Paste Special dialog box appears (see fig. 18.19).

7. From the list of formats, select OLE Embed.

The worksheet range appears in an Ami Pro frame that can be resized and reformatted. Use the commands on the Frame menu to change the appearance of the frame.

To edit the 1-2-3 worksheet data, double-click on the frame in Ami Pro or select the frame and press Enter. A 1-2-3 window opens and the data is loaded automatically. Make the changes you need, select File Update, and then select File Exit & Return to return to Ami Pro.

FROM HERE...

For Related Information

◀◀ "Using the Style Gallery," p. 228.

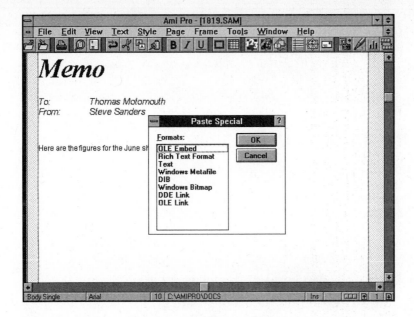

FIG. 18.19

The Paste Special
dialog box.

Using a 1-2-3 Chart in an Ami Pro Document

Although Ami Pro's charting capabilities let you create a simple chart
to graphically represent a set of numbers, you may want to make use of
the superior charting capabilities of a program dedicated to chart making. If you have the entire Lotus SmartSuite of Windows applications,
Freelance Graphics can offer sophisticated graphs that you can copy
into Ami Pro documents. You even can link 1-2-3 data to a Freelance
graph and then link the Freelance graph to an Ami Pro document. But
if you do not have access to Freelance Graphics, you still can create
professional-looking charts in 1-2-3 for Windows and use them in Ami
Pro.

As usual, you can copy the charts from 1-2-3 to Ami Pro in one of three
ways. The easiest is to perform a straight copy and paste by selecting
the chart in 1-2-3, copying it to the Windows Clipboard, switching to
Ami Pro, and then pasting the chart into the document. This method
creates no link between the original 1-2-3 data and the chart in Ami Pro.
To create a link, you must use either linking or embedding.

Linking a Chart

Use linking to copy a chart from 1-2-3 to Ami Pro when you plan for the Ami Pro file to remain on the current system, where it always has access to the 1-2-3 file in which you created the chart. When you link a chart from 1-2-3 to Ami Pro, the data remains in its original 1-2-3 worksheet file; only an image of the chart is copied to the Ami Pro file. To modify the chart, you must return to 1-2-3; any modifications to the 1-2-3 data automatically update the chart in Ami Pro, too.

To link a 1-2-3 chart into Ami Pro, follow these steps:

1. In 1-2-3, create and format the chart.

2. Save the worksheet file. This step is absolutely mandatory. You cannot link a chart if you have not saved it in a 1-2-3 worksheet file first.

3. Click on the chart's frame in 1-2-3 to select the chart, as shown in figure 18.20.

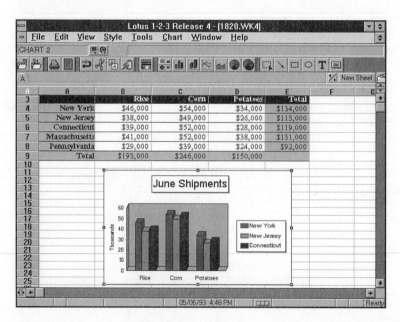

FIG. 18.20

A chart selected in 1-2-3 for Windows.

4. From the 1-2-3 menu, select Edit Copy or click on the Copy SmartIcon.

5. Switch to Ami Pro by using Alt+Tab or Ctrl+Esc, or by clicking on the Ami Pro SmartIcon.

6. Position the cursor in the Ami Pro document where you want the chart to appear.

7. Use Frame Create Frame to create a frame for the chart in Ami Pro.

8. From the Ami Pro menu, select Edit Paste Link. The chart appears in the Ami Pro document, as shown in figure 18.21.

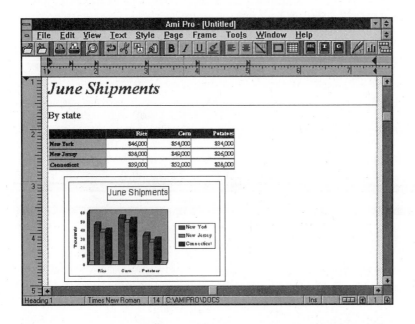

FIG. 18.21

A linked chart in an Ami Pro document.

Another approach to linking a chart is to create the chart in 1-2-3, select and copy it to the Windows Clipboard and then, in Ami Pro, select Paste Special from the Edit menu. When the Paste Special dialog box appears, select DDE Link or OLE Link from the list of formats. The DDE Link option copies the chart from 1-2-3 to Ami Pro and sets up an active link between the original and the copy. The OLE Link option performs the same action, but places the chart in an Ami Pro frame. You then can format the frame with the commands on the Ami Pro Frame menu.

To edit the chart, you can either manually switch to the 1-2-3 window and then modify the data, or you can double-click on the chart in Ami Pro to automatically switch back to 1-2-3.

When you save an Ami Pro document that contains a link to a 1-2-3 chart, the link information is saved in the Ami Pro document—but the data is saved in the 1-2-3 worksheet file. The next time you open the Ami Pro document, a message box asks whether to update the DDE links in the document. Click on Yes to have Ami Pro read and reflect any changes to the data in the 1-2-3 worksheet file saved on disk. These updates will occur whether you have created a DDE or OLE link. 1-2-3 does not have to be running or even installed for this update to occur successfully, but the 1-2-3 worksheet file with the changes must be on your system. Click on No to have Ami Pro open the document and display the data as it existed the last time the Ami Pro document was saved. To update the link, you can select Link Options from the Edit menu, select the link from the list of links that appears in the Link Options dialog box, and then click on Update.

Embedding a Chart

If you plan to transport the Ami Pro document to another computer (perhaps to copy it to a portable computer), you may want to embed a chart from 1-2-3 rather than link it. Embedding has the advantage of incorporating the data for the chart in the Ami Pro file so that you do not require access to the data in the original worksheet if the chart must be updated. You do need access to 1-2-3 on the destination computer to make any changes to the chart, however.

Think of embedding this way: Embedding places the data for the chart in Ami Pro along with information that the chart was created in 1-2-3. As long as 1-2-3 is available in the system, you can edit the chart. Double-clicking on the chart transfers the data to the copy of 1-2-3 on the current system only long enough for you to use 1-2-3's commands to modify the data. Then the data and revised chart are returned to Ami Pro where the chart is displayed.

You can embed a 1-2-3 chart in Ami Pro in one of two ways. If you already have created the chart in 1-2-3 and saved it in a worksheet file, follow these steps:

1. Click on the chart's frame to select the chart in 1-2-3.

2. From the 1-2-3 menu, select Edit Copy or click on the Copy SmartIcon.

3. Switch to Ami Pro by using Alt+Tab or Ctrl+Esc, or by clicking on the Ami Pro SmartIcon.

4. Position the cursor in the Ami Pro document where you want the chart to appear.

5. From the Ami Pro menu, select Edit Paste Special. The Paste Special dialog box appears (see fig. 18.22).

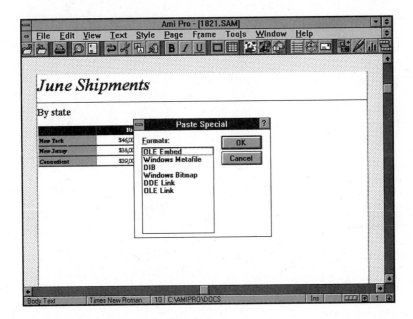

FIG. 18.22

The Paste Special dialog box in Ami Pro.

6. From the list of formats, select OLE Embed. The chart appears in a frame in the Ami Pro document.

To edit the chart, double-click on the frame or select the frame and then press Enter. The 1-2-3 window opens and shows the data for the chart. Edit the data, select File Update to update the chart in Ami Pro, and then select Exit & Return from the File menu to leave 1-2-3 and return to Ami Pro.

If you have not yet created the chart and want to create it on the fly, follow these steps:

1. Select Edit Insert.

2. Choose New Object... from the pop-out menu.

3. Select 1-2-3 Worksheet from the list of object types that appears.

4. When the 1-2-3 window opens, enter the data you need and create the chart.

5. Select File Update.

6. Select File Exit and Return to return to Ami Pro.

When you use this method, a snapshot of the 1-2-3 worksheet is embedded in Ami Pro, including both the data you've entered and the chart you created. By arranging the data and the chart in the 1-2-3 worksheet before you return to Ami Pro, you can get in Ami Pro an attractive display of both the 1-2-3 chart and the data that it portrays.

FROM HERE...

For Related Information

◄◄ "Creating a Chart," p. 537.

Embedding an Ami Pro Document in a 1-2-3 Worksheet

With object linking, you can link selected text from an Ami Pro document to a 1-2-3 cell so that any changes to the text are reflected automatically in the 1-2-3 file. But copying and pasting selected text from Ami Pro to 1-2-3 is probably just as helpful. Text in an Ami Pro document is less likely to be updated regularly (unlike a table of numbers in 1-2-3 that may be updated frequently, perhaps even hourly or daily).

You may find it more useful to embed—rather than link—an entire Ami Pro document into a 1-2-3 worksheet file. The document can provide a report on a particular aspect of the data shown in the 1-2-3 worksheet or add background information that someone should have when trying to interpret the 1-2-3 worksheet.

When you embed an Ami Pro document in a 1-2-3 file, an Ami Pro icon appears in a worksheet cell (the same icon you double-click on in the Windows Presentation Manager to start Ami Pro). Double-clicking on the Ami Pro icon in a 1-2-3 file opens Ami Pro so that you can read or print the Ami Pro document information embedded in the 1-2-3 file. To use the embedded Ami Pro information, you do not need the original Ami Pro document file on the system; however, you do need Ami Pro so that you can use the document information embedded in the worksheet.

To embed an Ami Pro document, you can either copy a preexisting document to 1-2-3 and use the Edit Paste Special command, or you can use the Ami Pro Edit Insert Object command to temporarily use Ami Pro to create an embedded object. Either way, an Ami Pro icon appears in the worksheet. Double-clicking on the icon loads the document in Ami Pro.

Embedding a Preexisting Ami Pro Document into 1-2-3

To embed a preexisting Ami Pro document in a 1-2-3 worksheet, follow these steps:

1. Make sure that the document is saved in an Ami Pro file.

2. Select any portion of the document. You can select as little as a single character. Figure 18.23 shows a document with a small portion of text selected.

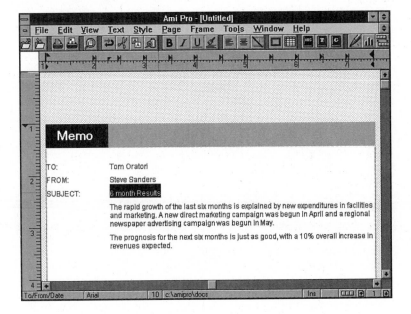

FIG. 18.23

A portion of text selected in an Ami Pro document.

3. From the Ami Pro menu, select Edit Copy or click on the Copy SmartIcon.

4. Switch to 1-2-3 for Windows by using Alt+Tab or Ctrl+Esc, or by clicking on the 1-2-3 SmartIcon.

5. Position the cell pointer near the data you want to document with the Ami Pro text.

6. From the 1-2-3 menu, select Edit Paste Special. The Paste Special dialog box appears.

7. From the list of Clipboard formats, select Ami Pro Document Object.

8. Click on the Paste button to embed the Ami Pro document object. An Ami Pro icon appears in the 1-2-3 worksheet, as shown in figure 18.24.

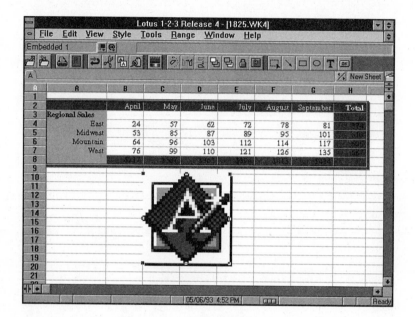

FIG. 18.24

An Ami Pro icon embedded in a 1-2-3 worksheet. It appears in a shadowed designer frame.

The Ami Pro icon appears at a fairly large size and in a designer frame. You can reduce the size of the icon by dragging a corner handle toward the center of the icon. You also can remove the designer frame by following these steps:

1. Select the icon.

2. From the 1-2-3 menu, choose Style Lines & Color or click on the Lines & Color SmartIcon.

3. In the Lines & Color dialog box, click on the Designer Frame check box to turn off the frame.

4. Click on OK.

A simple icon without a designer frame appears in the worksheet, as shown in figure 18.25. The icon shown has also been manually sized to make it small.

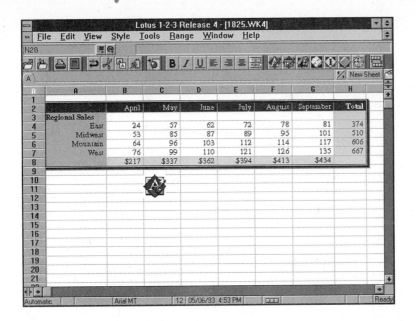

FIG. 18.25

A small icon
without a
designer frame.

Creating and Embedding an Ami Pro Document from within 1-2-3

The second method available for embedding Ami Pro documents in
1-2-3 worksheets is to create a new Ami Pro document "on the fly"—so
that the document is embedded in the 1-2-3 worksheet you are working on.

In the following exercise, you create a small 1-2-3 worksheet that tracks
the profits for a business over four quarters. Unfortunately, expenses
seem to be rising at a faster rate than sales, and profits have continually slipped. The explanation for this phenomenon has been ably
explained in an Ami Pro report. Before you send the 1-2-3 worksheet
containing the numbers to the members of the board, you decide to
embed the explanatory Ami Pro letter so that the board members can
read it after seeing the apparently gloomy picture depicted by the data.

To begin, follow these steps:

1. Create the small worksheet shown in figure 18.26. Type the labels
   and values into the cells, create the formulas that subtract expenses from sales, and then choose the B&W3 template from the
   Gallery to format the cells. (The Gallery command is on the Style
   menu.)

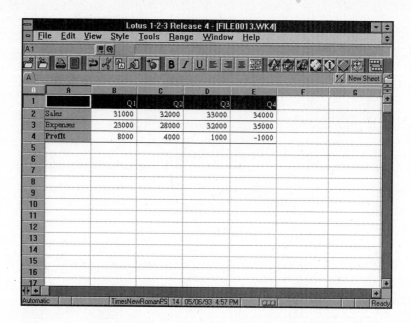

FIG. 18.26

The 1-2-3
worksheet,
showing falling
profits.

2. Type Note: in cell A6 to help the reader understand that the icon
   you will place next to the word Note: leads to a written explanation of something in the worksheet. Your next task is to use Ami
   Pro to create the explanatory letter document.

3. Switch to Ami Pro by using Alt+Tab or Ctrl+Esc, or by clicking on
   the Ami Pro SmartIcon.

4. Create a new document and then type the following short explanatory note:

   **The opening of 17 new branch locations contributed heavily to
   our expenses during the past year.**

   **For this example, leave the simple message at that. But imagine
   that the message was a multipage, detailed report on the expenses incurred while preparing each of the 17 new branch
   offices. Although the sample message is much shorter than such
   a detailed report, the result for the longer message is the same
   as for this example.**

5. Save the Ami Pro file.

6. Select any of the text in the file, as shown in figure 18.27. You can
   select as little as a single character, but at least some—if not all—
   text must be selected.

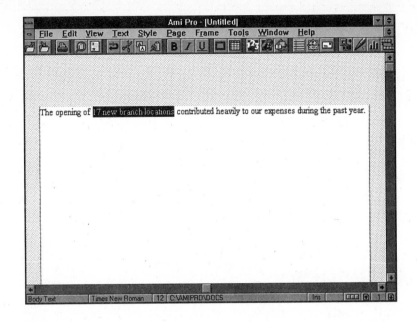

The opening of 17 new branch locations contributed heavily to our expenses during the past year.

FIG. 18.27

Selecting text in the Ami Pro document.

7. From the Ami Pro menu, select Edit Copy or click on the Copy SmartIcon.

8. Switch to 1-2-3 for Windows by using Alt+Tab or Ctrl+Esc, or by clicking on the 1-2-3 SmartIcon.

9. Position the cell pointer on cell B6.

10. From the 1-2-3 menu, select Edit Paste Special.

11. From the list of Clipboard formats in the Paste Special dialog box, select Ami Pro Document Object.

12. Click on the Paste button in the Paste Special dialog box. A large Ami Pro icon appears, as shown in figure 18.30.

   The Ami Pro icon that appears in 1-2-3 for Windows.

13. Use the handles of the icon to reduce the icon's size; drag the icon to position it next to the word Note: in cell A6. You can remove the designer frame from the icon as you learned in the preceding section.

To access the note from within 1-2-3, double-click on the Ami Pro icon. The Ami Pro window reopens with the note text loaded. After you read the text, choose File Exit & Return to close the Ami Pro window. Then switch back to the 1-2-3 window manually.

The alternative to using Copy and Paste Special to embed an Ami Pro document in a 1-2-3 worksheet is creating the worksheet within 1-2-3 and then selecting Edit Insert Object from the 1-2-3 menu (or clicking on the Embed Data SmartIcon). From the Insert Object dialog box that appears, select Ami Pro Document as the Object Type and then click on OK. When the Ami Pro window opens, type the note you want to embed into 1-2-3 and then choose File Update from the Ami Pro menu. To finish and return to 1-2-3, select File Exit & Return from the Ami Pro menu. You return to the 1-2-3 window where an Ami Pro icon representing the embedded document is in place.

Incorporating a Freelance Graphics Logo in a 1-2-3 Worksheet

Freelance Graphics for Windows, also from Lotus Development Corporation, is an easy-to-use but full-featured presentation graphics application. It makes creating professional-looking presentation handouts, overheads, transparencies, or slides simple and straightforward. In a single file, you can create a series of presentation pages: some with text and some with graphics, organization, and table charts.

Although Freelance excels at creating entire presentations, it also offers a comprehensive set of drawing tools and clip-art pictures you can use to create diagrams, designs, or logos. These tools surpass the basic drawing tools incorporated in 1-2-3 for Windows. Because Freelance is a Windows application, you easily can transfer a logo drawn in Freelance to a 1-2-3 worksheet. In addition to copying a drawn object to 1-2-3, you can even embed an entire Freelance presentation in a worksheet, a topic covered later in this chapter.

To transfer a logo drawn in Freelance to a 1-2-3 worksheet, complete the logo in Freelance first. Then select the logo and choose Edit Copy to copy it to the Windows Clipboard or click the Copy SmartIcon. After you switch to 1-2-3, place the cell pointer at the destination for the logo and use the Edit Paste command or click the Paste SmartIcon to transfer a copy to the worksheet. You can move and resize the logo and print it just as it appears on the worksheet.

Freelance does not enable you to establish an OLE link between a logo in Freelance and a 1-2-3 worksheet. You can only copy and paste the logo. That's because Freelance does not allow you to select only certain items on a presentation page to link or embed to other applications. You must link the entire presentation page to another application, instead.

Copying and Pasting the Freelance Logo into 1-2-3 for Windows

Here are the detailed steps for transferring a logo from Freelance to 1-2-3:

1. Create the logo in Freelance Graphics for Windows. You do not have to save the file because you do not create an OLE link.

2. Select the logo. You may want to use the Freelance Group command to group the Freelance drawing objects that comprise the logo into one object. (A grouped object is easier to select.) Figure 18.28 shows a selected logo in Freelance.

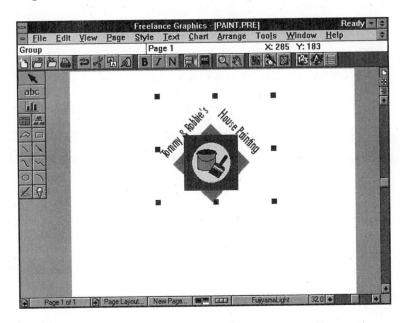

FIG. 18.28

A logo selected in Freelance.

3. From the Freelance menu, select Edit Copy or click on the Copy SmartIcon.

4. Switch to 1-2-3 for Windows by using Alt+Tab or Ctrl+Esc, or by clicking on the 1-2-3 SmartIcon.

5. Place the cell pointer on a cell at the approximate location for the logo.

6. From the 1-2-3 menu, select Edit Paste or click on the Paste SmartIcon. The logo appears in a worksheet cell.

To resize the logo, click on a corner handle and drag diagonally. To reposition the logo, place the pointer on the selected logo and drag the logo to a new position. After it is resized, the logo appears as shown in figure 18.29.

```
Lotus 1-2-3 Release 4 - [1833.WK4]
 File   Edit   View   Style   Tools   Range   Window   Help
L34

                     A        B        C        D        E    F    G    H
                                                                      New Sheet
 1
 2
 3            Tommy's Riddle   House Painting
 4
 5                            Revenue Sheet
 6
 7                            1988     1989     1990
 8   Revenues
 9        Exteriors          34000    46000    51000
10        Interiors          28000    24000    26000
11        Touch-ups           6500     4700     5100
12        Subcontracted       2400     3800     2900
13        Subtotal           70900    78500    85000
14
15   Expenses
16        Paint              14000    21000    35000
17        Supplies           19000    20000    24000
18        Uniforms            2000     3600     5100
19        Subtotal           35000    44600    64100
20
21        Net                35900    33900    20900

Automatic          Arial MT        12  05/06/93 5:02 PM              Ready
```

FIG. 18.29

The logo placed and resized in a 1-2-3 worksheet.

T I P   You can resize the logo proportionally (change its size without changing its shape) by holding the Shift key as you drag a corner handle.

The logo may appear in a 1-2-3 frame. To remove the frame, select the frame and then select Lines & Color from the Style menu. To remove the frame, set the Edge Line Style to None. The logo appears as a free-floating object on the 1-2-3 worksheet.

The following exercise creates a simple logo in Freelance Graphics and copies it to a 1-2-3 worksheet. In this exercise, you create the logo for Lola's Pet Care and place it next to the title of a small worksheet that analyzes Lola's breakdown of revenues by animal type.

1. Open Freelance Graphics for Windows.

2. Select <u>C</u>reate a New Presentation from the Welcome to Freelance Graphics dialog box that first appears; click on OK.

3. Click on the <u>S</u>martMaster with Blank Background check box in the Choose a Look for Your Presentation dialog box (this action selects a clear background design for the page); click on OK.

4. Choose [None] from the list of page layouts on the Choose Page Layout dialog box to get a clear page (a page without Click Here... blocks).

5. From the toolbox at the left edge of the window, choose the Symbol tool (the button showing a light bulb).

6. From the list of symbol categories in the Add Symbol to Page dialog box, select ANIMALS.SYM.

7. Click on the symbol of a reclining lion and then click on OK to transfer the symbol to the page. The symbol appears as shown in figure 18.30.

FIG. 18.30

The symbol placed on the page.

8. From the toolbox, click on the Text tool (the button showing the letters abc).

9. Click on the page just above the lion and type Lola's Pet Care, Inc.

10. Click on the OK button that is part of the text-entry box. The text appears on the page.

11. From the Text menu, select Font.

12. From the Font dialog box, choose Arial MT as the face and 48 as the point size; select Bold as an attribute.

13. Click on OK to see the changes to the text on the page.

14. To complete the logo, select Curved Text from the Font menu and then select the first shape at the upper-left corner (this shape starts the text at the 9 o'clock position); click on OK.

15. Select and then drag the curved text to surround the lion's head as shown in figure 18.31.

FIG. 18.31

The completed logo.

These next steps select both drawing objects that make up the logo and copy them to the Windows Clipboard:

1. Click on the text once, press and hold the Shift key, and click on the lion symbol. Both drawing objects should be selected.

2. From the Arrange menu, select Group to group the two drawing objects as one object. (This step is optional.)

3. Select Edit Copy or click on the Copy SmartIcon to copy the objects to the Windows Clipboard.

If you plan to use Lola's logo again, save it in a Freelance file. If not, close or minimize the Freelance window now: your work in Freelance is complete. Open a 1-2-3 window so that you can finish this exercise by following these steps:

1. In the 1-2-3 window, reproduce the small worksheet shown in figure 18.32.

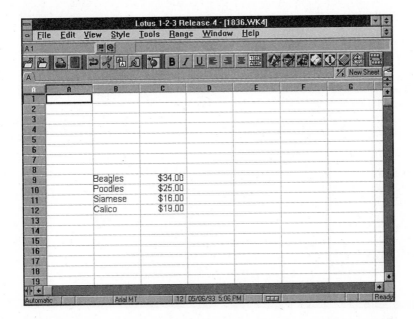

FIG. 18.32

The revenue breakdown worksheet for Lola's Pet Care.

2. Place the cell pointer in cell A1.

3. From the 1-2-3 menu, select Edit Paste or click on the Paste SmartIcon. The logo appears in cell A1 of the 1-2-3 worksheet.

4. Drag the lower-right handle of the frame surrounding the logo to resize the logo.

5. Remove the thin line that surrounds the logo's frame: with the logo still selected, choose Lines & Color from the 1-2-3 Style menu or click on the Lines & Color SmartIcon.

6. Set Line Style to None and then click on OK. Figure 18.33 shows the final result.

For Related Information

◄◄ "Enhancing the Appearance of Data," p. 217.

FROM HERE...

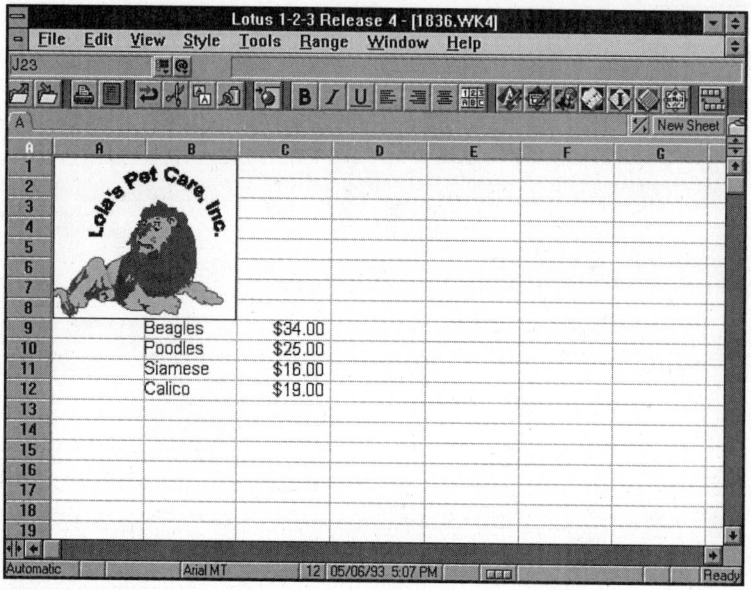

FIG. 18.33

The logo copied to the completed 1-2-3 worksheet.

Embedding a Freelance Presentation in a 1-2-3 Worksheet

By copying and pasting a logo from Freelance to 1-2-3, you can transfer a single graphic image. But you can also embed an entire Freelance presentation as an object in a 1-2-3 worksheet file. With this technique, you can embed a series of pages containing a mix of text and graphics that can explain the results shown in a worksheet file. While working in 1-2-3, you can double-click on the presentation object to open Freelance and view the presentation.

To embed a Freelance presentation, you can create the Freelance presentation and then use the 1-2-3 Edit Paste Special command to paste the presentation into 1-2-3 as an embedded object; alternatively, you can use the Edit Insert Object command (or click on the Embed Data SmartIcon) from within 1-2-3 to create an embedded presentation. You use the first method (Edit Copy and Edit Paste Special) to embed a preexisting presentation in a 1-2-3 worksheet. Use the second method (Edit Insert Object) to create and embed a Freelance presentation on the fly, as you're working in 1-2-3.

Embedding a Preexisting Presentation

To embed a preexisting Freelance presentation, follow these steps:

1. Create the presentation and save it in Freelance as a file.

2. Click on the Page Sorter icon at the right edge of the Freelance window to view the presentation in Page Sorter view. You must use Page Sorter view to select the single page that will be the one to display in 1-2-3 even though the entire presentation will be embedded in 1-2-3, too.

3. Select the page you want to appear in 1-2-3. (The data for the entire presentation is copied to 1-2-3 also.) Figure 18.34 shows a presentation in Page Sorter view with the title page selected.

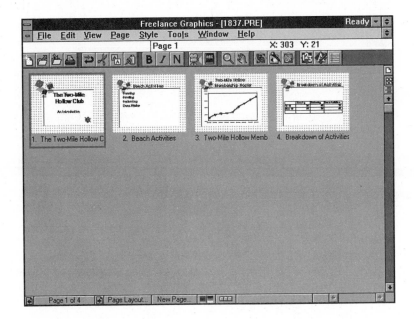

FIG. 18.34

A Freelance
presentation in
Page Sorter view.

4. From the Freelance menu, select Edit Copy or click on the Copy SmartIcon.

5. Switch to 1-2-3 for Windows by using Alt+Tab or Ctrl+Esc, or by clicking on the 1-2-3 SmartIcon.

6. Place the cell pointer on the cell where the presentation object should appear.

7. From the Edit menu, select Paste Special. The Paste Special dialog box appears.

8. Select Freelance Presentation Object and click on the Paste button. The selected page of the presentation appears on the worksheet, as shown in figure 18.35. Use the handles to resize and reposition the page.

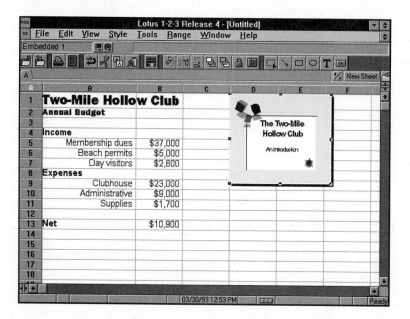

FIG. 18.35

The presentation embedded in 1-2-3.

To open the Freelance window and view the presentation at any time, double-click on the presentation page in the 1-2-3 worksheet.

Because all the Freelance presentation data is embedded in the 1-2-3 worksheet file, the worksheet file grows considerably in size. The advantage to embedding the presentation is that you can transfer the worksheet to another computer and view the presentation there (as long as Freelance Graphics for Windows exists on the other computer) without having to transport the Freelance presentation file also.

Creating an Embedded Freelance Presentation from within 1-2-3

While working in a 1-2-3 worksheet, you can temporarily switch to Freelance Graphics long enough to create a presentation. When you return to 1-2-3, the Freelance presentation and its data are embedded in the worksheet. From within 1-2-3, you can view the Freelance presentation, complete with charts, tables, graphics, sound, and animation by double-clicking the presentation page that appears in 1-2-3.

To create an embedded Freelance presentation from within a 1-2-3 worksheet, follow these steps:

1. Position the cell pointer in the 1-2-3 worksheet where you want the presentation object to appear (the embedded presentation will be represented by the display of a page from the presentation).

2. From the 1-2-3 menu, select Edit Insert Object.

3. From the Insert Object dialog box that appears, select Freelance Presentation as the Object Type and then click on OK.

4. Create the presentation pages as you normally would when the Freelance window opens.

5. From the Freelance menu, select File Update.

6. From the Freelance menu, select File Exit & Return to return to 1-2-3 and embed the completed presentation.

The following example gives you the chance to embed a Freelance presentation in a 1-2-3 worksheet. Although you create a presentation of only two pages, the same procedure works if the presentation is dozens of pages. To begin, open Freelance and follow these steps:

1. From the Welcome to Freelance Graphics dialog box, select Create a New Presentation.

2. From the Choose a Look for Your Presentation dialog box, select the BLOCKS.MAS SmartMaster set from the list and then click on OK.

3. From the Choose Page Layout dialog box, choose the Title page layout and then click on OK.

4. Click on the Click Here To Type Presentation Title block and type Lola's Expansion Plans.

5. Press the down-arrow key to move to the next Click Here... block.

6. Type 1994 and Beyond and then click on OK. Because you don't add a symbol to the title page, you can ignore the Click Here To Add Symbol block. It will appear in Freelance while you create the presentation, but not when you view the presentation later. Figure 18.36 shows the completed title page.

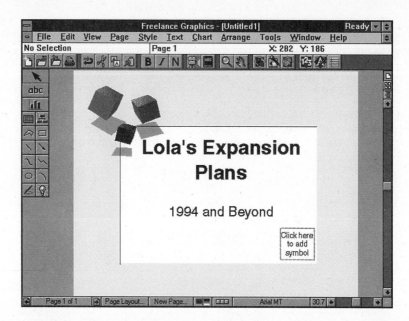

FIG. 18.36

The completed
title page.

To create a second presentation page, follow these steps:

1. Click on the New Page button at the bottom of the Freelance window.

2. From the New Page dialog box, select the Bulleted List page layout and then click on OK.

3. Click on the Click Here To Type Page Title block and type Expansion Plans.

4. Press the down-arrow key to move to the first bullet point.

5. Type the following list of bulleted text points, pressing Enter after each; click on OK to complete the list:

   Pet grooming service

   Pet sitting service

   Chain of retail pet supply stores

   Figure 18.37 shows the completed bulleted list page.

6. Click on the Page Sorter icon at the right edge of the Freelance window to switch to Page Sorter view.

7. Select the title page by clicking on it. The selected page is the one that displays when the presentation object is embedded in 1-2-3. You will see the second page when you view the presentation by

clicking on the title page that appears in 1-2-3. Figure 18.38 shows the presentation with the title page selected in Page Sorter view.

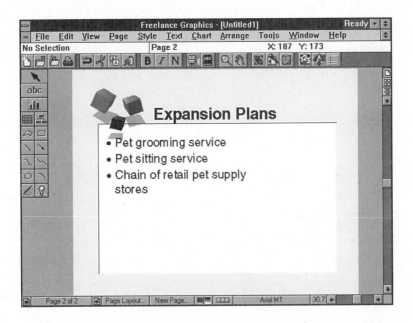

The completed bulleted list page.

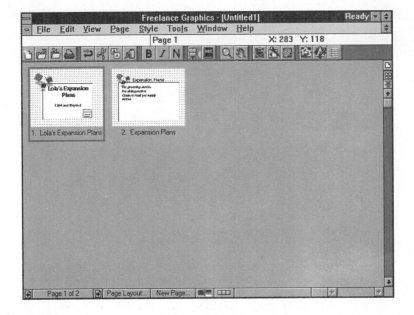

The presentation with the title page selected in Page Sorter view.

8. From the Freelance menu, select <u>E</u>dit <u>C</u>opy or click on the Copy SmartIcon to copy the presentation to the Windows Clipboard.

9. Switch to 1-2-3 for Windows by using Alt+Tab or Ctrl+Esc, or by clicking on the 1-2-3 SmartIcon.

In 1-2-3, you embed the presentation in the Windows Clipboard into a worksheet. Begin by following these steps:

1. Create the small, sample worksheet shown in figure 18.39.

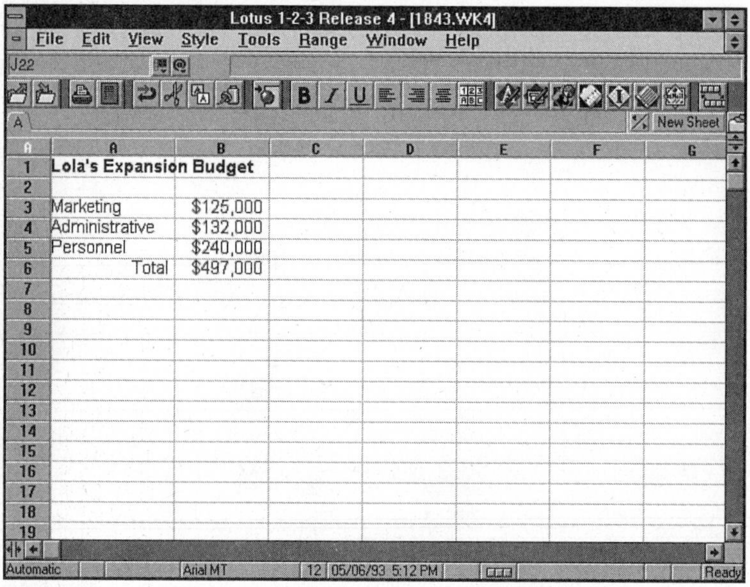

	A	B	C	D	E	F	G
1	Lola's Expansion Budget						
2							
3	Marketing	$125,000					
4	Administrative	$132,000					
5	Personnel	$240,000					
6	Total	$497,000					

FIG. 18.39

The sample 1-2-3 worksheet.

2. Position the cell pointer in a blank cell to the right of the worksheet title.

3. From the 1-2-3 menu, select <u>E</u>dit Paste <u>S</u>pecial.

4. From the Paste Special dialog box, select Freelance Presentation Object and click on the <u>P</u>aste button. The title page of the Freelance presentation appears in the 1-2-3 worksheet (see fig. 18.40). You can resize and reposition the page by dragging the handles surrounding the page.

To view the presentation from within 1-2-3, double-click on the presentation page showing in the 1-2-3 window. The Freelance Graphics window opens with the presentation loaded. Turn from page to page through the presentation or view the presentation as a screen show. When finished, select <u>F</u>ile E<u>x</u>it & Return from the Freelance menu to return to 1-2-3.

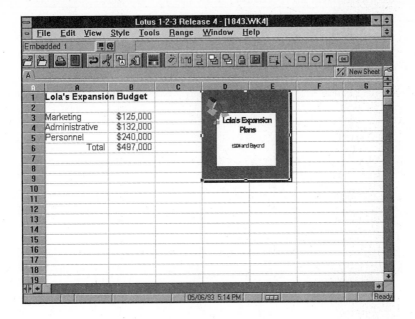

FIG. 18.40

The Lola presentation embedded in a 1-2-3 worksheet.

Using 1-2-3 Data in a Freelance Graphics Chart

The graphing capabilities in 1-2-3 for Windows are sophisticated enough that you may feel no need to use a separate graphics program like Freelance Graphics. But you may want to incorporate data from a 1-2-3 for Windows worksheet in a presentation you are preparing in Freelance. If so, you will find it easy to transport the data from 1-2-3 to Freelance—and easy to set up an OLE link between the two programs.

If you need to copy data from a worksheet to a Freelance chart and have no concern about whether the chart is updated if the 1-2-3 data changes, a straightforward copy and paste through the Windows Clipboard can do the job. After selecting the range of data in 1-2-3, copy the range to the Windows Clipboard and then switch to the Chart Data & Titles window of a Freelance chart. There, use Paste to retrieve the data from the Windows Clipboard. This procedure performs a one-time-only transfer of the data and does not set up a link.

With the copy-and-paste method, the data in 1-2-3 must be arranged the same way you want it to appear in the Chart Data & Titles window. The data sets you represent with lines or sets of bars must be arranged in columns rather than rows in the worksheet. Figure 18.41 shows a worksheet range that can be copied easily to Freelance because the series of numbers about each town is arranged in a column. Figure 18.42 shows the same worksheet with the series of numbers about each town arranged in rows. This second worksheet requires an additional procedure to transpose the rows and columns.

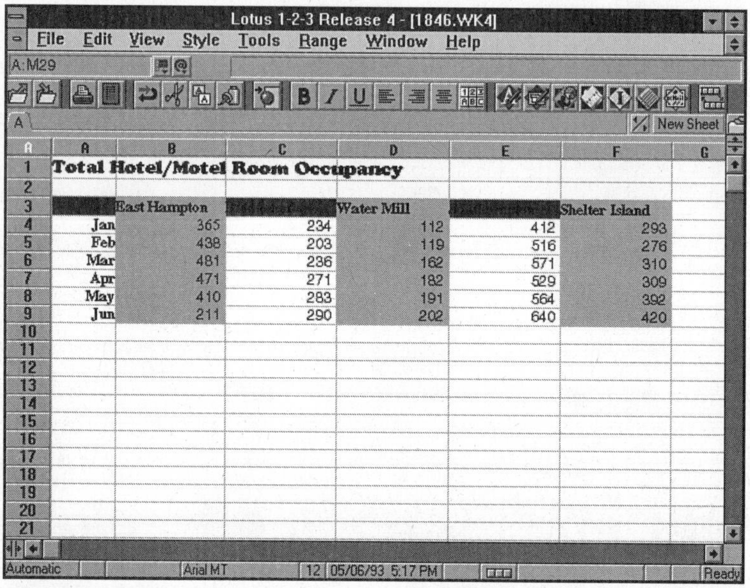

FIG. 18.41

An easily imported worksheet with sequences of data arranged in columns.

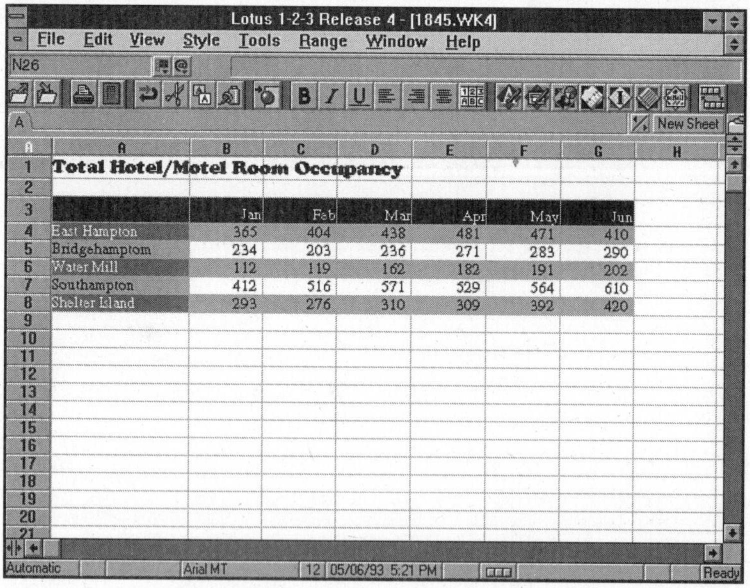

FIG. 18.42

The same sequences of data arranged in worksheet rows.

Copying 1-2-3 Data into a Freelance Chart

When data sets are arranged in worksheet columns and you do not need to create a link, follow this procedure to use 1-2-3 data in a Freelance chart:

1. Open the 1-2-3 worksheet containing the data.

2. Select the range of data you want to copy to a Freelance Graphics chart, such as range A3..D9 in figure 18.43. Include the column and row headers in the selected range.

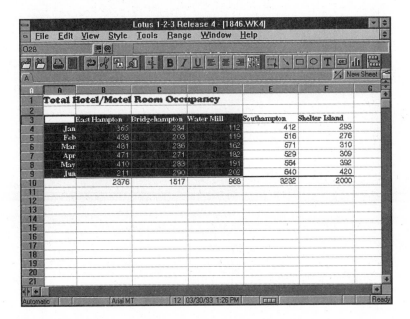

FIG. 18.43

A selected 1-2-3 range to copy to Freelance.

3. From the 1-2-3 menu, select <u>E</u>dit <u>C</u>opy or click on the Copy SmartIcon.

4. Switch to Freelance Graphics for Windows by using Alt+Tab or Ctrl+Esc, or by clicking on the Freelance Graphics SmartIcon.

5. Start a chart by clicking on a Click Here To Create Chart block, by selecting the Chart icon in the toolbox, or by selecting <u>N</u>ew from the <u>C</u>hart menu and then <u>D</u>ata Chart from the list of chart types. After you select a chart type and style, the Chart Data & Titles window opens (see fig. 18.44).

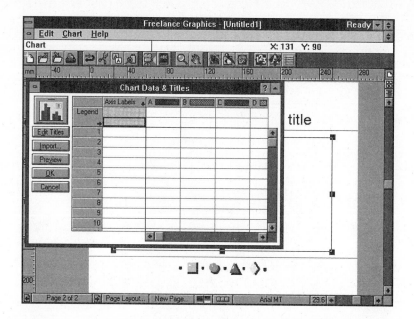

FIG. 18.44

The Chart Data &
Titles window
for a Freelance
chart.

6. Position the cell pointer in the Chart Data & Titles window where
   you want the data to appear. Place the pointer in the gray cell at
   the top of the Axis Labels column and at the left end of the Legend
   row (just outside the upper-left corner of the white data area as
   shown in figure 18.44) if you have selected the column and row
   headings in 1-2-3. Place the pointer in the first blank cell if you
   have selected only the data without selecting the column and row
   headings.

7. From the Freelance menu, select Edit Paste or click on the Paste
   SmartIcon. Figure 18.45 shows the data pasted in the Chart Data &
   Titles window.

8. Click on the Edit Titles button to add titles to the chart; click on
   and hold the Preview button to preview the chart; or click on OK
   to place the chart on the presentation page. Figure 18.46 shows
   how a stacked bar chart would look created from the data on the
   Chart Data & Titles window.

Linking or Transposing 1-2-3 Data
for a Freelance Chart

If you have to transpose the rows and columns of data in 1-2-3 before
you can use them in the Freelance graph, or if you want to link the 1-2-3

and Freelance data, you must use the Freelance Edit Paste Special command to retrieve the data from the Windows Clipboard.

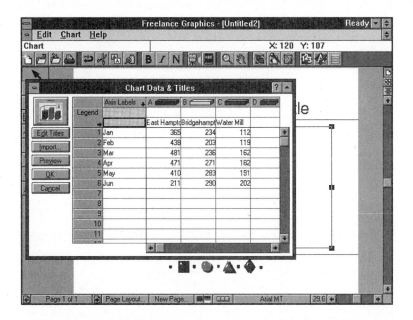

FIG. 18.45

The 1-2-3 data pasted into the Chart Data & Titles window.

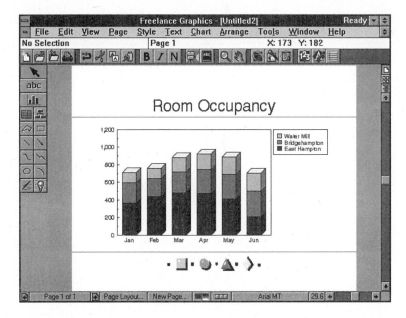

FIG. 18.46

A stacked bar created from the 1-2-3 data pasted into the Chart Data & Titles window.

After selecting a range in 1-2-3 and copying it to the Windows Clipboard
with the 1-2-3 Edit Copy command, switch to an open Chart Data &
Titles window in Freelance and select Edit Paste Special from the
Freelance menu. The Edit Paste Special window opens, shown in figure 18.47.

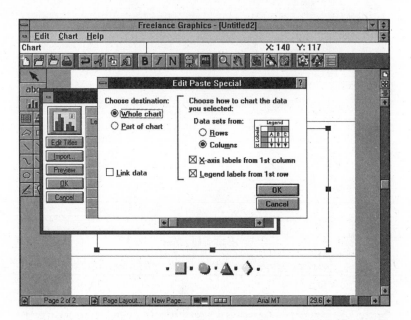

FIG. 18.47

The Edit Paste
Special window
in Freelance.

Freelance recognizes that the data on the Windows Clipboard is a range
of data from 1-2-3 for Windows; in the Edit Paste Special dialog box,
Freelance presents a number of options for importing the data.

If the selected 1-2-3 range is the complete set of data for the chart, select Whole Chart. A set of options at the right of the dialog box enables
you to specify whether the data sets in the 1-2-3 data are arranged in
rows or columns. If the data sets are arranged in columns, Freelance
imports them as-is to the Chart Data & Titles window. If the data sets
are arranged in rows, Freelance transposes the rows and columns before importing them. Two check boxes in the Edit Paste Special dialog
box let you indicate whether you have included the column and row
headings in the 1-2-3 range and whether to include them as x-axis labels
or legend entries in the Freelance Chart Data & Titles window. To create a link between the 1-2-3 data and the Freelance chart, click on the
Link Data check box. If a link exists, the 1-2-3 data in the Freelance chart
is automatically updated.

If you select a 1-2-3 range that contains only part of the data for a
chart—perhaps a single data set—select Part of Chart from the Edit

Paste Special dialog box. The dialog box shows a list of chart parts. By selecting one of these parts, you can determine where the 1-2-3 range goes on the Chart Data & Titles window. If you want to copy a data set with the Part of Chart option, you must type the legend or axis-label data manually. Only the Whole Chart option lets you automatically import X-axis titles and legend entries. Figure 18.48 shows the Edit Paste Special dialog box when you select Part of Chart.

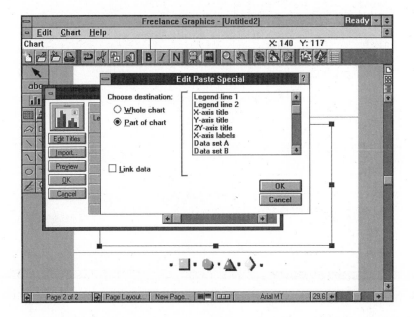

The Edit Paste Special dialog box when Part of Chart is selected.

You can use the Part of Chart option when you want to import only a portion of a 1-2-3 worksheet. You can select a single series of numbers in 1-2-3 and then select a data set from the list in the Edit Paste Special dialog box. The set of numbers is imported to that data set. You also can import only axis titles, legend entries, and chart headings and notes by selecting them in 1-2-3 and then choosing the appropriate chart part from the list.

T I P

Because the Part of Chart option enables you to pull selected data into a selected portion of a chart, you can use the option to consolidate sets of numbers from various 1-2-3 worksheets. You can select a range in one worksheet and then use Part of Chart to paste it into Data Set A. Then you can select a range from a different worksheet and use Part of Chart to paste it into Data Set B, and so on.

When you use the Part of Chart option, you can click on the Link Data check box to set a link between the range in 1-2-3 and the selected part of the chart. In one chart, therefore, you can have active links to several different ranges in several different worksheets. Changes to any of the worksheets are reflected in the Freelance chart.

Linking Data from Several 1-2-3 Worksheets

In this exercise, you import a range from a 1-2-3 worksheet into a Freelance chart. Then you add a range from a different worksheet and set up links between the data in 1-2-3 and the Freelance chart.

Begin by creating the small worksheet shown in figure 18.49 and save it in a file. Then select the column and row headings and the numeric data (range A6..D9)(see fig. 18.50). Do not include the cells along the bottom of the worksheet that contain calculations.

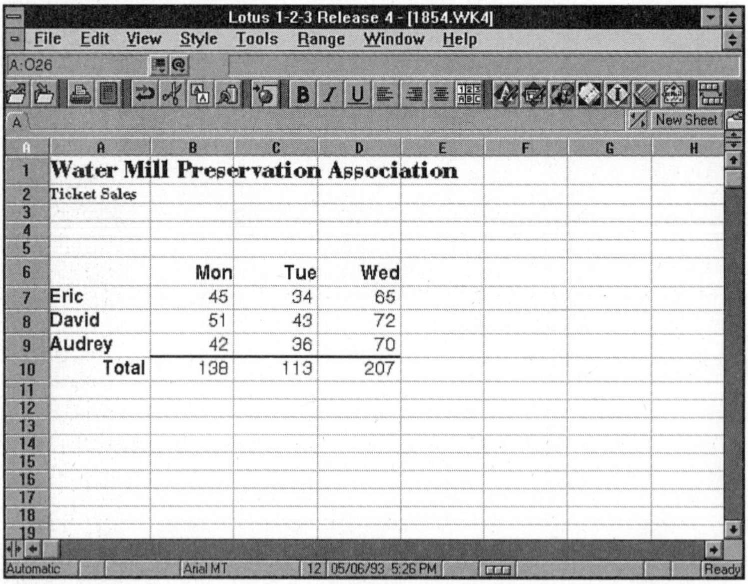

FIG. 18.49

The sample worksheet with data to be graphed in Freelance.

From the 1-2-3 menu, select Edit Copy or click on the Copy SmartIcon to copy the range to the Windows Clipboard. Then switch to Freelance Graphics and create a chart by following these steps:

1. From the Welcome to Freelance Graphics window that opens when you first start Freelance, select Create a New Presentation.

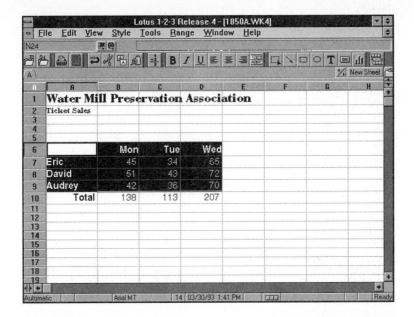

FIG. 18.50

The data selected
in the 1-2-3
worksheet.

2. From the Choose a Look for Your Presentation dialog box, select the 3LINE.MAS SmartMaster set and click on OK.

3. From the Choose Page Layout dialog box that appears, select the 1 Chart page layout and click on OK.

4. Click on the Click Here To Create Chart block.

5. From the New Chart Gallery dialog box, select 3D Bar and click on OK. Do not change the selected chart style. The Chart Data & Titles window opens.

6. Place the cursor in the lower of the two gray cells at the upper-left corner of the data area in the Chart Data & Titles window.

Now you use Edit Paste Special to import the data from 1-2-3 and create a link. Because each individual's numbers are arranged in a row in the 1-2-3 data, you use the controls in the Edit Paste Special dialog box to transpose the data so that each row of numbers in 1-2-3 appears in a column on the Freelance Chart Data & Titles window. As a result, each set of numbers is represented by a set of bars of the same color. The legend indicates which person is represented by each color. To use Paste Special, follow these steps:

1. From the Freelance menu, select Edit Paste Special.

2. Select Whole Chart from the Edit Paste Special dialog box to tell Freelance to import all the data in the Windows Clipboard as a complete set of data for a chart.

3. Select <u>R</u>ows to specify that the data in 1-2-3 is arranged in rows.

4. Make sure that the <u>X</u>-Axis Labels From 1st Row and Legend Labels From 1st Column check boxes are checked so that the row and column headings in the 1-2-3 data are imported into the Legend and Axis Label cells of the Chart Data & Titles window.

5. Click on the <u>L</u>ink Data check box to set up a DDE Link between the 1-2-3 data and the Freelance chart.

6. Click on OK. The data is imported into the Chart Data & Titles window; notice that the rows and columns have been transposed as shown in figure 18.51. The blue underlines in the Chart Data & Titles window indicate that it contains linked data.

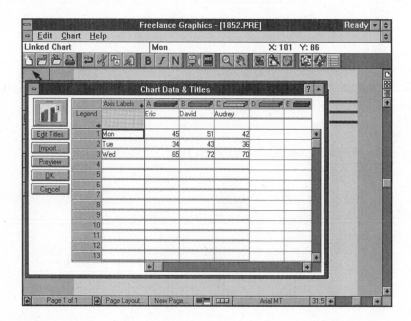

FIG. 18.51

The data after importing.

To see the chart that results from this data, click on and hold the Pre<u>v</u>iew button. After you see the chart, release the Pre<u>v</u>iew button to return to the Chart Data & Titles window.

To complete the chart, you need to add one more person's information. That person's data is kept in a different worksheet. Switch to the 1-2-3 window, take a moment to create a new 1-2-3 worksheet and enter the data shown in figure 18.52.

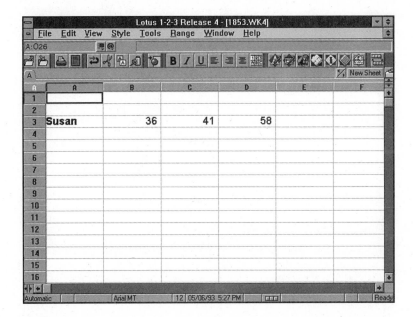

FIG. 18.52

The data for one last person.

Select only the numbers (do not include the row heading in cell A3); use the Edit Copy command or the Copy SmartIcon to copy the selected range to the Windows Clipboard. Switch back to Freelance and follow these steps:

1. From the Freelance menu, select Edit Paste Special.

2. Select Part of Chart from the Edit Paste Special dialog box and then select Data Set D from the list of chart parts.

3. Make sure that the Link Data check box is checked.

4. Click on OK.

To complete the chart, type the name Susan in the Legend cell at the top of Data Set D (in the cell to the right of Audrey). To see the chart that results from this addition, click on OK. Figure 18.53 shows the finished chart.

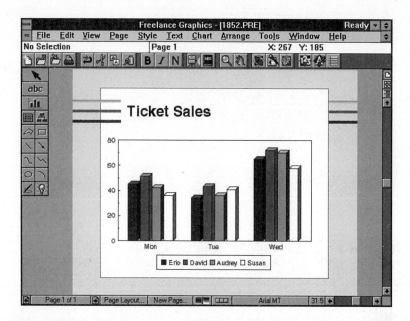

FIG. 18.53

The completed
Freelance chart.

Questions & Answers

In this chapter, you learned about integrating Lotus Windows applications. If you have any questions about any topic covered in this chapter and cannot find the answer in any of the help windows, scan this section.

Q: After I copy to the Windows Clipboard an object that I want to link, when I switch to the other application, the Paste Link command is not available on the Edit menu. When I try using Paste Special, instead, DDE Link is not one of the available formats. Why is this?

A: Probably because you have not saved the object in the source application in a file. You must save the data in a file before you can create a link.

Q: Why can't I link data between two applications if I have not saved the data in a file in the source application.

A: Because the data in a link must be stored in a file created by the application that was used to originate the data. The filename for the data is part of the information that is transferred to the destination application via the Windows Clipboard. This lets the destination application maintain a link with the data file even if the source application is not running, or even installed on the system.

Q: Even though I know the data in two applications are linked, changing the data in the source application does not change it in the destination application. Why?

A: The link may have been deactivated. To reactivate a link, select Links or Link Options on the Edit menu. Click the link on the list and then click Update.

Q: Every time I open a file with a link in a Lotus SmartSuite application, the application asks whether I want to update the DDE links. How can I get rid of this message?

A: By unlinking the data. This leaves the data in the destination application, but removes the link between the data in the original application and the data in the destination application. The drawback is that the data in the destination applicaton will no longer automatically change if the source data is changed.

Q: Should I use linking or embedding if I want to use data from 1-2-3 in an Ami Pro document.

A: Use linking if you want changes to the 1-2-3 data to update in Ami Pro, too. Use embedding if you plan to move the Ami Pro document among PCs. The 1-2-3 data will be embedded in the Ami Pro file.

Q: After I select Paste Special to embed an object I've copied in another Windows application, why do so many formats appear on the list?

A: Because when you copy an object to the Windows Clipboard, several different ways of representing the data are copied to the Clipboard simultaneously. This insures that the destination application will find a form of data on the Clipboard that it can accept. For example, when you copy a 1-2-3 table to the Clipboard, the numbers are copied to the Clipboard as text, as Rich Text in a table, and as a picture of the original 1-2-3 formatted table. If the destination application does not have the capability to edit numbers in a table, it can always use the plain text or the picture of the 1-2-3 table, instead.

Q: Can I embed a single object or group of objects from a Freelance page into 1-2-3?

A: No, you must embed an entire presentation. To transfer a single object, you can use Edit Copy and Edit Paste to transfer the object, or you can link the object into 1-2-3.

Q: Will the techniques I have learned in this chapter work equally well with other Windows applications?

A: They will work with other Windows applications that support OLE 1.0 as clients and servers. Consult the user manual for the application to see if it is OLE-compatible.

Q: After I have created a logo in Freelance that I will use often in 1-2-3 worksheets, is there a way to save the logo in a readily accessible place.

A: In Freelance, you can copy the logo to the Windows Clipboard and then save the Clipboard contents as a CLP file on the disk (by starting the Clipboard Accessory and then using File Save As). Then, to get the logo, you start the Clipboard and use File Open to retrieve the logo to the Clipboard. Then you can switch to 1-2-3 and paste the logo into the worksheet. You may find it easier and faster to open the Windows Clipboard to retrieve the logo than to open Freelance. In addition, you can copy the CLP file to any computer, whether it has Freelance installed or not, and use the logo in Windows' applications.

Summary

In this chapter, you learned how to combine the strengths of 1-2-3 and other Lotus Windows applications by simply copying and pasting information from one window to another or by using Object Linking and Embedding to set up links and dependencies among applications.

Using these techniques, you learned how you can combine the presentation powers of Freelance, the document preparation prowess of Ami Pro, and the data analysis and storage capabilities of 1-2-3 to create a powerful, integrated system that excels at managing text, images, and numeric data.

Appendixes

OUTLINE

Installing 1-2-3 Release 4 for Windows

Installing 1-2-3 Release 4 for Windows is almost automatic—after you start the program, you follow simple on-screen instructions. You must install this software on a hard disk—you can't run it from floppy disks.

Installing this software takes about 15 or 20 minutes. When you are ready to begin, turn on the computer and follow the instructions in this appendix.

Preparing To Install 1-2-3 Release 4 for Windows

1-2-3 Release 4 for Windows includes one set of high-density disks of either 5 1/4 inch or 3 1/2 inch. After you install 1-2-3 Release 4 for Windows, store the original disks in a safe location.

If the system is connected to a network, disconnect from the network before you start installation. At one point in the installation process, 1-2-3 for Windows scans the computer for available space on hard drives. If your computer is connected to a network, this step takes a long time because 1-2-3 for Windows scans every drive on the network.

Before you install this program, make sure that your computer meets the following hardware, storage, and memory requirements:

- A system with 80286, 80386, or 80486 architecture (an 80386 or 80486 is recommended)

- An EGA, VGA, or IBM 8514 monitor

- Microsoft Windows Version 3 or higher, running with DOS Version 3.11 or higher

- 3M of random-access memory (RAM) if you use Windows 3.0, or 4M of RAM if you use Windows 3.1

- 7M of available hard disk storage for 1-2-3 Release 4 for Windows program only; 15M of available hard disk storage to install the 1-2-3 Release 4 for Windows program, additional program features, help and sample files, and DataLens drivers

The following are optional:

- Printer (any printer supported by Windows 3.0 or 3.1)

- A mouse (highly recommended)

Using the Install Program

Because 1-2-3 for Windows runs only under Microsoft Windows, the Windows Program Manager must be active before you install 1-2-3 for Windows. Start Microsoft Windows and place the Install disk in drive A. (If you install from a different drive, substitute that drive's letter.) Choose File Run from the Program Manager menu and type **A:INSTALL** in the Command Line text box (see fig. A.1). Then choose OK. An on-screen message informs you that Install is copying working files to the hard disk. The Welcome to Install screen appears (see fig. A.2). Choose OK to proceed with the installation.

The 1-2-3 for Windows Install program displays as a series of dialog boxes. If you need help at any time during installation, select the Help button in the dialog box.

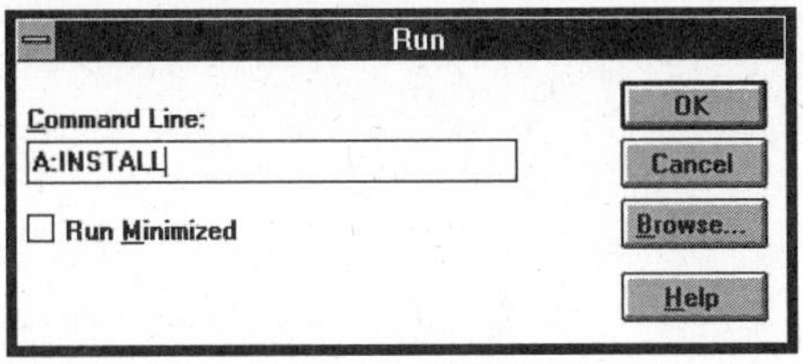

FIG. A.1

The Run dialog box of the Windows Program Manager.

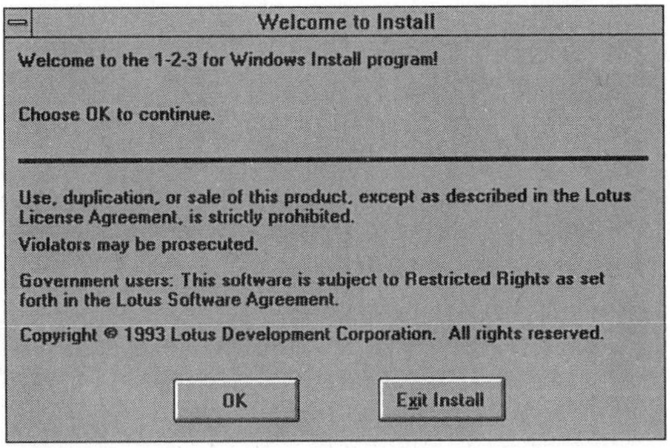

FIG. A.2

The Welcome to Install screen.

Registering Your Original Disks

To make the original set of disks usable, you must register them by entering and saving your name and company name on the Install disk (see fig. A.3). Type your name and press the Tab key, and then type the company name (you do not have to enter a company name if the program is licensed to you personally). Be sure that you type the information correctly. If everything is correct, choose OK. A dialog box appears with these selections—choose Yes to confirm or No to return to the preceding dialog box (see fig. A.4). After you choose Yes, your name and optional company name, along with an ID number, appear every time you start 1-2-3 for Windows.

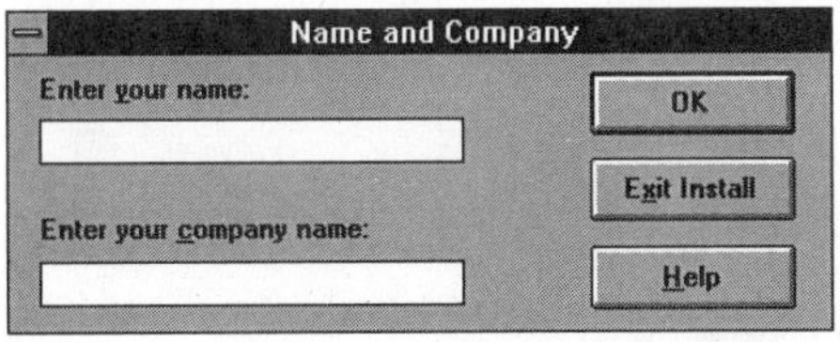

FIG. A.3

The screen on which you record your name and company name.

FIG. A.4

Confirming your name and optional company name.

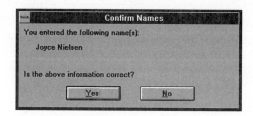

Choosing To Install with Defaults or Options

The 1-2-3 Release 4 for Windows Install main menu contains the following icons: Install 1-2-3, Install on a server, View product updates, and Choose country driver and sort order (see fig. A.5). If you need to select a country and sort order other than the default of US Numbers First, select the Choose country driver and sort order icon, make the selection, and choose OK. Next, select the Install 1-2-3 icon to continue with the installation process.

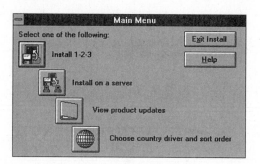

FIG. A.5

The 1-2-3 for Windows Install main menu.

A dialog box appears (see fig. A.6). To install 1-2-3 for Windows with the default settings, select the Default Install icon. To determine which options to install, select the Customized Install icon. Select the Install for Laptops icon to conserve the most disk space.

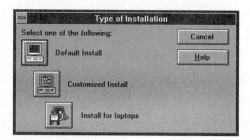

FIG. A.6

The Type of Installation dialog box.

If the Install program finds a previous release of 1-2-3 for Windows on your system, the dialog box in figure A.7 appears. You can choose to install the new version in a new directory, or to replace the existing version by installing the new version in the same directory. After you make your selection, click on OK to continue.

This dialog box appears if you already have 1-2-3 for Windows on your system.

If you install with the default settings, select the drive and directory to install 1-2-3 for Windows in the resulting dialog box. Then choose OK and choose Yes to confirm the creation of the new directory. Proceed to the following section.

If you use Customized Install, the dialog box shown in figure A.8 appears. Select the drive and directory to install 1-2-3 Release 4 for Windows. In the example, the default drive and directory is C:\123R4W. The available files to transfer and the amount of space needed for each of those files also appear in the dialog box.

Installing 1-2-3 for Windows with options.

Choose <u>A</u>dditional Features to display the dialog box shown in figure A.9. In this box, choose each of the optional features, such as <u>A</u>uditor, <u>B</u>acksolver, and so on, that you want to install. After you finish making the selections, choose OK.

<table>
<tr><td colspan="3">Select Additional Features to install</td></tr>
<tr><td colspan="3">Select one or more of the following:</td></tr>
<tr><td>☒ <u>A</u>uditor</td><td>28 K</td><td>OK</td></tr>
<tr><td>☒ <u>B</u>acksolver</td><td>36 K</td><td>Cancel</td></tr>
<tr><td>☒ <u>S</u>olver</td><td>678 K</td><td><u>H</u>elp</td></tr>
<tr><td>☒ <u>L</u>otus Dialog Editor</td><td>218 K</td><td></td></tr>
<tr><td>☒ <u>M</u>acro Translator</td><td>617 K</td><td></td></tr>
<tr><td>☒ <u>T</u>ranslate Utility</td><td>781 K</td><td></td></tr>
<tr><td>☒ Version manager for Lotus <u>N</u>otes</td><td>7 K</td><td></td></tr>
<tr><td>☒ S<u>p</u>ell Check</td><td>61 K</td><td></td></tr>
<tr><td>Space needed for selected files:</td><td>2426 K</td><td></td></tr>
<tr><td>Remaining space on drive:</td><td>7567 K</td><td></td></tr>
</table>

FIG. A.9

Selecting 1-2-3 for Windows optional features.

To display the dialog box shown in figure A.10, select Help and <u>S</u>ample Files from the Customized Install dialog box. In this dialog box, choose each of the optional files you want to install. To install the optional macro help file, for example, choose Detailed <u>M</u>acro Help. After you finish making the selections, choose OK.

<table>
<tr><td colspan="3">Help and Sample Files</td></tr>
<tr><td colspan="3">Select one or more of the following:</td></tr>
<tr><td>☒ <u>S</u>ample files</td><td>15 K</td><td>OK</td></tr>
<tr><td>☒ Detailed <u>M</u>acro Help</td><td>269 K</td><td>Cancel</td></tr>
<tr><td>☒ Detailed @ <u>F</u>unction Help</td><td>239 K</td><td><u>H</u>elp</td></tr>
<tr><td>☒ <u>T</u>utorial</td><td>185 K</td><td></td></tr>
<tr><td>☒ T<u>o</u>ur</td><td>4406 K</td><td></td></tr>
<tr><td>Space needed for selected files:</td><td>5114 K</td><td></td></tr>
<tr><td>Remaining space on drive:</td><td>7567 K</td><td></td></tr>
</table>

FIG. A.10

Selecting 1-2-3 for Windows help and sample files.

To display the dialog box shown in figure A.11, select Data<u>L</u>ens Drivers from the Customized Install dialog box. In this dialog box, select the DataLens drivers for each type of external database file you want to access. For example, select <u>P</u>aradox to enable use of Paradox database files. After you finish making the selections, choose OK.

Choose OK. If the specified program directory does not already exist, the install program offers to create it (see fig. A.12). Choose Yes to confirm the creation of the new directory.

Adding Icons to a Program Manager Group

The next dialog box enables you to determine which application icons to add to the Windows Program Manager and the group name to which you assign the icons (see fig. A.13). By default, the selected icons install in the Lotus Applications group window. To install the icons in a different program group window, you can choose the name you want from the drop-down list box. Choose OK when you finish.

1-2-3 for Windows has two different 1-2-3 Install icons. The one you see depends on whether you installed from 3 1/2-inch or 5 1/4-inch disks. The only difference is the disk shown on the icon.

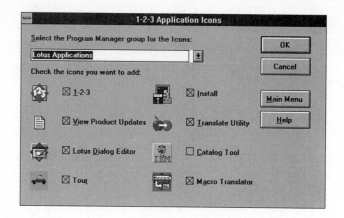

Selecting
application
icons to add to
the Program
Manager.

Selecting 1-2-3 Default Preferences

The User Preferences dialog box appears on-screen (see fig. A.14).
The following options are selected by default: Drag-and-Drop Cells,
Use Automatic Format, Save Files Every ___ Minutes, Undo, Run
Autoexecute Macros, and Beep On Error. You also can specify the num-
ber of previously used files to display, and determine whether to dis-
play the default Worksheet Directory. Choose OK when you finish.

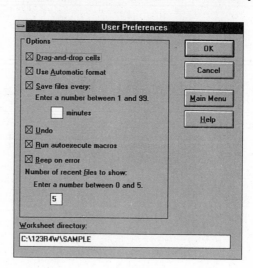

Selecting
the default
preferences.

Transferring Files

Install creates the directories (see fig. A.15) and then decompresses and transfers the program files from the Install disk to the hard disk. After Install finishes with the current disk, a dialog box appears and prompts you to insert the next disk. Continue to insert the appropriate disks as you are prompted. After installation is complete, a series of messages appears, followed by the Installation Finished dialog box (see fig. A.16). Choose OK.

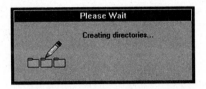

Installing the Adobe Type Manager

The next screen enables you to install the Adobe Type Manager, version 2.5 (see fig. A.17). A sophisticated program, the Adobe Type Manager improves the on-screen and printed appearance of fonts. Lotus recommends that you install ATM to use with 1-2-3 Release 4 for Windows. ATM includes several new font sets. 1-2-3 for Windows uses ATM when the program scales fonts—such as when compressing a worksheet to print on one page. Other Windows 3 programs can use this same copy of ATM. If you do not want to install ATM at this time, choose No and skip to the next section.

To install ATM now, select Yes; a dialog box prompts you to insert the ATM program disk in the appropriate drive. Choose OK to continue.

When installed, the Adobe Type Manager loads each time you start Windows.

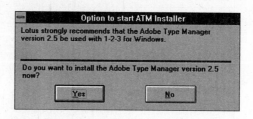

The Option to
Start ATM
Installer
dialog box.

 NOTE   If you use Windows 3.1, you do not have to install Adobe
Type Manager to take advantage of scalable fonts. Windows
3.1 has TrueType scalable font technology built in.

Completing the Installation

The next screen tells you that the Install program is complete. Choose
OK. If you chose to install the Adobe Type Manager, you now must
restart Windows before you begin using 1-2-3 Release 4 for Windows.
Refer to Chapter 2 for instructions on starting 1-2-3 Release 4 for
Windows.

At some point, you may need to change the Windows 3 configuration.
If you purchase a new printer or a new video display, you must
reconfigure Windows 3 for the printer or video display. You can modify
the configuration of Windows through the Program Manager Control
Panel. Refer to the Windows documentation for details.

You can run the 1-2-3 Release 4 for Windows Install program again from
the hard disk—access Windows and select the 1-2-3 Install icon.

Using the Dialog Box Editor

T he Dialog Box Editor enables you to create custom dialog boxes for use in 1-2-3 for Windows macro programs that use the DIA-LOG command. You can use custom dialog boxes to display messages, to prompt the user for input, or to present an entire series of options in a complex application.

The Dialog Box Editor is a separate program, usually installed when you install 1-2-3 for Windows. If you chose not to install the Lotus Dialog Box Editor when you installed 1-2-3 for Windows, see Appendix A for more information on installing the program.

Understanding Custom Dialog Boxes

Custom dialog boxes are dialog boxes you create for special purposes. You use the DIALOG macro command to display a custom dialog box. 1-2-3 stores any response the user makes in the worksheet so that macro programs can examine and use the stored information.

In many ways, custom dialog boxes are similar to the standard dialog boxes displayed in 1-2-3 or other Windows programs. They can use the same elements, such as push buttons, check boxes, and list boxes. Custom dialog boxes even look like standard dialog boxes. The primary difference is that you create custom dialog boxes to meet your special needs.

Understanding Dialog-Box Controls

You can add push buttons, default push buttons, radio buttons, check boxes, edit boxes, list boxes, static text, combo boxes, or group boxes to custom dialog boxes. Table B.1 describes each of these controls.

Table B.1 Dialog-Box Controls

Control	Description
Push button	Closes a dialog box
Default push button	A push button that is automatically selected when the dialog box is displayed
Radio button	Allows user to select one option at a time
Check box	Allows user to select options that are not mutually exclusive
Edit box	Allows user to enter up to 511 characters
List box	Allows user to pick one item from a list of items
Static text	Gives the user information
Combo box	Combines list boxes and edit boxes in a single control
Group box	Groups and labels related controls

 NOTE Although the Lotus Dialog Box Editor can create bitmap buttons, 1-2-3 does not display these types of dialog-box objects. Do not add bitmap buttons to dialog boxes you intend to use in 1-2-3 for Windows.

Creating a Custom Dialog Box

Creating a custom dialog box using the Lotus Dialog Box Editor is a fairly simple process—but one that requires a little planning if you want the dialog box to be useful.

For example, before you begin the creation of a custom dialog box, decide what type of output you expect. If the dialog box is intended to select program options, you will want to present the user with a predetermined list of options—perhaps using radio buttons or check boxes. On the other hand, if the dialog box is intended to solicit user input, you will want to provide an edit box in which the user can type variable information.

You also should decide whether a custom dialog box is really the proper approach to take. Although it may be tempting to create your own variations on standard dialog boxes (such as the File Open dialog box), consider whether this approach may confuse, rather than help, your application's users. Remember that you can use 1-2-3's built-in dialog boxes in your applications—without having to worry about making sure that they work correctly!

Finally, consider the layout of the objects in custom dialog boxes. If the objects in the dialog boxes don't line up, the appearance is anything but professional. Consider, too, the order of the objects in the dialog box: if possible, place edit boxes and other controls in a logical order so that the user can move easily from one object to the next.

Creating a New Dialog Box

To begin creating a custom dialog box, start the Lotus Dialog Box Editor. To start the Dialog Box Editor, click on the Lotus Dialog Box Editor icon in the Windows Program Manager. Alternatively, click on the Lotus Dialog Box Editor SmartIcon from within 1-2-3 for Windows. Figure B.1 shows the Lotus Dialog Editor window.

You use this window to create and edit custom dialog boxes. There are four drop-down menus: Use the File menu commands to create, save, and open dialog-box files and to exit the Lotus Dialog Box Editor. The Edit menu commands enable you to copy dialog-box descriptions to and from 1-2-3, cut, copy, and paste dialog-box objects (controls), and change the appearance of dialog-box objects. The Control menu enables you to select objects you want to place in a dialog box. The Options menu offers basic controls for how you use the Lotus Dialog Box Editor itself.

To start a new custom dialog box, select File New or click on
the Create File SmartIcon from the Lotus Dialog Editor window; the
New dialog box appears (see fig. B.2). The New dialog box creates
a basic dialog box that contains no objects. You later add objects to
the empty dialog box.

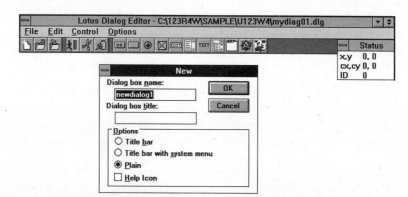

The name in the Dialog Box Name text box is the default name for the
new dialog box. You use this name in macros to refer to the custom
dialog box. The Lotus Dialog Box Editor supplies a default name (such
as newdialog1); for this example, accept the default name. If you include more than one custom dialog box in a worksheet application,
provide different names for each custom dialog box.

If you want the dialog box to display a title, enter the text of the title in
the Dialog Box Title text box. If you do not include a title, the title bar
does not appear on your custom dialog box. For this example, enter
Personal Data as the dialog-box title. If you include a title, it should
describe the dialog box's purpose.

Select Title Bar to display just the title; select Title Bar with System
Menu to include a system menu in the dialog-box title bar. Select Plain
to omit both the title bar and system menu. If you include a system
menu, the user can use the system menu to close or move the dialog
box. For this example, select Title Bar.

Click on OK or press Enter. Click the mouse anywhere in the Lotus Dialog Editor window to create the basic dialog box in the default size (see fig. B.3). If necessary, you can change the size of the dialog box by clicking inside the dialog box and then dragging the selection handles to the correct size.

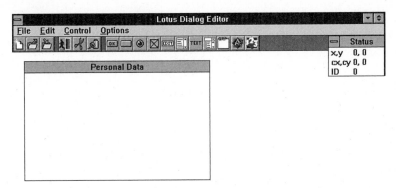

You add objects to the dialog box by selecting objects from the Control menu or by clicking on the appropriate SmartIcon and then clicking on the location where you want to add the object. Double-click on an object, such as static text, to edit the default text. The following table shows the applicable SmartIcons next to their corresponding Control menu options.

Table B.2 SmartIcons

SmartIcon	Control Menu Option
	Push Button
	Default Push Button
	Radio Button
	Check Box
	Edit Box

continues

Table B.2 Continued

SmartIcon	Control Menu Option
	List Box
	Static Text
	Combo Box
	Group Box

To complete the sample dialog box, add the four edit boxes, four static-text objects, the default push button (OK), and the push button (Cancel) shown in figure B.4. Edit the static text and the push button text to read as shown in the figure. To resize an object, click on the object to select it and drag the selection handles. For a professional appearance, carefully align the dialog-box objects.

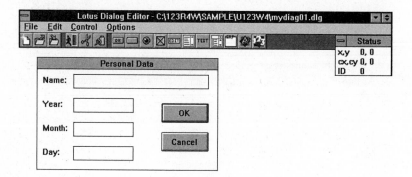

FIG. B.4

A new dialog box with added objects.

The sample dialog box is now ready to test—but first you should save it. Select File Save (or File Save As) or click on the Save File SmartIcon. Specify a name you can remember, such as **MYDIAG01**. You can use the File Open command or the Open File SmartIcon to open saved dialog-box files.

Copying a Dialog Box to 1-2-3

You transfer a custom dialog box from the Lotus Dialog Box Editor to 1-2-3 for Windows by copying the dialog box to the Clipboard and then pasting it into 1-2-3. You do not paste the actual dialog box into 1-2-3, however. Instead, you paste a *dialog-description table* (information used by 1-2-3 to duplicate the dialog box). 1-2-3 does not use the dialog-box file you saved in the Lotus Dialog Box Editor. The only way to add a custom dialog box to 1-2-3 is to copy it to the Clipboard and paste it into 1-2-3.

To copy the dialog box to 1-2-3, follow these steps (starting in the Lotus Dialog Box Editor):

1. Make certain that none of the individual dialog-box objects are selected. Although you can select the entire dialog box, this is not necessary.

2. Select Edit Copy.

3. Use Ctrl+Esc or Alt+Tab to return to 1-2-3 for Windows. If you have not already started 1-2-3 for Windows, return to the Program Manager and start 1-2-3 for Windows.

4. Select an empty location in the worksheet for the dialog-description table. This table uses 11 columns and 3 rows more than the number of objects in the dialog box. You may want to create a separate worksheet for dialog-description tables to keep from overwriting existing data.

5. Select Edit Paste. Figure B.5 shows the dialog-description table for the sample dialog box in figure B.4 (in this figure, column widths were adjusted to show all columns in the table on one screen).

Don't worry if your dialog-description table doesn't match the figure. Dialog box objects are listed in the order you created them, and so may not be listed in the same order in your dialog-description table. Also, if the objects you create are a different size or are positioned differently, their description lines will vary from the figure, as well.

Testing the Dialog Box

The next step is to test the dialog box to make certain that it works correctly. You use the DIALOG macro command to display a custom dialog box; you use the same command to test the dialog box.

Lotus 1-2-3 Release 4 - [DIAG01.WK4]

File   Edit   View   Style   Tools   Range   Window   Help

A15

	A	B	C	D	E	F	G	H	I	J	K
1	DIALOG	newdialog1									
2	-2.1E+09	10	15	35	156	84	""	""		"Personal Data"	2
3	108	28	40	16	1	1E+09	"button"	"OK"	0		
4	32	4	116	12	8000	1E+09	"edit"	""	0		
5	5	5	25	10	1000	1E+09	"static"	"Name:"	0		
6	32	24	52	12	8001	1E+09	"edit"	""	0		
7	5	25	20	10	1001	1E+09	"static"	"Year:"	0		
8	32	44	52	12	8002	1E+09	"edit"	""	0		
9	5	45	25	10	1002	1E+09	"static"	"Month:"	0		
10	32	64	52	12	8003	1E+09	"edit"	""	0		
11	5	65	20	10	1003	1E+09	"static"	"Day:"	0		
12	108	52	40	16	2	1E+09	"button"	"Cancel"	0		
13	END DIALOG										

Automatic   Arial   12 | 03/29/93 2:52 PM   Ready

FIG. B.5

The dialog-description table for the example dialog box.

First, create a range name for the dialog-description table. You can select Range Name Use Labels and choose To the left from the For Cells list to apply the name in cell B1, NEWDIALOG1, to the upper-left corner of the dialog-description table.

Then create a macro that contains the following single command:

```
{DIALOG NEWDIALOG1}
```

Name this macro \d and then run the macro. 1-2-3 displays the custom dialog box as shown in figure B.6.

To test the dialog box, add text to the edit boxes and then select OK or Cancel to close the dialog box and end the macro. When the macro ends, the dialog box is cleared from the screen. If the dialog box does not display when you run the macro, make certain that the macro refers to the correct range (the dialog-description table). In particular, make certain that the name of the dialog box is assigned to the cell containing the DIALOG label in the dialog-description table.

Using Custom Dialog Boxes

Although the sample dialog box seems to work, it is not very useful without a method to access the results. For example, after the user selects OK, you probably will want to know what information was typed in the edit boxes. You also will want to know whether OK or Cancel was selected.

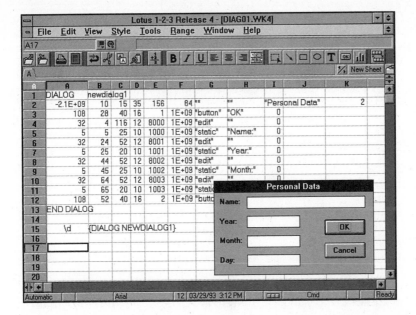

The custom
dialog box.

The key to accessing dialog-box results is understanding where 1-2-3 stores those results. Once you know that, you can use the information in worksheet formulas or macro commands.

Understanding the Dialog-Description Table

The first row of a dialog-description table must contain the label DIA-LOG in the first column. This label tells 1-2-3 that this is the beginning of a dialog-description table.

The last row of a dialog-description table must contain the label END DIALOG in the first column.

The second row of a dialog-description table describes the dialog box. Column 9 of the second row contains the dialog-box title. The rows below the second row describe the dialog-box objects.

The first nine columns of the dialog-description table hold the information 1-2-3 needs to display the dialog box and any objects it contains. The information in these columns is generated automatically when you paste the dialog box into 1-2-3 and should not be changed. Column 7 describes each object's type; column 8 shows the text (if any) displayed on the object.

Column 10 of the dialog-description table is called the *input column*. Values in this column describe the initial state of dialog-box objects. For example, if you add text to column 10 of a row that describes an edit box, the text you enter is displayed as a default value in the edit box. For the sample dialog box shown in figure B.6, typing **Brian** in cell J4 displays Brian as the default value in the edit box that follows Name. If you add **@NA** to a cell in column 10, the associated dialog-box object becomes unavailable. Typing **@NA** in cell J12 dims the Cancel button. If the object is a list box, the input column should contain the range name or address of a single-column range that holds the list of items to display in the list box.

Column 11 of the dialog-description table is called the *output column*. 1-2-3 stores the results from the dialog box in column 11. 1-2-3 stores the number of the push button used to close the dialog box in row 2, column 11 of the dialog-description table. If a radio button or check box is selected, 1-2-3 stores 1 in the output column of that object's row. If the object is a list box, 1-2-3 stores the offset number of the selected item (from the input range) in the output column. For example, if the list box shows five items, and the first item is selected, the output column shows a 0. If the second item is selected, the output column shows a 1, and so on.

Using Dialog-Box Results

One of the best ways to use dialog-box results is to name the cells in the output column (column 11 of the dialog-description table). Write your macro so that it tests the results when the macro continues after the user selects one of the dialog-box push buttons. For example, you can apply the range name USER_NAME to cell K4 in the sample dialog-description table. Then use the values the user enters to perform calculations or determine how the macro program should continue.

Custom dialog boxes are easy to create and easy to use. You will find that, with a little practice, you can customize your macro programs with your own dialog boxes—and create a more professional appearance for your applications.

The Lotus Multibyte Character Set

The Lotus Multibyte Character Set (LMBCS) enables you to display, store, and print characters you might not find on your keyboard. These special characters include monetary symbols, mathematical symbols, operator signs, and diacritical marks.

To enter a character that is not on your keyboard, press Alt+F1 (Compose) and then type a series of keystrokes, called a *compose sequence*. To create some characters, you can use one of several compose sequences. For example, to enter the British pound sterling symbol (£), you press Alt+F1 (Compose) and then type **L=** or **L-**.

Depending on your hardware, some LMBCS characters might not display on your monitor or print from your printer. If a character does not display, print a sample range to see whether the character is available from your printer.

Because not all LMBCS characters have compose sequences, you also can generate these characters by using the @CHAR function. For example, type **@CHAR(156)** to enter the British pound sterling symbol (£) into the worksheet.

If you frequently use some characters, you easily can create macros to enter the compose sequences for you. (See Chapters 15 and 16 to learn how to create macros.)

The tables that follow list the special characters with their LMBCS codes, the compose sequence(s) used to create each character (if available), a description of each character, and the actual character produced.

Group 0

Table C.1 defines the Group 0 LMBCS characters.

Table C.1 LMBCS Codes for Group 0 Characters

LMBCS Code	Compose Sequence	Character Description	Character
32		Space	(Space)
33		Exclamation point	!
34		Double quotes	"
35	++	Pound sign	#
36		Dollar sign	$
37		Percent	%
38		Ampersand	&
39		Close single quote	'
40		Open parenthesis	(
41		Close parenthesis	)
42		Asterisk	*
43		Plus sign	+
44		Comma	,
45		Minus sign	–
46		Period	.
47		Forward slash	/
48		Zero	0
49		One	1

LMBCS Code	Compose Sequence	Character Description	Character
50		Two	2
51		Three	3
52		Four	4
53		Five	5
54		Six	6
55		Seven	7
56		Eight	8
57		Nine	9
58		Colon	:
59		Semicolon	;
60		Less than	<
61		Equal sign	=
62		Greater than	>
63		Question mark	?
64	aa *or* AA	At sign	@
65		A, uppercase	A
66		B, uppercase	B
67		C, uppercase	C
68		D, uppercase	D
69		E, uppercase	E
70		F, uppercase	F
71		G, uppercase	G
72		H, uppercase	H
73		I, uppercase	I
74		J, uppercase	J
75		K, uppercase	K
76		L, uppercase	L
77		M, uppercase	M
78		N, uppercase	N
79		O, uppercase	O

continues

Table C.1 Continued

LMBCS Code	Compose Sequence	Character Description	Character
80		P, uppercase	P
81		Q, uppercase	Q
82		R, uppercase	R
83		S, uppercase	S
84		T, uppercase	T
85		U, uppercase	U
86		V, uppercase	V
87		W, uppercase	W
88		X, uppercase	X
89		Y, uppercase	Y
90		Z, uppercase	Z
91	((	Open bracket	[
92	//	Backslash	\
93	))	Close bracket	]
94	vv	Caret	^
95		Underscore	_
96		Open single quote	'
97		a, lowercase	a
98		b, lowercase	b
99		c, lowercase	c
100		d, lowercase	d
101		e, lowercase	e
102		f, lowercase	f
103		g, lowercase	g
104		h, lowercase	h
105		i, lowercase	i
106		j, lowercase	j
107		k, lowercase	k
108		l, lowercase	l

LMBCS Code	Compose Sequence	Character Description	Character
109		m, lowercase	m
110		n, lowercase	n
111		o, lowercase	o
112		p, lowercase	p
113		q, lowercase	q
114		r, lowercase	r
115		s, lowercase	s
116		t, lowercase	t
117		u, lowercase	u
118		v, lowercase	v
119		w, lowercase	w
120		x, lowercase	x
121		y, lowercase	y
122		z, lowercase	z
123	(-	Open brace	{
124	^/	Bar	|
125	)-	Close brace	}
126	--	Tilde	~
127		Delete	
128	C,	C cedilla, uppercase	Ç
129	u"	u umlaut, lowercase	ü
130	e'	e acute, lowercase	é
131	a^	a circumflex, lowercase	â
132	a"	a umlaut, lowercase	ä
133	a'	a grave, lowercase	à
134	a*	a ring, lowercase	å
135	c,	c cedilla, lowercase	ç
136	e^	e circumflex, lowercase	ê
137	e"	e umlaut, lowercase	ë
138	e'	e grave, lowercase	è

continues

Table C.1 Continued

LMBCS Code	Compose Sequence	Character Description	Character
139	i"	i umlaut, lowercase	ï
140	i^	i circumflex, lowercase	î
141	i'	i grave, lowercase	ì
142	A"	A umlaut, uppercase	Ä
143	A*	A ring, uppercase	Å
144	E'	E acute, uppercase	É
145	ae	ae diphthong, lowercase	æ
146	AE	AE diphthong, uppercase	Æ
147	o^	o circumflex, lowercase	ô
148	o"	o umlaut, lowercase	ö
149	o'	o grave, lowercase	ò
150	u^	u circumflex, lowercase	û
151	u'	u grave, lowercase	ù
152	y"	y umlaut, lowercase	ÿ
153	O"	O umlaut, uppercase	
154	U"	U umlaut, uppercase	
155	o/	o slash, lowercase	ø
156	L= l= L– *or* l–	British pound sterling symbol	£
157	O/	O slash, uppercase	Ø
158	xx *or* XX	Multiplication sign	×
159	ff	Guilder	ƒ
160	a'	a acute, lowercase	á
161	i'	i acute, lowercase	í
162	o'	o acute, lowercase	ó
163	u'	u acute, lowercase	ú
164	n~	n tilde, lowercase	ñ
165	N~	N tilde, uppercase	Ñ
166	a_ *or* A_	Feminine ordinal indicator	ª

LMBCS Code	Compose Sequence	Character Description	Character
167	o_ *or* O_	Masculine ordinal indicator	º
168	??	Question mark, inverted	¿
169	RO ro R0 *or* r0	Registered trademark symbol	®
170	–]	End of line symbol (Logical NOT)	¬
171	12	One half	$^1/_2$
172	14	One quarter	$^1/_4$
173	!!	Exclamation point, inverted	¡
174	< <	Left angle quotes	<<
175	> >	Right angle quotes	>>
176		Solid fill character, light	▓
177		Solid fill character, medium	▓
178		Solid fill character, heavy	█
179		Center vertical box bar	│
180		Right box side	┤
181	A'	A acute, uppercase	Á
182	A^	A circumflex, uppercase	Â
183	A'	A grave, uppercase	À
184	CO co C0 *or* c0	Copyright symbol	©
185		Right box side, double	╡
186		Center vertical box bar, double	║
187		Top right box corner, double	╗
188		Bottom right box corner, double	╝
189	c¦ c/ C¦ *or* C/	Cent sign	¢
190	Y= y= Y– *or* y–	Yen sign	¥
191		Top right box corner	┐

continues

Table C.1 Continued

LMBCS Code	Compose Sequence	Character Description	Character
192		Bottom left box corner	└
193		Bottom box side	┴
194		Top box side	┬
195		Left box side	├
196		Center horizontal box bar	─
197		Center box intersection	┼
198	a~	a tilde, lowercase	ã
199	A~	A tilde, uppercase	Ã
200		Bottom left box corner, double	╙
201		Top left box corner, double	╔
202		Bottom box side, double	╨
203		Top box side, double	╤
204		Left box side, double	╟
205		Center horizontal box bar, double	=
206		Center box intersection, double	╪
207	XO xo X0 or x0	International currency sign	¤
208	d–	Icelandic eth, lowercase	∂
209	D–	Icelandic eth, uppercase	Ð
210	E^	E circumflex, uppercase	Ê
211	E"	E umlaut, uppercase	Ë
212	E'	E grave, uppercase	È
213	i<space>	i without dot, lowercase	ı
214	I´	I acute, uppercase	Í
215	I^	I circumflex, uppercase	Î
216	I"	I umlaut, uppercase	I
217		Bottom right box corner	┘

LMBCS Code	Compose Sequence	Character Description	Character
218		Top left box corner	⌐
219		Solid fill character	■
220		Solid fill character, lower half	■
221	/<space>	Vertical line, broken	¦
222	I'	I grave, uppercase	Ì
223		Solid fill character, upper half	■
224	O´	O acute, uppercase	Ó
225	ss	German sharp, lowercase	ß
226	O^	O circumflex, uppercase	Ô
227	O'	O grave, uppercase	Ò
228	o~	o tilde, lowercase	õ
229	O~	O tilde, uppercase	Õ
230	/u	Greek mu, lowercase	µ
231	p–	Icelandic thorn, lowercase	Þ
232	P–	Icelandic thorn, uppercase	Þ
233	U´	U acute, uppercase	Ú
234	U^	U circumflex, uppercase	Û
235	U'	U grave, uppercase	Ù
236	y´	y acute, lowercase	ý
237	Y´	Y acute, uppercase	Ý
238	^–	Overline character	‾
239		Acute accent	´
240	–=	Hyphenation symbol	-
241	+–	Plus or minus sign	±
242	–– or ==	Double underscore	=
243	34	Three quarters	³/₄
244		Paragraph symbol	¶
245		Section symbol	§
246	:–	Division sign	÷

continues

Table C.1 Continued

LMBCS Code	Compose Sequence	Character Description	Character
247	,,	Cedilla accent	ç
248	^0	Degree symbol	°
249		Umlaut accent	¨
250	^.	Center dot	·
251	^1	One superscript	^{1}
252	^3	Three superscript	^{3}
253	^2	Two superscript	^{2}
254		Square bullet	■
255		Null	

NOTE If you use the @CHAR function with the numbers 1 through 31, the characters for LMBCS codes 257 through 287 are produced. These characters are listed in the Group 1 table.

Group 1

Table C.2 defines the Group 1 LMBCS characters.

Table C.2 LMBCS Codes for Group 1 Characters

LMBCS Code	Compose Sequence	Character Description	Character
256		Null	
257		Smiling face	☺
258		Smiling face, reversed	☻
259		Heart suit symbol	♥
260		Diamond suit symbol	♦
261		Club suit symbol	♣
262		Spade suit symbol	♠

LMBCS Code	Compose Sequence	Character Description	Character
263		Bullet	•
264		Bullet, reversed	
265		Open circle	○
266		Open circle, reversed	•
267		Male symbol	♂
268		Female symbol	♀
269		Musical note	♪
270		Double musical note	♫
271		Sun symbol	☼
272		Forward arrow indicator	►
273		Back arrow indicator	◄
274		Up-down arrow	↕
275		Double exclamation points	‼
276	!p *or* !P	Paragraph symbol	¶
277	SO so S0 *or* s0	Section symbol	§
278		Solid horizontal rectangle	▬
279		Up-down arrow, perpendicular	
280		Up arrow	↑
281		Down arrow	↓
282		Right arrow	→
283	mg	Left arrow	←
284		Right angle symbol	
285		Left-right symbol	↔
286	ba	Solid triangle	▲
287	ea	Solid triangle, inverted	▼
288	"<space>	Umlaut accent, uppercase	¨

continues

Table C.2 Continued

LMBCS Code	Compose Sequence	Character Description	Character
289	~<space>	Tilde accent, uppercase	
290		Ring accent, uppercase	°
291	^<space>	Circumflex accent, uppercase	^
292	'<space>	Grave accent, uppercase	`
293	´<space>	Acute accent, uppercase	´
294	"^	High double quotes, opening	"
295		High single quote, straight	'
296		Ellipsis	...
297		En mark	–
298		Em mark	—
299		Null	
300		Null	∟
301		Null	
302		Left angle parenthesis	<
303		Right angle parenthesis	>
304	<space>"	Umlaut accent, lowercase	¨
305	<space>~	Tilde accent, lowercase	
306		Ring accent, lowercase	°
307	<space>^	Circumflex accent, lowercase	^
308	<space>'	Grave accent, lowercase	`

LMBCS Code	Compose Sequence	Character Description	Character
309	<space>´	Acute accent, lowercase	´
310	"v	Low double quotes, closing	
311		Low single quote, closing	
312		High double quotes, closing	"
313	_<space>	Underscore, heavy	
314		Null	
315		Null	
316		Null	
317		Null	
318		Null	
319		Null	
320	OE	OE ligature, uppercase	Œ
321	oe	oe ligature, lowercase	œ
322	Y"	Y umlaut, uppercase	Ÿ
323		Null	
324		Null	
325		Null	
326		Left box side, double joins single	╞
327		Left box side, single joins double	╟
328		Solid fill character, left half	▌
329		Solid fill character, right half	▐
330		Null	
331		Null	
332		Null	
333		Null	

continues

Table C.2 Continued

LMBCS Code	Compose Sequence	Character Description	Character
334		Null	
335		Null	
336		Bottom box side, double joins single	╨
337		Top box side, single joins double	╤
338		Top box side, double joins single	╥
339		Bottom single left double box corner	╙
340		Bottom double left single box corner	╘
341		Top double left single box corner	╒
342		Top single left double box corner	╓
343		Center box intersection, vertical double	╫
344		Center box intersection, horizontal double	
345		Right box side, double joins single	╡
346		Right box side, single joins double	╢
347		Top single right double box corner	╖
348		Top double right single box corner	╕
349		Bottom single right double box corner	╜
350		Bottom double right single box corner	╛

LMBCS Code	Compose Sequence	Character Description	Character
351		Bottom box side, single joins double	±
352	ij	ij ligature, lowercase	ij
353	IJ	IJ ligature, uppercase	IJ
354	fi	fi ligature, lowercase	fi
355	fl	fl ligature, lowercase	fl
356	'n	n comma, lowercase	'n
357	l.	l bullet, lowercase	l·
358	L.	L bullet, uppercase	L·
359		Null	∓
360		Null	
361		Null	
362		Null	
363		Null	
364		Null	
365		Null	
366		Null	
367		Null	
368		Single dagger	†
369		Double dagger	‡
370		Null	
371		Null	
372		Null	
373		Null	
374	TM Tm *or* tm	Trademark symbol	™
375	lr	Liter symbol	ℓ
376		Null	
377		Null	
378		Null	

continues

Table C.2 Continued

LMBCS Code	Compose Sequence	Character Description	Character
379		Null	
380	KR Kr *or* kr	Krone sign	Kr
381	–[	Start of line symbol	
382	LI Li *or* li	Lira sign	₤
383	PT Pt *or* pt	Peseta sign	Pt

NOTE LMBCS codes 384 through 511 duplicate LMBCS codes 128 through 255. These codes are for use with code groups of other countries. Refer to Table B.1 for a list of these characters.

Symbols

D

F

O